D0781840

Founders of Modern Political and Social Thought

AQUINAS

Moral, Political, and Legal Theory

John Finnis

OXFORD UNIVERSITY PRESS

OXFORD

UNIVERSITY PRESS

Great Clarendon Street, Oxford OX2 6DP

Oxford University Press is a department of the University of Oxford.
It furthers the University's objective of excellence in research, scholarship,
and education by publishing worldwide in

Oxford New York

Athens Auckland Bangkok Bogotá Buenos Aires Calcutta
Cape Town Chennai Dar es Salaam Delhi Florence Hong Kong Istanbul
Karachi Kuala Lumpur Madrid Melbourne Mexico City Mumbai
Nairobi Paris São Paulo Shanghai Singapore Taipei Tokyo Toronto Warsaw

with associated companies in Berlin Ibadan

Oxford is a registered trade mark of Oxford University Press
in the UK and in certain other countries

Published in the United States
by Oxford University Press Inc., New York

British Library Cataloguing in Publication Data

Data available

Library of Congress Cataloging in Publication Data
Finnis, John.
Aquinas/John Finnis.
(Founders of modern political and social thought)
Includes bibliographical references and indexes.
1. Thomas, Aquinas, Saint, 1225?-1274—Contributions in political
science.   2. Thomas, Aquinas, Saint, 1225?-1274—Contributions in
social sciences.   I. Title.   II. Series.
JC121.T453F55 1998   320'.092—dc21   97-51411
ISBN 0-19-878084-2
ISBN 0-19-878085-0 (Pbk.)

3 5 7 9 10 8 6 4 2

Typeset by J&L Composition Ltd, Filey, North Yorkshire
Printed in Great Britain on acid-free paper by
Biddles Ltd, Guildford and King's Lynn

M.C.

R.A.
C.C.G.
M.F.

J-P.A.
J.G.
E.R.

T.M.

Preface

There are some serious flaws in Aquinas' thoughts about human society. A sound critique of them can rest on premises he himself understood and articulated better, I think, than his philosophical masters Plato and Aristotle, and much better than Machiavelli, Hobbes, and the other makers or heirs of the Enlightenment. This book does not, of course, undertake the comparisons needed to justify this hypothesis about the fundamental superiority of Aquinas' work in moral, social, political, and legal theory. It does try to clarify the criteria for such a comparison, and to indicate how far his thought illuminates and, in large measure, satisfies them.

Reasons for action, personal conscience, free choice and self-determination, human dignity, community, family, justice, and state law—these are perhaps the main matters that (for differing reasons which I shall not explore) became clearer to Aquinas than to the founders who preceded him or those who followed. In keeping with the purposes of this series, I focus on Aquinas' treatment of these and other matters of perennial concern, and leave in shadow the biographical, literary, political, or other influences on him, the origins or parallels of his views in earlier or contemporary writers, and the historical aftermath and effects of his work.

Aquinas' work is not ideological; all its presuppositions and premisses are treated by him as open to rational consideration and argument. Of course, his primary vocation as a scholar was to be a theologian. Still, he believed that this required sound, uncompromisingly critical philosophy. Philosophy done well is completed and supplemented by theology, which uses historically given information not available to philosophy (or to the other sciences of nature) as such. But he also thought, and showed in practice, that philosophical inquiry, argument, reflection, and judgement can go a long way without any reliance on theology or religious faith. In this book I shall concentrate on elements in Aquinas' work which are, in that sense, purely philosophical. Only my final chapter discusses some elements of his theology, and of the case for accepting them as the philosophical inquiry's appropriate completion and supplement.

Readers whose interest is restricted to ethics (rather narrowly conceived) could follow a short path through the book: Section II.1, the first four paragraphs of II.2, Chapters III–V, Sections X.3–4, and Section X.6. Legal theorists could focus on Chapter II, Sections V.1–2, VI.1–3, and VI.5, and Chapters VII–IX. But since politics embraces law and expands on ethics, readers concerned with social and political theory should find no part of the book irrelevant; any shortened ways through it must be their own.

My exposition quite often goes beyond what Aquinas says; statements in this book should not be ascribed to Aquinas unless signified as quotations or (as often in the footnotes) close paraphrases. However, when a statement is footnoted by citation to Aquinas, it can be assumed to be close to the words of at least the first citation, unless that begins 'see' (when the textual support will be less close). Phrases such as 'we may think that . . .' warn that I am substantially developing or amending Aquinas' views. Though the book says more about ethics than students of social and political thought may expect, it is far from giving a complete idea of Aquinas' account of morality.

I have worked from the Latin texts, in the latest critical editions where they exist. Since the critical editions made in recent decades are sadly too expensive and unwieldy for wide use, my citations often indicate the relevant place in formerly standard editions (whose text should not, however, be relied upon). All translations are my own; I comment on one feature of them in II.2 at n. 26 below. Aquinas' usage is very flexible, often informal, and always context-relative. So when quoting or paraphrasing I have often given, in curly brackets {to minimize italics}, the Latin word or phrase corresponding to the immediately preceding English word(s) or phrase, or indicating elements in the cited passage which supplement the elements picked out in my paraphrase. Readers surprised by this or that rendering of the Latin should consult the original, above all the original *argumentation*, as well as Aquinas' other uses of the relevant word or phrase—the last a task much eased by Busa (1992).

For the past thirty years or so, my work in moral, political, and legal theory has employed principles which seemed to me to be substantially those employed by Aquinas in his main writings on practical reason, natural law, *prudentia*, and justice. Grisez (1965) made clear the presence and sense of those principles in Aquinas. My *Natural Law and Natural Rights* (1980) set out an ethical theory rooted (as the preface made clear) in Grisez's re-presentation and development of classical arguments and (as was indicated elsewhere in the book) in my understanding of Aquinas on justice, law, and other matters. Since 1965 Grisez's major writings have not claimed to be interpretations of Aquinas, whose work he has regarded as the point of departure for a free-standing philosophical treatment of ethical theory. I have collaborated extensively with Grisez in this free-standing work (see especially Finnis *et al.* 1987; Grisez *et al.* 1987), while also pursuing my own investigations into Aquinas. Writing this book required of me a wider and deeper acquaintance with Aquinas' works. That has confirmed my previous understanding of the foundational principles (and Aquinas' subscription to them), and led me to think one-sided or wrong some common beliefs about his social and political thought (including some I held)—not least about his thought on rights, the structure of justice, the state's authority, sex and marriage, slavery, and tyrannicide, but also on ultimate human fulfilment.

Early drafts of virtually all chapters were read by Kevin Flannery SJ (who checked out and commented on hundreds of citations and texts) and Germain Grisez; they each improved the work greatly. I am indebted also to Gerard V. Bradley, Marie C. Finnis, Patrick Lee, and Joseph Pilsner CSB, who helpfully reviewed parts in draft.

January 1998

Contents

CONTENTS

Abbreviations and Conventions

Cross-references to chapters and sections in this book appear in the form
VII.3. Footnotes are numbered; endnotes to chapters are cued with lower-
case letters.

a.   article
c   corpus
c.   chapter
d.   distinction
ex.   exposition (of Peter Lombard's text, in *Sent.*)
obj.   objection
q.   quaestio
s.c.   sed contra
sol.   solution (to a subquestion in *Sent.*)
un.   unique (e.g. where a quaestio has only one article)
v.   verse

Paragraph numbers taken from editions are given in square brackets.

Works of Aquinas

The dates are in most cases conjectural and in some important cases
disputed; I generally follow Emery in Torrell (1996: 330–61) and Gauthier
in *Opera* 25/2. 479–500. For information on the English and French translations available, see Torrell (1996: 331–59).

Aet.   *De Aeternitate Mundi contra Murmurantes* (On the Question of
         the World's Eternity, against the Murmurers), 1271. *Opera* 43.

An.   *Sententia Libri De Anima* (Commentary on Aristotle's *De Anima*
         (On Soul), 1267–8. *Opera* 45/1. Paragraph numbering: Pirotta
         (1936).

Brev. *Breve Principium* (Short [i.e. first in a two-part] Inaugural Lecture,
         given on becoming a Master at the University of Paris), 1256.
         Paragraph numbering: Verardo (1954).

Cael. *Sententia super Librum De Caelo et Mundo* (Commentary on
         Aristotle's *De Caelo* (On the Heavens) to 3. 302b29), 1272–3.
         Opera 3. Paragraph numbering: Spiazzi (1952).

Car.   *Quaestiones Disputatae de Caritate* (*De Caritate*: Disputed
         Questions on Charity [Love]), 1269–72. *Opera* 24/2.

Caus. *Expositio super Librum De Causis* (Commentary on the pseudo-
         Aristotelian Neoplatonist treatise on Causes), 1272.

Cen.   'Homo quidam fecit cenam magnam et vocavit multos' (Sermon on Luke 14: 16–24) 1267–73. Page numbering: Bataillon (1983: 360–9).

Comp.   *Compendium Theologiae ad fratrem Reginaldum* (A Compendium of Theology), 1265–7 and 1272–3. *Opera* 42. Paragraph numbering: Verardo (1954).

Corr.   *Quaestio Disputata de Correctione Fraterna* (Disputed Question on Fraternal Correction), 1269–72. *Opera* 24/2.

Cred.   *Collationes Credo in Deum* (Sermon-Lectures on the [Apostles'] Creed [*In Symbolum Apostolorum*]), 1273. Paragraph numbering: Spiazzi and Calcaterra (1954).

Dec.   *Collationes de Decem Praeceptis* (Sermons on the Ten Commandments) (also called *De Duobus Praeceptis Caritatis*) (On the Two Precepts of Charity [Love]), 1273. Torrell (1985). Paragraph numbering: Spiazzi and Calcaterra (1954).

Decret.   *Expositio super Decretalem* (Commentary on Two Decrees of the Fourth Lateran Council (1215)), 1261–5. *Opera* 40. Paragraph numbering: Verardo (1954).

Div.   *Expositio super Dionysium De Divinis Nominibus* (Commentary on Pseudo-Dionysius' treatise on naming God), 1261–7. Paragraph numbering: Pera (1950).

Empt.   *De Emptione et Venditione ad Tempus* (On Buying and Selling on Credit), 1262. *Opera* 42. Paragraph numbering: Verardo (1954).

Ent.   *De Ente et Essentia* (On Being and Essence), 1252–5. *Opera* 43. Paragraph numbering: Spiazzi (1954).

Ep. Reg.   *Epistola de Regimine [Subditorum/Iudaeorum] ad Ducissimam Brabantiae [or ad Comitissam Flandriae]* (Letter to the Duchess of Brabant [or, more likely, Margaret Countess of Flanders] on [her questions about] Governing [Jews (and Christian usurers and others)]), 1269–72. *Opera* 42.

Eth.   *Sententia Libri Ethicorum* (Commentary on Aristotle's *Nicomachean Ethics*), 1271–2. *Opera* 47. References (e.g. IX. 7 n. 6 [1845]) are to the book, lectio, and paragraph number in Busa (1992), followed by the paragraph number in Spiazzi (1949).

Eth Tab.   *Tabula Libri Ethicorum* (Table of terms used in Aristotle's *Nicomachean Ethics*, as analysed in Albert the Great's first commentary, c.1250), 1270. *Opera* 48.

Fid.   *De Articulis Fidei* (Letter to the Archbishop of Palermo on the Articles [Clauses] of the Apostles' Creed), 1260–8. *Opera* 42. Paragraph numbering: Verardo (1954).

Gen.	*Sententia super Libros De Generatione et Corruptione* (Commentary on Aristotle's treatise *On Generation and Corruption* to book 1. 5. 322ᵃ33), 1272–3. *Opera* 3. Paragraph numbering: Spiazzi (1952).
Graec.	*Contra Errores Graecorum* (Expert opinion for Pope Urban IV, on certain theological errors of the Greek Orthodox), 1263–4. *Opera* 40.
Hebd.	*Expositio in Librum Boethii de Hebdomadibus* (Commentary on Boethius' treatise on the goodness of existing things), after 1259. *Opera* 50. Paragraph numbering: Spiazzi and Calcaterra (1954).
I, I-II, II-II, III	See *ST*.
Impugn.	*Contra Impugnantes Dei Cultum et Religionem* (Against those [in the University of Paris] who Attack the Religious Life [especially the mendicant orders]), 1256. *Opera* 41. Paragraph numbering: Spiazzi and Calcaterra (1954).
In I Cor.	*Commentarium et Reportatio super Epistolam Primam ad Corinthios* (Commentary on Paul's First Letter to the Corinthians), 1263–5. References are to the chapter and lectio, the biblical verse, and the paragraph number in Cai (1951a).
In Eph.	*Reportatio super Epistolam ad Ephesios* (Commentary on Paul's Letter to the Ephesians), 1263–5. References are to the chapter and lectio, the biblical verse, and the paragraph number in Cai (1951a).
In Gal.	*Reportatio super Epistolam ad Galatas* (Commentary on Paul's Letter to the Galatians), 1263–5. References are to the chapter and lectio, the biblical verse, and the paragraph number in Cai (1951a).
In Heb.	*Expositio super Epistolam ad Hebraeos* (Commentary on the Letter to the Hebrews), 1263–5. References are to the chapter and lectio, the biblical verse, and the paragraph number in Cai (1951a).
In Ioann.	*Reportatio super Ioannem* (Commentary on John's Gospel), 1269–72. References are to the chapter and lectio, the biblical verse, and the paragraph number in Cai (1952).
In Iob	*Expositio super Iob ad Litteram* (Commentary on the Book of Job), 1263–5. *Opera* 26.
In Isa.	*Expositio super Isaiam* (Commentary on Isaiah), 1249–53. *Opera* 28.

In Matt.   *Reportatio super Evangelium Matthaei* (Commentary on
            Matthew's Gospel), 1269–70. References are to the chapter,
            the biblical verse, and the paragraph number in Cai (1951*b*).

In Rom.   *Commentarium super Epistolam ad Romanos* (Commentary
            on Paul's Letter to the Romans), 1271–3. References are to the
            chapter and lectio, the biblical verse, and the paragraph
            number in Cai (1951*a*).

In I Thess. *Reportatio super Epistolam Primam ad Thessalonienses*
            (Commentary on Paul's First Letter to the Thessalonians),
            1263–5. References are to chapter and lectio, the biblical
            verse, and the paragraph number in Cai (1951*a*).

In I Tim.   *Reportatio super Epistolam Primam ad Timotheum*
            (Commentary on Paul's First Letter to Timothy), 1263–5.
            References are to the chapter and lectio, the biblical verse,
            and the paragraph number in Cai (1951*a*).

Mal.   *Quaestiones disputatae de Malo* (*De Malo*: Disputed
            [Debated] Questions on Evil), 1269–71. *Opera* 23.

Meta.   *Sententia super Metaphysicam* (Commentary on Aristotle's
            Metaphysics to book 12), 1269–72. References are to the book,
            lectio, and paragraph in Busa (1992), followed by the para-
            graph number in Cathala (1935).

Opera   *Opera Omnia Sancti Thomae Aquinatis Doctoris Angelici*,
            the 'Leonine edition' of the works of Aquinas (critically edited
            by the Commission (of Dominican scholars) established by
            Pope Leo XIII in 1879), projected in fifty volumes, the first of
            which was published in 1882 and twenty-one still remain to
            be done.

Perf.   *De Perfectione Spiritualis Vitae* (On the Perfecting of the
            Spiritual Life), 1269–70. *Opera* 41. Alternative chapter
            numbering, and paragraph numbering: Spiazzi and Calcaterra
            (1954).

Peri.   *Commentarium in Libros Perihermeneias* (Commentary on
            Aristotle's *Peri Hermeneias* (*De Interpretatione*: On Assertive
            Statements)), 1270–1. *Opera* 1* (revised 1989). Paragraph
            numbering: Spiazzi (1955).

Phys.   *Sententia super Physicam* (Commentary on Aristotle's
            Physics), 1268–70. *Opera* 2. Paragraph numbering: Maggiòlo
            (1954).

Pol.   *Sententia Libri Politicorum* (Commentary on Books 1 to 3. 5
            (1280ª6) of Aristotle's *Politics*), 1269–72. *Opera* 48. Refer-
            ences (e.g. Pol. III. 6 n. 5 [395]) are to the book, lectio, and
            paragraph number in Busa (1992), followed by a reference to

the paragraph number in Spiazzi (1951). Citations of the form *Politics* 3. 4. 1279ᵃ21 are to Aristotle, *Politics*.

Post.   *Expositio Libri Posteriorum* (Commentary on Aristotle's *Posterior Analytics*), 1271–2. *Opera* 1* (revised 1989). Paragraph numbering: Spiazzi (1955).

Pot.   *Quaestiones Disputatae de Potentia* (Disputed Questions on the Power of God), 1265–6.

Princ.   *De Principiis Naturae* (On the Principles of Nature), 1252–6. *Opera* 43. Paragraph numbering: Spiazzi (1954).

Ps.   *Postilla in Psalmos* (Commentary on Psalms 1–54), 1272–3. References are to the Psalm (numbered according to the Vulgate), the paragraph numbering in Busa (1992), and the biblical verse.

Q. An.   *Quaestiones Disputatae de Anima* (Disputed Questions on Soul), 1266–7. *Opera* 24/1.

Quodl.   *Quaestiones de Quolibet* (Disputed [Debated] *Quodlibetal* [Random] Questions), 1256–9 (VII–XI) and 1269–72 (I–VI, XII). *Opera* 25.

Rat.   *De Rationibus Fidei ad Cantorem Antiochum* (On the Reasons for the [Catholic] Faith, to a Cantor of Antioch), 1265–8. *Opera* 40. Paragraph numbering: Verardo (1954).

Reg.   *De Regno* [or *De Regimine Principum*] *ad regem Cypri* (On Government [or Kingship] [or: On the Rule of Princes/Political Leaders], to the King of Cyprus), *c.*1265. *Opera* 42. References are to *Opera* 42's divisions of books and chapters, followed by the different division(s) given in some earlier standard editions, followed by paragraphs first in Eschmann (1949) and then in Spiazzi (1954).

Retra.   *Contra Doctrinam Retrahentium a Religione* (*Contra Retrahentes*: Against the Teaching of those who Deter People from Entering the Religious Orders), 1271. *Opera* 41. Paragraph numbering: Spiazzi and Calcaterra (1954).

ScG   *Summa contra Gentiles* ('A summary against the Pagans'; more correctly entitled *Liber de Veritate Catholicae Fidei contra Errores Infidelium*, 'Treatise on the Truth of the Catholic Faith against the Errors of Unbelievers'), 1259–65. *Opera* 13–15, revised in Pera (1961). References are by book (I, II, III, IV), chapter, and paragraph number in Pegis *et al.* (1955–7), followed by the paragraph number in Pera (1961).

Secret.   *De Secreto* (On Secrets), 1269. Report of a commission of seven masters appointed by the Dominican chapter in Paris in 1269 to answer questions of principle about compelling the disclosure of secrets. *Opera* 42. Paragraph numbering: Verardo (1954).

Sens. *Sententia Libri De Sensu et Sensato* (Commentary on Aristotle's *Sense and Sensibilia*), 1268–9. *Opera* 45/2. Paragraph numbering: Spiazzi (1949*b*).

Sent. *Scriptum super Libros Sententiarum Petri Lombardiensis* (Commentary on the Sentences [Opinions or Positions of the Church Fathers] [Handbook of Theology] of Peter Lombard [*c*.1155]), I, 1253–4; II, 1254–5; III, 1255–6; IV, 1256–7. References are by book (I, II, III, IV), distinction (d.), question (q.), article (a.), and sometimes to the response (solution) to a subquestion (sol.) and to Aquinas' exegesis {expositio} of Lombard's text (ex.).

Sort. *De Sortibus ad Dominum Iacobum de Tonengo* (On Casting Lots, a short treatise for James of Tonengo, papal chaplain), 1268–71. *Opera* 43. Paragraph numbering: Verardo (1954).

ST *Summa Theologiae* (A Summary of Theology), I, 1265–8; I-II, 1271; II-II, 1271–2; III, 1272–3. *Opera* 4–5, 6–7, 8–10, 11. References (e.g. I-II q. 2 a. 2c and ad 2) are to the four parts (first, first-of-the-second, second-of-the-second, third), question (q.), article (a.), corpus (c) (i.e. the body of Aquinas' response), reply (ad 1, ad 2, etc.) to a particular, numbered objection (obj. 1, obj. 2, etc.) and/ or to the sed contra (s.c.) ('but against that . . .': a summary and preliminary response, to which Aquinas is not necessarily committed).

Sub. *De Substantiis Separatis* (On the Nature of Angels), 1271–3. *Opera* 40.

Supp. *Supplementum* (A Supplement to [or rather, a partial completion of] *ST*, posthumously and anonymously constructed from passages of IV Sent). *Opera* 12 (the best text of the relevant parts of IV Sent.).

Trin. *Super Boethium de Trinitate* (Commentary on Boethius' treatise on the Trinity), 1257–9. *Opera* 50.

Unit. *De Unitate Intellectus contra Averroistas* (Against the [Parisian] Averroists' Thesis of a Single [Separate] Intellect), 1270. *Opera* 43. Citations are to the line number in *Opera* 43, and then to paragraphs in McInerny (1995) and in Spiazzi (1954).

Ver. *Quaestiones Disputatae de Veritate* (*De Veritate*: Disputed [Debated] Questions on Truth), 1256–9. *Opera* 22.

Vercell. *Responsio ad Ioannem Vercellensem de Articulis 108* (Reply to the Dominican Master-General about 108 allegedly questionable passages in works of Peter of Tarentaise [later Innocent V]), 1265–6/7. *Opera* 42. Paragraph numbering: Verardo (1954).

Virt. *Quaestiones Disputatae de Virtutibus* (*De Virtutibus*: Disputed [Debated] Questions on the Virtues [in General (*De Virtutibus in Communi*)]), 1269–72.

Virt. Card. *Quaestio Disputata de Virtutibus Cardinalibus* (Disputed [Debated] Question on the Cardinal Virtues [practical reasonableness, justice, courage, and temperance]), 1269–72. *Opera* 24/2.

I

Life, Learning, Works

1.1. *Family and Politics*

Thomas Aquinas was born in 1225,[a] perhaps 1224 or early 1226,[b] as fourth and last son of Theodora, wife of Landulf, knight and master of Roccasecca castle.[1] In his letters he always calls himself Thomas de Aquino, 'Thomas of the Aquino clan'; the lords of Roccasecca were subordinate to their clan's more powerful branch, whose lands included the ancient town of Aquino less than five miles to the south of Roccasecca. Besides his three older brothers, he had five sisters (one of them killed by lightning near Thomas in the castle nursery). Towards the end of his life, when his strength suddenly began to fail in December 1273, he tried recuperating with his youngest sister, Theodora, countess of Sanseverino castle. The illness which ended in his death on 7 March 1274 took hold on a passing visit, in mid-February, to a favourite niece in her castle twenty-five miles west of his birthplace.

On a narrow mountain spur high above the village of Roccasecca, the family's home and fortress commanded a 360-degree view of mountain, hill, and valley; west to east across the wide plain below ran the ancient inland road from Rome to Naples. The place is about fifty-five miles north-west of Naples, a little closer to Naples than to Rome, and was just inside the Kingdom of Sicily and Naples. Ten miles north-west of Roccasecca, at Monte Sangiovanni,

---

[1] This chapter is thematic rather than chronological; a table of the principal events in Thomas's life is set out in n. a. For the events and works discussed in this chapter, see Torrell (1996), Tugwell (1988), Weisheipl (1983), Marc (1966).

the family had another castle. Though visible from Roccasecca castle on a clear day, this second high fortress was over the border, in papal territories which from there extended west-north-west for more than a hundred miles. North of these papal lands stretched the Holy Roman Empire, right up to the North Sea and the Baltic and east to Vienna. Since the end of the twelfth century the empire's German rulers, the Hohenstaufens, had also ruled the distinct kingdom of Sicily and Naples. Thomas's father Landulf gave his allegiance to young King Frederick II in 1210; in 1220, the year the Pope crowned Frederick emperor, he became the royal justiciar, the official responsible for maintaining the king's peace, administering justice, and collecting royal taxes, in the large region between Roccasecca and Naples.

While Thomas was a 6- or 7-year-old in his second year of elementary education with the Benedictine monks of Monte Cassino abbey (ten miles east along the flanks of the mountain), his eldest brother, Aimon, was on crusade in Frederick II's army. Held for ransom on Cyprus by a Christian warlord, Aimon was released through papal intercession in 1233, and from then on supported the papacy in its conflicts with Frederick.

The next eldest brother, Reginald, joined Frederick II's cosmopolitan court. In 1243–4 he was campaigning with the king's army against papal cities in Tuscany. But in 1245 the Pope released Frederick's subjects from their allegiance to the king-emperor. Reginald and Thomas's family more or less shifted their political allegiance to the papacy. In the following year, or soon after, Reginald was harshly (and in Thomas's view unjustly)[c] put to death—as was Thomas's brother-in-law William of Sanseverino—as an alleged conspirator against Frederick.

The confused and violent politics of thirteenth-century Italy affected Thomas and his dynastic family in many other ways. His years with the monks at Monte Cassino were brought to an end in 1239 when the abbey, one of Europe's most ancient and important monasteries, was harassed by imperial forces retaliating against Frederick II's excommunication. There is evidence that when Thomas was a student in Paris and his family were on the run from Frederick, in the late 1240s, he was able to raise ecclesiastical funds for them with papal support. In 1264 his work at Orvieto ended when his friend Pope Urban IV fled from the advancing imperial army and the uprisings within the city. Earlier that year Urban IV had appealed to Thomas's brother Aimon to defend

Monte Sangiovanni castle against the imperial forces. In 1266 Thomas's brother-in-law Count Roger of Sanseverino gave close support to Charles of Anjou at the grim battle, twenty-five miles north-north-west of Sanseverino and the same distance north-east of Naples, which effectively ended Hohenstaufen rule and gave Charles the crown of Sicily and Naples. The new king appointed Roger as his representative in Rome, and Aimon as justiciar in Sicily.

Family business—administering the tangled estate of another brother-in-law, and arranging the guardianship of the dead man's sons by Roger and Theodora of Sanseverino—took Thomas to King Charles's court near Naples in the autumn of 1272. After nearly thirty years' working in Paris, Cologne, Rome, and Orvieto (sixty miles north of Rome), he had just returned to his home country to establish a house of studies {studium} in Naples for his religious order. In Paris, which he left for the last time in June 1272, he had known the protection and hospitality of King Louis IX of France (who died on crusade in 1270). Charles was Louis's younger brother, and took the occasion of Thomas's visit to promise financial support for Thomas's theology lectures for the royal University of Naples. Thomas's last period of teaching was in the service of both his order and his homeland.

Yet the dealings of his era's kings, popes, and emperors leave almost no palpable trace in Thomas's writings. The Holy Roman Empire itself goes as unmentioned as the historical myths by which its authority was commonly defended. Almost unmentioned, too, are the crusades to win back and hold Jerusalem and the Holy Land, vast political ventures closely involving members of his family and vigorously promoted by associates such as Urban IV and his own teacher Albert.[d] The papacy's secular or political authority Thomas mentions only twice, in passages remarkable for their terse ambiguity (see x.5); it finds no place in his two main treatises on theology, and the claims of the political canon lawyers and decretalists might never have been made, for all that Thomas says. Like his treatise on law, the little tract on government (De Regno) which he undertook to compose for the young Norman king of Cyprus is silent about the political conditions, problems, and upheavals which marked their times.[e]

1.2. *The Great Conversation*

Instead, Thomas's readers overhear him, so to speak, engaging in a vast trans-temporal conversation. This extended far beyond the scholars of twelfth- and thirteenth-century Christendom, and embraced the masters of inquiry, reflection, and theory in classical Greece (Aristotle and through him the Pre-socratics and Plato), republican Rome (Cicero), the late imperial and post-imperial Roman provinces (Augustine and Boethius), eleventh-century Persia (Avicenna/Ibn Sina), and twelfth-century Islamic Spain (Averroes/Ibn Rushd) and Egypt (Rabbi Moses Maimonides), to mention only a few leading participants. Aquinas entered into this conversation not later than his fifteenth year, when in November 1239 he began studying at the University of Naples.

This school of general and legal studies was founded by Frederick II in 1224, to rival the papal university and law school of Bologna, and to train men for imperial service. For almost five years Thomas followed the course in liberal arts and philosophy. He presumably read logic in some of Aristotle's logic books (*Organon*) with Boethius' commentary, grammar in some classical Latin sources, rhetoric in Ciceronian treatises, arithmetic, music, and harmonic theory in Boethius, geometry in Euclid, and astronomy in Ptolemy. An Irish professor taught him from Aristotle's books of 'natural philosophy' (natural sciences), at that time excluded from public study in the leading university, the University of Paris. Doubtless it was at Naples that Aquinas began to understand how quite different sciences can converge on the same conclusion by different arguments and data—'as, for example, when the truth that the earth is round[f] is demonstrated by means of one premiss by the astronomer (i.e. by means of solar and lunar eclipses) and by means of another premiss by the natural scientist (i.e. by means of the motion of heavy objects towards the [earth's] centre)'.[2]

Greek, Latin, Jewish, and Moslem culture met and mixed at the court and university of Frederick II, *stupor mundi* ('wonder of the world'). In the early 1230s Frederick's court astrologer (astronomer-meteorologist) Michael Scot was producing Latin translations of many of Averroes' commentaries on Aristotle—a project he had begun in Toledo on the borders of Christendom and Islam, and carried forward in Bologna. Aquinas' earliest philosophical writing,

---

[2] *Post.* I. 41 n. 16 [371].

in about 1252, was closely engaged with, and considerably indebted to, the great Arab commentators.[g]

By that time, Aquinas had spent six or seven years studying with the polymath German philosopher, natural scientist, and theologian Albert. The first two or three (1245/6–48) were probably spent at the Dominican studium in Paris (perhaps also attending lectures in the University of Paris). The next three or four (1248–51) were spent at the Dominican studium which Albert had just founded in Cologne. Albert the Great was then in the early stages of his twenty-year project of making 'intelligible to the Latins' (the West) the whole corpus of human learning, as found in Aristotle, in the Arab commentators, and in 'new sciences'. We have versions of Aquinas' own notes from two of Albert's courses, one of them a commentary on Aristotle's *Ethics*.[h]

Aristotle presents his *Ethics* as the first part of a comprehensive 'philosophy of human affairs';[3] Thomas, who never took time out to learn much Greek (or French or German), had to wait until the early 1260s before reading the second part, the *Politics*. By then he had already published some observations on political theory, scattered about in his first major work, an immense and brilliant commentary (1252/3–7) on the standard theological compendium, Peter Lombard's *Sentences*. These observations for the most part reflect the views of human social and political life suggested by Aristotle's *Ethics* and *Metaphysics*.

1.3. *Among Mendicants and Professors*

Thomas's family had hoped their youngest son would become a Benedictine monk, and perhaps eventually, by joint papal and imperial appointment, abbot of the uniquely ancient and wealthy monastery of Monte Cassino, overlooking the Rome to Naples road only ten miles east of Roccasecca. But Thomas was of independent mind and will, and turned instead to the Dominicans, the Order of Preaching Friars founded in the first two decades of the century by the Spaniard Dominic de Guzman.

Life as a Dominican friar shared with monastic life the constant rhythm of choir and corporate prayer at seven or eight appointed hours of day and night, and the vows of personal poverty, chastity,

---

[3] Cf. *Nic. Eth.* I. 2. 1094^{b}11, I. 13. 1102^{a}12, 10. 9. 1181^{b}14–15.

and obedience to one's superiors in the order. It differed from monastic life in three important ways. Dominic's order, like the order founded in the same decades by Francis of Assisi, was intended to rely for its upkeep not on landed estates but on begging. Friars were, in principle, mendicants.[i] Second, they were not tied to one house, but were always liable to be moved about from one to another, or sent out for preaching or study. And third, they were preachers (or the teachers of preachers). Indeed, Dominic's was the first religious order founded specifically for preaching. The Dominican's vocation of expounding and debating Catholic teaching, in face of the doubts and denials which troubled the age,[4] was to be grounded in academic study, and carried forward in urban centres of intellectual ferment such as the new universities or studia of Bologna, Paris, Oxford, Naples, Montpellier . . .

Thomas's family vigorously opposed his Dominican vocation. When he joined the order towards the end of his studies in Naples, the family sought first to deflect him with a papally sponsored offer of appointment to some attractive Church office. Then, when Thomas was passing through Tuscany, heading for Paris with a group of senior Dominicans, his brother Reginald got Frederick II's leave to seize him. He was taken first to Monte Sangiovanni, then to Roccasecca, and for more than a year was restrained from leaving these castles. He is said to have put the time to good scholarly use, studying and doubtless largely committing to his immensely capacious memory the whole Latin Bible and Peter Lombard's compendium of the theology of the Church Fathers, tutoring some of his sisters, and corresponding with former classmates of his in Naples.

His release by the family in 1245 was accompanied, it seems, by another papal offer, the abbacy of Monte Cassino itself and permission to hold it even as a Dominican. Not for the first time or the last, Aquinas refused the papal offer; in 1265 he declined to be appointed archbishop of Naples.[j]

The way of life that he preferred to these positions of power, wealth, and relative ease was most austere, not so much in food and drink as in watching and wakefulness. We know the daily rhythm of his later years. Like other professors, Aquinas would regularly start his two or three hours of lectures each day in term at six in the morning. He began his day well before that, saying his

[4] See II-II q. 10 a. 7c and ad 3.

own mass and attending the mass said by his personal assistant; after lecturing he would write and dictate until the midday meal, which he would follow with private prayer and a short siesta. Having worked far into the night, he would pray in the chapel while others in the priory were asleep; as his confrères got up for the midnight services, he would slip back into his cell for a moment so that he could go in to choir with them. In less than twenty-five years, he wrote over eight and a half million words, in Latin's brevity, and in tightly disciplined[5] argument, much of it dense with citation, quotation, and allusion. He read widely, and kept up with the work of other scholars, constantly adapting his own expositions and arguments to the latest discoveries about texts, the most adequate new translations, and the arguments of other scholars.

Austere, but not a solitary life. True, he scarcely went out for walks, and often skipped refectory meals. But much of his writing was done with secretaries and personal assistants who were his companions in the order. After 1260 his role as a preacher-general required him to attend all governing council (chapter) meetings of the order's Roman province, and any meeting of the order's supreme governing council (general chapter) held in that province. The constitution of the Dominican order (though it wins no more attention than the Holy Roman Empire in Aquinas' works) was of the kind he calls 'well mixed', combining the merits of monarchy, aristocracy, and democracy:

the government of any city-state[k] or kingdom is best ordered when somebody appointed by virtue of personal excellence {secundum virtutem} presides over everyone, with subordinates similarly governing by virtue of and in accordance with their true merits {secundum virtutem}, and yet rulership belongs to everyone because anyone is eligible to be elected and each ruler is elected by everyone. For that is the best constitution, one well mixed out of monarchy (inasmuch as one person presides), aristocracy (in as much as the many who rule do so *secundum virtutem*), and democracy or the power of the

---

[5] But one must not exaggerate the precision and rigour; he worked always in a hurry, made many mistakes of composition, corrected some with care and left others surprisingly uncorrected. The golden rule for readers of his autographs as for interpreters of his work is: remain aware of a certain looseness ('souplesse'), even of a certain amount of approximation ('d'une certain dose d'à peu près'): Gils (1992: 201). Another of his most important 20th-century editors speaks of the mixture of carefulness and negligence, of clarity of thought and liberty of form, that characterize his intellectual physiognomy: Gauthier, in *Opera* 48. B51.

people (inasmuch as those who rule can be chosen from among the ordinary people, and this election of rulers belongs to the people as a whole).[6,l]

The government of Aquinas' order involved all this, as well as that constant rotation of rulers and ruled which he associates with good government.[7] So elections, voting, the debates of deliberative and governing bodies, and the accompanying give and take, must have become a regular part of Aquinas' cycle of activities.

And a considerable part of his life was spent on the road. Dominicans, unlike abbots and bishops, were meant to go everywhere on foot (except where one could go by boat). Aquinas, though notably big, heavy, and slow-moving, was a conscientious member of the order, and so must have hiked thousands of miles. Naples to Paris is about 1,100 miles, Paris to Cologne over 300, Paris to Valenciennes and back over 250, and Paris to Rome and back nearly 2,000, though Aquinas travelled parts of some of these journeys by ship and river boat. Every year's chapter meeting meant days on the Italian roads.

No trees overhang the roads from Naples to southern France today, but Aquinas' last illness came after a blow to the head from a branch, somehow, soon after leaving Naples for an eleven-week journey to Lyons. Thirteenth-century foot travellers faced many perils, such as floods, beasts, and outlaws. Their way took them, in the passing company of farm labourers, pilgrims, merchants, soldiers, players, and vagrants, back and forth between the old world of landed castles and monasteries and the new world of the trading cities.[m] Aquinas gives no more than hints of his aliveness to the different charms, opportunities, and dangers of these worlds. But the diversities of the human condition are not overlooked in his pages; his attentive reading (not least of the Old Testament) and his months of living on the road forbade naïvety.

Aquinas the mendicant friar became a regent master (full professor) in the University of Paris in 1256, about four years below the minimum age under university rules. His appointment met intense opposition. The Dominicans were nominating him to a chair they had gained in 1230 by non-participation in an academic strike. In the intervening twenty-five years, many professors had come to

---

[6] I-II q. 105 a. 1c (for the Latin, see n. l). See further VIII.2 at nn. 37–59 below.

[7] In 'political' as distinct from 'despotic' government, 'the roles {personae} of ruler and subject are interchanged {communantur} for the sake of equality and, moreover, many people are constituted as rulers either in one position of authority or in a number of such positions': *Pol.* 1. 5 n. 2 [90]. See III. 4 and VIII. 2 below.

8

reject the legitimacy of the mendicants' new-model religious life and their papally sponsored freedom from local episcopal control. During the winter of 1255-6 hostility among the masters spread among students and townspeople; Louis IX felt obliged to furnish a round-the-clock military guard for the priory where Aquinas lived (a few hundred yards south of the just-completed cathedral of Notre Dame). A papal letter to the university, dated 17 June 1256, deplores the efforts of masters and students to ostracize and disrupt the recent inaugural lecture of 'our beloved son friar Thomas de Aquino'. Over the next twelve months or so, the Pope sent a dozen or more letters, to the king, to many high officials of the French Church, to the chancellor and the leaders of the professorial opposition, demanding that the mendicant orders be accepted in the university and that Aquinas and the Italian Franciscan scholar Bonaventure be fully received into the consortium of regent masters {universitas magistrorum}. Not until the autumn of 1257 did the masters defer.[n] Aquinas then taught as professor of theology in the University of Paris until the end of the academic year in 1259.

Antagonism to the mendicants flared up again in Paris in the late 1260s, along with increasingly bitter controversy between the Dominicans and the Franciscans themselves. Aquinas had spent most of the decade teaching young Dominicans practical moral theology, writing commentaries on biblical texts, and undertaking scholarly projects for the papacy, first at Orvieto (north of Rome), and then as sole professor at a new Dominican studium in Rome. In mid- or late 1268 (perhaps soon after the studium was pillaged by the forces of the doomed Conradin, last of the Hohenstaufens) the order suddenly recalled him to Paris.

There new and more radical doubts and denials had emerged, along with a recrudescence of the old forms of opposition. Aristotle's works of natural philosophy had become compulsory in the arts (philosophy) faculty in 1255; in the late 1260s professors deeply influenced by Averroes' commentaries were theorizing about human intellect, and about the universe's eternity, in ways they themselves took to be contrary to Christian teaching. In 1269-72 Aquinas produced treatises on these diverse matters, defending the new patterns of religious life, refuting the Averroistic notion that we all share one intelligence, and showing that the universe's creation at some first point of time can neither be disproved nor proved by natural science or metaphysics.[o]

At points in these treatises Aquinas allows himself some expressions of passion {indignatio}[8] and polemic.[9] But the situation—perhaps not least the Franciscan opposition to Aristotelian positions in philosophy—also seemed to him to call for a complete and non-polemical commentary on all Aristotle's major works, then being freshly translated. In the late 1260s and early 1270s he produced line-by-line commentaries on twelve works, including the *Metaphysics* and the *Ethics* (both completed), and the *Politics* (not completed). Aquinas considered philosophy a necessary part of the project of Catholic theology, and judged that philosophy finds its appropriate completion in that theology. But he also considered that natural science and philosophy—not least the 'practical philosophy' by which we can better understand and direct our actions and our societies—can be authentically and, to a considerable extent, fruitfully pursued without appeal to the sources (x.5) which make possible that theological completion.

During the same four years, among many other teaching and writing projects, Aquinas continued work on his great theological treatise, *Summa Theologiae*, begun in Rome by 1266. In the forty-five months of his second Paris professorship, he carried it forward into its treatment of morality, law, and politics.

1.4. *Appealing to Reasons*

The *Summa Theologiae* sets out, sympathetically and plausibly, more than 10,000 objections to the positions it proposes and defends. Like no one before him and not many since, Aquinas takes the academic 'comprehensive textbook', keeps or even enhances its coherence and coverage, but re-creates it in disputation form.

Two sorts of disputation were central to the university of Aquinas' time. Regular disputations were structured by the master as a course, an orderly sequence of questions arising either from a set text (as we see in Aquinas' or Bonaventure's commentaries on Lombard's *Sentences*) or from the master's own understanding of some field of topics (as we see in Aquinas' extensive *Disputed Questions on Truth* (and other matters), *De Veritate*, and *Disputed*

---

[8] See *Unit.* v, line 397 [122] [266].
[9] Cf. II-II q. 38 a. 1c: 'contention' is admirable when it is 'a contesting of error, with appropriate pungency {impugnatio falsitatis cum debito modo acrimoniae}'.

Questions on Evil, De Malo). More occasional (and voluntary) 'quodlibetal' disputations, in Paris held before Christmas and Easter, required the master and his assistant to tackle questions about anything {de quolibet} raised by anybody {a quolibet} in the audience. Twelve sets of quodlibetal disputations by Aquinas survive; altogether they consider 260 topics, metaphysical, theological, or moral. One questioner asks whether Christianity would have been credible if Jesus had done no miracles, the next asks whether young Jewish children who want to become Christians can be baptized without their parents' permission; one questioner asks whether children are morally obliged to obey parental commands to do something not otherwise morally required, the next whether vendors are morally obliged to disclose latent defects in their goods. Does an erroneous conscience bind? Is something done in fear done voluntarily? Should you pay back to a friend the money you borrowed to ransom yourself from murderous bandits? And so on.ᴾ

Late in Aquinas' career as a professor in Paris, a quodlibetal question was put to him: Should professors of theology settle these or any other disputed questions by reason or by authority? His response indicates why his work remains relevant to non-believers. Here it is in full:

Any activity is to be pursued in a way appropriate to its purpose. Disputations have one or other of two purposes.

One sort is designed {ordinatur} to remove doubts about *whether* such-and-such is so. In disputations of this sort you should above all use authorities acceptable to those with whom you are disputing; with Jews, for example, you should appeal to the authority of the Old Testament; with Manichees, who reject the Old Testament, you should use only the New; with Christians who have split off from us, e.g. the Greek [Orthodox], who accept both Testaments but reject the teaching of our [Catholic] saints, you should rely on the authority of the Old and New Testaments and of those church teachers {doctores} they do accept. *And if you are disputing with people who accept no authority, you must resort to natural reasons.*[10]

Then there is the professorial academic disputation, designed not for

[10] A parallel passage, *ScG* I c. 2 n. 3 [11], adds that we are all 'compelled' {coguntur} to give our assent to natural reason (i.e. reasons accessible without reasoning from authority, i.e. reasons called 'moral or philosophical reasons' in another parallel passage: *Rat.* c. 1 [955]). Elsewhere, he had refined this: some of these reasons are strictly compelling, in that, once we have become aware of them, we simply cannot withhold our intellectual assent to them; others depend for their force on our dedication to truth, and we are psychologically capable of (often unreasonably) evading the argument and withholding assent (II *Sent.* d. 25 q. 1 a. 2c).

removing error but for teaching, so that those listening may be led to an understanding of the truth with which the professor {magister} is concerned. And here you must rely upon reasons, reasons which track down the root of the truth and create a real knowledge of how it is that your assertions are true. Otherwise, if professors settle questions by bare authorities, listeners are indeed told that such-and-such is so, but gain nothing in the way of knowledge or understanding {scientiae vel intellectus}, and go away empty.[11]

This is one of the few occasions when Aquinas feels no need to reply explicitly to the 'objections', the counter-positions which (perhaps following something proposed from the audience) he puts in the form of arguments, usually logically valid and more or less plausible, immediately after the question.

Aquinas ends his Paris tract against his professorial critics with the words: 'If any wish to write replies to my defence, I shall be delighted. For there is no better way of disclosing truth and refuting error than by opposing the opposition. "Iron sharpens iron; friend shapes up friend"'.[12] The proverb indicates the conditions under which disputation, being friendly collaboration[q] in seeking truth, yields understanding rather than illusory confirmation of prejudice or vain triumph over opposition.[13] Aquinas' reason for structuring his *Summa Theologiae* in disputation form is suggested by a remark in another of his last writings: 'Anyone who wants to really understand and know some truth will find it very helpful to know the *questions* {dubitationes} and objections raised about it. By resolution of puzzles {solutio dubitatorum} one discovers the truth, and so, if one is to know the truth about something, it is very important that one see the *reasons* for holding a contrary opinion.'[14] The transcriptions of his

---

[11] *Quodl.* IV (Mar.–Apr. 1271) q. 9 a. 3c (emphasis added, here as elsewhere unless otherwise indicated). On those specifically theological reasons which, being accessible only by faith (i.e. being warrantable only on the presupposition—which may or may not be independently reasonable—that God has somehow revealed them), are not 'natural reasons' and yet are far more reasonable than bare appeal to some authoritative statement, see X.1, X.5 below.

[12] *Perf.* c. 30 [26], lines 103–4 [734], quoting Prov. 27: 17.

[13] Aquinas also quoted it in his *Summa contra Gentiles* when defending Christian moral teachings with arguments addressed to non-believers; noting the dangers of solitary life and lonely thinking (see n. q), he added: 'people give each other mutual help in acquiring knowledge; one stimulates another to good or pulls the other back from bad. Hence the proverb, "Iron sharpens iron; friend shapes up friend"': *ScG* III c. 128 n. 2 [3002]. Cf. *In I Cor.* 11. 4 ad v. 18 [628].

[14] *Cael.* 1. 22 n. 3 [223]. See also n. 4 [224]: 'doubts emerge from reasons, and as long as one is still puzzled {dubitat}, with one's doubts unresolved, one's mind is like someone

---

lectures and Bible commentaries enable us to catch an echo of his voice; though these are not disputations, Aquinas' consideration of the text presses forward by proposing the questions, doubts, and interrogative objections to which he replies (sometimes by recalling the interpretations made by the Fathers of the early Church, sometimes simply in his own words and on his own authority). And in these lectures, the phrase 'Here there is a *quaestio*' means 'Here there is a difficulty, an objection, a source of dispute or doubt, and thus a question to be pursued, answered, resolved, as best we can.'

Edifices as vast and elaborate as the unfinished *Summa Theologiae*, or as Aquinas' writings taken as a whole, can call to mind the Gothic cathedral. The hundreds of cathedrals and great abbeys which were completed in Aquinas' lifetime, many of them in or near Paris, were among the loveliest of that supremely complex and powerful style. They make manifest the intelligence, energy, and strength of the individuals who conceived them, and the societies that built them, amid all the weaknesses, injustices, and disorder of the age. But if Aquinas was interested in the architectural developments of his time, he does not say so. *Claritas*—lucidity, splendour—is central to his thoughts about beauty, but the incomparable luminescence of the Gothic stained-glass windows is as absent as the Holy Roman Empire from his writings. Some of his main philosophical positions are nearer to Plato's than to Aristotle's (and it is said that he wanted to do a commentary on the *Timaeus*, the only available work of Plato's). But his philosophical discourse, though subtle and not without moments of eloquence, is very remote from the imaginative play of Plato's dialogues.[r] Aquinas intended all his work to emulate and surpass Aristotle's in persuading simply by its lucidity, by its clear statement of straightforward *reasons*, free from subtext and any esoteric purpose or 'art of writing'. Even his religious poetry, while dense in allusion, minimizes symbolism and appeals directly to intellect. Still, a keen sense of rhythm discreetly governs his prose, which achieves

tied up and unable to move.' Also *Meta.* III. I [338–45], which underlines the importance of considering doubts (puzzles, problems, difficulties) {dubitationes} wherever they come from, and characterizes *philosophy* precisely as the unrestricted consideration of truth {universalis consideratio de veritate} which therefore involves an unrestricted doubt-raising about truth {universalis dubitatio de veritate}, pursuing simultaneously particular and general doubt(s): n. 6 [343]. This is the *dubitatio*, not of scepticism but of inquiry and discernment {non infidelitatis sed admirationis et discussionis}: cf. III q. 27 a. 4 ad 2.

elegance by artful simplicity and a word-order designed to articulate the propositional structure, the sequence of thought, the
emphases required by the underlying argument.

In questions of philosophy, Aquinas was quite willing to be an
innovator, and to take and defend a position which virtually everyone, even friends and confrères, thought seriously mistaken and
dangerously misleading. Almost no one, for example, agreed with
his notion (see v.8 below) that the human soul—intellectual, animal, and vegetative all in one—is the form, the intrinsic organizing
principle, of the human body and of every level of one's life, one's
reality. (Only later did this conception of the distinctively human
unity of body and soul win the favour it deserves.) But more often
he was content to restate coherently a philosophical and theological tradition already two millennia long; the help persons can give
each other in reaching the truth includes, above all, the great help
one can get from all one's predecessors.[15] His theorizing's rational
soundness, explanatory power, and detachment from the conditions of his own time,[t] and even of his own life, contribute greatly
to its lasting worth. Where his positions seem in need of revision or
reversal, one may think that he deferred too readily to the assumptions and categories accepted in the great millennial conversation
and in the institutions of his era. But in debating with him as he
would have wished, one must be cautious about one's own presuppositions. We may accuse Aquinas of failing to subject conventional wisdom fully to evidence and argument, but we must also
allow his arguments to put our own age's conventional wisdom to
the test of reason.

Aquinas, then, would have had little interest in a chapter of this
kind; perhaps he would have sought what matter for reflection he
could find in the chapters which follow. The disputation format
which he so valued as the matrix of inquiry and exposition had this
motive: to meet questioners—listeners or readers—where they
were, as they were. Today's readers are not placed where his
were. So I shall constantly cut across the grain of his expositions,
to see how far the substance of his theory meets the questions to
which—we think today—a critical theory of political, social, and
legal thought must respond in any age.

---

[15] *Meta.* II. I n. 15 [287]. Philosophy suffers severe set-backs and regressions, sometimes from wars or natural disasters etc. (*Meta.* XII. 10 n. 30 [2597]), but can and does from
time to time get things clearer, not least under the stimulus of earlier mistakes (*Meta.* II.
I n. 15 [287]).

Notes

a. I adopt the following chronology, conjectural in various respects (see generally Tugwell 1988: 201–34, 291–324; Torrell 1996: 1–12, 18–25, 36–8, 96–101, 117–20, 142–4, 179–82, 247–9, 289–93; Marc (1966)).

1225	Birth at Roccasecca
1230/1–9	Oblate at Monte Cassino abbey
1239–44	Student at University of Naples
1244	Joins Dominicans (Order of Preachers)
1244–5	Detained by family at Monte Sangiovanni and Roccasecca
1245/6–8	Student at Dominican studium, Paris
1248–51	Student at Dominican studium, Cologne
1251–2/3	Lecturer on the Bible, University of Paris
1253–6	Bachelor in Theology, lectures on Lombard's *Sentences*, University of Paris
1256–9	Paris: Master (Professor) in Theology
1259/60	Southern France and northern Italy (Bologna)
1260–1	Dominican studium, Naples
1261–5	Orvieto: Lecturer in Dominican studium; scholarly work for papal curia
1265–8	Rome: establishing and teaching in Dominican studium
1268–72	Paris: University Master (Professor) in Theology
1272–3	Naples: establishing and teaching in Dominican general studium (lectures included in University of Naples curriculum)
1274	(7 March) Death at Fossanova Cistercian monastery

b. *Aquinas' birth* . . . The conventional dates are 1224 or 1225. Reasons for accepting 1226 are given in Tugwell (1988: 291–2). Weisheipl (1983: 3–4, 112, 411, 413, 465) is consistent with this, once Weisheipl's seemingly faulty arithmetic is corrected. But see Torrell (1996: 1), favouring 1225.

c. *Thomas and the execution of Reginald* . . . See Foster (1959: 41, 71, 108); Torrell (1996: 3).

d. *Crusades and crusaders* . . . Aquinas has a sentence defending the possibility of a religious society established to fight for the Holy Land (II-II q. 188 a. 3 ad 3), and a paragraph comparing the obligation to go on a crusade unfavourably with the obligation an individual may have undertaken by making a vow to become a monk or friar (q. 189 a. 3 obj. 3 and ad 3). Questioners in quodlibetal disputations ask him whether the spiritual benefits of vowing to go to the relief of the Holy Land are lost if one dies before reaching there (answer: not necessarily: *Quodl.* II q. 8 a. 2), and are even greater if one dies on the way back rather than the way there (answer: other things being equal, yes: *Quodl.* V q. 7 a. 2). Another such questioner asks about risking one's wife's chastity by going on crusade without her (Aquinas' answer: if she has good reason not to come, and is not willing to be chaste in your absence, you should not go: *Quodl.* IV q. 7 a. 2c). This last answer (Mar.–Apr. 1271) is more favourable to the spouses' interests in the marriage than his earlier, more conventional (see *Opera* 25/2. 331 n.) treatment of the question in IV *Sent.* d. 32 a. 4 (= *Supp.* q. 64 a. 4) ad 1, where he noted the ecclesiastical norm that the vow to go on crusade can be taken by a husband without his wife's consent, just as a husband has the right to go to war for his feudal lord without her consent—but that such a vow cannot be taken by the wife (though the wife's marital/sexual rights {ius} are preserved—it was thought—by the fact that she can accompany her husband on crusade). On equality within marriage, see v.7 below.

e. *Silence about political conditions of the time* . . . Eschmann (1949, xxx–viii) shows how, behind the text of *De Regno*, one can detect some awareness of the circumstances of Cyprus and its Norman king. But this should not be exaggerated; Genicot (1976) assembles much evidence for his conclusion that though the *De Regno* breathes 13th-century ideas and outlook, it scarcely reflects the political realities, or even the principal concerns of the age. The tract makes reference to many authorities and illustrative cases, but none of them is later than the 7th century AD. Another example: Aquinas' discussion of the dissolution of oaths and allegiance, in *ST* II-II q. 12 a. 2, is written only twenty-five years after the Pope spectacularly released Frederick II's subjects from their allegiance, but Aquinas refers to no event later than the 4th century AD and to no source more recent than 1184.

f. *'The earth is round' proved by convergence of arguments from different sciences* . . . The fable that medieval thinkers believed the world to be flat was invented by Enlightenment propagandists in the early 19th century (see Russell 1991); for a partial antecedent, see Hobbes (1651, c. 46 n. 42). That the earth is spherical was accepted by Augustine of Hippo, many other Church Fathers, and by all educated people; that it can be proved scientifically to be round {rotunda, sphaerica} is one of Aquinas' stock examples of scientific method: see e.g. I q. 1 a. 1 ad 2, I-II q. 54 a. 2 ad 2; *Post.* I. 41 n. 16 [371]; *Trin.* q. 5 a. 3 ad 7 (all making the point about the convergence of proofs from different sciences, some more mathematical, some more physical); for the detailed argument from lunar eclipses, see *Cael.* II. 28 nn. 2–3 [541–2]. The view is essentially Aristotle's, as is the corollary view that the earth must be small in comparison with the sun, the planets, and the stars: Aristotle, *De Caelo* 2. 13. 297^{b}3–298^{a}20.

g. *Aquinas' debt to Arab commentators* . . . See e.g. *Princ.* introd. in *Opera* 43, 5–6; Torrell (1996: 48–9).

h. *Aquinas' transcription of Albert's course on the Nicomachean Ethics* . . . See *Alberti Magni Omnia Opera* xiv, ed. W. Kübel (Münster, 1968); Gauthier in *Opera* 48, app. p. xvii, notes that one-third of young Thomas's time in Cologne must have been spent on this partly secretarial work for Albert.

i. *Friars as mendicants* . . . In Aquinas' time, Dominican begging had become restricted to an annual late-summer quest for funds; Franciscans, however, still went out to beg every day: Tugwell (1988: 623 n. 25).

j. *Aquinas' refusals of papal offers of ecclesiastical preferment* . . . See Tugwell (1988: 205, 207–8, 224). We should presume that St Thomas's refusals (if indeed there were such offers) were consistent with his own teaching (c.1256): 'Some say that the Pope cannot order someone to accept episcopacy, because consent should be free. But if this were the position, ecclesiastical order would be ruined {perire}. For unless people could be compelled {cogi} to accept the government of the Church {regimen ecclesiae}, the Church could not be preserved; for sometimes those suitable for a position will not accept it unless compelled {coacti}': IV *Sent.* d. 29 a. 4 (= *Supp.* q. 47 a. 6) ad 4. Likewise III *Sent.* d. 39 a. 3 sol. 1 ad 3: 'although fleeing from prelacy can sometimes proceed from good, it is always bad to resist it obstinately {pertinaciter}'. His final treatments, c.1271–2, put the position (though not the case for it) more tightly: it is in principle proper—and even praiseworthy if one is motivated by awareness of one's deficiencies—to decline appointment as a bishop where there is no emergency requiring one's acceptance for the well-being of the Church; but when the person calling one to this office makes the appointment an order {injunctio; praeceptum} it is not morally permissible to persist *finaliter* in one's refusal even if one's motive for refusing is one's dedication to the contemplative life: II-II q. 185 a. 2c and ad 1 and ad 3; *Quodl.* V q. 11 a. 2c. (Dominican life, Aquinas argues, is one sort—the best sort—of contemplative life: II-II q. 188 a. 6; and see IV.2 at n. 29 below.)

k. *'City-state'* . . . I shall sometimes use this expression to translate *civitas*; Aquinas' use of this term is rarely restricted to the city-states (characteristically not kingly) of classical Greece or medieval Italy, and is often best conveyed simply by the modern term 'state'. Still, it sometimes retains a nuance (whether of limited size or of republicanism) allowing it, as here, to be distinguished from the kind of state he calls a 'kingdom' {regnum}. See VII.1 at nn. 2–4 below.

l. *Mixed government is best* . . . 'Unde optima ordinatio principum est in aliqua civitate vel regno, in qua unus praeficitur secundum virtutem, qui omnibus praesit; et sub ipso sunt aliqui principantes secundum virtutem; et tamen talis principatus ad omnes pertinet, tum quia ex omnibus eligi possunt, tum quia etiam ab omnibus eliguntur. Talis enim est optima politia, *bene commixta* ex regno, inquantum unus praeest, et aristocratia, inquantum multi principantur secundum virtutem, et ex democratia, idest potestate populi, inquantum ex popularibus possunt eligi principes, et ad populum pertinet electio principum': I-II q. 105 a. 1c.

m. *Aquinas moved from the world of castles and monasteries to the urban world* . . . See Synan (1978). On his interest in military matters (to which the knightly world was ordered), see Synan (1988). On the opportunities and dangers of urban life, see *Reg.* II. 7 and 8 (II. 3 and 4) [137–48] [839–46].

n. *University resistance to papal directives to admit Thomas as a master . . .* Writing in 1256, between inception as a master and acceptance by the other masters, Aquinas expressed a severe view of resistance to papal authority, including papal authority over universities: *Impugn.* II c. 2 ad 8–10 [66–9].

o. *Aquinas' polemical treatises of 1269–72 . . .* See *Perf., Retra., Unit.,* and *Aet.* In IV *Sent.* d. 49 q. 1 a. 1 sol. 4c (*c.*1257), Aquinas is already denouncing the absurdity of the opinion that the soul which is the form of the human body is not essentially intelligence but only a kind of reflection {refulgentia} of an intelligence which is *separata* from one's soul and shared, as a *single* intellect, by everyone {unus [intellectus] communis omnibus}.

p. *Aquinas' quodlibetal questions . . .* The answers, put very briefly: (1) Yes (*Quodl.* II. q. 4 a. 1); (2) No (a. 2); (3) Only if the parental directive is within parental jurisdiction over the household or the child's education and morals (q. 5 a. 1); (4) Disclosure is not required by justice if the price is not higher than the thing, with its defect, is worth and the buyer is put to no unfair risk (a. 2); (5) Yes (*Quodl.* III q. 12 a. 2); (6) Strictly speaking, it is done voluntarily, but in a certain respect it is involuntary and necessitated (*Quodl.* v q. 5 a. 3); (7) Yes (*Quodl.* v q. 9 a. 1).

q. *Collaboration as opposed to solitary life and lonely thinking . . .* 'Woe to those who are alone' {Vae soli!}: see e.g. *ScG* III c. 128 n. 2 [3002]; *In Rom.* 1. 8 ad v. 31 [165]. On the desirability of friendship and companionship in intellectual projects as well as other sorts of activities, see *Impugn.* II c. 2c [53]: 'In all types of enterprise {negotii} which can be carried forward by a number of people, the *societas* of many {plurium} is very fruitful. So *Prov.* 18: 19 says "Brother helped by brother is a well-found city", and *Eccles.* 4: 9 says "It is better to be two together than one, for the two have the profit of their association {emolumentum societatis suae}." But pre-eminently in the acquiring of knowledge, the multiple association of many students all together is helpful . . .'; also *Eth.* VIII. 1 n. 3 [1540], x. 10 n. 16 [2096].

r. *Aquinas on Plato, metaphor, and imagery (versus Aristotle) . . .* See *Cael.* 1. 22 n. 8 [228]:

> Some people say [i] that these poets and philosophers, and above all Plato, did not mean {intellexerunt} what their words on the surface seem to mean {quod sonat secundum superficiem verborum} and that they wished to hide {occultare} their wisdom under stories and enigmatic sayings; and [ii] that it was Aristotle's practice, for the most part, not to object to their meaning, which was sound, but to their words (lest anyone fall into error from this way of speaking) . . . Alexander [of Aphrodisias], on the other hand, wanted to say [i] that Plato and the other ancient philosophers meant what their words seem to mean and thus [ii] that Aristotle was trying to argue not only against their words but also against what they [these authors] meant. But it matters little to us which of these views is right. For *philosophy's concern is not to find*

out what people have thought but what is the truth of the matters in question {studium philosophiae non est ad hoc quod sciatur quid homines senserint sed qualiter se habet veritas rerum}.

See also *An.* 1. 8 n. 1 [107], which is sharper:

Here we should note that in criticizing Plato's opinions, Aristotle often is criticizing them not as Plato intended them but as superficially understood {quantum ad sonum verborum: literally, 'according to the sound of the words'}. He does this because Plato had a bad method of teaching—for he says everything figuratively and teaches by symbols, meaning {intendens} by his words something other than the words themselves seem to mean {aliud . . . quam sonent}, as when he said that the soul is a circle.

The point had been made earlier by Averroes, Albert, and others: see *An., Opera* 45/1. 38n. Aquinas, at all events, shares Aristotle's view that poetic and metaphorical speech has no place in philosophy, and that the philosopher should teach without such extrinsic matter {ex propriis}: *Meta.* 1. 15 n. 7 [231]. On these issues, and on the philosophical intentions in Aquinas' style, see Chenu (1963: 117–23, 169–72).

II

Subject-Matter
and Method

II.1. *Beginnings: The Four Types of Order*

There are points in his work where Aquinas has a special opportunity to say just what he thinks a theory of human action and society is about.

One is the prologue to the second part of his *Summa Theologiae*. This whole part will, he says, be about people precisely as *principium*, source, of their own deeds, having free choice {liberum arbitrium; libera electio} and power {potestas} over those deeds.[1] Indeed, as he promptly adds, one's deeds (acts, actions)[2] are really human only if one is fully in charge—ruler, master, owner {dominus} of them.[3]

So the *Summa*'s hundreds of disputations and thousands of

---

[1] I-II prol.

[2] Some of what one does is not by free choice but is rather a matter of spontaneity (see e.g. *Ver.* q. 24 a. 12c), and Aquinas distinguishes such 'acts of a human being {actiones hominis}' from 'human act(ion)s': I-II q. 1 a. 1c. He is not concerned to establish a technical jargon, but rather to point to the substantive distinction, and even on the same page (ad 2) he calls a freely chosen action an *actio hominis*.

[3] I-II q. 1 a. 1c. One has this mastery or dominion {dominium} over one's own actions precisely in that one's will is not forced to one or another of opposing proposals: *Pot.* q. 3 a. 7 ad 12. Elsewhere he observes that to deny that human persons are each masters of their own acts is to assert something 'impossible, and destructive of all moral philosophy and social-political life {politicae conversationis}': *ScG* II c. 60 n. 5 [1374]; see likewise *Mal.* q. 6 a. un. c; *Unit.* III, lines 336–7 [81] [232]; *Peri.* I. 14 n. 5 [180]; *In Matt.* 2 ad v. 2 [170] ('regimen reipublicae destrueretur').

arguments on good and bad in personal and social life are thematized by three terms—freedom, power, mastery—each drawn from talk about society but here applied to one's own choices and chosen actions.

Another comparably significant point in Aquinas' work is the prologue to his commentary on Aristotle's *Ethics*. Aristotle presents his *Ethics* as the first part of the 'philosophy of human affairs', with his *Politics* the second part (1.2 above); Aquinas, unlike many of Aristotle's more recent readers, takes this plan seriously.[4] In this 750-word prologue, then, supplemented by the 750-word prologue to his *Politics* commentary,[a] Aquinas offers a fundamental account of the place both of that 'philosophy' in the whole field of human thought and of 'human affairs' in the whole scheme of things. Since much in Aristotle's treatment seeks to describe and explain the behaviour of individuals and societies, we have here Aquinas' most careful account of the proper subject-matter, point, and method of social theory, political theory, and legal theory, as well as of ethics and the theory of justice.

Central to that account is the conclusion that sciences {scientiae} are of four irreducibly distinct {diversae}[5] kinds: (1) sciences of matters and relationships {ordo} unaffected by our thinking, i.e. of the 'order of nature {rerum naturalium}' studied by the 'natural philosophy' which includes 'natural science' {[scientia] naturalis},[6] mathematics, and metaphysics; (2) the sciences of the order we can bring into our own thinking, i.e. logic in its widest sense;[b] (3) the sciences of the order we can bring into[c] our deliberating, choosing, and voluntary actions, i.e. the moral, economic, and political sciences compendiously called *philosophia moralis*; (4) the sciences of the multitude of practical arts, the technologies or techniques which, by bringing order into matter of any kind[7] external to our thinking and willing, yield 'things constituted by human reason'.

This account of types of sciences may seem very different from the claim about free choice made in the prologue to the second part

---

[4] e.g. *Eth.* I. 2 n. 13 [31].

[5] 'Diverse' means the very opposite of 'same', in as many senses as there are of 'same' (see *Meta.* v. 12 n. 2 [914]), and is appropriately used of things which differ from each other essentially (see *ST* I q. 31 a. 2c and ad 1), and/or in their way of originating (*Cred.* a. 2 [892]). [6] *Meta.* prol. n. 6.

[7] As, for example, in composing a poem, though 'poems, more than the other technical doings, belong to the reason which makes us the human beings we are {magis ad rationem pertinent secundum quam homo est homo quam alia mechanica opera}': *Eth.* IX. 7 n. 6 [1845].

of the *Summa Theologiae*. But it turns out to involve the same fundamental thesis: human actions, and the societies constituted by human action, cannot be adequately understood as if they were merely (1) natural occurrences, (2) contents of thought, or (4) products of techniques of mastering natural materials (even the materials of our bodily make-up). True, there are elements in human life and behaviour—indeed, specifically human elements—such as the workings of one's digestion, or one's instincts and emotions, which can and should be understood as objects (subject-matter) of natural science. Moreover, deliberate human actions both involve the rational art of logical thinking and exploit practical arts and technologies, often intending and producing a result assessable on its technical merits or demerits. But human actions and societies cannot be adequately described, explained, justified, or criticized unless they are understood as also, and centrally, the carrying out of free choices. For neither the making of free choices nor any of their consequences regarded as such are reducible to nature, logic, or technique. The personal and, in many cases, social self-determination[8] which is the intrinsic and immediate result of every free choice is not an event in the workings of nature, nor a kind of inference, nor the making of a product, though it has analogies with each of those. So, rational reflection on personal and social self-constitution can neither be reduced to, nor adequately modelled upon, a natural science, a logic, or a technology.

The main theorists from Hobbes down to today have more or less consciously rejected this methodological thesis, this anti-reductive conception of social and political theory, and even this conception of ethics. Today, indeed, almost all who write or teach political or social theory are in like case, refusing or failing to acknowledge the reality of free choice, and treating their subject-matter as if it were a natural substance or else a technique or product of technique. Aquinas' methodology offers a radical and, I believe, clearly superior alternative.

In exploring and reflecting upon this methodology, one might first consider Aquinas' beliefs about free choice. But I reserve that issue to the next chapter (III.3). For the moment let it suffice that one makes a free choice when, judging that one has reason(s) or other motives to adopt one possible course of action ('option'), and reason(s) to adopt some incompatible alternative, one adopts one

[8] See text and n. 68 below. Nothing, even internal to oneself, necessitates one's free choices: *Mal.* q. 6 a. un. c.

option (if only to 'do nothing') in preference to the other and so settles what (unless one changes one's mind) one will do.

II.2. *Social Theory Considers Groups and their Actions*

The acts {operationes} of groups and societies, as well as individual actions, fall within the subject-matter of *moralis philosophia*: that is the conclusion of Aquinas' *Ethics* prologue. Why does he think so? The answer can begin with two preliminary clarifications.

First, the name *moralis philosophia* or *philosophia moralis* is not of much moment for Aquinas. Throughout his work he is largely indifferent to academic labels. He is interested, of course, in the working language of educated people. For it provides a fund of reminders of relevant data, and a stock of insights which, when clarified and interrelated, can amount to the sort of intellectual knowledge that deserves to be called *scientia*—well-grounded and personally understood explanatory knowledge which is not merely well certified but includes insight into why the matter stands as it does. But he is not very interested in creating for philosophy, even for his own philosophizing, a unified and stable set of technical terms.[d] Still, it is important to be aware that 'moral philosophy' is not a completely adequate translation of *moralis philosophia*. 'The philosophy of self-determining human conduct' would be a fair rendering.[e] 'Self-determining' signals that *moralis philosophia* is only one of the two parts of 'practical philosophy' {practica philosophia}, the part which concerns actions which 'remain in the person who acts',[9] the other part being the theory or sciences of arts or techniques.[10]

Second: In saying that the philosophical consideration of certain

[9] *Pol.* prol. n. 6 [6]. See also *Eth.* prol. n. 3 [3]: 'The subject-matter of *moralis philosophia* is human action directed to some purpose {ordinata in finem} or again, the human person as someone who, by [free-]willing, acts for end(s) {homo prout est voluntarie agens propter finem}'.

[10] See *Pol.* prol. nn. 5–6 [5–6]: political theory {politica; politica doctrina; civilis scientia} is contained under *practica philosophia*, not as one among the technologies {factivae scientiae; artes mechanicae}, but rather as one among the moral sciences, of action {activae scientiae}, i.e. *scientiae morales*. And *Pol.* 1. 2 n. 12 [53]: '*actio* and *factio* are different in kind {specie}; for *factio* is the sort of doing {operatio} which makes something in matter which is external [to the mind and will] . . . ; *actio*, on the other hand, is the sort of doing which remains [lasts] in the doer {permanens in operante} and bearing on the doer's very life'. As a matter of word usage, the term *factio* can extend to include *actio*

types of social group is part of *moralis philosophia*, Aquinas is not saying that the resulting social theory—my term, not Aquinas'—should be regarded as reducible to, or part of, the theory of individual conduct or individual ethics. Indeed, his *Ethics* prologue denies that. Instead it contends that *moralis philosophia* is divided into three 'parts', two of which I am calling social theory or sciences. These three parts concern the activities of (1) individuals as such, (2) households as such, and (3) the 'civil group' as such (this last part, or type of theory, being called *politica*).[11]

Aquinas does not mean this subdividing of *moralis philosophia* to be taken too strictly; the intermediate theory or science called *oeconomica*, which the prologue treats as concerned with running a household (in Aristotle's Greek an *oikos*), is treated later in the *Ethics* as extending to 'economics' in a wider sense, involving wholesale and retail dealings within and between neighbourhoods and trade-groupings.[f] The important thing in each case is that the theory concerns human activities {operationes}, activities of a kind that should be called *actio* rather than *factio*, i.e. doing (considered precisely as self-determining) rather than making (considered precisely as shaping something outside the acting person's mind and will).

It is important to understand why and how Aquinas relates *groups* and *activities*. A group, association, society, or political community is, says his *Ethics* prologue, a kind of whole {totum}; actions, says his own treatise on justice, are of persons and wholes {suppositorum et totorum}.[12] But a group, Aquinas underlines, is not a unity of 'composition or conjunction {colligatio}[g] or continuity'; it is no more and no less than a unity of order. So the individuals who are 'parts' or members of an armed force not only do things which are part of the actions of that force, but also do things which are not the action or even part of the action of the force as a whole. Contrariwise, the armed force *does* things—surrounds the

of the last-mentioned kind (II-II q. 134 a. 2c), just as 'art' can be either distinguished from or treated as including *moralis philosophia* and practical reasonableness {prudentia}.

[11] *Eth.* prol. n. 6 [6]. Since *civilis* is simply the Latin for the Greek *politikē*, as *civitas* for *polis*, and since the *polis* is the city-state and *politikē* is the theory of such supposedly complete communities, 'civil group' {multitudo civilis} here signifies the sort of community which is or is capable of being a politically organized community and typically organized precisely as a state.

[12] II-II q. 58 a. 2c; also *Unit.* III, line 155 [69] [223]. Aquinas regards persons {suppositi} as wholes {toti} (see e.g. *Quodl.* II q. 2 a. 2), but the dictum in II-II q. 58 seems to extend also to groups as wholes.

enemy, occupies the town, wins the war—which none of the
human individuals who belong to it as its parts do.[13] Thus Aquinas
firmly discourages attempts to understand human societies as
organisms or substances.[14] There are analogies between organisms
and societies; 'the different people in different[15] jobs in a society
are *quasi* (like) the different members (limbs, organs) of a single
natural body';[16] but the disanalogies are fundamentally more
important.

What, then, is a human group's 'order'? Why does such order
make the group unified, one, a whole? Order of this kind has,
says the *Ethics* prologue, two kinds of element. There is (A) the
interrelationship(s), the co-ordination, between the members of the
group (the parts of the whole). More importantly and fundamentally, there is (B) the relation between the group and the purpose or
point (*finis*, 'end') of the associating-together and co-ordination by
its members which makes it a group.[17] But the primacy of (B) in
explanation (a primacy explored throughout this chapter) in no way
eliminates the importance of the factors co-ordinated.

Take, for instance, political theory {politica} and its subject-
matter. Political theory (says the *Politics* prologue) considers the
'parts and *principia*' of political communities (states). Here 'parts'
means elements such as individual persons, families, and neighbourhoods. And *principia* (literally 'principles') includes everything
else of explanatory significance, including origins, moving factors
such as emotions, shaping factors such as conventions and constitutions, and, above all, the ways in which all these elements
{singula}—the whole {totum} and its parts—can be brought to
fulfilment {perfici possunt}.[18] It is this last explanatory source
that is primary: understanding the possibility and process of fulfilment involves understanding (B)(1) the purposes of associating

---

[13] *Eth.* prol. n. 5 [5].

[14] I-II q. 17 a. 4c: many people constitute a single people {multi homines sunt unus
populus}; but this *totum* is *unum* not straightforwardly {simpliciter} (as a substance is) but
rather in a qualified sense {secundum quid}.

[15] Elsewhere, Aquinas notes that attempts to achieve an exaggerated unity in the
political community by homogenizing its members to one or a very limited number of
types will in fact destroy the polity: *Pol.* II. 1 nn. 13–16 [181–4].

[16] *Mal.* q. 4 a. 1c; II-II q. 108 a. 4 ad 1. A group {multitudo ordinata} is a body 'metaphorically' {in metaphoricis locutionibus; similitudinarie dictum} but is not the reality
{veritas rei} of a body': III q. 8 a. 1 ad 2.

[17] *Eth.* prol. n. 1 [1]. All other interpersonal unities of action, and of bodies or minds,
are consequential upon the primary unity of (shared) purpose: IV *Sent.* d. 27 q. 1 a. 1 sol.
1c.   [18] *Pol.* prol. n. 8 [8].

which are the point of doing so, and (2) the way in which this associating, if successful, constitutes or contributes (or is meant to contribute) to the well-being, the fulfilment, of the associating individuals (and of other 'parts', such as households and neighbourhoods).[19] Only by understanding (B)(1) and (2) can political theory, or other social theory,[20] adequately describe, account for, justify, or criticize (A): the patterns of association and co-ordination which provide its subject-matter.

The primacy of purposes (point) has implications, and raises questions, which need further discussion (II.3). (Modern economics gets going with Adam Smith's proposal that it be undertaken as a science of *side*-effects.[h]) But the prior question is why a theory of society or associations can be counted as part of *moralis philosophia*, why (that is to say) groups must be understood in terms of *actions*. And the answer to this question is now available. In the parts of *moralis philosophia* dealing with human societies including states, the social group is understood as an order of human persons considered as *acting* persons; indeed, the group is studied as an order—system, pattern, interrelationship, co-ordination—of voluntary (and thus also intelligent, even if misguided) actions, activities, *operationes*.[21]

No doubt that statement of social theory's proper subject-matter needs to be expanded to include certain pre-conditions of human action, conditions which generate options, particularly certain dispositions to act—above all, readiness to act as a member of the group. For such dispositions significantly contribute to the constituting and existence of the group even when no action is presently called for. But conditions which generate options are understood, precisely as such, by understanding possible actions (II.3), and specific dispositions by understanding the sorts of action they dispose one to. So the conclusion can fairly be stated without reference to such conditions and dispositions: Societies as well as individual actions are subjects of *moralis philosophia* precisely because *moralis philosophia* considers human actions {operationes}

---

[19] For (1) see *Pol.* prol. n. 8 [8]; for (2) see *Eth.* prol. n. 4 [4].
[20] e.g. legal theory: see I-II q. 90 a. 2.
[21] See *ScG* II c. 30 n. 14 [1076]: many acting persons {agentes} gathered together {congregari} to carry out one action (like rowers to propel a boat) are like a single agent {agens}, something constituted {qui fit actu} through their co-ordination {adunationem} towards a single action; also *Impugn.* II c. 2c [56]: 'a society {societas} seems to be nothing other than a co-ordination [association] {adunatio} of people {hominum} for doing some one thing in common {ad unum aliquid communiter agendum}'.

(in their relationship to each other and to purpose(s) {ordinatae ad invicem et ad finem}),[22] and human societies have their distinctive reality as orders of intelligent, voluntary, purposive action.[23]

Aquinas, as we have seen, has a quick, dialectical argument to show that human groups and societies are not natural bodies, organisms, or substances {unum per se}: some acts of group-members are not acts of the group and some acts of a group are not the act of any of its members. But then, one may ask, how can we say (as Aquinas does)[24] that there are *social acts*, group action or agency, as well as the acts of individual human agents, human persons (who after all are natural bodies)?

'The state is said to do whatever its ruler does.'[25] 'Is said to': the thought is part of common speech, common sense. Aquinas often articulates the thought in terms of a singular ruler, a king or president, but is happy to apply it to ruling bodies, large or small: 'acts done by the whole association, or by a majority {pluribus} in it, or by its head {princeps}, can pertain to you as a member of a society {collegium}, even though you did not do them yourself or of your own judgement and choice'.[26]

But this passage, like indeed the phrase 'is said to' in the other passages, provokes a doubt. Perhaps the notion of a social act is merely a legal or moral fiction, a 'manner of speaking' useful for ascribing to individuals, justly or unjustly, some culpability or liability for the acts of others? And here we can recall the different

---

[22] *Eth.* prol. n. 2 [2].

[23] 'Action' here means *actio* as distinct from *factio*; the state {civitas}, for example, is constituted by human reason {humana ratione constituta}, not (strictly speaking) made {facta} by human reason: see *Pol.* prol. n. 7 [7].

[24] See e.g. n. 21 above and n. 28 below.

[25] I q. 75 a. 4 ad 1; *Mal.* q. 4 a. 1c. Also *Perf.* c. 13 [630]: 'We [commonly] say {dicimus} that the *civitas* does what its leaders do.'

[26] *Mal.* q. 4 a. 1c; also *Eth.* ix. 9 n. 4 [1869]. Latin has the advantage that its word for human beings, *homines*, is distinct from its word for an adult male, *vir*; so I always translate *homo, homines,* by some ungendered expression such as 'human being' or 'we'. But Latin has the disadvantage that its pronouns are almost all gendered even when the meaning extends to persons of either sex. To avoid the nowadays disconcerting 'he' I usually employ the indefinite 'one' or the plural 'they', and occasionally, as here (to avoid misleading connotations in a passage about one leader and many members), I use the indefinite 'you'. In non-American English usage, the indefinite pronoun 'one' is implicitly in the first-person singular, and thus very helpfully replicates the 'internality' of one's practical deliberations, which is the proper perspective for doing practical philosophy and thinking about morality. There is of course some cost in avoiding 'man': no one synonym for *homo* so effectively conveys the interplay of individual, group, and the unity of the human race. And one should not overlook the imbalance in Aquinas' thought discussed in v.7 below.

but related moral or legal problem with which Aristotle wrestles perceptively but (as he confesses) inconclusively in *Politics* 3: If the identity of the state changes (as Aristotle thinks it does) when its constitutional order changes, can agreements entered into and debts incurred by the state under the previous constitution be rightly repudiated by the new state? (Aquinas reproduces Aristotle's discussion and carries it no further.)[i]

It may be that the question whether societies such as states have a reality such that they themselves, as well as their members, *act* is one needing a definite answer only in the context of questions about liability and responsibility. But even if that be so, those moral or legal questions deserve an answer which looks not to some self-'validating' fiction but to social reality as best we can understand it. Aquinas' judgement that, as a matter of social reality, there are identifiable social acts seems sound, even if more arguments for it would be welcome.

As we shall see (III.3), Aquinas analyses the elements of deliberation, choice, and action in highly political terms. This suggests a way of understanding social acts which is at least consistent with Aquinas' work and also provides a reason for affirming that there are such acts.[j] There is a social act, we can say, when some proposal for co-ordinated action is held out to relevant members of the society in such a way that they can, and some or all do, choose to participate in the proposed action precisely as the action thus, 'publicly', proposed. There is, then, no social act without the acts of individual human persons (just as there is no society without its individual human members).[27] Yet the social act is a real, not a fictitious resultant of the individual acts,[28] for there is indeed what I shall call a policy (however implicit, 'unstated', informal, and privy to the group itself), a policy which the relevant members choose to *participate* in carrying out.

This will also explain why acts of rulers (directors, coaches . . .) and their delegates can be acts of the group even when it is not obvious that some co-ordinated, joint action is under way. For it belongs to rulers and their delegates to initiate group action by words and deeds which define what shall be the public policy coordinating the future actions of relevant members of the group.

[27] And so Aquinas can say that 'every act is the act of a person {personae} (because acts are of individuals {singularium})': III *Sent.* d. 1 q. 1 a. 2 ad 6.

[28] '. . . there is *one* act when many people together are rowing a boat': III q. 35 a. 5 ad 3; also *Eth.* prol. n. 5 [5].

Indeed, the very fact that leaders and their functionaries are looked to (willingly or reluctantly, *de jure* or merely *de facto*) as authors of 'public policy' indicates that their seemingly isolated acts of making such a policy have their meaning and reality as parts of wider, lasting patterns of co-ordination of actions (and therefore, of course, of dispositions to act).

In this analysis I take the term 'public policy' from politics, particularly the law and politics of states; but it applies analogously (II.7) to every group capable of acting as a group. If states can be understood in the act-centred way envisaged in Aquinas' political theory, so too can other groups. Thus states, even when understood in this act-centred way, can correctly be understood as orders not only of the individual human persons who are their members (primarily, citizens), but also of the lesser societies and groups within them. Like Aristotle, Aquinas wants to understand the state, the political community, in both these ways.[k]

II.3. *Social Theory Understands Acts 'by their Objects'*

So states and other groups are to be understood by understanding their acts and, more fundamentally, the acts of their members. But how are such acts to be understood? Aquinas' answer has two elements, the one being common to all acts, the other specific to co-ordination of actions. This section concerns the first.

Nothing is more basic to Aquinas' idea of theory, science, or understanding in general than the following epistemological principle (strategy for getting knowledge): 'the *nature* of X is understood by understanding X's *capacities* or capabilities, those capacities or capabilities are understood by understanding their activations or *acts*, and those activations or acts are understood by understanding their *objects*'.[l] This principle Aquinas found in Aristotle's treatise on sensory and intellectual knowledge, the *De Anima*.[29] But from the first few pages of his first major work, the young Aquinas puts the principle to work in every context where the nature of some active reality is in question.

At first glance, the principle may seem an unattractive relic of

---

[29] *De Anima* 2. 4. 415a16–22; *An.* II. 6 nn. 6–10 [304–8], III. 14 n. 9 [803]. See also *ST* I q. 87 a. 3c; I *Sent.* d. 1 q. 1 a. 1 ad 3; d. 17 q. 1 a. 4 ad 4; III *Sent.* d. 23 q. 1 a. 2 ad 3.

Aristotelian methods which are thought to have hindered, not promoted, the natural sciences. Aquinas, expounding the principle for beginners, says that where a capacity {potentia} is passive, it is activated by an object which stands to that activation as source {principium} and moving cause; 'thus colour is the source of [the act of] seeing in so far as it moves [the capacity of] sight'.[30] But isn't this quite empty as an account of eyesight? Doesn't science make progress by looking to origins (chronologically prior), not ends? These are fair questions, and Aquinas would be happy to answer them; indeed, in this same exposition he begins by confronting his position with an objection: capacities surely can't be understood by looking to factors which are subsequent to them (as their acts are) or extrinsic to them (as their objects are)? He, like Aristotle, is keen to get clear about all the factors involved in seeing, e.g. the differences between 'coloured' (including white or black) objects and completely transparent objects, the role of the air as medium between object and eye,[31] the way in which colours somehow move the air all the way between object and eye,[32] the role of the sun in all this,[33] the importance of the pupil's transparency,[34] and in general whatever can be found out about the arrangement of parts of the body which results in seeing.[35] So he would doubtless welcome the new information available today about the relation between prisms and nerves and brain and so forth. But he would point out that both the scientific inquiry and its exposition are guided by the intention to show how these arrangements of body-parts enable green objects to be seen as green, flat objects as flat, receding objects as receding, accelerating objects as accelerating, and so forth. In an explanatory account of vision, all but only those features of the relevant organ(s), parts, and their movements will deserve a place which show how it is that seeing tracks the *visible* features of the *object* seen (whereas the operations of a diseased or traumatized eye fail to do so).

So even in the case of capacities that are essentially[m] 'passive', the principle that they are understood by reference to their objects holds good. Its relevance and validity are all the more evident in the case of capacities that are essentially active, capabilities to change and affect things, e.g. to heat, to generate, to build. And

---

[30] I q. 77 a. 3c. [31] *An.* II. 15 n. 6 [432]. [32] See *An.* II. 17 n. 8 [458].
[33] See *Q. An.* q. 5 ad 7. [34] See *An.* II. 15 nn. 6, 12 [432, 438].
[35] For the general programme, see e.g. *Sens.* 1 n. 7 [7]; for particular efforts to discover the bodily mechanisms involved, see e.g. ibid. 3 nn. 3–8 [35–42].

where the capability is to act by way of thought, deliberation, and decision, the principle takes on a special force.

We should not expect any principle to apply in just the same sense (univocally) across the four irreducibly distinct types of order which correspond to the four types of science or theory. If there are principles that apply in each of the four, they will apply analogically, i.e. with some patterned shift in their meaning and significance (II.7). There is an irreducible difference between (1) the way the parts of the eye and the relevant parts of the brain hang together to enable an animal to see something visible, (2) the way the parts of a sound argument hang together to establish its conclusion, (3) the way two leaders can bring together their conflicting reasons, their judgements, emotions, choices, and movements to make peace by shaking hands on the White House lawn, and (4) the way a band can follow a musical score to make their instruments render a national anthem. Yet in each case, one understands what is going on, in the relevant type of order (natural, logical, moral, technical), by relating the relevant elements to something which can rightly, but in an analogical sense, be called the object(ive) (or the goal . . . , the *finis*) of that 'going on'. In that way, Aquinas' principle applies, analogically, in all four types of order and theory.

In any event, in relation to *human acts*, whether of doing {actio} or making {factio}, we can accept that part of Aquinas' principle which is last in expression but first in application: acts are understood by their objects.[36] To find out and helpfully describe *what* someone is doing, the strategic question to ask and answer is always the question *why*: 'Why are you behaving like that?'[n]

For an example from Aristotle which Aquinas regularly uses, take: What are you doing? I'm going to the cupboard. Why? To get some herbs? Why? To mix a potion. Why? To lose weight. Why? Because that way I'll feel fit and be *healthy* again.[37] So, though my behaviour was indeed an instance of walking, *what* I was doing (in walking) was not taking a walk but preparing medicine (but also going to the cupboard and trying to lose weight and

---

[36] In so far as the principle also asserts that we understand human nature by understanding human capabilities, and understand these capabilities in turn by understanding human acts, I shall return to it in III.7, where I shall also explore some further implications of 'human acts are understood by their objects'.

[37] See *Phys.* II. 5 n. 6 [181] (on *Physics* 2. 3. 194^{b}35–195^{b}1); *Meta.* v. 2 n. 9 [771] (on *Metaphysics* 5. 2. 1013^{a}35–^{b}3); Finnis (1991a: 11–12); II.6 at n. 72 and III.3 n. 20 below.

perhaps following doctor's orders, and so on). Each question asked for, and was answered by reference to, the object, in the relevant sense of 'object'. My behaviour, simple as it was, turned out to have several, even many objects.

Such a set of objects can be put in their series, as relatively proximate (close in to the behaviour) or relatively remote. For example, lawyers might devise a jargon, according to which the 'further' objects (to get healthy, and/or to retain the doctor's respect) would be described as the 'motive(s)' while the close-in objects would be described as the 'intention' (what is intended). And such a jargon might be useful. But the point here is not what jargon to use, but how we can and do come to understand human behaviour, and get into a position to describe it.

And the point will apply equally to people's behaviour in groups, and the activities of the group. The example to which Aquinas returns dozens of times, not least in the prologue to the *Ethics*, is the co-ordination of soldiers in battle, in order to prevail over the enemy. Sometimes he expands the example to include various levels of co-ordination:

If we consider [1] the state president {rector civitatis} [say President Roosevelt in 1944] and [2] the army commander {dux exercitus} [General Eisenhower] and [3] one individual soldier [GI Private William Braher on 'Utah Beach', Normandy, on 6 June 1944], the president obviously has a priority in the relationships between these acting persons {in ordine agentium}; it was at his command {imperium} that the general went into the war, and it is in accordance with the latter's orders {ordinatio}[38] that the soldier is fighting with his hands. Now the objective {finis} of the soldier is to overcome the enemy [on and behind the beach] and that is further directed {ordinatur} towards the victory of the whole force {exercitus}, the victory which is the general's objective; and this objective in turn is further directed towards the well-being {bonum statum} of the state {civitatis vel regni}, which is the objective of the president or king. So, it must be the case that what stands as the ultimate objective {ultimus finis} in all this is the objective and outcome sought precisely by the action of the first of these acting persons [Roosevelt]. But although such objective is first in intention, it is last in realization {operatio}, and is the effect of other causes [not just of Roosevelt's directive] . . .[39]

[38] *Ordinatio* here signifies equally the 'order(s)' issued by the general and the general's plan and dynamic disposition-of-forces.

[39] *Pot.* q. 7 a. 2 ad 10. The term *obiectum* is not used here, but rather *finis*; but this is immaterial since 'the *obiecta* of active powers stand to the relevant activities as *fines*' (*An.* II. 6 n. 7 [305]).

32

If one reads such a passage after a detailed account of the Normandy campaign of 1944, one's first impression may be of naïve simplicity. Between Roosevelt and Eisenhower lay the Secretary of State for War and the Joint Chiefs of the Armed Forces, not to mention allied leaders such as Churchill and structures of allied co-operation such as the Combined Chiefs of Staff Committee. Between Eisenhower and a soldier storming the beach at Varreville (code-named 'Utah Beach') were nine levels of leaders (ignoring deputies and staff): Montgomery (21st Army Group) commanding Bradley (US First Army) commanding Collins (VII Corps) and then the commanders of the soldier's division, regiment, battalion, company, platoon, and section. Private Braher was a co-ordinated and co-operating part of at least nine groups {multitudines}, each group a 'part' of the one republic (a republic then acting in very close co-operation with other states such as Britain and Canada).

But the simplicity of Aquinas' account is not a naïve simplification. With one exception, the essentials of the historical facts are all accounted for in the quoted passage. Individual soldiers fighting 'by hand' (whether wielding a bayonet, firing heavy artillery, or driving a tank or bomber or ambulance) do, of course, typically want and hope for victory. In that sense, victory is the end each has in view. But 'end in view' can be taken more strictly. Although top commanders, if competent (unlike Hitler), do not attempt to plan all the way down, and leave subordinate commanders to plan and conduct the details of particular operations, the fact remains that the individual members of a large and complex force have *no plan* for the victory which will win the war,[40] no conception of how to bring it about, and typically little or no idea of what progress if any is being made towards it.[41] A few may entertain private plans of how they would conduct the campaign if they were in charge. But these 'plans' are not—or, at least, had better not be—what guides their own or anybody else's actions. Their conduct, save as

[40] So, though victory is the goal {finis} of the whole army rather than merely of its supreme commander {dux} (see I-II q. 19 a. 8c), Aquinas regularly says (e.g. *Eth.* prol. n. 1 [1]) that the order of the army's various units is 'for the sake of {propter}' the whole army's directedness {ordo} towards its commander, whose objective is precisely the victory of the whole army (and not of any of its units or personnel as such). And see IX. 3 n. 65 below.

[41] ''I really couldn't fathom the whole thing [the Normandy campaign]—I couldn't understand what it was all about. I never remembered seeing the battalion commander except at ceremonies." If all infantrymen in all armies share something of this feeling . . .': Hastings (1989: 248).

deserters, is guided by their standing role in the force and by the more particular orders they get, which carry into effect the real plans adopted by the supreme military commander.[42]

Is such a passage *describing*, in its explanatory essentials, what does happen, or *prescribing* what ought to happen? The answer must be that it is, and means to be, doing both. In depicting the co-ordinated interaction of (1) 'civilian' or 'political' direction of the armed forces, (2) unified military command of those forces,[43] and (3) disciplined personnel acting under orders, Aquinas is expressing a judgement about what is reasonable. As made, or taken seriously, by anyone wondering how political communities and their members *should* act in the face of hostile threat to their community's well-being, such a judgement is 'prescriptive' or 'normative', a judgement about what they should choose to favour, promote, and (so far as they can) put into effect. But the judgement also describes what happens very often and 'naturally'.

Still, as Aquinas insists, human affairs are distinguished from 'natural occurrences' (events in the first of the four types of order: II.1) precisely by being the result of more or less reasonable choices. So: to say (as Aquinas does) that such and such a pattern in human affairs is 'natural' does not, in this context, mean that it is 'usual', or 'normal' in a statistical sense, still less that it happens automatically unless prevented. Rather one means that intelligence and reasonableness favour it, so that, since people are more or less intelligent and reasonable, it tends to be the pattern adopted (or the resultant of adopted patterns) and in the relevant circumstances will be adopted save where (as may be very frequent) it is prevented directly by the prevailing of emotions over reason in choice, or indirectly by unreasonable institutions or practices themselves shaped by emotions, at the expense of reasonableness. This sense of 'natural', and this unconfused juxtaposing of prescription and explanatory description, will be revisited in II.7 below.

---

[42] On the circumstances in which it can be reasonable (and compatible with one's duty of proper respect for authority) to depart from one's orders as given, see e.g. II-II q. 64 a. 6 ad 3 (IX.2 n. 27 below); also III.4 nn. 56–63 below, VIII.2 n. 33 and VIII.3 at n. 104 below.

[43] See also *ScG* III c. 76 n. 7 [2523]: 'the political leader {politicus} gives rules and laws to the army leader, who lays down the law and makes rules for centurions and tribunes'; *Eth.* III. 8 n. 2 [474]: 'politicus, i.e. rector civitatis'.

II.4. *Social Theory's Account of Co-ordination*

The passage we have been considering articulates an understanding of the hierarchical co-ordination of president, commanding general, and individual soldier, in line with the hierarchy of their reasonable object(ive)s. It omits anything explicit about the more or less horizontal co-ordination among individual soldiers (and, *mutatis mutandis*, among individual units under the one supreme military command). In many places, including the *Ethics* prologue, Aquinas strips the matter down to barest essentials. Order within a group has two dimensions: co-ordination {ordo}[44] between part and part, member and member (including, we now may say, subgroup and subgroup); and an intelligible relationship {ordo} between that co-ordination and its *finis*, its end, purpose, objective, object, goal, point . . . The passage quoted shows that the latter 'relationship to end' {ordo in/ad finem} includes cases—surely the usual situation—where the end is more or less multiple. But what does Aquinas say about the former dimension, the members' co-ordination of their actions? His analyses can be summarized in seven points.

1. Such co-ordination, he says, must be understood like any other intelligible human action, by reference to its object. So this dimension is dependent on the other; the latter, relationship or directedness to end, is 'more important, because it is *first*'.[45] But 'object' refers not only to the ultimate end (well-being of the republic)[46] but also to every intermediate end (victory over Nazi Germany, recapture of France, defeating Rommel's Army Group B, establishing a bridgehead on Utah Beach, silencing this gunpost . . .), each of which is an end because it is a means to a higher, further end in the chain or ladder of means to that ultimate end.

2. Each of these more and less ultimate ends or object(ive)s can be the *ratio*, the directing object(ive), the rationale and primary source of co-ordination to achieve it. Why is this man running forward alongside that man while a third lies shooting at that sand dune? To silence that gunpost . . .

---

[44] For the synonymy of *ordinare* and *coordinare* in this sort of context, see e.g. I-II q. 100 a. 6c.   [45] *Eth*. prol. n. 1 [1] 'principalior quia primus'.

[46] It is important, and often overlooked, that Aquinas frequently uses the phrase 'ultimate end {ultimus finis}' in this relative and limited sense; e.g. where adultery is being committed for purposes of theft, the ultimate end of the act of adultery is theft: II-II q. 11 a. 1 ad 2.

3. At each level, co-ordination is either by constant unanimous agreement or, more likely, by following the directives or group/public policy determined, and made known to the other members, by some *dux* or *duces*, leader or leaders. A fuller account of how purposes give the direction essential to co-ordination will include an account of agreement, convention, authority, and law (VI.3, VIII. 3, X.3): a community's law, indeed, is essentially concerned with those actions and other external arrangements by which each of its members is co-ordinated {coordinatur} with the others.[47]

4. Co-ordination may be more or less limited in its objective and subject-matter, and in its duration. Aquinas mentions the co-ordination of students as an instance of temporary coming together; perhaps he is envisaging the co-ordination involved in arriving on time in the lecture hall, not shuffling disturbingly, asking pertinent and only pertinent questions. In the same context he instances the co-operation of military personnel as limited, too, in time and in objective and subject-matter, in contrast with the co-ordination of the members of a household or a *civitas* 'in life as a whole {in vita simpliciter}'.[48]

5. Limited forms of co-ordination such as these may be structured around an art, a technique, varying with both the object in view and the nature of the material (including in some cases the human body and psyche) to be mastered. The art of rowing an eight, the 'science of war',° the craft of the infantry platoon . . . Even relatively unlimited and open-ended forms of co-operation, such as political community, will usually involve common resort to arts and techniques such as language or, more technically, the practices and institutions (by no means *merely* technical) of law.

6. Co-ordination in human groups is by self-determining (and group-constituting) free choices, made for reasons not reducible to any art or set of arts. The third type of order cannot be reduced to the fourth. Social theory cannot be reduced to any number of crafts, however far-reaching their scope and refined the material whose mastery they teach. At every level of co-ordination, the

---

[47] II-II q. 58 a. 8c (which, like many other passages, makes in relation to justice a point elsewhere made about human law, namely its concern only with external acts and instrumentalities: see V.I at n. 28; VII.2–3).

[48] III *Sent.* d. 33 q. 3 a. 1 sol. 4c (for 'life as a whole', see also II-II q. 48 a. un. c: 'adunata ad totam vitam, sicut multitudo domus vel familiae'; *Pol.* 1. 2 n. 12 [53]: 'life, i.e. domestic affairs {conversatio domestica}'). For another limited group, see *Eth.* VIII. 10 n. 16 [1687]: companions in a hostel; cf. III.2 below.

choice is always open whether to participate or desert,[49] to forge ahead or hang back. An individual's participation or desertion may or may not affect any fourth-order project which the group is pursuing. But whether or not it does so—whether or not it alters the state of affairs on the field at the end of the day, and whether the day was won or lost—that individual choice has a distinct significance in the third order, on the person of the individual making it and on the interpersonal relationships {concordia,[50] communio, communicatio} it affirms or betrays, builds up or weakens, damages, or destroys.

7. So, though co-ordination almost always involves some leadership, some exercise of authority, it always requires the exercise of autonomy by the parties to the co-ordination, the members of the team or other group. Having 'mastery of their own action {dominium sui actus}', all who are subject to authority (be they servants or free citizen-subjects), in acting at the direction {per praeceptum} of others (the rulers, one, few, or many), are 'acting *of themselves* and by free choice {seipsos per liberum arbitrium}'.[51] And so, Aquinas concludes, the ruled as well as (though not in the same way as)[p] the rulers need that sort of practical understanding and good judgement {prudentia}—attentive to the group's common good—which is called political {politica}.[52]

II.5. *Social Theory can Describe 'Internally'*

Commanders and leaders, subordinates and teams adopt a plan or at least a policy. What makes sense to the leader can make sense to the led. What the group is doing, what it's up to, what its plan or policy is, can be understood by a newcomer, quite often without

[49] 'One of [Private Ascher's] group gazed around at Normandy for a few minutes after their landing, then declared decisively: "This is no place for me," and vanished from their ken for ever': Hastings (1989: 248).

[50] By *concordia*—not mere absence of strife, but practical like-mindedness, unity of hearts—people are sufficiently united {adunantur} to be able to pursue the state's common good {reipublicae bonum} and soldiers to act co-operatively {concorditer} for the victory which is their shared goal {communis finis}: *ScG* III c. 151 n. 3 [3236].

[51] II-II q. 50 a. 2c. This abstracts from, but neither denies nor overlooks, the profound differences between slaves or servants of a master or mistress and free citizens of a republic or commonwealth, on which see v.6 and v.7 n. 1 below.

[52] Ibid. and ad 1, 2, and 3; likewise q. 47 a. 12. Of course, if we are thinking of a domestic rather than a political group, the *prudentia* required of the members as such would rather be *oeconomica* than *politica*: q. 47 a. 11c, q. 50 a. 3.

instruction or any verbal communication at all. The outsider can understand the insider's intentions and know what's going on.

The plan, policy, and intention which others can be told about, or told to follow, or come to understand without being told, is itself 'practical'. It is about what *to do*. 'In order to achieve this, I or you or we *should* do that.' It is not about what is the case, nor even about what will be the case.

It is about what *is-to-be* the case, is-to-be (should be) done—a prescription and not, as such, a prediction. If one has an intention, one's knowledge of that intention is, first and foremost, *practical* knowledge, a knowledge of the end, the purpose one has, and the means, the purposeful conduct one has chosen. As practical knowledge, it is real knowledge, true and in its own way complete, even if the conduct is prevented and never takes place. And when one is acting on one's intentions and carrying out one's plan, one knows *what one is doing* without having to inspect one's conduct, without 'looking to see', even introspectively.

One can reflect upon what one is doing or (more likely) has done. Others can observe one's behaviour and, often enough, understand what one is doing. A newcomer can 'get the picture' before deciding to join in (or stay out). Such knowledge by intelligent observation and reflection is not itself practical. It is about the practical knowledge of an acting person or group, but is itself 'theoretical' or 'speculative'.[53] Neither of these English words is an entirely happy translation of Aquinas' *speculativa*; 'theoretical' suggests general and abstracted from concrete events, 'speculative' suggests uncertainty, and all such connotations must be eliminated to get the point. 'Descriptive-explanatory' is nearer. Such knowledge (or belief[54]) is about what is the case, that is to say about what the acting person's or persons' intention, plan, purpose (and thus practical knowledge) actually is. This sort of attention to the intentions, the reasons for acting, of acting persons is what Weber, Collingwood, H. L. A. Hart, and many others have called *adopting the hermeneutic or internal point of view*, and commended as essential to descriptive social theory.

---

[53] *Ver.* q. 3 a. 3 ad 4.

[54] Often one does not know what one thinks one knows, for one is more or less mistaken. So there is 'speculative' *belief*. And such belief can be more or less certain; it can be 'speculative' in the idiomatic sense of an adventurous inference, a hunch. Aquinas is well aware of such conjectural 'knowledge' or opinion: see e.g. I q. 57 a. 3c, q. 86 a. 4c, II-II q. 48 a. un. c, q. 95 a. 1c. But it is quite irrelevant to the distinction between practical and speculative.

So there can be historical understanding of human hopes, deeds, failures. Indeed, Aquinas uses the term 'historical' precisely to make a closely related point: the 'historical' interpretation of Scripture is the interpretation which, unlike allegorical or moralizing interpretations, identifies what the author of the passage intended.[55] (And some authors, including some biblical authors,[q] intend their work to narrate what they judge someone else to have meant to say and intended to do; the fact that they can be right, and that their readers can understand them aright, can be of the highest importance: Aquinas is willing to stake his whole faith and life on such historical understanding of intentions.[56])

But history, the narration, even the accurate and ample narration of deeds and sayings, leaves something to be desired; it certainly informs, and even explains;[57] but does it sufficiently clarify one's understanding of human affairs?[58] The question arises even when the intentions, deeds, and sayings narrated are well understood by both narrator and audience. It is the question whether, and how, anything both true and *general* can be said about human affairs— the question how there can be a political or social *theory*.

For human affairs are extremely variable, multiform, contingent. The contingency is not simply that things happen by chance, though of course chance occurrences are frequent in human affairs[59] as well as in non-human nature—a fact which Aristotelian natural science handles plausibly enough by attending (not unlike a modern science) to what happens generally.[r] The specific problem here is, rather, the *diversity of people's choices*, in the face both of the natural course of things (including their own inclinations and emotions) and of chance opportunity or predicament. To indicate this diversity Aquinas ransacks the language: 'multifarious',[60] '*omni*fariously',[61] 'indeterminate',[62] 'infinite'.[63]

Whatever the criteria of good and bad, the range of bad choices is infinite and the freedom to make them (for the good they promise) is real. Technological progress, being progress in an irreducibly

---

[55] I q. 1 a. 10c; *In Gal.* 4. 7 ad v. 24a [254].
[56] See III q. 5 a. 3c; see also I *Sent.* prol. q. 1 a. 5c; x.5 below.
[57] See *Meta.* VI. 3 nn. 7, 11, 31 [1197, 1201, 1222]; *Peri.* I. 14 nn. 11–12, 19 [186–7, 194]; Finnis (1992b: 9–10, 17).   [58] See II *Sent.* d. 11 q. 2 a. 3c.
[59] E.g. *Sort.* c. 4 [661].   [60] *Eth.* II. 7 n. 3 [321]; *In Matt.* 7 ad v. 13 [651].
[61] III *Sent.* d. 36 q. 1 a. 5c ('peccata contingunt omnifariam . . .').
[62] *Eth.* III. 10 n. 6 [493].
[63] II-II q. 10 a. 5c; *Eth.* II. 7 n. 2 [320]. Still, people's purposes, though infinite in number, are not infinite in types {specie}: I-II q. 60 a. 1 ad 3.

different type of order, is no guarantee of moral decency, and morally wrong options are always likely to retain their attraction. So there is no reason to expect that human history will follow any 'law of progress'. Still, good reasons will always be attractive to human intelligence, and rejection of bad ways of life and of their accompanying or originating or resulting political regimes is always possible. There is no reason to expect that history will follow a 'law of decline'. And although the gains from human goodwill, skill, and effort can be lost, and restored, and lost again, there is no sufficient reason to believe that history runs in pre-ordained cycles. In sum, there is no reason to predict the triumph of good or of evil in this world, whether in the long run or the medium term.[s] Social theory's generality is not to be found in charting overall human progress, decline, or eternal returns.

So the question remains. Truth about human affairs is accessible and the knowledge is genuine enough. But can there be any *general* and interesting knowledge of human affairs? Can knowledge of human affairs be more than an endless narrative of one thing after another? Can it have the structure of a science, a general theory?

II.6. *Social Theory is General because 'Practical'*

Aristotle's *Politics* offers a good deal of empirical but well-structured and general information about the conditions on which states, bad as well as good, can be expected to remain stable, and the conditions under which revolution, disorder, and collapse are more or less likely. The descriptive generalizations about cause and effect are based upon extensive historical-comparative research, whose existence Aristotle is proud to record in his advertisement for the *Politics* at the end of the *Ethics*.[64] He also recommends a programme of research into monopolies and other matters of economics.[65]

Still, neither Aristotle nor Aquinas doubts that a social science worthy of the name must be a practical science.[66] And 'practical'

---

[64] See *Nic. Eth.* 10. 9. 1181^{b}17–18. Aquinas takes the last paragraph of the *Ethics* as the programme of the *Politics*: *Eth.* x. 16 n. 17 [2180].

[65] *Politics* I. 11. 1259^{a}4–6; *Pol.* I. 9 nn. 12–16 [146–50].

[66] So Aquinas quietly clarifies Aristotle's phrase 'the philosophy of human affairs' (*Nic. Eth.* 10. 9. 1181^{b}15) as 'practical knowledge {scientia operativa} concerning human affairs': *Eth.* x. 16 n. 16 [2179].

here does not mean, simply, capable of being put to use, as 'practical mathematics' might be a selection of techniques useful for, say, architects or merchants. A science or theory is practical, in the full sense, if it is *about*, and *directs toward*, what it would be good to do, to have, to get, and to be. It is a practical *art* when its ultimate object is limited and, like the technique for achieving it, essentially external to the character of the practitioner.[67] It is practical[t] in the fullest sense when it is about, and prescribes, what is to be *done* {agenda}, in the open-ended field of human life as a whole, by choices and acts (which as deliberate and chosen are essentially self-determining—i.e. internal to and constitutive of an individual's character or a group's or community's identity and quality)[68] in view of objects, ends, *goods* that provide reason to act and lend point to individual or group life as an open-ended whole.[69] When it is made an object of reflective study, such a fully practical and unequivocally prescriptive social theory will be part (a supremely important part) of *moralis philosophia* (II.2). Nothing more important can be constituted by human reason than the *civitas*;[70] the highest and most general form of practical theory is political theory {politica}; the object or point {finis} of political theory subsumes[71] the object or point of all other parts of *philosophia moralis* and all arts, crafts, and technologies—though without eliminating the distinct character of those other parts and

---

[67] Aquinas from time to time uses the term 'art' to cover both third- and fourth-order dispositions and actions: e.g. *Pol.* prol. nn. 1–2 [1–2].

[68] Even though a single choice (Aquinas thinks) cannot form a habitual disposition in the strict sense (which is formed by reiteration of acts: I-II q. 51 a. 3), still a choice lasts in, and shapes, one's will(ingness) until one repudiates or repents of it (see e.g. *Ver.* q. 24 a. 12c). Although their emotional character and culture can be profoundly shaped before they reach the age of reason (on which, see VII.6 at n. 110 below), children cannot make free choices until they reach that age; and when one does reach it, one is immediately {statim} confronted with the rational necessity of deliberating, so far as one can, *about oneself* {de seipso} and about the direction, the integrating point, of one's whole life {salus sua}, so that one treats oneself as an end in oneself to which other things are related as quasi-means {de seipso cogitet, ad quem alia ordinet sicut ad finem}, and either does or fails to do 'what is in oneself {quod in se est}': I-II q. 89 a. 6c ad 3; II *Sent.* d. 42 q. 1 a. 5 ad 7; *Ver.* q. 28 a. 3 ad 4; and see *Mal.* q. 7 a. 10 ad 8.

[69] For this contrast between art (technique, in the fourth order) and unrestricted practical reasonableness (*prudentia*, in the third order), see e.g. I-II q. 21 a. 2 ad 2, q. 57 a. 4c and ad 1 and ad 3, a. 5c, II-II q. 47 a. 2 ad 1, a. 5c; and see IV.4 at nn. 90, 91 below.

[70] *Pol.* prol. n. 7 [7]: 'for the *civitas* is the most important {principalissimum} of those things which can be constituted {constitui} by human reason'. For Aquinas' qualifications about this priority, see VII.5 below. See also IV. 3 at nn. 58–60.

[71] 'Embraces, i.e. contains under itself': *Eth.* I. 2 n. 11 [29]; cf. VII.5 at nn. 76–83 below.

arts.[72] Political theory is *about* and *directs towards* the common good of the political community; its object—i.e. its subject-matter and its point as a human enterprise (i.e. as theor*izing*)—is 'human good', without restriction. 'The point of political theory is *human good*, that is, what is best in human affairs.'[73]

One understands, and can describe, what acting persons *are* doing when one understands their reasons for behaving as they do. The reasons people have for doing what they do can hang together to structure a social science just to the extent that *good* reasons—reasons good as reasons for action—hang together in a coherent set of principles and conclusions, general or strategic reasons, and particular or tactical applications. The reasons which, as a clear-headed theorist, one counts as good when considering human affairs in reflective social theory—even theory intended primarily as explanatory *description*—are the very reasons one counts as good reasons when considering what to do.

The conception of social theory which is articulated in the preceding sentence has implications for social theory's methodology (II.7–8), and raises a question to be considered in III.5–7: Can one, in truth, identify really good reasons for action?

II.7. *Social Theory can Describe 'Analogically'*

If social science, as Aquinas contends, is under the direction of, or indeed part of, an unabashedly moral theory, won't the realities of human existence be overlooked? Isn't idealism synonymous with naïvety? And even if social theory of this sort were to find a place for the facts, and the real patterns of cause and effect, how would it find the vocabulary to articulate the realities? If, for example, 'constitution' or 'law' are defined as decent systems of government

---

[72] See II-II q. 47 a. 11 ad 3: 'horse-riding and soldiering and politics differ in species, even though the purpose of [the first] is directed towards the purpose of the next [and so on]'. Here 'politics' translates *habitus civilis*; in a. 11c the word is *politica*, which here refers directly to readiness for active engagement in a political life which includes deciding issues of war and peace, but is also Aquinas' standard term for the corresponding practical theory, political theory.

[73] '[F]inis politicae est humanum bonum, id est optimum in rebus humanis': *Eth.* I. 2 n. 11 [29]. In Aristotle, this line of thought fits in with Aristotle's view that political action (the government of the *polis*) has amongst its proper functions to make citizens thoroughly good people—a view which Aquinas rejects (see VII.2–7).

or just directives, how can the theory have anything to say about most governmental or legal systems of government, which surely mix justice with injustice? When Plato says that enactments made for partisan purposes are not laws, or that fanatical partisans are not citizens,[74] doesn't he display the blinkered narrowness of moralism and idealism, and doesn't his dictum sound all too like the 'persuasive definition' of a rhetorician?

Aquinas accepted and deployed Aristotle's account[75] of the scope of sciences or theories, which Aristotle interwove with an account of the scientific or theoretical use of definitions and terms. The proper field of any science or theory properly includes everything which is relevantly *related to* one *central* type, and the relevant sorts of 'relationship to central type' include, *inter alia*, not only what generates things of that type but also their characteristic defects or corruptions (and the causes of such breakdowns). So a watered-down[76] or corrupted version of the type can rightly—scientifically as well as popularly—be called by the same name, not with the same meaning ('univocally', as Aquinas translates) nor merely equivocally, but by the sort of relationship-in-difference of meaning that Aquinas (changing Aristotle's vocabulary) calls *analogy*. Deviant or corrupted versions {Greek: parekbaseis} are not the only sorts of watered-down case: goodwill between passing strangers is not a rich instance of friendship, but it is all that the situation reasonably requires, and calling it friendship is neither senseless nor necessarily misleading.[77]

In Aristotle's vocabulary, 'analogy' {Greek: analogia} means proportionate equivalence; the model is: a:b = c:d; for example, insight stands to intelligence as seeing stands to eye.[78] Such proportionality or 'geometrical equality' is the conceptual structure of distributive justice (VII.1 n. a).[79] In Aquinas' vocabulary, this 'analogy of proportionality' is only one of two or more broad types of

---

[74] Plato, *Laws* 4. 715b. See likewise 712e–713a; *Statesman* 293d–e; *Republic* 4. 422e; Cicero, *De Legibus* 2. 5. 11; *De Republica* 3. 31. 43.

[75] *Metaphysics* 4. 2. 1003ᵃ32–ᵇ15; see *Meta.* IV. 1 [534–47].

[76] Aristotle's metaphor: see *Politics* 2. 1. 1262ᵇ16.

[77] See *Nic. Eth.* 8. 1. 1155ᵃ21–2; 9. 5. 1166ᵇ31–2; cf. IV.3 below. Indeed, Aristotle seems to contend (*Politics* 7. 1: 1301ᵃ25 ff.) that sometimes the social condition of a community requires the constitution to take a form which elsewhere (e.g. *Politics* 3. 7. 1279ᵃ22–31) he has described as one of the despotic and deviant forms {parekbaseis}.

[78] *Nic. Eth.* 1. 6. 1096ᵇ29, 5. 3. 1131ᵃ31; *Eth.* 1. 7 n. 13 [95].

[79] *Nic. Eth.* 5. 3. 1131ᵃ31, ᵇ8–12. Aquinas illustrates (*Eth.* v. 5 n. 4 [941]): £1 in wages for Plato who worked for one day = £2 wages for Socrates who worked for two.

analogy {Latin: analogia}.[80] The other is the one mentioned above: the unifying relationship of various things to one central case/type, a relationship which warrants a corresponding relationship of shifting meanings to one focal meaning.[81] Though Aristotle speaks of this in his discussion of the scope of sciences (and elsewhere),[u] neither he nor Aquinas has a special label for it.

But the discerning of central cases and focal meanings goes on more or less explicitly throughout Aristotle's work, not least in his analysis of types of friendship and of states or constitutions in *Nicomachean Ethics* 8, which Aquinas doubtless knew as well and as early as he knew *Metaphysics* 4. Aquinas later found it vigorously employed in the analysis of citizenship and constitutionality in *Politics* 3, as his own commentary reflects. We can take the early stages of that analysis as illustrative.

It is an analysis which, as Aquinas says, aims to make clear who is a citizen *simpliciter*—straightforwardly, without qualification—and who is a citizen only *secundum quid*—literally 'according to something', i.e. in some respect(s), relatively speaking, in a qualified sense.[82] It works its way to the conclusion that a citizen *simpliciter* is someone who can participate in government, whether in the courts (e.g. on juries) or in some sort of deliberative council, and whether on a restricted basis as in monarchical or aristocratic systems or an unrestricted basis as in a democracy {democratia}[v] (to which, indeed, the definition of citizen applies most plainly). But the analysis had to take into account that a definition of this sort will not be applicable to all constitutions alike. Aquinas' commentary at this point deploys, at least tacitly, each of the two broad types of analogical use of terms:

One must be clear, Aristotle says, that in any field, wherever there are items which differ in type, one being naturally primary, another secondary, and another related in some even remoter way, then *either* there is nothing common to them, as in equivocations, *or* there is something common only barely or to a certain extent. But constitutions, as will be said further on, differ in type, and some are 'prior' and others 'posterior'.[83] Those that are

---

[80] *Ver.* q. 2 a. 11c; cf. I q. 13 a. 5c. The distinctions drawn in these two texts (not to mention other texts) are not identical, and 'analogy' is itself an analogical term—i.e. its meaning shifts more or less systematically with context.

[81] See I q. 13 a. 5c. The metaphors 'central' and 'focal' (see Owen 1960; Fortenbaugh 1991: 229–30) are not Aquinas', who often employs terms such as 'prior' or 'primary', or 'maximal(ly)', to make the same point.   [82] See also I-II q. 105 a. 3 ad 2.

[83] Thus the distinction between types of constitution is a *divisio analogi*: see e.g. *Mal.* q. 7 a. 1 ad 1; *ST* I-II q. 61 a. 1 ad 1.

defective {vitiatae} and violate right constitutional order are naturally posterior to the non-defective—just as in every genus of things the perfect is
naturally 'prior' to the corrupt {corrupto}. And so in the various [types of]
constitution [good and bad] there must be a different meaning of 'citizen'
{ratio civis}.[84]

Let us take the two kinds of analogy one by one.

1. When he uses the term 'naturally' {naturaliter} with reference
to the priority and posteriority of types of constitutions, Aquinas is
implicitly deploying analogy of proportionality—$a:b = c:d$. (In II.3
we saw analogy of proportionality in relation to 'objects' in the four
types of order.) As he has made clear, political theory is not natural
science, and political communities are not natural organisms but
systems of acting by agents who act by intelligence and free choice
(II.1–2). So, in the philosophy of human affairs, when one predicates
'natural' or 'naturally' of such a community and its arrangements,
one does not (if one is speaking carefully and centrally!)[85] mean
'automatically', or 'by virtue of innate subrational inclination' or of
any other 'natural impulse'. Nor does one mean 'usually' or 'very
frequently' or '(statistically) standardly'. Rather, one means (says
Aquinas) 'rationally', i.e. as judged by the standards for judging our
actions reasonable or unreasonable, right or wrong: things are 'naturally' X for human persons when they are X 'in accordance with
right reason'.[86] The reasonable stands to human actions and
communities as the usual stands to the course of nature: normative,
normal, standard, natural—using each of those terms analogously,
not univocally. So, just as $1:2 = 3:6$ but 1 is not equal to 3, so the
natural-as-reasonable need not be at all usual. (In fact the reasonable, 'naturally prior' types of constitution are found relatively
rarely in practice.")

2. Judged by the standards appropriate for evaluating human
actions and communities as reasonable or unreasonable, some

---

[84] *Pol.* III. 1 n. 7 [354].

[85] Of course, one can use 'naturally', 'humanly', etc. in a sense that is, within political
theory, secondary, as when one says that it is natural and all too human for people to act
unreasonably under the influence of their emotions (even though, speaking focally, acting
in this way 'is neither natural nor human, i.e. reasonable {ratione regulata}': *Eth.* v. 13 n.
15 [1049]); see III. 7 at n. 154 below.

[86] *Eth.* I. 13 n. 3 [156], which also observes that things which for people of good
character (i.e. fully reasonable people) are naturally pleasurable because in accordance
with right reason are not found pleasurable by the majority of people (who are more or less
corrupt and swayed by contradictory desires, some for extravagance and excess, some for
meanness). See also e.g. *Eth.* x. 8 n. 14 [2063], and the texts quoted and cited in III.7 n. 150
below.

constitutions are central, rationally 'prior' cases of constitutionality and others are deviant, corrupt, secondary, rationally 'posterior'. We should understand 'citizen' focally in the way which will
fit with the central cases of constitutions; in the context of those
constitutions we can understand what it centrally is to be a citizen:
to be entitled to participate in government. People who are entirely
excluded from participating in government, and are simply and
solely subjects, are not citizens in the scientifically, philosophically significant sense of that term.[87]

Of course, as Aristotle and Aquinas immediately remark, such
people may well be conventionally called citizens, in the political
discourse of certain political communities. One can find popular
definitions such as: 'any descendant of two citizens is a citizen'.
But such superficial thoughts fail to get to the *ratio* of citizenship,
to what it is that constitutes and makes intelligible the relevant set
of practices and corresponding ways of speaking.[88] Still, what if the
state's own law defines 'citizen' in that superficial sort of way?
Well, philosophers and others engaged in scientific thinking should
not treat lawyers and their definitions as authoritative.[89]

The theorist's efforts to identify what, in human affairs, is 'naturally', i.e. rationally and morally, 'primary' or central will run into
difficulties and doubts. Political and constitutional arrangements
are a good deal more complex than theorists envisaged when they
proposed (as Aristotle did) a classification of states into types such
as monarchy, aristocracy, democracy, and their respective corruptions. Aquinas does not resolve in detail the terminological com-
plexities and substantive difficulties which Aristotle, more or less
consciously, gets into in his typology of constitutions. But he
shares Aristotle's stance: 'When one is philosophizing [theorizing]
in any practical matter {unaquaque arte}, one is considering the
truth and so is not concerned merely with what is useful in practice
{utile ad agendum}; one must not neglect or omit anything, but

---

[87] People who are not entitled to participate in government, but who are eligible to be
given (for merit or otherwise) such an entitlement and/or who are united as quasi-equals
and partners with citizens, and/or whose status is part of someone's ground for claiming
citizenship, are citizens not *simpliciter* but in a qualified sense {secundum quid}: see v.7
at n. 203 on women.   [88] See *Pol.* III. 1 n. 9 [356].
[89] Cf. *Retra.* 13 [829]: 'It seems unfitting and ludicrous for professors of theology to cite
the remarks of [ecclesiastical] jurists as authoritative, or to argue about what they mean.'
Though he never confuses philosophers with *professores sacrae doctrinae*, Aquinas would
clearly say the same about social philosophy's relationship to legal definitions, which
extend all the way to pure fiction.

46

rather must make the truth of the matter known in every particular.'[90]

So we can see some main lines of Aquinas' implicit response to the challenges posed at the beginning of this section. No part of human reality is to be dismissed. Social theory is not about ideal cases, still less about ideal worlds untroubled by wrongdoing, scarcity, misunderstanding, and fear.[91] It seeks not merely to classify non-ideal cases, but also to explain the characteristic causes of their deficiencies, and to identify the conditions in which corruption is comparatively likely to occur. Books 4 to 6 of Aristotle's *Politics* are an effort, well-informed for its day, at such explanatory description. By deploying the analogy of focal meaning, theoretical vocabulary can perspicuously accommodate the range of relevant realities, sound and corrupt. The deviant cases are not put out of sight, or 'persuasively' defined out of existence.[92]

II.8. *Social Theory can Describe from the Moral 'Point of View'*

The social theorist identifies the 'citizen' as one who is entitled to share in governing. In tyrannies, then, only the tyrants and possibly their cliques will really be citizens, in the focal sense of the term. But tyrants will often call their subjects citizens. So too they will usually call their decrees *laws*. And from several points of view, and in several registers of discourse, and for several practical purposes (e.g. when doing business in the tyrant's court), the decrees of tyrants are indeed laws. But just in so far as these 'laws' are made without regard to constitutionality, or human decency and the interests of the community as a whole, they are 'rather corruptions of law'.[93]

---

[90] *Pol.* III. 6 n. 5 [395].

[91] 'Ideal state' is not the best translation of 'best polity {optima politia}', the subject-matter of the last part of Aristotle's *Politics* as referred to in *Eth.* x. 16 n. 17 [2180].

[92] So: in so far as there is honour {fides} among thieves, there is a 'juridical order {ordo iuris}' and the gang has 'a kind of justice {aliquam formam iustitiae}': II *Sent*. d. 6 a. 4 ad 3; see also I-II q. 92 a. 1 ad 4. But one does not understand fidelity, law, right, justice, or human society most adequately by understanding these concepts, and the corresponding realities, as they are understood and lived out in the Mafia.

[93] II-II q. 60 a. 5 ad 1 {potius legis corruptiones}; I-II q. 95 a.2c ('non lex sed legis corruptio') (note that *corruptio* is not mere rhetorical denunciation; it is Aquinas' standard translation of Aristotle's word *parekbaseis*); *In Isa.* c. 10 ('perversa legislatio'). See further VIII.3 at nn. 90, 104–11 below.

In saying this, the theorist deliberately privileges, indeed adopts, one point of view. The noun phrase 'point of view' may have no precise equivalent in Aquinas' Latin, but it fairly represents the methodological thesis he takes over from Aristotle. Different people have widely differing views about what is important, worth while, pleasant, and so forth, whether in an individual or a social context. Different people use words somewhat differently, marking their differing evaluations, preferences, tastes. In deciding what *is* important in human affairs, what are worthwhile social structures and decent forms of co-operation in which to take pride and pleasure, philosophically clear-headed social theorists adopt quite consciously and explicitly a particular standard, a particular 'rule and measure', *kanon kai metron* (says Aristotle), *regula et mensura* (says Aquinas).[94] They use this standard even when intending primarily to describe and explain (rather than primarily to recommend or prescribe). And the standard is specified as: how things look, seem on reflection to be, to a certain sort of person.

'In all such matters, pertaining to human activities, it seems that the truth is: what seems to the *studiosus* (who judges rightly about such matters) to be the case.'[95] Now *studiosus* is simply a translation handed to Aquinas for Aristotle's key word *spoudaios*, the serious, morally weighty, mature person whose views and conduct deserve to be taken seriously—the right-minded person, a person of practical reasonableness and integrated character, a person who is (in that rich sense) truly virtuous. So *studiosus* is synonymous with *virtuosus*, and 'the measure according to which one is to judge about any and all human affairs is virtue, and the good person precisely as virtuous'.[96]

This raises a good many questions, and many of them cannot be resolved before considering Aquinas' theory of practical rationality, good and evil, right and wrong (III.5–7, IV.1–5). Here I shall make only some preliminary observations.

First, the appeal to the standard of the morally right-minded person is not viciously circular. Aristotle and Aquinas[97] on several occasions compare this standard to the standard we use to identify what is or is not, say, sweet. What is sweet is what *seems* sweet to a *healthy* person. Now this is only an analogy, and its point is not to

---

[94] *Nic. Eth.* 3. 5. 1113ᵃ32; *Eth.* III. 10 n. 7 [494].   [95] *Eth.* x. 8 n. 13 [2062].

[96] Ibid.; *Nic. Eth.* 10. 5. 1176ᵃ15–16. See also IV *Sent.* d. 29 a. 3 sol. 1c (= *Supp.* q. 47 a. 3c); *ST* I q. 1 a. 6 ad 3: 'the *virtuosus* is the rule and measure of human acts'.

[97] e.g. *Mal.* q. 1 a. 5 ad 10; *In Matt.* 19 ad v. 28 [1614]; see also I-II q. 1 a. 7c, q. 2 a. 1 ad 1.

suggest that right and wrong are matters of taste, or matters settled by experience as are matters of sensory qualities. Understanding and sound judgement are not matters of looking and seeing; 'point of *view*' is only a metaphor when applied, by analogy, to moral judgement and the use of moral judgement as the standard in social science. The point of the analogy with tasting was largely to indicate how there need be no vicious circularity in appealing to a certain type. What counts as being in good health is settled by many criteria besides tasting sugar as sweet; tasting sweet things as sour is only a sign, not the substance, of being in some way ill.

Second, whatever may be thought of the analogy with tasting sweet things, the issue confronting the social theorist is inescapable. Are, say, self-direction and participation in government really important and worth while (with the result that citizenship in the Aristotelian sense and constitutionality deserve a place in the philosophical account of human affairs)? Many people, perhaps the great majority,[98] may strongly feel that ready access to the pleasures {voluptates} of food, sex, and emotionally powerful music is more important. Should the theory of politics perhaps be replaced with a general theory of consumption and consumer-satisfying institutions? Should the theory of law be absorbed into a general theory of 'social engineering' or of 'markets'? One cannot answer such questions without ranking features of human existence in terms of importance. Aquinas' answer, with Aristotle, is (as we have seen) that when one is doing social theory, one's judgements of relative *importance* should be the same judgements one has to make when deliberating and deciding about one's own life, i.e. the practical judgements made by the sort of person one regards as a good example.

Third, the method does not eliminate from view, or render indescribable, those institutions, such as slavery, which seem to be, not deviant versions of something else, but flourishing examples of vicious attitudes and practices. What may seem the central case of slavery—say slavery in the early Roman empire or the *ante bellum* South—is an intelligible system stabilized by law which, however inadequately, mitigates the most radical consequences of the idea of treating one human being as the mere property and tool of another. The 'purest' cases of slavery are arrangements such as the forced-labour camps of wartime Nazi Germany, where the

---

[98] Cf. *Eth.* I. 5 n. 3 [57]: 'almost all ordinary folk {populares homines}'; III. 4 n. 44 below.

labourers are used up hugger-mugger like, or even as, mere material. Systems such as the Roman or the *ante bellum* American pay their own tribute to virtue in their self-interpretation: slavery is rationalized as no more than penal servitude (extended to guiltless children by a notion of family solidarity), or the facts of human dignity are set aside on false or irrelevant pleas alleging the substandard intelligence of the enslaved race. These systems are deviant versions of proper institutions such as penal detention, wage service, and inheritance. A good descriptive and explanatory account of them will be constantly attentive, however tacitly, to their departures from the decent social forms, their violations of basic human goods and rights.

Fourth, this social-theoretical strategy does not privilege conventional, unreflective *mores*. Who counts as virtuous and good is not settled for the philosopher prior to all philosophical reflection. True, moral philosophy starts from conventional moral judgements. But it subjects them to every relevant philosophical question. Such questions can concern the internal coherence of the conventional judgements, their clarity, their *truth*—their conformity with every aspect of reality which might affect rational judgement about the good and the right. The strategy can avoid the question-begging circularity of supporting a value or principle (say, political liberty) by reliance upon a character-type identified just by reference to that value or principle.

Indeed, fifth, Aquinas clearly recognized that Aristotle's appeal to the standard of the *spoudaios* cannot be treated as bedrock. It cannot settle the further questions: What really are the human goods, important by their presence or absence in the life of a person or a group? What types of human choice and action are truly reasonable and right? What response can be given to sceptical doubts about the objectivity of answers to those questions? When commenting on Aristotle's appeals to the standard constituted by the *spoudaios*, Aquinas makes it explicit that the appeal is sound because 'good character' (as in 'person of good character': *spoudaios* or *virtuosus*) 'is defined by reference to its being in line with right reason'.[99] In other words, identifying the *spoudaios* is a matter of critical judgement, which has standards. Nobody's

---

[99] *Eth.* III. 10 n. 7 [494]. See also *ST* I q. 1 a. 6 ad 3: if the *virtuosi* judge rightly by following inclinations (which, in them, are in line with reason), others can judge rightly (even without having the right inclinations) by following *doctrina* which is grounded in *principia*.

reason or reasoning, not even the intelligence and reasoning of thoroughly good people, is simply its own measure or entirely self-validating.[100]

So the lasting point of the appeal is this. If there are rational, philosophically warrantable standards of good and evil, right and wrong, they constitute for theorists not only the appropriate standards for conducting their own lives alone and with friends, families, business associates, and fellow citizens, but also appropriate criteria both for selecting matters for theoretical study and for articulating its results. (That, restated, is the point with which II.6 concluded.) The ultimately decisive criteria for 'concept-formation in social science' are the standards of unrestrictedly rational practical reasonableness, of right judgement about what to do (and what not to do).

In the wake of Hobbes, Hume, and Kant, late nineteenth- and twentieth-century social theorists attempted 'value-free' investigations of human affairs. I have analysed, elsewhere, the attempts made in a field familiar to me (general theory of law), and argued that they were fruitful on condition that they were not value-free.[101] The analysis supported a quite general conclusion:

There is thus a mutual though not quite symmetrical interdependence between the project of describing human affairs by way of theory, and the project of evaluating human options with a view, at least remotely, to acting reasonably and well. The evaluations are in no way deduced from the descriptions; but one whose knowledge of the facts of the human situation is very limited is unlikely to judge well in discerning the practical implications of the basic values.[102] Equally, the descriptions are not deduced from the evaluations; but without the evaluations one cannot determine what descriptions are really illuminating and significant.[103]

Notes

a. *Prologues to the commentaries on the* Ethics *and the* Politics . . . The former, unlike the latter, is not editorially defined as a prologue to the whole commentary, but both in form and in substance unquestionably is one. So I shall refer to it as *Eth*. prol. (nn. 1–6).

---

[100] See I-II q. 19 a. 4, q. 91 a. 2, a. 3 ad 2; and X.3 below.

[101] Finnis (1980: 4–18).

[102] Finnis (1980) uses the term 'values' to translate the term *bona* as used in the phrase *bona humana* in e.g. I-II q. 94 a. 2 and *Eth*. 1. 4 n. 1 [43], 12 n. 4 [142], VI. 4 nn. 11–12 [1172–3], etc. The present book speaks, with the same intended meaning, of (basic) human goods; see III. 2 n. d. and III. 5 below. [103] Finnis (1980: 19).

b. *Logic, in its widest sense* . . . Aquinas calls this, in *Eth*. prol. n. 2 [2], *ratio-nalis philosophia* and says that it includes not only the relationship {ordo} of principles to conclusions but also the relationship {ordo} of parts of speech to each other in so far as these are signs of concepts which are mean-ingful expressions {voces significativae}. But this need not be understood as bringing all aspects of language or linguistics under 'rational philosophy', i.e. into the second type of order. For expressions are not 'meaningful', in the sense that Aquinas usually considers relevant, unless they are so ordered as to make a statement affirming that such-and-such is true (or false), i.e. an assertion: *Peri*. prol. n. 3 [3b]; cf. n. q. below; v. 5 at nn. 117–22 below.

c. *Order we can bring into our thinking, doing, making* . . . In introducing these three types of order, Aquinas says, in each case, that 'reason, by/in considering, makes {ratio considerando facit}' the order in question. In *Pol*. prol. n. 2 [2] his formula is: reason is both knowing and making {et cognoscitiva et factiva}. My paraphrase (not a translation), 'can bring into', is intended to preserve the delicate balance, or path, between 'find-ing' and 'making'. See III.6 n. t below.

d. *Use of words in Aquinas* . . . 'People of sound judgement do not fuss about what things are called {sapientis est non curare de nominibus}': II *Sent*. d. 3 q. 1 a. 1c. 'A person of sound judgement does take care with words in so far as they signify some aspect of reality {proprietatem rerum} and not for their own sake': II *Sent*. d. 42 q. 2 a. 2 sol. 3 ad 1.

e. *'Moralis philosophia' as 'the philosophy of self-determining human con-duct'* . . . The word *moralis* in Aquinas often lacks the specifically norma-tive connotations of 'moral'. As to *philosophia*, note that, as in modern English the word 'ethics' signifies not only (1) the *theory* of the supreme standards for conduct but also (2) the *set of such standards* themselves and (3) the *relationship* between particular conduct or character and those standards, so too in Aquinas (whose Latin lacks any exact counterpart to the English word 'morality') the term *moralis philosophia* signifies not only (1) the *theory* of human conduct and society, but also (2) everything else signified by 'ethics'; see e.g. *Eth*. prol. n. 3 [3] (n. 9 above). Note: '*theoria*, id est consideratio vel speculatio de veritate': *Meta*. II. 1 n. 2 [274].

f. *Is oeconomica exclusively the theory of households* {domesticae multi-tudines}? . . . In *Pol*. I. 1 nn. 3, 19 [11, 27], etc., as also in *Reg*. I. 1 [1.2] [14] [749], the threefold distinction between individual, household, and *per-fecta communitas* is expanded to a four- or even fivefold distinction by the addition, between household {familia domus unius} and *perfecta commu-nitas*, of locality {vicus} where typically one will find one trade or craft.

g. *Unity of conjunction* {colligatio} . . . This is a good example of Aquinas' flexible use of terms, allowing context and argument and the nature of the subject-matter to stabilize the meaning. Here in the prologue to *Eth*., *colligatio* is contrasted with unity of order. So it obviously is to be taken in the sense it has in *Phys*. VIII. 7 n. 8 [1028] (parts of an animal are connected by *colligatio*), *Meta*. v. 3 n. 3 [779] (parts of a dwelling), *ST* I

q. 113 a. 5 ad 3 and III q. 68 a. 1 ad 2 (*colligatio* of child *in utero* with mother) or III *Sent.* d. 13 q. 2 a. 2 sol. 2c and *In Heb.* 4. 2 ad v. 12 [224] (members of the body are joined by nerves and joints or nerves and arteries). But in other places the *colligatio* which the *Ethics* prologue denies exists in human groups is predicated precisely of such groups: IV *Sent.* d. 24 q. 3 a. 2 sol. 3c. (political community), *ScG* IV c. 35 n. 7 [3731] (members of a household), and *Impugn.* II c. 2 ad 4 [61] (members of a college).

h. *Modern economics launched by Adam Smith as a study of side-effects . . .* See Finnis (1990: 194–5).

i. *State debts and undertakings after a change of constitution . . .* See *Politics* 3. 3. 1276^{a}7–^{b}15. Aquinas says (*Pol.* III. 2 n. 8 [364]) that the question still hanging at the end of the discussion will be 'settled in what follows'; but it is not, and he does not settle it when confronted by the issue as a claim of justice (by people expelled after a revolution) in *Quodl.* XII q. 15 [16] a. 1 ad 3. Aristotle's probable view (that such liabilities should normally be honoured) can be inferred from what he says in c. 40 of a treatise (unknown in Aquinas' day) on the Constitution of Athens: see Barker (1948: 100, 381 n. 2). See also Voegelin (1957: 326).

j. *Social acts . . .* See Finnis *et al.* (1987: 90, 120–3, 131, 276, 288–9); Finnis (1989).

k. *What is the political community an order of? Individuals? Or also of intermediate groups? . . .* Aristotle gives both answers: *Politics* 1. 2. 1252^b, 3. 1. 1275^b.

l. *X's nature is understood by understanding X's capacities, which are understood by understanding X's activities, which are understood by understanding their objects . . .* See Finnis (1983: 21–2). This fundamental element in Aquinas' strategy as a theorist is not so much rejected as completely overlooked in much modern work on Aquinas.

m. *Capacities 'essentially' passive or active . . .* The qualifier 'essentially' is to signify that powers of the soul, even when they are passive (e.g. the appetitive powers, including the will, which are passive in so far as they are moved by their objects and the apparent desirability of those objects), are also active: see *Ver.* q. 16 a. 1 ad 13.

n. *The answer to 'What are you doing?' by way of the further question 'Why are you behaving like that?' . . .* Here I employ (by stipulation) a useful terminological distinction between 'behaviour' (an event in the first order) and 'doing' or 'action' considered as the carrying out of a human choice, the adoption and execution of a proposal shaped in deliberation. On the significance of 'Why?' questions in this context, see Anscombe (1958: 9–36).

o. *'Military science' . . .* As a technique involving mastery of materials and the limited objective of victory in war, this is an art, in the fourth order. But just in so far as it makes no real sense unless brought into line with the common good of the state being defended, military science (the science of war)—particularly what the supreme commander needs—has rather the character of the third order and *prudentia*: II-II q. 50 a. 4; see VII.5 at n. 78 below.

p. *The* prudentia *required of subjects* . . . In II-II q. 47 a. 12c Aquinas contends that *as* subject or *as* servant one does not need *prudentia*, but only as a rational and free willing person. This does not seem to be right, for as q. 50 a. 3c observes, the self-directing choice *to obey or conform* calls for a kind of *prudentia*. Now such a choice seems to be made precisely as subject or as servant. Perhaps Aquinas, however, is thinking that this self-directing choice is a kind of threshold choice, by which one, so to speak, opts into the role of obedient servant or obedient subject, and thereafter simply acts in that role without *prudentia*. That would not be a satisfactory account of the dispositions and actions of free citizens or even of effective military personnel, who need to make the plan their own to the extent that they can depart from it, and from their orders, if that is called for by the situation, judged—in line with their leaders' reasonable objectives—by themselves and responded to on their own initiative. (It would be more like the situation of the slave, who—in extreme forms of *slavery*—does not know what the master is up to.)

q. *History and biblical writings* . . . Aquinas distinguishes between genres {modi} of biblical writing; e.g. some parts of the Bible are 'intended by way of historical narrative {per modum narrationis historicae proponuntur}', others are not. As to those parts which are, one must take as foundational the truth of the history {pro fundamento tenenda veritas historiae}; 'spiritual' commentaries are to be erected only on this foundation. See I q. 102 a. 1c. Caution: The meaning intended by the author is the 'historical' meaning even when the author did not intend to be giving a historical narrative. (Similarly, the 'literal' = 'historical' = intended meaning is often not literal but figurative, as in poetry (*Quodl.* VII q. 6 a. 3 ad 20); so by understanding the metaphor in a metaphorical passage one comes to understand the passage's literal meaning (I-II q. 102 a. 1 ad 1).) To gauge what the author meant one must consider *inter alia* the original audience; so, for example, Genesis was intended for a 'primitive people {rudi populo}' and shapes its account accordingly: I q. 61 a. 1 ad 1, q. 66 a. 1 ad 1, q. 68 a. 3c; II *Sent.* d. 14 a. 2 ad 2, a. 5 ad 1. Creation did not take 'six days' but was instantaneous: IV *Sent.* d. 43 a. 3 sol. 3 ad 1.

r. *Chance occurrences and Aristotelian natural science and historical knowledge* . . . See *Physics* 2. 4–6. 195^{b}31–198^{a}13; *Phys.* II. 7–10 [198–238]; *Metaphysics* 6. 3. 1027^{a}29–^{b}16; *Meta.* VI. 3 esp. nn. 1196–8; *Peri* I. 14 nn. 12, 19 [187, 194]; Finnis (1992b: 9–10). Also x. 2 at n. 25 below.

s. *No 'philosophy of history' (laws of progress, decline, or inevitable cycles)* . . . Theology, with sources of information not available to (though not opposed to) philosophy, can judge that history has, in a certain sense, a centre—an event of supreme importance, long prepared and rich in consequences. But nothing in theology, as Aquinas reasonably understood it, gives or even purports to give any firm basis for thinking that the truth or goodness embodied in history's centre will have become prevalent at any time up to and including the ending of the history of the human race.

t. *'Practical' theory* . . . See Finnis (1983, ch. 1).

u. *'Analogy' as relationship to central case or focal meaning* . . . One of Aristotle's most articulate discussions and deployments of this second sort of analogy is to be found in his analysis of types of friendship in *Eudemian Ethics* (7. 2. 1236ª16–30), a work largely unknown to Aquinas. Aristotle's modern commentators sometimes call this sort of analogy *pros hen* (literally 'towards something' or 'related to/with reference to one thing') homonymy, and Aquinas' neo-scholastic exponents often called it (somewhat confusingly) 'analogy of proportion'.

v. *'Democratia' in Aquinas' commentary on the Politics* . . . One must here use the critical Leonine edition of *Pol.*; in earlier printed editions Aquinas' term *democratia* was suppressed in favour of the anachronistic *status popularis*, people's or populist state; and correspondingly for *aristocratia* and *monarchia*.

w. *Good forms of constitution and political order are found relatively rarely* . . . Aristotle makes this bluntly clear in *Politics* 4. 11. 1295ª25–34, 1296ª37–40. Aquinas' commentary does not reach this passage, but he refers to these parts of *Politics* 4 in *Eth.* VIII. 10 n. 2 [1673] and certainly both knew and agreed with this opinion. In *Eth.* VIII. 10 n. 9 [1680] he says explicitly what Aristotle *ad loc.* says at most implicitly, that the good forms of constitution are corrupted 'easily'.

III

Freedom, Reason, and Human Goods

III.1. *Sceptical Doubts*

Aquinas is well aware of sceptical doubts. 'Since one is in charge of oneself {dominus sui}, it seems at first glance that, when one's actions affect only oneself, one is morally free to do whatever one likes.'[1] Indeed, what does it matter if my actions do affect others? *Many* think that we neither can nor should be really concerned about the well-being of others.[2] And when one goes beyond a 'first glance', and beyond social conventions, isn't it clear that 'justice' entirely 'arises from some human opinion' and 'consists in what *seems* or does not *seem*' to be right?[3] Look at the 'great differences' in these opinions; 'something considered immoral at one period or in one region is not considered immoral at all in another time or place'. Isn't it idle, then, to speak of the 'naturally right or naturally just'?[4] Surely there's no justice or injustice other than being in line or out of line with the (positive) law of some place and time?[5] Considered in themselves, independently of local and transient conventions, aren't all choices and actions morally

---

[1] II-II q. 122 a. 1c; likewise I-II q. 100 a. 5 ad 1.
[2] Ibid.; also II-II q. 47 a. 10c; *Eth.* vi. 7 nn. 9–10 [1203–4].
[3] *Eth.* v. 12 n. 3 [1018].   [4] *Eth.* i. 3 n. 2 [33]; *Mal.* q. 2 a. 4 obj. 13.
[5] *Eth.* i. 3 n. 2 [33], v. 12 n. 10 [1025]; *In Rom.* 5. 4 ad v. 14 [428].

indifferent'?[6] And, most fundamentally, how can anything be said to be 'inherently rationally desirable' or naturally or truly choice-worthy? Surely, what is desirable and choice-worthy for me is whatever seems desirable and choice-worthy to me (together with whatever seems to me prudent as a means of getting and keeping what I want)?[7]

Though sceptical relativism in his era lacked the prestige and institutional support (e.g. by educators) that it enjoys today, Aquinas articulated its essential positions and sources of popular appeal. When he first read the *Ethics*, perhaps in Naples in his teens, he will have seen Aristotle confronting it, early in the treatise.[8] And one must suppose that he noticed the inadequacy of Aristotle's explicit response.

That response could be sought in several places. In book 3 there is the appeal to the *spoudaios*, the person of good character, whose judgement should be accepted as sound rather as a healthy person's sense of taste is the criterion of what tastes sweet. As a standard of judgement within descriptive social theory this can be acquitted of vicious circularity (II.8). But it gives no help in responding to the question whether judgements identifying the *spoudaios* have any genuine truth value. Then in book 5, where the sceptical relativism of Aristippus is identified, Aristotle's appeal to 'natural right' is weak and confused; perhaps we have here only jumbled, gappy lecture notes. A final opportunity, in book 6's discussion of wisdom and insight {nous}, is passed up; Aristotle's talk of perceiving the truth in the concrete situation is disconcertingly reticent about whether there can be wisdom or insight into *general* 'practical' truths of ethics—something comparable to the wisdom and insight which there can and must be into 'theoretical' truths. And in this context Aristotle suggests something a neo-Humean could endorse: practical reasonableness {phronēsis} is about means, not ends. Doesn't this seem to concede that one's ends, one's basic purposes, are given to one's reason(ing) by one's desires and feelings (doubtless shaped by one's culture) about what is appealing? And doesn't that make nonsense of the *Ethics* as a whole?[a]

From the outset of his work in ethics and politics, Aquinas

---

[6] See *Mal.* q. 2 a. 4 obj. 13: 'So: nothing is naturally just or good, and consequently nothing is naturally unjust or bad. Therefore every act is in itself [morally] neutral {indifferens}.'   [7] *Eth.* III. 10 n. 4 [491]; also *Meta.* XI. 5 n. 14 [2224].
[8] *Nic. Eth.* I. 3. 1094^{b}14–17; cf 5. 7: 1134^{b}24–7; *Eth.* I. 3 n. 2 [33]; V. 12 n. 10 [1025].

articulates what he thinks needs to be said, to improve upon Aristotle's response to sceptical doubts. (His interest here as elsewhere is in the truth, not in repairing Aristotle's errors or omissions.)

III.2. *Self-Refutation of Sceptical Doubting*

The primary elements of a sound response to sceptical doubts about practical truth can be reached by understanding the making and carrying out of free choices. This understanding must not be reductive. It must not suppress aspects of deliberation and choice which the person deliberating and choosing engages with and is more or less aware of and reflective about. What choice or range of choices is selected for philosophical reflection and analysis should not matter; a structurally sound analysis of one choice will provide a basis, albeit in principle defeasible, for understanding all. In an analysis seeking to clarify the constant, central elements of Aquinas' understanding of free choice, reasons for action, and the first principles of practical reasonableness, any choice would do as subject-matter. But the choice I shall consider first is one which will allow us to pursue directly the dialectic with scepticism. It is a choice and act which Aquinas does not formally consider (doubtless because he did not have to address an audience impressed by sceptical denials of free choice): the choice to entertain the sceptical challenge, to treat it as a proposition to be taken seriously.[9]

What is going on when an ancient Greek, or a contemporary neo-Humean, responsibly entertains and affirms the proposition that the basic motivations for human action are feelings not reasons, passions not intelligent insights into or rational judgements about what is truly choice-worthy? Such an affirmation is meant to be, not an arbitrary opinion, but rather a true judgement made in the face of age-old prejudices and conventional 'wisdom'. Moreover, the proposition affirmed as true is meant to be a conclusion, not simply and immediately self-evident. So, defending it requires careful argumentation—work which one can *choose* to undertake or not.

Notice first that the proposition in question is not a statement of general scepticism. It does not claim, indeed it is inconsistent with

---

[9] See I-II q. 16 a. 1 ad 3: 'Putting one's theoretical understanding {ratio speculativa} to work in [the activity of] understanding and judging is a matter of will.'

the claim, that *all* opinions are mere opinions, and none are true (or false). (Any such general claim is inevitably and obviously self-refuting, falsified by what is involved in making it, as Aristotle and Aquinas underline.[10]) The proposition in question is an affirmation presupposing, and indeed asserting, that there is some truth at stake. And the main thing to notice is: Someone considering whether to agree with the proposition is supposing that it would be good, even if perhaps uncomfortable, to find out this truth, to get clear about whether such affirmations are or are not *correct*.

This sort of good is intelligibly good, not merely something emotionally appealing. We can understand the good of truth and knowledge even when attaining it seems likely to be thoroughly painful or upsetting. And the relationship between understanding and reality—the relationship we call truth (and knowledge)—is one which only intelligence can know. One's getting to know the truth about some topic, one's judgements and affirmations being correct—this is something of value, an intelligible and understood (not merely felt) good {bonum intelligibile; bonum intellectum}.[b] It gives point to the labour of reading or listening, of thinking, wondering, testing, and so forth (in preference to doing nothing, or doing something else). To say it gives point is to say that it is an end {finis}, an intelligent objective. Indeed, it is to say that it has its own point and is not *merely* a means to some other end. It is to say that one has a reason for acting thus (inquiring and so on).

This reason for acting is a motivation which is neither *exclusively* an urge or a drive for emotional satisfaction, nor merely instrumental to some other rational objective. To recognize this reason is to understand the worth, the intelligible good, of the possible purpose. It is to understand that if one's purpose were to be blocked, if one were to get into or remain in a muddle about this issue of scepticism, or if one scented the truth but refused to put aside prejudice, one would be so far forth deprived, deficient, badly off. (To say or think this is not to deny that remaining in ignorance might be emotionally more comfortable. Nor does it necessarily

---

[10] *Metaphysics* 4. 4. 1005^{b}35–1006^{a}28, 8: 1012^{a}29–^{b}18, 11. 5. 1062^{b}1–11, 6. 1063^{b}30–5; *Meta.* IV. 6 nn. 12–15 [607–10], 17 nn. 7–8 [742–3], XI. 5 n. 13 [2223], 6 n. 22 [2246]; *Post.* I. 44 n. 10 [404]; *Eth.* VI. 5 n. 8 [1182]. It is important to note that Aristotle claims no originality for this; arguments from self-refutation are not only sound and important but also part of any educated common-sense or simple and honest reflectiveness. Aquinas vigorously deploys argument from self-refutation against those (Latin Averroists) who held that there is only one human intellect, and denied that intellect is more than a mover of (rather than part of) one's individual reality. See v.8 at n. 212 below.

amount to the thought that neglect or refusal to understand would be immoral. It does not contradict the thought that one has things one should be doing other than reflecting on scepticism.) So, finding out is envisaged by the inquirer as a kind of 'perfection', limited but real, and failing to find out as a kind of imperfection. And thus, in all these ways, discovering the truth about ethical scepticism, or about the neo-Humean theory of motivation, is choice-*worthy*.

But in that case the claim that nothing is really choice-worthy is sufficient evidence of its own falsity. Similarly self-refuting are the claims that all opinions about good and bad in human action are mere arbitrary opinions, that practical reasoning is always the slave of the passions, that reasons as reasons have no power to motivate the will, and that human goods are not willed because understood to be good but thought to be good because desired or preferred.[c] The structure of self-refutation is in each case essentially the same: the reasonableness of taking the claims seriously and of treating them as giving one a reason to spend time reflecting on their content is inconsistent with that content.

Nor is this some logical trick. The core of the argument is the distinction between intelligence and feeling, between reasons for action[d] and mere spontaneous urges or 'passions'. One understands that distinction only by attending reflectively to the data of one's own deliberating and choosing. The concepts of reason for action, intelligible end, intrinsic point, and understood good implicitly define one another[11] (rather like the concepts of circle, radius, and circumference), but one cannot break into the circle of definitions without such reflective attention to data. The point of taking as an example the deliberation, choice, and action of the ethical sceptic (or of someone considering whether to examine and evaluate ethical scepticism) was simply that here the data were inescapably close to hand. One might take as matter for the reflection any other deliberate human action at all.

Consider the choices and actions in two other, different contexts. The first context was considered in II.3. At 9.45 p.m. on 4 June

---

[11] Thus in any practical deliberation and activity, 'the good intended . . . is that for the sake of which everything else [in that activity] is done. In medicine everything is done for the sake of health, in military affairs, for the sake of victory. But this good intended in an activity or choice is called an end [the activity's point] {finis}. For end [point] is simply that for the sake of which the other things are done': *Eth.* i. 9 n. 3 [105]; 'the reasons for possible actions which have point are identified by looking to their point {rationes eorum [operabilium] quae sunt ad finem, ex fine sumuntur}': I-II q. 14 a. 2c; and see the texts quoted in n. 31 below.

1944, despite well-founded predictions of poor weather in the Channel, Eisenhower overruled the contrary advice of his airforce commander and the doubts of his second-in-command, and confirmed the decision to invade France on the 6th: *'I don't like it*, but there it is . . . '.[12] His emotional repugnance was great, the reasons for postponing were very strong, but he chose to follow the very strong reasons for going then.[e] Once his decision was made, the detailed plans for D-Day became more or less immediate reasons for action for most[13] of the many thousands of people called upon, by reason of military commands and allegiance, to make their part of the invasion a success. The whole vast, co-ordinated venture was a means, interlocked with others and chosen as the most effective available (when thus interlocked), for achieving relatively early victory in Europe and then in the Pacific. Victory, and relatively early victory, was an intelligible good, and end. But its goodness and point was, in turn, as a means of protecting and promoting more ultimate and basic intelligible goods such as peace and justice, human life and health, truth and sharing in knowledge of it, and so forth, all to some extent damaged and threatened, in the United States and many other communities, by Nazi domination of Europe and the continuance of world war.

The other context I shall consider is one to which I shall return from time to time in the course of this book. It is suggested by Aquinas' occasional allusions to co-operation between students, and to the temporary groups constituted by people sharing a hostel. If we put these together (as Aquinas perhaps does at one point),[14] we can take as a conveniently imaginable subject for reflection various choices made in a university or college student hostel. The details of the context and the choices can be filled in as questions arise about individual and social existence.

[12] Hastings (1989: 71).

[13] Not everyone chose to follow those reasons for actions: 'Then, as they pulled away from the side [in their landing-craft], they saw their major waving farewell from the upper deck. He had decided to leave [Sergeant] Hertz and the others to explore Omaha [invasion beach] alone that day, and they never saw him again': Hastings (1989: 95).

[14] *Impugn.* II c. 2 ad 3 [60], considering a private student house, secular or religious, within the public studium or university. (These distinctions between private and public do not turn on questions of ownership of the place or the enterprise.)

III.3. *Reason and Will: Deliberation and Choice*

Aquinas reflected on the internal structure of deliberation and choice more carefully, it seems, than anyone before and almost anyone since. His analysis of the interplay of reason and will, of understanding and responsiveness, in that structured process is one of his most original theoretical achievements.[f] Several of its main elements have been rejected by many of his followers,[g] and many of those who profess to accept and expound it have misunderstood it. Aquinas himself contributed to the inherent difficulties in the subject-matter by setting out the results of his analysis in an *order*, a sequence, that invites confusion. Yet those results, once sorted out, are most illuminating.

The core of the analysis, as we shall see, is an understanding of *will* and *willing* in a precise sense, as one's intelligent *response* to what one *understands* as opportunity. It is an explanatory description of one's intelligence in action,[15] of the way in which reasons *motivate*. It does not assert that one acts only for reasons, or that one can act without the support of one's emotions. But it does assert, and make manifest, how reasons give one motives to act which are not merely, nor even predominantly, emotional.

Two other preliminary observations. First, the analysis is 'from the internal point of view' (II.5). But like any sound analysis, it proceeds not by trying to peer inside, or catch a glimpse of oneself in some kind of sideways or 'reflexive' 'look' by a kind of inner eye. It attends, like other analyses, to data which in this case are the data of one's own experience (and in *this* sense it can be called 'introspective'), the experience of someone who has made deliberate choices, and who knows of other people's deliberations, motives, and choices. Perhaps the most important evidence is the cases in which one begins the process of acting but does not complete it—where one decides to look for means of doing something but never gets round to considering them, or never identifies a specific proposal for doing what one was interested in, or never adopts one proposal in preference to all other options (including staying put and doing nothing of this sort), or never acts on one's

---

[15] 'For one's will is in one's intelligence {voluntas in intellectu est} . . . For the source of this sort of appetite is understanding {intelligentia}, i.e. the intellectual act {actus intellectus} which is somehow moved by something intelligible {ab intelligibili}' (*Meta.* XII. 7 n. 4 [2522]; see also nn. b and d); 'intellectus in agendo non distinguitur a voluntate' (*Vercell.* q. 22 [846]); *ST* I q. 57 a. 1, q. 87 a. 4; III. 6 n. 139 below.

choice when the time for action arrives and other pre-conditions are satisfied.[h]

Second, it is worth noticing from the outset how many of the elements in the analysed structure are named, by Aquinas but following ordinary language, with terms which are central to political discourse. Plato's guiding thought, that the *polis* is the human being writ large, and each of us a *polis* writ small,[16] here finds some common-sense confirmation. Moreover, as we should expect (II.2), the analysis will apply as well to social as to purely individual choices and acts.

Here is a group of eight students, occupying a corridor of eight rooms and a small kitchen in the college hostel. They are deciding whether or not to establish for themselves, by agreement, a curfew on cooking and kitchen conversation after 9.00 p.m. The walls are thin, the doors even thinner, voices and kitchen noises travel, some of the students find it hard to study at nights with these distractions. But they all enjoy company, and like relaxed night-time talking; and some of them get back late from libraries and would prefer to cook late. From time to time, most of them get really interested in the work, and want to read late and do the note-taking that brings comprehension. More constantly, they want to succeed in examinations, to get employment and the bundle of benefits loosely envisaged and named 'a future'. They see the point of getting along together, and understand how in this debate that cuts both ways. As an individual student in this situation, what are the elements in one's deliberating and choosing?

Take as a starting-point for the analysis not the beginning of the process but the central event, the choosing. Aquinas calls this *electio*, and the name is fitting. Whether it is the students reaching a collective decision by voting, formally or informally, or an individual student deciding which way to 'vote', the structure of this 'electing' is essentially the same. There is a preferring of one option to another. The choice may be between (i) a 9.00 p.m. curfew, (ii) a 10.00 p.m. curfew, and (iii) leave things *laissez-faire*. Each has its attractions, its point. None has all the merits of the others. And they are mutually incompatible—real alternatives. One is aware of what will be given up when one selects. Yet one can choose, and choose one does.

The choice is of certain means to an end. If one opts for the 9.00

---

[16] *Republic* 2. 10. 368d–369a; cf. 4. 11. 434d–435a; 8. 1. 544d–545a.

p.m. curfew, it is with the intention of increasing study time. 'Intention' can be used broadly, to include the whole package of end(s) and means, or any of its elements, as willed —'We intend to have silence after 9.00 p.m. so as to have more study time.' Or it can be used more narrowly, to pick out *end* as distinct from *means* —'We are enforcing silence with the intention of enhancing our academic work.' Aquinas from time to time uses *intentio* in the broader sense;[17] but he generally prefers to reserve the word *intentio* for end(s) as distinct from means. According to this specialized use, then, he will say: *electio* is of means,[18] *intentio* is of end.

Intentio and *electio* are analytically distinguishable elements in one's response to the benefits, as one understands them, of the proposal[i] one adopts. Analytically, there is the adopted proposal, the chosen plan—having a curfew from 9.00—and there is the plan's intended purpose and intended benefits—having more study time, doing better work, getting deeper understanding and/or better examination results, and so forth. The plan—proposed, debated, adopted, carried out—is a means. The purpose and the benefits it promises to realize are the ends. One could have opted for the socializing benefits of continued *laissez-faire*. Until one adopts a curfew plan (means), one need not have formed the intention to go for the benefit (end) of increased study time. If so, one forms that intention only, and precisely, in making that choice.[19] Choosing and intending are analytically distinguishable, as means and end are distinguishable, but they need not be chronologically or 'psychologically' separate.

The intended ends are no mere jumble; the plan's immediate purpose (increased study time) is itself intended and being chosen as a means to the intended benefits of better work and so forth. Similarly, the plan itself, the chosen means, is doubtless itself an end, in relation to various actions that need to be taken to put it into effect (putting up notices, getting a clock for the kitchen, reminding the forgetful . . .).[20] Devising the plan is a matter of

---

[17] e.g. II-II q. 64 a. 7c; *In Matt.* 7 ad v. 17 [661]. The distinction between the two senses of 'intention', and the applicability of the broader sense in which means *qua* chosen are included, along with end(s), in 'my intention', is clearly articulated in *Mal.* q. 2 a. 2 ad 8.

[18] 'Means' {id quod ad finem est} (literally: that which is *to* an end) here refers, not to instruments {organa} nor even to techniques precisely as fourth-order realities, but to some action of the chooser, an action chosen for the sake of its benefit(s). 'Choice is always of human acts': I-II q. 13 a. 4c. [19] e.g. I-II q. 12 a. 3c.

[20] Indeed, within the series which begins with the initiation of the proposal's execution and ends with the proposal's and action's consummation in the ultimate intended benefit,

intelligence, of seeing the point and envisaging means that have some likelihood of being effective in yielding benefits without unacceptable loss of other goods.

So: forming the intention to go for these benefits in this way by adopting this proposal is one's response to the reasons in favour of the proposal. Aquinas' name for one's ability to understand reasons (benefits), and to think up plans and proposals, is 'practical understanding' {intellectus practicus}. His name for one's ability to relate one sort of benefit to another, and to reason about the effectiveness of means and the respective merits of alternative plans, is 'practical reason' {ratio practica}, which often is used to include practical understanding, just as in any other context the terms 'reason(ing)' and 'judgement' include 'comprehension' or 'understanding'. For one's ability to respond to reasons for action, Aquinas uses the term 'will' {voluntas}.

'Reason' and 'will' are nouns, and reason and will are spoken of as doing this and that. But they are not like little persons—or machines—installed inside the acting person. They are factors in the acting of the single, unitary agent, the acting person (or group of persons). Aquinas makes an objector say that reason can't direct will to do anything because one's will, not being one's understanding, can't understand directions. Aquinas then gives the pertinent reply: I, the acting person, give *myself* directions, inasmuch as I am intelligent and willing.[21]

So intending and choosing are the central 'acts' of will.[22] Of these, choosing is the decisive act, being the occasion for the

every means is also an end (relative to the immediately preceding means), and every end is also a means (relative to the next further end). 'It is not only the ultimate end, for the sake of which the agent acts, that is called *end* in relation to what precedes it: *each* of the intermediate means which are between the primary agent and the ultimate end is called an end in relation to what precedes it {omnia intermedia quae sunt inter primum agens et ultimum finem dicuntur finis respectu praecedentium}': *Meta.* v. 2 n. 9 [771]; also *Phys.* II. 5 n. 6 [181]; *ST* I-II q. 1 a. 3 ad 3; Finnis (1991c: 10–14/1992a: 134–8); II.3 n. 37 above, IX.1 nn. 17–18 below. Reflection on this set of nested ends which are also means shows why 'means' has the meaning it has in this context and why it is generally a good translation of Aquinas' standard phrase *id quod ad finem est* ('that which is towards end'), provided one bears in mind the point made in n. 18 above and the further point that some 'means' are constituent parts or aspects of the relevant end.

[21] I-II q. 17 a. 5 obj. 2 and ad 2. Thus, though Aquinas will sometimes say that the will is master/mistress of its activity {domina sui actus} (*Virt.* q. 2 a. 10 ad 6), his usual statement is that I (the acting person) am master/mistress of my (voluntary) activity.

[22] But, once again, knowing, intending, choosing, etc. are not, strictly speaking, acts of one's powers but rather of oneself, the person {suppositum}, by virtue of one's capacities {per potentiam}: *Ver.* q. 23 a. 13 ad 7.

formation of the definitive intention as well as the making of the choice; to adopt a proposal is to prefer it as a package promising these benefits by these means, rather than a package offering the same benefits (and perhaps more) but different means (say, 10.00 p.m. curfew) or a package offering different benefits and different means (say, continued *laissez-faire*).

But intention and choice are not the only aspects of the will's activity (i.e. of one's responsiveness to reasons). One has to choose precisely because one confronts not simply a single attractive proposal, but alternatives (including the status quo), each offering intelligible benefits. The choice is not between all proposals that one's restless intelligence brings to mind. It is between proposals that interest one, proposals that remain interesting after one has thought about one's situation, problem, or opportunity. So Aquinas' analysis identifies two further factors. There is precisely this thinking—deliberation—about the practical possibilities in the situation; Aquinas names this with another political term: *consilium*, taking counsel whether with oneself or with one's associates in the group—the specifically deliberative part of the whole process of deliberation. And there is the responding with interest, and sustained interest, to one or more of those possibilities as an interesting proposal, a live option or options. For this Aquinas' name is *consensus*, a kind of assent[23] to more or less specific options as really eligible. If one were in a situation where one proposal offered all the benefits of alternative proposals, and some more benefit, then (as Aquinas observes[24]) one would not need to choose; the alternatives would drop out of consideration, leaving one proposal as (in a modern jargon) 'dominant', and one would simply assent to this proposal and start acting on it. Choice {electio} as distinct from assent {consensus} is a matter of preferring *one* amongst alternative proposals *both* or *all* of which win one's assent as promising benefit and so remain interesting.[25]

---

[23] Strictly speaking, intellect/reason 'assents' to propositions, will (which is accompanied by some response of one's senses or imagination: I-II q. 75 a. 2c) 'consents' to what reason judges to be (at least in some significant respect(s)) good: III *Sent.* d. 23 q. 2 a. 2 sol. 1 ad 1. But 'it is customary to use the terms interchangeably {unum pro alio}': I-II q. 15 a. 1 ad 3.

[24] I-II q. 15 a. 3 ad 3 (where Aquinas also observes that one's assent to this uniquely attractive proposal could still be called 'choice', inasmuch as this proposal would still, in a sense, be being 'preferred' to the unattractive alternative).

[25] *Electio* in the strict sense (unlike consensus) always involves a preferring: II *Sent.* d. 7 q. 1 a. 1 ad 1, d. 24 q. 1 a. 2c ('to choose is to prefer one thing to another {alterum alteri praeoptare}'); I-II q. 12 a. 3c (*praeeligit*); q. 13 a. 4 ad 3 (*praeeligi*); q. 15 a. 3 ad 3 (*praefertur, praeeligitur, praeaccipimus*).

This assent of the will is one's response, in each case, to one's judgement that a proposal makes sense, offers practicable benefits, hangs together as a package of means to end(s). So Aquinas has a name for the acts of reason in which one forms these judgements of practicability and suitability: each of them is a *sententia*. That was the Roman juridical term for judgement, and Aquinas sometimes calls this sort of deliberative judgement just that, a *iudicium*.

Choice, then, is more than a matter of forming a judgement. We have to choose when, however long we deliberate, we do not conclude that one proposal is 'dominant', i.e. offers all the benefits of alternatives plus some more benefit. In the absence of such a conclusion, our deliberating (reasoning) is brought to an end only by will, by the act of choosing. Nevertheless, in the act of choosing, analysis can still discern the will's defining characteristic, of responding to *reasons*. In choosing, one not only intends the intelligible benefits of the means one is adopting. One also, it seems, is bringing one's rational deliberations to a close in a final judgement, a judgement of preference which can be called *iudicium electionis*, the judgement 'of', i.e. in, the very choosing.[j]

Before concluding this section by going back to the very sources {principia} of one's choosing, it will be convenient to sketch Aquinas' analysis of choice's aftermath, execution of choices in action. We shall have occasion to return to it more than once (VIII.1). The analysis has the same pattern: *will* is one's *response to reason(s)*. The choice was of an intelligible proposal; adopted, that proposal becomes a plan of action. But though the plan, once adopted by choice, is directive for one's activities, it is a directive which may not become fully operational until the relevant occasion or set of circumstances arises. When that condition is fulfilled (which may be immediately or at some more or less predictable time in the future), one must hold one's adopted plan in view, in one's mind's eye, and—unless one rejects its directiveness by changing one's mind, choosing to reverse one's former choice, and abandoning one's intention—then and there put it into effect. One will do so by employing not only one's limbs and one's strength, but also perhaps various techniques and skills and perhaps also other people.[26] *Imperium*, command, is Aquinas' once again highly political name for such guiding, directing, and shaping of actions by this sort of conditional directive and its re-presentation, to oneself, of one's

---

[26] See I-II q. 17 a. 3 ad 1, II-II q. 83 a. 1c; IV *Sent.* d. 15 q. 4 a. 1 sol. 1c.

adopted plan.[27] The response of one's psychosomatic make-up, in well-directed activity, he calls *usus*, the use or employment of one's bodily powers in *one's action*. The two elements are more clearly evident in social acts. When the group have agreed, whether by an accepted majority or unanimously, on a 9.00 p.m. curfew as from next Monday, they need to treat that decision, that *electio*, as constituting the rule, the way-things-are-to-be-done-around-here. They have to start treating the plan as no longer a mere proposal but as directive, an *imperium*, effective when the relevant pre-condition is fulfilled ('it's now Monday'). By shutting down on conversation and cooking at 9.00, they put it into effect, make use {usus} of their capacities to execute it.

If the plan works, if the action yields, at least to some extent, benefit as hoped for, the response of those who committed themselves to it by choice will be some measure of satisfaction, which Aquinas names *fruitio*. There may or may not be emotional satisfactions, pleasure palpable to the feelings (and such pleasure will be good and acceptable if the act is good, bad and corrupting if the act is morally bad).[28] But there will be the rational satisfaction—or contentment {quies}[29]—of understanding that one's intended purpose has been fulfilled. Here, as at every other point, the response—the delight[30]—is of will, one's responsiveness to reason(s).

In thus appreciating one's success, one is relating what one's action accomplished back to the benefits which it was intended to realize. Those benefits were the intelligible point, and one's understanding of them was the intelligent source, of the whole sequence of deliberation, choice, and action.

What are the benefits, the intelligible human goods understood {bona intellecta} by a student thinking about the situation? Various broad types of benefit come to mind: knowledge, for example, and friendship or companionship. Fairness, too, perhaps as part of companionship, perhaps distinct—no need to enter into that question at this stage in the analysis (see IV.3–5). As a 19-year-old student, one's understanding, awareness, of such possible benefits—one's

---

[27] I-II q. 17 a. 1; *imperium* is absent from the activities of subrational animals: a. 2.

[28] IV *Sent.* d. 31 q. 2 a. 3c (= *Supp.* q. 49 a. 6c); I-II q. 34 a. 1c.

[29] *Quies* is almost synonymous with *fruitio* and signifies the *resting* in fulfilment by which motion (i.e. action, or development) is completed; often contentment, or 'being content with': e.g. I *Sent.* d. 1 q. 4 a. 1 ad 5; I q. 5 a. 6c, I-II q. 67 a. 5c.

[30] 'There is a delight {delectatio} which follows reason's awareness . . . a delight which is in one's intellectual appetite, i.e. in one's will': I-II q. 31 a. 4; n. 75 below.

intellectus finium,[31] understanding of ends—goes far wider and deeper than this situation. In childhood, one came to understand that in indefinitely many situations knowledge and/or friendship (not to mention other broad types of benefit) can be involved, whether as types of opportunity, or as goods being achieved (realized, instantiated), or as what is lost in various types of potential or actual harm. The respectable arguments one would now deploy in discussion of the situation, appealing however tersely and implicitly to benefits of this sort, use premises that one uses and hears used in countless other sorts of situation. The particular sorts of benefit that would give point to (be *fines,* ends, for) a curfew, or for keeping to *laissez-faire,* are also the point, the *fines,* for much that one does, much of what we group together to do.

Corresponding, responding, to this awareness of various benefits is one's constant openness to and disposition to become interested in such benefits, and one's corresponding negative attitude toward their opposites. Aquinas labels this underlying intelligent responsiveness *voluntas* or *voluntas simplex,* will or simple willing.[k] The label is not altogether happy, since *voluntas* or will is the general word for one's responsiveness in all the other, more specific ways: interest in possible action in *this* situation, assent to *these* specific proposals, intention to get peace and quiet, an intention perfected and given effect in choosing to adopt this curfew, in willingness to adjust one's life to the curfew, and in rational satisfaction when the plan works out.

Those, then, are the main elements in Aquinas' analysis of freely chosen human action. It can be set out in tabular form. But one refinement or complexity should first be noted. As sketched in the foregoing paragraphs, the analysis presents the forming of intention as logically prior to but chronologically and causally one with[32] the choosing of the means. So it often is. And Aquinas insists that intending is not just being interested in and favouring some possible end, but rather is favouring (willing) an end *as the*

---

[31] *Ver.* q. 5 a. 1c. See also I-II q. 56 a. 3c ('the *principia* of this *ratio agendorum* . . . are *fines*'); *Virt.* q. 5 a. 2c ('the *principia* for actions {agibilium} are *fines,* for it is from these ends that we get the *ratio agendorum*'); I-II q. 3 a. 4c ('from the outset we want to follow an intelligible end {finem intelligibilem}, but we follow it by virtue of the fact that an act of our understanding {intellectus} makes it present to us') and ad 3 and 4, q. 9 a. 1, q. 10 a. 1.

[32] Somewhat, perhaps, as emitting sound is logically or naturally prior to but chronologically simultaneous with singing a song (ii *Sent.* d. 12 a. 2c: 'sonus praecedit cantum natura sed non tempore').

69

point or objective of some means, some possible action for the sake of it.[33] But he also explicitly envisages the forming of an intention without yet the choosing of means, and any table of the elements of deliberation and action tends to suggest that this can be so. The two positions can, however, be reconciled as follows.[34]

Sometimes one has a good in view and considers pursuing it or not. One can make a kind of preliminary or procedural choice: I will look for means and will pursue this good if I find means that are acceptable.[35] The forming of an intention 'without having determined the means which are the object of choice'[36] is made precisely by making that kind of preliminary choice, a choice which initiates deliberation—debate about the pros and cons of a curfew—but may or may not result in a substantive choice and intent to pursue the good by actions going beyond deliberation.

Still, the point of setting out Aquinas' analysis of action in tabular form is not to take a position on fine details of the analysis. It is rather to display vividly the grounds for Aquinas' fundamental proposition about human freedom: that it is through one's will that one's reason has the power to move one to action,[37] and one's 'will' is one's capacity to shape oneself by responding to reasons.[38] But the table will be misread unless one attends steadily to our freedom's very root {radix libertatis}: the fact that one's reason puts before one *more than one reason* for action, and more than one way of acting (option) that is good in some intelligible respect.[39]

---

[33] See I-II q. 12 a. 1 ad 3 and 4.   [34] See I-II q. 12 a. 4 ad 3.

[35] This sort of procedural 'thinking about deciding {ratio ratiocinatur de volendo}' and 'willing to deliberate {voluntas vult ratiocinari}' seems to be referred to in e.g. I-II q. 17 a. 1c.   [36] Ibid.

[37] I-II q. 90 a. 1 ad 3: 'ratio habet vim movendi a voluntate'.

[38] I q. 19 a. 1c, q. 82 a. 3c and ad 1 and 2 (understanding is prior to will, as motivating factor is prior to what is moving *qua* moving {sicut motivum mobili} and the active is prior to the acted upon {activum passivo}; for it is understood good—a *conception* that something is or would be good—that moves the will); a. 4c; also II *Sent.* d. 39 q. 2 a. 2c (what inclines one to good is one's rational will in so far as it follows one's natural understanding of the universal principles of right {iuris}); and see nn. 172, 139, 149 below.

[39] I-II q. 17 a. 1 ad 2: the subject-matter of one's freedom is one's will, but the cause of one's freedom is one's reason, because one's will is free precisely in that it can be brought to bear on diverse possibilities {diversa}, and this in turn is possible only because one's reason can grasp diverse intelligible goods {conceptiones boni}. One's will's object is always: good grasped as intelligible {bonum apprehensum per formam intelligibilem}: I q. 19 a. 1c. See also e.g. *ScG* I c. 72 n. 2 [618], II c. 48 n. 6 [1246].

REASON one's understanding and reasoning {RATIO}	WILL one's responsiveness to reasons {VOLUNTAS}
understanding basic ends/goods {intellectus finium}[i]	basic openness to these {voluntas simplex}[ii]
envisaging a possible purpose for action {apprehensio finis}[iii]	interest in pursuing that purpose; in some cases, provisional resolution to act if deliberation finds acceptable means {intentio}[iv]
deliberation (when needed)[v] about means: devising of possible options as increasingly specified conceptions of eligible purposes {consilium}[vi]	assent to increasingly specified conceptions of eligible purposes as interesting and acceptable, an assent which becomes increasingly specific, until it is an
judgements that options *A, B* ... are each practicable/suitable for me/us here and now {sententiae, iudicia}[vii]	assent to options *A, B* ... as each sufficiently interesting to be live options for me/us now {consensus}[viii]
judgement of preference made in choosing ('This is the thing for me/us to do') {iudicium electionis}[ix]	formation of definitive intention and adoption of one proposal by choice {electio}[x]
self-direction by using the chosen proposal as a 'rule of action' and directive to act {imperium}[xi]	exertion of one's capacities in carrying out choice {usus}[xii]
knowledge of action's success in achieving its end {cognitio finis in actu}[xiii]	taking satisfaction in action's achieving its end {fruitio}[xiv]

[i]   *Ver.* q. 5 a.1c; see also I-II q. 94 a. 2, II-II q. 47 a. 6c; *An.* 1. 8 n. 13 [119].

[ii]   I-II q. 12 a. 1 ad 4, q. 15 a. 3c; and see q. 10 a. 1c.

[iii]   I-II q. 6 a. 2c, q. 15 a. 3c.

[iv]   I-II q. 12, especially a. 1 ad 4, a. 4c and 2 and 3; and see q. 8 a. 3.

[v]   Sometimes judgement about means needs no prior deliberation: I-II q. 14 a. 4 ad 1.   [vi]   I-II q. 14.

[vii]   I-II q. 13 a. 1 ad 2, a. 3c, q. 14 a. 1 ad 2, a. 4 ad 1.   [viii]   I-II q. 15.

[ix]   See n. j.   [x]   I-II q. 13.

[xi]   I-II q. 17; IV *Sent.* d. 15 q. 4 a. 1 sol. 1 ad 3; *Quodl.* IX q. 5 a. 2c. Often also called reason's directive {praeceptum} about acting: II-II q. 153 a. 5c.   [xii]   I-II q. 16.

[xiii]   See I-II q. 11 a. 1 ad 2, a. 4c.   [xiv]   I-II q. 11.

III.4. *Reason's Civil Rule over the Emotions*

Before turning to Aquinas' account of the most basic or primary reasons for action, it will be as well to allay a doubt. Isn't his theory of action excessively rationalistic and, in particular, indifferent to the role of emotion in human life? Isn't Hume nearer the mark in insisting that, at bottom, reason is the slave of the passions?

Aquinas would reply that Hume has misunderstood both reason and passion. Neither sort of motivation need be the slave of the other. One device he employs to convey his subtle and realistic understanding of this matter is a political analogy taken from a remark in Aristotle's *Politics*. 'Despotic' and 'civil [political] or kingly' governance should be distinguished, says Aristotle; masters rule slaves despotically (not necessarily, he thinks, unjustly), but free people are ruled in a civil or kingly way.[40] Aquinas will apply this thought in his account of 'limited government' (VIII.2). But he employs it more insistently in his efforts to clarify the role of reason and reasons in human action.

Mind, he says, rules body despotically; unless impeded by some internal or external factor,[41] one's limbs will naturally move in conformity with one's mind's directives. Like a slave considered precisely as slave, they cannot resist such directives. But one's emotions are ruled by one's reason in the way that free people are ruled by their king or other leader. Free citizens {liberi cives} or free people generally {liberi homines} can oppose and resist {obviare} their ruler's directives {imperium}.[42] Like free citizens, emotions can resist their rightful ruler's directives not merely by blocking them, but also in an active way by acting on (as) motivations of their own. Indeed, they are capable of inclining their own appointed ruler, the rational will, to the ends to which *they* are attracted.[43]

This analogy with non-despotic government focuses on capacity to *resist*, but leaves it unclear whether such resistance is or is not contrary to reason (and thus contrary to the natural order, properly

---

[40] *Politics* I. 2. 1254^{b}5–7.   [41] *Virt*. q. 1 a. 4c.

[42] *Mal*. q. 3 a. 9 ad 14; cf. e.g. *Pol*. I. 3 n. 9 [64]: appetite can in some matters 'contradict {contradicere}' reason. For the political/legal theory, see VIII. 2 at nn. 21–38 below.

[43] See I-II q. 9 a. 2 ad 3, q. 17 a. 7c, q. 56 a. 4 ad 3; *Eth*. X. 10 n. 3 [2082]. Not that the will can be rendered a slave, or instrumentalized, in the most radical sense; where there is will at all, it cannot but be free: I q. 115 a. 4c, I-II q. 6 a. 4c; *Comp*. I c. 128 [255]; for nothing in this world but the persuasion of understood good can move one's will: *ScG* III c. 88 n. 2 [2638].

so called[44]). On the one hand, the very idea of resistance or 'repugnance'[45] to reason suggests an unreasonable motivation, and one of Aquinas' most constant themes is that defections from—or inconsistency {repugnantia} with or 'repugnance' to[46]—reason's governance and sway are the very essence of *wrongful* choice and action.[47] On the other hand, the analogy is, on its face, a comparison not with rebels but with free citizens, and sometimes Aquinas characterizes them, precisely for the purposes of this analogy, as 'free people who *have the right* {ius} and [rightful] power {facultas} of resisting *some* of the ruler's precepts'.[48] Here the suggestion is that, in line with the proper constitution of human persons, emotion may *appropriately* (and thus not wrongfully) resist reason's directives, directives which are going presumably beyond somehow their proper scope.[49] How might this be so?

Aquinas' thought on these matters can be integrated and perhaps developed in four theses.

First: allowing one's emotions sway over one's reasons for action is indeed the paradigmatic way of going, and doing, wrong. (Indeed, in Aquinas' specialized vocabulary, one has 'moral', as distinct from intellectual, virtues precisely in so far as one's emotions do

[44] Recall that what is properly speaking natural, in human affairs, is not what is usual: 'most people follow the impetus of their emotions and bodily inclinations . . . only the wise, who are few, resist {obviare} such emotions by reason': *ScG* III c. 154 n. 14 [3268]; similarly *ScG* III c. 85 n. 6 [2602]; *Ver.* q. 5 a. 10 ad 7; *Comp.* I c. 128; II. 8 n. 98 above.

[45] See I q. 81 a. 3 ad 2 ('rationi repugnari'); *Eth.* II. 8 n. 3 [335] ('resistere et repugnare rationi'—taken to be the essence of what virtue and right reason(ableness) has to overcome). See also I-II q. 92 a. 1c: the virtue of the emotional capacities consists in their obedience to reason. [46] See *Eth.* IX. 4 n. 21 [1817]; cf. n. 13 [1809].

[47] So emotion is the root of all wrongful choices and dispositions {passio . . . est radix peccati}: II *Sent.* d. 42 q. 2 a. 1c. The self-love {amor sui} which is the cause of all immorality {principium omnis peccati} (I-II q. 77 a. 4) is a *passio* of the sensitive appetites: q. 77 introd. The 'justice, metaphorically speaking {metaphorica iustitia}' which is a synonym for virtue is so named because virtue is a matter of the right relationships within the community of elements in one's inner make-up, especially reason, will, and the emotions: see I-II q. 46 a. 7 ad 2; IV. 4 n. e below.

[48] *Virt.* q. 1 a. 4c: 'sicut reges et principes civitatum dominantur liberis, qui habent ius et facultatem repugnandi quantum ad aliqua praecepta regis vel principis'. See also I-II q. 58 a. 2c ('ius contradicendi'); VIII. 2 at n. 21 below.

[49] See also *Virt.* q. 1 a. 4c: 'lower appetite [e.g. emotional inclination or aversion] has a natural and proper tendency {propriam inclinationem ex natura sua} whereby it does not obey superior appetite [i.e. will] at the nod {ad nutum} but sometimes resists {repugnat}'. Note: what one has at one's nod {ad nutum} are the possessions which one can freely use for one's own benefit {suam utilitatem}: I *Sent.* d. 2 a. 5 ex., III *Sent.* d. 23 q. 1 a. 1c; *Meta.* 1.3 n. 9 [60]; II-II q. 66 a. 1c; and 'it pertains to the status of masters [domini] that at their nod they direct the actions of their subjects': II *Sent.* d. 10 a. 3c; see also I-II q. 56 a. 4 ad 3, q. 58 a. 2c.

not have that sway.[50]) And passion's sway over reason makes choices culpable not when emotion swallows up or sweeps away reason (rendering one's behaviour non-voluntary and subhuman),[51] but rather when emotions make reason their ingenious but corrupted servant.[52] Reason in passion's service does its master's bidding by inventing intelligent and attractive but, in the last analysis, specious and imperfectly intelligent *rationalizations*[1] for doing what one (emotionally) wants, against some reason or reasons for not so acting.[53] By 'rationalization', here as elsewhere, I mean reasons which one recounts to oneself or to others, for doing an action that one in fact is undertaking for emotional satisfaction, for emotional 'reasons' that are not the reasons which intelligence understands and reason affirms and develops.[54]

Second: though they are the usual more or less proximate cause of wrongful choice and action, emotions are inherently good, natural, and desirable. They *serve* reason and rational will by helping to move one to act intelligently and indeed reasonably;[55] 'good desires {concupiscentiae bonae} work against a perverse reason'.[56] (Eisenhower's fear of the disaster that might well result from his decision to invade in dodgy weather may have been uppermost in his feelings, but emotions do much of their work below the level of dominant feelings, and his emotional responses to the imaginable bad consequences of postponements, his soldierly zeal, and his aversion to shame, or suchlike, will certainly have been supporting

---

[50] I-II q. 64 a. 1c; IV. 2 at nn. 17–19, 22–3 below.

[51] See I-II q. 10 a. 3c, q. 77 a. 7c; *Ver.* q. 17 a. 1 ad 4; *Mal.* q. 3 a. 3 ad 9.

[52] See I-II q. 10 a. 3c: then, 'somehow disposed by passion, one judges something to be appropriate and good which one would not have so judged, but for the passion'; also *Mal.* q. 3 a. 9c, a. 10 ad 1 and ad 2. The rationalization may be more plausible than the stock example adduced e.g. in I-II q. 77 a. 2 ad 4.

[53] So 'from the beginning, so as to be able to pursue and enjoy their desires freely, people have thought to find reasons {cogitaverunt invenire rationes} why fornications and other sexual pleasures are not wrong', but the reasons they have offered seductively to themselves and each other have been unreasonable {sine ratione}: *In Eph.* 5. 3 ad v. 6 [282].

[54] On such *persuasio*, cf. I-II q. 80 a. 1. See also at nn. 78–9 below.

[55] See e.g. III *Sent.* d. 33 q. 2 a. 4 sol. 2 ad 6. Indeed, as Aquinas says in I q. 20 a. 1 ad 1: 'the intellectual appetite which is called will moves, in us [unlike in God], by way of our sentient appetite(s) {mediante appetitu sensitivo}. So the close-in motivating factor moving us to bodily activity {proximum motivum corporis} is sentient appetite. . . . "Love", "joy", and "pleasure", in so far as they signify acts of sentient appetite, are "passions [emotions]", but not in so far as they signify acts of our intellectual appetite [will].' 'One's will is midway between one's reason and one's desirous sensory appetite {media inter rationem et concupiscibilem}, and can be moved from both directions': II-II q. 155 a. 3 ad 2. On pleasure as sometimes reinforcing and sometimes deflecting reason, see e.g. I-II q. 33 a. 3c and 4c.   [56] II-II q. 155 a. 1 ad 2.

his giving of the order to go.) Emotions enhance the goodness of good choices and actions.[57] Any ideal of passionless, unemotional rational action is constantly repudiated by Aquinas.[58] Indeed, he is so convinced of the goodness and importance of human emotion that in the *Summa* he puts his whole elaborate discussion of *love* under the heading of a treatment of the emotions, those motivating factors which are generically common to human and subhuman animals.[59] This, it must be said, was a perilous and almost inevitably confusing move.[60] For one can and must speak of love which is precisely intelligent and rational {amor intellectivus seu rationalis}[61]—and such love, being of intelligible and understood goods, especially goods intrinsic to human persons, has a proper name: will![62] Still, Aquinas' decision to treat love as primarily a passion (emotion) underlines his opposition to any rationalistic downgrading of human feeling, of emotional desires and satisfactions, or of the inclinations or other motivating factors which underlie consciousness and feelings. He willingly expounded, and removed all ambiguity from, a teaching of St Augustine: if humankind had not wrecked, by sinful choice, their inner harmony of feelings with reason,[63] reasonable sexual intercourse would be experienced

---

[57] See I-II q. 24 a. 3c: 'an aspect of the perfection of the morally good is that the acting person be moved to good not only by will {secundum voluntatem} but also by sentient desire {appetitum sensitivum}'; see also ad 1: 'it is more praiseworthy to do a charitable [loving] act as a result of rational judgement than from the emotion of mercy *alone*'. Also I-II q. 34 a. 4 ad 3 (a good act cannot be perfectly good without *delectatio*); q. 77 a. 6 ad 2: 'good emotion {passio}, following reason's judgement, increases merit'. He adds: 'If, however, emotion takes precedence over reason's judgement, in the sense that the acting person is motivated more by emotion than by rational judgement, such emotion diminishes the action's goodness and praiseworthiness.'

[58] See I-II q. 24 a. 3; *Ver.* q. 26 a. 7; *Mal.* q. 3 a. 11, q. 12 a. 1c. The thought was and is attributed to the Stoics, but Aquinas thinks that their dictum that all emotions are bad, though very objectionable and misleading as a dictum (see e.g. *Eth.* II. 3 n. 8 [272]), probably had a more innocuous meaning (namely that emotion unmoderated by reason is bad): I-II q. 24 a. 2c. [59] See I-II q. 6 introd., q. 22 introd., q. 26 introd.

[60] Aquinas seeks to avert the danger by appropriating the word *dilectio* for love which is a matter of intelligence and will {libera electio}, not emotion: I-II q. 26 a. 3; *Div.* IV. 9 n. 9 [402] but his account of *dilectio* seems narrow, since he makes it follow not on understanding (or even consenting to) an intelligible good, but on rational judgement and choice (I–II q. 26 a. 3c and ad 4).

[61] I-II q. 26 a. 1c and ad 1. The same is true of every other emotion which has a counterpart, going under the same name, in the intellectual dynamism which we call will—e.g. anger: *Mal.* q. 12 a. 2 ad 1.

[62] I-II q. 26 a. 1c. This rational, volitional love—a matter of will—is to be called an emotion {passio} only 'by an extended manner of speaking {extenso nomine}': a. 2c.

[63] On the lost *harmonia* of the feelings and emotions with reason, see I-II q. 82 a. 2 ad 2 with *In Rom.* 5. 3 ad v. 12 [416].

---

with even greater intensity of pleasure than it now is.[64] In short, the subjection of passions (emotions) to reason, a subjection which for Aquinas is of the essence of moral and political soundness, involves not their suppression, elimination, or even diminution, but rather their integration with reasons, i.e. with the intelligible goods instantiated in persons.[65] In virtuous action, emotions are taken up into reason {assumuntur a ratione};[66] their felt strength will then be a sign of one's (will's) commitment to one's morally good purposes.[67]

Third: one's emotions appropriately resist one's reasonable self-direction when they are motivating one towards one's real good *as a sentient being*. Soldiers risking their own destruction by storming a beach to overthrow a genocidal tyranny, or nurses, advocates, and presidents risking their health to fulfil their responsibilities, Jesus of Nazareth in the garden on the night before his death, all have natural, appropriate, feelings of fear or of aversion from carrying on,[68] and yet may rightly choose to carry on. The fact that one's emotions in this way resist {repugnant} one's reason 'does not prevent them from obeying it'.[69]

Fourth: Aquinas' political analogy suggests also that sometimes (perhaps even often) feelings must be accepted as legitimate guides to choices between options which, though all of them rational and reasonable, are none of them *required* by reason (none is 'dominant'). So, as a student in our imaginary hostel, one might reasonably

[64] I q. 98 a. 2 ad 3, developing Augustine, *De Civitate Dei* XIV. c. 26. See also II-II q. 153 a. 2 ad 2 and IV *Sent.* d. 26 q. 1 (=*Supp.* q. 41) a. 3 ad 6: marital intercourse (the one reasonable type of human sexual intercourse) need not be contrary to reasonableness {rationis ordo} when, even if the intensity of pleasure during the act means that the spouses are not then and there being directed by reason, their choice to engage in marital intercourse was shaped by reason (as well as emotion). Also d. 31 q. 2 a. 1 (=*Supp.* q. 49 a. 4) ad 3; v.3 at nn. 58, 63–70, 91 below.

[65] Thus the reason why marriage can be a remedy for the dis-integrating pull of sexual desires and emotions {concupiscentia} is not that it gives them an outlet (for that would only make them the more insatiable: IV *Sent.* d. 2 q. 1 a. 1 sol. 2c; *Eth.* III. 22 n. 12 [646]) but rather that it enables them to be integrated with reason, by being directed to the *intelligible goods* of marriage (notably procreation and mutual commitment {fides}) which are instantiated in the determinate persons, my spouse, myself, and (we hope) our children: IV *Sent.* d. 26 q. 2 (=*Supp.* q. 42) a. 3 ad 4; *In I Cor.* 7. 1 ad v. 3 [318] ('in remedium concupiscentiae ... coarctatur ad determinatam personam'). See v.4 at n. 58 below. [66] IV *Sent.* d. 17 q. 2 a. 3 sol. 1c; cf. also *In Ioann.* 11. 5 ad v. 34 [1535].

[67] I-II q. 24 a. 3 ad 1, q. 30 a. 1 ad 1, q. 59 a. 3c and 5c.

[68] Note: one's aversion from what one understands or takes to be bad is always a result of its opposition to some real or supposed good one loves: e.g. *ScG* III c. 151 n. 4 [3237].

[69] I q. 81 a. 3 ad 2.

judge that as between a curfew at 9.00 p.m., or a later curfew, and no curfew (*'laissez-faire'*) there is no rational consideration which settles the matter—each of these incompatible alternatives is better than the others in some irreducible respect—and that therefore one is entitled to make the required choice by following one's own feelings. Reason would still be in charge, exercising a constitutional supervision over one's deliberations (as well as over the group's voting procedures), in two ways. Negatively: reason would forbid one to allow any influence whatever to certain emotional motivations which, but for their unreasonableness, might influence one's vote (say, the desire to hurt a student whose appearance or mannerisms one despised, or to seduce another student). And positively: one's judgement that an option is more harmonious with one's relevant emotional inclinations gives one a *reason* to favour that option; indeed, reasons of this quasi-procedural kind have a particular importance in making certain kinds of choice, choices which yield the hoped-for benefits only if one's commitment is whole-hearted and in line with one's whole personal constitution, one's individual susceptibilities and inclinations.[70]

It remains that, as Aquinas makes clear, any adequate critical account of ethics (and, therefore, of politics) must acknowledge the profound difference between rational and emotional motivation. And one's grasp of that difference will not be adequate unless one understands both the inherent independence of rational motives (reasons for action), *and* the way such motives can be either supported and reinforced *or* undermined and disrupted by emotional motivations. The difference between acting for reasons and acting on emotions which have subjugated reasons to their objectives (as rationalizations) is a difference so impressive that Aquinas—that most stalwart defender of the *unity* of human nature[71]—will even say that in the human person 'there are two natures, the intellectual and the sentient {sensitiva}'.[72]

This duality of types of motivation—a duality which reason's

---

[70] Aquinas is willing to say that each of us has an individual nature: I-II q. 51 a. 1c (unhealthy or healthy); q. 63 a. 1c; *Eth.* III. 20 n. 9 [621]; IV *Sent.* d. 44 q. 1 a. 3 sol. 2 (size) and sol. 3 ad 3 (male or female); *Virt.* q. 1 a. 8c (indisposed or disposed to follow the good of practical reasonableness); *Ver.* q. 25 a. 6 ad 4 (see n. 150 below).

[71] See v.8 at nn. 208–17 below.

[72] I-II q. 10 a. 3 ad 2; each of us 'is composed of a double nature, an intellectual and a sentient nature': II-II q. 165 a. 2c; see also III *Sent.* d. 29 q. un. a. 5c; *Virt.* q. 2 a. 12 ad 6. For 'each power of the soul is a form or nature' (I q. 80 a. 1 ad 3) and 'since what is apprehended by the understanding [e.g. intelligible, universal human goods such as

'civil rule' (*prudentia*: III.5) can make into a harmony or unison of inner peace,[73] motivating with a kind of unity {uniformiter}—is obscured by the ordinary language of motivation, as much in English as in Latin. There are two radically distinct (though analogous) senses of 'motiv(ation)', of 'opt(ing)', and of 'prefer(ence)', and certainly of 'love'[74] and 'satisfaction'.[75] A similar duality of meaning is found in every other word commonly employed to describe human action and its motivational antecedents[76] and concomitants. A word forged primarily for describing emotional life, such as 'desire', will be co-opted for the account of rational motivation;[77] words forged primarily for describing the latter, such as 'will' and even 'reasons', will be co-opted by extension for describing activity motivated and directed emotionally.

The vital philosophical task of distinguishing is made the more difficult by emotion's capacity for harnessing reason to its service,[78] inverting the proper (fully reasonable) relationship between the two sorts of motivation, and disguising its success behind the smoke-screen of rationalizations. So, for example, rationalization may advance the thesis that freedom consists in doing what one wants (desires, finds emotionally appealing)—a freedom that in truth is 'not genuine but apparent {non vera sed apparens}', and really servitude.[79]

Philosophical discourse, for the sake of clear explanation, needs a stability greater than common language's. So by 'reason for action' I shall consistently mean a reason understood by intelligence and attractive to will, and by 'will' one's capacity to respond precisely to such reasons.

---

knowledge or virtue, or bads such as any life of thievery] and what is apprehended by sense are generically different, the intellectual appetite [and power] is distinct from the sentient appetite [and power]' (a. 2c with ad 2). This distinction must not be confused with another, namely the distinction, within one's intellectual nature, between intellect as such and the general rational appetite for (responsiveness to) intelligible goods, i.e. will. See e.g. *An.* III. 15 n. 4 [821]; *Mal.* q. 8 a. 3c.

[73] See II-II q. 29 a. 1c.

[74] On *amor sensitivus* as distinct from *amor intellectivus seu rationalis*, see I-II q. 26 a. 1.

[75] On perfect (rational) and imperfect (subrational) *fruitio*, see I-II q. 11 a. 2. On the joy, which is not an emotion {*passio*}, of doing justice (by acts of will, which are not emotions, since will is not emotion), see q. 59 a. 5c (the insistence is Aquinas').

[76] e.g. 'hope': there is the hope created by an 'inclination of sentient appetite' and the hope which 'is an act of will': III *Sent.* d. 26 q. 2 a. 2c.

[77] e.g. IV *Sent.* d. 15 q. 4 a. 1 sol. 1c.

[78] See e.g. I-II q. 75 a. 2 ad 1, q. 77 a. 1c, q. 80 a. 1c and a. 2c; nn. 52–4 above.

[79] *In Rom.* 6. 4 ad v. 20 [509].

III.5. *The Basic Reasons for Action*

Analysis of the options before an individual or group, such as our students, brings to light intelligible human goods, instances of broad types of benefit realizable by intelligent action (III.3). Are there, then, a number of basic human goods, not fully reducible to any one most fundamental good? Aquinas maintains that there are.

The English verb 'founded upon', and the parallel adjectives 'basic' and 'fundamental', have their meaning from a spatial-structural metaphor. Aquinas uses the same verb[80] and noun.[81] Adjectivally he employs a numerical metaphor to make the same point; in the quest for someone's reasons for action, one eventually reaches reasons which are 'first' or 'primary' {prima}, i.e. 'ultimate'[82] in the sense that they direct one towards 'ends in themselves' and are not means to any yet further ends. So Aquinas' discussion of the *'first* principles of practical reason' concerns basic reasons for action, the sorts of ends and goods that are not means to or derived from other ends or goods.

Working as a theologian, Aquinas composed no treatise on ethics or politics, and his discussions of the basic reasons for action always occur in the context of some other matter in hand. And these other matters—relations between sensory and intellectual appetites,[83] the natural structure of our affections {amor},[84] necessity and freedom in our willing,[85] the difference between Aristotle's and the Roman jurists' notions of natural law,[86] the reflective question whether practical reason (deliberation towards choice and action) has one or several 'first principles'[87]—all are matters set more directly in the 'first order', the domain of metaphysics (which Aquinas explores sometimes with no more than philosophical resources and more often with the further sources and methods

---

[80] I-II q. 94 a. 2c.

[81] His use of our metaphor is rare, but telling: 'the desirable that is naturally desired is the source and foundation {principium et fundamentum} of other desirables. But in desirables, end is foundation and source of means, since those things which are for an end are desirable only by reason of the end' (*Ver.* q. 22 a. 5c). The end on which one fixes one's intention is, so to speak, one's foundation {fin[is] . . . est quasi fundamentum} (*In Matt.* 7 ad v. 26 [673]).

[82] I-II q. 94 a. 2c. So the ultimate reason {ultimus finis} why someone is preparing a medicine may be health {sanitas}: I-II q. 12 a. 3c.   [83] 1 *Sent.* d. 28 q. 1 a. 4c.

[84] *Perf.* c. 14 [13], lines 50–4 [627].   [85] I-II q. 10 a. 1; *Ver.* q. 22 a. 5c.

[86] *Eth.* v. 12 n. 4 [1019].   [87] I-II q. 94 a. 2.

of theology). As a result, he never offers in any one place a complete inventory of the basic reasons for action.

Still, his discussions take the reflective identification of basic reasons for action far beyond the point reached by Aristotle,[m] indeed to a degree of clarity not, I think, reached again until such discussions were resumed in a 'third order' mode quite recently.[n] Fittingly, the last of Aquinas' discussions is the fullest. It is in his treatise on law, in the *Summa Theologiae*, where he raises the question whether the natural law {lex naturalis} contains one precept or many. His answer is that there are many precepts of natural law, all of them unified, however, by their relationship to the one absolutely (i.e. unqualifiedly) first precept which is their common root: the precept that 'good is to be done and pursued, and bad avoided'.[88] 'And on this are founded all other precepts of the law of nature; and thus all those things-to-be-done (or to-be-avoided) which practical reason naturally *understands to be human goods* [or their opposites] pertain to the precepts of the law of nature.'[89]

In this context the terms 'natural law' or (synonymously) 'law of nature' refer, of course, to the third order (of deliberation and morally significant choice), not to the first order (of the natural sciences and metaphysics) (II.1). These 'precepts of the natural law' are precisely, as Aquinas said a few sentences earlier, 'first principles of human actions' {prima principia operum humanorum}.[90] The 'human goods' {bona humana} directed to by these first principles must—precisely because they are the subject-matter of *primary* (underived) practical principles—be the primary or basic human goods. Since 'good and 'end' are interdefinable,[91] they are equally our basic ends.[92]

---

[88] Ibid. c ('Hoc est ergo primum praeceptum legis, quod bonum est faciendum et prosequendum, et malum vitandum'), and ad 1 and 2.   [89] Ibid. c.

[90] I-II q. 94 a. 1 ad 2.   [91] Ibid. a. 2c: 'bonum habet rationem finis'.

[92] I-II q. 56 a. 3c (the principles of practical reasonableness's direction of actions {rationis agendorum} are ends {fines}). These ends of human life {fines humanae vitae} are more basic than (and give point to) all the virtues, being 'pre-existent' in our practical reason as 'naturally known principles' prior to (and making possible) the development of any virtue: II-II q. 47 a. 6c, q. 56 a. 1c; likewise *Ver.* q. 5 a. 1c. 'Just as in theoretical reason there are innate principles of demonstrations, so in practical reason there are the innate ends connatural to human beings {innati fines connaturales homini}': III *Sent.* d. 33 q. 2 a. 4 sol. 4c. Aquinas frequently refers to these ends with the singular noun, 'end {finis}', which is often mistranslated as 'the end'. I-II q. 58 a. 3 ad 2 is one of the texts which show directly that by *finis* he often means ends: 'the intellectual excellence {virtus intellectiva} which makes reason go well in morally significant deliberation {circa moralia} presupposes right interest in end(s) {appetitum rectum finis}, so that one may reason rightly

Aquinas then recalls that to understand a possibility as *good* is to understand it as an intelligible *purpose* (object of interest and inclination) {finis}. So, what practical reason 'naturally understands as goods {bona} (and thus as to-be-pursued-by-action(s) {opere prosequenda})' are what human beings have natural inclinations towards.[93] And so, he goes on, 'corresponding to the order of our natural inclinations there is an order in the precepts of the law of nature'. The order Aquinas here has in mind is a metaphysical stratification: (1) what we have in common with all substances, (2) what, more specifically, we have in common with other animals, and (3) what is peculiar to us as human beings.[94]

So (1) we have the inclination to preserve ourselves in existence as the sort of beings we are; and we understand *human life* {vita hominis} to be a good° to be served and preserved {conservatur}.[95] Elsewhere Aquinas refers to this good as conservation of oneself {conservatio individui},[96] and refers to the good(s) most intrinsic to life (and to its conservation) as health[97] and bodily integrity.[98] The basic good in question can, then, be described as human life, in (if possible) maturity, integrity, and health.

about the principles, i.e. the ends {principia, id est fines}, from which reason reasons'. Similarly e.g. III *Sent.* d. 33 q. 2 a. 4 sol. 4c.

[93] I-II q. 94 a. 2c; 'quia vero bonum habet rationem finis . . . inde est quod omnia illa ad quae homo habet naturalem inclinationem ratio naturaliter apprehendit ut bona'.

[94] I-II q. 94 a. 2c. For a slightly different metaphysical ordering (in terms of (1) and (2)), see IV *Sent.* d. 33 q. 1 (= *Supp.* q. 65) a. 1c.

[95] Ibid.; *Eth. Tab.* s.v. 'sentire': 'vivere est secundum se ipsum bonum'.

[96] II-II q. 155 a. 2c.

[97] I *Sent.* d. 48 q. 1 a. 4c: 'we have in us a kind of natural will whereby we desire {appetimus} what is intrinsically {secundum se} a good for human beings as human beings {bonum homini inquantum est homo}. This natural will follows reason's understanding in so far as it considers something without reference to specific purposes and circumstances {absolute considerans}: as when we will knowledge {scientiam}, virtue, health {sanitatem}, and suchlike.' Health is intrinsically {secundum se} good: *Meta.* III. 4 n. 6 [374]; it is one of a number of 'goods needed by human beings {bona homini necessaria}' like 'wisdom, bodily health, and suchlike': *ST* I-II q. 2 a. 4c. It is a natural good (*Ver.* q. 26 a. 8 ad 2), 'the natural good of the human body' (*Div.* 4. 21 n. 4 [551]). It is the 'form of the body' (as knowledge is the form of the intellectual soul) (*Unit.* 1, line 199 [10] [180]); it is caused by the 'principles of life' (*ScG* IV c. 72 n. 2 [4067]) and consists in a sort of interior harmony {harmonia quaedam humorum} appropriate to our nature as an animal {quaedam commensuratio humorum per conventientiam ad naturam animalis}: *ScG* II c. 64 n. 3 [1424]; I-II q. 73 a. 3c; 'sanitas commensurationem debitam in partibus corporis importat': IV *Sent.* d. 17 q. 1 a. 1 sol. 3c; also I-II q. 54 a. 1c.

[98] On bodily integrity {consistentia} as the basic good of which being and living are, in a sense, components, see I-II q. 10 a. 1c; on this *consistentia* see also I-II q. 35 a. 6c, II-II q. 61 a. 3c; III *Sent.* d. 34 q. 2 a. 2 sol. 2 ad 2, IV *Sent.* d. 32 a. 1 ad 2.

Then (2) we have a more specifically animal-human inclination towards what we also understand as the goods of 'the mating of male and female, and the bringing up of children, and such like' {coniunctio maris et feminae,[p] et educatio liberorum, et similia}.[99] In an earlier work he had spoken of an inclination to a single though complex good[100] which is naturally attractive to our *reason*,[101] a good which includes both personal sexual union and the procreation and education of children: the 'natural inclination to *marriage*'.[102] The later text does not deny that this is *one* good but prefers to point to its elements, elements which in some other animals are naturally separate.

Finally (3) we have inclinations which are specifically human because their objects are appreciable only by rationality {secundum naturam rationis}. One understands, for example {sicut . . . }, the good of knowing the truth about God, and the good of living in fellowship or companionship {in societate} with others—with persons who can share in such goods.[103]

This whole passage gives rise to two obvious questions: Why does it speak of the good of knowledge about God rather than simply the good of knowledge? And what other basic human goods, if any, might Aquinas have mentioned here or indeed earlier in his stratified list?

The answer to the first question must remain conjectural. Aquinas frequently identifies, simply, *knowledge* as a basic or primary good,[q] and the present passage's specification to truth *about God* is immediately followed by a reference to the good of avoiding *ignorance* (not just about God).[104] So the specification should perhaps be

[99] I-II q. 94 a. 2c; likewise *Eth.* v. 12 n. 4 [1019].

[100] For the singular (non-plural) form 'good of marriage', see e.g. IV *Sent.* d. 26 q. 1 (=*Supp.* q. 41) a. 3 ad 4, d. 33 q. 1 a. 3 sol. 1 ad 5.

[101] IV *Sent.* d. 26 q. 1 a. 1c (=*Supp.* q. 41 a. 1c): natural reason {ratio naturalis} inclines one to marriage {matrimonium}—for two reasons {causae}: the good of children procreated, nurtured, and educated to full maturity and human accomplishment {ad perfectum statum hominis}, and the good of the union, complementarity, and assistance which a man and a woman can give each other by their association in home life. These two reasons constitute a *single* good, marriage: d. 27 q. 1 a. 1 sol. 1c (=*Supp.* q. 44 a. 1c); v. 4 n. 58 below.

[102] IV *Sent.* d. 26 q. 1 a. 2c (=*Supp.* q. 41 a. 2c): 'inclinatio naturae ad matrimonium'.

[103] I-II q. 94 a. 2c. Although there is a sense in which goods like life and mating are 'shared' with other animals, it is important to note that only rational beings, capable (at least radically) of participating in these goods by understanding, deliberation, and free choice, can in the focal sense *have* goods and so, by sharing them, live *in societate* and friendship with each other: II-II q. 25 a. 3c.

[104] See also *ScG* III c. 39 n. 4 [2170]: 'A large part of human misery is error and deception.'

understood as making clear several points about the knowledge that is a basic human good: that it is specifically intellectual knowledge, of a kind that no other animal could even be interested in, let alone attain; and that it is knowledge not of truths which, however brilliant the feats of intelligence required for their discovery, are *unimportant* (e.g. of the number of ink molecules on this page) but rather of truths which matter.[105] For, knowledge of the right answer to the questions whether God does or does not exist (a question whose answer Aquinas firmly declares is not self-evident but needs to be reached by reasoning),[106] and what is to be thought about God's nature, is obviously very significant knowledge.[107] The inclination with which the good of knowledge matches up is the natural desire, not to know random facts, but to investigate, discover, and make oneself at home with things' deepest explanations.[108]

The answer to the question about the exhaustiveness of the list of basic goods or primary practical principles in q. 94 a. 2 is not conjectural. Aquinas would certainly add to the list. In the very next article he refers to another distinct natural inclination: to *act* according to reason.[109] The corresponding basic good he mentions very frequently and centrally. It is the good of (practical) reasonableness {bonum rationis; bonum secundum rationem esse}, the good of ordering one's emotions, choices, and actions by intelligence and reason.[1] The *bonum rationis* is both an intelligible good in which a reasonable person is interested *and* the good of that person's being interested in it and sufficiently well integrated

---

[105] See I q. 22 a. 3 ad 3: since we cannot know everything, knowledge of worthless things, though good in itself (I-II q. 35 a. 5 ad 3) is better avoided, since it impedes our consideration of more important truths.

[106] I q. 2 a. 1 and a. 2. Still, since the reasoning is readily available, knowledge of conclusions such as 'God exists' can be said to be 'natural' or 'naturally introduced in each of us {naturaliter omnibus inserta}': 1 *Sent.* d. 3 q. 1 a. 3 ad 8, III *Sent.* d. 24 q. un. a. 3 sol. 1; *ST* I q. 2 a. 1 obj. 1, q. 12 a. 12 ad 3; *Brev.* c. 1. But this knowledge by natural reason, though real and grounded, is also much in need of clarification and amplification {confusa}: *ScG* III c. 38 n. 1 [2161]; *Ps.* 13.1 ad v. 1. See also IV. 5 n. 113 below.

[107] Indeed it is the supremely significant knowledge, and just as Rome or Jerusalem could be called, antonomastically, 'the City', so truth about God could be called antonomastically the truth: see *ScG* I c. 1 n. 4 [7]. And see x.4 below.

[108] '[T]he rational creature's natural desire [to know] is to know ... the types and families of things and their explanation {species et genera rerum et rationes earum} ... not individuals as such {singulares} ... ': I q. 12 a. 8 ad 4; also I-II q. 3 a. 8c. And see II-II q. 167 a. 1 ad 1.

[109] I-II q. 94 a. 3c: 'naturalis inclinatio inest cuilibet homini ad hoc quod agat secundum rationem'. Cf. q. 91 a. 2c: 'rationalis creatura ... habet naturalem inclinationem ad debitum actum et finem'; and q. 93 a. 6c, q. 94 a. 4c.

(mind integrated with will and each with subrational desires and powers)[110] to choose it and put it into practice.[111] Another name for it, then, is the good of virtue, *virtus*.[112] This is not some prim conformity to convention or rule, but excellence and strength {virtus} of character involving a disposition and readiness to act with *intelligent* love in pursuit of *real* goods—the basic human goods towards which the primary practical principles direct—and successful resistance to the ultimately unreasonable lure of bad options.[113] When this good is actually instantiated in the character of some person or group, it can be given the name of its central element, the virtue—the directive and integrating disposition—of *prudentia*, perhaps least misleadingly translated *practical reasonableness*. As Aquinas says, 'all moral virtues involve a sharing in the good of practical reasonableness {bonum prudentiae}';[114] and

---

[110] This inner orderliness of emotions, inclinations, and dispositions with each other and with the goods acknowledged by reason is inner peace {pax interior}—see *In Matt.* 5 ad v. 9 [438, 443]; II-II q. 29 a. 1c and ad 1—not to be confused with complacency of sentiment ('feeling good'). [111] See III *Sent.* d. 33 q. 1 a. 2 sol. 1c.

[112] I-II q. 94 a. 3c; *Car.* a. 2c (to have virtue, there is required a love of the sort of good for the sake of which virtue does what it does {amor boni ad quod virtus operatur} . . . but the virtue which pertains to human beings *qua* human does what it does for the sake of good of a kind connatural to human beings; so there naturally is in human wills a love of that kind of good, which is the good of [practical] reason[ableness] {huius boni amor, quod est bonum rationis}). On the natural inclination to the practical reasonableness of virtue, see e.g. *ScG* III c. 63 n. 3 [2379a] (the desire that the whole of a human being's life be disposed according to reason, which is to live according to virtue); I-II q. 58 a. 4 ad 3 (the natural inclination to the good of virtue {bonum virtutis} is a kind of incipient virtue {inchoatio virtutis} but not virtue complete. And the stronger it is, the more dangerous (the more poisonous: III *Sent.* d. 36 a. 1c) it can be, unless joined to a reason which not merely aspires to be but truly is right); q. 85 a. 1c; a. 2c (a natural *inclinatio* to virtue is appropriate to us because we are rational, which involves acting according to reason— which is acting according to virtue) and ad 3; *Pol.* I. 11 n. 3 [164]; IV. 2 below.

[113] So virtue is to be valued precisely as one's actualizing the good of reasonableness {bonum rationis ex quo laudatur virtus}: II-II q. 155 a. 4 ad 3; *Eth.* IV. 9 n. 2 [751].

[114] II-II q. 53 a. 5 ad 1. 'There is in human beings a natural inclination {inclinatio quaedam naturalis} to the act of practical reasonableness {actum prudentiae}, which is called natural virtue . . . but this inclination can work itself out either to goods or to bads, and so it is not itself the virtue [of practical reasonableness]': III *Sent.* d. 36 a. 1c. It will amount to the virtue only when it is integrated with the other elements of good character: justice, courage, and self-control: each of these four cardinal virtues is a strategic way of instantiating the *good of practical reasonableness*, in one's deliberations (*prudentia*), one's dealing with others (justice), and one's inner integration of emotions with reasons (temperance): I-II q. 61 a. 3c. Similarly, we have natural inclinations towards these 'moral goods', but these inclinations, too, will result in bad character unless they are integrated with the inclination to practical reasonableness: 'moral inclinations without *prudentia* fall short of real virtue' (Virt. q. 5 a. 2c; also *Quodl.* XII q. 14 a. un. c; also I-II q. 65 a. 1 ad 1: 'natural inclinations lack the perfect character of virtue if *prudentia* is lacking'). So the intrinsic, basic good under consideration here is best described as the *good of virtue*, as in I-II q. 94 a. 3c. '[All human] virtues pre-exist in one's natural

'the good of practical reasonableness {bonum prudentiae} is instantiated in acting persons themselves, who are perfected precisely in their acting (for practical reasonableness is right reason in *doing* [as distinct from making])'.[115]

Are there other basic human goods? Friendship {amicitia} is a good frequently mentioned by Aquinas as the object of a natural inclination.[116] But this is no more and no less than the central case of the *in societate vivere*, the living in fellowship, which Aquinas included in his primary listing. Justice, too, is the object of a natural inclination and love,[117] and thus an intrinsic aspect of the basic good of *societas*.[118] But it also involves rejecting any *unreasonable* willingness to make choices which, even as a side-effect, prejudice other people, and is thus intrinsic to the basic good of practical reasonableness and *virtus*.[119] Harmony with the transcendent source of the universe's existence and order is a good which Aquinas judges basic and the object of natural inclination;[120] it probably should not be reduced either to 'knowledge about God' or to *societas* and friendship, for it goes beyond knowing and loving to becoming like {assimilatio} (x.4). So that can be added to the list. Finally, there is *beatitudo* or *felicitas*, happiness in the sense of *fulfilment*. But this turns out to be, not so much an item to be added to the list of basic human goods, as rather a kind of synthesis of them:[121] satisfaction of all intelligent desires and participation in all the basic human goods (whatever they are), and

---

orientation towards the good of virtue {naturali ordinatione ad bonum virtutis}, which exists in one's reason in so far as one is aware of this kind of good, and in one's will in so far as one is naturally interested in that good, and also exists somehow in one's lower powers in so far as they are naturally subject to one's reason; and some people have this combination [of integrating factors] in such a way that they are less resistant [than other people] to the good of [practical] reason[ableness] {ad bonum rationis} . . . ': III *Sent*. d. 33 q. 1 a. 2 sol. 1c.

[115] I-II q. 57 a. 5 ad 1.

[116] e.g. III *Sent*. d. 27 q. 2 a. 2 ad 1; *Virt*. q. 2 a. 8 ad 7; *Eth*. VIII.1 n. 4 [1541]; *Perf*. c. 15 [14], lines 27–9 [637] (IV. 3 n. 36 below).   [117] e.g. II-II q. 183 a. 4c.

[118] *Societas* involves living in harmony (harmonia . . . concordia . . . consensus: *Div*. XI. 2 n. 16 [908]) with one's fellows, i.e. peace [pax], and so the point of justice is peace (e.g. *In Heb*. 12. 3 ad v. 14 [687]) though justice is not a mere extrinsic means to, but rather a component of, that basic good. See further VII.2 at nn. 36–49 below.

[119] See IV.4 especially at n. 80, and v. 2 and IX. 1 at nn. 13–14 below.

[120] e.g. *Perf*. c. 14 [13], lines 173–4 [634] {instinctum naturae}.

[121] See *Ver*. q. 22 a. 5c: 'what one's will is interested in necessarily (as if determined to that by natural inclination) is a last end: *beatitudo* and those things included in it: existence, knowledge of truth, and some other such things {finis ultimus, ut beatitudo et ea quae in ipso includuntur, ut esse, cognitio veritatis, et aliqua huiusmodi}'.

thus a fulfilment which is complete and integral (integrating all its elements and participants) (IV.2; X.4).

III.6. *Understanding First Practical Principles*

Before considering how basic reasons for action are interrelated as components of human fulfilment and sources of moral judgement about right and wrong, we may take stock.

Aquinas gave his fullest account of basic human goods in the context of considering the 'first principles of human actions'.[122] The question he directly posed was whether there is only one such first principle or many. His answer was that there are many, though one of them is the 'foundation' of all the others {supra hoc fundantur omnia alia} because—just as the principle of non-contradiction gives rational thought its form, excluding all simultaneous affirmation and negation (of the same thing in the same respect)—this unqualifiedly 'first principle of practical reason' gives practical thought its form: 'good is to be done and pursued, and bad is to be avoided {bonum est faciendum et prosequendum,[s] et malum vitandum}'.[123] So the goods {bona} which he proceeds to identify will all be referred to in principles of the form: *X* (say, human life) is a good, to be pursued and preserved {vita conserva[nda]}, and what damages *X* is a bad, to be avoided; actions that are good as means to realizing such basic human goods are to be done; actions bad as harming a basic good are to be avoided.

Neither grammatically nor substantively are practical principles indicative (stating what is or will be the case). Nor are they imperative (giving commands or orders). They are directive; the Latin gerundive form 'fac*iendum* et prosequ*endum* et . . . vit*andum*' exactly captures this directiveness to what '*is-to-be* done . . . pursued . . . avoided' in the sense, not of 'will be' but of 'ought to be'.

This *ought* is intelligible in a sense which is not *moral*. Even people quite indifferent or hostile to all moral claims can and, if they are intelligent, do recognize and use (albeit defectively) some

---

[122] I-II q. 94 a. 1 ad 2, a. 2; n. 88 above.

[123] I-II q. 94 a. 2c. Though the principle as here articulated puts *faciendum* before *prosequendum*, and is often mistakenly rendered by commentators in the form *bonum est faciendum* (or, even worse, as the imperative 'Do good and avoid evil!'), it is *prosequendum* that gives the primary and essential sense of the principle. See n. s below.

at least of the first principles of practical reason.[124] The moral sense of 'ought', understood critically, not merely conventionally, is reached—as we shall see (IV.5)—when the absolutely first practical principle is followed through, in its relationship to all the other first principles, with a reasonableness which is unrestricted and undeflected by any subrational factor such as distracting emotion. In that sense, the 'ought' of the first principles is incipiently or 'virtually', but not yet actually, moral in its directiveness or normativity.[125] Just in so far as they are each a first principle, the 'ought' that each affirms—even the ought of 'is-to-be-avoided'[126]—is nothing more nor less than the intelligible, propositional content of the attractiveness of that basic human good towards which the principle in question directs.[127]

Though practical principles, and the practical norms and judgements derivable from them, state what ought to be (is-to-be) rather than what is or will be, and though they cannot be reduced to 'speculative', i.e. non-practical, principles, they are true (not false)[t] and direct us to the basic goods *as true* goods.[128]

The first principles of practical reason are 'indemonstrable' and 'self-evident'.[129] This does not mean that they are data-less intuitions, or 'felt certainties', or that one cannot be mistaken about them,[u] or that they cannot be defended by rational considerations. On the contrary, Aquinas firmly holds that they are understood by what he calls 'induction' of principles,[130] by which he means insight into data of experience (data preserved, after the direct experience, in the memory). 'To reach a knowledge of them [first

---

[124] See *Ver.* q. 16 a. 2 ad 6 (sinful operations of practical reason are attributed, like practical reason's virtuous operations, to one's grasp (but misuse) of the first principles of practical reason, i.e. to *synderesis*); also II *Sent.* d. 7 q. 1 a. 2 ad 3, d. 39 q. 3 a. 1 ad 1 and ad 5, IV *Sent.* d. 50 q. 2 a. 1 sol. 1c (= *Supp.* q. 98 a. 1c). Not just every right judgement but 'every judgement of practical reason proceeds from certain naturally known principles': I-II q. 100 a. 1c.

[125] So these first principles are sometimes called principles of common 'right' {iuris communis}, while at the same time it is being stated that to know them is not yet to be able to make right moral judgements or have moral virtues (but only, rather, the seeds of the virtues): e.g. I-II q. 51 a. 1c, q. 58 a. 5c.

[126] For 'desiring good is the reason for avoiding bad {appetitus boni est ratio quare vitetur malum}': I-II q. 25 a. 3c.

[127] Hence the primacy of 'to be pursued {prosequendum}' over 'to be done {faciendum}' (see nn. 123 and s).

[128] See I q. 79 a. 11 ad 2, q. 82 a. 3 ad 1; *Eth.* VI. 2 n. 17 [1140]; *Ver.* q. 22 a. 10 ad 2.

[129] I-II q. 91 a. 3c {principi[a] indemonstrabil[ia]}; q. 94 a. 2c {principia per se nota}; *Eth.* v. 12 n. 3 [1018] {principia indemonstrabilia}; II *Sent.* d. 24 q. 2 a. 3c {principi[a] per se not[a]}.

[130] e.g. *Eth.* VI. 3 n. 7 [1148].

principles, whether of speculative or of practical reason] we need sensory experience and memory.'[131] And though not grasped as conclusions from reasoning, they can be defended by argument.[132] Such arguments can be called dialectical; they will, for example, point out to sceptics the ways in which their own deliberations and actions are directed by their understanding and acceptance of reasons for action, precisely as goods and reasons.[v]

'Self-evident' {per se notum} ('known through itself'), means no more than: not known by virtue of knowing some 'middle term'[133]—i.e. not *deduced* by syllogistic reasoning from some prior, more evident *proposition*.[134] A proposition thus knowable *per se* is only known, however, when its terms (and what they refer to) are understood,[135] and this understanding cannot be had without experience. In discussing the first principles of practical reason, Aquinas indicates that we will understand and accept them only if we have the experience and other relevant knowledge needed to understand their terms; for he points out that there are some practical principles (not perhaps absolutely *first* principles) which, though *per se nota*, are known only to people who are wise.[136]

The first practical principles are not, properly speaking, innate;[w] babies do not know them at all, and young people come to know them more or less gradually.[137] One cannot, for example, understand that knowledge is a human good unless one has had both the experience of wondering whether . . . or why . . . and of finding an answer to one's question, and has noticed that answers suggest more questions, and that the answers to questions tend to hang together as 'knowledge', and that other people share this ability

---

[131] II *Sent.* d. 24 q. 2 a. 3c. See also *Post.* II. 20 n. 11 [592], stating that our knowledge of principles, in 'every art and science', arises from previous 'sense', or, more precisely, sense and memory and 'experience', i.e. awareness of similarities and correlations among the items sensed and remembered; likewise *ScG* II c. 83 n. 26 and n. 32 [1674b, 1679].

[132] Indeed, wisdom is a matter not only of drawing conclusions from, but also of making judgements about, indemonstrable first principles, and of *rebutting* {disputando} *those who deny them*: I–II q. 66 a. 5 ad 4.

[133] In a syllogism ('Fido is a dog, but all dogs are mortal, therefore Fido is mortal') the middle term, i.e. the term which links Fido to the mortality affirmed of him in the conclusion, by linking both the premisses to the conclusion without itself appearing in the conclusion, is 'dog'.

[134] Thus self-evident propositions, not being known as conclusions of a deduction, are 'principles', sources for deductive argumentation: see I-II q. 57 a. 2

[135] 'Self-evident principles {principia per se nota} are those which, once their terms are understood, are immediately {statim} known because the predicate is contained {ponitur} in the definition': I q. 17 a. 3 ad 2; also q. 2 a. 1c, I-II q. 94 a. 2 ('praedicatum est de ratione subiecti'); *Ver.* q. 10 a. 12c.   [136] I-II q. 94 a. 2c, I q. 2 a. 1c. See also n. 135 above.

[137] I-II q. 94 a. 1 ad s.c.

---

and opportunity. Anyone who has this sort of ordinary experience can readily go beyond it by ordinary intellectual acts of the kind we simply call 'understanding' {intellectus}—the kind of simple insight which in every field of human knowledge is needed to provide the premises for all reasoning and every conclusion. These acts of insight yield new concepts, and propositions about universals that can be instantiated in inexhaustibly many particulars: so *knowledge* (and not merely the answer to this question that grips me now) is a good for any being like me; and *human life* (not just my survival in this present danger) is a good; and so forth.[138]

Since they are 'first principles', and 'per se nota', and 'indemonstrable', they cannot possibly be deductions from propositions such as 'One should follow natural inclinations' or 'One is entitled to satisfy one's desires' or 'One should act in conformity with human nature'. If such propositions are true at all, it can only be as more or less unilluminating or even misleading ways of referring to the set of genuine first practical principles identifying specific types of basic human good as to be realized, pursued, and respected—and of those genuine principles' entailments.

Nor, of course, can the genuine first practical principles be 'speculative' ('theoretical', i.e. non-practical) propositions about what is the case, e.g. about human nature. Some commentators on Aquinas have imagined that they are such propositions, on which a 'practical', i.e. directive, character is conferred by the intervention of some act of will.[x] Such a view not only contradicts Aquinas' conception of the first practical principles as 'founded on' an absolutely first practical principle whose form—the form which makes every practical principle and proposition *practical*—is neither indicative nor imperative, but gerundive and directive.[y] It also hopelessly contradicts his basic and pervasive understanding of will—that it is response to reasons.[139] Practical intelligence is not slave

---

[138] Aquinas has a name for the stock {habitus} (the acquired understanding and stable capacity to make use) of such practical, directive, universal propositions which anyone is likely to have acquired in childhood, by such entirely ordinary non-deductive insights: *synderesis*. See e.g. I-II q. 94 a. 1 ad 2, I q. 79 a. 12, II-II q. 47 a. 6c and ad 1 and 3; II *Sent.* d. 24 q. 2 a. 3c, d. 24 q. 2 a. 4c, III *Sent.* d. 33 q. 2 a. 4 sol. 4c. But nothing whatever turns on that curious early medieval word; precisely for this stock of insights, Aquinas is often content to use the same name as he (like Aristotle) uses for the acquired grasp of first principles in non-practical matters: *intellectus* (*nous*): e.g. II-II q. 49 a. 2c; *Ver.* q. 5 a. 1c. The practical principles, once understood, are etched {inscribuntur} on one's mind (even when one is not thinking of them) in the way that the principles of geometry are etched on the mind of someone who understands geometry: see II *Sent.* d. 24 q. 2 a. 3 ad 3.

[139] Basic texts: I q. 59 a. 1c, q. 87 a. 4c; I *Sent.* d. 1 q. 1 a. 2c, II *Sent.* d. 25 a. 1c.

---

to the will any more than it is the slave of the passions. It moves our wills just in so far as, and in that, reasons can and often do *motivate* us. We are intelligently attracted by goods which are attractive to reason by reason of their intelligible goodness, i.e. by the benefits their instantiation promises. That goodness, precisely as opportunity, as is-to-be, is the source of all genuine moral normativity—that is, all normativity in the third order, i.e. in deliberation towards choice and action.

In short, the 'ought' of first practical principles is not deducible from 'is', whether from 'is willed by God' or from 'has been prescribed by me myself'.

Equally, an 'ought' worthy of being acknowledged by critical intelligence cannot be rightly understood as a projection or manifestation or other resultant of desires or impulses of will or emotion. Humean and neo-Humean denials that reasons can be basic motivations are sheer misunderstandings of practical reason and will—not least, of the motivations of any well-motivated, i.e. knowledge-seeking, defence of those denials (III.2).

Such, I believe, would be the thrust of Aquinas' response to doubts and denials which he was not pressed by his audience to consider and refute.

III.7. *The Way to Understanding our Nature*

Still, the basic human goods and first practical principles pertain to human nature. So, where's the mistake in supposing that they must be deduced from the *is* of a metaphysical-anthropological account of persons as human? Why else call the principles principles of *natural* law or *natural* right, or even 'the law of nature'? And if first practical principles, as I have argued, are not deduced from any non-practical proposition, why does Aquinas' principal discussion of them make constant reference to non-practical propositions about natural inclinations? These three questions can be answered together.

One understands human nature by understanding human capacities, those capacities by understanding human acts, and those acts by understanding their objects. That is Aquinas' primary methodological or, if you like, epistemological principle for considering the nature of an active being (II.3). But the objects of humanly chosen acts are precisely the basic purposes {fines}, i.e. goods {bona}, with which Aquinas is concerned, as we have seen, in his most elaborated account of first practical principles.[140] So the epistemic source of the first practical principles is not human nature or a prior, theoretical understanding of human nature (though a theoretical knowledge of the efficacy, as means, of certain choosable conduct is relevant to our knowledge of first practical principles). Rather, the epistemic relationship is the reverse: any deep understanding of human nature, i.e. of the capacities which will be fulfilled by action which participates in and realizes those goods, those *perfections*, is an understanding which has amongst its sources our primary, undemonstrated but genuine practical knowledge of those goods and purposes.

This has two relevant consequences. First (and less important): it is not unfitting to use the word 'natural' to refer to the practical principles ('law', *qua* directive) which identify and direct towards those human goods and thus[141] that human nature.

Second: the goods to which practical reason's first principles direct us are not abstract, 'ideal' or 'quasi-Platonic forms'. They are perfections, aspects of the *fulfilment*, flourishing, completion, full-being, of the flesh-and-blood human beings (and the palpable human groups or communities) in whom they can be instantiated.[142] Everyone who understands the relevant sense of the word 'good' understands it in the sense of 'good for', 'beneficial for', 'more or less perfective of'.[143] In the principles which state the basic reasons for human choice and action, 'good' refers to a possible

---

[140] See *An.* II. 6 n. 7 [305] (II.3 n. 39 above); *An.* III. 14 n. 9 [803]: 'Will is the only appetite in *reason*. Now powers are differentiated by the character of their objects. But the object of an appetitive power is perceived good(s) {bonum apprehensum}', i.e. in the case of a rational as distinct from a sensitive power, understood good(s).

[141] 'Moral precepts are in accord with {consequuntur} human nature *because* they are the requirements/prescriptions of natural reason {cum sint de dictamine rationis naturalis}': IV *Sent.* d. 2 q. I a. 4 sol. I ad 2; likewise, repeatedly, I-II q. 71 a. 2c (e.g. 'virtues . . . are in accordance with human nature just in so far as they are in line with reason; vices are against human nature just in so far as they are against the order of reasonableness'); also q. 94 a. 3 ad 2, q. 18 a. 5c, q. 78 a. 3c, II-II q. 158 a. 2 ad 4 ('the activity [of the capacity for anger] is natural to human beings just in so far as it is in accordance with reason; in so far as it is outside the order of reasonableness it is contrary to human nature'); etc. See also v. 3 nn. 91–2, VII. 7 at n. 138 below.

[142] On the tight conceptual link between *good* as in 'good is what all things desire' and *perfection*, see I q. 5 a. Ic and ad I (p. 108 n. 20 below), a. 3c and a. 6c; *Ver.* q. 21 a. Ic; *Comp.* II c. 9 [575].

[143] This does not mean that the basic goods are mere useful goods rather than intrinsically worth while {honesta}. On the contrary, they are 'goods intrinsically and without qualification, which are desired as ends for their own sake, even when they lead to something else {bona simpliciter et per se, quae tanquam fines appetuntur *sui gratia*, etsi in aliud ducant}': II *Sent.* d. 21 q. I a. 3c.

perfection—at least partial, *pro tanto* fulfilment—of a human person or community. How could there be a practical knowledge of the first practical principles that did not amount to an understanding, however informal, of the nature of the persons and groups who can be benefited by actions directed by those principles?

Metaphysicians—whose knowledge comes last in the proper sequence for acquiring scientific knowledge[z]—can deploy the knowledge they glean from epistemologically prior sciences such as ethics (*philosophia moralis*). The metaphysician will rightly observe that the order of ontological dependence is in some respects[144] the converse of the epistemological principle. Nothing can be a human good, benefit, or perfection, or an object of or reason for human action, save what can be realized by human action; and human actions can accomplish nothing beyond human capacities; and human capacities are what they are precisely in that we have the nature we have. So a metaphysical account of these matters—such as Aquinas'—can give a certain emphasis to the capacities intrinsic to human nature. And the most immediate expression of any such capacity (i.e. of an active potentiality) is a 'natural inclination'.[145]

As the various references to natural inclinations in *Summa Theologiae* I-II make clear, Aquinas has in mind three sorts of inclination:[146] tendencies, dynamisms, or dispositions which can be influential even without consciousness of their working and are essentially dispositions of a person's parts and powers towards their own actualizations;[147] tendencies which make themselves felt, more or less constantly, as sensory appetites (including aversions), i.e. as emotions or passions;[148] and tendencies which are precisely in the will, as natural forms of responsiveness to *reasons* and intelligible human goods.[149] The discussion in I-II q. 94 a. 2 is not concerned to make clear which of these types of natural

---

[144] But not all: 'goods have a kind of attractive force {bonum habet quasi virtutem attractivam} . . . A good, therefore . . . causes in the appetitive capacity [whether sensory/ emotional or intellectual/will: q. 29 a. 1, q. 35 a. 1] a certain inclination (or readiness {aptitudinem} or connaturality or love {amor}) to that good . . . {bonum . . . causat . . . inclinationem}' (I-II q. 23 a. 4c). Or again: 'the right ends {fines} of human life are fixed {determinati}. And so there can be natural inclination(s) in relation to those ends' (II-II q. 47 a. 15c). [145] See e.g. I q. 80 a. 1c and ad 1 and ad 3.

[146] See I-II q. 26 a. 1c and the texts cited in the next three footnotes.

[147] e.g. I-II q. 1 a. 2c, q. 6 a. 4c, q. 29 a. 1c.

[148] e.g. I-II q. 35 a. 1c; q. 41 a. 3c (desperation and crippling fear are 'natural' to some people).

[149] e.g. I-II q. 62 a. 3c, q. 85 a. 1c, q. 93 a. 6c; and see III.4 esp. n. 72 above. Indeed, the will itself is a natural inclination: q. 6 a. 4c.

inclination Aquinas has in mind in advancing his thesis—not epistemological but metaphysical and doubtless also theological—that the goods to which the first principles of practical reason and natural law direct us are the objects of natural inclinations.[150] But the important point to understand is that the discussion neither asserts nor implies that one knows *which* inclinations are 'natural inclinations' (in the relevant sense) *prior* to or independently of an understanding of the intelligible goods which are their objects. On the contrary, Aquinas is clear that there are common (and in that sense 'natural') inclinations—such as desperation, and fear which disarms all resistance to harm or other evil—which, in the sense which here concerns him, simply are 'not natural'.[151] Indeed, he maintains, precisely as a metaphysician, that the goods cause the inclinations.[152] Where the object of an inclination—e.g. to hurt or to have *more than others* (precisely as such)—makes no sense as a *human good*, the inclination is not natural within the meaning of q. 94 a. 2.[153] 'There is in us a natural inclination towards what is appealing {conveniens} to bodily feelings {carnali sensui} against the good of practical reasonableness {contra bonum rationis}':[154] the object of that 'natural' inclination is not a basic human good or *reason* for action.

Had Aquinas been concerned here with the epistemological questions which preoccupy us today, he might well have described the kinds of *experience* of inclination or interest (or 'natural loves')[155] in which we first come to understand that this or that object of present interest to me is only an instance of a general (in the logical sense 'universal') form of good, of human opportunity which is open-ended in that it can in principle be instantiated in the actions and lives of any human person and is in principle as

---

[150] Clearly, however, 'natural inclinations' here does not refer to characteristics which some people have and other people do not, characteristics which he elsewhere calls natural inclinations, e.g. 'natural inclinations to certain sins' (inclinations which arise from a corruption of a human person's nature) (I-II q. 78 a. 3c) or inclinations 'natural' to some individual but not to the human species as such (III *Sent.* d. 36 a. 1c; *Ver.* q. 25 a. 6 ad 4). See the general discussion in I-II q. 31 a. 7c, on the various forms of corruption of body or custom or habituation which make it 'natural {connaturalis}' for some people to like eating coal or other people, or copulating with beasts or with humans of their own sex, etc.—pleasures which in themselves (i.e. considering what is appropriate to human beings in reason) are 'in the focal sense unnatural but in a secondary sense connatural {innaturales simpliciter sed connaturales secundum quid}'.

[151] I-II q. 41 a. 3c. See also nn. 70, 148 and 150 above.   [152] See n. 144 above.

[153] Thus 'natural inclinations in a human being as human being never run counter to the good of virtue, but are always in line with it': III *Sent.* d. 29 a. 3c.

[154] *Mal.* q. 16 a. 2c.   [155] See I-II q. 23 a. 4c, q. 29 a. 1c, q. 41 a. 3c.

---

beneficial and worth while for others as it is for me. Such a discussion would have more easily and firmly focused on the third-order perspective of *moralis philosophia*, concerned with reasons for action precisely as reasons. The shift in theoretical perspective would not, however, have eliminated all reference to the 'theoretical' (non-practical) knowledge which is presupposed by practical understanding. For one cannot understand that a possibility (e.g. of acquiring knowledge or becoming a friend) is an opportunity, a good, to-be-pursued, unless one first knows, to some extent, that it is a possibility (e.g. that questions sometimes have answers, or that one can communicate and interact with another person). Still, since the goods of human existence are each open-ended, the practical knowledge of basic human goods will outrun, by anticipation, the theoretical knowledge it presupposed. (By reflection, the theoretical can appropriate what was known practically.)

In any event, when Aquinas' largely first-order discussion is transposed (as in this chapter) into its third-order equivalent, it can be seen to contain the outlines of a response to the sceptical doubts with which this chapter began. In so far, however, as most of those doubts were framed as doubts about moral right and wrong, rather than about the prior issues of *ought* and *is*, a response to them should be made in the context of considering how first practical principles develop into fully fledged moral principles and virtues (see IV.5). Outlining that development is a main concern of the next chapter.

Notes

a. *Neo-Humean interpretations of Aristotle* on phronēsis, *means, and ends* . . . The issue here is not how the *Nicomachean Ethics* should in truth be interpreted (as to which, see e.g. Wiggins 1975) but how a sceptic may capitalize on certain statements in *Nic. Eth.* 6. 12. 1144^{a}9, 6. 9. 1142^{b}33 (or indeed in II-II q. 47 a. 6c, with which contrast I-II q. 66 a. 3 ad 3 and *Eth.* VI. 8 n. 17 [1233]).

b. *Intelligible and understood goods* . . . the plural term *bona intelligibilia* is not rare in Aquinas: e.g. *Comp.* II c. 9 [576]; *ST* III q. 60 a. 4c; *Rat.* c. 4 [966]; plurality of intelligible goods is plainly implicit in the singular form used in e.g. I-II q. 30 a. 1c, q. 31 a. 5c; *Meta.* XII. 7 n. 4 [2522]. Though Aquinas sometimes uses the term in a narrow way to signify goods of intellect or spirit as such, the last-mentioned text (quoted in n. c) establishes its general equivalence to 'intelligible good' and 'understood good' {bonum intellectum}. The plural term *bona intellecta* is not used by Aquinas; but the plurality of understood goods implicitly referred to by his very frequent phrase *bonum intellectum* is evident in many passages, notably I-II q. 19 a. 3; *ScG* III c. 88 n. 2 [2638]; *Virt.* q. 1 a. 5 ad 2, a. 8 ad 13; *Eth.* VI. 11 n. 3 [1277]; cf. also I-II q. 9 a. 1c, q. 10 a. 1c, q. 94 a. 2c.

c. *'Good is what all things desire'* . . . This dictum from *Nic. Eth.* I. 1. 1094^{a}2–3 is often quoted by Aquinas, and will be completely misunderstood (especially in a neo-Humean way) unless taken in the light of *Metaphysics* 12. 7. 1072^{a}29: 'we desire things because they seem good to us; it is not that they seem good to us because we desire them'. The point is emphasized by Aquinas; see e.g. *Meta.* I. 4 n. 3 [71]: what is *end* is 'in itself desirable {per se appetibile}, by reason of which it is called good'; *Meta.* XII. 7 n. 4 [2522]: 'something which is desirable to sensory appetite {concupiscibile} but is not an intelligible good {intelligibile bonum} is an apparent good. A primary good must be willable, i.e. desirable by intellectual appetite (for will is in understanding {voluntas in intellectu est}, and not merely in the appetite of sensory desire). . . . But what is desired by *intellectual* appetite is desired because it seems good in itself {secundum se}. For the source {principium} of this kind of appetite is intelligence, that is, the act of understanding which is somehow moved by the *intelligible*.' In short, in understanding *X* as good one understands it as 'to be pursued {prosequendum}', i.e. as desirable, and thus (in so far as one is an intelligent and integrated being) one desires it. See further IV. 2 n. 20 below.

d. *'Reasons for action'* . . . Though Aquinas has no word or phrase literally corresponding to 'reason for action', and does not use the adjectival metaphor 'basic', he is clear that there are basic reasons for action. And though he never formally addresses the question 'Which are the basic reasons for action?', and never offers to set out a complete list of them, his work identifies such reasons with unprecedented explicitness and care. All chosen behaviour is 'for a purpose', *ad finem* (to some end); choice is always of means to end, to the end or ends one intends. 'In human actions *ad finem*, the reasons for them derive from the end(s)': I-II q. 14 a. 2c. So, though Latin idiom did not encourage Aquinas to speak literally of 'reasons for action', his constant talk of the ends of chosen action is most accurately understood in just those terms. End {finis} is relevant to chosen actions because it has (really or apparently) the intelligible character of *good* {ratio boni}; the good that is of interest to one's intelligent interest (i.e. to will, intention, and choice) is always a good that one considers an *intelligible* or *understood good* {bonum intellectum}; to understand a purpose {finis} as good is to understand that it gives one a reason for action. Practical thinking's most abstract and basic or primary principle gives the connection between goods and reasons for action the same sort of tightness as the principle of non-contradiction. For the first principle of practical reason is: '*Good* is to be *done* and *pursued* and evil avoided {bonum est faciendum et prosequendum et malum vitandum}': I-II q. 94 a. 2c: one is to interest oneself in and act to instantiate intelligible good(s). Such reasons make possible one's practical reasoning; they provide the premisses for deliberation. Thus they provide any intelligent action with its *principia*—both its sources or bases, as intelligent action, and its articulate or articulable 'guiding principles'.

e. *Eisenhower's decision to go for 6 June* . . . His statement went on 'I don't see how we can possibly do anything else': Hastings (1989: 71). Like many another idiom, this is misleading if taken at face value. It is elliptical for something like: If we don't go on the 6th, the whole thing will have to be put off for months and may become impossible because of loss of surprise, enhanced German beach defences, public unrest, etc.; but the goods to be achieved by an invasion are such that it ought not to be abandoned; therefore even high risks do not warrant putting it off.

f. *Originality of Aquinas' analysis of deliberation, choice, and action* . . . He creatively developed a long tradition of reflection: see Gauthier (1954).

g. *Rejection of important elements in Aquinas' act-analysis* . . . See Finnis (1980: 339).

h. *Sound act-analysis is not by 'introspection'* . . . See Donagan (1982: 654). But if Donagan had reflected more carefully on his own insight into the significance of interrupted acting (on which see also I-II q. 8 a. 3 ad 3), he would have seen that his rejection (651-3) of Aquinas' post-choice elements, *imperium* and *usus*, results from overlooking conditional choices (see Finnis 1994), as to which (i) their execution need involve no new choice (cf. 651) and (ii) the time for executing them will usually be separated, sometimes widely, from making them.

i. *'Proposals' for adoption by choice* . . . This conception of the intelligible content of options is used a great deal by Aquinas, albeit usually in verb form. Thus: 'intelligence moves will in the way an end is said to move (motivate), i.e. inasmuch as one's intelligence first conceives the intelligible benefit of some purpose {praeconcipit rationem finis} and *proposes* it to one's will': *Ver*. q. 22 a. 12c; also I-II q. 10 a. 2c, q. 13 a. 1c, a. 5 ad 1, a. 6 ad 3, q. 19 a. 1c, q. 20 a. 1 ad 1.

j. *'Iudicium electionis'* . . . The term is found only in early works (see II *Sent*. d. 24 q. 1 a. 3 ad 5, q. 2 a. 3 ad 4; *Ver*. q. 16 a. 1 ad 15, q. 17 a. 1 ad 4 and ad 17). But the idea—that choice includes, so to speak, a judgement in it—is present in the discussions of *electio* in Aquinas' last writings: see *ScG* II c. 48 n. 6 [1246]; *ST* I-II q. 13 a. 1c: 'the act in which one's will tends [definitively] to something proposed to it as good, being an act directed to an end by one's reason, is materially an act of will, though formally an act of reason'. Aquinas' almost invariable term for free choice or freedom of choice is *liberum arbitrium* (=*libertas arbitrii*), and he treats this idiom as synonymous with *libera electio* (=*libertas electionis*): see e.g. IV *Sent*. d. 20 a. 5 sol. 4 ex.; d. 38 q. 2 a. 2 sol. 1 ad 1; *In Gal*. 5. 4 ad v. 17 [314].

k. *Responsiveness: interest and aversion* . . . One's constant underlying aversion to the evils (harms, deficiencies, etc.) opposite to benefits is given by Aquinas (I-II q. 8 a. 1 ad 1) the name *noluntas* (from *nolle*, to be unwilling)—

a name that has not made its way in the world. As intelligent responsiveness to reasons for and against action, *voluntas* extends to cover the negative as well as the positive.

l. *Reason in the service of emotion produces rationalizations* . . . See Grisez *et al.* (1987: 123–5). Since one's will responds only to intelligible goods {bonum intellectum}, wrongful choice must be of objectives which are in some respects intelligible (intelligent); one's grasp of the offensiveness to reason which makes them wrong must be marred by some ignorance or error which arises either directly from some inclination of feeling, or from a settled disposition {malitia; vitium} which was originally shaped under the distorting influence of feeling but now, even without the present influence of feeling, can make one judge an unreasonable objective reasonable (I-II q. 78 a. 1; II *Sent.* d. 43 q. 1 a. 1c and 2c); in these ways, passion dominates ('binds' {ligat}) reason, without eliminating or silencing it: see I q. 63 a. 1 ad 4, I-II q. 10 a. 3c. 'In this way passion brings one's reason to a particular judgement opposed to what one knows as a general proposition {in universali}': I-II q. 77 a. 2c; *Eth.* VII. 3 n. 20 [1347]. (Even the understanding of general truths can be lost or prevented by, for example, seduction playing on passions: II *Sent.* d. 22 q. 1 a. 2 ad 1 and a. 3c.) Aquinas' account of the content of rationalizations remains, however, disappointingly thin, e.g. 'pleasure is what's worth going for {sectanda}': I-II q. 77 a. 2 ad 4.

m. *Aristotle on first practical principles* . . . Cf. II *Sent.* d. 24 q. 2 a. 3c, III *Sent.* d. 33 q. 2 a. 4 sol. 4c. Gauthier (*Opera* 47. 267*) says that what Aquinas says about natural law/right and about 'first natural principles' owes more to 13th-century jurists and theologians than to Aristotle, and (ibid. 88 ad *Eth.* II. 4 n. 7 [286]) quotes William of Auxerre (professor in Paris c.1230), *Summa Aurea* II tr. 8 q. 1: 'sicut in speculativis sunt quaedam quae per se sunt nota quae sunt pura natura speculationis. Ita in agendis sunt quaedam principia agendi per se nota in quibus ius naturae consistit.'

n. *Recent discussions of first practical principles* . . . See Grisez *et al.* (1987) and the bibliography therein.

o. *The basic good of human life* . . . We are like every living thing in having a dynamism towards preserving our life; but human life includes, when it is healthy, the functioning and integrated *capacity* not only to eat and digest and reproduce and feel and move about, but also to think and to act rationally: thinking and choosing are aspects of the developed and healthy human *organism*. See e.g. II-II q. 179 a. 1c. It does not, of course, follow that life in immaturity or ill health is devoid of value; it continues to instantiate the basic intelligible good of life, albeit in a reduced way.

p. *The basic human good of marriage* . . . It is clear that in *ST* I-II q. 94 a. 2c, when speaking of *coniunctio maris et feminae*, Aquinas is inviting his readers to think of marriage. For in this sentence he quotes a few words from a passage in Justinian's *Digest* (AD 533) which also expressly refers to marriage {matrimonium} as a *maris et feminae coniunctio*: that reference, as quoted by Thomas in IV *Sent.* d. 26 q. 1 (= *Supp.* q. 41) a. 1 s.c., reads: 'ius naturale est maris et feminae coniunctio, quam nos matrimonium appellamus'. See also II-II q. 154 a. 2c; *ScG* III c. 123 n. 8 [2966]; *In Matt.* 19 ad v. 4 [1549] ('[Jesus] intends to prove that marriage {coniunctio maris et feminae} was established by God.') *Coniunctio* here connotes sexual intercourse but primarily the whole conjoining of lives in marriage, a consortium and community of two lives that is appropriate to the conception, gestation, and education of children by their parents and is in any case a natural form of human friendship (see v.4 at n. 56 below). Early printed editions of *ST* replace *coniunctio* here with *commixtio*, a word which tends to be more narrowly focused on sexual intercourse. The text offered with some recent English editions likewise uses *commixtio*; but the Leonine edition, which those editions purport to be following, rejects the word *commixtio* here, since it has no support at all in the 13th-century manuscripts on which that edition rests. *Coniunctio* is, moreover, the term used in the parallel passage in *Eth.* v. 12 n. 4 [1019]; and see *ScG* III c. 123 n. 7 [2965]; *In Matt.* 19 ad vv. 4, 5 [1549, 1551]; IV *Sent.* d. 26 q. 1 (= *Supp.* q. 41) a. 3 ad 4.

q. *Basic good of knowledge* . . . See e.g. II-II q. 109 a. 2 ad 1 and I-II q. 9 a. 1 ad 3 ('ipsum verum quod est perfectio intellectus continetur sub universali bono ut quoddam bonum particulare'); q. 10 a. 1c ('naturaliter homo vult . . . cognitionem veri'); *Eth.* VII. 13 n. 14 [1511]; *Phys.* 1. 10 n. 5 [79] ('interdum intellectus hominis quadam naturali inclinatione tendit in veritatem licet rationem veritatis non percipiat'). Of course, though knowledge is *per se* good, it can *per accidens* be bad, e.g. because it induces in someone unreasonable pride or enables someone to devise and carry out some wrongful choice: II-II q. 167 a. 1c and ad 1 and ad 2.

r. *The basic good of (practical) reasonableness* . . . Sometimes *bonum rationis* is synonymous with *bonum intellectum*, an intelligible and more or less understood good (e.g. I-II q. 30 a. 1c), i.e. the benefit, real or apparent, which is the will's object (e.g. q. 80 a. 1c). But there are many strategic passages in which the only reasonable translation is something like 'the good of practical reasonableness', signifying that the good he has in mind is the good of *reason's successfully extending its directedness-by-reasons (first practical principles)* (and by all of them taken together in a reasonable way, in their integral directiveness) *into the domain of passions and actions* which, but for this rule by reason, would result in unreasonable dispositions and/or choices and actions: see e.g. I-II q. 55 a. 4 ad 2 (read with *Div.* 4. 22 [577–8]); q. 59 a. 4c ('the good of practical reasonableness {rationis bonum} to which moral virtue directs the appetitive part of one's soul is precisely that which [namely passions, and operations of the will] is moderated or directed by reason'); q. 61 a. 2c ('the good of practical reasonableness {rationis bonum} can be considered in two ways: (1) inasmuch as it consists in reason's very activity {in ipsa consideratione rationis consistit}; in this way there is one principal virtue, called *prudentia*. (2)

inasmuch as reason's order is brought into something else {circa aliquid ponitur rationis ordo}; and this something else may be actions (and so we have justice) or emotions [and so we have two further virtues, courage and temperance]'). Also *Eth.* II. 3 n. 8 [272] (it belongs to the *bonum rationis* that the sensitive appetite, whose movements are the passions, be regulated by reason {eam [rationem]}). This translation is confirmed by the close conjunction of the *bonum rationis* with the thought in Pseudo-Dionysius, *De Divinis Nominibus* c. 4, that human good involves acting according to reason {bonum hominis est secundum rationem vivere}: e.g. III *Sent.* d. 29 a. 1 s.c., d. 33 q. 1 a. 1 sol. 1c. The *bonum rationis* is impeded (*a*) by what is contrary to reason {contrarium rationi}, and (*b*) by what takes away one's use of reason. The former is always morally bad, but the latter—e.g. in chaste but exciting marital intercourse (see v.4 at nn. 58, 67, 69 below)—need not be: see II-II q. 150 a. 3 ad 2.

s. *The priority of* prosequendum *to* faciendum . . . Aquinas makes this clear in the next sentence but one: 'everything to which people have a natural inclination reason naturally understands as good and consequently as to be pursued in action {opere prosequenda}'. As he says in another mature text, *Mal.* q. 10 a. 1c: 'all acts of an appetitive capacity [such as the will] come down to two common matters, pursuit {prosecutionem} and flight (as the acts of an intellectual capacity come down to affirmation and negation); so pursuit {prosecutio} is in appetite [particularly, willing] what affirmation is in intellect. . . . And good has the character attractive {attractivi}, since "good is what everything desires {appetunt}" (*Nic. Eth.* I. 1. 1094^{a}2–3).' (In an effort to clarify the absolutely first principle of practical reason, I-II q. 94 a. 2c appeals to the same—ambiguous and so not too helpful: see n. c—Aristotelian tag.) Texts treating *prosequendum* as the positive directiveness of practical reason (and *vitandum* as the negative counterpart) include I-II q. 84 a. 4c, II-II q. 125 a. 1c, q. 147 a. 1 ad 2; *ScG* I c. 90 n. 2 [750]; *Virt. Card.* a. 1c; *Meta.* v. 1 n. 14 [762]; *Eth.* VI. 2 n. 5 [1128]. See also II–II q. 47 a. 8 ad 1. *Bonum . . . faciendum* is very much less frequent; indeed, outside I-II q. 94 a. 2c it is found only in relatively marginal texts, almost all concerned with moral or other laws: II-II q. 79 a. 3 ad 3 (praecept[a] affirmativ[a] pertinent ad faciendum bonum); *In Rom.* 7. 4 ad v. 23 [586] (lex inducit ad bonum faciendum); 13. 1 ad v. 3 [1030].

t. *Practical principles, norms, and judgements can be true* . . . Aquinas' own discussion, in *Eth.* VI. 2 n. 8 [1131], begins with a general conception of practical truth as conformity to right appetite, and notes that appetite is right by its conformity to true reason {rationi verae}, so that there is evidently a vicious circle {circulatio}. Aquinas offers to resolve the problem by stating merely that whatever end (as distinct from means) appetite is concerned with is determined for human beings by nature {determinatus est homini a natura}. (Cf. II-II q. 47 a. 15c: 'the right ends of human life are determined/determinate {determinati}'.) This does not say that the truth of practical knowledge consists in conformity to human nature or to non-practical truths about nature, an apparently simple thought—all too simple!—which Aquinas could readily have stated had he shared it. But it is not at all clear how the circle is being broken. The answer seems to lie in the direction indicated by Grisez *et al.* (1987: 115–20/Finnis 1991b: i, 253–8): human beings do not *find* and know initially by non-practical knowledge the possible fulfilment to which the is-to-be of practical knowledge points. (Nor of course do they *invent* and fashion their own fulfilment's very possibility, as if there were some sort of creative art or technology for living human life.) Rather, beginning from first practical principles which they neither select nor fashion, human persons *develop* their fulfilment's possibility; and in this developing of possibility, practical knowledge has its truth—and in particular the first practical principles have their truth—by *anticipating* the fulfilment whose realization is possible through actions in conformity with those principles. Not only the realization but also the specification and projection of one's possible human fulfilment depend on more than *given* human nature; for human nature includes the capacities of practical reason and the response of free will, so that what we *can be* through free choices and actions depends on practical knowledge (understanding of practical principles) rather than the practical knowledge being true by conformity to some prior reality, actual or possible. On this understanding, the truth of practical reason is radically diverse from that of non-practical knowledge; but this is analogy, not equivocation, because in both cases there is a conformity of the human mind, and its objects, with the mind of God (cf. *ScG* III c. 47 n. 7 [2243]; x.3 below). And this may be what Aquinas is driving at with his reference to human ends being determined, taken together with his manifest unwillingness (and see I–II q. 57 a. 5 ad 3) to reduce 'practical truth' to a special case of theoretical truth by treating it as ultimately a conformity to human nature. Human ends and fulfilment are *more fully* known to us practically, i.e. by anticipation of what is-to-be, because unlike the ends and fulfilment of other animals, they are open-ended, not fully determinate. On this incomplete determinacy of human nature, cf. *ScG* IV c. 83 n. 18 [4188a].

u. *Error about first principles (speculative or practical)* . . . Aquinas often says that no one makes mistakes about principles, or first principles (e.g. I-II q. 79 a. 12 ad 3, q. 100 a. 11c, II-II q. 180 a. 6 ad 2; *Mal.* q. 3 a. 12 ad 13; II *Sent.* d. 24 q. 3 a. 3 ad 2, d. 39 q. 3 a. 1 ad 1). But this must be understood narrowly, since (often nearby in the same works, and sometimes in the same passage) he also says that error about even first principles is possible (and can be difficult to overcome, for want of more obvious considerations by which to disprove the mistaken belief): e.g. I-II q. 72 a. 5c, q. 88 a. 1c, II-II q. 156 a. 3 ad 2; *Mal.* q. 3 a. 13c; II *Sent.* d. 39 q. 3 a. 1 ad 1, d. 43 q. 1 a. 4c. For on the way from principles to conclusions, one can easily be misled by pleasure or by any of the emotions {passiones}, or even by mistakes of reasoning (e.g. II *Sent.* d. 39 q. 3 a. 1 ad 1) or by assuming something false (*Ver.* q. 16 a. 2 ad 1) or imaginary (*Mal.* q. 7 a. 5 ad 6); and if one chooses and acts on a false practical conclusion one can acquire the corresponding wrongful disposition {vitium}, and will accordingly become inattentive to any true principle which would undermine one's vice, and will tend to replace it with some principle which, though actually false, would if true support the wrongful choices one now habitually favours (see e.g. III *Sent.* d. 36 a. 1c). Thus by a kind of corruption of one's nature (see *ScG* IV c. 95 n. 2 [4273]) one will be *de facto* erring 'about principles', and this error can become explicitly an error 'of principle' if and when one goes on to deny principle(s) which are true and assert principles which are false. But these 'malicious' denials of true principles are really a kind of lying (see *Eth.* VI. 10 n. 18 [1274]), because like everyone else one does in fact have at least a general {in universali} understanding of true principles (an understanding reached without reasoning) and this understanding cannot be suppressed but constantly works, at some level, to oppose what one is asserting and living out (see II *Sent.* d. 39 q. 3 a. 1c; *Ver.* q. 16 a. 2c and ad 1). Note that when Aquinas wants to exemplify the principles about which 'one cannot err', he usually adduces what one may call 'formal' principles: e.g. that one should not do wrong {iniuriam} (*Quodl.* III q. 12 a. 1c [line 43]) or harm (*An.* III. 15 n. 9 [826]) to anyone, or that God is to be obeyed (II *Sent.* d. 39 q. 3 a. 2c). Aquinas' statement, at I-II q. 94 a. 4c (similarly *ScG* III c. 47 n. 7 [2243]), that the truth of general principles of reason, including practical principles {communia principia rationis, sive speculativae sive practicae} is *equally known to everyone* must be understood as stating what is the case 'in principle' or under favourable conditions, and is in any case said incidentally, while discussing the very different question whether natural law's content is the same for everyone.

v. *Defence of first principles of practical reason . . .* See *Post.* 1. 20 n. 5 [171]. Such a defence can be called 'dialectical', in one sense of that rather protean (even in Aquinas) word: *Meta.* 1. 10 n. 14 [164]; cf. *Post.* 1. 20 nn. 5 and 6 [171–2]. A model for such defences is Aristotle's critique of general scepticism: *Metaphysics* 4. 4. 1005^b35–1006^a28, 8. 1012^a29–b18, 11. 5. 1062^b1–11, 6. 1063^b30–5; and see III. 2 n. 10 above.

w. *The first practical principles are not, properly speaking, innate . . .* There are no concepts naturally given, *ab initio*, in the human mind: *Q. An.* q. 8c. Aquinas often says that first principles are naturally 'given' {indita} to us; but he means that we are given an understanding, an intellectual 'light', whereby we can understand these principles as soon as we have the relevant experience of the world and of our sentient (emotional) appetites. It is this 'rational light' which is innate (*Trin.* q. 3 a. 1 ad 4), and by transference Aquinas will sometimes say that the principles are innate and/or that the ends to which the principles direct us are innate (e.g. III *Sent.* d. 33 q. 2 a. 4 sol. 4c). But all our knowledge begins with the senses: *Eth.* II. 1 n. 2 [246], including our knowledge of first principles: *ex sensu acquiruntur* (III *Sent.* d. 25 q. 2 a. 1 sol. 4 ad 1, IV *Sent.* d. 9 q. 1 a. 4 sol. 1c; I-II q. 94 a. 1 s.c.). Shortly before discussing the *principia iuris communis*, Aquinas says that knowledge of principles comes to us from the senses {cognitio principiorum provenit nobis a sensu}: I-II q. 51 a. 1c.

Our knowledge of such principles is 'natural' not because given at birth but because acquired spontaneously, without investigation (*Ver.* q. 16 a. 1c; *Virt.* q. 1 a. 8c), 'naturally, not from effort {studio} or from our willing' (*ScG* III c. 43 n. 2 [2203]). Human intellect begins as a *tabula* on which 'nothing is written': I q. 79 a. 2c; 1 *Sent.* d. 39 q. 2 a. 2 ad 4. Even what we know 'without investigation' we cannot come to know without getting something from the senses: *Ver.* q. 16 a. 1c.

x. *First practical principles are not theoretical principles given practical force by an act of will* . . . The erroneous claim that they are is often advanced today, but can also be found, in essence, within a few years of Aquinas' death, in Peter of Auvergne's continuation of the commentary on the *Politics*: see *Pol.* VII. 2 [1083].

y. *First practical principles are not indicative or predictive but gerundive and directive* . . . In another context, considering the *imperium* which guides the execution of one's concrete choice, Aquinas calls the gerundive in 'This *is to be done* by you {Hoc est tibi faciendum}' 'indicative': I-II q. 17 a. 1c. But this is only in order to contrast it with the imperative 'Do this! {Fac hoc}'. The gerundive-indicative does not state what is the case, or what will be the case, but rather, as he says in explaining the point, directs {ordinat} someone *to* something to-be-done {ad aliquid agendum}.

z. *Scientific (explanatory) metaphysical knowledge comes last* . . . See *Eth.* VI. 7 n. 17 [1211]; *Meta.* I. 2 n. 11 [46]; *Trin.* q. 5 a. 1 ad 9.

IV

Fulfilment and Morality

IV.1. *Basic Reasons for Action: The Further Questions*

There are many basic reasons for action. So how are they inter-related, ordered? Each directs one to a basic good which is intrinsically good for any human being. And each can be instantiated in indefinitely many ways in one's own life and one's own communities, as well as in the lives of other people and other communities. But one's time and capacities, like those of even the wealthiest and most powerful community, are limited. So how is one to decide which instantiations to try to bring about by choice and action, whether individual or communal?

Each of the basic reasons directs us towards an intrinsic good—a good which is intelligible as an end in itself and provides a sufficiently explanatory answer to the question 'Why are you doing that?' ('Because otherwise we'd be in danger'; or 'Because I'd like to find out the truth about . . .'; or 'Because we're friends'; and so on—no further answer need normally be given.) But it is equally true that, even if richly instantiated in my life or the life of my communities, none of the basic goods amounts, by itself, to complete human well-being or fulfilment. Moreover, a sufficiently explanatory answer to the question 'Why are you doing that?' may not be a completely satisfactory answer, for it may fail to show that the choice to do this was not only intelligent but also fully reasonable.[1]

---

[1] One can have an immoderate, unreasonable desire for or interest in acquiring knowledge: II *Sent.* d. 22 q. 1 a. 1 ad 7.

'Because I'm trying to find out the truth about . . .' explains sufficiently why a scientist has decided to inject a group of prisoners with
syphilis. 'Because I'm trying to escape from death row' explains
sufficiently why a prisoner is attacking a warder. But neither statement answers further pertinent questions about what is-to-be-done
by scientists, condemned prisoners, or anyone else.[2] If there are first
practical principles which direct us towards truly interesting goods,
are there also principles which guide our choices and priorities
amongst those goods and amongst their possible instantiations?

Aquinas responds to these questions in his discussions of three
broad topics: (1) happiness as fulfilment {beatitudo}, (2) virtue
(rational and therefore moral excellence of choice, action, and
character) and its structuring and unifying principle, practical reasonableness {prudentia} both individual and political, and (3) the
highest morally binding principle. In considering those three topics
we can also consider his ideas of common good and general justice.

IV.2. *Available Human Fulfilment*

Since human goods (intrinsically desirable purposes) and opportunities (eligible instantiations of those goods) are multiple, the question arises whether there is a human condition, conceivably
attainable in or by one's willing and acting, which could be called
fully satisfactory. This human condition would be not so much
another, additional basic good as, rather, a state of affairs which, by
excluding all lack and bad (deficiency in attainment of basic goods)
and fulfilling every desire (for intelligible, basic goods), would be
fully satisfactory ('perfect'), and *lacking nothing desirable* ('complete'). For the concept of such a state of affairs, and prior to
investigating whether the concept has any counterpart in attainable reality, Aristotle adopted the word *eudaimonia*, and Aquinas
beatitudo (or, synonymously,[3] *felicitas*).

We could translate those words by 'happiness', provided we
meant not simply a state of good feeling. (Though pleasure is by

---

[2] See II-II q. 69 a. 4 obj. 1 and ad 1: to the objection that one's natural inclination to
resist one's destruction justifies one in using force to resist even just execution; Aquinas
replies that 'what nature inclines one to is to be pursued not indiscriminately {passim} but
reasonably {secundum rationis ordinem}'. (Contrast Hobbes (1651, c. 14 paras. 1, 8, 18, 29,
etc.) on the 'inalienable right' of defending oneself against even just punishment.) See
further IX.2 at nn. 44, 45.   [3] See e.g. I q. 62 a. 1c; *ScG* III c. 25 n. 14 [2068].

no means excluded, the fully satisfactory may involve perfections of which one is not aware in one's experience and whose worth is simply not measured by feeling's glow.) What is important is that at this point in the philosophical reflection in which these words are being used, their meaning be identified in the way just indicated. The relevant concept is at this stage a formal one, not yet filled out with any content or reference save this: a complete or perfect good {bonum perfectum et sufficiens}[4] which includes nothing bad and fulfils all desires.[5] What such a good state of affairs consists in—whether it involves only me, or also my friends, or in principle everyone, and what it 'would be like to be in it'—remains as yet undetermined. So a sounder translation would be 'flourishing' or 'fulfilment', understood in this formal way.[6]

Now Aquinas is very clear that no state of affairs in this world can fully correspond to or instantiate the general idea of *beatitudo*, of a good complete and fully satisfactory for human persons. Such a good is quite beyond our powers; there is no need to labour the points he makes about the evils which ineluctably afflict our present life, and our incapacity to satisfy our desires before the death we naturally abhor.[7] And fulfilment in some other, say future, life 'goes beyond anything we can find out by inquiry and reasoning'.[8]

Yet Aquinas does not conclude that moral philosophy must do without the concept of *beatitudo*. Rather, he retains the concept in

---

[4] I-II q. 5 a. 3c and a. 4c; see also q. 1 a. 5c ('bonum perfectum et completivum sui ipsius'); q. 3 a. 3 ad 2. Also called by Aquinas an 'integral good' {bonum integrum}, presumably to signify that the perfection is of a good made up of many goods (see I-II q. 3 a. 2 ad 2) which stand to the integral good somewhat as parts stand to whole: *Eth.* 1. 9 n. 5 [107]. *Sufficiens* or *per se sufficiens* translates Aristotle's *autarkēs*, 'self-sufficient', i.e. lacking in nothing.

[5] I-II q. 5 a. 3c and 4c. 'All desires' means all that we desire by a 'natural appetite', i.e. a desire which can be coherent with one's other desires and reasonable: see e.g. q. 5 a. 8 ad 3. Since the fulfilment of desires in operation includes pleasure {delectatio}, Aquinas sometimes says that the general idea of *beatitudo* involves three 'conditions': good which is complete {perfectum consummatum}, lacking in nothing {per se sufficiens}, and pleasurable {cum delectatione}: e.g. *Mal.* q. 13 a. 3c.

[6] This formal concept Aquinas calls the 'general idea {communis ratio} of *beatitudo*'; he distinguishes this use of the word from its use to refer specifically {secundum specialem rationem} to whatever actual or possible state of affairs is judged to correspond to or instantiate that general idea. See I-II q. 3 a. 2 ad 2, q. 5 aa. 3c and 8c; and also q. 1 a. 7c; earlier, IV *Sent.* d. 49 q. 1 a. 3 sol. 3c (see also II *Sent.* d. 38 a. 2 ad 2); *ScG* IV c. 95 n. 7 [4278]. See further VII. 1 n. 13 below.

[7] I-II q. 5 a. 3c; *ScG* III c. 48; *Eth.* 1. 10 n. 12 [129]; IV *Sent.* d. 43 a. 1 sol. 1c: 'varietas fortunae, et infirmitas humani corporis, scientiae et virtutis imperfectio et instabilitas, quibus omnibus beatitudinis perfectio impeditur'; *Reg.* 1. 9 [63] [782].

[8] *Eth.* 1. 9 n. 11 [113]: 'felicitas alterius vitae omnem investigationem rationis excedit'; likewise II *Sent.* d. 2 q. 2 a. 1c. But see x.4 below.

---

a specific though secondary sense, which he expresses by the term *beatitudo imperfecta*, incomplete fulfilment. The term is, on its face, paradoxical; since *beatitudo* has been defined as a perfect good, *imperfecta beatitudo* means an imperfect perfect good, a somewhat less than fulfilling fulfilment. Still, in the analogy of beatitude, the incomplete fulfilment which Aquinas has in mind is not radically inadequate for its role, like various popular conceptions of happiness or fulfilment which he passes in review. The unsatisfactoriness of riches, honours and fame and glory, power, length of days, and bodily pleasures—their incapacity, too, to make unifying sense of a whole life—is shown by a series of arguments[9] which get their force in large measure from an implicitly 'internal' perspective, an appeal to what makes sense to the reasonable deliberating subject[10] who recalls, for example, how possession of wealth and other temporal goods only shows up their insufficiency.[11]

Why, then, does Aquinas retain the idea of human fulfilment, albeit with this reduced and puzzling meaning? The answer must be that reason seeks—i.e. it is unintelligent not to seek—a more complete and coherent guidance-by-reasons-for-action than is supplied by a set of reasons for action considered *one by one*. Each of the first practical principles is 'primary'; each directs towards an intrinsic and basic human good that is only one amongst others and thus is incomplete. And each of these goods is realizable in countless different ways, ways not all of which, however, are consistent with acting for other basic goods or with the realizing (instantiating; making actual) of the same or other good(s) by and/or in some other person or persons or group(s).[12] Reason, then, seeks a more complete—one may say, integral—directiveness, the directiveness not of each first practical principle taken on its own but of all taken together.[13] That is to say, it is obviously desirable to make all one's

---

[9] I-II q. 2 aa. 1–6; also *ScG* III cc. 27–33.

[10] The immediate appeal is to the standard, the model for thinking, provided by wise people {sapientes}, the very same people as are the subject of the first sentence of the *Ethics* commentary {. . . sapientis est ordinare}; in both cases the relevant 'ordering' is the third type of order, the getting in order of one's own deliberating.

[11] I-II q. 2 a. 1 ad 3. The point is clear to the 'wise', if not to 'fools', rather as matters of taste (which these questions are certainly not) are to be adjudicated by people with olfactory organs in good order: a. 1 ad 1 (on the limits of this analogy, and Aquinas' awareness of them, see 1.8 above). *In Matt.* 5 ad vv. 3–10 [404, 406] extends the point to getting ahead and dominating, and to doing whatever one likes.

[12] The problem of bringing unity and determinacy into one's willing, in face of the multiplicity and diversity of intelligible goods, is explicitly noted in I-II q. 50 a. 5 ad 3.

[13] The whole set of first practical principles {lex naturalis} is 'directive by and of reason {directivum ex parte rationis}': I-II q. 91 a. 4c.

choices, actions, states of mind, and feelings harmonize with *all* the first practical principles taken integrally, i.e. in their *combined* guiding force. This desirability is a source, a principle, of the integral directiveness of practical reason. Aquinas (as we have seen: III.5) calls it the good of (practical) reason or reasonableness {bonum rationis}; its significance for us is such that Aquinas can say that it is the proximate goal of our existence.[14] Those who instantiate this good in their character and action have its intrinsic result, the good of virtue {bonum virtutis}.[15]

Accordingly, we reach Aquinas' central definition of the human fulfilment which moral and political philosophy identify as here and now the organizing *point* of individual and social choice, as something attainable (so far as is possible in one's circumstances) by one's own or our own actions as we are. It is this: *virtue in action*.[16] And that means practical reason in *action*, successfully extending its directiveness to all one's emotional and voluntary dispositions and activity.[17] For virtue simply is the *perfection* of the human capacities involved in action, i.e. the powers of understanding and responding to intelligible goods and of choosing and carrying out one's choices well—a perfection which involves bringing those powers of intelligence, will, and (as sharing in rational choice and action) emotion into

---

[14] III *Sent.* d. 33 q. 2 a. 3c: 'finis proximus humanae vitae est bonum rationis in communi'. See generally III. 8 at nn. 109–15 and n. r.

[15] '. . . the natural human inclination to act according to reason, that is, according to virtue': I-II q. 94 a. 3c; 'the good towards which human virtues are immediately ordered is the good of reason(ableness)': III *Sent.* d. 33 q. 1 a. 1 sol. 1c; '*prudentia* is included in the definition of the other virtues, a definition in which is found first the good of reason(-ableness) and thence [by participation {per participationem}] the essence of virtue {per prius bonum rationis, et per consequens ratio virtutis}': a. 1 sol. 2 ad 1.

[16] I-II q. 5 a. 5c: 'the imperfect *beatitudo* attainable in this life can be acquired with natural human capacities, in the way that people can acquire virtue, in whose working out in action it [imperfect fulfilment] consists {virtus, in cuius operatione consistit}; likewise q. 4 a. 6c and a. 7c and 8c; also II-II q. 181 a. 2c (practical reasonableness itself {prudentia} is oriented towards the *vita activa* which consists in the workings of the virtues {operationes virtutum moralium}); *Eth.* I. 13 nn. 1 and 11 [154, 164], 16 n. 1 [187], etc. Note that these moral virtues have a point, people's 'civil and natural good {bonum civile et naturale hominis}', to which one's will has a pre-moral natural inclination: III *Sent.* d. 33 q. 2 a. 4 sol. 3c. 'Civil' here connotes both temporal and political. In his early writings, what Aquinas later will call *beatitudo imperfecta* is often called *felicitas civilis*: e.g. II *Sent.* d. 41 q. 1 a. 1c.

[17] See I-II q. 4 a. 5c. See also the last passage quoted in n. 15 above; and III.5 nn. 112–15 and n. r above. Also *ScG* III c. 63 n. 3 [2379a]: 'there is a certain human desire . . . which is principally this, that the whole of human life be lived reasonably {secundum rationem disponatur}, which is: living according to virtue'. And it is by 'acting in accordance with the [first] principles of practical reason [that] one makes oneself actually [i.e. in operation] virtuous': *Eth.* II. 4 n. 7 [286].

co-operative[18] harmony with each other and with the human goods.[19]

In short, Aquinas locates the immediate principle (source) of unity in moral life (and thus in political life, too) in the unity—the essential coextensiveness—of (1) the good of complete reasonableness in one's willing of human goods with (2) the good of *imperfecta beatitudo*. Both (1) and (2) are essentially a matter of fullness of participation in human goods, so far as that participation can be chosen or otherwise willed by a human person or group.

The centrality of this *fullness* in Aquinas' thought about morality is made clear by his most official definition of 'good' as 'desirable fulfilment {perfectio appetibilis}'.[20] But it is also and more directly made clear by his formal account of good and evil {malitia} in any willed human act: the act's goodness consists in its fullness of being {plenitudo essendi}, its badness in its deficiency of being.[21] For what measures this fullness or deficiency? Nothing other than reasons, directing one to choose intelligible human goods in the way directed by the integrating intelligible good of one's being reasonable.[22] Suppose one's willing is mastered and deflected {deducatur}[23] by passion, so that one chooses or otherwise wills an instantiation of good which, by contrariety to practical reasonableness (the *bonum rationis*), is deficient in the intelligible good one could have willed. In that case, one's act—and thus oneself as a person shaping oneself in and by that act—falls short of *pleni-*

---

[18] Though practical reasonableness {prudentia} directs all the other moral virtues, one cannot actually be practically reasonable unless one's emotions {passiones} are in harmony with one's reason; in this sense, *prudentia* depends on the other moral virtues: I-II q. 58 a. 5. On the necessary interdependence of all the virtues {connexio virtutum}, see III *Sent*. d. 36 a. 1c ('oportet virtutes omnes esse simul'); I-II q. 65 a. 1; *Virt. Card*. a. 2.

[19] I-II q. 55 a. 1c and ad 1, 2, and 4, a. 2c and ad 1 and 2, a. 4c and ad 2 and 3, q. 56 a. 4c and ad 1, 3, and 4.

[20] I q. 5 a. 1c and ad 1: 'The goodness of something consists in its being desirable {appetibile}; hence Aristotle's dictum that "good is what all things desire". Now desirability is consequent upon completion/fulfilment {secundum quod est perfectum}, for things always desire their completion/fulfilment {perfectionem}. . . . the term "good" expresses the idea of desirable completion/fulfilment {bonum dicit rationem perfecti quod est appetibile}.'   [21] I-II q. 18 a. 1c and ad 1.

[22] See I-II q. 18 aa. 5c, 8c, and 9c, q. 19 aa. 3c, 4 (read with q. 91 a. 2c), 5c (choosing what one believes to be contrary to practical reasonableness is inevitably deficient in reasonableness even if one's belief that one's proposal is unreasonable be mistaken and unreasonable), and 6c.

[23] e.g. II-II q. 155 a. 1c: it is of the essence of virtue that one's reason be steadfast {firmata} against emotions {passiones} by which reason itself might be led away {deducatur}.

tudo essendi, of the fulfilment attainable not by luck but by acting.

Fulfilment as virtue in action, the imperfect[24] yet in a sense sufficient unifying or ordering point of human life, will provide— when further explained—the conception of fulfilment relevant to Aquinas' political theory as discussed in Chapters v to ix. But before explaining and exploring the implications of this conception of *beatitudo imperfecta*, we should note that Aquinas also entertains another, different conception of it.

For he quite often says that incomplete fulfilment consists not only in the just-mentioned 'working of practical intelligence bringing its order into human actions and emotions',[25] but also, and 'primarily and principally', in contemplation—to which the life of practical reasonableness and virtue is 'secondary'.[26]

It must be admitted that Aquinas, being much more interested in perfect than in imperfect human fulfilment, never fully clarified *imperfecta beatitudo*, and in that sense never resolved the tensions within Aristotle's accounts of human flourishing. It is clear, however, that he never treated the life of practical reasonableness and virtue as a mere means to a fulfilment found essentially in a state of contemplation paralleling as closely as possible, in this life, the contemplation of God. That is to say, it is clear that for Aquinas the life of practical reasonableness and virtue is itself always somehow *beatitudo*, albeit *imperfecta*. And Aquinas never treated contemplation as an organizing or integrating principle of social and political theory.

Indeed, even in his conception of personal ethics, contemplation has an uncertain role. He is clear that one cannot enter into a

---

[24] Even virtue, when not fully integrated with an orientation to the real, ultimate *beatitudo perfecta*, is imperfect (though still real {vera} virtue): II-II q. 23 a. 7c.

[25] I-II q. 3 a. 5c: 'in operatione practici intellectus ordinantis actiones et passiones humanas'.

[26] Ibid., citing *Nic. Eth.* 10 (presumably 10. 7–8. 1177ª12–1178ᵇ7). Also *Trin.* q. 6 [lect. 2 q. 2] a. 4 ad 3: 'the imperfect human felicity attainable in this life, which Aristotle discusses, consists in contemplation of the [most noble intelligibles] by the *habitus* of wisdom' (read with *Q. An.* q. 16c, lines 246–53, 269–73). Also *ScG* II c. 83 n. 28 [1675]; IV *Sent.* d. 49 q. 1 a. 1 sol. 4c ('one is fulfilled {perfectus} principally in the goods of speculative [theoretical] reason, and secondarily in the goods of practical reason; and Aristotle reaches conclusions {determinat} about this fulfilment {de felicitate} in the Ethics, neither asserting nor denying the fulfilment {beatitudinem} which is after this life'). *In Matt.* 5 ad v. 3 [404], however, attributes to Aristotle the view that *perfecta beatitudo* consists in the virtues of the life of contemplating the highest things {in virtutibus contemplativae vitae, scilicet divinorum et intelligibilium}, and bluntly describes this view as false. Cf. n. 43 below.

---

contemplative way of life, except very imperfectly, until one has first attained 'perfection in the active life'—for would-be contemplatives will otherwise find difficulty in acting morally and will have to leave off contemplating in order to devote themselves completely to getting the virtues in action; and, correspondingly, the more perfectly one is in the *vita activa* of operative virtues, the more one can be occupied with both action and contemplation.[27, a] His model was the exemplary bishop who can 'receive from God through contemplation and hand on to his people through action';[28] or again, the model of his own religious order, aspiring to 'hand on to others the fruits [doctrine and preaching] of contemplation'.[29] So Aquinas' alternative account of attainable fulfilment, in which contemplation is 'primary' and the active life 'secondary', is not what it might seem. For even on this account active virtuous living is not only foundational and never dispensable[30]—never reasonably left behind—but is also included in the best possible fulfilment of the contemplation which is somehow action's fulfilment.[31] In the last analysis, contemplation is a form of action and had best issue in (further) action, indeed 'public' action.[32]

In any event, Aquinas never suggests that either families or political communities should be wholly directed towards facilitating contemplation by their members.[33] All in all, *beatitudo imperfecta* can plausibly serve as a moral principle for social and political theory only when it is understood as the life of practical reasonableness in action, not forgetting that at least one of the basic human goods to be pursued and realized by practically reasonable choices and actions is a good necessarily involving contemplation: knowledge.

---

[27] III *Sent.* d. 35 q. 1 a. 3 sol. 3c, quoted in n. a. So the contemplative life of the philosophers, rooted in concern for the philosopher's fulfilment as a knower, proceeds from a flawed self-love {ex amore sui}, unlike the contemplative life of the saints who are in love with the object of their contemplation: III *Sent.* d. 35 q. 1 a. 2 sol. 1c.

[28] III *Sent.* d. 35 q. 1 a. 3 sol. 3c.   [29] II-II q. 188 a. 6c: 'contemplata aliis tradere'.

[30] II-II q. 182 a. 4 ad 1.   [31] III *Sent.* d. 35 q. 1 a. 4 sol. 2c and ad 2; x.4, 6 below.

[32] See *In Matt.* 13 ad v. 1 [1079]: from the private [domain] of contemplation to the public [domain] of teaching [others].

[33] *ScG* III c. 37 n. 7 [2158] only says that freedom from external disturbances, to which all civil government is directed {ad quam ordinatur totius regimen vitae civilis} [and see VII.3 below], is a pre-condition for contemplation {requiritur . . . quies}.

IV.3. *Egoism, Self-Fulfilment, and Common Good*

Many today[34] think that the fundamental problem of ethical and political theory is to escape egoism—to show how and in what sense one can be required, in reason, to give weight to others' interests against one's own, and to recognize at least some moral duties to other people. Theories are constructed to expound the rationality and/or natural primacy of egoistic 'prudence', and to explore the question how we may 'bridge the gap' between such prudence (on the near bank) and morality (on the farther shore). In Aquinas' view, such thoughts and theories are radically misconceived.

For: the only *reasons* we have for choice and action are the basic reasons, the goods and ends to which the first practical principles direct us. Those goods are *human* goods; the principles contain no proper names, no restrictions such as 'for me'.[35] So it is not merely a fact about the human animal, but also and more importantly a testimony to people's practical understanding, that they can be interested in the well-being of a stranger, whom they will never meet again but now see taking the wrong turning and heading over a cliff;[b] for it is the same good(s) that the stranger can share in or lose and that I can: specifically human good(s).[36]

Moreover, every such response, in which one is moved by the intelligible good one can instantiate or protect in the existence of another person, also creates or reaffirms a relationship between us, additional to the relationship which consists simply in our both being human. This willed relationship Aquinas calls *societas*, and it is itself a basic human good: harmony[37] among human

---

[34] Sidgwick (1902: 198): 'in the modern ethical view, when it has worked itself clear [of Greek moral philosophy], there are found to be two [regulative and governing faculties recognized under the name of Reason],—Universal Reason and Egoistic Reason, or Conscience and Self-Love'.

[35] See II *Sent.* d. 3 q. 4 a. 1 ad 2: my will's intrinsic object is *good*, not *mine*. And the good is the good of all who share the same *nature*: see II-II q. 31 a. 2 ad 2, q. 64 a. 6c (quoted v.3 n. 38 below); nn. 36, 64 below.

[36] See *ScG* III c. 117 n. 5 [2899]; *Eth.* VIII. 1 n. 4 [1541]; *Car.* q. un. a. 8c and ad 7; *Div.* IV 9 n. 13 [406]; *Perf.* c. 15 [14] lines 27–31 [637]: 'because all human beings share in the nature of the species {conveniunt in natura speciei}, every human being is naturally a friend {amicus} to every human being; and this is openly shown in the fact that one human being guides, and aids, in misfortune, another who is taking the wrong road'. (This is not contradicted by the next sentence, affirming that 'one naturally loves oneself more than another person'.) *Eth.* IX. 5 n. 2 [1821] says that goodwill towards strangers is not friendship, meaning not 'friendship' in the focal sense.

[37] 'Harmony {harmonia} is the fittingness of order {convenientia ordinis}' (*Div.* V. 1 n. 45 [650]); and 'Good consists in order; but people are rightly ordered to other people in

---

persons—friendship, whether in its central or in one of its second-ary forms, neighbourliness, fraternity.[38]

One can choose to be an egoist. But one has no choice whether harmony among persons, or friendship, is a basic good, intrinsic to human flourishing; nor about whether harmony is blocked, and friendship negated, by egoism. The choice to be a thoroughgoing egoist sets itself against reason; for it treats the basic reasons for action as if they directed me, not towards a universal human good which includes my own good as one amongst other instantiations, but rather just towards my good—as if the principle came specified with a proper name (mine!). And my choice to be an egoist also sets me against a basic reason for action, the reason directing me to a good in which I could otherwise have participated: friendship and harmony amonst persons. For there can be no friendship or real harmony between persons where one fails to recognize, or to take as a reason for action, the good of the other person(s) as worth pursuing and respecting as an end in itself, for the sake of the other(s) rather than merely for one's own sake.[39]

So egoism, misconstruing all the basic goods, and condemning the basic good of *societas*, radically severs one from the good of practical reasonableness itself. And a theoretical description of human society which treats all human action as fundamentally egoistic quite misunderstands the principles of human motivation. Not that reasonable motivation is 'altruistic', mindful only of the good of other people. On the contrary, there is a reasonable love of self {dilectio sui ipsius} which has priority over, and is a foundation for, love of others.[40]

But here a different and perhaps even more important doubt and misunderstanding can arise. 'Self-love' is the popular name for the dominant motivation of people who help themselves, and exploit others, to get a superabundance of money, honours, food, and sex[41]—people whose principle, if they had one, we could today call egoism. Since such people are turning their backs on goods

mutual dealings {in communi conversatione} both in words and in actions, so that each relates to each as is proper; [and] this fittingness of [interpersonal] order {convenientia ordinis} [is a special type of intelligible good {specialis ratio boni}]' (II-II q. 114 a. 1c); 'in intelligent/intelligible {intellectualibus} [i.e. human] loves there is not only order but also the fittingness of order' (*Div.* IV 12 n. 7 [457]).

[38] 'Neighbour', 'brother {frater}', and 'friend', in this context, all denote the same *affinitas* and the same rational motive: II-II q. 44 a. 7c.　　[39] See e.g. II-II q. 44 a. 7c.
[40] II-II q. 44 a. 8 ad 2, q. 26 a. 5; n. 92 below.　　[41] *Eth.* IX. 8 n. 9 [1863].

of reason {bona rationis} and thus of virtue,[42] their condition is truly misery, the antithesis of fulfilment.[43] Correspondingly, if one is *really* a friend to oneself, one will want a superabundance of the goods of reason and virtue—of genuine fulfilment so far as it is possible in this world.[44] But then, does not the life of virtue—even a virtue that spurns egoism, acknowledges the claims of justice, and includes true, unselfish friendship—seem to be no more and no less than a very refined form of self-love? Should not *beatitudo*, perfect or imperfect, be translated 'self-fulfilment'? And is that a truly worthy {honestum} good?

This doubt goes very deep in the self-interpretation of the Western civilization—Greek, Jewish, Roman, and Christian—in which Aquinas is a central figure. The pervasiveness of the doubt, or misinterpretation, is the most important reason for judging 'happiness' an unsafe and unsatisfactory translation of *beatitudo*. But 'fulfilment', without more, is liable to a similar misunderstanding: to be read as 'self-fulfilment'.

So it is necessary to make a careful distinction. Aquinas says we each want—indeed cannot not want—to *be* happy {felix}.[45] He says we want not only the goods of reason in action, and the necessary pre-conditions of practical reasonableness (especially sanity),[46] but also the many bodily and circumstantial goods which depend on good fortune—health, wealth, offspring, and so forth—and the pleasure that perfects good action.[47] But equally, and consistently with all that, he insists that the fulfilment, the *beatitudo* or *felicitas* to which all one's reasonable deliberation, choice, and action are directed, is a *common good*.[48] How could it be otherwise, given that one's basic reasons for action are goods for any human being, and that they include friendship and every form of harmony between persons?

One's own fulfilment, then, takes its place within—is part

---

[42] Ibid. n. 11 [1865].

[43] *Eth.* I. 16 n. 1 [187]: for fulfilment {felicitas} consists essentially, principally, and predominantly, in the workings of virtue {in operatione virtutis} (as well as in the goods external to practical reasonableness itself, which are subject to good or bad luck).

[44] *Eth.* IX. 8 n. 11 [1865].   [45] e.g. *Mal.* q. 3 a. 3c; II *Sent.* d. 25 q. 1 a. 2c.

[46] *Eth.* I. 16 n. 11 [197], a point not being made here by Aristotle.

[47] I-II q. 33 a. 4c; 'good' action here means 'good at least apparently or in some respect': q. 34 a. 2. See also III.4 n. 57 above. Having offspring is one of the goods of fortune which are organically related {quare conferunt organice} to *beatitudo imperfecta*: II *Sent.* d. 33 q. 1 a. 2c.

[48] See *ScG* III c. 44 n. 4 [2215] I-II q. 90 a. 2c and ad 3; cf. I-II q. 3 a. 2 ad 2. Cf x. 6 n. 169 below.

---

of—common fulfilment, *felicitas communis*.[49] This common good, which as an individual's or group's end or intention—principle—provides the most satisfactory and fully reasonable direction in choosing and acting, is indeed the good of a complete community, a *communitas perfecta*.[50] What is a 'complete community', and which communities are complete? The answers will prove to be much more complex than is often thought (see VII.6–7). Here it is sufficient to observe that any answer must be relative. For many purposes, and in many contexts, the complete community relevant to one's life of practical reasonableness is the political community within which one lives, with one's family: 'complete community = *civitas* {perfecta communitas civitas est}'.[51] But a *civitas*, complete in its own way, may be unable to defend itself; so, beyond family and *civitas*, there rises a third level of community, communities of *civitates* organized for mutual defence {compugnatio}; they may amount to a realm {regnum}[52] or a province {provincia}[53] or simply to a condition of friendship between states {amicitia inter civitates}.[54] But the mind's eye cannot rest there; *politica* is for the sake of the *civitas*[55] but also for 'human good, that is, the best in human affairs'.[56] And *politica*'s primacy over all other bodies of practical thought and knowledge 'comes from the very nature of its end':

For . . . if the good for one human being is the same good [i.e. *human good*] as the good for a whole *civitas*, still it is evidently a much greater and more perfect thing to procure and preserve the state of affairs which is the good of a whole *civitas* than the state of affairs which is the good of a single human being. For: it belongs to the love which should exist between human persons that one should seek and preserve the good of even one single human being; but how much better and more godlike that this should be shown for a whole people and *for a plurality* of *civitates*. Or: it is lovable that this be shown for one single *civitas*, but much more godlike that it be shown for the whole people embracing many *civitates*. ('More godlike' because more in the likeness of God, who is the universal cause of all goods.) This good, *the good*

---

[49] I-II q. 90 a. 2c.   [50] Ibid.; and a. 3 ad 3.   [51] I-II q. 90 a. 2c; and see VII.1 below.
[52] *In Matt.* 12 ad v. 25 [1011]; the Marietti edition (Cai 1951b) improbably also calls this a *communitas consummationis*; one may suspect a mistranscription of *compugnationis*.
[53] *Reg.* I. 1 [I. 2] [14] [748].
[54] *Eth.* VIII. 4 n. 9 [1593]. Aristotle's text here was talking about friendship between citizens {cives}, but the translation used by Aquinas read *civitates* in lieu of *cives*. See also *Eth.* IX. 6 n. 7 [1836] ('the friendship between diverse states {civitates} seems to be the same as *concord* . . . for it is a political friendship concerned with matters of advantage {utilia} and with things needed for human life').
[55] *Eth.* I. 2 n. 11 [29].   [56] Ibid. n. 12 [30].

common to one or many civitates, is what the theory, i.e. the 'art' which is called 'civil', has as its point {intendit}. And so it is this theory, above all—as the most primary {principalissima} of all practical theories—that considers the ultimate end of human life.[57, c]

The supreme practical science of ethics and politics[58] seeks to unfold the directiveness of practical reason. Is Aquinas, in the passage just quoted, tracking that directiveness no further than the flourishing of a nation-state which, like the France of his friend King Louis IX, integrates many formerly independent political communities? The logic of the passage is not so restricted. If followed through, it points to nothing short of the fulfilment of all human persons and communities[59] (what has recently been called 'integral human fulfilment').[60]

We tend to read such passages without appreciating their force, thinking that *of course* politics and political theory are concerned with a wide common good, and forgetting that here political theory is being expounded from a fully 'practical', internal point of view. If the human good with which political theory should be concerned is this integral fulfilment of all persons and communities, then that is equally the human good with which any reasonable human person should be concerned and in which—in senses and ways to be explored—each of us should locate our own, our family's, and our state's fulfilment.

The quoted passage appeals first to the universality of human good, realizable in the lives of one or many—of you all as well as me.[d] It appeals secondly to a love which is unrestrictedly 'amongst people' {inter homines}. (The 'should exist' is not an appeal to some

---

[57] Ibid. nn. 11–12 [29–30] (Latin in n. c). See also *Eth.* VI. 7 n. 7 [1201]; and *Ver.* q. 5 a. 3c, where, having noted that the paterfamilias governs the household and the king governs the *civitas* or *regnum*, Aquinas immediately adds that what is common to both sorts of government is that 'common good is higher {eminentius} than individual good {singulare}', and that 'as is pointed out in the beginning of the *Ethics*, the good of a people {gentis} is higher {divinius} than the good of a city-state or family or individual person {personae}'. See also x. 4 at n. 107 below.

[58] 'The fundamental principles {principia} of political theory are given here [sc. in the inquiry which embraces both the *Nicomachean Ethics* and the *Politics*]': *Eth.* I. 19 n. 2 [225].

[59] Aquinas says that the human community as a whole is a part of the universe as a whole, to which human good stands as part stands to whole (see I-II q. 2 a. 8 ad 2, q. 19 a. 10c); but he also considers the good of subrational creatures to be subordinate and instrumental to the good of other components of the universe, notably human beings: I q. 96 a. 1c; x. 4 at n. 86 below.

[60] Finnis *et al.* (1987: 283–4); Grisez *et al.* (1987: 128, 131–3). Cf. *Mal.* q. 4 a. 1c: 'the whole multitude of human beings [of all times and places] is to be considered as like one community {quasi unum collegium}'; also x. 4 at n. 150 below.

moral rule presupposed to exist independently of the good sense, the intelligibility, of that love.) The two appeals are interdependent. Every intelligent love has not only its accompanying (perhaps initiating)[61] emotional element but also its intelligible ground, its *ratio*.[62] Here the ground for the love is, first, that other people, precisely as people {homines} (one or many, individual or grouped), can participate in, and instantiate, human good; and then that the human good includes, as one of its constituents, a type of intelligent, freely chosen[63] relationship, the love we call friendship— which includes what Aquinas elsewhere calls a natural good, friendship of all human persons for each other {amicitia omnium hominum ad invicem} by reason of their likeness in specific nature.[64]

The essence of any friendship, even so thinned out and extended a friendship as here, is that A is interested in B's well-being for B's sake; and B is interested in A's well-being for A's sake; and A is interested in A's own well-being not only for its own sake but also for B's sake; and B likewise. Thus the interest of neither person comes to rest solely on that person's own well-being, nor solely on the other person's well-being.[65] So their relationship of interest (will, choice, action, and affection) is, and is directed towards, a truly common good—not simply two individual goods of the same 'common' type, nor the sum of those goods. It is that truly *common* good which gives their relationship, their sharing {communicatio}, its *ratio*, its intelligible ground or point. Neither person's well-being is instrumentalized to the other's. Self-love is, so far forth, transcended. This is the answer to the fear that my choices, even my good choices, must all be primarily and/or fundamentally for my own sake, for my own self-fulfilment.

What is true of the intelligible structure of friendship between A and B remains true when the interest in others' well-being for its

---

[61] *Eth.* IX. 5 n. 5 [1824].

[62] On *ratio diligendi*, rational ground for loving, see II-II q. 23 a. 5 ad 2, q. 26 a. 2 ad 1, a. 4c, a. 7 ad 3, a. 8c, q. 44 a. 7c, q. 103 a. 3 ad 2.   [63] *Eth.* VIII. 1 n. 1 [1538], 5 n. 8 [1603].

[64] *Eth.* VIII. 1 n. 4 [1541]; also *Car.* q. un. a. 8c ('ratio dilectionis . . . in omnibus hominibus invenitur') and ad 7 ('ex natura homo omnem hominem diligit'); and n. 36 above. In *Eth.* VIII. 1, as in some other passages, the position is obscured by an apparent assimilation (here found in Aristotle's text) with the natural friendship of birds or other animals (for their young).

[65] II-II q. 44 a. 7c; *Eth.* VIII. 5 n. 10 [1605], IX. 4 n. 3 [1799].

own sake—for their own sake—is extended to many and even to all human beings. Friendship is between equals;[66] to say that everyone can rightly have a kind of friendship with every other human person is to affirm a fundamental equality of human persons, precisely and simply as members of the one race each able to participate in some measure in *human* goods, notwithstanding all the inequalities that obstruct the formation of friendships of more particular kinds.[67]

To point to the horizon of integral human fulfilment and universal friendship is not to suggest that one is directed by practical reasonableness to leave behind particular, limited relationships with one's family, neighbourhood, or workplace, one's city and country, or one's special friends. On the contrary.[68] In view of many limitations and specializations of one's capacities, and the particularities of one's origins, interdependencies, and (as we shall see) commitments, there is a necessary and reasonable prioritizing of types of interpersonal relationships and of community.[69] Friendships must be compatible with one's responsibilities—most obviously with what one owes to others as their due. For justice, as we shall soon see, covers the same field as friendship.[70] Where someone is in direct need {extrema necessitas}, one's ordinary responsibilities (e.g. to care for one's parents) and one's rights (particularly of property) are overridden by duties of assistance, even when the person in need is a mere stranger.[71]

---

[66] *Eth.* VIII. 5 n. 10 [1605], 7 n. 8 [1631–2]. There can be friendship between people who are unequals; though real and important, it is friendship *secundum analogiam* and by the analogous ('geometrical') equality of proportionality: 7 n. 6 [1629], 8 n. 1 [1639], IX. 1 n. 2 [1758], etc.

[67] And see v. 8. Aristotle could see this equality in his discussions of slavery: *Nic. Eth.* 8. 11. 1161^{b}5–6; see also *Eth.* VIII. 11 n. 13 [1700]. A real friendship, precisely by acknowledging the equality, runs counter to {contrariatur} the condition of slavery (*In Ioann.* 15. 3 ad v. 14 [2014]) and makes the slave free {caritas de servo facit liberum et amicum} (*Dec.* prol. [1151]).   [68] See II-II q. 31 a. 3; *Eth.* I. 9 nn. 10–12 [112–14].

[69] *Car.* q. un. a. 8c: there is a *ratio dilectionis* in respect of each and every human person; but since we cannot even think of everyone in particular, let alone render everyone some particular service, we are bound to do something in particular only for those who are joined to us by a reason for friendship {ratio amicitiae} which is more particular than simply that they are human persons. Commitment and friendship: v. 4 at nn. 51–60 below.

[70] *Eth.* VIII. 9 nn. 2 and 8 [1658, 1664], 11 n. 1 [1688].

[71] II-II q. 31 a. 3c and ad 3; see also VI.2 at nn. 20–32 below.

IV.4. *Further Modes of Reason's Directiveness: General Justice and* prudentia

So practical reasonableness, the integral directiveness of all the practical principles, directs one not only towards one's own fulfilment but also to a set of wider wholes of which my fulfilment is in each case a constituent part: the common good of human fulfilment as such, and the common good of every community, group, and friendship that can be integrated into human fulfilment. If 'virtue in action' is the core of imperfect fulfilment, we can now see why Aristotle[72] and Aquinas maintain that another suitable name for virtue is: *general justice.*[e]

Aquinas' explanation of this now forgotten sense of the word 'justice' begins with the observation that 'one who serves some community serves each of the people {omnibus hominibus} contained within it'.[73] But the members stand to their community (whatever sort of community it is) as parts stand to whole. Since parts are parts *of* the whole, a part's good bears on {est ordinabile in} the whole's good (and thus, as the first point indicated, on the good of all the other parts).[74] So whether one's virtue-in-action bears on oneself or on other individuals {alias personas singulares}, it can be for the sake of *common good* {est referibile ad bonum commune}. This willingness to treat common good—in particular the common good of a relevant group or community—as the point of one's actions as they bear on individuals (including oneself) is called 'general justice'.[75] (The basis for this all-embracing justice is, once again, the fact that the human good(s) to which practical reason directs us are good(s) for human beings as such, and so for every human being.)[76]

So this virtue is not one virtue among others. Like *beatitudo imperfecta*, it is simply the whole set of virtues-in-action—lived morality—considered in a particular light (or as Aquinas would say, under a particular formality or *ratio*). Moral norms {moralia praecepta} state 'what is inherently right {secundum se iustum} according to the general justice which is virtue as a whole {omnis virtus}'.[77] If *beatitudo imperfecta* is virtue considered precisely as the effective content of someone's actual life, general justice is virtue considered as *explicitly* and precisely oriented to the good of

---

[72] See *Nic. Eth.* 5. 1. 1130ᵃ8–14.   [73] II-II q. 58 a. 5c.   [74] Ibid.
[75] Ibid., q. 79 a. 1c.   [76] See II-II q. 58 a. 5 ad 2.   [77] I-II q. 100 a. 12c.

other persons precisely as persons with whom one is in community. For in all of them there are instantiated the human goods which practical reasonableness {bonum rationis} directs one towards.[78] Still, as Aquinas' explanations of this justice also emphasize, the common good of a community is not something over against the good of its members.[79] And beyond every more specific community is the community one has with every human person who could be affected by one's choices; so justice, unlike (say) generosity {liberalitas} or mercy, can extend to everyone.[80]

A third way into the meaning and content of morality, and thus of politics, is provided by Aquinas' reflections on *prudentia*, practical reasonableness. Much could be said about this highest-level excellence of intelligence and character, this virtue at once intellectual and moral, by which one brings right order into one's concern with every human good, integrates the rational content of the moral and political sciences into one's character and will,[81] and does so for the sake of the human good of reasonableness itself {bonum rationis}.[82] *Prudentia*, directing every virtue, embodies (so to speak) as an active disposition of mind the very meaning, force, and content of the moral *ought*. But I shall focus narrowly upon *prudentia*'s bearing on the questions already raised in this chapter.

Aquinas has framed and confronted the relevant challenge. Not the most sceptical, relativist, egoist, or other neo-Humean denials that practical reasonableness can be more than the executive servant of subrational desires or sheer conventions. But rather the milder claim that reason requires no more than concern for one's

---

[78] So virtue is a matter of serving and preserving the *bonum rationis*, which as its object has the truth (about human goods) and as its characteristic effect general justice (II-II q. 124 a. 1c), which is a matter of bringing rational order into all human affairs (q. 123 a. 12c). [79] See II-II q. 58 a. 5c.

[80] See II-II q. 58 a. 12 ad 1 (the resources wherewith to exercise one's generosity would be exhausted long before one had been generous to everyone); q. 71 a. 1c (no one has what it would take to help everyone in need, so one can render assistance according to considerations of proximity in time and place and relationship; and lawyers or doctors are not morally obliged to render all their services without fee); VI. 4 at nn. 78–81 below.

[81] For *prudentia* is not simply a matter of reason {non est in ratione solum} but is partly a matter of interest, desire, and disposition {sed habet aliquid in appetitu}; in so far as it is in one's reason alone, it is called 'practical sciences', namely ethics, economics, and political theory {ethica, oeconomica et politica}': *Eth.* VI. 7 n. 6 [1200]. *Prudentia* involves bringing one's actual deliberations, choices, *and* actions under the real direction of the truths which those sciences consider: II-II q. 53 a. 2c and ad 2, a. 4c, a. 5c.

[82] Thus, for example, the moral virtue of self-control {temperantia} restrains one from bad pleasures 'for the sake of the good of reasonableness {propter bonum rationis}': I-II q. 68 a. 4 ad 1; the moral virtues of steadfastness {fortitudo}, gentleness, etc., are similarly for the sake of that same strategic good: III *Sent.* d. 34 q. 1 a. 2c.

---

own good and that prudence is concerned not with the common good of any of one's communities, but simply with one's own good {bonum proprium}.[83]

This position is unreasonable, Aquinas replies. It commends a proposal to be intelligently concerned exclusively with the *good of one* person (me), and not with helping to realize human goods in the lives of others, except where doing so would be a means to the good of that one—someone who would thus not be instantiating any form of genuine as opposed to imitation friendship or communion. Contrast that with the proposal to be concerned with *common good*, human good participated in by a number of persons in community, friendship, and general justice. Right reason {recta ratio}—that is to say, reason undeflected by emotions—considering these alternatives simply 'judges that common good is *better* than the good of one',[84] and thus that the first alternative proposes, unreasonably, to prefer an inferior to a better concern, an inferior to a better form of life. If one exerts oneself for the well-being and good order {salus et regimen} of other people, one is in fact loving oneself more, and 'reserving for oneself the better part', than if one cared only 'for oneself'.[85]

The statement that common good is better than the good of one is easily misunderstood. It does not mean that *societas* is a good more basic, or intrinsically better, than other basic goods (life, knowledge, marriage or procreation and education . . .). It does not mean that the choice to save a group or community by choosing to kill or rape one human being is better than the choice to respect the life and integrity of all, whatever the side-effects of that choice (VII.6). The common good that is better than an individual's good is a good consistent with all the moral principles implicit, as we shall see, in allowing the first practical principles their combined directiveness—an integral directiveness pointing us towards the practical reasonableness, justice, and virtue involved in 'moral' goodness, a goodness complete as the basic human goods and practical principles are not if considered one by one or compared one to one with each other.

---

[83] II-II q. 47 a. 10c.

[84] Ibid.; and see n. 57 and accompanying text above. Also *ScG* II c. 45 n. 5 [1223]: 'many goods are better than one [finite] good, for they have all the latter good and some further good(s)'.

[85] III *Sent.* d. 35 q. 1 a. 3 sol. 1 ad 2: for it is more godlike (see n. 57 above and x.4 at n. 107 below) to be a source of good activity for oneself *and others* than for oneself alone.

What then is meant by the proposition that common good is better than individual good? Responding to the objection that concern for common good frequently results in neglect of one's own, Aquinas makes two replies. (1) One's own good cannot be realized apart from the common good of one's family or *civitas* (or other political realm). Being part of a winning team is a good for the contributing member; Aquinas appeals to the pagan saying that a Roman would rather be poor in a rich empire than rich in a poor one. (2) One simply is a part of a household and a state, and it makes no sense to consider one's own good in isolation from the good of those groups; parts cannot do well save in relationship to a relevant whole, and a part incongruent with its whole is morally low-grade {turpis}.[86]

So blunt an assertion that we human persons, with the high dignity of free choosers, are none the less 'parts' of 'wholes' is certainly harsh to modern ears. But, as we have seen, it is central to Aquinas' thought.[87] It should not be understood as promoting any kind of totalitarianism. Aquinas considers that justice itself demands that, save perhaps in occasional emergencies, the individual members of a community must be left to fulfil their responsibilities on their own self-directed initiative.[88] And in any event, a coherent political conception of partnership, participation, or sharing is bound to contain, under its perhaps smoother surface, the very implication to which Aquinas gives such explicit and repeated prominence.

The students on their corridor (III.3) are each parts of a whole; if they play their parts in a co-operative way, each can flourish as a student and, quite probably, as a friend or at least a friendly associate[89] and good neighbour to the others. If each proceeds without concern for the common good, so that their little state is rendered poverty-stricken by noise, dirt, kitchen odours, electrical overloads, quarrelling, resentment, and other forms of discord and disarray, the success—not to mention the all-round happiness and well-grounded self-respect—of even the most 'prudent' (skilfully self-interested) among them is likely to be quite inferior to the

---

[86] II-II q. 47 a. 10c, I-II q. 92 a. 1 ad 3.

[87] See text at n. 74 above. See also e.g. *Eth.* VI. 7 n. 7 [1201] paraphrased in n. 57 above; and II.2 at nn. 12–20 above.   [88] *ScG* III c. 71 n. 4 [2470]; see further VII.5–7 below.

[89] This sort of association Aquinas treats as a form of 'civic friendship' (translating Aristotle's *philia politikē*); and to Aristotle's examples Aquinas adds association between students: *Eth.* VIII. 12 n. 3 [1704].

fulfilment attainable by all in a corridor whose members consistently see themselves, and accordingly act, as parts of a little whole. (The full sense of such a relationship will become clearer when the dependence of co-ordination and authority on an idea of the common good is explained: VIII.3.)

So the good which *prudentia* seeks to instantiate—by its reasonable adjudications about what the first practical principles, taken all together, direct—is the 'common end of the whole of human life {communis finis totius humanae vitae}'[90] or 'the whole of living-in-a-good way {totum bene vivere}'.[91] Even as an individual who wants[92] to live one's life well as a whole, one cannot have an ultimate horizon of concern for human goods which is narrower than: the goods of all persons and communities. But one also is reasonably a member of communities very much smaller than the human race. So 'the common good' takes on a more limited, and more practicable, reference to communities such as states, churches, cities, trade associations, families.

Now groups of these types can deliberate and act (II.2). Those individuals whose co-ordinated deliberations, choices, and/or actions are also the deliberations, choices, and actions of the group need a practical reasonableness specialized to the purposes and conditions of the action of their sort of group. Aquinas thinks the problems and group purposes, and thus the groups themselves and the corresponding forms of *prudentia*, fall into really distinct types.[93] There is individual prudence (not, however, closed to common good),[94] domestic (familial) prudence {oeconomica}, and political prudence;[95] indeed, there is also military *prudentia*, distinguished from the prudence of business enterprises because it, unlike them, is concerned with the safeguarding of 'the whole common good'.[96]

Here, as in countless other places, Aquinas employs the term 'common good' with a quite specific reference: to that 'complete community' {perfecta communitas} which on most occasions he calls the *political* community, meaning thereby a *civitas* or *regnum* or *provincia* or, more generally, any body which has a

---

[90] II-II q. 47 a. 13c; see also a. 2 ad 1, I-II q. 21 a. 2 ad 2; *Eth.* VI. 8 n. 17 [1233].

[91] II-II q. 47 a. 2 ad 1; *Eth.* VI. 8 n. 17 [1233]; and see II–II q. 50 a. 3 ad 2; VII.6 at n. 124 above.

[92] And one should want to do so, and therefore ought {debet} to love oneself more than any other human person {magis diligere, post Deum, quam quemque alium}: II-II q. 26 a. 4c; n. 40 above. [93] II-II q. 47 a. 11c. [94] Ibid. ad 3. [95] Ibid. a. 11c.

[96] II-II q. 50 a. 4c and ad 2, q. 48 a. un.

public as distinct from a private character and thus is (as a city-state, a realm, or a province each in its own way is) a *republic* {respublica}.[97]

But it is precisely in discussing the different 'types' of *prudentia* that Aquinas makes it quite clear that there is not just one common good, the political common good. Rather, there is also, for example, the common good of a household or family,[98] a common good that is 'private' but still common (though *less* 'common' than the public common good, the common weal [status communis]).[99] And what is for some purposes complete can for other purposes be incomplete, less 'common'.[100] Practical reasonableness directs us towards a common good that even philosophy can set no narrower than 'the common good of the whole of human life'.

IV.5. *The Principle and Point of the Moral Ought*

It may have seemed strange to consider 'complete virtue', 'general justice', and the supreme intellectual and moral virtue of *prudentia*, before considering moral principles. For without practical propositions identifying what types of choice are reasonable, with more specificity than the first practical principles, a consideration of virtue(s) gives little guidance to deliberation and conscience.[101]

---

[97] *Impugn.* II c. 2c [56]: 'A society is called public [as distinct from private] when people communicate and deal with each other in constituting a *respublica*: e.g. the people of one *civitas* or of one *regnum* are associated in one *respublica*.' For other references to republics as the generic type of political community, see e.g. I-II q. 100 a. 5c ('communitas seu respublica'); II-II q. 43 a. 8c. In other places, *respublica* retains the Roman connotation of that public good, that common weal, which a political community has, and which needs to be defended, cared for, etc.: II-II q. 40 a. 1c (the care of the *respublica* being in their charge, leaders have the responsibility of guarding the *respublica* of the *civitas* or realm or province subject to them); q. 102 a. 3c (one can show respect to people in positions of dignity in two ways; for the sake of the common good, when e.g. one serves that person *in administratione reipublicae* . . .). Almost all Aquinas' references to *respublica(e)* are in the context of speaking of the common good, or of some public good. See further VII.2, VII.5 below.   [98] II-II q. 47 a. 11c.

[99] See I-II q. 19 a. 10c. Similarly, there is the 'private' (though still common) good of a religious order, as distinct from 'the common good of the whole Church': *Impugn.* II c. 1c [26].   [100] See IV.3 at nn. 51–7 above.

[101] One's conscience is the judgement {sententia} one reaches in trying to *apply* practical principles (ultimately the first practical principles, i.e. natural law/right) to particular (types of) situations in which one is deliberating about, or at least contemplating, acting, or is reflecting on what one did: I q. 79 a. 13c, II *Sent.* d. 24 q. 2 a. 4c; VIII.1 n. 4. An erroneous conscience is morally binding simply because to the person in error it seems to

Prudentia itself is part of the definition, content, and influence of every other moral virtue;[102] by it one judges where a virtue ends and becomes a vice; and it enables one to do so by applying principles, ultimately the first practical principles.[103] So principles, propositional practical truths, are more fundamental than virtues;[104] for virtues are the various aspects of a stable and ready willingness to make good choices, and, like everything in the will, are a response to reasons, and reasons are propositional.[f]

The preceding sections of this chapter have advanced a partial explanation of the way in which first practical principles, which even the amoral and the immoral take guidance from,[105] can yet be the ultimate source of a specifically moral directiveness which, when accepted in dispositions of character, shapes *virtues*—dispositions to do the *right* (and avoid the *wrong*) without excessive difficulty or delay. The explanation has focused upon the possible unitary or integral directiveness of the first principles when taken, not one by one, but all together, and not as instantiatable in one person or arbitrarily selected group but in all human

be stating the truth, and so (however monstrous my error) I cannot defect from my conscience without being guilty of a willingness to act *contrary to the truth*: I-II q. 19 a. 5c; *Ver.* q. 17 a. 4c.

[102] e.g. I-II q. 65 a. 1c, q. 66 a. 3 ad 3, II-II q. 47 a. 7; III *Sent.* d. 33 q. 1 a. 1 sol. 2 ad 1, q. 2 a. 3c, p. 108 n. 18 above.

[103] I-II q. 58 a. 5c; II-II q. 47 a. 6c: 'certain things pre-exist in practical reason as naturally known principles, and the ends of the virtues are of this kind ... and some things are in practical reason as conclusions, and the means which we arrive at on the basis of those ends {ex ipsis finibus} are of this kind. And the latter are the concern of *prudentia*, applying the universal principles to particular conclusions about what to do {ad particulares conclusiones operabilium}'; ibid. ad 3: '*synderesis* moves *prudentia*, as the understanding of [first] principles moves knowledge {synderesis movet prudentiam sicut intellectus principiorum scientiam}'; *Ver.* q. 5 a. 1 ad 3, q. 14 a. 2c. Since it supervises the whole way down from first practical principles to specific moral norms and particular acts, *prudentia* 'directs the moral virtues not only in choosing means but also in establishing ends {praestituendo finem}. For the end of each moral virtue is to attain the mean in its own subject-matter, and this mean in turn is determined according to *prudentia*'s right reason': I-II q. 66 a. 3 ad 3; likewise II-II q. 47 a. 7c and ad 3. (On the role of *prudentia*, in a broad sense, in establishing ends as well as means, see also II *Sent.* d. 41 q. 1 a. 1 ad 6, III *Sent.* d. 33 q. 2 aa. 3c and 5c.) And this rational, moral mean between too much (e.g. foolhardiness) and too little (e.g. timidity) is settled by natural reason's norms {regulae}, some of which are affirmative and others negative: *Mal.* q. 2 a. 1c.

[104] 'The intention of anyone acting virtuously is to follow reason's rule {ut rationis regulam sequatur}': I-II q. 73 a. 1c. 'Any and every virtue consists in attaining some *rule* {regula} of human knowing or doing' (II-II q. 10 a. 5c; also q. 23 a. 3c); and the relevant rule or measure is reason: 'the good of moral virtue consists in fitting the measure of reason' and 'the good of anything which is measured {mensurata et regulata} consists in conforming to its rule {regula}' (I-II q. 64 a. 1c); and 'moral virtue . . . brings one's passions into line with the rule of reason {passionem reducit ad regulam rationis}' (ad 1).

[105] See III.6 n. 124 above.

persons and communities. That integral directiveness was what implicitly thematized Aquinas' discussions of 'imperfect' fulfilment, of general justice, of the friendship {amicitia} possible between all human persons, and of *prudentia*. In every case, the appeal was to the intelligible good of taking the basic human goods and ends, not as principles for envisaging and pursuing purposes arbitarily limited and shaped by subrational motivations, but as principles for a *fully* reasonable response to the *attractiveness* of intelligible human good, the *integral* well-being of human persons. If the moral 'ought/not' is not to be a mere reflection of convention or upbringing, or mask for desire (e.g. to dominate), it must be explicable in terms of the intelligibilities emphasized in the preceding (very summary) sentence.

Consider a norm or precept[106] indubitably moral in type (leaving aside, here, the question whether it be true or not): for example, the norm prohibiting killing innocent people, or (one of Aristotle's favourite examples[107]) the norm against adultery. These appear in the Decalogue of Jewish and Christian faith, but Aquinas is clear that (if true) they are in any case truths of practical *reason*, of natural law knowable in principle by anybody without appeal to any divine revelation.[108] And he is also clear that norms such as these are not *per se nota* but are conclusions. No doubt they are, he thinks, very proximate to first principles, and are very easily and promptly {statim} reached; but they are none the less conclusions from prior principles of practical reason.[109]

---

[106] I shall use 'norm' and 'precept' synonymously. Aquinas prefers the latter and rarely uses the former, but 'precept' today seems legalistic. Each has disadvantages; 'norm' can be misunderstood (though rather grossly) as having something to do with averages or 'normality'.

[107] *Nic. Eth.* 2. 6. 1107[a]8–17, 5. 2. 1130[a]24–32, 1131[a]1–6, 6. 1134[a]17–23, 11. 1138[a]24–6; *Eudemian Ethics*. 2. 3. 1221[b]18–26.

[108] I-II q. 100 a. 1c, q. 108 a. 2 ad 1: 'the moral precepts of the law [of the Old Covenant] {moralia legis praecepta} are prescriptions of reason {de dictamine rationis}'. For the phrase 'moral precepts of natural law', referring to norms of this sort, see *Quodl.* IV q. 8 a. 2c.

[109] I-II q. 95 a. 2c: 'Some things are *derived* {derivantur} from common principles of the law of nature in the manner of *a conclusion* {per modum conclusionis}, as 'one should not kill' can be *derived as a kind of conclusion* {ut conclusio quaedam derivari potest} from 'one should do harm/evil {malum} to no one'. Also q. 100 a. 1c, a. 3c and ad 1, a. 6c, a. 11c and ad 1, q. 94 a. 6c; v. 2 at nn. 31–2 below. There are passages in which Aquinas speaks of moral norms of this type as if they were at the highest level and *naturaliter* or *per se nota*: e.g. I-II q. 100 a. 1c, II-II q. 122 a. 1c and 4c. But these are in contexts in which the distinction between such norms and the principles from which they are derived is of less importance than the distinction between (i) all such norms and (ii) norms knowable only by the wise or (iii) norms which have their validity from their positive enactment.

What then are these higher, and indeed highest, most primary *moral* principles? In discussing the status of moral precepts of natural law as conclusions from principles, Aquinas refers neither to the unqualifiedly first principle identified in I-II q. 94 a. 2 ('good is to be done and pursued and bad avoided'), nor to any of the positive first principles ('life is a good to be pursued' etc.) implied by that article's argument, nor even, it seems, to the two negative or avoidance principles articulated there ('one should avoid ignorance' and 'one should not offend those people with whom one should have dealings {debet[110] conversari}'). He does, however, refer to some principles which he says are primary and *per se nota*. One is this: 'One should not do harm to any other human being {nulli debet homo malefacere}'.[111] The proper understanding of that principle will concern us in IX.1–3. More important now is another principle: 'One should love one's neighbour {proximum tuum}[112] as oneself'.[113]

This principle, says Aquinas, is not only a 'first and common precept of the law of nature' and 'self-evident to human reason', but also a principle from which all moral principles and norms, pre-eminently[114] those concerning other people, can (given further premisses) be inferred as either implicit in or conclusions from it.[115] And, most interesting, it is a kind of end, *finis*, of all those

---

[110] See nn. 36, 64, 92 above.   [111] I-II q. 100 a. 3c.

[112] Who then is my neighbour, my *proximus*? If 'people in Ethiopia or India', as Aquinas says (Virt. q. 2 a. 8c), can be benefited by my prayer, they are my neighbours, though he mentions them to his 13th-century audience as people so *remote* that we cannot and therefore morally need not seek to benefit, i.e. to love, them in any other way. As he explains in his discussion of the neighbour-as-oneself principle in II-II q. 44 a. 7c, 'neighbour' is synonymous here with 'brother' (as in 'fraternity') or 'friend' or any other term which points to the relevant affinity {affinitas}, which consists in sharing a common human nature {secundum naturalem Dei imaginem}. 'We ought to treat every human being as, so to speak, neighbour and brother {omnem hominem habere quasi proximum et fratrem}': II-II q. 78 a. 1 ad 2.

[113] I-II q. 99 a. 1 ad 2, q. 100 a. 3 ad 1, q. 100 a. 11c, II-II q. 44 a. 2. In the latter three places, this principle, precept, or command is paired with the command to love God, and in q. 99 a. 1 ad 2 and II-II q. 44 a. 2c and ad 4 the latter command is said to be implicitly contained in the precept of love of neighbour (as end is implicit in what is relative to end {quod est ad finem}, i.e. means). See x.4 at nn. 88–92 below. Note that the existence and nature of God are said by Aquinas to be not *per se nota* (though provable by argument): I q. 2 a. 1 and a. 2; cf. III.5 at n. 106 above, and x. 3 n. 41 below.

[114] But not exclusively; Aquinas rejects the opinion he ascribes to Aristotle, that only what is harmful to others is morally bad in the strict sense, and holds instead that anything contrary to right reason is wrong even if (like the prodigal's dissipation) it harms only oneself: I-II q. 18 a. 9 ad 2.

[115] I-II q. 100 a. 3 ad 1, a. 11c. It is the 'root': *In Matt.* 19 ad v. 19 [1585].

other moral norms.[116] Significantly, the article of the *Summa* which introduces this principle is the article to which Aquinas has reserved his explanation of the unmistakably moral 'ought': the 'obligatory {obligatorium}' is what 'ought {debet} to be done' and *this* 'comes from the necessity of some *end*'.[117]

The importance of the neighbour-as-oneself principle in explaining not merely the content but the very meaning of morality thus becomes evident. Here, in this principle, is the proposition of reason which is moral in content but stands to other moral norms in the same position—i.e. as what gives point[118]—as *beatitudo imperfecta*, and the common good *qua* point of general justice and of prudence, stand to the virtues (and thus to morality). The principle gives, indeed, the summary propositional content of reason's directiveness towards common good; it articulates, normatively, what is meant by *common* good. It provides an articulation of what is meant by '*Good* is to be done and pursued', once 'good' has been given the reference given it by the other first practical principles. And in all this it provides an *end* of the kind needed to make sense of the 'ought' in any and every other moral principle or norm.

'One should love one's neighbour.' But to love a person volitionally (not simply emotionally)[119] is to will that person's good. So, to love one's neighbour is to will the neighbour's good—and not just this or that good, but good somehow integrally; and nothing inconsistent with a harmonious whole which includes one's own good (likewise integrated in itself and with others' good). Thus the love-of-neighbour principle tends to unify one's goals. Moreover, the love of neighbour required by this principle need not be a 'particular friendship'.[120] Rather, as beings each of whom one can love like oneself, every human being is like every other. (For the root of this equality, see v.8.) So the principle of neighbour-love directs

---

[116] I-II q. 99 a. 1 ad 2, q. 100 a. 5 ad 1, a. 11c, q. 105 a. 2 ad 1; III *Sent.* d. 37 q. 1 a. 2 sol. 2 ad 2 (where, moreover, its status is taken to be analogous to the status of the principle of non-contradiction); *In I Tim.* 1. 2 ad v. 5 [13] (one is put in a right relation to other people by all realizations of the virtues {per omnes actus virtutum ordinatur homo unus ad alium}). [117] I-II q. 99 a. 1c.

[118] The end or point is, of course, not the proposition itself but that to which it points, one's neighbours: 'when we do something for the sake of our neighbour's advantage {propter utilitatem proximi}, the precept's point is the neighbour {finis praecepti est proximus}': *In Ioann.* 4. 4 ad v. 34 [642]. [119] See III.4 at nn. 61–2, above.

[120] The love involved in a particular friendship {amor amicitiae} does have at its core, however, one's willingness as a friend to treat the friend as one treats oneself {amans se habet ad amatum, in amore amicitiae, ut ad seipsum}: II-II q. 28 a. 1 ad 2; cf. n. 69. above.

---

towards the widest, ultimately all-embracing community of persons.

Here then is a first, architectonic, and master principle of morality (of *philosophia moralis* and of *prudentia*), a principle conceived by Aquinas—or at least ready to be interpreted by his careful reader—as the import, the specifically moral significance, of the first practical principles when taken together, integrally.[g] Aquinas will, of course, be the first to raise some further questions. The answers to these questions are to enhance both the content and the normativity of even this master principle of morality by reference to an even more ultimate principle, directing us towards some even better good, for the sake of which all human persons—self and communities of neighbours—should be loved. But these questions arise in relation to every other fundamental element in our knowledge, and we can leave them for later reflection (x.4). Provided those further questions and their answer are not suppressed, Aquinas is content to say that moral principles and norms—and the moral ought—are *all* implicit in or referable to this one principle.[121]

The way from first practical principles to specific moral norms about murder, adultery, theft, and so forth is a way which runs through the 'neighbour as oneself' principle. The logic of that specification is explored in later chapters (v.2–6; vIII.3). But Aquinas himself loses no time in pointing out a first implication of the neighbour principle. The Golden Rule (as we call it)—'Do to (and for) others as you would wish them to do to (and for) you'—is, he says, a 'kind of standard {regula} for love of neighbour', implicit in, and explicating, the master principle.[122] He reads the Golden Rule into Aristotle's thought about the relation between *philia* of others and towards oneself,[123] thereby making plain his conviction that in the master principle he has found the point where philosophical and theological sources meet in a truth evident to reason whether aided or unaided by divine revelation. And he similarly transforms Aristotle's thought about proportionate reciprocity (proportionately returning good for good and evil for evil) as the cement of

---

[121] I-II q. 99 a. 1 ad 2, with q. 91 a. 4c and q. 100 a. 2 and a. 3. See n. 113 above.

[122] I-II q. 99 a. 1 ad 3 (quoting both *Nic. Eth.* 9. 4. 1166ª1–3 and Matt. 7: 12). The Golden Rule is a principle of natural law or reason {praeceptum legis naturae}: I-II q. 94 a. 4 ad 1; Iv *Sent.* d. 33 q. 1 a. 1 ad 8. No one is ignorant of it: *Dec.* prol. [1129] (mentioning it in its negative form, 'Do not do to others what you wish them not to do to you'). Aquinas does not use the name 'Golden Rule'. [123] *Nic. Eth.* 9. 4. 1166ª1–3.

interpersonal relations, converting it into the rather different thought that such relationships are preserved by everyone's willingness to do for their fellow citizens whatever they want for themselves.[124]

The way to specific moral norms, which begins with the absolutely first practical principle, and runs through that principle's specifications in 'first principles of practical reason' identifying basic goods whose fully reasonable pursuit the moral master principle directs, is a way beset with the risk of deviations. Any confusions at the level of principle, perhaps small in themselves, get magnified and greatly extended at the lower levels of specification and application.[125] So: diversity of moral beliefs and practices has nothing like the implications which sceptics assert (see III.1 above). In an intelligent but passionate species it is a sign, not of error's impossibility (because 'there is no moral truth'), but of the variety of truly reasonable options and forms of life and the ready possibility of error on the long way from first principles to specific norms and choices. Like all the great exponents of natural law and moral objectivity, Aquinas expects immoral customs and practices to predominate.[126] Each member of the human species begins as a *tabula rasa*, a sheet on which nothing has yet been written,[127] needing to learn what is and is not intelligent and reasonable, truly desirable and lovable. Any oversight, distortion, or suppression will result in bad practices whose rationalizations will be transmitted and perpetuated in language, education, law, and the other institutions or modes of action around which families, associations, and political communities shape themselves.

Notes

[a.] *Contemplative virtue requires perfection in the active life* . . . III *Sent.* d. 35 q. 1 a. 3 sol. 3c: 'Quamdiu homo non pervenit ad perfectionem in vita activa, non potest in eo esse contemplativa vita, nisi secundum quamdam inchoationem imperfecte; tunc enim difficultatem homo patitur in actibus virtutum moralium, et oportet quod tota solicitudine ad ipsos intendat, unde retrahitur a studio contemplationis. Sed quando iam vita activa perfecta est, tunc operationes virtutum moralium in promptu habet, ut eis

[124] *Eth.* v. 8 n. 9 [973]: 'per hoc enim commanent homines adinvicem, quod sibiinvicem faciunt quod quaerunt'; cf. *Nic. Eth.* 5. 5. 1132^{b}33.

[125] See *Ent.* prol. [1]; *Cael.* 1. 9 n. 4 [97].

[126] See I-II q. 99 a. 2 ad 2, II *Sent.* d. 39 q. 2 a. 2 ad 4.

[127] e.g. I q. 79 a. 2c; *Unit.* IV, line 165 [93] [242]; III. 6 n. w above.

non impeditus libere contemplationi vacet. Tamen secundum quod homo est magis vel minus perfectus in vita activa, circa plura vel pauciora occupari potest activae vitae simul cum contemplativa.'

b. *Interest in the well-being of strangers* . . . See Cicero, *De Officiis* 3. 5 (cited by Aquinas, II-II q. 77 a. 1c, in another connection) and 1. 50–2, stressing that to have and act upon such concern is a duty flowing from 'natural principles of human fellowship {societas} and community'.

c. *The universal common good* . . . *Eth.* 1. 2 n. 12 [30] (quoted at n. 57): 'Et ideo, si idem est bonum uni homini et toti civitati: multo videtur maius et perfectius suscipere, id est procurare, et salvare, id est conservare, illud quod est bonum totius civitatis, quam id quod est bonum unius hominis. Pertinet quidem enim ad amorem qui debet esse inter homines quod homo quaerat et conservet bonum etiam uni soli homini, sed multo melius est et divinius quod hoc exhibeatur toti genti et civitatibus. Vel aliter: amabile quidem est quod hoc exhibeatur uni soli civitati, sed multo divinius est quod hoc exhibeatur toti genti, in qua multae civitates continentur. Dicit autem hoc esse divinius, eo quod magis pertinet ad dei similitudinem, qui est universalis causa omnium bonorum. Hoc autem bonum, scilicet quod est commune uni vel civitatibus pluribus, intendit methodus quaedam, id est ars, quae vocatur civilis. Unde ad ipsam maxime pertinet considerare ultimum finem humanae vitae: tamquam ad principalissimam.'

d. *Human good is realizable in many lives* . . . The opening and closing phrases of the passage quoted from *Eth.* 1. 2 nn. 11–12 [29–30] are (like much else) quite incompatible with the kind of 'eudaimonism' which many today (e.g. Murphy 1996: 54) attribute to Aristotle and Aquinas.

e. *General justice* . . . Plato's conception of justice as essentially order in the soul (on which, see IV *Sent.* d. 17 q. 1 a. 1 sol. 1c) suggests a conception of 'general justice'; and see III. 4 n. 47 above. But the 'general justice' (for this term, see I-II q. 100 a. 12c, II-II q. 79 a. 1c) that is essentially concerned with bringing all one's virtues into relation with other people and the common good of one's communities is distinguishable from that more metaphorical sense of general justice (ibid., and II-II q. 58 a. 2), and is more usually called by Aquinas 'legal justice'—a term I shall not use (simply to avoid confusion) (see II-II q. 58 a. 5 and a. 6). 'General' is the more convenient qualifier because Aquinas, following Aristotle, divides justice into 'general' (= 'legal') and 'particular' (or 'special': II-II q. 79 a. 3c): see *Eth.* v. 3 n. 6 [918]; but cf. VI.1 below.

f. *Knowledge of first principles is conceptual and propositional* . . . Jacques Maritain maintained that there is a knowledge which is 'connatural' or 'by affinity or congeniality' or 'through inclination' *rather than conceptual* (Maritain 1951: 91–4; 1986: 30). As he conceded (1951: 91) in relation to the expression 'knowledge through inclination', such terms are never used by Aquinas in discussions of the principles of natural law. In fact, 'knowledge by connaturality' in Aquinas' work refers only to the way in which someone with the right emotions and dispositions will be able to judge rightly in moral matters. Nowhere does Aquinas even suggest that the content of such a judgement is non-conceptual. On the contrary, Aquinas is clear that there is no non-conceptual human understanding: *Ver* q. 4 a. 2 ad 5 ('we cannot understand without expressing some conception . . . in this sense, *all* understanding in us is, strictly speaking, "saying"'); and he unambiguously states the conceptual, propositional character of our understanding of first principles: *Post.* 1. 5 n. 7 [50]; *Hebd.* lect 1, lines 169–70 [18]. (Nor does Aquinas resort to any sort of non-conceptual knowledge as an intuitionistic source of confessedly inexplicable exceptions to moral norms, as Maritain did (e.g. 1986: 155–6).)

g. *Neighbour-as-self as a master principle of morality* . . . The neighbour-as-oneself principle functions in Aquinas' ethics rather like the 'categorical imperative' of the kingdom of ends in Kant; and in content though not in literary form like the 'first moral principle' in the moral theory outlined in Grisez *et al.* (1987: 121, 127–9/Finnis 1991*b*: i, 259, 265–7): 'In voluntarily acting for human goods and avoiding what is opposed to them, one ought to choose and otherwise will those and only those possibilities whose willing is compatible with a will towards integral human fulfilment.'

V

Towards Human Rights

v.1. *The Point of Justice: Right {ius} and Rights {iura}*

The basic good of practical reasonableness {bonum *prudentiae*} summons one to treat the good of other people as a reason for action in one's own practical deliberation and choosing. For: the direction the first practical principles give one's deliberation is towards goods one can share in along with others, and it has no rational stopping-place short of a universal *common good*: the fulfilment of all human persons. The rational, normative content of that directiveness is adequately articulated in the principle of *love of neighbour as oneself*. Those who, guided by that principle, are positively open to that integral or universal common good in all their deliberations have the good and fully reasonable disposition (virtue) which Aquinas calls *general justice*.

Those conclusions of Chapter IV invite us to find a way from such highly general principle to specific norms of the kind everyone calls 'moral', and to make much more specific the idea of common good. There are political institutions (state government and law) which have as their entire justifying point the identification and promotion of the common good of those complex communities of households which we call political communities, or states. Chapter VII will show that, in Aquinas' opinion (often misunderstood), no human person or body has responsibility for, or any genuine authority over, all aspects of the fulfilment of the members even of one state, let alone of the human race as a whole. The specifically political common good, or public good, is but one stratum in a layered complex which includes, as intrinsically valuable and more primary, both individual good and the common good of households and other groups.

Common good is the object of general justice.[1] General justice can be specified into the forms of *particular justice*,[2] primarily fairness in the distribution of the benefits and burdens of social life, and proper respect for others {reverentia personae}[3] in any conduct that affects them. The object of particular justice (henceforth simply 'justice') is the other person's right(s) {ius}.[4] It follows, therefore, that one cannot respect or promote common good without respecting and promoting rights. Respect for rights is the specific form which respect for common good and for the 'bond of human society'[5] must take.

Such is the first fruit of Aquinas' analysis of justice and its object. It is somewhat obscured from view by aspects of the Latin vocabulary with which he worked. This obscurity has occasioned much needless excitement and confusion in twentieth-century reflections on Aquinas and on the history of political thought. The word *ius* (which can be spelled *jus* and is the root of 'just', 'justice', 'juridical', 'injury', etc.) has a variety of quite distinct though related meanings. When Aquinas says that *ius* is the object of justice, he means: what justice is about, and what doing justice secures, is the *right* of some other person or persons—what is due to them, what they are entitled to, what is rightfully theirs.

This meaning of *ius* is made clear in the Roman law definition which Aquinas adopts: justice is the steady willingness to give others what is *theirs*.[6] For the definition is given with two formulae which Aquinas uses entirely interchangeably: 'what is theirs {quod suum est}'[7] and 'what is their right {ius suum}'.[8] What is theirs, or their right, is: what, as a matter of equality, they are entitled to {quod ei[s] secundum proportionis aequalitatem debetur}.[9] *Almost always* this 'something due (owed) {debetur}' is to the advantage of the person who has the right {ius} to it.[10] But Roman

---

[1] II-II q. 58 a. 6c.   [2] II-II q. 58 a. 7, q. 61 a. 1. Cf. VI. 1 below.   [3] II-II q. 62 a. 1 ad 2.
[4] II-II q. 57 a. 1c, q. 58 a. 1c, q. 60 a. 1c.
[5] II Sent. d. 42 q. 1 a. 4c, IV Sent. d. 33 q. 1 a. 3 sol. 2c (= Supp. q. 65 a. 4c) (the bond {foedus} of friendship between human persons {amicitiae hominis ad hominem}).
[6] II-II q. 58 a. 1c.   [7] II-II q. 58 a. 1 ad 5, a. 11, etc.; II Sent. d. 42 q. 1 a. 4c.
[8] II-II q. 57 a. 4 ad 1, q. 58 a. 1c, etc.   [9] II-II q. 58 a. 11c; also q. 57 a. 1c and a. 2c.
[10] A few examples to add to the *ius contradicendi/repugnandi* discussed in III.4 at n. 48 and VIII.2 at n. 28: a right of entering on one's inherited estate (III Sent. d. 10 q. 2 a. 1 sol. 1c and ad 2); the right [or power] of giving baptism {ius/potestas dandi baptisma; ius

law, and still, vestigially, the language of Aquinas' time, accepted that a liability might also be a *ius*; to be given the appropriate penalty is a malefactor's *ius*.[11] Today we would scarcely speak of a malefactor's right to punishment (unless we meant to point out an advantage, e.g. in being punished rather than subjected to 'reformative' lobotomy or detention in a 'psychiatric clinic'). This shift in linguistic usage is of little significance.[a] Equally unimportant, in substance, is the relative rarity of *iura*, the plural of *ius*, with the meaning 'rights'. It seems clear that Aquinas, while occasionally using *iura* to mean 'rights',[12] feels no pressure to do so; for the singular form *ius* includes a plural meaning, just as in his usage *bonum* very often means not the good but a good or goods, *finis* equally often means not the end but end (i.e. an end or ends), and *persona* often means persons. So he is content to use the word *iura* more frequently with another meaning: 'the laws'.

Indeed, the major complication in the semantics of *ius* is that it has also the distinct meaning: law (and thus laws {iura}). Aquinas often uses it with that meaning. Of course, he also has another word for law: *lex*. Some twentieth-century commentators have thought that Aquinas had in mind a distinction in meaning between *ius* used in this sense and *lex*. But he had no interest whatever in making such a distinction, and there is no masked teaching to be found below the surface of his discussions of *ius* and *lex* (or anywhere else in his work). The many passages in which he uses *ius* and *lex* interchangeably make this entirely clear, as does the flow of argument in many other passages in which one or the other term is used.

These two main meanings of *ius*—right(s) and law(s)—are rationally connected. To say that someone has a right is to make a claim

baptizandi} (IV *Sent*. d. 6 q. 1 a. 3 sol. 3 ad 2; *ST* III q. 67 a. 2c); a right to consecrate {ius consecrandi} (IV *Sent*. d. 13 q. 1 a. 1 sol. 3 ad 1); a right to receive eucharistic communion {ius in perceptione eucharistiae} (IV *Sent*. d. 9 a. 5 sol. 1c); a right to receive tithes {ius percipiendi/accipiendi decimas} (IV *Sent*. d. 25 q. 3 a. 2 sol. 3 ad 4; *Quodl*. II q. 4 a. 3 ad un.); a right to ask one's spouse for intercourse {ius petendi debitum} (e.g. IV *Sent*. d. 34 a. 5c (= *Supp*. q. 58 a. 4c)); a right of possession {ius possidendi} (II-II q. 66 a. 5 ad 2; a complainant's right that a guilty defendant be punished {ius ut reus puniatur} (II-II q. 67 a. 4c); the right of the people to make their own arrangements about their monarch {ius multitudinis sibi providere de rege} (*Reg*. 1. 6 (1.7) [49] [770]); and texts cited in n. 12 below.

[11] See Finnis (1980: 209); II-II q. 108 a. 2 ad 1.

[12] e.g. the rights of rulers {iura princip[um]} (*In Rom*. 13. 1 ad v. 7 [1042]); episcopal rights and responsibilities {iura et officia} (*Impugn*. II c. 3c [75] quoting Gratian); rights of a [local] church {iura ecclesiae} (*Impugn*. II c. 3 ad 8 [463] (on Thomas Becket's defence, in AD 1170, of the Church's rights and goods, undertaken in awareness that it might well provoke the King of England into wrongful counter-measures)).

about what practical reasonableness requires of somebody (or everybody) else.[13] But one's practical reasonableness is guided and shaped by principles and norms, in the first instance by the principles of natural reason, i.e. of natural law—*lex naturalis* or, synonymously,[14] *ius naturale*—and then by any relevant and authoritative rules which have given to natural law some specific *determinatio* for a given community: positive law, i.e. *lex positiva* or, synonymously,[15] *ius positivum*, usually *ius civile*. So, if I have a natural—as we would now say, human—right I have it by virtue of natural law {ius naturale}; if I have a legal right I have it by virtue of positive law {ius positivum}, usually the law specifically of my own state {ius civile}. Thus law, natural or positive, is the basis for one's right(s) {ratio iuris},[16] precisely because the proposition 'X has such-and-such a right' cannot rationally be other than a conclusion from, or a *determinatio* of, practical reason's principles.

The same result follows from Aquinas' primary definition of *ius*: that act, forbearance, or other thing which is just.[17] For *what is just* is what the virtue of justice requires the relevant person(s) to give to, or do for, or abstain from in relation to, someone else. And what justice requires is settled by law—moral (natural) or positive.[18]

Still, though law thus has a kind of priority to rights, rights have

---

[13] In making or acting in acknowledgement of such a claim, one is following what one judges reason settles {ratio determinat} and asserting and/or following a kind of (highly specified) rule of practical reasonableness {quasi quaedam regula prudentiae}: II-II q. 57 a. 1 ad 2.

[14] See e.g. II *Sent*. d. 24 q. 2 a. 4c ('"natural law" means precisely the universal principles of right {lex naturalis nominat ipsa universalia principia iuris}'); III *Sent*. d. 37 q. 1 a. 3c ('the laws embedded in reason itself are called "natural law/right" {leges quae ipsi rationi sunt inditae . . . ius naturale dicuntur}'); IV *Sent*. d. 15 q. 3 a. 2 sol. 1c, d. 33 q. 1 (= *Supp*. q. 65) a. 1c ('so the natural understanding embedded in one, whereby one is directed to appropriate action, is called "natural law" or "natural law/right" {ideo naturalis conceptio ei indita, qua dirigatur ad operandum convenienter, lex naturalis vel ius naturale dicitur}'); *ST* I q. 113 a. 1 ad 1, I-II q. 94 a. 4 ad 1, a. 5c and ad 3, II-II q. 88 a. 10 ad 2; *Quodl*. VII q. 7 a. 1c [lines 119, 120]; *Impugn*. II c. 4 ad 1 [186] [c. 5 lines 463–4] ('since the norms of the natural law {praecepta legis naturae} bear on everyone in common, this precept of natural law/right {hoc naturalis iuris praeceptum} about manual labour extends to people of all kinds'). And compare I-II q. 95 a. 2 ad 1 with II-II q. 147 a. 3c.

[15] e.g. IV *Sent*. d. 15 q. 3 a. 1 sol. 4c (ius positivum . . . le[x] positiva), d. 36 a. 5c.

[16] II-II q. 57 a. 1 ad 2: the relevant law thus stands to the right as the plan in the builder's mind stands to the building. (This response to an objection is complicated by the specialized Roman law use of *lex* to mean written, i.e. statutory, law. Consequently, *ratio iuris* has sometimes been mistranslated 'expression of law'; but the argument as a whole makes the sense clear.)

[17] II-II q. 57 a. 1c: 'iustum dicitur aliquid, quasi habens rectitudinem iustitiae, ad quod terminatur actio iustitiae . . . et hoc quidem est ius'; ad 1: 'nomen *ius* primo impositum est ad significandum *ipsam rem iustam*'; a. 2c: 'ius sive iustum est aliquod *opus adaequatum alteri*'. [18] II-II q. 109 a. 3 ad 3.

a kind of priority to law, even to the moral norms (though not the first principles) of natural law. This is obvious in relation to positive law {ius positivum}; if a statute declares permissible something which, contrary to natural law {ius naturale}, violates someone's natural right(s), the statute is overridden by the right(s), fails to make such conduct just, and cannot succeed in giving anyone the right to engage in it.[19] But, more interestingly, the rights that people have by virtue of natural law itself are not mere resultants of the norms of natural law which articulate them, or of the natural duties which correspond to them. For to say that person A has a right *vis-à-vis* person B is to say that A has a kind of *equality with B*.[20] If the right in question is a natural right, the equality must be a natural equality, not merely a 'status' conferred by the norms of natural law. The ultimate normative (third-order) foundation of natural right(s) is the principle of neighbour-as-self love, and the primary principles of practical reason on which that supreme moral principle rests. But the ultimate ontological (first-order) foundation of natural rights is the radical equality of human beings, as all members of a species of beings of a rational nature and thus all persons (v.8).[21]

Though he never uses a term translatable as 'human rights', Aquinas clearly has the concept.[b] He articulates it when he sums up the 'precepts of justice' by saying that justice centrally {proprie dicta} concerns what is owed to 'everyone in common' or 'to everyone alike {indifferenter omnibus debitum}' (rather than to determinate persons for reasons particular to them {ex aliqua speciali ratione}).[22] For, as he goes on to say, what is owed to everyone alike, in the great 'republic under God'[23] in which every human being is a member, includes at least: not to be intentionally killed by another private person, or in any other way physically {in personam} harmed, or cuckolded, or subjected to loss or damage of property, or falsely accused or in any other way defamed.[24] Such a list of *iniuriae*—violations of right(s)—is implicitly a list precisely of rights to which one is entitled simply by virtue of one's being a

---

[19] II-II q. 57 a. 2 ad 2. Note that adultery typically violates not only chastity but also justice, by violating the cuckolded spouse's right(s): II-II q. 61 a. 3c, q. 65 a. 4 ad 3, q. 154 a. 12c.

[20] I-II q. 114 a. 1, II-II q. 58 a. 10c, III q. 85 a. 3c and ad 2; *Eth.* v. 11 nn. 4–5 [1003–4].

[21] 'A person is an individual substance of a rational nature': I q. 29 a. 1c; 'of an intelligent nature {in intellectuali vel rationali natura}': ScG iv c. 35 n. 1 [3725]. The word 'person' is particularly frequent in the sections of II-II on justice.

[22] II-II q. 122 a. 6c   [23] I-II q. 100 a. 5c.   [24] II-II q. 122 a. 6 ad 1 and ad 2.

---

person. Aquinas would have welcomed the flexibility of modern languages which invite us to articulate the list not merely as forms of right-violation (in-iur-iae) common to all, but straightforwardly as rights common to all: human rights.[25]

Aquinas' discussions of wrongs {iniuriae} are implicitly discussions of rights. A good example is his treatment of the presumption of innocence, which he puts very early in his treatment of justice. When one judges 'things', what is at stake is simply the rightness of one's judgement (the benefit of being in truth not error). But when one passes judgement on other persons—particularly, but not only, if one is a judge in court—what is at stake is chiefly {praecipue} their well-being, which will be damaged by one's condemnatory opinion, an opinion by which they are wronged {iniuria[n]tur} if it is formed without sufficient grounds. Love of neighbour requires that one give others the benefit of doubt.[26] Perhaps one will very frequently {frequentius} be deceived? So be it. 'Better to err often by thinking well of bad people than to err even rarely by thinking badly of someone good. For the latter, not the former, involves wronging someone {iniuria alicui}.'[27] Of course, the principle only states a presumption, and the vulnerability of third parties in the event of a mistaken judgement of innocence might be ground to lower the burden of proof. But the implicit structure of Aquinas' argument is clear enough: when a right is at stake, ways of thinking about the foreseeable outcome of one's acting which are appropriate when no right is involved can be ruled out by justice—i.e. by concern and respect for right(s).

Still, isn't what's primary in Aquinas' thought the duty owed, not the corresponding right? Isn't Aquinas primarily interested in the moral uprightness, the just character, of the duty-bearer, not in the right(s) of the one to whom the duty is owed? Not at all. Although Aquinas' main discussion of right(s) is in the context of justice considered as a virtue—as an aspect of good character—he takes care to exclude these suppositions. For he makes it clear that justice's primary demand is that the relevant 'external acts' *be done*; they need not be done out of respect for justice, or as a

---

[25] See also II-II q. 58 a. 11 obj. 3 and ad 3: injuries {iniuriosae actiones} such as homicide are ways of giving people less than is theirs {suum} (and thus less than their ius).

[26] Indeed, 'in any matter, one should presume the good rather than the bad unless the contrary is proved': IV *Sent.* d. 27 q. 1 a. 2 sol. 4 (= *Supp.* q. 45 a. 4) ad 2.

[27] II-II q. 60 a. 4 ad 1.

manifestation or result of good character.[28] So: the good of justice {bonum iustitiae} is not the 'clean hands' (better: clean heart) of those who are to do justice but rather—what Aquinas puts at the head of his treatise on justice—justice's very object: the *right(s)* of the human person entitled to the *equal treatment* we call justice.[29] Aquinas' morality and politics is a matter of rights just as fundamentally as it is a matter of duties and of excellences of individual and communal character.

v.2. *Rights' Foundation: Deducing Specific Moral Norms*

The moral norms which answer the question what human rights every person has, and what responsibilities one has in relation to oneself [30] and others, must be specifications of that supreme principle of practical reasonableness, love of neighbour as oneself. Indeed, Aquinas says, they must be deductions from it.[31] But he never sets out such a deduction. He has no general discussion of the way from the highest moral principle(s) to moral norms such as the exclusion of killing the innocent, adultery, perjury. He says that the way is short,[32] but however short it needs more than one premiss, and the needed premisses he does not systematically display. He did not have to confront the claims of utilitarianism and its theological counterpart, proportionalism; or of the Kantian ethic which knows the *bonum rationis* but no other basic,

---

[28] I-II q. 64 a. 2c, II-II q. 58 a. 10, 11 *Sent.* d. 27 a. 3 ad 3; VII.3 at nn. 58–9 below.

[29] II-II q. 57 a. 1c. See also *Eth.* v. 2 n. 10 [909]: the good of (my doing) justice (unlike the good of the other virtues) is not my good but the good of others {alienum bonum}. Note, too, that the moral wrong in injustice is always serious except when the person whose right has been violated by the action or (omission) in question is neither hurt nor put out and can reasonably be presumed not to have been unwilling for it to be done (or omitted): II-II q. 59 a. 4c and ad 2.

[30] One has no rights *vis-à-vis* oneself, and in that strict sense no 'duties to oneself' and cannot do oneself a wrong {iniuria} or injustice: see II-II q. 57 a. 1c, q. 59 a. 3 ad 2. But many of the responsibilities entailed by the good of practical reasonableness concern conduct which has no direct relationship to others (and in an extended sense of justice one's duties to oneself—e.g. of cleanliness and, more important, of regulating oneself by reason's rule {sibi debet munditiam et ordinationem sui sub regimine rationis}—are duties of 'justice': 11 *Sent.* d. 42 q. 2 a. 2 sol. 2c).

[31] See I-II q. 99 a. 2 ad 2; 11 *Sent.* d. 24 q. 2 a. 3c; also IV.5 at n. 109 above.

[32] Ibid., e.g. I-II q. 100 a. 3c. But it is long enough for some of the conclusions (especially those where the wrongness of a type of act does not consist in injury to other people) to be *evident* only to people of sound judgement {sapientes}, who therefore need to *teach* other people: *Mal.* q. 15 a. 2 ad 5.

intelligible human good; or of the Nietzschean ideal of a self-creative life. Many of his successors have neglected to consider the issue, and have proposed that moral norms of the type just mentioned have the self-evidence of first principles. Others have proposed premisses which, though suggested by some of Aquinas' argumentation or remarks, are unsatisfying and plainly incoherent with Aquinas' general theory. 'Natural functions are not to be frustrated', for example, commingles the third, moral order with the first, natural-science order. To make progress, we should set aside some of the *ad hoc* arguments which Aquinas offers when defending specific moral norms upheld in the tradition, and return to the deepest elements in his account of morality—elements we sketched at some length in earlier chapters.

The moral norms we are considering will be directive of chosen acts. They will consider those acts not simply as means adequate or inadequate for achieving some defined end: that is the role of some technology or 'art', not of the *philosophia moralis* which is oriented to nothing less than the whole of human life. They will direct deliberation towards choice. Deliberation considers ends, means, and circumstances including foreseeable outcomes or consequences.[33] The moral norms will state what reasonableness requires of the choosing person in all the circumstances. So the likely outcome of acts will be of great importance, but only in the way(s) that outcomes are considered in deliberation towards choice and action. So it will matter whether an outcome is one's intended end, or a means to some further end which one intends, or is neither an end nor a means but a foreseen side-effect which, whether it is welcome (a bonus) or unwelcome, one does nothing *to* bring about. Foreseeable side-effects will not be outside one's responsibility, but the moral norms will bear on them in different ways. Some moral norms may concern precisely what is intended and/or chosen, and not side-effects. Other moral norms may be largely concerned with side-effects.

And the moral norms will be specifications of practical reason's first principle: good is to be done and pursued, and bad avoided.

---

[33] See e.g. I-II q. 6 a. 2c (having become aware of an end, and then deliberating about the end and about means to it {deliberans de fine et de his quae sunt ad finem}, one can be either moved or not moved to pursue it); 1 *Sent.* d. 48 q. 1 a. 4c (the passage quoted in III.5 n. 97 above continues: 'We also have in us a kind of deliberated will(ing) which follows reason's act of deliberating about end(s) {voluntas deliberata consequens actum rationis deliberantis de fine} and about various circumstances . . . ').

Since human good is as multiple as human nature is complex, the specifications will so direct choice and action that each of the primary, basic aspects of human flourishing (basic human goods) will be respected and promoted to the extent required by the good of practical reasonableness. What does that good require? That each of the basic human goods be treated as what it truly is: a basic reason for action (respect, promotion) amongst other basic reasons for action whose *integral* directiveness is not to be cut down or deflected by subrational passions. The principle of love of neighbour-as-self, and its specification in the Golden Rule, immediately capture one element in that integral directiveness: the basic goods are good for any human being, and I must have a reason for preferring their instantiation in my own or my friends' existence. The other framework moral rules, specifying fundamental human rights and responsibilities, will give moral direction by stating ways in which more or less specific *types of choice* are immediately or mediately contrary to some basic good and thus contrary to reason's integral directiveness, the *bonum rationis* which is the content of the *bonum virtutis*.

The next three sections consider the ways in which Aquinas derives three sets of norms integral to the framework of his morals and politics: the norms against killing, non-marital sex, and lying—norms promoting the goods of human life, marital friendship, fecundity, and care of children, and authenticity in communication. At first glance, some of these norms may seem remote from the topic of rights. But they are not.

v.3. *Respecting the Good of Human Life*

Human life itself, which is lost or destroyed by death, is a basic human good, and the subject-matter of a primary reason for action (first principle of practical reason and natural law).[34] Some types of act are contrary to that good, and so are picked out in a moral norm as: not to be chosen.[35] What sorts of act? Acts which kill more people than they save? Or which do more harm than good, overall

---

[34] I-II q. 94 a. 2c.

[35] II-II q. 154 a. 3c (fornication is *against the good* of any human being who may be conceived {contra bonum hominis nascituri} but homicide is *against the good* of the already born human being {contra vitam hominis iam nati}) (or indeed of the unborn child: II-II q. 64 a. 8 ad 2; *Dec.* 7 [1263]); *In Matt.* 19 ad v. 18 [1584]).

and in the long run? Or which use inhumane or ignoble methods of killing? Or are against the will of the person killed? No, but rather: every act which is intended, whether as end or means, to kill an innocent human being;[36] and every act done by a private person which is intended to kill any human being.[37] 'For in every person, even an evildoer, we ought to love the nature . . . which is destroyed by killing.'[38] The reference to 'the nature' here is a reference to the person killed's very being, considered as a fitting object of intelligent love, and the usual name for an animate creature's very being is *life*.[39] So the norm excluding a private person's choosing to kill any human being can be deduced, we may say, from the requirement of love of neighbour-as-self, via the premiss that an intrinsic aspect of one's neighbour's and one's own good is the basic good of life, and the premiss that no more than in one's willing of ends may one choose means which are contrary to a basic human good. There are no exceptions to the norm when it is accurately stated in all its terms ('private', 'intending' . . .). It does not, however, exclude lethal acts of defence against serious attack, provided that in defending oneself (or another) one (a) is not motivated by private desire {privata libido} for revenge or by feelings of hatred, and so (b) does not intend the destruction of the attacker, whether as an end (revenge or hatred) or as a means.[40] Still, even if the norm excluding choosing (i.e. intending) to kill is adhered to, one's defence will be unjust if one employs means of defence which are more destructive than is needed for one's legitimate purpose, preservation of one's own or another's life.[41]

---

[36] II-II q. 64 a. 6 and texts cited IX.3 n. 75 below.

[37] II-II q. 64 a. 3 (private person killing non-innocent); a. 5 (killing oneself); a. 6 (killing any innocent); a. 7 (killing by a private person as a side-effect of defence using means available and necessary to stop attack). Universally: 'morally significant acts {moralia} get their [moral] character {species} not from what happens as a side-effect {per accidens}, outside one's intention {praeter intentionem}, but from precisely what it is that one intends {per se intentum}': II-II q. 150 a. 2c. Even more generally: 'what is *per se* in human acts and conduct is what is *intended* {secundum intentionem}', and what is incidental {per accidens} is what is a side-effect {praeter intentionem}: II-II q. 37 a. 1c, q. 38 a. 1c; cf. II-II q. 73 a. 8c.

[38] II-II q. 64 a. 6c: 'in quolibet, etiam peccatore, debemus amare naturam quam Deus fecit, quae per occisionem corrumpitur'. On the opposition between (the object of) intelligent, natural love and choosing to kill, see also II-II q. 64 a. 5c; IV. 3 n. 35 above, X. 4 n. 85 below.

[39] 'To "live" is simply: being in such-and-such a nature {vivere nihil aliud est quam esse in tali natura}, and "life" means the same, but abstractly': I q. 18 a. 2c.

[40] II-II q. 64 a. 7c; IX.1 below.

[41] II-II q. 64 a. 7c; and n. 42 below. Of course, one ought also to minimize the bad effects of an act which is unreasonable even apart from its side-effects, and one's culpability in

---

Within the one, verbally undifferentiated norm against 'homicide', Aquinas distinguishes between the exclusion of all private killing with intent (i.e. all choices *to* kill) and the requirement of due diligence {debita sollicitudo; debita diligentia}, i.e. the duty to take all due care—all the care that the Golden Rule requires in the circumstances—to avoid causing death as a side-effect of some otherwise reasonable choice.[42] The distinction is implied, moreover, by his general theory of virtue, i.e. of goodness and badness, right and wrong, in human acts. Acts are good (right) in type {ex genere; secundum se; de se} when their object, i.e. their proximate and defining purpose, is in line with practical reasonableness: say, making a charitable gift. These are types of act good by reason of their 'appropriate [or: due] matter {ex debita materia}';[43] i.e. *what they are about* is in line with reason. But a particular act of a generically good *type* will be bad if its further purpose (motive) and/or other circumstances in which it is chosen make it out of line with reason: say, making a charitable gift merely to gain a reputation for generosity, or making it at the expense of neglecting the safety or remuneration of one's employees. And acts will be bad of their type if the object, the immediate purpose[44] by which they

respect of bad side-effects (*a*) is not eliminated by the fact that they were not intended, (*b*) is greater than it would have been had one's act been otherwise legitimate (in which case one might have been morally entitled to cause and accept them), (*c*) may vary depending on whether they were foreseen, or unforeseen but inherently inevitable, or unforeseen but foreseeable with reasonable diligence, and (*d*) varies also with the gravity of one's wrongful intention: I-II q. 73 a. 8c, q. 20 a. 5c.

[42] II-II q. 64 a. 8c; IV *Sent*. d. 25 q. 2 a. 2 sol. 2 ad 3. Unfortunately, he does not make the distinction fully explicit when discussing justified and unjustified lethal acts of self-defence (II-II q. 64 a. 7), though it is clearly implicit since the wrongfulness of means which, though not intended to kill, are disproportionate to the needs of self-defence and thereby cause death leaves the death still a side-effect, unintended {praeter intentionem}; and see IX.1 at nn. 13–22 below.

[43] II *Sent*. d. 36 a. 5c (a fundamental and clear exposition of the relation between object {obiectum = materia}, further end(s) and (other) circumstances in determining the moral rightness or wrongness (= goodness or badness) both of types of act and particular acts); *Mal*. q. 7 a. 1c ('exterior acts differ generically from each other by reason of their *objects*; hence it is commonly said that a [type of] act bearing on due *matter* {cadens super debitam materiam} is good of its kind, and an act bearing on undue matter is bad of its kind'); q. 2 a. 4 ad 5: 'the matter of an act is called its object'; and ad 9 ('ends are of two sorts: proximate [close in] and remote [further out]. An act's close-in end is the same thing as its object, and from this it gets its specific type. Its further end(s) does not give it its specific type; but the act's directedness to such end (or ends) is one of its circumstances {duplex est finis: proximus et remotus. Finis proximus actus idem est quod obiectum, et ab hoc recipit speciem. Ex fine autem remoto non habet speciem; sed ordo ad talem finem est circumstantia actus}'); a. 6c and a. 7 ad 8, q. 10 a. 1c, I-II q. 20 a. 1 and a. 2.

[44] That is, the 'proximate object', the close-in 'means', the 'matter' of the act: II *Sent*. d. 38 q. 1 a. 5c.

are, for moral purposes, defined is a purpose out of line with reason: they 'bear on inappropriate matter {indebitam materiam}';[45] e.g. a private person's choosing—having as object/matter—the killing of a human being.[46]

Thus the way down to the single undifferentiated precept against homicide clearly runs through two different implicit premises, two different, relatively specified moral principles or norms. There is one principle which excludes types of act defined by their object/matter: choosing to destroy a basic good (here, human life). There is another which excludes neglecting fair care for others (here, for their lives).

v.4. *Marriage, Sex,* fides, *and Integrity*

A second example of the derivation of specific moral norms: the set of norms about sex. Many, if not all, of these norms are derived by considering different ways in which a choice to engage in a sexual act[47] can be contrary to the basic human good of marriage.[48] So, throughout this section, we are dealing not merely with a question of 'personal morality', but with the intelligibility of a basic social institution, the family and its household. The best approach to understanding what Aquinas does and does not mean by 'contrary to the good of marriage {contra bonum matrimonii}' is to look first at the question of sexual morality which he treats far more often than any other: a certain kind of non-marital sex between a married couple.

To understand this, it is necessary first to be clear about Aquinas' view of marital intercourse—a view often misunderstood. A virtuous choice to engage in an act of marital intercourse need not be motivated by the hope of having children.[c] Another distinct,

---

[45] See e.g. II-II q. 100 a. 1c.

[46] See II *Sent.* d. 40 a. 2 (and the exegesis in Finnis 1991a: 65–6) showing that the wrongness is never a matter of the behaviour considered as a physical performance and/or outcome, but is always a matter of the will's orientation to its immediate (if not also its further) object. Synonymous with 'bear on inappropriate matter' is 'are inherently linked with a bad end {secundum se sunt coniuncti malo fine}'.

[47] Essentially an act intending to lead to one's own or another's sexual satisfaction {delectatio completa mentem suffocans} or 'pleasure like that in coitus': see IV *Sent.* d. 33 q. 3 a. 1 ad 4 and ad 5; II-II q. 152 a. 1c and ad 4; and acts intending sexual arousal and partial satisfaction and manifesting one's assent {consensus} to such pleasure: q. 154 a. 4.

[48] That marriage is a basic human good: I-II q. 94 a. 2c; III.5 at nn. 99–102 and n. p above.

---

sufficient, and entirely acceptable reason is: 'to give one's spouse the bodily co-operation, in *marital* [sexual] intercourse, to which he or she is entitled' {ut debitum reddat}.[49] Does this mean acting out of a sense of duty? Or only in response to one's spouse's claim of right or other initiating request? Not at all. There is nothing unreasonable about either party taking the initiative and asking for or tacitly seeking intercourse.[50] Appropriately making and acting on and/or in response to such a request, the spouses will indeed '*each be giving the other* what he or she is entitled to {ut *sibi invicem* reddant}'—one's bodily co-operation in marital sexual intercourse. But doing so has a point; it need not be at all a matter of choosing 'to do one's duty' or even 'to give him what he's entitled to' or 'give her her rights'. Rather the point will be, says Aquinas, the good of marital *fides* {bonum fidei}.[51]

What, then, is *fides*—literally 'fidelity' or 'faithfulness'— in this context? It is the disposition and commitment of each of the

[49] IV *Sent.* d. 26 q. 1 (= *Supp.* q. 41) a. 4c, d. 31 q. 2 a. 2c (= *Supp.* q. 49 a. 5c), d. 39 (= *Supp.* q. 59) a. 2 ad 5; III q. 80 a. 7 ad 2; *Mal.* q. 4 a. 1 obj. 17 and ad 17.

[50] Nowhere does Aquinas suggest that it is in any way wrong for, say, the woman to seek {petere debitum} or demand marital intercourse {exigere debitum}. On the contrary, he is clear that standardly (i.e. leaving aside anomalous cases where one spouse had previously taken a 'simple' vow not to marry, or had fornicated with a sibling of the other) there is nothing wrong either in seeking or in providing due bodily co-operation in marital intercourse {non peccaret mulier *neque exigendo* neque reddendo debitum}: *Quodl.* III q. 7 a. 1 ad 1. And if the man notices that she is interested in intercourse but embarrassed to express her wish, he should do the asking himself, thus himself both seeking and giving the due bodily co-operation in marital intercourse {sic vir *petendo reddit*}: *Quodl.* x q. 5 a. 3c [line 36]. See also IV *Sent.* d. 32 a. 2 sol. 1c (= *Supp.* q. 64 a. 2c): often the spouses will ask *each other* explicitly {verbis *invicem* [debitum] petunt}, but a wife may prefer to give non-verbal signs of being interested in marital intercourse; in either case she is *both* 'seeking what is due' {debitum petat} *and* showing her own 'willingness to provide it' {quando expressa signa in uxore apparent voluntatis debiti *reddendi*}; similarly d. 38 q. 1 a. 3 sol. 2 (= *Supp.* q. 53 a. 1) ad 4. See also *In I Cor.* 7. 1 ad v. 3 [321] (*mutuo debent sibi debitum reddere*}. In fact *reddere/petere debitum* is often no more (and no less) than a phrase for 'have/request [marital] intercourse': see e.g. I-II q. 19 a. 6c; *Sent.* d. 34 a. 5 ex.

[51] *Supp.* q. 49 a. 5c (cf. IV *Sent.* d. 31 q. 2 a. 2c): 'when spouses come together with a view to procreation, *or* so that they can give what they owe each other, which is a matter of *fides*, they are totally free from wrongdoing {quando coniuges conveniunt causa prolis procreandae, *vel* ut sibi invicem debitum reddant, quod ad fidem pertinet, totaliter excusantur a peccato}'; and ad 2: 'giving what [sexual intercourse] is due . . . is a matter of the good of *fides* {redditio debiti, quae ad bonum fidei pertinet}'. Equally clearly d. 39 (= *Supp.* q. 59) a. 2 ad 5: there is nothing wrong about marital intercourse {reddere debitum} 'for the sake of {propter} the good of offspring or {aut} the good of the *fides*' by which even unbelieving spouses are bound to one another.

spouses to 'cleave to {accedere}'[52]—precisely, to *be maritally united with*—the other and no other person.[53] So, besides the negative
commitment not to be maritally or in any other way sexually
united to anyone else ('fidelity'), *fides* even more basically includes
a positive commitment and willingness,[d] a reason *for* action.[54]
This is the key to understanding Aquinas' understanding of sexual
morality. *Fides* is, indeed, the characteristic proximate object(ive)
or 'appropriate matter about which {debita materia [circa quam]}'
we are engaged when we choose and engage in marital intercourse,
even on those occasions when we also have explicitly or implicitly
the hope of procreating.[55] This positive *fides* is the willingness and
commitment to belong to, and be united in mind and body with,
one's spouse in the form of *societas* and friendship[56] which we call
marriage.[57]

---

[52] *Accedere* has a wide range of meanings around 'approach' and 'adhere to', and
importantly includes 'have sexual intercourse with' (e.g. as in fornication: I-II q. 73 a.
7c; *ScG* III c. 122 n. 1 [2947]). Its meaning in respect of marital *fides* is clearly very closely
analogous to its meaning in one of Aquinas' central theological propositions, that it is by
fides that we adhere to {accedere} God (IV *Sent*. d. 45 q. 1 a. 2 sol. 1c (= *Supp.* 69 a. 4c); I-II
q. 113 a. 4c, II-II q. 7 a. 2); and it is virtually synonymous with the *adhaerere* by which
man and woman leave their respective parents and 'cling/cleave to each other and
become two in one flesh' (Gen. 2: 24; Matt. 19: 5): see II-II q. 26 a. 11c and ad 1 and s.c. [4].
[53] IV *Sent*. d. 31 q. 1 a. 2c (= *Supp.* q. 49 a. 2c) (see n. 55 below); *In I Cor.* 7. 1 ad v. 2 [318].
[54] IV *Sent*. d. 31 q. 1 a. 2 ad 3 (= *Supp.* q. 49 a. 2 ad 3): 'as the promise involved in
marriage includes that each party will not go to {accedere ad} anyone else's bed, so too it
includes this: that they *will give* each other due bodily co-operation in marital intercourse
{quod sibi invicem debitum reddant}—and *this latter is the more basic* {principalius},
since it follows precisely from the mutual power which each confers on the other. And so
each [of the two obligations, positive as well as negative] is a matter of *fides*.'
[55] IV *Sent*. d. 31 q. 1 a. 2c (= *Supp.* q. 49 a. 2c): the act [of marital intercourse] is a
morally good kind of act because it has an appropriate object, namely the *fides* by which a
man cleaves to his wife and to no other woman [and a woman to her husband and no other
man] {actus . . . est bonus in genere ex hoc quod cadit supra debitam materiam; et sic est
fides, per quam homo ad suam accedit, et non ad aliam} (for the translation of *supra
debitam materiam*, see II *Sent*. d. 36 a. 5c and the other texts cited in nn. 43–4 above); and
see IV *Sent*. d. 31 q. 2 a. 1c and a. 2c (= *Supp.* q. 49 a. 4c and a. 5c), where what is said in IV
Sent. d. 31 q. 1 a. 2c (= q. 49 a. 2c) about the nature and good of *fides* in relation to
marriage itself is shown to be equally and explicitly applicable to the 'marital act' of
intercourse. *Pace* Noonan (1967: 344).
[56] IV *Sent*. d. 41 a. 1 sol. 1c (= *Supp.* q. 55 a. 1c). *Eth.* VIII. 12 nn. 18–24 [1719–25]
explains in terms of friendship {amicitia} the whole justice, usefulness, pleasure {delec-
tatio in actu generationis}, and delight {amicitia iucunda} in shared virtue which can be
found in a good marriage with its division of complementary roles. IV *Sent*. d. 33 q. 1 a. 1c
(= *Supp.* q. 65 a. 1c) recalls this treatment when identifying *fides* as one of the two natural
goods and ends of marriage. So *fides* is essentially marital friendship. See also n. 65 below.
[57] IV *Sent*. d. 33 q. 1 a. 1c and a. 3 sol. 3c (= *Supp.* q. 65 a. 1c and a. 5c).

This *societas* is a unique type of relationship; it is unified by its dual point {finis}: the procreation, nurture, and education of children, and the full sharing of life in a home.[58] It is a companionship {societas}[59] which should, Aquinas thinks, be 'the greatest friendship, for they are united to each other not only in the act of bodily uniting in sexual intercourse {carnalis copulatio}, which even among lower animals creates a kind of delightful {suavis: sweet} *societas*, but also in mutual help {mutuum obsequium} in sharing together in the whole way of life of a household {ad totius domesticae conversationis consortium}'.[60]

So, *fides* is a motive, a reason *for* many co-operative acts intrinsic or incidental to a sharing in the 'whole life' of the marital household. As *motive (reason) for* choosing to participate in an

---

[58] IV *Sent.* d. 27 q. 1 a. 1 sol. 1c (= *Supp.* q. 44 a. 1c): marriage is oriented to 'some one thing {ad aliquod unum}', but the one thing is two things, each radically unifying and mutually reinforcing as, together, the point of marriage: *una generatio et educatio prolis* and *una vita domestica*. These two 'ends' of marriage define it, but there are other benefits intrinsic to it (other 'secondary' ends besides mutual help); one of these is the multiplication of friendship by non-incestuous marriages which link two families: IV *Sent.* d. 40 (= *Supp.* q. 54) a. 3c. But the most important or intrinsic of these supplementary secondary ends or benefits is 'the healing of one's desires {remedium concupiscentiae}': d. 33 q. 2 a. 1 (= *Supp.* q. 67 a. 1) ad 4. This is not a matter of simply providing sexual release; on the contrary, desires which are simply 'given an outlet' only grow in strength (II-II q. 151 a. 2 ad 2, a. 3 ad 2; IV *Sent.* d. 2 q. 1 a. 1 sol. 2c, d. 26 q. 2 (= *Supp.* q. 42) a. 3 ad 4). Rather it is a matter of integrating sexual desire with reason, which is what one does when one chooses intercourse in order to actualize and experience the good of marriage, i.e. for the sake of begetting children and/or of marital *fides*. When sex is thus made marital by integration with the marital goods {bona matrimonii} it is 'healed' by being given intelligent meaning, and then the satisfaction it can give does 'restrain' the desire which now is directed by reason(s) {ratione ordinatur}: d. 26 q. 2 (= *Supp.* q. 42) a. 3 ad 4. Desire so 'restrained' by integration with reason can issue in satisfaction (pleasure) of the most intense kind: I q. 98 a. 2 ad 3; II *Sent.* d. 20 q. 1 a. 2 ad 2; III.4 at nn. 64, 65 above.

[59] See VII.6 at nn. 112–20 below.

[60] *ScG* III c. 123 n. 6 [2964]. On the tight link between conjugal friendship/love {amicitia}—the mutual love or even love affair {mutua amatio} between spouses—and that mutual help in life which is the marital benefit peculiar to the spouses, see IV *Sent.* d. 26 q. 2 (= *Supp.* q. 42) a. 2c, d. 29 q. 1 a. 3 sol. 2 (= *Supp.* q. 47 a. 4) ad 1. On the tight link between mutual help and the good of offspring (such that the former can be regarded as a secondary end implicit in the latter), see IV *Sent.* d. 31 q. 1 (= *Supp.* q. 49) a. 2 ad 1. On the love {dilectio} that properly exists between spouses—the strongest of all forms of love between human beings—see also II-II q. 26 a. 11c; *In Eph.* 5. 9 ad v. 29 [328]. On marital intercourse (*understood always as a kind of continuation, expression, and experiencing of the common commitment to a shared and procreative life*) as a cause of marital friendship, see IV *Sent.* d. 41 a. 1 sol. 1c (= *Supp.* q. 55 a. 1c); as a cause of love {amor ex commixtione}, II-II q. 154 a. 9c; as a primary motive for the love between spouses, II-II q. 26 a. 11 ad s.c. [4]. For Aquinas' remarkable analysis of the passionate *effects* of love, an analysis implicitly but manifestly on the paradigm of spousal love as fitting cause of marital intercourse, see I-II q. 28 a. 5. On beauty as an appropriate cause of sexual attraction inviting to good marriages (which outlast bodily beauty): III *Sent.* d. 2 q. 2 a. 1 sol. 1c.

---

act of marital intercourse it is simply, we can say, the intended good of experiencing and in a particular way actualizing, and enabling one's spouse to experience and in a particular way actualize, the good of marriage—of our marriage precisely as our being bound,[61] and belonging, to each other in *such* an exclusive and permanent co-operative relationship.[62] Each of us is entitled to the other's co-operation in such acts, provided there is no reason[63] for abstaining. So, truly marital intercourse is literally an act of justice.[64] But that does not prevent it from being also an act of love.[65] It is an act which we can enter into with joy {laetantes};[66] the fact that it can give the greatest of all[67] bodily pleasures {delectatio intensissima} in no way makes it unreasonable;[68] there is nothing wrong at all with our welcoming assent to such pleasure in the marital act;[69] nor in our being motivated towards such an act by the prospect of giving and sharing in that delight as token of our marital commitment.[70]

---

[61] See *ScG* IV c. 78 n. 5 [4123]: *fides*, by which man and wife are bound to each other {sibi invicem obligantur}.

[62] Because marriage is a type of relationship unified and specified by a single, basic human good, it makes sense even when one aspect of that complex good happens to be unattainable. So a man and a woman past the age of child-bearing can marry for the sake of marriage, and the integration of their sexual desires by this good makes their marital sexual intercourse reasonable and morally good: IV *Sent.* d. 34 a. 2 (= *Supp.* q. 58 a. 1) ad 3.

[63] e.g. the health of either party: IV *Sent.* d. 32 (= *Supp.* q. 64) a. 1c and ad 2; and see IV *Sent.* d. 32 (= *Supp.* q. 64) a. 7c and n. 86 below.

[64] IV *Sent.* d. 26 q. 1 (= *Supp.* q. 41) a. 4c, d. 31 q. 1 a. 2 (= *Supp.* q. 49 a. 2) ad 2; see also d. 38 q. 1 a. 3 sol. 2 (= *Supp.* q. 53 a. 1) ad 3.

[65] The spouses' mutual commitment {pactio} which *fides* serves is properly a bond of love {vinculum amoris} (*In Isa.* 7 ad v. 14, line 436); indeed 'spouse' is a word for signifying love (*In Matt.* 9 ad v. 15 [769]). Since *fides* is not merely negative but also positive, to speak of greater *fides* is to speak of greater love {fidelior amor}: see *ScG* III c. 123 n. 8 [2966]; n. 56 above.

[66] *In I Cor.* 7. 1 ad v. 5 [325]. Note: this thought—that spouses who have been abstaining will return to marital intercourse with joy—is Aquinas' own contribution, not suggested by the text on which he is there commenting; for other sources of the thought, see ibid. ad v. 2 [319]; I-II q. 105 a. 4c (on Deut. 24: 5).

[67] II-II q. 152 a. 1c; and see *Quodl.* XII q. 13 a. un. c, q. 14 a. un. c [line 53].

[68] II-II q. 153 a. 2 ad 2; IV *Sent.* d. 26 q. 1 a. 3 ad 6 (= *Supp.* q. 41 a. 3 ad 6), d. 31 q. 2 a. 1 ad 3 (= *Supp.* q. 49 a. 4 ad 3); I-II q. 34 a. 1 ad 1. And see n. 58 above and III.4 at n. 64 above.

[69] See *Mal.* q. 15 a. 2 ad 17.

[70] See IV *Sent.* d. 31 q. 1 a. 1 ad 1 (= *Supp.* q. 49 a. 1 ad 1): as hunger makes us interested in eating {ad excitandum ad comestionem}, so divine providence has attached pleasure to marital intercourse to interest us in engaging in generative types of act {ad excitandum ad actum}; d. 26 q. 1 a. 4 obj. 5 and ad 5 (= *Supp.* q. 41 a. 4 obj. 5 and ad 5); *Supp.* q. 65 a. 4 ad 3 (cf. IV *Sent.* d. 33 q. 1 a. 3 sol. 2 ad 3). See also *Ver.* q. 25 a. 5 ad 7: when what is rightly desired has been settled by reason [sc. intercourse between us as soon as appropriate, as an act of marital *fides*], then even though one's bodily appetite is aroused towards it there is nothing wrong with all that {tametsi sensualitas in id feratur, nullum erit peccatum}.

All this enables us to understand various ways that a spouse can act, sexually, 'against the good of marriage'. Clearly by adultery.[71] But suppose that one spouse, say the woman, gives the other permission to commit adultery, say by taking a mistress {concubina}? And suppose she gives it in the hope of preserving the marriage as an ongoing state of affairs? Aquinas' answer is clear: giving such permission, too, is wrong, because against the good of marriage {contra matrimonii bonum}.[72] The answer does not depend upon an assessment of all the circumstances and likely consequences. It looks rather to the object, the close-in intention, the 'matter' of the choices—the husband's choice to have sex outside marriage, and the wife's to give her consent to it. Further intentions, and (other) circumstances, can make an act wrong, but they cannot make it right if its object is morally bad.[73]

Another type of choice contrary to the good of marriage is frequently mentioned by Aquinas. One (or both) of the spouses, say (for simplicity) the husband, chooses to engage in intercourse[74] with motives that do not include *fides*: perhaps he wants intercourse *simply* for the pleasure of it,[75] or perhaps his motive is simply to mitigate his own temptations to extra-marital sex,[76] or

---

Universally, 'part of the fullness of the morally good is that one is moved to the good [with which a particular act is concerned] not only by one's will but also by one's sense appetites, one's flesh': I-II q. 24 a. 3c. And universally, 'it is natural to us as rational animals that our power of desiring {[vis] concupiscibilis} be drawn towards what is sensually enjoyable {in delectabile sensus} in line with reasonable order {secundum ordinem rationis}': *Mal.* q. 4 a. 2 ad 4 [or: ad 1].

[71] II-II q. 154 a. 8 ad 2 and ad 3 ('contra bonum matrimonii').

[72] IV *Sent.* d. 33 q. 1 a. 3 sol. 1 (= *Supp.* q. 65 a. 3) ad 5.

[73] For: an act is morally good only if all its elements are good—all the intentions with which it is chosen, including the proximate intention we call its object or matter, must be right and it must not be morally inappropriate in the circumstances. If any one of these elements or factors is out of line with practical reasonableness, the choice is wrong. As Aquinas puts it summarily (quoting an old tag): 'Bonum ex integra causa, malum ex quocumque defectu' ('good from unflawed contributing factors, bad from any defect'): see I-II q. 18 a. 4 ad 3, q. 19 a. 6 ad 1, q. 71 a. 5 ad 1, II-II q. 79 a. 3 ad 4; *Mal.* q. 2 a. 1 ad 3, a. 4 ad 2; *Eth.* II. 7 n. 2 [320].

[74] Or indeed, to marry. Aquinas thinks that in his day {nunc} the majority of people enter upon marriage with the same intent with which people in pre-Christian times engaged in extra-marital sex: IV *Sent.* d. 33 q. 3 a. 3 ex.

[75] The 'simply' is vitally important (see n. 70 above), and is explicit in the article expressly devoted to the question, IV *Sent.* d. 31 q. 2 a. 3c (= *Supp.* q. 49 a. 6); and see a. 6c obj. 1 {intendens *solam* delectationem}. It is implicit though not explicit in other texts, e.g. IV *Sent.* q. 26 q. 1 a. 4c (= *Supp.* q. 41 a. 4c); *In I Cor.* 7. 1 ad v. 6 [329]; *Quodl.* VIII q. 6 a. 5.

[76] IV *Sent.* d. 31 q. 2 a. 2 (= *Supp.* q. 49 a. 5c) ad 2.

---

perhaps he is interested only in his health.[77] In any such case, Aquinas discerns two possibilities. This man's indifference to *fides* as a positive reason may coexist with some concern for *fides* as a ground for restraint; he may be wholly unwilling to have sex with anyone other than his wife. Or he may be indifferent to *fides* altogether, and would prefer and/or be willing to be having sex with some other more appealing woman if she were available—but only his wife is here and now available. In either type of case he is choosing to have intercourse with her without any intention either of making their marriage procreative or of expressing marital affection for his spouse and enabling the two of them to experience and actualize their marriage. So he is acting—most obviously where his motive is simply pleasure—as if he were with a call-girl {meretrix}.[78] In either type of case, says Aquinas, his act is contrary to {contra}, and disconnected from {extra}, the good(s) of marriage—above all from person-to-person *fides*—and so it savours of adultery even though fidelity in a merely behavioural sense has been preserved.[79]

In each of these cases,[80] this man's act is wrong; in cases of the second type the wrongfulness, and the wrong to his wife, is in principle grave. The judgement that such acts are wrong does not depend upon their likely or foreseeable consequences. It looks to the act's object or 'matter' (what it is *about*), which no longer is to express *fides* by sexual union, but rather is: to have sex, get release, or something else similarly de-personalized. Of course, the act's contrariety to the good of marriage is not the same kind of contrariety as an act of killing's contrariety to the good of life. Aquinas' account would be much clarified by some sorting out of different ways in which one's choosing and acting are contrary to practical

---

[77] Ibid. ad 4. Aquinas envisages a further way in which intercourse between spouses might be morally defective because unhinged from the good of *fides*, namely where either or both of them engage in it solely to signify something which in itself is extrinsic to their own marital commitment: IV *Sent.* d. 31 q. 2 a. 2c (= *Supp.* q. 49 a. 5c).

[78] See IV *Sent.* d. 31 q. 2 a. 3 ad 1 (= *Supp.* q. 49 a. 6 ad 1): in his intercourse with his wife he is not concerned with anything about *her* other than what he would be concerned with in a prostitute {nihil aliud in ea attendit quam quod in meretrice attenderet}.

[79] II-II q. 154 a. 8 ad 2. Likewise the converse (and bizarre) case considered in *Mal.* q. 3 a. 8c and it seems in II *Sent.* d. 22 q. 2 a. 2c, where a man thinks he is having intercourse with his wife and is then glad to find that it was with someone else.

[80] Also in the further case envisaged (along with the aforementioned types of case), in IV *Sent.* d. 31 q. 2 a. 3c (= *Supp.* q. 49 a. 6c), where one's state of mind in choosing intercourse is such that one would be *willing* (not merely emotionally inclined) to have intercourse with this person (one's spouse) even if one were *not* this person's spouse.

reasonableness, not least in relation to sex and marriage; but such a clarification seems not to have been offered until recently.[81]

There are other ways besides this in which sex between husband and wife can be non-marital—in Aquinas' phrase, contrary to the good(s) of marriage. For the intrinsic point of marriage includes procreation, which is primary at least in the sense that without procreation (and the complex and ambitious project of raising of children which is procreation's completion), the other aspects of marriage's point, and marriage's other benefits, would provide no sufficient ground for marriage's characteristic unity, exclusiveness, and permanence. So their sexual acts will not allow spouses to experience and actualize their *marriage* unless they are acts of the procreative type.[e] This, and only this, is the type of act by which they are really 'one flesh'[82] and have the unity which is the essence of marriage, a unity of minds and emotions and bodies in an act which has the unique oneness of a reproductive type of act.[83] As individuals, the woman and the man are complete in respect of all their other capacities and acts; but with respect to sexual reproduction each is only a part of a mated pair which together makes up the *unum*—we may say, the one organism— which can reproduce. Even if marital intercourse occurs (as it usually does) at a time when reproduction will not in fact follow, the spouses' choice to unite sexually in the reproductive way[84] makes them that organic *unum*; then, if their intentions are not contrary to the marital good in the way discussed in the preceding paragraph, their intercourse will really be what they intend it to be,

---

[81] See Grisez (1993: 553–752). But it has always been clear that a choice not to marry (whether not to marry this person now, or in the future, or not to marry anyone), if made on the ground that doing so would have the effect of impeding the realizing of other basic goods one hopes to participate in and share with others, need not be a choice against, or disrespecful of, the good(s) of marriage, and can (especially if made for the reasons indicated in x.5–6 below) be the choice of the better option: see e.g. II-II q. 186 a. 4c.

[82] IV *Sent.* d. 41 a. 1 sol. 4 (= *Supp.* q. 55 a. 4) ad 2; and see *ScG* III c. 122 n. 5 [2951].

[83] See III *Sent.* d. 8 a. 1c (in coitus they are like a single generative principle {unum generans}: two in one flesh); I q. 92 a. 1c (by coitus the man and the woman temporarily become—are made into—*one*, as in a plant in which male and female are conjoined all the time; man and woman are bodily conjoined into one for the generative act {generationis opus}); *In I Cor.* 6. 3 ad v. 16 [304] (from two they become one in the generative act); *In Matt.* 19. ad v. 5 [1553]; *In Eph.* 5. 10 ad v. 31 [333] (in the generative act {actus generationis} their activity [sc. intercourse {carnalis coniunctio}] is like what in plants is done by one and the same body). And see n. 84 below.

[84] See *ScG* III c. 122 n. 5 [2951]. Thus, even those who (e.g. from old age) cannot generate may be able to engage in the generative act {actus generationis}: *Quodl.* XI q. 9 a. 2 ad 1. So *actus/opus generationis* here means 'generative act' (act of the generative type) rather than 'act of generation'; see also e.g. IV *Sent.* d. 42 q. 1 (= *Supp.* q. 56) a. 2c.

and have the meaning and *honestas* they intend it to have: marital union.

But if the spouses choose sexual activity which, in either of the two broad ways we have been discussing, is non-marital—is not integrated with the basic good of marriage itself—they have broken the link between sexual activity and the good of practical reasonableness itself. In so doing they deliver over their sexual capacities and acts to the rule of emotional desire and satisfaction, of *libido* and *concupiscentia* which go astray not (to repeat) by being very strong, but by being dis-integrated from reason.[85] Spouses may invent forms and limits of many kinds for their sexual activity, or take them from some culture. But none of these forms or limits will have intrinsic intelligibility, as the integration of sexual choices and dispositions by the good of marriage has.[86] None will provide a rational critique of sex's de-personalization in promiscuity, or of the thought that bodily and emotional satisfaction, pleasurable experience, unhinged from basic human reasons for action and posing as its own rationale, is the best thing that human existence can offer.[87]

Not being coherently ordered around the good(s) of marriage, all these *ad hoc* or cultural sexual mores will tend to deprive marriage itself of its central element[88] by disabling the spouses from understanding their sexual intercourse as specifically nothing other than—and therefore nothing less than—the experiencing and actualizing of their marital *fides*.[89] For one cannot understand

---

[85] See n. 68 above.

[86] Of course, the two-sided good of marriage itself provides many reasons, intelligible in themselves without invention, for spouses to abstain from sexual intercourse, e.g. when either of them is disinclined or unwell, or they lack the time or privacy appropriate, or when abstaining for a time will intensify mutual satisfaction, and so forth; n. 63 above.

[87] See II-II q. 153 a. 5; *In I Thess.* 4. 1 ad v. 5 [80]; *Mal.* q. 15 a. 1c (ad fin.) and a. 4c; II *Sent.* d. 7 q. 1 a. 2c.

[88] See IV *Sent.* d. 28 a. 4c (= *Supp.* q. 48 a. 1c): while marriage {coniugalis copula} is not, essentially, the [marital] sexual intercourse itself, it is, essentially, 'the associating of man and wife *for* sexual intercourse {in ordine ad carnalem copulam} *and* for the other things which properly belong to them *in consequence* [of such intercourse]'; and see II-II q. 26 a. 11 ad s.c. [4].

[89] Remember: *fides* is the object of marital intercourse (n. 55 above); the parties can have the explicit further intention of doing what they thereby can to procreate, but often their openness (as we can say) to procreation is quite implicit (see IV *Sent.* d. 31 q. 2 a. 2c (= *Supp.* q. 49 a. 5c) with ad 1 {actu vel habitu}) and is essentially an element in their *fides*. For this *fides* is the constant and steady will to uphold and respect their sharing in a type of association (and institution) which as a type has procreation as its primary defining point.

---

one's act of intercourse as an act expressing and actualizing marital *fides*—i.e. expressing and actualizing one's marriage itself—if one also holds that sexual acts can rightly be chosen for some other, non-marital motive. And such an impediment {*impedire*} to the intelligibility of the marital association— and thus to the appeal of marriage itself (and of their own marriage) to the wills of spouses or potential spouses—must, and manifestly does, damage and impede wider common goods, by wounding the marital commitment to children in their conception, bringing to birth, nurture, and education to the maturity, freedom, and virtue on which the political community depends.

In short: The well-being of children, and so of the whole set of human communities, depends on the unreserved, long-term commitment of pairs of persons fitted by their biological, emotional, dispositional complementarity—as persons of opposite sex—to be parents (which includes the generation, gestation, nurture, education, and care of 'this child, these children, of *ours*'). But this commitment needs to be expressed, experienced, and actualized in the marital intercourse which unites the two spouses at all levels of their being. Now spouses cannot engage in truly *marital* intercourse if willing, even hypothetically or conditionally, to seek sexual satisfaction in any one or more of the various extra-marital ways. And anyone who judges that it can be reasonable for human beings to seek sexual satisfaction in an extra-marital way is hypothetically/conditionally willing to seek it in some such way. So nobody who is a spouse, or who considers it reasonable for human beings to become spouses, can judge that it can be reasonable for human beings to seek sexual satisfaction in an extra-marital way. And anyone who has a reasonable concern for the well-being of children must reject the opinion that it can be reasonable for human beings to seek sexual satisfaction in an extra-marital way. That is why all extra-marital sex {*luxuria*} both is *contrary* to the good of marriage and offends against love-of-neighbour,[90] and for both reasons is against

---

[90] See *Mal.* q. 15 a. 2 ad 4; IV *Sent.* d. 33 q. 1 a. 3 sol. 2c (= *Supp.* q. 65 a. 4c).

reason,[91] and consequently against nature.[92]

The reasons for judging some 'marital' i.e. inter-spousal sex bad are thus also reasons for judging bad (immoral) the unchastity {luxuria} involved in every other type of sexual misconduct. Various sorts of morally bad sex involve other wrongs besides unchastity; rapes, adulteries, seduction of children, all violate justice as well as chastity.[93] But the specifically sexual vice in morally bad sex is in every case measured by the chosen act's deviation—and the extent of its deviance—from truly marital intercourse {secundum quod magis distat a matrimoniali concubitu},[94] intercourse which is wholly uncoerced on both sides,[95] generative in type in its chosen behaviour, and genuinely motivated by that *fides* which in its central case is a true friendship.

The stakes, Aquinas thinks, are high. If we treat these powerful desires which (like various other desires and aversions) we share with other animals as having no rational connection—to be preserved integrally in every good choice—with our reason's first practical principles, then we treat our human existence as lacking the dignity which is presupposed in every claim of *right*.[96] Similarly, if the rational connection between acts, as defined by their

[91] That the vice of all extra- and non-marital sex is its opposition to the principles of practical reasonableness (i.e. to the intelligible human goods) is put at the forefront of Aquinas' accounts: e.g. II-II q. 153 a. 2c, a. 3c, q. 154 a. 1c, a. 2 ad 2, a. 11c; *ScG* III c. 122 n. 2 [2948]; IV *Sent.* d. 26 q. 1 (= *Supp.* q. 41) a. 1c. (Aquinas' moral arguments never run from 'natural' to 'therefore reasonable and right', but always from 'reasonable and right' to 'therefore natural'; and see III.7 at n. 141 above.) 'Against reason' does *not* refer to the fact that one cannot think clearly in the pleasure of sexual acts; this is true of marital intercourse but (because such intercourse is integrated with—chosen in view of—one or more goods and *reasons* such as *fides*) does not make it in any way morally flawed: e.g. IV *Sent.* d. 26 q. 1 (= *Supp.* q. 41) a. 1c, a. 3 obj. 6 and ad 6, d. 31 q. 2 a. 1 (= *Supp.* q. 49 a. 4) ad 3. But morally disordered sexual desires, *consensus*, and activity are perhaps uniquely likely to disrupt and dissolve reason's constitutional rule and dis-integrate the acting person, and hinder reason's own operations: e.g. II-II q. 153 a. 5c; *Mal.* q. 15 a. 4c.

[92] All extra-marital sex (and even conditional assent {consensus} to it) is contrary to nature *inasmuch as it is contrary to reason*'s requirements: e.g. *Mal.* q. 15 a. 1 ad 7; *In Rom.* 1.8 ad v. 26 [149]; n. 91 above. Some extra- or non-marital sex is *also* unnatural in a narrower sense, namely every act in which sexual satisfaction is sought and which is not an act of the generative type (see n. 84 above): II-II q. 154 a. 11c.

[93] IV *Sent.* d. 41 a. 4 sol. 1c; see also I-II q. 73 a. 5 ad 1, a. 7c. Obviously, raping a woman is worse than fornicating or committing adultery with her: II-II q. 65 a. 4 ad 3; rape is one of the traditional set of four most serious harms to the person: 'rape {stuprum}, slavery, flogging, death': IV *Sent.* d. 29 a. 2 (= *Supp.* q. 47 a. 2) ad 2.

[94] IV *Sent.* d. 41 a. 4 sol. 3c; see also *Mal.* q. 15 a. 1c.

[95] IV *Sent.* d. 41 a. 4 sol. 3c.

[96] See e.g. IV *Sent.* d. 27 q. 3 a. 1 sol. 1c (= *Supp.* q. 66 a. 1c): 'by concupiscence the whole human being is turned into [mere] flesh {totus homo caro efficitur}'; likewise d. 31 q. 2 a. 3 ad 4 (= *Supp.* d. 49 a. 6 ad 4).

objects, and the first principles of practical reason is a connection wholly subject to circumstances as assessed and valued on utilitarian, proportionalist, or (say) Nietzschean lines, again the claims implied by the assertion of basic human rights cannot be rationally sustained and will be surrendered or traded off for purposes shaped ultimately—below all rationalizations—by the desires of individuals or groups who have the power (capacity and determination) to satisfy, in one or another form, their *libido*, their *concupiscentia*.

In line with all this, we can say that the premiss needed to get from love of neighbour-as-self to the specific moral norms excluding the various types of non-marital sexual activity is something like: it is contrary to one's good as a human person, and to the good of one's communities and dependants, for one's choices to express, or be inherently productive of, a *duplicitas* or inner dis-integration of one's self, namely the dis-integrity of emotional motivation and intelligible goods.[97] (That is why Aquinas judges that a most important benefit intrinsic to marriage's point is the healing of this inner dis-integrity {remedium concupiscentiae}.)[98] In the following section, we shall see that implicit in Aquinas' explanation of the moral norm excluding lying is a rather similar premiss, identifying as contrary to human good the *duplicitas* or inauthenticity of an act which (we may say) divides one's inner from one's outer self.

v.5. *Truth, Assertion, and Authenticity*

It is always wrong to lie.[99] It is wrong to lie to enemies in war.[100] It is wrong to lie to save oneself[101] or one's client[102] from unjust conviction and execution. Or to save some other person or group from destruction by genocidal killers who have no right to be told

---

[97] So non-marital sexual desires and conduct result in a division of the self {duplicitas animi} (II-II q. 53 a. 6 ad 2), and dissolve the self {animum solvunt} (II-II q. 153 a. 1c: the essence of the vice of *luxuria*). *Animum* in Aquinas means not just intelligence and will but also emotions (see e.g. II-II q. 157 a. 3 ad 1)—i.e. all that needs to be integrated if bodily action is to be morally good. [98] See n. 58 above.

[99] II-II q. 110 a. 3 (and such lies—as also in Machiavelli, *The Prince* (1513; 1st pub. 1532) c. 18—include the making of promises while having no intention of keeping them: II-II q. 110 a. 3 ad 5, q. 40 a. 3c); III *Sent.* d. 38 q. un. a. 3; *Quodl.* VIII q. 6 a. 4c.

[100] II-II q. 40 a. 3c; see VI. 3 n. 70, VII.1 at n. 9 below.

[101] II-II q. 69 a. 2c. And the wrongness of lying, whatever the truth in issue, can be a reason for accepting martyrdom: II-II q. 124 a. 5 ad 2. [102] II-II q. 71 a. 3 ad 3.

the truth.[103] Yet it can be right to ensnare the enemy's forces by deliberately deceptive manœuvres, ruses, and ambushes.[104] Even those who have committed criminal offences can rightly conceal their guilt by remaining silent.[105] As for killers to whom one must not lie, one normally has a strong obligation to frustrate their purpose by silence, defiance, concealment, distraction, force, or any other morally acceptable means.[106] Why then should we hold that one may never lie? What moral basis did Aquinas have—as someone well familiar, by family experience and personal reflection, with military and political exigencies—for this radical opposition to a mainstay of every Machiavellian, 'realist' politics (and of consistent Machiavellians' 'realistic' pursuit of their purposes within their own business, their political party and other associations, and even their own family and perhaps their teaching . . .)?

Aquinas' premiss is not, as many have hastily supposed, that lying is contrary to the natural function of tongue or speech.[107] There are several reasons why that could not be a ground for Aquinas' position; most obviously, it is incompatible with his acceptance that much speech has nothing to do with truth or falsity;[108] and it jars with his thesis that one can lie with a nod, a wink, a movement of one's finger.[109] So, if not all speech is capable of being a lie, and conversely any conduct intended to be taken as

---

[103] See II-II q. 110 a. 3 ad 4; III *Sent.* d. 38 a. 3 ad 6; *Ps.* 5.3 ad v. 3; *Dec.* 10 [1314].

[104] III *Sent.* d. 38 a. 3 ad 5 (fleeing in pretended defeat, so as to draw the enemy's forces into an exposed position and/or an ambush); II-II q. 40 a. 3c (ambushes are directed {ordinantur} to deceiving {ad fallendum}); q. 71 a. 3 ad 3.

[105] II-II q. 69 a. 2c; however, one who is asked by a court acting within its jurisdiction and on the basis of evidence legally sufficient to ground a justified suspicion can be legally (as in Roman law) and morally obliged to answer, even if the answer involves a confession of guilt: ibid.; *Quodl.* v q. 8 a. 2.

[106] See II-II q. 110 a. 3 ad 4 (distraction or concealment {dissimulatione}); see also II-II q. 71 a. 3 ad 3., and nn. 131–3 below.

[107] The supposition is based on the dark statement in II-II q. 110 a. 3c that since 'spoken words {voces} are naturally signs of what one understands {intellectuum}, it is unnatural and undue {indebitum} for one to signify by speech what one does not have in one's mind'—a statement which needs to be read in the context established by qq. 109–13. At the equivalent moment in III *Sent.* d. 38 a. 3c the premiss is that speech {locutio} was invented 'for expressing conceptions in one's heart'; this is more satisfactory than the premiss offered in *Eth.* IV. 15 n. 7 [837], that signs were instituted to represent things as they are. Also *Quodl.* VIII q. 6 a. 4c; the formulations in *ST* synthesize those in III *Sent.* and this early *Quodlibet* (1257), which in turn appeals to the analysis in *Peri.* 1. 7 (see n. 115 below). See also n. 123 below.

[108] *Peri* 1. 7 and nn. 115, 119 below. Even statements in the present indicative, when made, for example, by poets, novelists, playwrights, and actors, are not (or not directly) the asserting of anything as true.   [109] II-II q. 110 a. 1 ad 2; *Quodl.* VI q. 9 a. 3c.

---

communicative can be a lie,[110] what are the wrong-making features of a lie? We can begin where Aquinas begins his full-dress
treatment of lying, with the virtue of veracity or truthfulness.

This virtue is not part of justice in the central sense, but is part of
the sphere or zone of justice, or closely linked to justice.[111] It is not
a matter of something owed to someone else as a matter of legally
defined right, but rather of personal decency (uprightness, honour-
ableness) {honestas}.[112] Its object, i.e. the human good with which
it is concerned, is truth precisely as a perfection of understanding,
i.e. as knowledge.[113] But veracity itself is the disposition to say
what is true, to tell the truth by proffering certain signs (exterior
words or deeds) which conform to reality.[114] Must one be telling
the truth all the time and in all circumstances? In all one's communicative expressions? By no means.[115] Veracity is a *due* ordering
of signs.[116] But as in all reflections on virtues, nothing yet said
about veracity's classification and object makes clear what precisely is due. Discussions of the virtue, unless they are guided by
consideration of the underlying norm of practical reason, provide
no sufficient indication whether or not a *specific type of act*, spe-
cifiable in terms which do not presuppose its rightness or wrongness, is wrong (contrary to virtue), and if wrong generally is also
wrong universally.

Still, Aquinas' consideration of veracity as a virtue does furnish
important clues to answering the question about lying as a specific
type of act. For in discussing communication {manifestatio},
which is veracity's generic subject-matter, Aquinas repeatedly indicates what he thinks most relevant: when one communicates by
asserting something,[117] one actually or purportedly communicates
something *about oneself*, namely what one understands, believes,

---

[110] II-II q. 111 a. 1c and ad 4, a. 2 ad 1 and 3: e.g. politicians who go through the motions
of worship or contribute to Church funds not for God's sake but simply to communicate
(assert) the (false) message that they are of upright character (a. 2 ad 1).

[111] II-II q. 109 a. 3.   [112] Ibid. c.   [113] II-II q. 109 a. 1, a. 2 ad 1.

[114] Ibid. a. 1c and ad 3.

[115] Ibid. ad 2 (speaking the truth is something which is generically good—has a good
proximate object—but can be rendered morally bad by circumstances including intentions); 4c. And there are many types of expressive communication in which truth or
falsity need not be in issue, e.g. requests, commands, questions, and the vocative (summons to attention): *Peri.* 1. 7 n. 5 [86].   [116] II-II q. 109 a. 2c.

[117] On the importance of assertions (assertings) as the specific kind of act with which
veracity is concerned, and which alone can be a lie, see II-II q. 69 a. 2c ('falsitatem
proponere'); q. 110 a. 1c ('voluntas [verum vel] falsum enuntiandi', and ad 1 ('intendens
dicere falsum'); a. 3 ad 1, q. 111 a. 1 ad 1; III *Sent.* d. 38 a. 5 ad 1 and ad 3.

has in mind.[118] The 'exterior signs' by which I make assertions bring the person with whom I am communicating into a relationship not simply to certain meanings and certain things directly meant {significat[a]} but also to me. For my asserting a proposition[119] states precisely—indirectly (performatively) but necessarily—*that I believe it* to be true; to assert it as probable is to state that *I think it* probable, and so forth. Assertion is an act of self-disclosure[f] (and veracity is a matter of personal authenticity).

When one is lying, the mind one professes to reveal to those one is addressing is not one's actual mind. For one lies if and only if one asserts a proposition as true, believing it to be false, and thus communicating something about oneself—'I believe this to be the case'—which is false even if the proposition asserted happens, contrary to one's belief, to be true.[120] This is one reason, it seems, why Aquinas maintains, against Augustine and most of the theological tradition, that what defines lying is not intention to deceive, but simply intention to *assert* the false.[121] The division of oneself—into the counterfeit self (heart, mind) fabricated exteriorly by the false asserting, and the true self hidden interiorly—is fully effected in such an act of falsely asserting. Of course, assertion involves communication, and the intention to assert the false proposition and to profess the counterfeit mind will also be an intention that some recipient be deceived. So, as Aquinas says, deception—the impressing of falsehood on the mind of another—is a kind of completion of the lie,[122] without which it

---

[118] II-II q. 109 a. 2 ad 2, a. 3c and ad 3, q. 110 a. 3c, q. 111 a. 1c; *Eth.* IV. 15 n. 5 [835]. So his first treatment of veracity in *ST* (I q. 16 a. 4 ad 3; likewise III *Sent.* d. 33 q. 3 a. 4 sol. 1c) says that it is a matter of showing *oneself* (by words and deeds) *as one is* {homo . . . ostendit se ut est}.

[119] On the distinction between the proposition asserted and the statement(s) by which it is asserted, see e.g. I q. 29 a. 3 ad 1. In figurative discourse the proposition asserted may lie well below the surface of the words: II-II q. 110 a. 3 ad 1 and ad 6; III *Sent.* d. 38 a. 3 ad 5. What appears to be an assertion may be no more than a report of someone else's views (e.g. I q. 77 a. 5 ad 3: 'non asserendo sed recitando'), or a statement of a hypothesis (e.g. I q. 100 a. 2 ad 2: 'non dicit asserendo sed opinando').

[120] II-II q. 110 a. 1c. So the assertion of something which happens to be true but which one believes to be false is an act of lying even if we would not say that *what was said* was 'a lie': III *Sent.* d. 38 a. 1 ad 1. [121] II-II q. 110 a. 1c; cf. *Quodl.* VI q. 9 a. 3c.

[122] II-II q. 110 a. 1c; III *Sent.* d. 38 a. 1c. In the odd, marginal category of joking lies {mendacium iocosum}—the only clear example Aquinas mentions is pointless exaggeration unlikely to be believed (III *Sent.* d. 38 a. 2 obj. 3 and ad 3)—there is, Aquinas seems to be saying, intent to make a false, deceptive assertion but no intent that anyone shall remain deceived beyond the duration of the joke: III *Sent.* d. 38 a. 1 ad 5 and a. 2 ad 1). Aquinas has nothing against jokes, e.g. playful insults unlikely to wound their object: II-II q. 72 a. 2 ad 1.

would be pointless and insignificant. But the moral significance of the lie consists in its character precisely as false *self*-expression: what is signified, assertively and communicatively, *as being in one's mind* is in fact not in one's mind.[123] Its intrinsic moral significance is not so much in the fact (important as this typically is) that someone comes to believe the false proposition directly asserted. Its significance is rather, we may say, in this: what purports to be a relating of mind to mind and thus of person to person—the relationship whereby self discloses self to another—is in reality made to be[124] not that relationship at all but an act of *duplicity*, the presentation to another person of a pretended mind and heart.[125]

As we have said, and Aquinas makes clear, there are countless occasions when one has no obligation to make any self-disclosure or indeed any communication at all to others or to some other(s),[g] and many occasions when one has an obligation, sometimes very strong, not to do so.[126] One can rightly 'hide oneself'[127] by one's silence. But *if* one does make an act of communication which, because assertive in its meaning, is purportedly self-disclosing, one should never make it the duplicitous act of projecting for acceptance (belief) a phony self while actually remaining hidden behind one's pretended self-disclosure.

What, then, about the pretended flight designed to deceive—that is, to lead the pursuing enemy into ambush? Though done in the hope that it will be taken as *evidence* of a state of mind (belief that

---

[123] This is the sense and point, it seems to me, of the argument against lying in the passages cited and quoted in n. 107 above, not least *Eth.* IV. 15 n. 7 [837] (which seems anomalous and unhelpful until read with nn. 5–6 [835–6] which are concerned precisely with disclosing oneself, in one's words and deeds, as what one actually is). The premiss about the 'natural' or 'invented' purpose of speech is best taken as pointing to the fact that, given this natural or well-established context, a communication which is meaningful in that context *as* an assertion, will *inevitably* be meaningful also as (purportedly) heart-disclosing.

[124] What matters is that I am *choosing* to make my assertive ('truth-conveying') behaviour a deviation from the truth. Of course, I may be mistaken in thinking that my statement is false; but I cannot be mistaken in thinking—and making it the case—that what it secondarily asserts about me is false. See III *Sent.* d. 38 a. 1c; n. 120 above.

[125] See II-II q. 109 a. 2 ad 4 (veracity is opposed to duplicity {duplicitas} 'whereby one pretends one thing and intends another'); q. 111 a. 3 ad 2 ('intends one thing inwardly and externally holds out {praetendat} another thing'); *Ps.* 11.2 ad v. 2: '. . . double heart {duplex cor}: they show with their mouth that they have one thing [in mind], but in the heart they have something else'. [126] e.g. II-II q. 70 a. 1.

[127] II-II q. 69 a. 2 ad 3; this freedom to evade stating one's mind on the precise question at issue is subject, however, to the moral responsibility one may have, e.g. as a witness in court: ibid. 2c.

the battle is lost and flight necessary), it is not in fact, and does not even pretend to be, an act *of communication*. Rather there is a real flight (and a real hiding of the ambushing troops), carried out with the intentions—intentions hidden from the enemy—(1) that the enemy, in pursuing, will fall into the ambush, and quite possibly (2) that the fleeing troops will stop and turn upon the enemy once the ambush has been sprung.[128] Its substance is acts of concealment, i.e. deliberate non-disclosure, of plans, and in war one is not morally obliged to disclose one's plans or intentions to the enemy.[129] Politicians who hypocritically go to church, by contrast, are in an ongoing communicative relationship with those whom they wish to impress, such that their conduct is not simply a deed accompanied by a concealed intention but is intended to be, and is, a sign which makes an assertion—duplicitously.[130]

But if lying is always wrong, as Aquinas maintains (with Aristotle and Augustine), what should one say when the Gestapo come to the door demanding to be told the whereabouts of *X* and *Y* (friends whom one has hidden in one's attic), to take them off to the extermination camp? The young Aquinas recycles Augustine's counsel: If one is stopped in the street and asked whether one knows where any persons of a certain type (say, Jews or gypsies) are hidden, a fitting reply is that one would never reveal the whereabouts of such people even if under torture; but if one is at home and is asked specifically whether particular persons are here in this specific place {in illo loco determinato}, one should reply 'I know where they are, but I am not going to say where.'[131] Doubtless we can think of equally or more subtle responses which are yet free from all falsity of assertion;[132] the older Aquinas says

---

[128] See Jos. 8: 3–23, cited in II-II q. 40 a. 3 s.c.

[129] II-II q. 40 a. 3c: 'such concealment {occultatio} bears on the rationale and morally relevant character {ratio} of the ruses {insidiarum} which it is morally permissible to use in just wars'.

[130] II-II q. 111 a. 2c and ad 1 and 2. In general: worship is a sign of interior devotion, and so if you offer worship with words or other signs which are contrary to what you hold in your heart and mind, your inauthenticity {falsitas} is a form of pernicious lying; so it is wrong to sacrifice to idols even in time of lethal religious persecution: II-II q. 94 a. 2c. Paris is not worth a (charade) mass, and Sir Thomas More (within three years of the publication of Machiavelli's *The Prince*) chose to accept ruin and conviction as a traitor rather than lie on oath about Henry VIII's marriage.

[131] III *Sent.* d. 38 ex.

[132] Raymond Pennafort, master-general of the Dominicans while Aquinas was a student in Paris, dealt with the case in his *Summa de Paenitentia* (c. 1235) and recommended silence; if that would disclose the victim's whereabouts, change the subject; if that fails, then respond with an equivocal expression such as the Latin words which mean either

one 'may rightly hide the truth reasonably under some concealment {sub aliqua dissimulatione}'.[133] But it seems clear that what
underlies the classic position is a conception of human dignity and
worth {honestas}, precisely as it bears on the interpersonal act of
communication.

Those who lie to the Gestapo enter, so far forth, into the Nazis'
politics of manipulation. Those who instead refuse to make any
communication which would violate their own duties of non-
disclosure, and who remain silent or state a truth about themselves
but not about the victim's whereabouts, by their silence or their
(strictly limited) truth-telling affirm the human dignity of everyone
concerned, including even the Nazis, who have no right whatever
to be given the answers they are demanding. The good consequences of such an affirmation (and of refusing to join and promote
the culture of the liars) cannot be estimated, but should not be
overlooked when considering the bad consequences—equally
incalculable though more palpable and affecting—risked in rejecting the option of lying.

How serious is the wrongfulness of lying to save someone from
unjust physical or moral harm? The tradition followed by Aquinas
called such lies 'duty-related' {officiosa}[134] and holds that their

---

'He is not here' or 'He does not eat here': *Summa de Paenitentia*, 1 introd. 10 n. 6.
Equivocation is speech which expresses more than one proposition, so that the proposition which the speaker intends—and thus the mind and heart of the speaker—remains
unasserted: 'mental reservation'. Aquinas does not propose such ways of dealing with
situations of competing responsibilities, but his explanations of certain things said by
people presented in the scriptures as persons of complete virtue amount to accepting
some forms of equivocal speech and mental reservation—e.g. his analysis of Abraham's
statements (Gen. 12: 13–19, 20: 2–5) that his wife Sarah (whom Aquinas thinks was also
his niece—a kind of 'sister') was his sister: II-II q. 70 a. 1 ad 1, q. 110 a. 3 ad 3.

[133] II-II q. 110 a. 3 ad 4; substantially the same wording, in each case qualified by
'reasonable' or 'reasonably' {prudenter}, appears at q. 71 a. 3 ad 3 in relation to the
general's ruses in warfare and, by implication, non-disclosure of relevant facts by litigants. *Dissimulatio* (which in Aquinas most commonly means turning a blind eye) here
means keeping something hidden and should not be translated 'dissimulation', which in
English has lost the contrast with pretence {simulatio} and includes asserting a falsehood. For the whole point of q. 110 a. 3 ad 4 is to teach that asserting a falsehood is to be
shunned even if the consequences seem likely to be disastrous. A reply at least as subtle
as the Augustinian pair might include: 'You don't expect me to tell you that sort of thing.
Go ahead and search for yourselves if you want to.' Most discussions of such cases greatly
exaggerate the likelihood that the pursuing axeman or Nazi is willing to be blocked or
deflected by the householder's response. Distortion of this kind is endemic in utilitarian,
proportionalist, or other consequentialist hypotheticals, as in their 'calculations' or
'assessments' or 'weighings' of overall net good or harm.

[134] See II-II q. 110 a. 2c. The usual translations, 'officious' or 'useful', are unacceptable,
and even 'serviceable' seems inadequate; for such lies are not intermeddling, and are quite

wrongfulness, though real, is in itself[135] not serious.[136] Their moral deformity (wrongfulness) is not, as such, an injustice to others.[137]

Does that mean that the moral norm which excludes them is a mere ideal of lofty character? No. It is a moral directive of reason, an implication of the good of reason itself {bonum rationis} as that good involves (we may say) the person's integrity or authenticity—harmony of inner with outer aspects of the person—precisely as that integrity or authenticity bears on and indeed makes possible interpersonal communication. Such communication is central to the good of *societas* and is a requirement of love of neighbour as self. So the norm against the type of action summarily called lying—the type or species of action which we have now specified with more precision—excludes actions of that type because they cannot be willed without violating those higher principles requiring preservation of authenticity in communication. The resultant norm is not, 'Try to improve so that one day you will be able to live up to this ideal'. Nor is it, 'If you depart from this directive, your fault need not have been great'—true though that non-deliberative reflection may be. Rather, its content is simply, 'Exclude from your deliberations every option which includes the choice to lie'.

The principle on which even duty-related lying proceeds is implicitly, we may say, the consequentialist principle that one should assess ('weigh') the alternative future states of affairs which one anticipates as resulting from alternative options, and should choose the option from which one anticipates greater good or lesser bad results. And in the open horizons[138] of third-order, morally significant deliberation and choice, such an assessment is not rationally possible. For the results of such choices include the

different from lies which may well be useful to the liars but are not motivated by concern for fulfilling moral responsibilities {officia}.

[135] It may be made serious by being unfair or in breach of obligations which in fairness prevail over the presumptive duty to prevent harm to the person(s) whom one seeks to protect by lying. So a lie to save one's friend from conviction and execution by due process of law would always be a serious wrong, though the wrongfulness of a lie to save someone from unjust conviction (e.g. conviction based on false witnesses or biased judge or jury) would not (if not on oath) be serious: II-II q. 70 a. 4c and obj. 2 and ad 2.

[136] II-II q. 110 a. 4c, q. 70 a. 4c; III *Sent.* d. 38 a. 4c and ad 4, a. 5 ad 3 (generically even less serious a wrongdoing—though more of a lie—than idle exaggeration or practical joking {iocosum mendacium}). For the tradition from Augustine, see Gratian, *Decretum*, 2. 2. 22 q. 2, esp c. 14.

[137] See *In Isa.* 59 ad v. 3 (lines 31–3); II-II q. 70 a. 4c; n. 143 below; cf. 1 *Sent.* d. 43 q. 2 a. 2c ('one cannot lie without injustice'—at least some offence against general justice: see ad 4). [138] See *ScG* III c. 12 n. 7 [1964]; II. 6 at nn. 68–73 above.

determining of oneself, of one's character—and that of one's communities and of all who approve of one's actions—around their rational content (specific norm and 'justifying' principles). The impact of such determination of character on the whole lives of individuals and communities far outruns any assessment we could undertake to make by reason; there is no one unit of assessment available for measuring the value of whole lives. So the consequentialist principle can never do more than 'rationalize'—give the deceptive appearance of rational judgement to—choices motivated by something other than that principle. Even duty-related lying is on a slippery slope. To say this is not to make some sort of 'sociological prediction' or to allege some 'abuse of the moral principle', but is precisely to point to the absence of any principled stopping-point. Lower down the slope are the lies people tell to gain some advantage, or to inflict some harm, or out of indifference or hostility to the truth about important matters—all of which are more or less incompatible with love of neighbour as oneself and indeed with the very substance of human association,[139] and so are injustices and seriously wrongful.[140]

The unconditional, exceptionless negative norm excluding lying from upright deliberation and choice is part of the backbone of morality and law. But some forms of fraud and dishonest dealing involve no lying. One's responsibility not to conceal (leave hidden) facts which it is unfair to conceal can be both wide and serious.[141]

As for one's strong but affirmative and therefore not exceptionless responsibility to be a person of authenticity {virtus veritatis}, showing oneself in word and deed as the person one really is,[142] it too has radical implications. Systematically manipulating others to allow and afford one the satisfactions one wants is a life-project which—as Plato's and Machiavelli's amoralists make plain—requires that one profess fairness and decency, and conceal one's

---

[139] II-II q. 109 a. 3 ad 1: 'people cannot live together unless they believe each other as people communicating truth to each other'. Without this trust 'human *societas* cannot survive' (ibid.)—which is not a prediction that every lie will result in open anarchy and violent war of all upon all, but a sober assessment of lying's intrinsic detrimental impact on, and incompatibility with, the fellowship—and trust {fides} (*Trin.* q. 3 a. 1, lines 98–105 [lect. 1 q. 1[3] a. 1c]—which is the substance of any decent relationship that might exist between one person and another, i.e. between the liar and the person or persons deceived (not to mention the relationships between those other people whose trust in each other's communications is damaged by the liar's act).   [140] II-II q. 110 a. 4c.

[141] e.g. II-II q. 77 a. 2c and a. 3; VI. 4 n. 92 below (non-disclosure by sellers).

[142] I q. 16 a. 4 ad 3 (n. 118 above).

manipulative purposes. To notice the tawdriness of this inauthenticity[143] is to acknowledge a good which beckons one towards a life
actually lived in line with the fairness and decency one has been
professing, and no doubt often demanding of others.

v.6. 'Prudence', 'Virtues', and Exceptionless Specific Norms

There is wide opposition today to Aquinas' thesis that some true
moral norms exceptionlessly exclude certain types of act specifi-
able not in terms already morally loaded (such as 'cruel') but simply in terms of their object, i.e. proximate intention (such as to kill
an innocent, to copulate outside marriage, to assert what one does
not believe). The opposition takes various forms, partly cumula-
tive, partly incompatible with each other.[h]

One strategy is to deny that Aquinas held the thesis, or at least to
deny that it is compatible with his own deeper principles. The text
most often cited to support this denial concerns, indeed, the general issue we have been considering: the way down from highest
practical and moral principles to specific moral norms. General
principles {communia principia} of practical reason, says Aquinas,
have the same truth and correctness for everyone {apud omnes},
but specific conclusions {propria[e] conclusiones} of practical reason do not. It is right and true for everyone that one should act
reasonably, and it does follow as a specific conclusion from that
principle that what one has been lent for safe-keeping one should
return on demand. But although this conclusion is true for most
situations {ut in pluribus}, there are occasions when it would be
harmful and unreasonable to return what one is keeping, e.g. if the
thing deposited was a weapon and the depositor wants it back to
use in attacks on one's own people. And Aquinas here states, quite
generally, that because practical reasoning deals with non-necessary matters {contingentia}, its propositions become more and
more subject to exception the further one descends from high-level
general principle to specific conclusion.[144] Is he teaching that the
moral norms which elsewhere he seems to propose as exceptionless

---

[143] The lie is something morally tawdry {turpe} even when not harmful to anyone else:
Eth. iv. 15 n. 9 [839].

[144] I-II q. 94 a. 4c: 'quanto magis ad propria descenditur, tanto magis invenitur
defectus'.

are really no more than generalizations, true in general {ut in pluribus} but not always?

By no means. In fact, his own statement here—that moral norms are generalizations and are subject to exceptions—is no more than a generalization subject to important exceptions. Aquinas makes this clear in many ways, above all by distinguishing between affirmative and negative moral norms. Some moral norms are negative, directing us *not* to do acts of a more or less specific type. But most are affirmative, directing one *to do* such and such. Affirmative moral principles and norms hold 'always but not for every occasion {semper sed non ad semper}'. So, for example, the obligation to return things deposited for safe-keeping is in a sense universal, always a factor in moral deliberation about the things in one's possession. Yet there are occasions—those of the kind mentioned by Aquinas—when it should not (and therefore, properly understood, does not) govern those deliberations but is superseded by other obligations of justice. Such norms, though always somehow[145] relevant, leave it to one's moral judgement to discern the times, places, and other circumstances of their directiveness.

But negative moral norms can be, and a number in truth are, binding and governing always and on every occasion {semper et ad semper}.[146] Negative moral norms of this sort are, in short, both specific—immediately applicable without further moral reasoning—and exceptionless. Aquinas' generalization that norms become more subject to exception as they become more specific is just that, a generalization subject to a class of exceptions on which Aquinas himself firmly insists: the negative exceptionless specific moral norms. And it is these norms, relatively few in number, which give social life and just law their backbone. They make some of one's rights inalienable and, in an important sense,

---

[145] At least as a matter of one's dispositions (character; readiness in principle): *Mal.* q. 7 a. 1 ad 9: 'habitualiter'; III *Sent.* d. 25 q. 2 a. 1 sol. 2 ad 3: 'de actibus virtutum'.

[146] For this distinction between affirmative norms (e.g. honour your parents; do good to your neighbour; feed your children)—norms essential to a morally good life, always somehow relevant, but leaving to one's good judgement the discerning of the times, places, and other circumstances in which they will be decisively directive (they oblige 'always but not for every occasion {semper sed non ad semper}'—and negative norms binding *semper et ad semper* (because specifying and excluding acts which are 'bad in themselves and in no way can be rightly {bene} done'), see e.g. II-II q. 33 a. 2c, q. 79 a. 3 ad 3; *Mal.* q. 7 a. 1 ad 8; *Corr.* a. 1c and obj. 4 and ad 4; III *Sent.* d. 25 q. 2 a. 1 sol. 2 ad 3, IV *Sent.* d. 17 q. 3 a. 1 sol. 4 ad 3; *In Rom.* 13. 2 ad v. 9 [1052] (negative norms are more urgent and obvious as implications of the supreme principle of love of neighbour as self); n. 163 below.

absolute (though Aquinas uses neither of these words to make the point).

Some people have thought that the norms proposed by Aquinas as exceptionless naïvely attribute moral evil to items of physical behaviour (e.g. speaking knowingly falsely; or engaging in sodomy) and therefore cannot be true. Others, by contrast, have claimed that these norms are exceptionless only because they contain a tacit moral qualifier which makes them true tautologously—necessarily and therefore exceptionlessly. So 'Adultery is always wrong' is exceptionlessly true (they say) because 'adultery' *means* 'a married person's *unjustified* extra-marital intercourse'; 'Lying is always excluded' is exceptionlessly true because 'lying' unlike 'speaking falsely {falsiloquium}' refers to those falsehoods which are unwarranted; and so on. Thus a position which, on the first view, seems one of 'noble simplicity',[147] perhaps harsh, unworldly, or naïve but at least substantive and worth controverting, dissolves, on the second view, into mere exhortation ('paraenesis') to do what is right and avoid what is wrong, offering no definition of the line between them.

The first view was clearly envisaged and rejected by Aquinas at the outset of his writings on morality. In the second quarter of the twelfth century, Peter Abelard had argued, ambiguously, that behaviour is morally indifferent and the morality of acts depends entirely on intention. He was widely understood as denying that there are exceptionless, non-tautologous negative norms. So within a decade or two Peter Lombard's great Parisian textbook, the *Sentences*, attacked Abelard's position by contrasting it with passages from Augustine's treatises against lying, interpreted by Lombard as teaching that the acts specified in the exceptionless negative norms of Jewish and Christian tradition are called wrong 'in themselves' {mala in se} precisely because their wrongfulness does *not* come from the purpose, will, intention, or motivation of the person who does them. Aquinas magisterially disagrees with both Abelard (as widely understood) and Lombard. There are indeed acts each of which is wrong in itself and cannot in any way be rightly done {de se malus, qui nullo modo bene fieri potest}. But such acts are wrongful precisely by reason of the acting person's will, intention,

---

[147] Strauss (1953: 163); a 'simplicity' which (whether or not it confuses physical patterns or biological teleology with moral kinds, which is not Strauss's concern) does, in Strauss's view, 'considerably restrict' statesmanship (164) and overlooks the 'sad' exigencies of the common good (160); cf. Finnis (1996b: 3).

purpose. When I do such an act there may be nothing wrong with my further or general intentions {voluntas intendens}, my ultimate motivating purpose {finis ultimus}, e.g. to give money to the poor. What is wrongful (and what is picked out for exclusion by the relevant negative norm) is, rather, my choice, my *electio* or *voluntas eligens*, my immediate purpose {obiectum proximum; finis proximus}, e.g. to forge this testament. The goodness or badness, rightness or wrongness, of my 'exterior act' (i.e. everything I do to carry out my choice, even what lies entirely within my mind, as in wrongful thought) depends entirely on the goodness or badness, rightness or wrongness, of my will, my choice, my immediate purpose, my proximate intention, i.e. on what I choose and try to do, including what I choose and attempt as a means to my ultimate or ulterior purpose(s).[148] Sodomy, fornication, and masturbation, for example, are always wrong because any choice to get or give sexual satisfaction in such a way deviates inevitably (and widely) from, and indeed is opposed to, the goods of marriage and inner integrity (v.4 above).

As for the second view, that acts excluded by exceptionless moral norms are immoral merely 'by definition', it is obviously incompatible with Aquinas' discussions of killing the innocent, sexual deviations, and lying (v.3–5 above). To the analyses already given, add a single passage of unmistakable clarity. One of Aristotle's Greek commentators had argued that acts which are generally 'base', such as lying and adultery, become morally acceptable when chosen for their beneficial effect {pro utilitate}, e.g. having sex {misceri} with the wife of a tyrant so as to overthrow him.[149] Aquinas takes up this position as an objection: 'Whatever is intrinsically {ex genere} wrongful may not be done for any purpose however good . . . But as a commentator on the *Ethics* says, an equitable, i.e. morally good, man will commit adultery {adulterium} with a tyrant's wife, so as to kill him and liberate his homeland. So adultery is not intrinsically {secundum se} wrong.'[150] The objection

---

[148] II *Sent.* d. 40 a. 2c and ad 2 and ad 3; and see *Mal.* q. 2 a. 2 ad 8. Aquinas never wavers from his teaching that behaviour's moral character depends totally on the moral character of the deliberating and choosing which makes that behaviour voluntary and thus 'morally significant action' {actus in genere/specie moris} of some specific sort: see e.g. *Mal.* q. 2 a. 2 ad 13; *ST* I-II q. 20 a. 2c (where *ex actu volito* is synonymous with *ex obiecto proprio [voluntatis]*); q. 72 a. 8c: a wrongful act belongs to a specific kind by virtue of the act itself *according as it is directed towards the [proximate] object(ive) which the wrongdoer intends.*   [149] See Finnis (1991a: 34).

[150] *Mal.* q. 15 a. 1 obj. 5.

treats 'adultery' as meaning, not unjustified or unwarranted sex, but a class of sexual act describable in morally neutral terms; on this basis, then, the objection contends that adultery (an act of that type-description) is sometimes justifiable or good and right. Aquinas accepts this use of the term 'adultery' and simply rejects the claim that acts of that description can ever be justified even by the intention of averting such great evils. 'On this matter that commentator is not to be supported. For one ought not to commit adultery for any benefit {utilitate} whatever, just as one should never lie whatever the benefit.'[151] And this does no more than repeat positions central to Aquinas' treatise on killing and lying: 'every lie is wrong . . . it is not morally acceptable {licitum} to tell a lie even when doing so would free someone else from peril, whatever the peril [even death]'.[152] 'In no case and in no way is it permissible {licet} to kill an innocent.'[153] One can never rationally judge that killing the innocent, lying, committing adultery, etc. are truly 'the lesser evil' which might rightly be chosen for the sake of 'greater good'.[154]

Some people have hoped to soften these positions by appealing to Aquinas' acceptance of Aristotle's conception of *phronēsis*—in Aquinas' Latin, *prudentia*—as the virtue of practical reasonableness which in (and only in) the concrete situation 'has an eye for' what will be the right course of action, a 'seeing' (so to speak) which is no mere deduction from general rules.[155] Some people add that, since Aquinas' *prudentia* is itself radically dependent upon the possession of the other moral virtues, the moral life can in no way be assimilated to the application of rules such as might be taught by some book, or 'doctrine'; and so, they conclude, the apparently exceptionless moral norms do not really exclude from deliberation any options attractive to a prudence which considers *all* the circumstances. Others again claim to detect in Aquinas an

---

[151] *Mal.* q. 15 a. 1 ad 5: 'ille commentator in hoc non est sustinendus: pro nulla enim utilitate debet aliquis adulterium committere, sicut nec mendacium dicere debet aliquis propter utilitatem aliquam . . .'
[152] II-II q. 110 a. 3c and obj. 4 and ad 4; also q. 69 a. 2c: 'it is in no case permissible for anyone to assert a falsehood {falsitatem proponere in nullo casu licet alicui}'.
[153] II-II q. 64 a. 6, introd., and c, I-II q. 88 a. 6 ad 3; *Mal.* q. 13 a. 4 ad 11 ('never {nunquam}'). See also *Eth.* III. 2 n. 4 [395].
[154] In every context in which a moral issue of this kind is to be resolved, Aquinas refuses the invitation to resolve it by identifying the lesser evil: IV *Sent.* d. 6 q. 1 a. 1 sol. 1 ad 4 (with obj. 4) (killing); d. 9 a. 5 sol. 1 ad 3 (with obj. 3); *ST* II-II q. 110 a. 3 obj. 4 and ad 4 (lying); q. 68 a. 11 obj. 3 and ad 3 (killing); III q. 80 a. 6 obj. 2 and ad 2. See also *Corr.* a. 1 ad 4; IV *Sent.* d. 9 a. 4 sol. 2 ad 3. [155] *Nic. Eth.* 6. 12. 1143^{b}11–14.

esoteric distinction between an imperfect morality (for rogues or children) of necessarily over-simplified law (*lex*) and a higher and always more supple and equitable morality of right (*ius*).[i]

All these views foist on Aquinas a set of false contrasts. For Aquinas, the good of virtue—any virtue, including the moral and intellectual virtue of *prudentia*, and the virtue (justice) whose object is *ius*—is a good (the *bonum rationis*) to which we are directed by one of the first principles of practical reasonableness and natural law. And the way down from first and most general principles to specific moral norms is a way which will not be clear to those in whom a habit of vice has supplanted *prudentia*.[156] *Prudentia* is nothing other than the disposition to guide one's choices and actions by practical reasonableness. So it is informed and directed at every stage by every relevant practical principle and true moral norm.[157] What else could those principles and norms ever guide? And in the first instance *prudentia* will be guided by the norms which identify and exclude wrongful killing, adultery, false witness, and other offences against justice.[158] Such injustices cannot be justified by concern for the common good;[159] indeed, the common good is inherently preserved and promoted by the good (e.g. the life) of innocents so injured.[160]

Of course, affirmative moral norms leave much to be *discerned*, in relation to their bearing on particular situations and relationships. This conscientious discernment {aestimatio},[161] which far outruns any 'application' of rules comparable to the working out of theorems from axioms, will go well only when one's dispositions and feelings are constitutionally ordered by all the virtues. The question what *should* be chosen and done here and now always

---

[156] See e.g. I-II q. 94 a. 6c: depraved customs and corrupted dispositions have blinded some peoples to some of the specific norms {praecepta secundaria} of the natural law, e.g. those which exclude robbery, bestial or homosexual sex acts, or prostitution (IV *Sent.* d. 33 q. 1 a. 3 sol. 1 (= *Supp.* q. 65 a. 3) ad 2 (with obj. 2)).

[157] Every immorality involves a failing in *prudentia*, and every failing in *prudentia* involves a deviation from one or more of the relevant moral norms {divertens a regulis quibus ratio prudentiae rectificatur}: II-II q. 53 a. 1c.   [158] See II-II q. 56 a. 1c and ad 1.

[159] II-II q. 68 a. 3c: 'nullus debet alicui nocere iniuste ut bonum commune promoveat'.

[160] II-II q. 64 a. 6c; IX. 2 at n. 41. This makes sense only if *the common good* is taken to include exceptionless respect for the good—and the rights—of all the members of the community considered one by one as ends in themselves (and see n. 167 and x. 4 n. 85).

[161] See e.g. IV *Sent.* d. 29 a. 2c (= *Supp.* q. 47 a. 2c); II-II q. 47 a. 13 ad 2, q. 49 a. 2 ad 1 and ad 3, a. 4; and n. 162 below.

goes beyond what could be stated in a general norm,[162] and calls for such full-blooded *prudentia*. But prior to[163] this perfecting of deliberation by all the virtues, the virtue of *prudentia* should have played its other essential role: of excluding from one's deliberation all those options which involve the violation of specific negative moral norms and are therefore unjust—a violation of rights—and/ or unchaste or duplicitous . . .

The interplay of negative and affirmative moral norms in the life of virtue can be illustrated by the role of the good of *fides* in the largest individual and social project and commitment most people ever make: marriage. The negative norms of fidelity exceptionlessly exclude, most importantly, adultery but also, quite significantly, the de-personalized sexual use of one's spouse for one's own pleasure. The affirmative norms of fidelity direct one to creative and loyal co-operation in the conduct of the household and all the family affairs, above all the discharge of all the duties of parents to their children. These norms, though in their differing ways stringent and demanding, call for the constant exercise of judgement, inventiveness, alertness to need and advantage, discipline and relaxation, and all the other intellectual and moral virtues or aspects of virtue. Anything less violates the rights of spouse and children. There is thus a deep, mutually reinforcing continuity of rationale and significance between the negative and the affirmative;[164] a legalistic attitude to conjugal and domestic morality does not measure up.

The same interplay of affirmative and negative is manifest in the other fields of human fulfilment, loss, and harm. Those who most strictly teach the inviolability of innocent human life and the

---

[162] See e.g. II-II q. 140 a. 1 ad 2 ('*what should be done* in situations of danger cannot be inferred from anything general {ea quae sunt agenda in periculis non possunt ad aliquid commune reduci} in the way that *what should not be done* can {sicut ea quae sunt vitanda}'); *In Gal.* 6. 1 ad v. 1 [343] ('it cannot be determinately known {sciri determinate} when affirmative precepts create a definite obligation'). Still, *acts of virtue* are the subject not only of negative but also of affirmative norms which call for much judgement of many circumstances {praecepto affirmativo praecipitur actus virtutis, ad cuius rectitudinem multae circumstantiae concurrunt}: *Corr.* a. 1c; see also II-II q. 31 a. 3 ad 3 (one must make an assessment {aestimatio} which cannot be settled by any general rule {quae non potest communi regula determinari}): II-II q. 53 a. 4 ad 3.

[163] The negative requirements of morality, though ultimately the less important (II-II q. 79 a. 1c and ad 3), are always to be satisfied before the affirmative: I-II q. 72 a. 6 ad 2 (which also notes that the affirmative and negative precepts do not belong to different virtues, but to different levels of virtue {gradus virtutis}); q. 100 a. 7 ad 1.

[164] An affirmative norm (e.g. look after, and return, what you have borrowed) is often implied or included {comprehenditur} in a negative (e.g. do not steal): I-II q. 100 a. 4 ad 3.

---

wrongness of lying can quite naturally—reasonably—be found promoting the most far-reaching arrangements for medical treatment and the nursing of the sick, and founding and maintaining schools for everyone and universities, libraries, archives, and astronomical observatories for free scholarly and scientific inquiry.

For, in sum, reason's negative, exceptionless moral norms give to one's deliberations—and to morality and law themselves—their rightful firm boundaries {termini},[165] and thereby delineate indispensable protective human rights. But reason's affirmative norms, being open-ended in their application, call for the full play of all the virtues under the shaping direction of that *prudentia* by which one pursues the good of practical reasonableness along with all the other aspects of the flourishing of persons, the personal goods to which reason's first practical principles direct us.

v.7. *Persons as Ends in Themselves: Freedom and Equality*

In Aquinas' understanding of justice, rights are as fundamental as duties, and duties as fundamental as rights. We have duties which are not duties of justice, so *duty* is the wider concept. But when a duty is to another human person, it is a duty of justice, and that other person's right is its very object or point.

And justice is between equals. By nature—that is, precisely as human persons—all human beings are both free and equal.[166] 'Free' here refers both to the radical capacity for free choices, in which one is master of oneself, and to one's freedom from any justified domination by other human persons; to be free is to be—unlike a slave—an end in oneself.[167]

---

[165] II-II q. 79 a. 2c.

[166] 'Omnes homines natura sunt pares': II-II q. 104 a. 5c; 'natura omnes homines aequales in libertate fecit': II *Sent.* d. 44 q. 1 a. 3 ad 1; 'ad naturalia omnes sunt pares': IV *Sent.* d. 36 a. 2 ad 1.

[167] II *Sent.* d. 44 q. 1 a. 3 ad 1: 'nature made all of us {omnes homines} equal in liberty . . . for whatever is free is . . . an end in itself. For by our nature none of us is ordered to another as to an end {liberum . . . est quod *sui causa* est. Unus enim homo ex natura sua non ordinatur ad alterum sicut ad finem}'; also ibid. a. 3c; *ST* I q. 96 a. 4c; *ScG* III c. 112 n. 2 [2857]. Since 'cause' includes 'final' cause (= end) as well as efficient, formal, and material causes, the idea that one is free inasmuch as one is 'cause of oneself {causa sui}' includes the notions that (1) one is the source of one's own freely chosen actions and is not simply pushed or pulled by outside forces, and (2) that one acts for one's own sake and on one's own account and not *merely* for the benefit of and as instrument of another

There are many differences—inequalities—between persons, and some of them can give reason for one person to be subject to another's justified governance {praelatio; dominium}. Precisely in those respects, relations between these persons are relationships of justice, in a qualified, not central sense of justice.[168] So relationships between parents and children are not straightforwardly relationships of justice and right.[169] Still, Aquinas' statements to this effect must be understood very narrowly. Children are *owed*—and so have a right to—nurture, education, and moral formation {disciplina} by their parents.[170] More basically, children have as much right as anyone else not to be deliberately killed, raped, lied to, etc. by their parents—in each case an unqualified and exceptionless or absolute right. Indeed, it is only within a (wide but) limited range of matters that the person who is a child stands to the persons who are its parents *as child* {inquantum filius} to *parent*. Outside those matters—the range of matters involved in the common good of the family and the needs of the child's nurture, education, and *disciplina*—the child, even the pre-pubertal child, stands to parent as one free and equal person to another {inquantum est homo}:[171] fully entitled to disobey.[172]

Similarly, Aquinas' statements about the subordination of women must be read with great caution (though even then they seem seriously flawed).[j] The starting-point is that the mind {mens}, the intellect and will,[173] which makes us images of the divine—our human kind of soul or spirit[174] (v.8 below)—belongs, *without*

---

person (as a slave does): see *Meta*. I. 3 n. 7 [58]; I q. 83 a. I ad 3; III *Sent*. d. 9 q. I a. I sol. I ad I; *Reg*. I. I [I. 2] [10] [746]. See also IX. 2 at n. 33, x. 4 at nn. 85–6 below.

[168] II-II q. 57 a. 4c: 'non simpliciter iustum'.

[169] e.g. II-II q. 57 a. 4c and ad 2 ('*inquantum filius* est aliquid patris'); III q. 85 a. 3c. The same is true of relations between master and servant {servus}; see generally n. l.

[170] *Quodl*. II q. 5 a. Ic [line 53]: '*debet* pater filio non solum nutrimentum sed etiam disciplinam'.

[171] II-II q. 57 a. 4 ad 2 (and in this respect the duties to the children—or servants—are indeed 'in a certain way {aliquo modo}' duties of justice *simpliciter*; indeed, in these relationships we can be said to be concerned with justice and right in the full sense {perfecta ratio justi vel juris}; see also I q. 21 a. Ic, II-II q. 58 a. 7 ad 3).

[172] *Quodl*. II q. 5 a. Ic [line 42]: the child's duty of obedience extends only as far as the parent's right to rule {ius praelationis}; II-II q. 104 a. 5c; VII. 6 n. 101 below. Minimally, the child is never bound to obey a parental order to do something wrong: see *In Rom*. 13. I ad v. 2 [1028].   [173] I q. 93 a. 7c.   [174] *In I Cor*. 11. 2 ad v. 7 [604].

distinction[175] or difference,[176] to the males and females of the human species;[177] it is found 'as much in man as in woman {tam in viro quam in muliere}'.[178] All the rights which belong to us as human persons belong to females equally with males, including not only the rights not to be physically harmed, cheated, robbed, defamed, deceived, and so forth, but also the right to choose a vocation such as marriage or the 'religious life' and to decide for oneself *which* spouse, religious 'house', etc.,[179] and the right to subscribe or refuse to subscribe to a religious faith.[180] Women have legal and moral rights of ownership, management, and disposition of property.[181]

Turning to the affairs of the family household, Aquinas ascribes a limited governing responsibility and authority to the husband. Every complex co-ordination requires unanimity or, in default of unanimity, authority. In dealings with children, domestic servants, and persons outside the family, a rule requiring agreement between the spouses for every binding decision would sometimes result in paralysis and default to a very bad outcome. The responsibility of making decisions in default of agreement among partners, where the partnership's common good is seriously in issue and dissolution of the partnership is not a reasonable option, may be assigned by prior agreement—a possibility which Aquinas neglects to consider—but failing that must in the last analysis rest with someone identifiable independently of agreement. Aquinas' argument for locating this final authority with the husband appeals to a number of factual generalizations. At least one of these relies on evidence rendered unreliable by cultural patterns—of education, learned expectations, and so forth—tending to exaggerate inevitable sexual ('gender') differences.

One of Aquinas' generalizations is that a mother puts more of

---

[175] I q. 93 a. 6 ad 2: the image of God is common to both sexes {utrique sexui est communis} because it consists in our minds, in which there is no distinction between the sexes {cum sit secundum mentem, in qua *non est distinctio sexuum*}.

[176] IV *Sent*. d. 25 q. 2 a. 1 sol. 1 (= *Supp*. q. 39 a. 1) ad 2: 'women do not differ from men in matters pertaining to the soul {secundum rem, in his quae sunt animae mulier non differt a viro}'; *In I Cor*. 11 ad v. 7 (unpub. Leonine text, Busa 1992): 'vir . . . non diffe[rt] secundum spiritum a muliere'.

[177] *In I Cor*. 11. 2 ad v. 7 [607]: 'esse imaginem Dei commune est viro et mulieri'.

[178] I q. 93 a. 4 ad 1; *In I Cor*. 11. 3 ad v. 10 [614]: 'tam mulier quam vir est ad imaginem Dei . . . mulier est imago Dei sicut et vir'.   [179] See VII.6 at nn. 96–8 below.

[180] e.g. IV *Sent*. d. 39 a. 4 ad 4: at puberty, a child can freely opt for unbelief {poterit libere sequi . . . matrem infidelem}.

[181] e.g. II-II q. 32 a. 8 ad 2; see also IV *Sent*. d. 49 q. 4 (= *Supp*. q. 95) a. 1 ad 1, a. 3c.

herself {magis de suo} into the children than a father does.[182] Another is that men have the greater physical strength for confronting, for example, unruly children,[183] not to mention other persons with whom the family must deal. A third generalization is his claim that naturally men have *judgement* {discretio rationis} which is the less deflected by emotion and better adapted to giving instruction.[184] Here Aquinas is using the term 'naturally' in the way characteristic of first-order (natural-scientific) discourse, namely to signify what holds in the majority of cases {ut in pluribus}.[185] He accepts that in some cases the woman will have the steadier and better judgement (*use* of reason) and will.[186] As we have seen, he is clear that the intelligence and will of men and women is generically equal {communis}.[187] But there remains his claim that in women this intelligence and will is more subject—by and large {ut in pluribus}—to the unsteadying influence and flux of the emotions.[188] Given that the ultimate disposition of the household's affairs needs a firmly rational direction, and that the general, constitutive norms of an institution like marriage and domestic life must be apt for what holds more often than not, rather than for less common cases,[189] this claim about the influence of emotions serves as the final, more vulnerable premiss for his conclusion that

---

[182] III *Sent.* d. 29 a. 7 ad 4.

[183] *ScG* III c. 122 n. 8 [2954]. Still, though both parents should be involved in education, instruction, nutrition, and discipline (IV *Sent.* d. 33 q. 1 a. 3 sol. 1c), women have the greater role {feminis maxime incumbit} in this: IV *Sent.* d. 27 q. 1 a. 1 sol. 2c.

[184] I q. 92 a. 1 ad 2, II-II q. 156 a. 1 ad 1 ('iudicium rationis firmum'); *Eth.* VII. 5 n. 9 [1376].

[185] *Eth.* VII. 5 n. 9 [1376] particularly stresses this sense of 'naturally' as 'generally but subject to exceptions', precisely in asserting women's comparatively greater tendency (caused by physiological factors) to be led, to give in to cajoling and pressure, and so forth.

[186] II-II q. 156 a. 1 ad 1. In the trials and agonies of martyrdom, some women have shown themselves the equal of men in inner human strength {interioris hominis virtute viros aequaverunt}, and others have shown themselves stronger than men {fortiores viris}: III q. 72 a. 8 ad 3 (quoting Chrysostom). 'One comes across women who in soul are better than many men': IV *Sent.* d. 25 q. 2 a. 1 sol. 1 ad 1. One finds among women extremes of piety and extremes of cruelty: *In Matt.* 14 ad v. 8 [1228].   [187] See n. 175 above.

[188] II-II q. 156 a. 1 ad 1; *Pol.* I. 10 n. 9 [159]. So the relative weakness is bodily {propter imperfectionem corporalis naturae} (*Eth.* VII. 7 n. 9 [1376]) rather than intellectual or moral (understanding and will, as such). Thus, in heaven, when people's bodily make-up will reflect and respond to the quality of their soul (intellect and will), males and females will still be different, but the differences between persons in bodily and spiritual *quality* will not be correlated with sexual differences (but on merit) and no one will be deficient by reason of being female rather than male (or vice versa): see II *Sent.* d. 21 q. 2 a. 1 ad 2, IV *Sent.* d. 44 q. 1 a. 3 sol. 3 ad 3; x. 6 at n. 167 below.

[189] See *ScG* III c. 122 n. 7 [2953]; *Mal.* q. 15 a. 2 ad 12.

---

that ultimate leadership should be the husband's, as a responsibility owed to the wife[190] and children.[191]

Aquinas' standard statements about leadership within the family[192] certainly do not sufficiently deploy his own understanding of the complementarity of male and female, and of the equality and mutuality proper between spouses.[193] The model of unitary command appropriate for co-ordination in battle is applied to a sphere of *prudentia* much farther removed from the technical.[194] The assumptions and social forms of his era, and his corroborating Aristotelian generalization about domination by emotion, provide a distorted image of the domestic partnership of man and woman—and can have as their side-effect the surrender by husbands to their own deflecting emotional urges: to dominate, take the easier course, follow self-preference, and the like. Still, Aquinas' principles, and even his particular conclusions taken as a whole, do not underwrite domination and exploitation of wives by husbands. For him, authority is always responsibility, and is justified only so far as it is exercised for *common* good—in this case the good common to the spouses and their children. Moreover, authoritative decisions must follow deliberation, part of which is the gathering of information and the sharing of experience; so any important judgement about the household's affairs should, except no doubt in some emergencies, be informed by the experience and mature judgement of all concerned. Where discussion yields consensus, authority need not be exercised by anyone. And Aquinas himself accepts that there is a natural—rational—division of managerial roles and

---

[190] IV *Sent.* d. 32 a. 3c: '*tenetur* vir uxori in . . . dispensatione domus ad id quod viri est'. [191] See n. 170 above.

[192] e.g. II-II q. 164 a. 2 ad 1; and some incidental statements, e.g. IV *Sent.* d. 37 q. 2 a. 1 (= *Supp.* q. 60 a. 1) c and ad 4.

[193] In those matters which do not concern the ultimate direction {dispositio; dispensatio} of the household—'or matters of that sort supplementary {superaddita} to household management [e.g. selling oneself into another's service]' (IV *Sent.* d. 36 a. 3 (= *Supp.* q. 52 a. 3) ad 3)—Aquinas is clear that neither spouse can properly exercise authority over the other. Here man and woman, precisely in marriage—and, above all, in relation to marital intercourse, 'and in matters which concern one's organic integrity and sustenance {ad naturam spectant}' (ibid.: 'husband and wife are to be judged as equals {ad paria}')—have equal rights and responsibilities: II-II q. 32 a. 8 ad 2 ('aequalis in actu matrimonii'); *In I Cor.* 7. 1 ad v. 3 [321] ('ad paria iudicantur'); IV *Sent.* d. 32 a. 3c (= *Supp.* q. 64 a. 3c) ('aequales in reddendo et petendo debitum'; the concerns about nobility in the action are not repeated in the later works cited). There is no double standard in relation to marital intercourse or to non-marital sex, or in relation to the separation which can be an appropriate response to misconduct: IV *Sent.* d. 35 a. 4 ('ad paria iudicari'); ad 5.

[194] See VII.5 at nn. 76–9 below.

responsibilities within the family,[195] that good leaders do not take what fittingly pertains to those whom they lead,[196] and that the reasonable husband does not usurp {praeripit} roles which belong to his partner {socia}[197] in the domestic, marital friendship {amicitia}.[198] The husband's authority in relation to the wife is a paradigm case, he says, of non-plenary, limited, constitutional authority;[199] it leaves the wife responsible for directing and managing many things. First and last, their relationship is a friendship between free, equal, and complementary people[200] whose common good includes and is focused upon their children.[201]

As to the wider community, Aquinas makes no objection to the current {nunc} possibilities for the exercise of secular (e.g. royal) authority by women.[202] On the other hand, he accepts without complaint the near-universal traditional constitutional arrangements in which women, albeit citizens, had no right to participate in elections as candidates or voters or to exercise judicial power.[203] He seems content with the generalization that men have better and more efficacious practical judgement, and draws no political conclusions from the fact—which he acknowledges[204]—that, even if the generalization be true, there must be many women who have better practical judgement than many men, and some whose soundness of judgement is superior to most men's. He makes no challenge to Aristotle's judgement (as he reads it) that women are needed for household management and so should 'always abstain' from political activities {operibus civilibus}.[205, k] The conclusion does not follow from the premiss with anything like the universality he seems to take for granted. So this, like his very thin account of the role of the mother in the centre of a family, his unbalanced statements about authority in the household, and his mildly liberal but insufficiently radical account of servitude,[1] is a

---

[195] *Eth.* VIII. 12 n. 20 [1721].   [196] *Eth.* VIII. 11 n. 7 [1694].

[197] The wife (unlike a mistress {concubina}) is fellow partner in the management of the family and the sharing out of tasks: IV *Sent.* d. 33 q. 1 a. 3 sol. 3c. See also *Eth.* VIII. 10 n. 13 [1684].   [198] *Eth.* VIII. 11 n. 7 [1694] (Leonine text).

[199] *Pol.* I. 10 n. 2 [152]; and see VIII.2 at n. 26 below.

[200] *ScG* III c. 124 nn. 4 and 5 [2972–3] (polygamy violates this equality and freedom from servility).

[201] IV *Sent.* d. 33 q. 2 a. 1c: 'proles sit commune bonum viri et uxoris'.

[202] IV *Sent.* d. 25 q. 2 a. 1 sol. 1 ad 2; and see VIII.2 at n. 26 below.

[203] It does not belong to women as such to be citizens in the full sense {non competit simpliciter esse cives}, although full citizenship can be given to women of excellence {virtutis}: I-II q. 105 a. 3 ad 1; II. 7 at n. 82 above.   [204] See n. 186 above.

[205] *Pol.* II. 5 n. 12 [218]; and see n. k below.

part of his social and political theory open to notable improvement. The principles for the necessary revision are all, as we have seen, available in his account of human freedom and equality.

v.8. *The Root of Human Dignity: Our Bodies' Formative Principle*

Every member of the human species is entitled to justice. So, since the object of justice is always someone's right {ius}, there are rights which every member of our species is entitled to: human rights. But it would be equivocal and misleading to say, without clarification, that we have these rights *because* we are human. Rather, we each have them because every individual member of the species has the dignity of being a person.[206] And this is not a 'status' to be conferred or withdrawn, but a reality to be acknowledged. It is a truth already grasped in one's understanding of basic reasons for actions: goods good for me and anyone like me—anyone who shares my nature, any human being.

This, then, is an essential thesis of morality and *politica*. But what are its own bases, *principia*? What is the ground, the *ratio*, of human dignity? The thesis rests on premisses some of which belong primarily, not to practical reason's 'third-order' sciences or discourses (see II.1), but to 'first-order', 'speculative' sciences of the realities that are given to us prior to our deliberation and choosing. Still, those premisses are accessible in the very experience of practical reasoning, deliberation, choice, and action. Although their elaboration and defence take us out of the practical into the theoretical, a starting-point and constant reference point of such an exploration and defence can suitably be that practical experience. In showing briefly how this is so, I deploy in relation to *willing* a strategy which Aquinas constantly employs in relation to *understanding*, a deployment which he invites and fully authorizes[207] but never himself makes.

---

[206] The word and concept *persona* entails *dignitas*, and so is applicable to every individual of a rational nature: e.g. I q. 29 a. 3 ad 2; I *Sent*. d. 23 a. 1c, d. 26 q. 1 a. 1c. (If there are extra-terrestrial rational beings, they are persons, with the dignity and rights of persons.) It is the nobility or dignity of the species {natura} that counts, not the individual's present accomplishments or loss or immaturity of capacities, because (as this section explains) that specific nature is not merely a classification but subsists in the very form and actuality—soul—of each individual of the species.
[207] See I q. 87 a. 4 with a. 3.

We are in a difficult situation. I have considered the options and decided to lie. Now the time has come to state my position, and I am asserting what I believe to be false. I understand the question put to me, and the expectations of the questioner, and some of the benefits we might gain by my lie, and the meaning of what I am asserting. In the very act of telling my lie I also understand that my telling it is the carrying out of a choice *which I made* with those benefits in mind. And in the same act I hear my own voice speaking, see the faces of the hearers register their comprehension of my answer, feel my anxiety and its current effects in the dryness of my tongue and weakness of my knees, remember parental disapproval of a 4-year-old's fibs, and hope that my story now will do the trick. This experience *of the unity (including continuity)* of my being— as a feeling, willing, observing, remembering, understanding, physically active and effective mover or cause of physical effects and equally an undergoer and recipient of such effects—is a datum which the philosophical exploration of human and other natural realities can adequately account for only with great difficulty and many a pitfall.[208] Still, prior to all accounts of it, this intelligible presence {praesentia}[209] of my many-faceted acting self to myself is a datum *of understanding*; one and the same I—this human being {hic homo}—who am understanding and choosing and carrying out my choice and sensing, etc., is a reality I already truly understand,[210]

---

[208] I q. 87 a. 1c: diligens et subtilis inquisitio (and many do not know, and many have been mistaken about, the nature of soul).

[209] 1 *Sent.* d. 3 q. 4 a. 5c; and n. 211 below.

[210] Thus, while I q. 76 a. 1c says that in understanding something 'one *experiences* {experitur unusquisque} that it is oneself who is understanding {seipsum esse qui intelligit}', and that 'it is the very same person who *perceives* that he or she is both understanding and feeling {ipse idem homo est qui percipit se et intelligere et sentire}', q. 87 aa. 3 and 4 call precisely this *percipere* an initial but real understanding: e.g. 'one's act of will is *understood* {intelligitur} by one's intellect, both in so far as one perceives oneself willing and in so far as one knows [if one does] the nature of this act' (a. 4c). So the later Aquinas has not shifted away from the earliest: 'in one and the same operation I understand something intelligible and understand that I am understanding': 1 *Sent.* d. 1 q. 2 a. 1 ad 2. (See likewise ScG II c. 75 n. 13 [1556].) The late work *Unit.* v, lines 238–9 [112] [257] strikingly says: 'When my intellect *understands* that it is understanding, it understands a certain particular act {quando intelligit se intelligere, intelligit quemdam singularem actum} . . . For it is not particularity {singularitas} which is repugnant to intelligibility, but materiality'; see also II *Sent.* d. 17 q. 2 a. 1 ad 3: 'I understand that I am understanding, even though that understanding of mine [which I understand] is a particular activity {intelligo me intelligere, quamvis ipsum meum intelligere sit quaedam operatio singularis}'. (On the latter point, see similarly I q. 86 a. 1 ad 3.) On the presence-to-one's-understanding of the acts of one's other powers and dispositions (will, memory, sense, feeling, locomotion), see III *Sent.* d. 23 q. 1 a. 2 ad 3. On the inerrancy of understanding, precisely as such, see I q. 85 a. 6.

albeit not yet fully (explanatorily, with elaboration). (Indeed, it is by virtue of this primary understanding of my understanding, willing, and so forth, that I can and typically do value such understanding, voluntariness, unity of being, and so forth.[211]) So any theory which (like Plato's, as Aquinas thinks) denies the unity of the person (I, the bodily self) who lives, wants, chooses, tries, understands, senses, feels, moves, and is moved, and any theory which (like the Presocratic, Hobbesian, Humean, and other materialists') denies this acting being's (my) ultimate complexity of unity, will be inconsistent with both the data it seeks to explain and its own performance in offering its purported explanations.[212]

As Aristotle and Aquinas argue, the explanation of these data is this: The very *form* and lifelong *act(uality)*[m] by which the matter of my bodily make-up is constituted the unified and active subject (me myself) is a factor, a reality, which Aristotle calls *psychē* and Aquinas calls soul {anima}. In the human animal, from the very outset of its existence as human,[n] it is this one essentially unchanging factor, unique to each individual, which explains (1) the dynamic unity in complexity—in one dimension, we can say, the programme—of the individual's growth as embryo, foetus, neonate, infant . . . and adult,[213] (2) the unity and complexity of the individual's activities, (3) the relatively mature individual's understanding of universal (e.g. generic), immaterial objects of thought (e.g. classes, or truth and falsity, or soundness and unsoundness in reasoning), and interest in voluntarily bringing about universal (generic) benefits (e.g. health or justice), and (4) this unique individual's generic unity with[214] every other member of the species. In animals of other species, the corresponding factor is both vegetative and animal; in plants it is only vegetative (which already

[211] See e.g. 1 *Sent.* d. 3 q. 4 a. 4c: 'ipsa anima [est] naturaliter sibi praesens. . . . quantum se intelligit, tantum se vult et diligit'.

[212] See Aquinas' argument from the self-refutation of those who held that there is but one intellect: *Unit.* III, lines 28–9, 316–17 [62, 79] [216, 230]; III.2 at n. 10 above.

[213] See e.g. *ScG* IV c. 81 n. 7 [4152a]: 'Bodiliness {corporeitas}, since it is the substantial form in a human being, cannot be other than the rational soul, which—since it is the act of a body—requires that its own matter have three dimensions.' For the argument, see e.g. *ScG* II cc. 56–72, 83–4. Of course, the soul itself is immaterial and dimensionless: see e.g. *Caus.* 14; I q. 93 a. 3c ('a human soul is all {tota} in the whole human body, and is also whole {tota} in any and every part of that body'); *Ps.* 5. 6 ad v. 6 ('one's soul contains, and is a kind of foundation of, one's body').

[214] As I lie to you, I know with certainty that you hear me, understand me, may care whether I am lying, and might judge me with contempt if you found me out. Our unity of genetic species, morphological development, etc., only confirms this first-order truth available to practical reason (in the thought: if good for me, good for you) from its outset.

includes the remarkable features of generation); in members of our species the one factor unifying and activating the living reality of each individual is at once vegetative, animal (sentient and self-locomotive), and intellectual (understanding, self-understanding, and, even in thinking, self-determining by judging and choosing).[215] The manifold activations of these bodily and rational powers are variously dependent upon the physical maturity and health of the individual. But the essence and powers of the soul are given to each individual complete (as wholly undeveloped, radical capacities) at the outset of his or her existence as such.[216] This is the root of the dignity we all have as human beings.[217]

For *dignity* connotes both superiority (e.g. in power,[218] excellence, status) and intrinsic, non-dependent worth.[219] The radical capacity and act(uality) which each human being has by virtue of his or her individual rational soul makes each of us superior in the straightforward sense that we thereby have and instantiate every level of being—the physical solidity and dynamisms of a star or a galaxy, the chemical and biological complexity and self-directedness of a tree or a lion, *and more*: the capacity to understand all these other realities, to reason about them and about reasoning itself, to replicate and transform other beings on all those levels of reality, and with self-mastery's freedom to choose how to live.[220] In their inherent worth, our living, knowing, playing, and loving

[215] Thus: 'the principle by which we understand is intellect . . . so this must be united to one's body as form, not indeed in such a way that the capacity of understanding is the act of some organ, but because it is a power of one's soul, which is the act of a physical and organic body': *Unit.* III, lines 229–35 [80] [231]. On *soul* as the primary 'act' of a living, physically organized body, see e.g. *ScG* II c. 61 n. 2 [1397]; I q. 76 a. 1c and a. 4 ad 1; *An.* II. 1 n. 17 [227–9].

[216] The intellectual (and sensory and vegetative) soul by the creation of which I came into existence—existence as already a person—is not itself a person but only a 'part' (uniquely, the organizing part and indeed the very form and act(uality)) of me: I q. 29 a. 1 ad 5, q. 75 a. 4 ad 2; x.4 n. 106 below.

[217] 'From the essence of the soul flow powers which are essentially different . . . but which are all united in the soul's essence as in a root' (II *Sent.* d. 26 q. 1 a. 4c); 'the essence of the soul is simple, and is whole in each of its powers; hence the saying that the whole soul of Christ [on the cross] was experiencing fulfilment (inasmuch as one's soul is root of one's higher reason), and his whole soul was suffering (inasmuch as one's soul is the act of one's body and the root of one's lower powers)' (*Quodl.* VII q. 2 a. un. c).

[218] Especially of governing to governed: e.g. I q. 26 a. 4c.

[219] '"Dignity" signifies something's goodness for its own sake {propter seipsum}': III *Sent.* d. 35 q. 1 a. 4 sol. 1c.

[220] See e.g. *ScG* III c. 111 n. 1 [2855]; on our superiority to the stellar bodies, ibid. c. 120 n. 17 [2934].

are indeed paradigms of worth, as is the worth we grasp in our friend's (and thus[221] in every human person's[222]) very being.

Materialism's denials or determined agnosticism about *soul* and *species* radically misrepresent our experience as choosers—an experience internal and private, but shared in kind, common to us all, and in that sense in the public domain of philosophical reflection and discussion. Materialism likewise devastates the case for holding that 'by nature all human beings are equal', and that there are human rights and requirements of justice which do not discriminate between male and female, intelligent and dull, race and race, young and old, healthy and infirm.

Notes

a. *The modern language of rights . . .* As employed by Hobbes, this language is certainly different from Aquinas' in very significant ways. See Finnis (1980: 208).

b. *Having concepts without specific words . . .* Cf. I q. 29 a. 3: 'although the noun {nomen} *person* is never used about God in either Old or New Testaments, *what the noun signifies* is asserted of God in many scriptural passages'.

c. *Marital intercourse need not be motivated by hope of having children . . .* Noonan (1967: 300) cites only IV *Sent.* d. 31 q. 2 a. 2 (= *Supp.* q. 49 a. 5) ad 2 to support his claim (also 352) that for Aquinas 'only a procreative purpose freed marital intercourse from sin'. But the cited reply ad 2 says merely that choosing intercourse only to avoid one's own temptations to fornication (extra-marital sex) is (lightly) wrong; it says nothing whatever about procreative purpose; and the main reply to this very article (a. 2c)—not to mention the set of texts cited in n. 49 above—clearly contradicts Noonan by stating that *either* procreation or *fides* suffices as a reasonable motive for marital intercourse, *and* that in the latter case both spouses can be acting wholly faultlessly when they give each other the bodily co-operation each other is entitled to in marital intercourse. Noonan's entire, influential account is flawed from top to bottom by his failure to observe (1) that *seeking* the 'giving of what is due' (the 'rendering the debt', as he lamely translates *reddere debitum*) is never condemned by Aquinas even in contexts when procreation is out of the question, (2) that *fides* is the object not only of marriage but also of marital sexual intercourse, (3) that intercourse for the sake of 'what is owed' ('the debt'), i.e. by reason of *fides*, has a sufficient justifying reason alternative to procreative purpose, and (4) that marriage is a 'healing of concupiscence' not by providing release for

---

[221] And see IV.3 at nn. 35–6, 64, 66–7 above.

[222] It is perhaps because of the etymological and other semantic links between 'dignity' and 'person' that human beings—all bodily beings of a rational nature—are called *persons*: I q. 29 a. 3 ad 2.

lusts but by integrating sexual desire with intelligible good(s) and such an integrating good may but need not be the good of procreation, and when not procreation as such is the good of *fides*. See further Parmisano (1969).

d. Fides *as a positive commitment and reason for action* . . . Note that when thinking of *fides* as faith in God, Aquinas says both that it is by this *fides* that we cling to {accedere ad} God, and that *fides* is inherently a *motus*, i.e. a movement towards and/or motivation to shaping one's conduct towards union with God: e.g. IV *Sent.* d. 17 q. 1 a. 3 sol. 3c, d. 9 a. 3 sol. 6c; *In Heb.* 11. 2 ad v. 6 [575]. Indeed, by [religious] *fides* one's soul is wedded {coniungitur} to God 'because by faith the Christian soul makes a kind of marriage with God {quasi quoddam matrimonium cum Deo}': *Cred.* 1 [prol.] [860].

e. Acts of a generative (or: procreative) type . . . The biology and physiology of his day taught Aquinas that in female sexual activity (see IV *Sent.* d. 33 q. 3 a. 1 ad 5) a kind of 'seed {semen}' is emitted in the woman's genital tract; so his account of the generative type of act involves 'mixing of seeds {commixtio seminum}': IV *Sent.* d. 41 a. 1 sol. 4 ad 2. But he follows Aristotle in judging (rightly) that *this* type of seminal emission by the woman makes no contribution at all to generation and thus (unlike the emission of the man's semen) is not relevant to the act's being of a generative kind: III *Sent.* d. 3 q. 5 a. 1c; *ST* III q. 31 a. 5 ad 3. So *commixtio seminum*, as what defines acts as being *of a generative kind* uniting the parties in one flesh, means no more and no less than the man's depositing and the woman's taking his semen into her generative tract. (Aquinas is well aware that there can be no actual generation without the contribution of appropriate matter from the woman's generative system; not knowing about the ovum, he thinks of a kind of menstrual blood: ibid. But that is not relevant here; see nn. j, n below.)

Contraception: If the parties take steps, before, during, or after intercourse, to prevent this act of theirs from resulting in generation, their act is thereby removed from the class of acts of a generative kind, and so is wrong because contrary to the good(s) of marriage; indeed, it is not an act capable of allowing them truly to experience *marriage*: see *ScG* III c. 122 nn. 5 and 8 [2951, 2954]; IV *Sent.* d. 27 q. 2 (= *Supp.* q. 43) a. 1c, d. 31 q. 2 a. 3 ex.

f. Assertion and truth . . . 'In none of [the other four kinds of speech (questions, requests, commands, addresses/summons)] is there found [except as some sort of consequence] the true or the false, but only in assertions {oratio enunciativa}, which signify what *the mind* [of the speaker] thinks about things {id quod mens de rebus concipit}': *Peri.* 1. 7 n. 5 [86]. Again, 'an assertion {enunciativ[a] oratio} signifies things *according as their truth is in the mind* {res secundum quod earum veritas est in anima}': ibid. n. 6 [87]. (For the practical equivalence of *enunciatio* and *assertio*, see e.g. III *Sent.* d. 38 a. 5 ad 1.) These statements from Aquinas' commentary on Aristotle's treatise—which, as Aquinas says, ibid. prol. n. 3 [3], is a treatise on assertion—are particularly significant for present purposes because only a few sentences earlier (*Peri* I. 7 n. 2 [83]) Aquinas makes the more general statement that '*every* significant expression {vocis significativae} is used to signify understanding's conception [of something]'. It is this more general statement that Aquinas uses at a key point in his treatment of lying (e.g. II-II q. 110 a. 3: 'expressions {voces} are naturally signs of things understood {intellectuum}'). But it is on the more specific force of assertions, as asserting (indirectly but necessarily and inherently) something precisely about the speaker's mind, that Aquinas' moral analysis of lying actually depends. On assertion as a stating of the heart's inward conception, see also IV *Sent.* d. 38 q. 1 a. 1 sol. 1 ad 1.

g. *Situations in which there is no obligation to make any communication* . . . Because such situations are common, the theory developed under Grotius' auspices, that one lies only when one asserts a falsehood to someone who *has no right to the truth*, licenses lying in a very wide range of circumstances. For A 'has a right to X' when someone else *has the obligation* to give X to A (or to do X for A, etc). And such situations are generally far outnumbered by situations in which telling A the truth is, if not wrongful, at least a matter of discretionary choice. Grotius' own theory, as initially stated by him with cautious hedging and obscurity (Grotius 1625, III c. 1 sect. xi par. 1), but applied even by him to allow the deliberate assertion of falsehoods in many situations (sects. xii–xvii) (though not in promising, even to enemies! sect. xviii), is that making a statement which one knows to be, in all its meanings, false and contrary to one's mind is a lie only when doing so is 'repugnant to the existing and continuing right {repugnantiam cum iure existente ac manente} of the person addressed', the right in question being 'nothing other than the liberty in judging {iudicandi libertas} which speakers are understood to owe, as if by a kind of tacit promise {quasi pacto quodam tacito} to their interlocutors'. The subsequent discussion does not much illuminate the phrase 'liberty in judging'. In Grotius' opinion, people in authority (e.g. physicians and government officials) have a wide licence to lie to those over whom they have authority (sect. xv).

h. *Forms of opposition to Aquinas' thesis that there are exceptionless moral norms* . . . For the claim that Aquinas did not hold this thesis, or was inconsistent in holding it, see discussion and some bibliography in Finnis (1991a: 90–1). For the claim that the acts excluded by the exceptionless moral norms he defends are defined in terms of physical behaviour, see discussion and bibliography, ibid. 37–40, 94. For the claim that his exceptionless moral norms are tautologous, see ibid. 31–7, 67 n. For bibliography and discussion, see also Grisez (1991).

i. *Ways of softening Aquinas' exceptionless moral norms* . . . (1) 'Aristotelian *phronēsis*': see Finnis (1991a: 101–5). (2) '*Prudentia* considers all circumstances and departs from rules': ibid. (3) 'An equitable morality of *ius* not *lex'*: for this interpretation (refuted implicitly in v.1 above) see Goerner (1979, 1983).

j. *Subordination of women* ... Modern biological information has eliminated at least one important reason for thinking the subordination natural, namely the Aristotelian view that (1) in the biological processes of human generation, the male semen plays the active role and the female contribution is by way only of distilled menstrual blood which, though appropriately formed for its role in generation, is almost entirely passive in that role (e.g. III *Sent.* d. 3 q. 2 a. 1c; *ScG* IV c. 11 n. 19 [3479]); and that consequently (2) the child, though its bodily matter is wholly or almost wholly the contribution of the mother, can be described as the changed and completed semen (see e.g. *ScG* IV c. 45 n. 3 [3818]). As we now know, male and female gametes contribute equally to the genetic, chromosomal constitution of the conceptus, and the ovum is at least as formative in its contribution to the new being that begins at the insemination of the ovum. There remain aspects of the active v. passive (recipient) natural symbolism in the relations between male and female gametes (and persons).

The statement, drawn from Aristotle's *On the Generation of Animals* 2. 3. 737^{a}27, that the female is 'congenitally an, in a sense, anomalous male' seems to have been taken by Aquinas as a challenge to his Aristotelianism (Bonaventure ignores it and Albert passes it by). Aquinas accepts the biological basis of the claim: since (Aristotle believes) the male semen is the sole active principle in generation, and like makes like, the natural result of insemination must be the production of a male; females are thus anomalous, and result from some weakness of the semen or some outside factor such as the weather. So from the point of view of the generative power in semen {'per respectum ad naturam particularem' 'id est huius virtutis quae est in hoc semine'}, the female is a happenstance and deficient {aliquid deficiens et occasionatum}: I q. 92 a. 1 ad 1; *ScG* III c. 94 n. 11 [2695(a)]. But Aquinas rejects any suggestion that she is less a part of the grand divine scheme of nature than the male is: 'from the point of view of nature as a whole, woman is not a happenstance {per comparationem ad naturam universalem, femina non est aliquid occasionatum}' (I q. 92 a. 1 ad 1), because universal nature 'requires each of the sexes for the perfection of the human species {ad perfectionem humanae speciei utrumque sexum requirit}', and in heaven, where there will be both men and women, no one will be deficient by reason of their sex {nec ex sexu erit ibi aliquis defectus} (IV *Sent.* d. 44 q. 1 a. 3 sol. 3 ad 3).

k. *Aquinas' reading of Aristotle's views on women in politics* ... In IV *Sent.* d. 19 q. 1 a. 1 sol. 3 ad 4 he reads *Nic. Eth.* 8. 10. 1161^{a}1–3 (which says that the rule of heiresses over their husbands, being a matter of wealth or power not virtue, is oligarchical) as asserting that it is a corruption of constitutional order {corruptio urbanitatis} for rulership in general {dominium} to come to women—a hasty reading not repeated in *Eth.* VIII. 12 n. 14 [1685] *ad loc.* (Still, in *In I Tim.* 2. 3 ad v. 12 [80], he says, a little more accurately though still evidently from imperfect memory, that Aristotle teaches that the rule {dominium} of women is a corruption of *family*, as tyranny is a corruption of the state.) In any event, when Aquinas eventually read *Politics* 2. 6. 1269^{b}19–1270^{a}12 on the domestically and politically damaging corruption and insolence endemic among Spartan women, he may have thought it some confirmation of his political generalization: see *Pol.* II. 13 n. 7 [303 tertio]; I-II q. 105 a. 2 obj. 2 and ad 2. Given the instances one can readily find of corruption and insolence in the rule of men, the generalization still seems rash.

1. *Servitude* {servitus} . . . Aquinas has no general treatment of *servitus*, the status (II-II q. 183 a. 1c), state, or condition of being a *servus*. The terms are not to be automatically translated 'slavery' and 'slave'. Sometimes they clearly mean that, and on such occasions (e.g. IV *Sent.* d. 28 a. 3 (= *Supp.* q. 45 a. 5) ad 1) Aquinas is usually discussing the institution as a fact of life in many societies, without implying that he considers it morally acceptable (though disconcertingly passing up many an opportunity to challenge such an institution at its root: see e.g. I-II q. 105 a. 4 obj. 1 and 2 and ad 1 and 2). On the occasions when he treats the institution or condition as morally acceptable, it is subject to such severe legal and moral restrictions that it is better described as service or bond-service or perhaps (e.g. at II *Sent.* d. 44 q. 2 a. 2c, apparently postulating a liability of a *servus* to pay a levy {tributum} to the *dominus*) serfdom. The rest of this note considers what Aquinas says of *servitus* in this latter, ameliorated sense. (There are other, even more reduced, senses, e.g. the *quasi servitus* of those who, in utmost freedom, have made religious vows or exchanged the promises of marriage, thereby giving up their *libertas faciendi quodlibet*, their freedom to do what they will: e.g. *Quodl.* III q. 6 a. 3c [lines 133, 145]; *Perf.* c. 29 [25], line 50 [720].)

This *servitus* exists by positive, not natural, law and right; by nature, all people are equal in liberty, each of us ends in ourselves and none ordered to another as an end (see v.7 at n. 167 above); the only sense in which it may be natural is if it is useful for a *servus* to be ruled by someone wiser (II-II q. 57 a. 3 ad 2). Being a mere matter of positive law and positive right, it is morally limited by the requirements of morality and 'cannot override what is a matter of natural law {non potest praeiudicare his quae sunt de lege naturali}' (IV *Sent.* d. 36 (= *Supp.* q. 52) a. 2c; II-II q. 10 a. 12 ad 3 = III q. 68 a. 10 ad 2).

The liberty surrendered by those who sell themselves into *servitus* is a priceless good {inaestimabile bonum} (IV *Sent.* d. 36 (= *Supp.* q. 52) a. 3 ad 1; see also II-II q. 189 a. 6 ad 3), and wrongfully to reduce someone to *servitus* is one of the very gravest wrongs (*Reg.* 1. 11 [87] [803]). As an institution, it exists only as a result of human wrongdoing; it would not have existed in Paradise (I q. 96 a. 4c), and was introduced as a penalty not to be imposed without fault (IV *Sent.* d. 36 a. 1 (= *Supp.* q. 52 a. 1) ad 2 and 3). (But Aquinas does not challenge the noxious logic whereby, since the fruits of property belong to its owner, the 'penalty' of slavery extends, as a matter of human positive law, to the innocent children of female *servae*: ibid. a. 4c.) The *dominus* is owner as well as master; the *servus* can be bought and sold. But: (1) what is owned, bought, and sold is only the service {servitium}; for (2) the *servus* or *serva* retains morally and legally the freedom (right) to eat, sleep, marry, perform other natural functions, and to choose and maintain a religious faith without needing the permission, and notwithstanding the opposition, of the *dominus* (IV *Sent*. d. 36 (= *Supp*. q. 52) a. 2c and ad 1 and 2, and a. 3c; II-II q. 10 a. 12c and ad 3); (3) *servi* (male) and *servae* (female) must not be sold if the sale would separate spouses or make their married life very onerous (IV *Sent*. d. 36 (= *Supp*. q. 52) a. 2 ad 4), and (4) everything required for a decent marriage and married life prevails over the orders of the *dominus* (ibid. a. 3 ad 1 and ad 2); indeed, if a *servus* (say) has married with the consent of the *dominus*, he can proceed on the basis that he has the right to set aside his duties of service whenever his marital responsibilities so require; if he has married without the master's or mistress's consent, he should give his duties of service priority except where a reasonable assessment of the many factors in the situation enables him to conclude that his marital responsibilities justly take priority (ibid. a. 2 ad 3; the same norms hold for *servae*). A master can forbid a *servus* to become a priest, since the two forms of service are scarcely compatible; if the master allows the ordination, the *servus* is automatically freed; if the ordination went ahead without the master's knowledge, the master must be compensated by the bishop or out of the funds {peculium} of the *servus*, failing which the man reverts to *servitus* even though this prevents him from performing his priestly functions: IV *Sent*. d. 25 q. 2 a. 2 sol. 1c and ad 5.

As already stated, *servitus* does not deprive anyone of other basic human rights such as not to be killed, deliberately harmed, raped or used for any extra-marital sexual services (see IV *Sent*. d. 33 q. 1 a. 3 sol. 1 (= *Supp*. q. 65 a. 3) ad 4), lied to, robbed or cheated (e.g. of *peculium*), etc. Moreover, the servitude in no way extends to the mind or interior life of the *servus*: II-II q. 104 a. 5c and a. 6 ad 1, q. 122 a. 4 ad 3; VII.6 at n. 92 below. So it is only precisely in respect of the *servitus* of the *servus* that the relationship of master to *servus* is not a relationship of justice in the strictest sense but one of *ius dominativum* (II-II q. 57 a. 4 ad 1); in all other respects, as we have seen (nn. 169–72 above), this relationship between the two persons is properly a relationship governed by justice and mutual rights. Though falling (we should say) distinctly short of the requirements of human rights, this *servitus* is not the inhuman institution of slavery of republican Rome or the *ante bellum* United States; it differs radically from the 'absolute dominion and arbitrary power' of master over slave defended as part of the 'right of nature' by Locke (1689, vii. 85; xv. 172; xvi. 189; but cf. 182–3 rejecting enslavement of the slave's children).

m. *Soul as a body's act(uality), i.e. form and existence* . . . The refrain of *Unit*. is: 'soul is the act(uality) of the body {anima est actus corporis}': e.g. I, lines 487, 493–4 [27, 28] [191], III, line 334 [80] [231] ('act(uality) of the physically organized body {actus corporis physici organici}'). For this sense of 'act {actus}' as synonymous with 'actuality {actualitas}', i.e. existence {esse; existens} considered precisely as the actualizing of potentiality, see e.g. *ST* I q. 3 a. 4c, q. 4 a. 1 ad 3, q. 5 a. 1, q. 14 a. 3c; *Pot.* q. 5 a. 8c (some bodies have less actuality {de actualitate} than others because their whole potentiality {potentialitas} has not been brought to act(uality) {completa per actum}, since the matter which underlies their form as one thing retains the potentiality to have some other form {eo quod materia substans uni formae remanet in potentia ad formam aliam}); q. 7 a. 2 ad 9; *Peri.* 1. 5 n. 22 [73]; *Princ.*, lines 42–4 [340]. See also x.2 at nn. 22–5, 28–32 below.

n. *The outset of a human life . . .* Taking his natural science (biology, embryology, etc.) largely from Aristotle's empirical studies, Aquinas was unaware of the role of the male and female gametes in human generation. Since he envisaged it as resulting from the active, formative influence of male semen on essentially passive and inanimate (though not formless) female menstrual blood (n. j above), he supposed that it must naturally take some time (about forty to sixty days from the outset of conception) for the process of generation to yield a body sufficiently elaborated {complexionatum} and organized {organizatum} to receive and be organized anew by the rational, specifically human soul. See e.g. *ScG* II c. 30 n. 12 [1074], c. 89 n. 6 [1740], IV c. 44 n. 5 [3814]. It seems clear that, had he known of the extremely elaborate and specifically organized structure of the sperm and the ovum, their chromosomal complementarity, and the typical, wholly continuous self-directed growth and development of the even more elaborate and specifically organized embryo or embryos from the moment of insemination of the ovum, Aquinas would have concluded that the specifically human, rational (and sensitive and vegetative) animating form and act (soul)—and therefore personhood {personalitas: *ScG* IV c. 44 n. 3 [3812]}—can be and doubtless is present from that moment. If in some cases a single embryo divides to become twins, he would equally have understood this as an unusual (though not in any other sense unnatural) form of generation, either of two new embryos from one now deceased or of one new one from the older one which began a few days earlier and now continues as the newer one's sibling-parent. (On nonsexual generation by division in some animals, see *ScG* II c. 86 n. 3 [1708(b)].)

VI

Distribution, Exchange, and Recompense

VI.1. *Justice: Forms or Issues?*

Aquinas' discussions of justice are illuminated, but also confused, by his adherence to Aristotle's framework for discussing it, and by the structure of the *Summa Theologiae*.

The *Summa*'s expositions of morality are arranged within a classification, not of the goods to which rational acts are directed, nor of types of act, nor of practical reason's norms, but of virtues—aspects of character, of one's stable and ready[1] willingness to act in reasonable ways. The decision to make virtues the principle of arrangement was understandable. (The reflective theologian wishes to depict and explain the flourishing or deviations of human beings within a vast cosmological and historical account of the whole movement of creatures from their origin to their fulfilment[2].) But this superstructure can obscure morality's foundations. In conscientious deliberations, one wants and needs to understand what reason requires, what acts are consistent with pursuing human goods and avoiding evil. In such deliberations, virtues are not the issue at stake; they are consequences of resolving such issues rightly. To be concerned about justice is to be concerned

---

[1] II-II q. 32 a. 1 ad 1: the disposition to deliberate, choose, and *prompte et delectabiliter* act rightly; but even without being just (i.e. having such a disposition), one can act justly by virtue of natural reason {ex naturali ratione} (or out of fear, or hope of gain).

[2] See e.g. I q. 1 a. 3 ad 2; II *Sent.* prol.; *ScG* II c. 46 n. 2 [1230], IV c. 21 n. 2 [3576].

about treating other people in the way they are entitled to. Requirements of justice are identified not by reflecting on one's own
character but by considering what will establish or preserve a
reasonable relationship of proportionate equality between us, in
relation to some *act*, forbearance, arrangement, or other subject-
matter which is external, other-regarding (other-affecting).[3]

In any event, Aquinas' efforts to follow Aristotle in classifying
types of justice—its species, parts, and associated forms—yield no
really clear and stable analytical pattern.[a] The effort to understand
and work with the distinctions—say, between 'distributive' and
'commutative'—sheds little light on the substantive issues of justice. When will everyone, some people, or someone, be entitled to
some action or forbearance of mine, or to some thing which I
should provide, respect, or restore? Some of these issues and entitlements concern fairness in giving others their share of some pool
of benefits or burdens involved in living in community with each
other, in carrying out my own share of such burdens and responsibilities, and in managing, exploiting, and disposing of natural
resources. Some concern the wrongness of choosing to impose
some harm or loss on another or others. Some concern the wrongness of not avoiding such imposition of harm or loss. Some concern
fairness in bargaining and exchange, especially (but not only) in
recompensing others for what they lose in conferring some benefit
upon one. Some concern the requirements of fairness in compen-
sating those upon whom one has imposed some harm or loss without their free and informed consent. Some concern the
appropriateness of denouncing and punishing offences. These concerns provide topics for this chapter, not necessarily the headings
for a complete treatise on justice.

VI.2. *Property: Private Right and Social Responsibility*

The essential equality of all human beings is the presupposition for
all reasonable claims of right and so for all duties of justice.
Nowhere is this more evident than in Aquinas' account of rights
to things: property.

The 'things' {res} that can be the subject of ownership

---

[3] II-II q. 58 a. 11c; v. 1 at nn. 9, 20, 25, 29 above.

{dominium} or of other, lesser property rights (e.g. to possession, use, or 'fruits') include an indefinitely expandable range of more or less abstract entities such as monetary debts, transferable entitlements to delivery of goods or services, and so forth. But the value of all such artificial, fourth-order entities is derived from natural, first-order entities: the resources of land, waters, air, and all the other naturally given sources of material fruitfulness. The derivation may be more or less direct. A loaf of bread is indeed an artefact, a human product. So too is a marketable option on the contractual right to delivery of next season's wheat. But the option is valuable because people will still need nourishment next year, and the bread nourishes because of the chemistry of its elements, chemistry and elements that are part of the vast order of natural resources, which we find, and have the capacity to make use of, but not to create.[4]

All the components of the order of nature, other than persons themselves,[5] are resources which can rightly be used, and indeed used up, *for the benefit* of persons.[6] No subpersonal entity can have rights.[7] The moral or juridical relationships to such an entity that we call property rights are relationships to other people. They are matters of interpersonal justice. Arguments for founding property rights on alleged 'metaphysical' relationships between persons and the things with which they have 'mixed their labour', or to which craftsmen have 'extended their personality', are foreign to Aquinas. Though Aquinas has no formal treatment of ways in which property rights are acquired, he recognizes 'taking possession {occupatio}' as a legitimate mode of acquisition. But he does so on the basis that this appropriation of 'what from the outset was common' (i.e. available to all) is precisely a means whereby the owner to whom things have been appropriated 'gets things ready for', and 'shares them with, other people {aliis communicat}'.[8]

Indeed, all the justifications for appropriation of resources to

---

[4] See II-II q. 66 a. 1c and ad 3.
[5] Aquinas does not think that one owns or has any other property right in or over oneself. On *servitus*, see pp. 184–5 n. 1 above.
[6] II-II q. 66 a. 1c and ad 1. The benefit is a matter of utility (see *ScG* III c. 127 n. 3 [2995]: 'utilia homini'), of reasons not mere whim.
[7] See I-II q. 102 a. 6 ad 8; *ScG* III c. 112 n. 12 [2867]; but it is natural to feel pity for the sufferings of subpersonal animals, and failure to do so is a sign (and can also be a cause) of cruelty or unmerciful indifference to human beings: I-II q. 102 a. 6 ad 1 and ad 8; *ScG* III c. 112 n. 13 [2868]. On the significance of belonging to a species of persons rather than of subpersonal entities, see v.8 above.   [8] II-II q. 66 a. 2 obj. 2 and ad 2.

particular owners (or holders of lesser property rights) are based on 'general' justice, i.e. on the advantages which such appropriation is likely to bring to all members of the community. Property rights concern our handling of resources in two basic dimensions: (1) their management and distribution {potestas procurandi et dispensandi}; (2) their use for consumption. As to (1), appropriation of resources to the ownership (or lesser property rights) of particular individuals or groups is appropriate and even necessary, for three reasons: where something is held in common, or by many people, it tends to be neglected, and the work involved in managing it tends to be shirked; its management tends to be relatively confused, misdirected, and inefficient; and the whole situation tends to provoke discord, quarrelling, and resentment.[9] So the devising of a division and legal regulation of possessions brings great benefits to a community.[10] As to (2), the ultimate use of resources in consumption must remain fundamentally 'common' (unappropriated). Any appropriation of resources to particular owners is always subject to this reservation.[11]

But how is this reservation consistent with the very idea of ownership, and with the incentive-based advantages which make ownership useful and necessary? We may concede that everyone has a natural right to a fair share in the consumption of natural resources, and that no thing, no resource naturally belongs to some one person or group rather than another.[12] We may further concede that any scheme for appropriating to particular persons or groups the management and distribution of things, though not contrary to nature, will equally be not natural,[13] and so has moral or legal validity only by virtue of moral or legal principles and norms which, like all authentic moral or legal norms, are for *common* good. But what, we may wonder, is the value and substance of property rights which are *subject* to the always subsisting claim

---

[9] II-II q. 66 a. 2c. As to the third reason, see *Pol.* II. 4 nn. 2–3 [197–8], 5 n. 8 [214].
[10] I-II q. 105 a. 2c and ad 3; limitless accumulation in a few hands is to be prevented (ad 3). [11] II-II q. 66 a. 2c. [12] II-II q. 57 a. 3c; and see ad 2, q. 66 a. 2 ad 1.
[13] II-II q. 66 a. 2 ad 1: 'secundum ius naturale non est distinctio possessionum. . . . proprietas possessionum non est contra ius naturale sed iuri naturali superadditur per adinventionem rationis humanae'. This 'devising {adinventio} by human reason' is a paradigmatic field for *determinatio* (VIII.3 below). Also I-II q. 91 a. 3c, q. 94 a. 5 ad 3. Aquinas' location of the institution of property in the domain of *ius gentium* (II-II q. 57 a. 3c; and see n. 76 below) does little or nothing to clarify matters.

of each and every human being to a share, so that all one's possessions are 'in some respects common [to all]'?[14]

Aquinas' answer, in establishing the moral limits of property
rights, equally establishes the sense and limits of the proposition
that what one owns—even what one owns as part of one's personal
patrimony, and not (as we would say) in trust[15]—one holds 'as
common'.[16] The answer turns on the distinctions between (a)
resources one needs for the very survival of oneself and one's
dependants, (b) resources one needs in order to fulfil one's
responsibilities for the support and education of one's relatives
and household, for maintaining one's business[17] or profession or
other vocation, for launching one's children in such ways of life,
for paying one's debts,[18] and other such genuine responsibilities,
and (c) resources which are left over {superflua} after one has
made reasonable provision for both type (a) 'absolute necessity'
and type (b) 'relative necessity {necessitas conditionata}'.[19] Then
Aquinas' theorem is twofold: (1) *everything* one has is 'held as
common (or in common)' in the sense that it is morally available, as a matter of right and justice, to *anyone* who needs it to
survive; (2) one's *superflua* are all 'held as common', in the sense
that one has a duty *of justice* to dispose of them for the benefit
of the poor.

1. For anyone in dire necessity, nothing belongs to anyone in
particular: 'for anyone in that condition, all resources become *common resources*'.[20] That is to say, people who find themselves or
their dependants in such life-threatening[21] need are morally
entitled to take anything which will relieve that need, and this
entitlement overrides anyone else's otherwise legitimate title or

---

[14] *Pol.* II. 4 n. 5 [200]: 'oportet enim possessiones simpliciter quidem esse proprias
quantum ad proprietatem dominii, sed *secundum aliquem modum communes*'.

[15] Those in charge of ecclesiastical property hold it in trust for ecclesiastical purposes;
but their own wealth {patrimonium proprium} they can rightly dispose of in a much
wider range of ways: see III *Sent.* d. 29 a. 6 ad 3.   [16] II-II q. 66 a. 2c.

[17] See II-II q. 32 a. 6c: 'secundum proprium statum et negotia occurrentia'.

[18] See II-II q. 31 a. 3 ad 3; IV *Sent.* d. 15 q. 2 a. 6 sol. 3c.

[19] IV *Sent.* d. 15 q. 2 a. 1 sol. 4c; likewise, without the *absoluta/conditionata* terminol-
ogy, II-II q. 32 a. 5c.

[20] IV *Sent.* d. 15 q. 2 a. 1 sol. 4 ad 2 ('quando alius est *in statu extremae necessitatis*,
efficiuntur sibi *omnia communia*'); similarly II-II q. 32 a. 7 ad 3, q. 187 a. 4c.

[21] They need not wait until they are at death's door and incapable of helping themselves: IV *Sent.* d. 15 q. 2 a. 1 sol. 4 ad 4.

property right.[22] Correspondingly, if I am aware[23] of another person's extreme, evident, and urgent need,[24] and there is no one else to give relief in time,[25] I have a duty of strict justice (not merely 'charity')[26] to relieve that need by handing over resources that I own even though they are not *superflua* but rather are needed in a type (b) sense, i.e. for fulfilling my proper responsibilities to myself and others.[27] My duty does not require that I reduce myself or my dependants to type (a) extreme necessity.[28] If my dependants and I are already in or on the brink of such dire necessity, I am entitled to hold onto anything which I own (or legitimately possess) and need to preserve us.[29] In such conditions of dire necessity on *both* sides—essentially like the plank which will support one but not two people in a shipwreck[30]—there is no single rule or measure which identifies one pattern of action or outcome as the right one for all parties

---

[22] II-II q. 32 a. 7 ad 3. Such people are morally entitled to use force or stealth to get what they need; their acts may be 'theft' or 'robbery' in positive law and conventional discourse, but morally, and 'properly speaking', are neither robbery nor theft and—provided they respect the moral rights of others in similar need, and the exceptionless moral norms against lying, adultery, deliberately killing or injuring the innocent, etc.—are fully justified and right: II-II q. 66 a. 7c and ad 2, q. 110 a. 3 ad 4; IV *Sent.* d. 15 q. 2 a. 1 sol. 4 ad 2. A law or judicial order requiring them to be punished is an unjust law (see I-II q. 96 a. 4c and ad 3) and lacks moral force.

[23] But I need not go looking throughout the world for need which I might relieve; it is enough if I meet the needs of those I meet: II-II q. 71 a. 1c.

[24] Present or probable in future: IV *Sent.* d. 15 q. 2 a. 1 sol. 4 ad 4; cf. II-II q. 71 a. 1c: it is enough if one relieves present need.

[25] II-II q. 32 a. 5 ad 3, q. 71 a. 1c: though it can be praiseworthy to do so, I need not give help if it seems likely that those in need can be assisted by others who are more closely connected to them or who have more resources than I do.

[26] Misleadingly (in some respects), Aquinas' main treatment of the duty to make one's goods available to the poor (II-II q. 31 a. 3, q. 32 aa. 5–10) is under the heading of 'charity' (love of God and neighbour) rather than 'justice', though it is outlined again under justice (II-II q. 66 a. 7). Of course, there is praiseworthy alms-giving which is not a duty of justice but a work of supererogation: IV *Sent.* d. 15 q. 2 a. 1 sol. 4 ad 1; II-II q. 32 a. 5c {consilia}.

[27] *Quodl.* VIII q. 6 a. 2c; II-II q. 32 a. 5c and ad 3, a. 6c.

[28] II-II q. 32 a. 5c; IV *Sent.* d. 15 q. 2 a. 1 sol. 4c. Both texts conclude that 'one must [i] give alms out of one's *superflua*, and [ii] give alms to anyone who is in extreme necessity'; the context establishes that [ii] clearly means: to relieve extreme ('absolute') necessity one must be willing to give up parts of one's holdings which are not *superflua* but needed for type (b) ('relative') necessities. Here *superflua* means: what is not needed for either one's type (a) or type (b) needs. Sometimes, as in II-II q. 32 a. 5 ad 3, *superflua* seems to mean: what is not needed for one's type (a) necessities. Aquinas' imprecision here (taken with the last sentence of a. 6c) has caused confusion, but taken as a whole his texts yield the stringent theorem of justice stated in the text above.   [29] See II-II q. 31 a. 3 ad 3.

[30] Aquinas does not, I think, discuss this scenario. It might be thought that it differs from the case of the starving who beg from (say) a landowner whose own family faces starvation, in that the latter has a just and legal ownership, a title, which the sailor first to

to pursue and accept; the judgement of the person of practical reasonableness will often if not always identify some such pattern of action or conduct.[31] There is a very strong presumption that owners who are in extreme necessity should not be giving away what they and their dependants need to survive, but one may rightly set the presumption aside—even at lethal risk to oneself or one's dependants—to save some 'great personage who is vital to the Church or the state'.[32]

2. In situations where no one confronts extreme necessity, the right of owners and other property-holders to keep their property extends just as far as their type (b) need to maintain themselves (with their dependants) in the form of life which they have reasonably adopted. All their *further* resources {residuum; superflua} are 'held in common': all[33] these resources should be made available to those ('the poor') who, though not in extreme necessity, lack the resources to satisfy their type (b) needs. The poor have a natural right that the whole of this *residuum* be distributed in their favour.[34]

Of course, the level of resources which it is just for owners to regard as needed and not *superflua* is rather indeterminate; in any given case much could doubtless be added, or subtracted, leaving one still within this zone, in which owners have the prior right to consume their own property.[35] Regarded as formulas for a norm legalistically treated, Aquinas' references to 'superfluities' and 'appropriate status or position in life {proprius status}' leave plenty

reach the plank cannot appeal to. But remember that Aquinas' axiom is: in situations of extreme necessity, everything becomes common, i.e. ownership or other legal title is morally superseded for the duration of the situation.

[31] See II-II q. 31 a. 3 ad 3: 'in such situations no universal rule can be given, since the individual cases are so various'. Need one rule out the hypothesis that there can, in such cases, be two or more courses of action which are each morally acceptable even though they are incompatible and lead to quite different outcomes and perhaps to a collision or trial of strength? Since neither of the persons involved need be acting wrongly, the hypothesis is not contrary to Aquinas' sound thesis (I-II q. 18 a. 9; also II *Sent*. d. 40 a. 5c and ad 4) that, though there are types of acts which are generically neither morally good nor morally bad, every particular act, as chosen and done in its particular situation, is either morally good and right or wrong and bad.

[32] II-II q. 32 a. 6c {magna persona per quam Ecclesia vel respublica sustentaretur}.

[33] II-II q. 87 a. 1 ad 4: '*omnia* superflua'.

[34] II-II q. 66 a. 7c: 'res quas aliqui superabundanter habent, *ex naturali iure debentur* pauperum sustentationi'.

[35] II-II q. 32 a. 6c; IV *Sent*. d. 15 q. 2 a. 4 sol. 1c: 'even with much added, one would not exceed the wherewithal for one's position in life {status sui conditionem}, and with much subtracted the wherewithal for that position would still be properly maintained'.

of scope for owners to rationalize the holding and consumption of their wealth. But the true measure of one's needs is not the emotionally motivated expectations and patterns of consumption conventional among one's social class,[36] nor exaggerated fears about possible future penury,[37] but the bona fide[38] judgement of a practical reasonableness which includes, as always (IV.4), general justice and love of neighbour as oneself. This judgement is uprightly made when it looks along not just one dimension (e.g. how closely this person is related to me) but several (e.g. how great is this relative stranger's need). The incommensurability of such dimensions defies resolution by any general rule, and in a certain sense, the question to which the judgement responds 'cannot be settled by reason'.[39] Still, the question remains within the domain of reason, but reason's 'mean' is here a zone with vague boundaries[40] rather than a point, and the final judgement is remitted to the virtues of the reasonable[41] rather than to rules.

Resources needed for the investment and other expenses reasonably arising in one's legitimate business enterprises are not *superflua*.[42] Nor is one obliged to forgo proper savings for future use in consumption by oneself, one's dependants, or the poor.[43] One important way in which owners may be able to discharge their responsibility for distributing their *superflua* is by offering employment for wages.[44] The right of the household and its head to govern and manage the economy of the perhaps extended household—a right which depends for its significance on the powers that go with ownership of capital (goods not themselves needed for early consumption)—is, in fact, the foundation for a kind of liberty which Aquinas more takes for granted than discusses: the liberty to confront the state's rulers with the firm and rightful claim that their authority is limited (see VII.6, VIII. 2). In general, the responsibility

---

[36] See II-II q. 169 a. 1c (fancy dressing); *Eth.* IV. 7 n. 14 [732].

[37] IV *Sent.* d. 15 q. 2 a. 1 sol. 4 ad 4.   [38] See *Quodl.* VI q. 7 a. un. c and ad 1.

[39] Ibid. ad 1 (line 100): the question when someone is in such necessity that a *dispensator* must give the property away cannot be settled by reason {non potest ratione determinari} but is left to the prudence and faith of the *dispensator*.

[40] They 'cannot be defined with complete certainty': *Quodl.* VI q. 7 a. un. c (lines. 77–8).

[41] II-II q. 31 a. 3 ad 1: 'non potest universali regula determinari cui sit magis subveniendum, quia sunt diversi gradus et indigentiae et propinquitatis; sed hoc requirit *prudentis* iudicium'.   [42] See II-II q. 32 a. 6c: 'negotia occurrentia'.

[43] II-II q. 117 a. 3 ad 2, a. 4 ad 3.

[44] See I-II q. 105 a. 2 ad 6: wage labourers are presumptively among the poor to whom distribution of *superflua* is owed in justice.

for judging what the household and its members need (types (a) and (b)), and for deciding *how* to make *superflua* available to the poor, is the owner's.[45]

Of course, making such a decision involves dividing one's wealth between *proprium* and *superfluum*; this division in turn presupposes that one has discharged one's debts,[46] and one's debts include one's tax liabilities.[47] Aquinas tends to speak of taxes as a kind of stipend for governing.[48] But he teaches that rulers have a responsibility to provide, for each of their subjects, whatever they would otherwise lack to sustain them in their respective conditions and status in life.[49] More clearly, he goes along with Aristotle's clear and repeated teaching that it is appropriate for the state's rulers and laws to make provision for the fair distribution of goods for use in consumption, so that that use be truly 'common'.[50] In Aquinas' own theory this amounts to saying that the distribution by owners of their *superflua* is an appropriate subject for legislation to avoid backsliding, arbitrariness, and inequity. So payment of taxes imposed for redistributive purposes will be a primary way in which owners discharge their duty of distribution.

At first glance it seems naïve of Aquinas to say that if some are too rich, others must be too poor.[51] After all, economics is not a zero-sum game; riches may be gained in productive enterprises which to some extent enrich all concerned, employees and consumers alike. But Aquinas is right: if some have a *super*abundance—more than they need for their business, their legitimate savings, and their other responsibilities—then others *must*, in the real world, be

---

[45] II-II q. 66 a. 7c: 'committitur arbitrio uniuscuiusque dispensatio propriarum rerum, ut ex eis subveniat necessitatem patientibus'; I-II q. 105 a. 2c: 'optimum est quod possessiones sint distinctae, et usus sit partim communis, partim autem per voluntatem possessorum communicetur'.

[46] II-II q. 31 a. 3 ad 3; IV *Sent.* d. 15 q. 2 a. 6 sol. 3c: 'semper magis reddendum est debitum quam beneficium impendendum'.   [47] See II-II q. 66 a. 8 ad 3.

[48] See e.g. II-II q. 62 a. 7c (and so if rulers fail to provide proper service—e.g. fail to suppress burglary or banditry—they owe their subjects compensation by way of restitution: ibid. and ad 3); *Dec.* 9 [1292]; *In Rom.* 13. 1 ad v. 6 [1039]: 'quasi stipendia sui ministerii, non autem . . . pro praemio'. The only earthly *reward* that rulers are entitled to is honour and glory: ibid.; *Eth.* v. 11 n. 12 [1011]; cf. *Reg.* 1. 7 [1. 8–9] [53–66] [773–85]. II-II q. 66 a. 8 ad 3 postulates that taxation is 'for upholding common good {propter bonum commune conservandum}'.

[49] II-II q. 77 a. 4c: 'householders {oeconomic[i]} and *rulers of states* {politic[i]} *have to make provision for* {providere de} *the necessities of life for their* household or *state*'; see also *Reg.* II. 2 [I. 13–14] [100] [812]; VII.2 at n. 47 below.

[50] I-II q. 104 a. 1 ad 1, q. 105 a. 2c and ad 3; *Pol.* II. 4 nn. 5–6 [200–1] ad *Politics* 2. 3. 1263ᵃ24–5.

[51] II-II q. 118 a. 1 ad 2.

going short of what they are entitled to. For if we set aside the possible world in which everyone everywhere has enough to meet all their needs, *superflua* truly belong to others; anyone who keeps them is depriving, and indeed stealing[52] from, those to whom they should, by one means or another, have been made available.[53]

VI.3. *Contract: Freedom,* fides, *and Reciprocal Benefit*

Making a contract which courts will treat as binding and enforceable is participating in a practice, a convention, a social and often a legal institution. But one participates in a social practice also when one makes a promise of a kind that binds not legally, but only in conscience.[54] As with other social practices or institutions such as language, or the use of a conventional 'medium' of exchange (money),[55] so too with promises: there is a sense in which but for the pre-existence of the general practice(s), the making of a particular promise or contract would be in a certain sense meaningless and impossible.[56] And the practice has been introduced[57] because its existence makes available important benefits for individuals and their communities.

But, as with language, there is also an important sense in which the practice is not truly fundamental, but rather draws its intelligibility and even its existence from principles and insights which are prior to the practice. Even in the absence of any established practices of showing gratitude, of recompensing (if one can) a Good Samaritan, or of keeping promises to render a service, the meaning and effect of the Golden Rule includes the thoughts that one good turn deserves another,[58] and other people's reliance upon their

---

[52] II-II q. 118 a. 4c; if violence is used to retain the *superflua*, the injustice is robbery {*rapina*}: ibid.

[53] 'Superabundance', in this context = *superflua*: see II-II q. 66 a. 7c.

[54] Some agreements which do not bind *in foro contentioso* do bind in conscience: IV *Sent.* d. 27 q. 2 a. 1 (= *Supp.* q. 43 a. 1) ad 2.

[55] So money can be altered in value, or even rendered valueless, by change (deliberate or otherwise) in the practice of using and accepting it: *Eth.* v. 9 n. 5 [982]; *Pol.* 1. 7 n. 10 [120].

[56] So *pacta sunt servanda* ('agreements are to be performed') is a principle or norm not precisely of natural law, but of *ius gentium* (which is, however, a matter of natural law/ right: n. 76 and VIII. 3 at n. 88 below): *Eth.* v. 12 n. 4 [1019].   [57] II-II q. 77 a. 1c.

[58] On the 'debt of gratitude', which is not a 'legal' debt, but owed only *ex debito honestatis* or *ex debito iustitiae amicabilis*, to be discharged *gratis et liberaliter*, see

expectation of my assistance gives me morally significant reason to do what they expect. Moreover, what is introduced for social benefit is introduced for *common* benefit {introducta pro communi utilitate utriusque}, the benefit of *each* of us in relation to what as individuals or families we need from each other.[59] So institutions or practices such as sale (the paradigm of all non-gratuitous promises or contracts)[60] ought in each case to preserve and promote *equality* between the parties in respect of the subject-matter (the 'thing' and its price).[61] A practice which did not respect and demand such equality in loss and gain would be an unjust practice, incapable of doing what all other such practices do: grounding obligations in conscience. Finally, the social benefits available through the acceptance of practices are the benefits of collaboration, which would in principle be available, in the absence of the practice, by sheer unanimity about ends and means—unanimity which could arise and be maintained by simple coincidence in desire and judgement lasting all the way through the initiation, execution, and completion of common projects. (Practices of recognizing the authority of contracts, or more generally, of laws and other social rules, are substitutes for that practically unattainable constancy in coincidence of desire and judgement about common projects.) So behind all these practices, and supporting all conventional obligations of particular justice, is the obligation implicit in the basic human goods of friendship and practical reasonableness, and the requirement of general justice.

Promises and contracts engage one's fidelity,[62] one's good faith. It is worth exploring how that virtue resembles the virtue of veracity, truthfulness, authenticity in speech. (That there is such a resemblance is suggested by the phrases 'good faith' and 'bad faith', which extend to both dishonesty in the making and infidelity in the observance of a contract.[63]) It is not difficult to see that making a promise without any intention of keeping it is a form of lying.[64] But there is no such lie if one made the promise intending to keep

---

II-II q. 106 a. 1 ad 2; *Impugn.* II c. 6 [344]; *Mal.* q. 13 a. 4 ad 5. See also *Eth.* VIII. 13 n. 13 [1738].

[59] II-II q. 77 a. 1c.   [60] II-II q. 100 a. 1 ad 5.

[61] Ibid. See VI.4 at nn. 82–103 below.

[62] II-II q. 88 a. 3c; IV *Sent.* d. 31 q. 1 a. 2 (= *Supp.* q. 49 a. 2) ad 2.

[63] See II-II q. 189 a. 3c; IV *Sent.* d. 38 q. 1 a. 3c sol. 1c ('cum contractus bonae fidei inter homines factus obliget ad necessariam observationem').

[64] II-II q. 40 a. 3c, q. 110 a. 3 ad 5; V.5 at n. 99 above.

it, but later changed one's mind.[65] Still, a change of mind will be an act of infidelity—betrayal—unless the promise was of a kind which it was morally wrong to have made, or the circumstances of the parties (so far as they affect the subject-matter of the promise)[66] have changed so that it is inappropriate to carry out the promise. So we can wonder what precisely is the vice—the unreasonableness—in infidelity.

Like law-making, promising (whether contracting or making a vow) is more fundamentally an act of intelligence and reason than of will.[67] For it projects an order, a set of relationships between a person or persons and some act or other 'thing', and setting things in order is always fundamentally the work of practical understanding and more or less creative reason. As a kind of order envisaged for the future by present understanding, what is promised is affirmed[68] by the expression of the promise (or vow). The affirmation is not only an assertion of one's present intention to do what is promised. More importantly, it is also an assertion of one's present intention to undertake and acknowledge the *obligation* to do so[69] and the corresponding *right* of the promisee, such that the benefits or service of the promisor's performance can be counted, as from *now*, among the promisee's *sua* (belongings, goods) or *iura* (rights).

Now the latter intention (to undertake, by promising, such an obligation) makes sense. Forming, communicating, and acting

[65] II-II q. 110 a. 3 ad 5.
[66] Some promises (or oaths or vows) are to do something of a kind that should never be done; they have no validity or binding force: II-II q. 89 a. 9 ad 3, q. 110 a. 3 ad 5; *Quodl.* III q. 5 a. 2c. Some are to do something of a kind which can rightly be done, but which it was wrong for the promisor to promise. Others can be rightly made by this promisor, but in the circumstances prevailing at the time for performance would lead to an outcome which ought not to be brought about. These, too, should not be performed and do not bind (except to the extent necessary to be fair to the other party): IV *Sent.* d. 38 q. 1 a. 3 sol. 1 ad 3 (oaths and vows which would have a worse outcome {deteriorem eventum} if performed than if not performed should not (or at least need not) be kept, whether or not this outcome was or could have been foreseen at the time of the promise): II-II q. 89 a. 7 ad 2. Some promises are such that it is reasonable to keep them and reasonable to break them {licitum est et servare et non servare}: a. 9 ad 3. See also VIII. 2 at n. 36 below.
[67] II-II q. 88 a. 1c; IV *Sent.* d. 38 q. 1 a. 1 sol. 1c.
[68] See II-II q. 88 a. 3 ad 2 and 3; this intention is affirmed both as *asserted* and as 'made firm' ('privatum condictum . . . firmatur aliquo pacto') (II-II q. 57 a. 2c; also q. 89 a. 7c; *Quodl.* IV q. 12 a. 1 ad 4).
[69] Doubtless it is to make clear to all concerned, including the promisor, that precisely *this* intention is being expressed that (as Aquinas says: *Perf.* c. 16 [656]) formalities and *solemnitates* are introduced to make a contractual arrangement more firm {firmior}. *Any* promise creates an 'obligation of natural right' as a matter of decency {secundum honestatem}, but for a positive law promissory obligation {obligatione civili} something more is required (at least in Roman law): II-II q. 88 a. 3 ad 1.

upon such intentions makes available great mutual benefits and is in line with love of neighbour, general justice, and the Golden Rule. And the communicating of such an intention can be a lie. So, for both these reasons, the promise *rationally* affirms not just intention to act in a certain way but intention to be bound so to act—bound in the sense that the promisor's future performance is owed to the promisee and is a present right of the promisee, capable of being counted in the promisee's stock or wealth. As promisor, one's mere change of mind about performing will be a motive but cannot be a *reason* for one to deny that one now, after a change of heart, has the obligation that one, in promising, asserted one would have at every time from promise to performance.

Where a promissory obligation truthfully undertaken is repudiated (whether by refusal to acknowledge the obligation or by brazen disregard for acknowledged obligation), there is thus a kind of division of the self—of one's present self and one's former self whose intent one projected and affirmed in the promise. This division is one kind of untrustworthiness or bad faith, analogous to the division of inner and outer self which constitutes the untrustworthiness and bad faith involved (both as cause and as effect) in lying (including false promising) and related forms of inauthenticity.[70] The division of the self by this untrustworthiness—infidelity—presupposes that one's original expressions of intent and consent to undertake promissory obligation were freely given exercises of self-mastery. So promissory obligations can be undertaken only by persons who are adult and competent {sui iuris}, and uncoerced.[71] It is also a repudiation of the interpersonal relationship which that undertaking both projected as, and instituted to be, a good and mutually beneficial ordering of the parties and their affairs.[72] As we saw in the case of the supremely significant contract of marriage (v.4), the *fides* involved in contract is precisely the commitment to, and acknowledgement and expression of commitment to, that relationship.

---

[70] On the closeness of this analogy, and the stringency of the norm against violations of promissory obligations, see II-II q. 40 a. 3c (breaking promises to enemies is fraudulent and wrongful—provided, presumably, that pre-conditions such as absence of coercion are satisfied: see at n. 71 below).   [71] See IV *Sent.* d. 28 a. 3 (= *Supp.* q. 45 a. 5) ad 2.

[72] Because contract is a relationship between persons, contracts of the kind we are considering {materiales contractus} can only be entered into by mutual expression of willingness to do so: IV *Sent.* d. 27 q. 1 a. 2 sol. 1c and sol. 2c (= *Supp.* q. 45 a. 1c and a. 2c).

vi.4. *Commerce, Capital, and Credit*

If I acquire things to dispose of them with profit, I am engaged in commerce {negotiatio}.[73] In Aristotle's view, those who engage in commerce are seeking not so much the well-being of a household but rather the limitless increase of their own wealth; commercial activity for profit is thus fundamentally unnecessary, unnatural, and rather low.[74] This view Aquinas rejects. Commerce considered without regard to motives does have something sordid about it. But people can in fact involve themselves in trade and commerce for moderate rather than infinite gain, and with decent motives such as sustaining their households or helping the poor, or for the public benefit {publica utilitas} of ensuring that their country is supplied with what it needs. It is usually decent to seek moderate profit for such reasons; it is recompense for services rendered by work {quasi stipendium laboris}.[75]

There remains the interesting and important question, which types of commercial transaction are fair, and which are inherently unjust. A sound system of 'private law' (i.e. state law regulating private transactions) will track the moral judgements which answer that question.[76] Underlying those judgements is always the principle of equality (equivalence) in the exchange.[77]

Of course, one may give one's services, or things one owns, gratuitously—a work of mercy rather than justice. As a lawyer, a doctor, or other provider of services, one is morally bound to do such works of mercy whenever one stands in the position of proximate neighbour to people whose need for the service is great, and who cannot acquire or arrange for it in any other obvious way.[78] But no lawyer or other provider of services is bound always to provide them free.[79] Fees for services are (like salaries or wages) a

---

[73] II-II q. 77 a. 4 ad 2.

[74] *Politics* 1. 3. 1257^{b}1-1258^{a}18; cf. Aquinas' (strong) warning in *Reg.* II. 7 [II. 3] [139–40] [841–2] about the moral and political dangers of excessive interest in trade.

[75] II-II q. 77 a. 4c. The complete city-state {perfecta civitas} will make moderate use of merchants: *Reg.* II. 7 [II. 3] [142] [843]; VII. 2 n. 47 below.

[76] Legal institutions such as sale, contract, and property are matters of positive law, but at least in their general structure are so necessary to a just social life that they are a matter of deduction from basic moral (natural law) principles (and so are included in that part of a state's positive laws which is a matter of natural law and can be called *ius gentium*—law common to all peoples—as distinct from *ius civile*): I-II q. 95 a. 4c and ad 1, II-II q. 57 a. 3c and ad 3; *Eth.* v. 12 n. 4 [1019].   [77] II-II q. 61 a. 3c.

[78] II-II q. 71 a. 1c; n. 25 above.   [79] II-II q. 71 a. 4c; IV. 4 n. 80 above.

kind of price {pretium};[80] they should be moderate, and the measure of their fairness takes into account the situation of both provider and recipient, the nature of the transactions and the work {labor} involved, and the customs of the country.[81]

Sale is the paradigm example of exchange.[82] In any sale, buyer and seller act justly (leaving aside any question of fraud) if the price[83] received by the seller and paid by the purchaser is neither more nor less than what the thing sold is worth. For then the transaction respects the requirement of *equality* in mutual benefit {communis utilitas}; sellers are recompensed for what they have given up (their costs including fair wages for their labour, expenses incurred in transportation, etc.),[84] and buyers are likewise compensated for the price they have paid, by the value of what they acquire.[85]

In the context of justice, the measure of anything's 'value' is human need.[86] And one needs something if one cannot achieve one's end(s) without it.[87] So the value at stake in justice is use-value: in the order of nature a mouse, having senses and locomotion, is of greater worth {dignitas} than a pearl, but in terms of utility—what people need for their use—a pearl has a higher value {pretium}.[88] But utility is relative to circumstances: in a situation of necessity {necessitatis}, a loaf of bread (or even, *in extremis*, a mouse) will reasonably be more highly valued {praeeligeretur}, and fetch a higher price, than the most precious pearl.[89] The normal manifestation of need {indigentia} is preference {praeeligere}: so 'need' amounts in these contexts to 'demand'. The conventional institution of money {numisma} enables us to measure demand, i.e.

[80] I-II q. 114 a. 1c, II-II q. 71 a. 4 ad 3. [81] II-II q. 71 a. 4c.

[82] II-II q. 61 a. 2c.

[83] Whether the price is in money or (as in barter) things does not affect the principles (*Eth.* v. 9 n. 13 [990]; II-II q. 77 a. 4c); money is for facilitating the measuring (comparison) of the value of what passes between the parties, and thus for facilitating the exchange/sale: *Eth.* v. 9 n. 2 [979]; n. 90 below. [84] II-II q. 77 a. 4 ad 2; n. 118 below.

[85] So the guiding principle in setting a fair price—equality in *recompense* (compensation)—is the guiding principle in all voluntary and non-voluntary transactions, the matter of commutative justice: see II-II q. 61 a. 3c and a. 4c. And see at n. 102 below.

[86] *Eth.* v. 9 nn. 4–5 [981–2]. [87] II *Sent.* d. 29 a. 1c.

[88] *Eth.* v. 9 n. 4 [981]. And enormous money-wealth may have no utility to individuals in their situation (as when Midas' touch turns food to gold and he starves to death), or to anyone (as when a government or a people decide to nullify a currency: *Pol.* 1. 7 n. 10 [120]). But money is a normal measure of worth {dignitas} (II-II q. 117 a. 2 ad 2) and of a comparison, by price, which is at once conventional and rational (IV *Sent* d. 15 q. 2 a. 1 sol. 1 ad 1, d. 25 q. 3 a. 2 sol. 1c and a. 3c). [89] *Quodl.* 1 q. 7 a. 2c.

the demand of the buyer who has money and of the seller who needs {indiget} money and has what meets the buyer's demand {indigentia}.[90] The normal measure of something's value, therefore, will be the price it would currently fetch 'in the market {secundum commune forum}',[91] i.e. in deals between any willing sellers and buyers in the same locality and time-frame, each party being aware of the thing's merits and defects.[92]

This general fair market price—normally a range rather than a point[93]—will be mutually recompensing, so far as circumstances allow; sellers who bring to market goods for which there is no demand at a price which covers their costs and labour cannot expect to recover those costs.[94] And it will inevitably vary from place to place and time to time, according as the commodity in question is scarce or plentiful.[95] Sellers who use no deceit do not violate justice if they sell at the going price knowing that it will soon fall when other sellers come to market.[96] This acceptable variability has limits, however, in fairness. If to some particular buyer the thing is worth a lot more than the general market price, *and* the particular seller will incur some appreciable loss (not *merely* diminished profit) from parting with the thing at the general market price, then a fair price can significantly exceed the general market price.[97]

Now suppose that the buyer, having a pressing need, would willingly pay more than the general market price, but at that price the seller would incur no real *loss* in relinquishing the property (the open market price would fully cover what the seller invested in the thing;[98] or the seller is wealthy and has no unmet real economic

---

[90] *Eth.* v. 9 nn. 5, 9, 11–12 [982, 986, 988–9]. Money is the normal measure of the price of 'things which promise me what I need in life {ea quae sufficentiam in vita promittunt}': II *Sent.* d. 5 q. 1 a. 3 ad 1; it is an institution established {inventa} to enable commensuration of what is given with what is received in exchanges: II-II q. 61 a. 4c.

[91] See *Empt.* ii [722]; III *Sent.* d. 37 a. 6 ex.; II-II q. 77 a. 4c and ad 2.

[92] See II-II q. 77 a. 1; the measure is often imprecise (ad 2); but non-disclosure of latent defects is fraudulent, if it results in sale of the thing for more than the just price (or puts the puchaser in peril of harm or loss), and obliges the seller to make restitution: q. 77 a. 3c; *Quodl.* II q. 5 a. 2c.

[93] II-II q. 77 a. 1 ad 1.

[94] Conversely, unless the price covers the seller's labour and expenses {in labore et expensis}, goods will not be supplied for exchange, and there will be no trade: *Eth.* v. 9 n. 3 [980]. On the tension between 'current fair market price' and 'compensation for seller's costs, risks, and labour', see Baldwin (1959: 74–80), observing (79) that 'cost is the competitive price in the long run'.

[95] II-II q. 77 a. 2 ad 2: 'secundum diversitatem copiae et inopiae rerum'.

[96] II-II q. 77 a. 3 ad 4.   [97] II-II q. 71 a. 1c.

[98] Including all the seller's proper expenses (e.g. on transport), but not charges negligently or immorally incurred by the seller: *Empt.* iii [723].

needs—i.e. has *superflua*). In such a case the seller cannot rightly take advantage of the buyer's particular need, and must not set a price more than the going rate. Need(s) of one party, if not matched by needs of the other party which are comparable in value (though not necessarily in any other way), cannot justly be counted as changing the just, market price.[99] In a certain sense, a buyer in this situation gains more than the seller does. But this surplus value derives not from the seller but from the buyer's own situation {conditio}, and sellers cannot rightly *'sell' what is not theirs* or claim recompense for what is to them no loss.[100]

Exacting an unfair, i.e. 'unequal', price, even from a 'willing'[101] buyer, is indeed selling what is not one's own to sell. The just price is one at which all parties to the transaction are, so far as possible, compensated proportionately for what they are giving up. This is the pair of thoughts which—given the Golden Rule[102]—guides the moral analysis not only of the transactions which in law and common speech are sales of goods or services but also of the many types of investment in which 'lenders' charge for the use of their capital. (They are thoughts which Hobbes and many after him rejected, claiming that the only condition for justice in exchanges is that the parties have agreed the price[103]).

In some common types of loan, the owners retain their ownership and sell only the use of the thing. I hire out a horse or a book, or lease a house or a factory. The risk—the possibility that the thing itself will be destroyed or lost—remains with me, as owner.[104] Correspondingly, I as owner retain the power to sell the thing itself as distinct from its use.[105] That use goes to the

---

[99] II-II q. 77 a. 1c; *Mal.* q. 13 a. 4 ad 7; III *Sent.* d. 37 a. 6 ad 4.

[100] II-II q. 77 a. 1c: Aquinas adds here that, if the buyer in this situation is in a position to volunteer more than the due price, making such a supererogatory payment will be a decent thing to do. But in any other case, a seller who has taken advantage of a buyer's special need owes the buyer restitution of any notable surplus received above the market price: II-II q. 77 a. 1 ad 1.

[101] The freedom involved in such willingness is always watered down by the coercion arising from the buyer's need: see *Mal.* q. 13 a. 4 ad 9.

[102] II-II q. 77 a. 1 s.c.: no one wishes to buy something for more than its worth, therefore . . . The Golden Rule grounds a critique of excessive prices, even though everyone would like (fairness aside) to 'buy cheap and sell dear' (ibid. ad 2; *Quodl.* II q. 5 a. 2 ad 2).

[103] Hobbes, *Leviathan* (1651), xv. 14: 'The value of all things contracted for, is measured by the appetite of the contractors and therefore the just value, is that which they be contented to give.'

[104] Unless the loss resulted from their fault, hirers will not be liable to restore to the owner the value of the thing: Justinian, *Institutes* 3. 24. 5.

[105] See *Quodl.* III q. 7 a. 2c.

---

lessee or borrowing hirer, along with any fruits or profits arising from the use. In all such cases it is legitimate to make a charge (the rent, the hire, etc.) which compensates the owners for what they have given up in giving up the use of the thing,[106] while giving full credit to the users for any work they need to put into making the thing yield fruits. The charge is in effect the price for selling the thing's *use*.[107] The temporary users (borrowers, tenants, etc.) are justly liable not only to return the thing at the agreed time but also to pay this fair charge—just price—for use.[108]

In the case of money, however, use cannot be split off from ownership.[109] As we saw, its use as money is *disposal*—to be *spent* in exchange for goods or services or promises. When it is spent it is gone; someone else is now its owner.[110] If I allow you to use my money precisely as money (i.e. for use in exchange), I allow you to transfer the ownership of the money to someone else; so my grant of the use is also a grant of the thing (the money) itself—of ownership inseparably with the right to use.[111] In the law and logic of property, any promise by you (B) to 'repay the money' to me (L) is a promise, not that you will return that money to its owner, but rather that you will pay me (the former owner) a sum equivalent to the money which was transferred out of my ownership into your (doubtless temporary) ownership.[112] The risk of loss passes with ownership, from me to you and then on to anyone to whom you transfer it. In a contract of loan of money for B's use, B's obligation

---

[106] The price, i.e. the rent or other hire charge, is a charge for the use forgone and so can rightly exceed the depreciation in the thing's value through wear and tear over the period of lease or hire: *Mal.* q. 13 a. 4 ad 4; III *Sent.* d. 37 a. 6c. There is nothing necessarily wrong about living off rents: see I-II q. 105 a. 2 ad 6.   [107] *Quodl.* III q. 7 a. 2c.

[108] II-II q. 78 a. 1c.

[109] Of course, coins or notes could be lent not *as* money but as objects for display; in such a case, ownership and use (display) can be split up, and so the coins and notes can be hired out for a fee which is a sale precisely of their *use*: II-II q. 78 a. 1 ad 6; *Mal.* q. 13 a. 4 ad 15. The same can be true of other things typically consumed in use; a bottle of wine might be lent for display, hired as a stage-prop, and so on. And I could even rightly *hire* out a sealed bag of coins to you, with a view to your pawning it (i.e. depositing it as security against a loan to you from the pawnbroker); the sealed bag of coins here functions not as money but like a silver jug which, for a fair fee, I might hire to you for use, including use as a pledge for the pawnbroker: *Mal.* q. 13 a. 4 ad 15.

[110] See *Mal.* q. 13 a. 4c and ad 5 and ad 15.

[111] III *Sent.* d. 37 a. 6 ad 5; *Quodl.* III q. 7 a. 2c. A loan of money is strictly speaking a sale of the money, the purchase price being payable at the end of the loan.

[112] This is particularly obvious when a banker 'lends B money' by extending an overdraft or similar facility and then crediting a third party to B's order (e.g. by honouring the cheque B has given to that party).

to 'repay'[113] L remains the same whether B spends the money on consumption or investment or loses it by fire, theft, or unsuccessful trading.[b]

What charges, then, can I fairly make for the use of my money? Aquinas points out two broad types. (1) *Share of profits in joint enterprise*. If I 'lend' my money to a merchant or craftsman on the basis that we are in partnership {societas} (perhaps only for a single venture), so that I am to share in any overall losses or profits, my entitlement to my dividend of the profits (as well as to the return of my capital *if its value has not been lost by the joint enterprise*) is just and appropriate.[114] (2) *Recompense or indemnity {interesse} for losses*. In making any loan I can levy a charge on the borrower in order to compensate me for whatever expenses I have outlaid or losses I have incurred by making the loan.[115] And the terms of a loan can include a fee or charge which is payable if you fail to repay the principal on time, and is sufficient to compensate me for the losses I am liable to incur if the principal is not repaid on time[116] (while also deterring you from such default).

To make any other or further charge[117] in respect of the loan of money is unjust, and the name for this sort of charge—this sort of wrong—is *usury*. It is unjust because in making any such other or further charge I am demanding a price for something that is not mine to sell. For (as we saw) in making a loan of this sort I willy-nilly transfer ownership (and thus the risks of loss)[118] along with

---

[113] II-II q. 62 a. 6c {restitutio; recompensare}.

[114] II-II q. 78 a. 2 ad 5: Aquinas says that I retain ownership (as a part(ner)-owner), and that the merchant or craftsman does business at my [proportionate] risk {periculum}. The second point is the substantial one and is correct (though Roman law had allowed anomalous 'leonine' partnerships in which, by agreement, some of the partners were not liable for net losses; even in such partnerships, however, all partners would be liable for the proper expenses of the *societas*: Justinian, *Institutes* 3. 25. 2); the first point is true only if taken broadly, since strictly speaking the money passes from me to the *societas* and then on to further recipients with whom the *societas* does business.

[115] II-II q. 78 a. 1 ad 5, a. 2 ad 1. But I cannot rightly charge you for losses which result, during the period of the loan, from my own miscalculation of my own financial situation: *Mal.* q. 13 a. 4 ad 14. On the proper measure of compensable losses, see at nn. 127–32 below.

[116] *Mal.* q. 13 a. 4 ad 14; see also II-II q. 78 a. 2 ad 1; IV *Sent.* d. 15 q. 1 a. 5 sol. 2 ad 4; n. 132 below. Aquinas calls this fee *interesse* (i.e. an indemnity: see *Quodl.* III q. 7 a. 2c).

[117] Such illicit charges can take many forms besides monetary interest: e.g. higher prices for delayed payment of purchase price; promises to perform services or to make corresponding loans in future; and in general anything which can have a price: II-II q. 78 a. 2 ad 4 and ad 7; *Empt.*

[118] The *de facto* risk that the borrower will not only default but become insolvent or abscond is to be covered by taking security and/or insurance against default (and the

use.[119] The two cannot be separated; to transfer the one is to transfer the other,[120] and to use a thing of this sort is to 'consume' it, i.e. to lose both possession and ownership of it, either by transfer to someone else (in the case of money as such) or by destruction of the thing 'lent' (as in the case of bread or wine). In short: to use money as money (i.e. in exchange) just is to dispose of it—to confer ownership of it on someone else. Now: the value *to you* of the money I have transferred to you is identical to the amount of money I have lent. The value *to me* is the same. So I am fully compensated if you in due course return that same amount plus any expenses or other losses I necessarily incurred in (or as a result of) making the loan.[121] The only fair basis on which I can claim a share in any profit you make—or any value you add—is by sharing the risks of loss, by being (we might say) an equity partner in a kind of joint enterprise. This sharing transforms a mere *loan* into something essentially different.

Just as a buyer's urgent need and willingness to pay more than the current general market price does not justify the seller in charging more than that just (market) price, so the real needs of private or public borrowers—and thus the good consequences of lending to these persons—do not justify lenders in charging usury (i.e. interest above an indemnity {interesse} for their expenses and necessary losses).[122] True, those needs can, on occasion, justify borrowers in borrowing even at the usurious rates charged by such lenders, and governments in permitting usury (and borrowing from usurers) where the public interest would otherwise suffer.[123] Still, the usury charged by these usurers remains liable to be confiscated as an ill-gotten gain, and returned to the original borrowers

insurer's premium [fee] is a genuine expense of making the loan, and therefore chargeable to the borrower: see n. 128 below; see also at n. 84 above: among the grounds for buyers to recompense sellers is 'on account of the risk {periculum} to which sellers expose themselves in transferring the thing from place to place': II-II q. 77 a. 4 ad 2).

[119] The essential point can be variously expressed: I sell what does not exist {id quod non est} (II-II q. 78 a. 1c and ad 5; *Mal.* q. 13 a. 4c; *Ps.* 14. 5 ad v. 5); I sell the same thing twice (*Quodl.* III q. 7 a. 2c; *Mal.* q. 13 a. 4c); I sell you what already belongs to you as borrower (III *Sent.* d. 37 a. 6c and ad 5). [120] *Mal.* q. 13 a. 4c.

[121] See n. 115 above.

[122] II-II q. 78 a. 4c. If a borrower *genuinely* wishes to make a voluntary donation to the lender in return for the loan, it is permissible for the lender to accept it: *Mal.* q. 13 a. 4 ad 10.

[123] *Mal.* q. 13 a. 4 ad 6 (for borrowing, even at usurious interest, can sometimes result in many benefits {multae commoditates}) and ad 17; II-II q. 78 a. 1 ad 3; cf. the condemnation of laxity in permitting usury, in *Ep. Reg.* a. 2c.) See also VII. 5 n. 84 below.

if they can be found or, if they cannot be traced, distributed to the poor or spent on some other worthy public purpose.[124]

Aquinas' principles of justice in relation to property, work, and recompense are sound, and his argument applying them to money loans is valid.

His conclusions turned out to be compatible with the development of a just market in loans of money at a market rate of interest. This development was made possible by the linking of the two principles which Aquinas had identified as just bases for recovering something in excess of the principal: (1) association in the borrower's enterprise and thus the borrower's risk, and (2) indemnity for the lender's expenses and necessary losses. For with the development of a genuine investment market, in which stocks and shares (i.e. association in the risks of productive and other commercial enterprise) are traded alongside bonds (transferable money loans), it becomes possible to identify a rate of interest on bonds and other loans which compensates lenders for what they are reasonably presumed to have lost by making the loan rather than investing their money, for profit, in shares. Indeed, an efficient market will tend to identify this indemnifying rate of interest automatically. The remainder of this section explains the normative basis for this development rather more fully.

Aquinas' analysis of usury's injustice is sometimes said to have assumed that the loans in question were made in one-off transactions (outside any market) and for purposes of consumption[c] rather than commerce or investment. But nothing in his discussion manifests such assumptions, which are inherently unlikely. In discussing the needs of buyers or borrowers, which motivate their acceptance of an unjust purchase price or a usurious borrowing charge—the sale of something the seller or lender 'has not got'—Aquinas never indicates that he is thinking of a starving household rather than a merchant caught short of commodities and/or of funds with which to purchase them. His own earliest argument against usury attended explicitly to the fact that borrowers often transform the borrowed money into some other thing by their own

---

[124] *Ep. Reg.* a. 1c. (In saying this, Aquinas is not committed to saying that the rulers who borrowed at usury could rightly use state power to confiscate the interest they had agreed to pay; but there is some tension between his position on legal toleration in II-II and *Mal.* and his position in *Ep. Reg.* aa. 1 and 2.)

ingenuity and judgement {sagacitas} and industry (e.g. labour).[125] And he notes that involvement in usury may well be motivated by the desire for expanded business {maiores mercationes}.[126] Nor can he have been unaware of the money-lending markets flourishing in his day.[d]

More interesting is the question whether Aquinas should simply have accepted that interest charged at a market rate is a just charge. A market in which lenders are providing for themselves and their households out of the proceeds of their loans will simply be a network of usurers competing to practise injustice, *unless* their activities can reasonably be regarded as nothing but the provision of a service (a benefit to the borrower) which necessarily involves them in expenses and losses (including loss of profits) for which they can rightly seek recompense from the borrower. Aquinas freely grants that the activity is a service,[127] and that lenders can rightly include in the loan-contract a term requiring the borrower to recompense them for any loss {damnum} they incur by making the loan.[128]

What then is 'loss'? Aquinas has a general theory, which he deploys in his various general accounts (see VI.5) of compensation {restitutio}. I suffer loss from X when, as a result of X, I have less than I ought to {minus habeo quam debeo habere}. And this occurs in two different ways: (a) my being deprived of what I already actually have (as when someone destroys my house), and (b) my being impeded or prevented from getting what I was on the way to having {in via habendi} (as when someone digs up the seed I have sown). For loss or damage of type (a), I should receive the full value of what I lost. For loss of type (b), however, the compensation to which I am morally entitled is the value I realistically had in view, *discounted* to make fair and realistic allowance for the fact that, quite apart from the wrongdoer's conduct, what I potentially {virtute} possessed might in many ways have been prevented or impeded {multipliciter impediri} from actually {actu} becoming

---

[125] III *Sent.* d. 37 a. 6c and ad 4 (part of an argument not further used by Aquinas). Aquinas notes that lenders, too, often put their usurious gains to productive use (and so, though they are bound to make restitution of the money they charged on borrowers as usurious interest, they are generally entitled to keep the fruits of that interest, for those fruits are the product of their labour {propter suam industriam}): II-II q. 78 a. 3c and ad 3.

[126] *Empt.* iii [723].

[127] *Mal.* q. 13 a. 4 ad 5 and ad 6; III *Sent.* d.37 a. 6 ad 2; II-II q. 78 a. 4c.

[128] II-II q. 78 a. 2 ad 1.

mine in full measure or at all.[129] The seed I sowed might well have yielded little or no harvest. Who could know whether the crows would be unusually troublesome in the spring, or the summer be especially dry?

This general theory of compensable loss is presupposed in Aquinas' account of just compensation to money-lenders. They are entitled to compensation for losing what they ought to have {quod debe[n]t habere}.[130] So, on the general theory which Aquinas' phrasing here unmistakably recalls, they should be entitled to claim not only for (a) the whole amount of their expenses and costs but also for (b) an amount proportionate to the gain (profit) their investable funds brought within their reach, not actually {actu}— nor merely by some bare, abstract, unquantifiable possibility—but at least potentially {virtute} and realistically {in via}.[e] Aquinas *seems* to deny the last-mentioned type of compensation: the profit one might have made with the money one lends cannot, he says, be charged for, since one should not sell what one does not yet possess and may in many ways be prevented or impeded {impediri multipliciter} from getting.[131] What he should have said, and perhaps did mean by his surely deliberate phrasing, is that any charge made for loss of profit from available alternative investment (manufacturing, trading, share-holding, etc.) of the funds loaned ought to be *discounted* to allow for the multiple uncertainties involved in such investment.[132]

But one makes precisely that sort of discount, in effect, if one takes as the measure of loss of profit (i.e. lost alternative income) the general or average return on morally acceptable investments in a genuine capital market available to the lender. And morally acceptable investments include, as we have seen, risk-bearing

---

[129] II-II q. 62 a. 4c and ad 1 and ad 2; likewise q. 62 a. 2 ad 4 (the appropriate discount can be settled by some independent person of sound judgement {secundum arbitrium sapientis}). So the proper measure of damages (restitution) for digging up my seed is not the value of the full crop I hoped for, but the premium people would customarily pay for a field sown as mine was at the time of the wrong: IV *Sent.* d. 15 q. 1 a. 5 sol. 2 ad 4.

[130] II-II q. 78 a. 2 ad 1.

[131] Ibid.; the phrasing is precisely that used in q. 62 a. 4 ad 1 and ad 2; n. 129 above.

[132] Aquinas clearly accepts that borrowers who are late in repaying the principal may rightly be charged *interesse* for loss of the income that would have been available to the lender from the overdue principal, though that loss of prospective income must be discounted to an extent sufficient to take into account its uncertainty and the costs (e.g. labour) that would have been incurred in generating it: II-II q. 62 a. 4 ad 2; IV *Sent.* d. 15 q. 1 a. 5 sol. 2 ad 4; n. 116 above.

shares in commercial and productive associations {societates}. Thus there has become available an appropriate measure of fair charges (interest) for money loans. This measure adequately relates interest to risk and real productivity; it is thus quite different from any circular, bootstrapping claim which lenders may make to be 'recompensed' by this borrower for the gains they might otherwise have gained—as lenders in a network of mere usurers—from other borrowers.

Aquinas' account of usury, taken with his general theory of compensation, thus identifies *principles* (not rules made up by moralists or ecclesiastics) which enable us to see why in his era it was unjust for lenders to make a charge (however described) in the nature of profit, but with the development of a capital market for both equities and bonds it was to become fair and reasonable to make precisely such a charge, correlated with (which is not to say identical to) the general rate of return on equities.

VI.5. *Compensation and Punishment*

The distinction between laws we call *civil* and laws we call *criminal* is no more clearly marked by Aquinas than by Aristotle or by Jewish[133] or Roman law. But Aquinas does identify the basis for that distinction: the difference between one's duty to compensate and one's liability to punishment. Equally clearly he identifies the fundamental similarity of purpose: each of these branches of law concerns the restoration of an upset equality, the elimination of an unjustified inequality between persons; the restoration which justice requires can in either branch be called a recompense {recompensatio}. But the one branch looks to the losses incurred by specific persons, the other to a kind of advantage gained over all the other members of a community. For compensation {reparatio; restitutio; satisfactio} is essentially a matter of restoring to specific losers—to those who now have less than they ought[134]—what they

---

[133] See e.g. I-II q. 105 a. 2 ad 9, explicating Exod. 22: 1–9 on theft's penalties, e.g. return {reddere} of double or fourfold amounts. [134] II-II q. 62 a. 4c; VI. 4 at nn. 128–9 above.

have been deprived of.[135] But punishment {poena; retributio[136]} is essentially a matter of removing from wrongdoers a kind of advantage they gained, precisely in preferring their own will to the requirements authoritatively specified for that community's common good.[137] So in litigation of the kind we call civil, the court has the duty to give plaintiffs their rights {ius suum}, everything to which they are entitled as compensation for their injurious losses.[138] But in proceedings of the kind we call criminal, the court can be authorized to impose, relax, remit, or withhold penalties with a view to wider considerations of public good {publicae utilitati}.[139]

Aquinas sees 'recompense' or 'compensation' as a spectrum which includes (1) many (though not all) questions about what forms of transaction are fair (e.g. what is a just wage or, more generally, a just price), (2) all questions about how wrongdoers should compensate victims for the losses which unfair transactions or other forms of wrongdoing have imposed, i.e. how the rights (including dignity rights) of the unjustly treated are to be restored, and (3) all questions about the punishment of offenders for their violation of the equality which just laws establish between all of a community's members. This spectrum of shifting meanings of

---

[135] II-II q. 62 a. 5c. Sometimes Aquinas distinguishes compensation {satisfactio} for wrongful acts from return {restitutio} of something which has been, or would otherwise be, wrongfully detained: IV Sent. d. 15 q. 1 a. 5 sol. 1c. But often restitutio is a synonym for reparatio as the general category of civil compensation. The loss for which it would be unjust not to make restitution need not have resulted from the defendant's fault {iniustitia}: II-II q. 62 a. 3c. See also n. 152 below.

[136] Caution: retributio, unlike the English word 'retribution', extends to reward of merit as well as punishment for guilt (see e.g. I-II q. 21 a. 3c); like so many other key terms in Aquinas it takes its meaning-in-use from its context.

[137] See e.g. I-II q. 87 a. 6c and ad 3.

[138] II-II q. 67 a. 4c: note that the plaintiff is here called accusator and the defendant a guilty person {reus} who is to be penalized {puniatur} by the award of damages; moreover ad 3 states that victims of wrongdoing can be harmed by unwarranted remission of punishment, inasmuch as part of the compensation {recompensatio} to which they are entitled is a kind of restitution of a dignity interest {restitutio honoris} through the punishment of the injurer(s). Note also: the civil court's order to pay compensatory damages or to return goods does no more than reaffirm a moral obligation which the defendant ought already to have discharged; but in respect of any (civil or criminal) penalties, defendants are morally entitled to await the court's order: II-II q. 62 a. 3c. But where there was an offence, the ruptured relationship between the parties (wrongdoer and victim) is not fully restored by restitution of what the victim lost; there must be some further making amends, some specific humilitas, by the wrongdoer: IV Sent. d. 15 q. 1 a. 5 sol. 1 ad 1.

[139] IV Sent. d. 38 q. 2 a. 4 sol. 1 ad 1; II-II q. 67 a. 4c. Being an aspect of the overall 'care of the community', punishment can be imposed only by the authority of the supreme ruler(s): ibid., I-II q. 21 a. 4c.

recompensatio is not fully clarified by Aquinas. But it is no mere glissade of equivocation. It can illuminate by, for example, bringing to light the fact that to make restitution or to pay compensation is in each of the three contexts to terminate (or at least forestall) the wrong of withholding due recompense.[140] Aquinas' accounts of contractual obligations (VI.3), just prices, and compensation for usury (VI.4) illustrate issues (1) and (2) sufficiently for present purposes. What, then, is his account of punishment, as distinct or distinguishable from compensation for victims?

In any state of affairs capable of being improved by it, punishment's justifying point is to make an improvement. In Aristotle's phrase, which Aquinas everywhere adopts, punishment is 'a kind of [or: like a] *medicine* [remedy, cure]'.[141] But in Aquinas' thought this 'cure' involves far more than the possible reform[142] of the offender, and includes also the restraining[143] and the sheer deterrence of the offender[144] and of everyone else who needs deterring from wrongdoing and coercive inducement to decent conduct.[145] Above all, it includes the healing of a disorder—an unjust inequality, a *defectus in statu reipublicae*—introduced into the whole community by the wrongdoer's conduct. It is the remedying of this social disorder that gives punishment its defining characteristics.

For it is of the essence of punishments that they subject offenders to something *contrary to their wills* {contra voluntatem}.[146] This,

---

[140] IV *Sent.* d. 15 q. 1 a. 5 sol. 1c: 'to make restitution is precisely to put an end to an offence {ab offensa cessare}, the offence of holding on, without consent, to something to which someone else is entitled {rem alienam}'. One may have come by that something without any wrongdoing, e.g. as borrower or depositee: II-II q. 62 a. 3c.

[141] *Nic. Eth.* 2. 3. 1104^b17; *Eth.* II. 3 n. 6 [270]; II *Sent.* d. 42 q. 1 a. 2c, III *Sent.* d. 19 a. 3 sol. 2c; *ScG* III c. 144 n. 9 [3184]; II-II q. 43 a. 7 ad 1; etc. In a future state of affairs not susceptible of improvement (see x.6 below), the point of 'punishment' will be *retributio* without the remedial character it now has: see II-II q. 66 a. 6 ad 2; q. 68 a. 1c; but note that in II *Sent.* d. 36 a. 3 ad 3 even this ultimate 'ordering of fault by penalty' is counted as a *medicina*.

[142] This reform seems uppermost in *Eth.* II. 3 n. 6 [270]; see also III *Sent.* d. 19 q. 1 a. 3 sol. 2c, IV *Sent.* d. 46 q. 1 a. 2 sol. 3 ad 3; *ScG* III c. 158 n. 6 [3310]; I-II q. 87 a. 6 ad 3.

[143] II-II q. 108 a. 1c: *cohibitio*, which includes, however, deterrence (see a. 3c) as well as physical restraint.

[144] See IV *Sent.* d. 15 q. 1 a. 4 sol. 1c; I-II q. 87 a. 8 ad 2, II-II q. 33 a. 6c. This type of remedial purpose, like the reformative type, is absent in capital punishment (see IX.2 below): II *Sent.* d. 36 a. 3 ad 3; I-II q. 87 a. 3 ad 2.

[145] IV *Sent.* d. 46 q. 1 a. 2 sol. 3 ad 3; I-II q. 87 a. 8 ad 2, II-II q. 33 a. 6c ('unius exemplo alii deterrentur'), q. 99 a. 4c. See also VII.2 at n. 20 and VII.7 at n. 144 below on the need for coercion in the education and discipline of (especially) the young.

[146] II *Sent.* d. 42 q. 1 a. 2c; I-II q. 46 a. 6 ad 2: 'est de ratione poenae quod sit contraria voluntati'; likewise I q. 48 a. 5c, I-II q. 87 a. 2c and a. 6c; *Mal.* q. 1 a. 4c; *ScG* III c. 140 n. 5

---

not pain, is of the essence. Why? Because the essence of offences is that in their wrongful acts offenders 'yielded to their will more than they ought',[147] 'followed their own will excessively',[148] 'ascribed too much to their own preferences'[149]—the measure of excess being the relevant law or moral norm for preserving and promoting the common good.[150] Hence the proposition foundational for Aquinas' entire account of punishment: the order of just equality in relation to the offender is restored—offenders are brought back into that equality—precisely by the 'subtraction' effected in a corresponding, proportionate[151] suppression[152] *of the will which took for itself too much* (too much freedom or autonomy, we may say).[153] In this way punishment 'sets in order' the

[3149]. Still, punishment can be undergone and accepted voluntarily and freely (libenter), on one's own account or on behalf of one's friend: IV *Sent.* d. 21 q. 1 a. 1 sol. 4c.

[147] I-II q. 87 a. 6c (plus voluntati suae indulsit quam debuit), III q. 86 a. 4c (same); *Rat.* c. 7 [998] (same).   [148] II-II q. 108 a. 4c (peccando nimis secutus est suam voluntatem).

[149] *Comp.* I c. 121 [237] {plus suae voluntati tribuens quam oportet}. At the time of his *Sent.*, Aquinas seems not to have understood the will's offence in terms of excess, and so did not squarely identify punishment as subtraction in the field of willing: see e.g. IV *Sent.* d. 15 q. 1 a. 4 sol. 1c; but II *Sent.* d. 42 q. 1 a. 2c and ad 5 gets very close to the clarity of the late works.

[150] So the criminal's criminal offence is not, as such, against the victim so much as against 'common justice', like the case discussed in II-II q. 66 a. 5 ad 3: I lend you something and, when its return is overdue, I take it back by force or stealth instead of persuasion or due process of law; this conduct 'does not harm {gravet} [you] but is an offence against common justice, inasmuch [I am] usurping to [myself] the judgement on the matter and setting aside the due process of law {iuris ordine praetermisso}'.

[151] II *Sent* d. 42 q. 1 a. 2 ad 5: 'to the extent {tantum} that one has obeyed one's own will by transgressing the law . . . to that extent {quantum} one should compensate in the opposite direction {in contrarium}, so that thus the equality of justice may be respected'.

[152] I-II q. 87 a. 1c: the essence of punishment, whether by one's own conscience in remorse, or by some external governing authority, is this suppression {depressio} by or on behalf of the order against which the wrongdoer was in insurrection. Note that, by contrast, the principal purpose of restitution (which is always to the victim) is 'not that someone who has an excess {plus quam debet} should cease to have it, but that the person who has a deficiency {minus} should have it made good': II-II q. 62 a. 6 ad 1.

[153] II-II q. 108 a. 4c: 'the equality of justice is restored {reparatur} by punishment inasmuch as they undergo something contrary to their will'; *Comp.* I c. 121 [237]: 'there is a restoring {reductio} to the order of justice by punishment, through which something is subtracted from the will'; I-II q. 87 a. 6c = III q. 86 a. 4c: 'through punishment's recompense {recompensationem} the equality of justice is restored {reintegretur}'; *Rat.* c. 7 [998]: 'to restore them to the order of justice, something that they want needs to be taken away from {subtrahitur} their will—which punishment does by taking away goods they want to have or imposing bads they are unwilling to undergo'. See also *Eth.* v. 6 n. 6 [952], dealing simultaneously but to some extent distinctly with criminal punishment and civil compensation. Relevant goods which punishment takes away (corresponding to bads which it imposes) are: life, bodily security, liberty, wealth, homeland, and honours {gloria}: II-II q. 108 a. 3c.

guilt[154] whose essence was wrongful willing; and this (re)ordering {ordinativa} point of punishment can either be accounted remedial {medicinalis},[155] or contrasted with the remedial (deterrent, reformative).[156] The debts from which just punishment liberates the offender[157] are not debts to the victims whom the offender has indeed wronged (in one way or another *wilfully*) and who therefore might be plaintiffs in a civil proceeding or might understandably but wrongly desire revenge. Rather, we may say, those debts are the advantage—the inequality—which, in the willing of an offence, is wrongly gained *relative to all the offender's fellows* in the community against whose law, and so whose common good, the offence offends:[158] the advantage of freedom from external constraints in choosing and acting.[159]

Only offenders, therefore, can rightly be punished.[160] The punishment is only for their offence.[161] Basically or generally speaking it should be measured not by the harm that happens to have been done[162] but by the scale of the offender's fault[163]—as we may say, by the extent of the offender's manifested self-preference in disregard of the path marked out by law which others constrain themselves to follow. Other factors can, within just limits, be counted as justifying more, or less, severe punishment.[164] Punishment, though merited, need not be imposed when its imposition would

---

[154] *ScG* III c. 146 n. 1 [3193].   [155] As in e.g. II *Sent.* d. 36 a. 3 ad 3.
[156] As in e.g. II-II q. 108 a. 4c.   [157] *Comp.* 1 c. 226 [470].
[158] So one merits reward or deserves punishment (which can only be rightly imposed by persons responsible for a community, administering its law) precisely as someone who is (or, like a visitor, is reasonably taken to be) a part of a community: I-II q. 21 a. 3 ad 2, a. 4c and ad 3, q. 92 a. 2 ad 3. There is, in the focal sense, no punishment (or reward) of subhuman animals: *Comp.* 1 c. 143 [285].
[159] So punishment cures and removes this inequality: IV *Sent.* d. 15 q. 1 a. 1 sol. 3c; *ScG* III c. 146 n. 5 [3149]; and n. 153 above.
[160] 'The natural law {ius naturale} prescribes that punishment be imposed for fault, and that no one may be punished without fault {nullus sine culpa puniri debeat}': IV *Sent.* d. 36 a. 1 (= *Supp.* q. 52 a. 1) ad 3; see also II *Sent.* d. 33 q. 1 a. 2 ad 4; I-II q. 87 a. 8c (but cf. ibid. ad 2).
[161] II-II q. 108 a. 4c: 'poena non debetur nisi peccato'. There can be punishment without fault but not without *causa*, sc. reasons provided by the commission of the offence: ibid.
[162] IV *Sent.* d. 18 q. 1 sol. 3 ad 1: 'the quantum of culpability {culpae quantitas} is measured not by the harm {nocumento} one does but by the will {voluntate} with which one does it'.
[163] IV *Sent.* d. 20 a. 2 sol. 1c: 'quantitas poenae radicaliter respondet quantitati culpae'.
[164] *Quodl.* 1 q. 9 a. 2 ad s.c. Sentencing is Aquinas' usual paradigm case of that sort of discretionary judgement and choice (within the framework of the moral requirements of *prudentia*) which he calls *determinatio* of *ius naturale* or *lex naturalis*: see I-II q. 95 a. 2c; and VIII.3 at nn. 78–84 below.

cause disproportionate harm to others;[165] punishment is a matter of fairness {aequitas},[166] and the measure of that fairness is the common good for the whole community. Sometimes Aquinas speaks of punishment's justice as distributive,[167] sometimes as commutative.[168] These broad categories fail, once more, to capture the subtle relationship between the wrong criminals do to their victim, the wrong they do to the community and its members as a whole, and the healing and prophylaxis such wrongdoing warrants and makes just.

The justice of retribution, like the determination and supervision of restitution, and the maintenance of rights of property and contract, calls for a kind of social organization which can rightly claim a special, if not unique, completeness and priority: the state.

Notes

a. *Aquinas' unstable classifications of justice* . . . In I-II q. 60 a. 3 ad 3, as late as 1271, Aquinas seems to be still uncertain whether distributive justice and commutative justice are two distinct species of virtue. In III *Sent.* d. 33 q. 3 a. 4 sol. 1c and sol. 2c they had been distinct species of justice, but only two among others which included also *vindicatio*, the vindicative justice of repelling and punishing wrongdoing, *observantia*, the justice of appropriate obedience and, more generally, fulfilment of affirmative responsibilities and undertakings, and *innocentia*, the justice of not depriving or otherwise harming others. The *Summa*'s eventual vast treatment of justice presents *distributive* and *commutative* justice as the two 'species' of the 'particular' or (synonymously) 'special' justice (see II-II q. 58 a. 7c and a. 8 ad 2, q. 61 a. 1c) which (unlike 'general justice') is one of the four 'cardinal [hinge] virtues' and so is 'justice properly so called'. But on its last page, Aquinas subdivides justice quite differently. Here (1) justice's 'parts' (which would include its 'species') concern the entitlements of people to whom one is under an obligation 'for some special reason or in some special respect {ex aliqua speciali ratione}'. This would include many if not all 'distributive' entitlements to a fair share of some common benefit or burden, and surely all 'commutative' entitlements to recompense. But (2) 'justice properly so called' concerns what is due to everyone without distinction {indifferenter omnibus}, that is (we may say), as a matter of fundamental human rights. (II-II q. 122 a. 6c, paralleled in I-II q. 100 a. 12c, where the *per se iustum* of general justice is contrasted with

---

[165] II-II q. 43 a. 7 ad 1; contrast *Mal.* q. 5 a. 4c (judges need not look to some side-effects of their sentences). [166] *In Isa.* 24 ad v. 5.

[167] *ScG* III c. 142 n. 2 [3164]; *In Heb.* 2. 1 ad v. 2 [95].

[168] II-II q. 80 a. un. ad 1, q. 108 a. 2 ad 1; IV *Sent.* d. 14 q. 2 a. 1 sol. 2 ad 2; and see III *Sent.* d. 33 q. 1 a. 3 sol. 2 ad 2.

the special or particular justice which concerns arrangements {contractus} which people have made with each other; and see v.1 at nn. 22–5 above). Everyone, for example, has the right not to be plundered or intentionally killed by a private person; the counterpart of this right would be a duty which pertains to 'justice properly so called', not to a mere 'part of justice'.

Yet the injustice of homicide (and of the many other wrongs one individual can do to another) was treated by Aquinas as a vice opposed to a 'part' of justice, namely, commutative justice: see II-II q. 63 introd., q. 64 introd. And that was problematic, even leaving aside Aquinas' final remarks about justice 'properly speaking'. For the central or characteristic act of commutative justice was presented by Aquinas (II-II q. 61 introd. and a. 3c and a. 4c) as A's act of making recompense {restitutio; compensatio} to B for losses incurred by B—an obligation which, in the many cases of 'involuntary interaction {commutatio}', presupposes that A has *already wronged* B. Aquinas did not for a moment give support to the notion of Economic Analysis of Law, that anyone willing to pay compensation is entitled to deliberately harm another person! So in these many cases the primary focus of Aquinas' discussions 'of commutative justice' is actually not the duty of recompense, compensation, or restitution but the prior question whether A's act (e.g. of killing B in self-defence) is or is not a wronging of B. The term 'commutative justice' thus swings back and forth. A loose, wide sense extends to rights and wrongs in any interaction (or dealing) {commutatio} between individuals {singulari} or neighbours. A more precise sense extends only to the mutuality of making recompense, whether in 'exchange' for (as a *commutatio* of) the loss A has (wrongly) imposed on B or in exchange for a good voluntarily transferred (but not simply donated) by B to A.

The instability in Aquinas' classifications of justice suggests that he does not take them too seriously. The very distinction between general and particular (or special) justice is fragile. General justice is one's fundamental orientation towards common good; but Aristotle called it 'legal justice' and Aquinas usually follows suit. It is thus the justice of acting according to a *common* rule (II-II q. 157 a. 2 ad 2), i.e. according to all relevant laws, divine or human (II-II q. 79 a. 1c and 3c)—in the first instance according to their letter, but more fundamentally and ultimately according to the intent (always to be assumed to be just and reasonable) of their author(s): the radical justice of equity {aequitas, *epieikeia*} which departs from the common rule in its common (usual) meaning in order to uphold the rule in its true sense all things considered (see II-II q. 120 (de epieikeia) aa. 1 and 2; on the 'good judgement {virtus iudicativa}' needed for such departures from the 'common rule', see e.g. II-II q. 57 a. 6 ad 3; and see VIII.2 n. 30 below). Now, laws fit to be adhered to are, of course, made for common good. And everything required by the common good of some group is required according to some rational standard, i.e. some 'law' in the most general sense of the term. But, as Aquinas himself makes clear, acting 'for the common good [according to right reason]' is sometimes by

no means the same as acting 'according to a common [or: general] rule': see
e.g. II-II q. 80 a. un. ad 4, q. 157 a. 2 ad 2.

Again, the explanation which Aquinas suggests for the difference
between general (or legal) and particular (or special) justice—that the
former regards (the good of) a whole (group, community), while the latter
regards (the rights of) parts (individuals; neighbours)—is very elusive. For
in respecting and promoting the rights of each of the 'parts' (members) of a
group, one is acting for the good of that group (see v.6 at nn. 159–60 above)
and of 'other people in general {alium in communi}' (see II-II q. 58 a. 5c:
'iustitia ordinat hominem in comparatione ad alium . . . uno modo ad
alium singulariter consideratum [= particular justice], alio modo ad alium
in communi [= general (or: legal) justice]'). And, 'in serving some community one serves each of the people contained within it': II-II q. 58 a. 5c; IV.4
at n. 73.

Finally, it seems very likely that Aquinas' leading 16th-century commentator, followed by the subsequent tradition of interpretation down to
the mid-20th century, misunderstood and misapplied Aquinas' distinction
between general justice and the two species of particular justice—reducing
it to a distinction between the individual's duty to the state, the state's
duty (distributive) to individuals, and individuals' duties (commutative) to
each other: see Finnis (1980: 184–8, 196–7). The pleasing symmetry of this
tripartite distinction obscures from view the distortion involved (i) in
treating distributive justice as a responsibility and virtue only of the state
(or its rulers), as if individuals as such do not also have duties of fair
distribution, and (ii) in treating the state (rather than any and every community to which one is related) as the only direct object of general justice.
Note, incidentally, that where a community itself owes someone recompense for services rendered to it (e.g. as soldier or member of the government: ScG III c. 135 n. 15 [3090]), the obligation is one of commutative not
distributive justice.

b. *Money as coinage* . . . It is sometimes argued (e.g. Langholm 1984: 80, 84,
86, 151) that Aquinas' position on usury depends upon considering money
exclusively as coinage (or notes) which can be lost by fire, misplacement,
or theft by asportation. But nothing in Aquinas' argument seems to turn
on such an assumption, and much that he says about usurious charges
takes for granted that the principal in respect of which such charges are
levied can be quite abstract (e.g. a purchase price increased over what it
would otherwise have been). When we say that money is lost by fire, theft,
or unsuccessful trading, we shift between the physicalist sense of money
as coinage (or notes) and the abstract sense of liquid funds as entitlements
of a certain kind.

c. *Is it usury to charge for loans entered into by borrowers for commercial or
other non-consumptive purposes?* . . . Beware of the equivocation: when
Aquinas says that money is necessarily 'consumed' in use, he does not
mean that it is used for consumption *rather than* investment. Langholm
(1984: 87–8) rightly stresses that money borrowed by a merchant to invest

in a business venture is *consumed* in Aquinas' sense. (Langholm (89) unfortunately assumes that this is only because 'the physical pieces of coin borrowed are gone and thus consumed'. In fact, Aquinas' argument about consumption in use, and the inseparability of ownership and use of money as such, applies to money in any sense of the word, e.g. a credit balance in a banker's books.)

d. *Money markets in Aquinas' day* . . . The First Council of Lyons, in 1245, ordered ecclesiastical persons to avoid taking usurious loans wherever possible, and never to borrow at fairs or public markets {in nundinis vel mercatis publicis}.

e. *Application to money loans of Aquinas' general theory of loss* . . . See the full, careful, and frank analysis by Cajetan in his commentary (c.1517) on II-II q. 78 a. 2, *Opera* 9. 160–3; in demanding, rightly, that the lender's opportunity of alternative investment in trading activities be more than merely a bare general and incalculable possibility {in potentia communi non aestimabili}, Cajetan adds, too cautiously (and without any support in Aquinas), that the borrower's request for a loan must have been a kind of neighbourly interruption of the neighbourly lender's investment plans.

VII

The State: Its Elements and Purposes

VII.1. *'Complete Communities': States with Law*

Aquinas' most important treatment of political matters is perhaps his treatise on law (I-II qq. 90–108), a discussion shaped by a methodological decision and a theoretical thesis. The thesis is that law exists, focally or centrally, only in complete communities {perfectae communitates}. The methodological decision is to set aside all questions about which sorts of multi-family community are 'complete', and to consider a type, usually named *civitas*, whose completeness is simply posited. It is not a decision to regard the *civitas* as internally static or as free from external enemies. Revolutions and wars, flourishing, corruption, and decay are firmly on the agenda. But not the question which people are or are entitled to be a *civitas*.

Civitas and synonymously *communitas politica*[1] or *communitas civilis*,[2] in Aquinas, can usually be translated by 'a state', 'states', or 'the state', but never mean 'the State' as government, organs of government, or subject of public law. Though aware of the distinctions, Aquinas is not generally concerned to differentiate between nation and state or political community, or between

---

[1] I-II q. 21 a. 4 ad 3; *Eth.* v. 2 n. 4 [903]; *Pol.* I. 1 n. 3 [11], III. 6 n. 5 [395]; likewise *societas politica*: *Impugn.* II c. 2c [57].
[2] I-II q. 100 a. 2c; *Pol.* I. 1 n. 33 [41], II. 8 n. 6 [259]. Likewise *communitas civilis*: *Eth.* VIII. 12 n. 19 [1720].

the state's structure of governing offices and the particular rulers or office-holders.[3] And *civitas* and its synonyms are used consistently by Aquinas to signify the whole large society which is organized politically by the sorts of institutions, arrangements, and practices commonly and reasonably called 'government' and 'law'.[4]

The methodological decision which shapes Aquinas' central treatment of politics has important consequences. He is well aware that in his own world, though there are some city-*states* {civitates}, there are also many cities {civitates} which make no pretention to being complete communities but exist (perhaps established rather like castles to adorn a kingdom) as parts of a realm; and *civitates*, kingdoms, and realms may be politically organized in sets,[5] perhaps as 'provinces' (of which he often speaks) or empires (about which he discreetly remains almost wholly silent). He is well aware of the idea, and the reality, of peoples {gentes; populi} and nations {nationes}[6] and regions {regiones}. As we have seen, Aquinas is willing to raise his eyes to relationships of friendship between states,[7] and to the widest horizons of human community,[8] and he envisages treaties and other binding sources of law or right even between warring states.[9] His methodological decision allows him to abstract from all this.

It also allows him to abstract from a number of deep and puzzling questions: how—and indeed by what right—any particular *civitas* comes into being (and passes away); how far the *civitas* should coincide with unities of origin or culture; and whether and what intermediate constitutional forms there are, such as federations or international organizations. Liberated from such questions,

---

[3] So *civitas* in the treatise on law is treated as synonymous with *gens* (e.g. I-II q. 105 a. 1c) and *populus* (q. 96 a. 1c with q. 98 a. 6 ad 2).

[4] What I throughout call the state and Aquinas the *civitas* or *societas/communitas civilis/politica* is called by (e.g.) Maritain the body politic; what I call government and Aquinas *princeps/principatus, praelatus/praelatio*, etc., Maritain calls the State, that part of the body politic which specializes in the interests of the whole, a set of institutions entitled to use coercion, and so forth: Maritain (1951: 8–11). Much the same distinctions are being drawn, but, precisely in terms of those distinctions, the word 'state' is used in opposing senses, each rooted in common speech.

[5] He speaks, for example, of what we would call quasi-federal arrangements whereby a single king governs a number of different *civitates* each ruled by different laws and different ministers: I q. 108 a. 1c.

[6] *Reg.* II. 5 [II. 1] [123, 126] [829, 832]; *Pol.* II. 4 n. 1 [196]; *Meta.* II. 5 n. 3 [333].

[7] See IV.3 at n. 54 above.   [8] See IV.3 at nn. 55–60 above.

[9] II-II q. 40 a. 3c ('there are certain laws/rights of war {iura bellorum} and treaties which, even between enemies, are to be kept {foedera etiam inter ipsos hostes servanda}'); see IX.3 at nn. 61–3 below.

Aquinas will consider the *civitas* rather as if it were, and were to be, the only political community in the world and its people the only people.[10] All issues of *extension*—of origins, membership, and boundaries, of amalgamations and dissolutions—are thereby set aside. The issues will all be, so to speak, intensional: the proper functions and modes and limits of government, authoritative direction, and obligatory compliance in a community whose 'completeness' is presupposed.

Can a state's common good, being the good of a complete community, be anything less than the complete good, the fulfilment—*beatitudo imperfecta* if not *perfecta*[11]— of its citizens? That is the question with which this chapter is largely concerned; it will be answered with a distinction: Yes, and No. At the outset, however, it is sufficient to note that the question seems equivalent to another: What type of direction can properly be given by governments and law? Aquinas treats the questions as substantially equivalent, because he has stipulated that a state is a complete community[12] and given *complete community* the purely formal[13] description: a community so organized that its government and law give *all* the direction that properly can be given by human

---

[10] Though treating the state very much as if it were the only politically organized people in the world, Aquinas' account also holds that the state-wide common good which the state's laws are to promote and protect is but part of a wider common good. For this community is but part of a wider whole (see *Eth.* 1. 2 n. 12 [30]) and ultimately of the whole community of the universe {tota communitas universi} (I-II q. 91 a. 1c). Lawmakers' *prudentia*, justice, and fully reasonable directiveness towards the common good of their own *communitas perfecta* must be informed by, and consistent with, the law of a universal community—a law which as understood and shared in by us is called the natural law {lex naturalis; lex naturae; ius naturale}. What the organization of that universal community really is remains, philosophically speaking, to be determined. But it must extend at least as wide as the whole of humanity, present and future. That is not to say that Aquinas is articulating a duty to future generations, or envisaging an international law, or an actually world-wide government; nor that any or all of these would exhaust the significance of the open-endedness of the common good even of a community stipulated to be 'complete'.

[11] See I-II q. 5 a. 5c: 'the imperfect *beatitudo* attainable in this life can be acquired with natural human capacities, in the way that people can acquire virtue, in whose working out in action it [imperfect *beatitudo*] consists {virtus, in cuius operatione consistit}; likewise q. 4 a. 6c, a. 7c and a. 8c; *Eth.* 1. 13 nn. 4–7 [157–60].

[12] See I-II q. 90 a. 2c: 'perfecta communitas civitas est'; q. 90 a. 3 ad 3, II-II q. 65 a. 2 ad 2; *Reg.* 1. 2 [14] [749]; *Pol.* 1. 1 n. 23 [31]: 'civitas est communitas perfecta'; see also II-II q. 50 a. 1c: 'communita[s] perfecta civitatis vel regni'.

[13] Aquinas' implicit procedure hereabouts is similar to his explicit procedure in relation to *beatitudo* (see IV.2 at nn. 4–6): give first a merely formal description, a *communis ratio*, a general or formal idea (thus: 'whatever satisfies all desires'); then find the appropriate *specialis ratio*, the critically defensible, morally substantive account attainable by attending to the human goods at stake and their directiveness.

government and coercive *law* to promote and protect the common good, that is, the good of the community and thus[14] of all its members and other proper elements.

VII.2. *The State's Specific Common Good: Public and Limited*

It is easy to read Aquinas as holding that the state's common good is the fulfilment (and thus the complete virtue) of each of its citizens, and that government and law should therefore promote that fulfilment. Of course, Aquinas teaches the unwisdom of legislating against every act of vice,[15] and the need to proceed gradually in inculcating virtue by law,[16] not attempting the impossible.[17] But it is easy to read him as holding that such legislation, though unwise, is not *ultra vires*—does not reach beyond the state's common good or the purpose, functions, and jurisdiction of state government and law.

This reading can begin with Aristotle's critique of the Sophists' social-contract or mutual-insurance theory of the state. The law 'should be such as will make the citizens good and just',[18] since: 'a *polis* is a community [partnership] {communicatio} [koinōnia] of households and families in living well, with the object of a complete and self-sufficient [autarkēs] life . . . it must therefore be for the sake of truly good [kalōn] actions, not of merely living together'.[19]

Surely, one may ask, Aquinas didn't dissent from Aristotle here? Doesn't the *Summa Theologiae* reaffirm Aristotle's teaching that our need for state law is primarily to ensure the effective promotion of *virtue*, by way of laws enforced with penal sanctions, where parental capacity runs out?[20] And surely parents rightly try to

---

[14] See II-II q. 58 a. 5c; IV.4 above.   [15] I-II q. 91 a. 4c.

[16] I-II q. 96 a. 2 ad 2; VII. 6 at n. 90 below.   [17] I-II q. 93 a. 3 ad 3.

[18] *Politics* 3. 9. 1280^{b}11–14 (Aquinas' commentary stops at 1280^{a}6, but see *Pol.* prol. n. 4, I. 1 n. 23 [31]; and, more clearly, *Reg.* II. 3 [I. 14] [106] [817](n. 74 below)). See also *Politics* 7. 12. 1332^{a}28–^{b}12; *Nic. Eth.* 5. 2. 1130^{b}23–6; 10. 9. 1179^{b}32–1180^{a}5; Miller (1995: 225, 360); George (1993: 21–8).   [19] *Politics* 3. 9. 1280^{b}33–5, 1281^{a}1–4.

[20] I-II q. 90 a. 3 ad 2. See *Nic. Eth.* 10. 9. 1179^{b}31–1180^{a}22; *Eth.* x. 14 nn. 13–18 [2149–54]. Other passages affirming that the point of law is to use its coerciveness in the promotion of virtue include *Eth.* I. 14 n. 10 [174], II. 1 n. 7 [251]. Passages making the same sort of point without special reference to the coercive power of law: *Eth.* I. 19 n. 2 [225], v. 2 n. 5 [904], 3 nn. 12–13 [924–5].

educate their children into complete, all-round virtue and fulfilment? Doubtless, parents will exceed their authority if they try to
reinforce their education with coercive measures of the kind the
state can use.[21] But in all other respects, surely state law holds the
same place in the state as parental precepts hold in the family,[22]
precisely because it has the same purpose and jurisdiction of
promoting fulfilment and therefore inculcating virtue, without
restrictions of *goal*?

Plausible as it is, as a first reading of many passages, this interpretation of Aquinas must be rejected. No passage requires to be
read in this way, and it is inconsistent with a number of clear
passages in mature texts.

Clearest, perhaps, are the passages in which Aquinas argues that
'The purpose {finis} of human law and the purpose of divine law
are different':[23]

---

[21] *Eth.* x. 14 n. 17 [2153].

[22] *Eth.* x. 15 n. 4 [2158] and n. 5 [2159]: 'this is the only difference, that a paternal
precept {sermo} does not have the full coercive authority of a royal [or other public]
precept {sermo}'.

[23] I-II q. 98 a. 1c. This important thesis was elaborately and clearly set out by Aquinas
in his first version of *ScG* III c. 121, one of about nine whole chapters which he later
decided to eliminate from his draft treatment of divine law and government in *ScG* III.
Amongst the material suppressed was a triplet of chapters contrasting divine law with the
rule of (1) tyrants, (2) just kings, and (less sharply) (3) human fathers. The chapter stating
the disanalogy with just 'kings' (i.e. with the very idea of state government) ran as follows
(the emphases here as elsewhere are mine):

> God's law does not require merely that one behave well in relation to other people {sit
> bene ordinatus ad alios}, as the laws of just kings do.
> It is not merely that divine rule is dissimilar to the rule of tyrants who for their own
> advantage exploit those subject to them. Rather, divine rule also greatly differs from the
> rule of kings *who intend their subjects' advantage*. For kings are constituted to pre-
> serve *interpersonal social life* {ad socialem vitam *inter homines* conservandam}; that
> is why they are called 'public persons', as if to say promoters or guardians of *public
> good*. And for that reason, the laws they make direct people *in their relationships with
> other people* {secundum quod *ad alios* ordinantur}. Those things, therefore, which
> neither advance nor damage the *common good* are neither prohibited nor commanded
> by human laws.
> God, however, is concerned not only with ruling the human multitude, but also with
> what is in itself good for *each person individually*. For he is the creator and governor of
> nature, and the good of nature is realized not simply in the multitude but also in
> persons in themselves—each one. And so God commands and prohibits *not only those
> things by which one human being is related* {ordinatur} *to another*, but also those
> things according to which human persons are, in themselves {secundum se}, disposed
> well or badly. Here what St Paul says is relevant: 'The will of God is that you be made
> holy {sanctificatio}'.
> In this way we exclude the error of those who say that only what *harms or corrupts
> one's neighbour* {quibus proximus aut offenditur aut scandalizatur} is sinful.

For *human law's purpose is the temporal tranquillity of the state* {temporalis tranquillitas civitatis}, a purpose which the law attains by coercively *prohibiting external acts* {cohibendo exteriores actus} to the extent that those are evils *which can disturb the state's peaceful condition* {quantum ad illa mala quae possunt perturbare pacificum statum civitatis}.[24, a]

In other words, divine and civil government, in Aquinas' view, differ in method—the latter's prohibitions, unlike the former's, being restricted to external acts—because they differ in purpose. This double difference is insisted upon repeatedly:

The form of community {modus communitatis} to which human law is directed {ordinatur} is different from the form of community to which divine law is directed. For human law is directed to *civil community*, which is a matter of people *relating to one another* {quae est hominum ad invicem}.[25] But people are related to one another {ordinantur ad invicem} by the *external* acts in which they communicate and deal {communicant} with each other. But this sort of communicating/dealing {communicatio} is a matter of *justice* {pertinet ad rationem iustitiae}, which is properly directive in and of human community {directiva communitatis humanae}. *So human law does not put forward precepts about anything other than acts of justice* [and injustice] {non proponit praecepta nisi de actibus iustitiae};[26] if it prescribes acts of other virtues, this is only because and in so far as they take on the character of justice {assumunt rationem iustitiae} . . .[27]

Opera vol. 14. 46* col. 1 (for the Latin and the provenance, see n. a); the quoted passage's final sentence is in *ScG* III c. 121 n. 6 [2946].

The passage clearly affirmed that just state law neither prescribes nor prohibits thoughts, dispositions, intentions, choices, or actions which affect only the person whose will or deed they are. State law does not properly have as its responsibility the preservation or promotion of the all-round virtue, let alone the sanctification, of the individual subject, precisely as such. Its role is only to preserve and promote the common good, understood not as every true good in which human beings can share, but as the public good—a matter of interpersonal dealings, of specifically social life.

[24] I-II q. 98 a. 1c; see further n. b.

[25] As the deleted *ScG* passage (see n. 23) put it: 'kings are constituted to preserve interpersonal social life {ad socialem vitam inter homines conservandam} . . . For that reason the laws they make direct people [only, unlike divine government,] in their relationships with other people {secundum quod ad alios ordinantur}.' See also II-II q. 140 a. 1c: divine law's goal is that people join God, but 'human laws are directed {ordinantur} to certain this-worldly goods {aliqua mundana bona}'.

[26] So it is unlike divine government, which, as the deleted *ScG* passage stated, 'commands and prohibits not only those things by which one human being is related {homo ad alium ordinatur} to another, but also those things according to which human persons are each, in themselves, disposed well or badly' (see n. 23 above).

[27] I-II q. 100 a. 2c. Aquinas here appeals to *Nic. Eth.* 5, perhaps (as the Leonine editors suggest) 1. 1129^{b}14–25, but more likely 2. 1130^{b}25 (and see *Eth.* v. 2 n. 5 [904], 3 nn. 12–13 [924–5]), though nowhere does Aristotle make with any clarity the points which Aquinas

Aquinas' point in the last sentence is: derelictions of duty by soldiers, police, and emergency service personnel can readily be caused by want of courage; the injustices of adultery, child-abuse, or other sexual assaults typically arise from lack of sexual self-control, and so forth; so the law can rightly require choices characteristic of other virtues besides justice. But the law of the state cannot rightly regulate the full range of choices required by practical reasonableness:[28]

Types of virtue are distinguished by their objects, and each virtue's object can be related either to someone's *private good* or to the *common good* of the group. Take courage, for example: one can act out of courage either to save the state or to preserve the rights {ius} of one's friend. But law is for the common good. So, although there is no [type of] virtue the acts of which cannot be prescribed by law, *human law does not make prescriptions about all the acts of all the virtues, but only about those acts which are relatable {ordinabiles} to the common good, whether immediately* (as when things are done directly for the common good) *or mediately* (as when things are regulated {ordinantur} by the legislator *as being relevant to the good education* {pertinentia ad bonam disciplinam} *by which citizens are brought up to preserve the common good of justice and peace*).[29]

In this passage Aquinas clearly affirms that within a state there are 'private goods' (of individuals and small groups, e.g. of friends) whose good (e.g. whose right) is not part of the common good

---

is here concerned to assert about law's restricted purpose and content. At any event, the point was equally clear to Aquinas in his early writings: see e.g. III *Sent.* d. 37 a. 2 sol. 2c: 'civil law's precepts direct people in communications and dealings {communicationibus} which are other-directed {ad alterum}, in accord with the character of political life (which can only be of one human person to another) {secundum vitam politicam, quae quidem non potest esse nisi hominis ad hominem}' (i.e. which cannot reach into our *societas* with God). See likewise I-II q. 99 a. 5 ad 1, q. 104 a. 1 ad 1 and ad 3; *Quodl.* XII q. 15 [16] a. 2 [3] c.

[28] 'Practical reasonableness': the virtue of *prudentia*, the instantiating of the good of reason(ableness), the *bonum rationis*: see e.g. III *Sent.* d. 33 q. 1 a. 1 sol. 1c and sol. 2 ad 1; I-II q. 94 a. 3c; IV.4 above.

[29] I-II q. 96 a. 3c. *Disciplina*, moral education, is at least primarily a matter of the young {minores}: II-II q. 16 a. 2 ad 2. What sort Aquinas has in mind is indicated, for example, in I-II q. 105 a. 2 ad 1: law should seek to accustom people to getting along together easily {assuefacere ut facile sibi invicem sua communicarent}, which involves give and take (not being too concerned if someone passing through one's vineyard eats some of the grapes); people who are well brought up {disciplinati} are not disturbed by this sort of thing; indeed their *amicitia* with their fellow citizens is strengthened by it, and easy getting along together {facilis communicatio} is thereby confirmed and encouraged. It goes without saying that the *disciplina* includes many negative elements, such as the vigorous discouragement of acts such as homicide, theft, and so forth, which prejudice the maintenance of any decent *societas humana* (I-II q. 96 a. 2c) unless both prohibited and discouraged.

specific to the state—is not, I shall say, part of the specifically political common good.

That is only one of the ways in which Aquinas makes plain his view that, notwithstanding the 'completeness' of political communities, their specific common good is limited. Two other important limitations can be indicated without taking up the question of religious liberty.[30] The specifically political common good does not include the common good of another community in which the state's members will do well to participate, the community—like the state a *perfecta communitas*[31]—of the Church. Moreover, the common good of the political community does not, as such, include certain important human goods which essentially pertain to individuals in themselves, such as the good of religious faith and worship; the fact that such individual goods are goods for many people, or for everyone, does not convert them into the good of community:

> in human affairs there is a certain [type of] common good, the good of the *civitas* or people {gentis} . . . There is also a [type of] human good which—[though it] benefits not merely one person alone but many people—does not consist in community but pertains to one [as an individual] in oneself {humanum bonum quod non in communitate consistit sed ad unum aliquem pertinet secundum seipsum}, e.g. the things which everyone ought to believe and practise, such as matters of faith and divine worship, and other things of that sort.[32]

Aquinas' clearest name for this limited common good, specific to the political community, is *public good* {bonum publicum}.[33] It is distinct from the private good of individuals and the private common good of families and households, even though the political community (in Aquinas' most usual account) is comprised precisely of individuals and families. As the public good, the elements of the specifically political common good are not all-round virtue but goods (and virtues) which are intrinsically interpersonal,

---

[30] On which see IX.2 n. b; x.5 n. 137 below.

[31] So Aquinas treats *ecclesia* and *respublica* in parallel: II-II q. 31 a. 3 ad 3, q. 43 a. 8c; *Impugn.* c. 3, lines 475–98 (II c. 2 ad 10) [67–8]; III *Sent.* d. 9 q. 2 a. 3 ad 3. The Church resembles the political rather than the domestic {oeconomica} community {ecclesia similatur congregationi politicae}: IV *Sent.* d. 20 a. 4 sol. 1c. See x.5 below.

[32] *ScG* III c. 80 nn. 14, 15 [2559–60]. See n. c.

[33] See n. 23 above and at n. 55 below; and *In Rom.* 13. 1 ad v. 6 [1040]: 'kings take responsibility {sollicitudinem habent} for the *public good* in relation to secular {temporalibus} goods'.

other-directed {ad alterum},[34] person to person {hominum ad adinvicem}:[35] justice and peace.

'Peace', of course, should not be understood thinly.[36] In its fullest sense, peace {pax} involves not only concord (absence of dissension, especially on fundamentals) and willing agreement between one person or group and another,[37] but also harmony {unio} amongst each individual's own desires.[38] And Aquinas will make related observations: 'the principal intention of human law is to secure friendship between people {ut faciat amicitiam hominum ad invicem}',[39] and efforts to maintain peace by laying down precepts of justice will be insufficient without foundations in mutual friendship or love {dilectio}.[40] But, in the context of the passages about public good, it is clear that 'peace' refers, directly, only to (1) absence of words and deeds immorally opposed to peace, such as disorderly contentiousness,[41] quarrelsome fighting,[42] sedition,[43] or war,[44] (2) concord, i.e. the 'tranquillity of order'[45] between persons and groups which includes amongst its necessary but not sufficient conditions a love of neighbour as oneself,[46] along with the avoidance of collisions (e.g. in road traffic) and dissensions such as occur without personal fault, and perhaps also (3) a sufficiency of at least the necessities of life.[47] In short, it is the peaceful condition needed to get the benefits {utilitas} of social life and avoid the burdens of contention.[48] It is a peace which falls short of the complete justice

[34] III *Sent.* d. 37 a. 2 sol. 2c (n. 27 above).

[35] I-II q. 100 a. 2c (text at nn. 25 and 27 above).

[36] On the senses in which justice is and is not for the sake of peace, see II-II q. 29 a. 3 ad 3; *ScG* III c. 34 n. 2 [2139], c. 128 n. 6 [3006]. Cf. *In I Tim.* 6. 4 ad v. 20 [280]: 'the peace of the state consists in justice'. [37] e.g. *ScG* III c. 128 nn. 3–4 [3003–4].

[38] II-II q. 29 a. 1c and ad 1, a. 2 ad 2; see III.4 n. 47, III. 5 nn. 110, 118 above.

[39] I-II q. 99 a. 2c. [40] *Opera* 14. 43*.

[41] II-II q. 38 a. 1c; a serious form of immoral *contentio* is deliberately attacking truth and justice {veritatem iustitiae} in court: ad 3. [42] II-II q. 41 a. 1c and ad 3.

[43] II-II q. 42 a. 1. [44] II-II q. 40 a. 1.

[45] II-II q. 29 a. 1 ad 1, q. 45 a. 6c. See also IV *Sent.* d. 49 q. 1 a. 2 sol. 4c (citing Augustine, *De Civitate Dei* 19) absence of disturbance of that right order of the state which is secured by the government's will. Concord—agreement of wills—is only good when the shared intention is good; when that intent is bad the discord which prevents it is good: II-II q. 37 a. 1 ad 2.

[46] II-II q. 29 a. 3c: for 'this [neighbour-love] involves being willing to do one's neighbour's will even as one's own'.

[47] The state's rulers {politici} have a responsibility for providing their *civitas* with these economic necessities (see VI.2 at n. 49 above), though the provision itself will normally be by traders {negotiatores} who act not so much because they have a duty as for profit {propter lucrum quaerendum}: II-II q. 77 a. 4c; and see n. 146 below, VI. 4 n. 75 above.

[48] *Reg.* 1. 2 (1. 3) [17] [750]. It is a peace which is compatible with even tyranny: *Reg.* 1. 6 (1. 7) [44] [768].

which true virtue requires of us. An example: legislatures, *in the interests of peace*, provide that adverse possession for a length of time gives a good title even to squatters who took possession in bad faith—but a squatter who so acted never becomes morally entitled, in good conscience, to rely on this title.[49]

Still, even when all that is taken into account, Aquinas' position remains firmly outlined (though in its key terms susceptible of various interpretations or applications): those vices of disposition and conduct which have no significant relationship, direct or indirect, to justice and peace are not the concern of state government or law.[50] The position is not readily distinguishable from the 'grand simple principle' (itself open to interpretation and diverse applications) of John Stuart Mill's *On Liberty*.

VII.3. De Regno: *For Heavenly Fulfilment or Public Good?*

But can this reading of Aquinas be reconciled with the way he treats the question in his treatise on government (*De Regno*), or with his frequent assertion that inculcating virtue is a primary and proper rationale of law and state, or with the 'completeness' of the political community, or with the primacy of *politica* among the parts of *moralis philosophia*?

The *De Regno*, an openly theological little treatise written in a style unlike Aquinas' academic works in philosophy and theology,[51] but probably authentic,[d] includes some main elements of Aristotle's position that states are appropriately organized, and legally regulated, with a view to making their citizens truly good. Early in the *De Regno*'s exposition of the common good, or ultimate end, for which a king is responsible, we hear unmistakable echoes of *Politics* 3. 9 on the object of the *polis*, echoes inflected by the Christian understanding of history's point. Civil society

---

[49] *Quodl.* XII q. 15 [16] a. 2c: 'intendit civilis legislator [unlike the ecclesiastical makers of canon law] pacem servare et facere inter cives'; a. 3 ad 1: 'although owners so dispossessed may have no valid claim according to civil law, they have one according to divine law, whose goal is the salvation of souls'.

[50] I-II q. 96 a. 3c (n. 29 above); see also q. 99 a. 5 ad 1; *Eth.* v. 3 n. 13 [925].

[51] See *Reg.* prol. [1] [739]; this dedication to the King of Cyprus states that the exposition will be 'according to the authority of the holy scriptures and the teachings of philosophers, as well as the practice of worthy princes' and will rely throughout on the help of God, who is King of Kings, etc.

{congregatio civilis} is gathered together not simply to live but to live *well* {ad bene vivendum} and *in virtue* {vivere secundum virtutem}. Though its ultimate end and good—*beatitudo perfecta*, as Aquinas elsewhere calls it[52]—is in some sense beyond the reach of human virtue and attainable only by divine power {virtus}, it none the less is appropriately the fulfilment of human virtue, and so

it belongs to the authority and responsibility {officium} of a king to promote {procurare} the good life of the group in such a way that it is in line with the pursuit of heavenly fulfilment {congruit ad celestem beatitudinem consequendam}; so the king may *prescribe* {praecipiat} *whatever things lead to such fulfilment* and forbid, as far as possible, the contraries of those things.[53]

And Aquinas' advice on this question concludes:

Thus a threefold responsibility {cura} lies on the king. [1] First, in relation to the replacement of those who hold various offices: just as divine rule preserves the integrity of the universe by arranging that corruptible, transient things are replaced by new ones generated to take their place, so the king should be concerned to preserve the good of the group subject to him {subiectae multitudinis} by conscientiously arranging how new officials are to succeed those who fail or drop out. [2] Second, *by his laws and decrees, punishments and rewards, the king is to restrain his subjects from immorality and lead them to virtuous action* {ab iniquitate coerceat, et ad opera virtuosa inducat}, thereby following the example of God, who gave us law and who requites with reward those who follow and with punishments those who violate it. [3] Thirdly, the king is responsible for keeping the group subject to him safe against enemies; there would be no point in avoiding internal dangers, if the group were defenceless against external dangers.[54]

Don't the statements here underlined clearly propose an ambitious purpose for state rule, and acknowledge no limit on the inherent scope of that purpose?

No. The immediate context of the passages quoted shows in each case that Aquinas has several restrictions in mind. Take first the last passage, about the king's triple responsibilities, (1) supervising succession of offices, (2) restraining immorality and leading subjects to virtue, and (3) defence. As is signalled by its opening word 'thus' ('therefore'), it follows from a wider argument. That

---

[52] e.g. IV *Sent.* d. 49 q. 1 a. 2 sol. 2 ad 4; I-II q. 3 a. 2 ad 4 and a. 3; see IV.2 above.

[53] *Reg.* II. 4 [I. 15/16] [115] [823]. Since reaching this most ultimate end is the subject-matter of a set of governing arrangements {regimen} not human but divine, kings must regard themselves as subject to that divine regimen. On the consequent intersection of the secular, earthly, temporal authority of the state's rulers and the spiritual authority of priests (not least of the Pope), see *Reg.* II. 3 [I. 14/15] [110–11] [820–1]; and x.5 below.

[54] *Reg.* II. 4 [I. 15/16] [120] [826].

argument develops a careful parallel between what is needed for an individual's good life and what is needed for a community's. What an individual's good life {bona unius hominis vita} requires, above all, is virtue-in-action {operatio secundum virtutem} (secondary and quasi-instrumental requirements are the bodily goods necessary for action). So a group's—the political community's—good life, too, requires that the group act well. But there is a pre-condition for acting well: the unity of the acting being's parts. In individual human beings, this pre-condition is secured by nature. But in communities, the needed unity of life, the unity called 'peace' {pax}, has to be procured by governance {per regentis industriam}. So the community counterparts to individual virtue-in-action as primary element in an individual's good life are (1) the constituting of the community in the unity of peace, and (2) the directing of the peacefully united group towards well-doing {ad bene agendum}. The king's next {consequens} problem is to maintain and preserve these two primary elements of the group's good life.

At precisely this point Aquinas shifts from group 'good life' {bona vita in multitudine constituta} to 'public good' {bonum publicum}, treating them as synonymous. The *De Regno*'s treatment of our questions will be misunderstood unless one notices the effortlessness of this shift, and the synonymity and equivalence thus signalled.

There are, Aquinas is saying, three things incompatible with lasting public good, with that group good life whose primary elements are peace and acting well {tria quibus bonum publicum permanere non sinitur}. And the triple responsibility {cura} whose second element—'restraining subjects from immorality and leading them to virtuous action'—is our present concern is nothing other than the appropriate response to these three 'things incompatible with lasting public good'. The first 'incompatible thing' is unsuitable public officials, and the third is the incursions of enemies. The second is 'an internal impediment *to preserving the public good*: perversity of people's wills—their laziness in doing *what the public weal requires* {ad ea peragenda quae requirit res publica}, or again their harmfulness to the group's peace, their *disturbance of others' peace* by their violations of justice'.[55]

So, the second concern or responsibility {cura} of rulers, a

---

[55] *Reg.* II. 4 [I. 15/16] [119] [826].

responsibility proposed by Aquinas precisely as the appropriate response to *these* just-mentioned 'things incompatible with lasting public good', is not: of leading people to the *fullness* of virtue by coercively restraining them from *every* immorality. It is no more than: of leading people to *those* virtuous actions which are required if the public weal is not to be neglected, and of upholding peace against unjust violations.

What about the passage stating that rulers have the duty to promote heavenly fulfilment? This, too, should be taken to assert much less than appears on a first, non-contextual glance. For it too rests on the distinction between individual and group 'good life'. Promoting the *group's* good life is the king's concern. But Aquinas never supposes that such groups can attain perfect, i.e. heavenly fulfilment. So what he says here is: the group's good life is to be in line with {congruit} the 'pursuing of heavenly fulfilment {coelestem beatitudinem}'; by promoting group good life in that way, rulers are like swordsmiths or house-builders, whose role is to make an instrument suitable for others to put to their own good purposes. Thus the good life for which rulers are responsible is a *public* good, the justice and peace (rooted in citizens' characters rather than merely in fear of royal troops and judges) which in turn facilitate the domestically and ecclesially fostered individual virtue which is the human contribution to perfect *beatitudo*. The statement that rulers are to 'prescribe those things that lead to [perfect] fulfilment' (and 'to forbid their contraries *so far as is possible*') must be read as asserting a responsibility and authority no wider than the responsibility and authority for which Aquinas argues in the complex and carefully thought-out paragraphs by which the statement is flanked. And those paragraphs, as is now clear, deny rather than assert that a ruler should impose on individuals a legal duty to pursue their ultimate happiness or to abstain from choices which block that ultimate happiness without violating peace and justice. That denial will, as we have seen, be made much firmer and more explicit by the *Summa Theologiae*'s repeated differentiation of scope between divine governance and human governments' limited responsibility for their subjects' virtue.

VII.4. *The Virtue Required for Peace and Just Order*

Still, how should one understand those many texts, in many parts of Aquinas' work,[56] which flatly say that law and state have amongst their essential purposes and characteristics the inculcation of virtue by coercively requiring (within the limits of practicability) abstention from acts of vice?

The answer seems to be this. Human law must inculcate virtues because it will only work well as a guarantor of justice and peace if its subjects internalize its norms and requirements and—more important—adopt its purpose of promoting and preserving justice. The public good cannot be well preserved if people are untrustworthy, vengeful, willing to evade their taxes and other civic duties, biased in jury service, and so forth. So the preservation of public good needs people to have the *virtue*, the inner dispositions, of justice.[57]

This objective of inculcating virtue for the sake of peace and just conduct is coherent with Aquinas' constant teaching[58] that government or law, while rightly demanding of subjects that they do what is just and abstain from doing what is unjust, cannot rightly demand of them that they do so with a just mind and will, cannot require that they be just in the central, character-related sense of 'be a just person'. For just acts and forbearances are distinctly less likely to be chosen in the absence of a just character {habitus}. So it is a legitimate hope and important aim {finis} of government and law that citizens will come to have the virtue of justice and act out of that particular excellence of character.[59]

And if that is a legitimate purpose, then it must be at least a legitimate interest of government that citizens have other virtues too. Practical reasonableness is essentially all of a piece;[60] those who violate or neglect its directiveness in 'private' choices are thereby weakened in their rational motives, and their dispositions, for following its directiveness in 'public', other-affecting choices.[61]

---

[56] e.g. I-II q. 95 a. 1c; *ScG* III c. 121 n. 3 (n. b below); *Eth.* II. 1 n. 7 [251], v. 3 n. 12 [924].

[57] So an alternative to the standard dictum that, 'as the Philosopher says [in *Nic. Eth.* 2], the intention of legislators is to make their subjects good/virtuous' is: 'as philosophers say, the intention of all legislators is to make people just' (*In Rom.* 10. 1 ad v. 4 [819]).

[58] IV *Sent.* d. 15 q. 3 a. 4 sol. 1 ad 3; I-II q. 96 a. 3 ad 2, q. 100 a. 9 ad 1.

[59] I-II q. 96 a. 3 ad 2, q. 100 a. 9 ad 2; II *Sent.* d. 28 a. 3c and ad 3, IV *Sent.* d. 15 q. 3 a. 4 sol. 4 ad 3; *Eth.* II. 1 n. 7 [251].

[60] On the unity or connectedness (interdependence) of the virtues, see IV.2 n. 18 above.

[61] See e.g. *Virt. Card.* a. 2 ad 4.

Moreover, it seems clear that government and law—but does Aquinas ever affirm this directly and unambiguously?[62]—can rightly, for reasons ultimately of justice and peace, require and enforce a *public* morality going wider than issues of justice and peace. For parents have a primary educative responsibility in respect of their children,[63] and this responsibility—which, unlike public authority, includes a responsibility not only for peace and justice but also for seeing to the all-round character of the children[64]—may well be frustrated unless it is given some assistance and support by state government and law.[65] Those who corrupt children (drugs, sex, lying, greed, sloth, etc.) do them a great injustice.[66] But so too does anyone who neglects the child's nutrition, nurture, and education {disciplina}; making provision for such matters therefore falls within the responsibility of government {ad eum qui regit rempublicam}.[67] But even in seeking to promote justice-related virtues by requiring patterns of conduct which should habituate its subjects to the acts of these virtues,[68] the law cannot rightly demand that people acquire, or be motivated by, these virtuous

---

[62] A clear statement, but one directly concerned with ecclesiastical jurisdiction, is *In I Tim*. 5. 3 ad v. 20 [221]: 'The role of judges is public {iudex gerit personam publicam}, and so they ought to have as their goal the common good {intendere bonum commune}, which is harmed by public wrongdoing—because many people are corrupted {scandalizantur} by the example this gives. And so ecclesiastical judges ought to impose public punishments of a kind that will instruct and encourage others {ut alii aedificentur}.' Aquinas' constant references to conduct which is corruptive of character ('scandalizes' in the theologian's sense of that word), not least the reference at the end of the excised *ScG* text quoted above in n. 23, now the final sentence of *ScG* III c. 121 [2946], suggest this, though falling short of proving it.

[63] *Eth*. VIII. 11 nn. 4–5 [1691–2]; IV *Sent*. d. 26 q. 1 (= *Supp*. q. 41) a. 1c; cf. *Eth*. X. 15 n. 2 [2156].

[64] See e.g. the chapter on paternal authority in the deleted section of *ScG* III: *Opera* 14 app. pp. 46*–48* (and see n. 23 above). Here Aquinas argued that, unlike the rule of just kings, paternal rule over and responsibility for children extends 'not only to matters in which the child relates to other people but also to matters which pertain to the child as such {pater curam habet de filio non solum quantum ad ea in quibus ordinatur ad alios, sicut rex, sed etiam quantum ad ea quae pertinent ad ipsum secundum se}' (pp. 46*–47*); or Pera (1961: iii. 449–50). Parental rule is still restricted (unlike divine rule) to what is externally apparent, since hearts remain hidden from human beings, even parents, though some aspects of the child's disposition will doubtless be externally expressed and the parents can be concerned with these {quatenus per exteriores actus interior dispositio explicatur}. But see also p. 323 at n. 132; p. 240 n. 96; p. 241 n. 101.

[65] State law can rightly prohibit conduct which is an occasion of evils: see IV *Sent*. d. 15 q. 3 a. 1 sol. 4c.

[66] Not injustice in the central sense (relationship between equals) but real enough, and proper matter for laws: II-II q. 57 a. 4 ad 2; and see v.7 at nn. 170–2 above.

[67] *Impugn*. II c. 2 ad 10 [68]; *Eth*. X. 14 n. 13 [2149]; IV *Sent*. d. 15 q. 3 a. 1 sol. 4c.

[68] I-II q. 95 a. 1c, which treats this purpose as the ground for saying that human law is useful.

states of character or disposition. As Aquinas reiterates, the law's requirements (though not its legitimate objectives) are exhausted by 'external' compliance.[69]

Aquinas' thesis that state law is in these ways restricted in legitimate jurisdiction helps explain the disconcertingly formal character of his treatment of the questions—to which he gives some prominence—whether law seeks to make its subjects good,[70] and whether a good citizen must be a good person.[71] One expects something richer than Aquinas' answers, which are: (1) even wicked laws and rulers seek to make their subjects good (so that they be not merely obedient but readily obedient {bene obedientes} and thus good *as* subjects[72] and relative to the purposes of *that* regime);[73] and (2) in bad states a good citizen need not be a good person (though in all states a ruler, to be a good ruler, *should* be a good person). These answers make reasonable sense if Aquinas is taking the usual question about law and virtue to be one about the conditions for securing justice and peace by sufficient co-ordination of social life through law. The non-formal, substantive question, whether the point of such co-ordination is to make people *really* good persons *all round*, is simply not the issue in these passages.

VII.5. *Specifically Distinct Responsibilities for Common Good*

One may still wonder how far all this can be reconciled with the Aristotelian critique of social-contract and mutual-insurance conceptions of the state, a critique which the *De Regno* puts thus:

the ultimate purpose {ultimus finis} of a community {multitudo} gathered together {congregatae} is to live in accordance with virtue; for *people gather together* {congregantur} to *live well*, which someone living alone cannot attain; but *good life* is life in accordance with virtue, and so *virtuous life is the purpose of human gathering together* {congregationis}. . . . the only people who are counted as a community are those who, under the same laws and the

---

[69] I-II q. 96 a. 3 ad 3, q. 100 a. 9; IV *Sent.* d. 15 q. 3 a. 4 sol. 1 ad 3.
[70] e.g. I-II q. 92 a. 1; *Eth.* I. 19 n. 2 [225].   [71] e.g. *Eth.* v. 3 n. 14 [926]; *Pol.* III. 3.
[72] I-II q. 92 a. 1c: 'inducere subiectos ad propriam ipsorum virtutem'.
[73] Ibid.: 'non bonos . . . simpliciter, sed secundum quid, scilicet in ordine ad tale regimen'.

same governing arrangements {regimen}, are directed towards living well {diriguntur ad bene vivendum}.[74]

Are such statements about the purpose of political community (statements often parallelled in Aquinas' other works[75]) really consistent with the idea that governments' or lawmakers' responsibility to promote virtue does not authorize them to require more than the actions and forbearances necessary, directly or indirectly, for maintaining public and interpersonal good? I shall argue that they are, and that Aquinas' differentiation of three diverse kinds of practical reasonableness {prudentia}, individual, domestic, and political, helps make clear his whole, complex thought about the state's virtue-promoting responsibility and authority.

If one is a reasonable individual, one wants to 'gather together' with other individuals, households, and associations into political community; and is willing to direct oneself by laws, for the sake of the help that this community, this *congregatio*, can give one in one's own unrestricted purposes: *beatitudo* at least *imperfecta*, involving 'general justice' and love at least of neighbour as oneself. If one is a reasonable parent, one wants one's family to participate in the political community so that the family may flourish in every practicable way and its members co-operate with a view to that same *beatitudo*. If one is a reasonable citizen-voter or other participant in state government, one wants the law and the government to fulfil—i.e. to act in a way that advances and does not fall short of—these purposes of individuals and families. Thus there is an important sense in which the common good of the political community is all-inclusive, nothing short of the *beatitudo* of its members and the fulfilment of their families. This all-inclusive common good of the state includes the all-round virtue of every member of the state.

But it simply does not follow that lawmakers and other participants in state government are responsible for directing and

---

[74] *Reg.* ii. 3, lines 58–73 (i. 14/15) [106] [817]. The next paragraph [107] [817] looks beyond the imperfect beatitude of living virtuously and concludes that the ultimate end of the community, which is the same as the ultimate end of an individual, is to attain the fruition of perfect beatitude {per virtuosam vitam pervenire ad fruitionem divinam}.

[75] e.g. I-II q. 107 a. 2c: 'the purpose of any law is that people become just and people of virtue {iusti et virtuosi}'; ii *Sent.* d. 44 q. 1 a. 3c: 'a [third] purpose of government {praelatio} is the rectification of conduct {corrigendum mores}, as when bad people are punished and coercively brought to acts of virtue' (the first two functions of government being to give people direction in their activities; and to make up for weaknesses (as when peoples are defended by kings)).

commanding all the choices that need be made if this all-inclusive good is to be attained. It may well be that their responsibility—and thus their authority and right—is more limited, leaving families and individuals with a range of responsibilities whose carrying out, within the requirements of justice and peace, is not directed by government and law. If so, the goods which define the range of lawmakers' and other rulers' responsibility—say, the goods of peace and justice—can be called the common good of, specific to, the political community or state. This is the common good of, or specific to, a type of community which includes individuals and families, but whose successful ordering, while assisting individuals and families to attain fulfilment, does not supersede their responsibility to make good choices and actions on the basis of their own deliberation and judgements. These choices and actions are 'private'; the political community does not make, perform, or even stipulate them; they can be constitutive of *beatitudo imperfecta* more directly and immediately than any action by or on behalf of the political community can be (precisely as public, political action). There is, then, a specifically political common good whose content is understood in understanding what it is that political community, organization, government, and law can— and cannot—properly contribute towards the *beatitudo* of the state's members.

Accordingly, the reasonable pursuit of the 'all-inclusive' common good is stratified, into three distinct specializations of responsibility. Individual practical reasonableness (*prudentia*, without trace of selfishness), domestic practical reasonableness, and political practical reasonableness are three irreducibly distinct {diversi}[76] species of *prudentia*, three distinct 'parts' of moral practical reasonableness.[77] *Each* of these species of *prudentia* is

[76] Cf. the similar use of *diversi* in respect of the irreducibly distinct types of *ordo* and *scientia* discussed in *Eth.* prol. n. 1 [1–2]: 'secundum hos diversos ordines . . . sunt diversae scientiae' [2]. See II.1 at n. 5 above.

[77] II-II q. 48 a. un. c, q. 47 a. 11 ('the good of individuals, the good of families, and the good of *civitas* or realm are different ends {diversi fines}; so there are necessarily different species of *prudentia* corresponding to this difference in their respective ends: (1) *prudentia* without qualification {simpliciter dicta}, which is directed {ordinat[ur]} towards one's own good, (2) domestic prudence directed towards the common good of household or family, and (3) political prudence directed towards the common good of state or realm'); q. 50 a. 1c (the form of political prudence which is proper to state rulers is the most perfect form of prudence because it extends to more things and attains a further end than the other species of prudence).

concerned not (like military prudence[78]) with some special project which can be finished off but with, in a certain sense, 'the whole of life {tota vita}'.[79] The specifically political *prudentia* which is paradigmatically and principally, though not exclusively, the viewpoint of legislators[80] neither absorbs the other two nor even includes, directly, the whole of their content. Although rulers are in many respects in charge of their subjects, their jurisdiction as rulers is only, as we have seen, over the promotion of *public good*.

Public good is a part or aspect of the all-inclusive common good. It is the part which provides an indispensable context and support for those parts or aspects of the common good which are private (especially individual and familial good). It thus supplements, subserves, and supervises those private aspects, but without superseding them, and without taking overall charge of, or responsibility for, them. 'Neither in one's whole being nor in all one's belongings is one subordinate to the political community.'[81] And here we may add Aquinas' partial anticipation of the principle of subsidiarity:[82] 'it is contrary to the proper character of the state's governance {contra rationem gubernationis [civitatis]} to impede people from acting according to their responsibilities {officia}—except in emergencies'.[83]

Still, the justice and peace which rulers must maintain *are* for the sake of individual and familial well-being and cannot be identified and pursued without a sound conception of individual

---

[78] II-II q. 48 a. un. c, q. 50 a. 4. If military prudence deserves its place as a fourth species of *prudentia*, it is because it shares in the open-endedness of political prudence—is, so to speak, the extension of political prudence into the external hazard of war in which the whole life of the *civitas* and its elements is at stake: see II-II q. 50 a. 4 ad 1 and ad 2.

[79] II-II q. 48 a. un. c; 'tota vita' is short for 'the common end of the whole of human life' {communis finis totius humanae vitae} and 'the good of the whole of life' {bonum totius vitae}: q. 47 a. 13c and ad 3.

[80] II-II q. 50 a. 2 (note that in the introd. to q. 50, the prudence of rulers {regnativa} is called the prudence involved in law-making {legispositiva}; VIII. 1 at n. 16 below.

[81] I-II q. 21 a. 4 ad 3: 'homo non ordinatur ad communitatem politicam secundum se totum, et secundum omnia sua'; 'and so not all one's acts are meritorious or culpable by virtue of their relationship to that community'.

[82] Namely, that it is unjust for more extensive associations to assume functions which can be performed efficiently by individuals or by less extensive associations, since the proper function of instrumental associations is to help their members help themselves: see Finnis (1980: 146, 159).

[83] *ScG* III c. 71 n. 4 [2470]. What are these responsibilities? Marriage is one natural responsibility {officium naturae humanae} with which human law is rightly concerned (IV *Sent.* d. 27 q. 1 a. 3 sol. 1 ad 1, d. 31 q. 1 a. 2c and a. 3 s.c. 2, d. 39 a. 2 ad 3) and is a community responsibility {in officium communitatis} (d. 34 a. 1 ad 4).

and domestic responsibilities.[84] The *politica* which is the highest {principalior, principalissima} practical knowledge[85] must be *politica* in the sense that it includes, along with the specifically political, the considerations called by Aquinas *oeconomica* (see VII.6 below) and *monostica* (the individual-centred *Ethics* which precedes[86] the society-focused *Politics*). Because the *prudentia* of political rulers must comprehend, though without replacing, the *prudentia* of individuals and families, it is the most complete {perfectissima},[87] and though people who are not good persons can be good citizens (qua *subjects*), they cannot be good rulers.[88] The immediate and direct measure of individual and parental responsibility is not the directives of political authority, but remains the practical reasonableness of individuals and of heads of households.

In sum: The common good attainable in political community is thus a complex good attainable only if the state's rulers, its families, and its individual citizens all perform their proper, specialized and stratified roles and responsibilities. This common good, which is in a sense *the* common good of the political community, is *unlimited* (the common good of the whole of human life). But there is also a common good which is 'political' in the more specific sense that it is (1) the good of using government and law to assist individuals and families do well what they should be doing, together with (2) the good(s) which sound action by and on behalf of the political community can add to the good attainable by individuals and families as such (including the good of repelling and overcoming harms and deficiencies which individuals and families and other 'private' groupings could not adequately deal with). This, and only this, specifically political common good is what the state's rulers are responsible for securing and, by legislation and lawful governmental actions (judicial and administrative), should require their subjects to respect and support.

---

[84] Government and law may leave unprohibited the acts of certain vices (e.g. selling at unfair prices; or sex between unmarried consenting adults) without thereby approving them: I-II q. 93 a. 3 ad 3, II-II q. 77 a. 1 ad 1; n. 146 below.

[85] *Eth.* I. 2 n. 12–13 [30–1]; *Pol.* prol. 7 [7]; see IV.3 at nn. 55–60 above.

[86] See IV *Sent.* d. 2 q. 1 a. 3 ad 3.

[87] II-II q. 50 a. 2 ad 1; see also *Eth.* VI. 7 n. 7 [1201]. Similarly, general justice is *principaliter* a virtue of rulers {in principe} and *secundario et quasi administrative* in subjects: II-II q. 58 a. 6c. But note that individuals and heads of households are not merely subjects of the state's government and laws. So their justice is not merely administrative.

[88] I-II q. 92 a. 1 ad 3.

This specifically political common good is *limited* and in a sense *instrumental.*[89] It is what Aquinas, as we have seen, calls public good.

VII.6. *The State's Elements, Private and Public*

Aquinas' treatment can thus be understood as coherent. But there remains the challenge of principle. Are there good grounds for judging that the state's specific common good is this limited public good of justice and peace? If a government or legislature should, as Aquinas certainly thinks, ascertain and adhere to the truth about human fulfilment and morality, why shouldn't it use its public powers, and law's coercive pedagogy, to require of all citizens the acts and forbearances which will advance their fulfilment and complete virtue? Aren't rulers obliged to do so by *moralis philosophia*'s master principle, general justice or love of neighbour as oneself? Of course, if bad side-effects are too serious—if blowing one's nose too hard draws blood[90]—the effort should doubtless be made more gradual and perhaps indirect. But why judge the effort wrong in principle, an abuse of public power, *ultra vires* because directed to an end which state government and law do not truly have?

Aquinas' answers to such demands for justification are not as clear as we may wish. (When Kant and Mill announce positions similar to Aquinas', their attempted justifications are, at bottom, at least as sketchy.) Responding to the question whether there are limits (of subject-matter) to what can be required of subjects by their rulers, he denies that human law and government can have any obligation-imposing authority over 'matters which concern the inner life of the will {in his quae pertinent ad interiorem motum

---

[89] In other contexts, too, Aquinas will use the term 'common good' to refer to some good which falls short of, and is instrumental to, a more ultimate common good. Thus he will say that 'the army's leader intends a common good, that is to say [not peace and the state's common weal, nor even victory, but rather] the whole army's order {intendit bonum commune, scilicet ordinem totius exercitus}' (I-II q. 9 a. 1c), an order which is obviously only instrumental (see II.2, 3 above).

[90] I-II q. 96 a. 2 ad 2, citing Prov. 30: 33, and arguing that human law is to bring people to virtue gradually, lest, being pushed too hard, they break out into worse wrongdoing. See also *Mal.* q. 13 a. 4 ad 6; II-II q. 78 a. 1 ad 3.

voluntatis}'.[91] In such matters we are subject only to God.[92] Ground for this denial perhaps emerges in the next sentences, where Aquinas further denies that one can be morally obliged to obey human rulers in relation to certain matters of actual bodily behaviour, namely those which pertain to the nature of one's body {ea quae pertinent ad naturam corporis}.[93] In such matters, too, we are subject only to God—and this time a reason is assigned, the fundamental equality of human persons: 'for we are all, by [or: in our] nature, on a par {quia omnes homines natura sunt pares}'.[94] None of us stands to our neighbour as end stands to means, so there is no need, and no justification, for rulers to make rules requiring us to conform our dispositions or our self-regarding conduct to the interests of our neighbours.[95] The matters thus outside state power include the matters (e.g. whether and whom to marry) which elsewhere he says are beyond the power of even the highest authority in a *perfecta communitas*[96] because in these matters 'one is so much [a] free and independent [person] {ita liber sui}'.[97] And Aquinas mentions other such matters.[98]

[91] II-II q. 104 a. 5.

[92] He appeals, ibid., to Seneca's teaching that even the servitude of the Roman slave does not righly include the better part {melior pars} of the human being: one's mind {mens}, which is in charge of and responsible for itself {sui iuris}.

[93] II-II q. 104 a. 5c; he mentions the preservation {sustentatio} of one's body, and propagation. See also IV *Sent.* d. 36 (= *Supp.* q. 52) a. 2c: servants/serfs/slaves {servi} are not subject to their masters in any way that would restrict their freedom to eat, sleep, and 'do other things like that, pertaining to the body's needs'—or their power to marry. See also v.7 n. l (p. 185) above.

[94] II-II q. 104 a. 5c. For this proposition see also I q. 113 a. 2 ad 3; II *Sent.* d. 44 q. 1 a. 3 ad 1 (quoted v.7 n. 167 above); and likewise *Ver.* q. 11 a. 3c; *In Rom.* 9. 3 ad v. 14 [766].

[95] I-II q. 104 a. 1 ad 3: 'homo non ordinatur ad proximum sicut in finem, ut oporteat eum disponi in seipso in ordine ad proximum'.

[96] Among the matters in which one's freedom can rightfully prevail over all human command is the decision not to marry someone: ibid. Of course, marriage necessarily concerns justice, not least because it is likely to result in children; so state laws can regulate the general conditions of marriage (*Mal.* q. 15 a. 2 ad 12; IV *Sent.* d. 39 (= *Supp.* q. 59) a. 2 ad 3—minimal age, incest bounds, and so forth—if they do so with fairness and humanity and in ways genuinely related to the true 'political good' (*ScG* IV c. 78 n. 2 [4120]). But even if doing so would advance some public policy or the well-being of a family or Church or state, neither the state's officials nor any domestic or religious authorities can rightly compel anyone to marry, or to marry this person, or forbid the marriage of two consenting adults who are not within the classes of persons reasonably disqualified or forbidden to marry (*ST* II-II q. 104 a. 5c; IV *Sent.* d. 29 a. 4 (= *Supp.* q. 47 a. 6), d. 36 (= *Supp.* q. 52) a. 2.

[97] IV *Sent.* d. 38 q. 1 a. 4 sol. 1c. For the same reason (each of us being a free person {liber sui}), no one can rightly be subjected, even by God, to a spiritual penalty in their will on account of another person's wrongdoing: II-II q. 108 a. 4 ad 1.

[98] Another matter outside the rightful power of state government and law is the decision to take religious vows, e.g of virginity; here 'private good' is more weighty

Sometimes Aquinas identifies them compendiously as 'matters that concern one's person {ea quae pertinent ad suam personam}'.[99] It is no coincidence that the status of freedom, self-possession,[100] and equality—the metaphysical reality and normative entitlement which he is appealing to—is the status of *persons*.[101] This is the status which Aquinas seems to be taking for granted[102] when he puts forward the arguments to which we now turn, arguments which concern the competence of government.

The first argument points to the inability of state rulers to *succeed* in supervising movements of the human spirit which are inherently beyond their knowledge.[103] We can often reasonably judge the intentions with which someone is acting, but never the furthest and deepest interests and dispositions underlying the action chosen.[104] The lack of competence (capacity) is ground for denial of competence (jurisdiction, authority, right): God, not any human ruler, is the judge of secrets.[105] The rulers or directors of human communities, e.g. a religious congregation or a state, have absolutely[106] no right or authority to require anyone to disclose a secret sin which does not affect that community's public well-being. Only the effect on public well-being is the concern of human judges. A secret immorality may have this effect either intrinsically

{potius} than, preferable {excellentior} to, public or common good, because it belongs (Aquinas judges) to a different, higher genus than the common good of continued bodily propagation of the human species: II-II q. 152 a. 4 ad 3.

[99] II-II q. 88 a. 8 ad 2; IV *Sent.* d. 38 q. 1 a. 1 sol. 3 ad 2.

[100] See II.1 at n. 3 above. But this is not an 'autonomy' which exempts one from serious moral responsibility for one's freely chosen self-regarding acts; suicide is a more serious type of wrong than murder: I-II q. 73 a. 9 ad 2.

[101] Those who are free can 'freely dispose of their own persons {libere de sua persona disponere}' (II-II q. 189 a. 6 ad 2); a daughter is not her father's maidservant {ancilla}, and he has no power over her body (and so—from the age of puberty: II-II q. 88 a. 8 ad 2—she can make her own decision to (e.g.) enter religious life without parental consent) 'because she is a free person' (IV *Sent.* d. 28 a. 3 (=*Supp.* q. 45 a. 5) ad 1). Even if parents have promised their daughter's hand in marriage, and sealed the promise with an oath, the daughter has no duty to obey her parents' command that she fulfil the engagement: IV *Sent.* d. 29 a. 4 ad 2. See also v. 7 n. 172 above, x. 5 n. 132 below.

[102] He of course defends and explains this status—human dignity—elsewhere: see v.7 and 8 above.

[103] e.g. I-II q. 100 a. 9c: 'it does not belong to human beings to judge any save external acts, for "human beings see [only] those things which show" (1 Kgs. 16: 7)'. So even parental rule—which resembles divine government more closely than state rule does (because unlike state rule it can rightly concern itself with its subjects not merely as citizens but as what they are {secundum quod in sua natura subsist[unt]})—is restricted to 'those things which are externally evidenced about someone {illa . . . quae in homine apparent exterius}': *Opera* 14. 47* (=Pera 1961: iii. 449), excised from *ScG* III after c. 121.

[104] See e.g. II-II q. 89 a. 1c.; see also *Mal.* q. 16 a. 8c.

[105] II-II q. 33 a. 7 ad 5; *Secret.* 2 [1217].   [106] See *Secret.* 1–3 [1216–18].

(e.g. plotting to betray the state to its enemies[107]) or extrinsically, as when it has become a matter of public notoriety {infamia} or of formal and responsible accusations.[108] Only in cases thus stamped with a public character may a judge or other ruler override the legitimate privacy of wrongdoers or those who know their secrets, and require disclosure.

This line of thought assumes that judges and lawmakers appropriately have only limited responsibility and authority. That assumption is elaborated in a second argument, which develops more broadly the positions sketched in the preceding section, about the different viewpoints, responsibilities, and strata of the common good. This argument, which I shall develop in the remaining portion of this chapter, asks the questioner to go behind the proposition that states are complete communities, and to consider the grounds for it, on the tacit assumption that the institutions which give the community its completeness—law and government—need justification in the face of the natural equality and freedom of persons, and need to show just why and when their authority overrides the responsibility of parents and the self-possession[109] of free persons above the age of puberty.[110]

The state is not an organism, but an order of co-operative action for some purpose.[111] But what is that purpose, and why does it differ in *kind* from the purposes of other groups which might be constituted for far-reaching economic, educational, or defensive purposes? What makes the political community 'complete', rather than merely higher on a scale of increasingly inclusive membership and extensive objectives?

Prior to or independently of any politically organized community, there can exist individuals and families and indeed groups of neighbouring families. Any such groups of families are contingent

---

[107] II-II q. 33 a. 7c: 'those secret sins which are physically or spiritually harmful to one's neighbours, e.g. . . .'; *Secret.* 6 [1222] instances theft or arson in a [communal] house. Aquinas' six colleagues on the 1269 Dominican consultative commission were less willing than him to regard the public interest as overriding the entitlement to keep secrets private. See also II-II q. 68 a. 1 ad 3.

[108] II-II q. 33 a. 7 ad 5; *Quodl.* IV q. 8 a. 1c; *Secret.* 4 and 5 [1219, 1221].

[109] II-II q. 88 a. 8 ad 2 {suae potestatis}, q. 189 a. 5c {propriae potestatis}, a. 6 ad 2.

[110] Puberty (usually about 14 in males, 12 in females) is significant for these purposes as being the age by which most people can make proper use of reason {debitum usum rationis}: II-II q. 189 a. 5c.

[111] *Eth.* prol. n. 5[5]; *ST* I-II q. 17 a. 4c, III q. 8 a. 1 ad 2; in *Mal.* q. 4 a. 1c note the *quasi*. See II.2 above.

in their size, interactions, and common purposes and activities, if any. Families, in their central form, are not in that way contingent.

No doubt families are contingent in the sense that each is formed by free choices—in the central case, by the free choice of a man and a woman to enter upon that sort of reproductive and educative partnership, which is also the 'closest form of friendship'.[112] But families are non-contingent in the sense that they directly instantiate a basic human good[113]—the good probably best described as marriage itself.[114] And for a lengthy period in the life of all human infants families are the direct and practically indispensable means of instantiating the basic good of life and health and, almost as directly and indispensably, the goods of knowledge, friendship {societas}, and practical reasonableness, at least in their beginnings. No one is born without a mother and a father; the nurture without which no one survives cannot be more perceptively, lovingly, and fittingly provided than by a virtuous and capable mother and father, this mother and this father.[115] Love of neighbour as oneself has its perhaps most immediate and far-reaching demands right here, in the nurture of children to at least[116] the point where they become what the parents were when they made by free choice the commitment of marriage: truly self-standing, each free {*liber* or *libera sui*} and master or mistress of his or her own acts {*dominus* or *domina sui actus*}.[117]

'Human beings are by nature more conjugal than political.'[118] The family, essentially husband, wife, and children, is antecedent to, and more necessary than, political society (because oriented around {ordinatur ad} acts of procreation and nurture necessary for life itself).[119] The complementarity of man and woman in domestic life is the basis for an exclusive and fully committed friendship which not only assumes the necessary heavy responsibilities and

---

[112] *ScG* III c. 123 n. 6 [2964]: between husband and wife there is evidently the greatest friendship {maxima amicitia}; v.4 at nn. 56–60 above.

[113] That is, one of the human goods {bona humana} directed to by the first principles of human action {prima principia operum humanorum}: I-II q. 94 a. 1 ad 2, a. 2c; also II-II q. 47 a. 6c, q. 56 a. 1c; *Ver.* q. 5 a. 1c; III. 5–6, IV. 5 above.

[114] See III.5 at nn. 99–102 and n. p above.

[115] Critique of alternatives to marriage and family: *Pol.* II. 1 n. 7 [175] and 5 n. 2 [208].

[116] Parental duties of education and financial support last in some form for the whole life of the children: IV *Sent.* d. 33 q. 2 a. 1c (=*Supp.* q. 67 a. 1c).

[117] See IV *Sent.* d. 26 q. 1 a. 1c, d. 29 q. un. a. 4c and ad 1: in these matters, as the parent {pater} is free so is the son or daughter {filius}.

[118] *Eth.* VIII. 12 n. 19 [1720]; also n. 18 [1719]; *Nic. Eth.* 8. 12. 1162^{a}17–18.

[119] Ibid. [1720].

burdens but also (with good fortune) is useful, sexually enjoyable, and delightful simply as a friendship of virtue, a sharing of life and human goods {communicatio} which, Aquinas indicates, makes good sense even if children fail to be born or do not survive.[120] The life of the family and its household {domus} has such a far-reaching sufficiency of independent ends and such stability in patterns of effective means that it is the subject of a distinct discipline or practical science, *oeconomica*.

Aquinas knows that one can detach resource-management from the household in order to make it simply the art of accumulating wealth on a scale as wide as the *civitas*, or wider.[121] He knows of economists who do this, 'thinking that their function is the same as that of money-dealers [who seek cash {denarios} for its own sake], conserving and multiplying cash *in infinitum*'.[122] But in a reasonable conception of economics, accumulated money-wealth is merely instrumental to the good of persons—primarily and directly, of households,[123] the good of the *totum bene vivere* in shared domestic life {secundum domesticam conversationem}.[124] (The wealth of a household is properly held and administered for the common good of the household and thus for the benefit of the family members,[125] primarily and directly for spouse, children, and other members of the family, secondarily and indirectly for the benefit also of the person responsible for this administration and distribution.[126]) Even if, unlike Aquinas, one envisages economics as an understanding of capital formation, production, and consumption on a scale as wide as the political community, if not of regional and world-wide markets, Aquinas' household-oriented conception of the basic human purpose of economic activity can reasonably be sustained.

So Aquinas reaches the concept of 'complete community' only by attending to the deficiencies of such a community's elements or

---

[120] *Eth.* VIII. 12 nn. 22–5 [1721–4]; IV *Sent.* d. 34 a. 2 (=*Supp.* q. 58 a. 1) ad 3.

[121] *Reg.* II. 3 [I. 14] [106] [816]: 'if the ultimate end [of the human multitude] were abundance of wealth {divitiarum affluentia}, the economist {oeconomus} would be king'.

[122] *Pol.* I. 8 n. 4 [125].

[123] II-II q. 50 a. 3 ad 2; *Eth.* I. 1 n. 15 [15]; *In I Tim.* 3. 2 ad v. 5 [104]: 'wealth is not the end of economics but an instrument'.   [124] II-II q. 50 a. 3 ad 2; IV. 4 n. 91 above.

[125] So the other and more basic meaning of 'economist' {oeconomus} is 'a family's *procurator* and *dispensator*', the person who nurtures and distributes the family's goods: *Pol.* I. 1 n. 5 [13]. 'The one in charge of a family {gubernator} is called a *dispensator* as being the one who with due weight and in due measure distributes to each member of the family the tasks and necessities of [their common] life': I-II q. 97 a. 4c.

[126] *Pol.* III. 5 n. 5 [388].

'parts'—fundamentally, individuals and families. These parts are prior to the complete community not historically but in a more important way: in their immediate and irreplaceable instantiation of basic human goods. The need which individuals have for the political community is not that it instantiates an otherwise unavailable basic good. By contrast, the lives of individuals and families directly instantiate basic goods, and can even provide means and context for instantiating all the other basic goods: education, friends, marriage, virtue . . . As for the *non*-basic goods needed to support life and other basic goods—notably the instrumental goods of produce and exchange—Aquinas regards them as goods which, at least primarily and directly, are appropriately within the control of *private* persons and groups {potestati privatarum personarum subduntur res possessae},[127] dealing sometimes 'in public'[128] and sometimes in private. Their instrumentality is essentially in the service of households. As we shall see, a state's government and law can protect and greatly enhance the utility of these instrumental goods. Law and government thereby serve basic human goods which they in other ways serve more directly and immediately. The justice they can restore by the 'private law' regime of *reparatio* or *restitutio* and the 'public law' regime of *retributio* (VI.5 above) is doubtless an aspect of the basic good of *societas*, and in respect of that justice one may perhaps say that the specifically political common good is more than merely instrumental. But in all other respects, at least, the common good which is interdefined with the jurisdiction of state government and law seems indeed to be an instrumental good or set of goods, albeit of pre-eminent complexity, scope, and dignity among instruments.

VII.7. *Law and Government as Supplements*

Contrary to what is often supposed, Aquinas' many statements that we are 'naturally political animals' have nothing particularly

[127] I-II q. 105 a. 2c: 'and so private persons can have voluntary dealings with each other in relation to these possessions, e.g. buying, selling, making gifts, and other things of that sort'. The article proceeds to explain the need for state law to remedy the difficulties that arise in connection with such dealings. Thus, as q. 104 a. 1 ad 1 says, 'rulers {princ[ipes]} have authority not only to regulate {ordinare} matters in dispute but also the voluntary contracts which people make, and indeed everything which pertains to a people's common life and governing arrangements {communitas et regimen}'; also VI. 2 at n. 50.

[128] Thus a large trade fair or market is a public association (albeit temporary) of traders: *Impugn.* c. 3, lines 268–74 [II c. 2 [57]].

to do with *political* community.[129] So they cannot be pressed into service as implying that the state or its common good is the object of a natural inclination, is an intrinsic and basic good. Strikingly, they do no more than assert our *social* not solitary nature,[130] our need to have interpersonal relationships for necessities such as food and clothing,[131] for speech,[132] and in general for getting along together {convivere};[133] or the need for various social but not peculiarly political virtues, such as good faith in promising and testifying, and so forth.[134] On the other hand, Aquinas accepts Aristotle's opinion that we are 'naturally civil animals' because we are *naturally* parts of a *civitas*,[135] which stands to other natural communities[136] as an end.[137]

In human affairs which are matters of deliberation and choice, what is natural is settled by asking what is intelligent and reasonable.[138] That in turn is settled by looking to the first principles of practical reason, to the basic human goods.[139] So the *civitas* could be called 'natural' if participation in it (a) instantiates in itself a basic human good, or (b) is a rationally required component in, or indispensable means to instantiating, one or more basic human goods. Aquinas' opinion, rather clearly, is that it is the latter. At the relevant point in his lists of basic human goods he mentions nothing more specific than living in fellowship {in societate

---

[129] The only seeming exceptions to this are one or two texts where his commentary tracks Aristotle's argument that we are more naturally conjugal than political. Here 'political' does refer to the political whole of which marital communities are parts: *Eth.* VIII. 12 nn. 18–19 [1719–20].   [130] I-II q. 72 a. 4c; IV *Sent.* d. 26 q. 1 a. 1c.

[131] *ScG* III c. 85 n. 11 [2607].   [132] *Peri.* I. 2 n. 2 [12].

[133] *Eth.* IX. 10 n. 7 [1891]; see also *Reg.* I. 1 [4–8] [741–4].

[134] I-II q. 61 a. 5c (and see ad 4); *Trin.* q. 3 a. 1 s.c. 3.

[135] Outside the commentary on the *Politics*, the notion that individuals and/or households are (naturally) parts of the *civitas* is stated at I-II q. 90 a. 2c, a. 3 ad 3, q. 92 a. 1 ad 3, II-II q. 47 a. 11 ad 2, q. 50 a. 3c, q. 59 a. 3 ad 2; *Impugn.* II c. 2 ad 3 [60]. It seems that *ST* I q. 60 a. 5c ('if one were {si homo esset} a natural part of this *civitas*, this inclination [of good citizens to expose themselves to danger even of death for the preservation of the whole state {totius reipublicae}] would be natural to one {esset ei naturalis}') casts doubt on the appropriateness of calling people naturally parts of a *civitas*.

[136] At the relevant point in *Pol.* I. 1 n. 20 [28], the neighbourhood community is judged natural, alongside (or between) the family and the *civitas*.

[137] 'Animal naturaliter civile' translates the same Greek phrase as 'animal naturaliter politicum' (*Politics* I. 2. 1253ᵃ2–3). It is used only in *Eth.* I. 9 n. 10 [112]; *Pol.* I. 1 nn. 24, 26, 28, 29 [32, 34, 36, 37]. The naturalness of the *civitas* is stated in *Pol.* I. 1 nn. 23, 24, 29, 32 (which also states that we have within us a natural impetus to political community {communitas civitatis} as we have to the virtues) [31, 32, 37, 40].

[138] See e.g. I-II q. 71 a. 2c, q. 94 a. 3 ad 2; III. 7 n. 141 above.   [139] See n. 113 above.

vivere}[140]—something that is done also with parents and children, spouse, friends, and other people in various more or less temporary and specialized groups (of pilgrims, of students, of sailors, of merchants, and so forth).[141] The thought that we cannot live reasonably and well apart from a *civitas*[142] is consistent with the proposition that the common good specific to the *civitas* as such—the public good—is not basic but, rather, instrumental to securing human goods which are basic (including other forms of community or association, especially domestic and religious associations[143]) and none of which is in itself specifically political, i.e. concerned with the state. If that proposition needs qualification, the qualification concerns the restoration of justice by the irreparable modes of punishment reserved to state government.

Consider both the proposition and the possible qualification. What is it that solitary individuals, families, and groups of families inevitably cannot do well? In what way are they inevitably 'incomplete'? In their inability (1) to secure themselves *well* against violence (including invasion), theft, and fraud,[144] and (2) to maintain a fair and stable system of distributing, exploiting, and exchanging the natural resources which, Aquinas thinks,[145] are in reason and fairness—'naturally' (not merely 'initially')—things common to all. That is to say, individuals and families cannot well secure and maintain the elements which make up the *public good* of justice and peace—a good which, with good fortune, will also include prosperity.[146] And so their instantiation of basic goods is less

---

[140] I-II q. 94 a. 2c. See also *Impugn.* c. 3 [II c. 2c [55–6]]: 'societas nihil aliud esse videatur quam adunatio hominum ad unum aliquid communiter agendum. . . . adunatio hominum ad aliquid unum perficiendum . . . divers[ae] communicationes . . . nihil aliud sunt quam societates quaedam . . . [or] amiciti[ae]'.   [141] Ibid. [57]; *Eth.* 1. 9 n. 10 [112].

[142] So the whole complex of human goods can be called our 'civil and natural good {bonum civile et naturale hominis}', to which our will (i.e. our response to understood goods) has a natural, pre-moral inclination: III *Sent.* d. 33 q. 2 a. 4 sol. 3c. *Civilis* in this sense is a common 13th-century theological term for 'secular', referring to this world as distinct from our heavenly *patria*. Still, as q. 1 a. 4c makes clear, Aquinas welcomes the 'political' connotation of *civilis* even in this sort of context; for in one's spiritual life one is *civis civitatis Dei*, citizen in a realm which, unlike our earthly *civilitas* (polity), will not be left behind {evacuabitur} but rather perfected: x.6 at nn. 150–69 below.

[143] State laws or arrangements impeding the associating of citizens {quae adunationes civium impedi…

civium impediert} should be reformed whenever they involve arbitrary restrictions on membership (e.g. of universities) and thereby create disunity {scissura} in the political community: *Impugn.* c. 3, lines 386–90 [II c. 2 ad 4 [61]].

[144] The paternal power (authority) of admonition is inadequate in the face of rebels and contumacious offenders: I-II q. 105 a. 4 ad 5.   [145] VI. 2 at nn. 4–16 above.

[146] See *Reg.* 1. 2 [I. 3] [20] [753]: the fruits of good government are peace, justice, and economic abundance {affluentia rerum}; and n. 47 above. For the sake of economic

secure and full than it can be if public justice and peace are maintained by law and other specifically political institutions and activities, in a way that no individual or private group can appropriately undertake or match. Individuals' and groups' need for political community is *that* need, and the political community's specific common good[147] is, accordingly, that *public* good.

Suppose nobody was badly disposed, unjust, recalcitrant. Would there be need for states with their governments and laws? Aquinas is clear that in such a paradise there would still be need for 'government and direction of free people', since social life requires some unity of social action and where there are many people—intelligent and good people—there are many competing ideas about what actions should be done for the sake of the common good.[148] But he does not say that in such a state of affairs there would be need for specifically *political* government or law,[149] and his discussion, important and clarifying as it in some respects is, does not really carry further the question why there is need for states, political government, and state law.

Consider that question in the context of, say, violence within the household. Why can't this be dealt with by, say, paternal power? Is it merely that, say, the son may grow stronger than his parents, or outrun them? That is perhaps a relevant consideration.[150] But why does Aquinas say that neither the father nor any other non-public person can rightly threaten or impose penalties that are fully

benefits {commoditates}, government and law can rightly permit (though never promote) certain economic injuries (e.g. unjust transactions such as usurious loans): *Mal.* q. 13 a. 4 ad 6; II-II q. 78 a. 1 ad 3; see n. 84, VI.4 at nn. 123–4 above.

[147] Sometimes called the civil good {bonum civile}; see e.g. *Virt. Card.* q. un. a. 4 ad 4: the purpose of legislation (and of the military art) is the preservation of the civil good {conservatio boni civilis est finis et terminus militaris et legis positivae}.

[148] I q. 96 a. 4; cf. II *Sent.* d. 44 q. 1 a. 3c (omitting this reason for *dominium* and *praelatio* in paradise). The difference between these two texts—and between 'Augustinian' and 'Thomistic' political theory—is often exaggerated (as e.g. by Markus 1970: 221–30). See also VIII. 2 at nn. 65–6, VIII.3 at nn. 91–3 below.

[149] Indeed, in his commentaries touching on this matter incidentally rather than directly and for its own sake, Aquinas sometimes reports, without contesting, the view (which he ascribes to Aristotle) that if people were disposed well enough to comply with parental admonitions there would be 'no need for kings and judges' (*Ps.* 44. 5 ad v. 5), and the proposition that 'law is for the unjust, not the just' (*In I Tim.* 1. 3 ad v. 9 [23]). [150] See *Eth.* prol. n. 4 [4].

coercive?[151] Why can there be no law, in the focal sense,[152] within families or neighbourhood groups of families?

Aquinas here does not explain as much as we may wish. He is insistent about distinguishing public from private. He does so in many contexts: self-defence, war, resistance to tyranny, intra-familial discipline, ecclesiastical order, forms of justice, correction of wrongdoers, and so on. But he treats it rather as if axiomatic.[e] Still, if we bear in mind the content or force of the distinction, we may discern its purpose just below the surface of his texts.

What is matter for public authority is matter for law: the sword and the balance. It is matter for judgements, with often irreparable finality of outcome, given by impartial judges representing the *princeps*[153] before whom all who seek justice are equal.[154] None of us can rightly be simultaneously prosecutor, judge, and witness.[155] Private persons and bodies are not equipped for *judgement*, especially judgement according to publicly established *law*,[156] and so cannot rightly impose the irreparable measures which may be needed to restore justice and peace. So they are incomplete, *imperfecta*, and in need of completion by the order of public justice. When a society not only has individuals flourishing in families and other private associations and dealings but also is equipped for public justice, it is in principle complete, *perfecta*.

The irreparability of various measures often needed to restore justice plays a large part in the argument. The family or household (including domestic servants) is an *imperfecta communitas* and within it there is a *potestas coercendi*, a limited coercive authority

---

[151] *Eth.* x. 14 n. 17 [2153]; II-II q. 67 a. 1c, I-II q. 90 a. 3 ad 2 ('a private person {persona privata} does not . . . have the coercive authority {vim coactivam} which law should have'). Note that a leader of the domestic community (an *imperfecta communitas*) has the 'incomplete' coercive power of imposing rather light penalties, penalties which do no irreparable harm (beating): I-II q. 87 a. 8 ad 3, II-II q. 65 a. 2 ad 2; IV *Sent.* d. 37 q. 2 a. 1 ad 4. But fundamentally, paternal discipline is by admonition {monitiones; potestas admonendi}: I-II q. 95 a. 1c, q. 100 a. 11 ad 3, q. 105 a. 4 ad 3; see also *In I Tim.* 1. 3 ad v. 9 [23].

[152] In a secondary sense of 'law', the household or family is governed by the order imposed by its leader's 'law and precept {ordo per legem et praeceptum}' (*Meta.* XII. 12 n. 8 [2634]), 'precepts or standing orders {praecepta vel statuta}' which [because not fully coercive] do not strictly speaking {proprie} have the character {ratio} of law (I-II q. 90 a. 3 ad 2 and ad 3).

[153] The *custodia iustitiae*, as a response to wrongdoing, is a *commune bonum* which is committed to a ruler {praelatus} as *persona publica*: IV *Sent.* d. 19 q. 2 a. 1 ad 6; II-II q. 67 a. 4c; it is to bring the unjust to justice that state governments {princip[es] terrae} rule with *public* power: II-II q. 62 a. 7 ad 3. The *princeps* is the supreme judge: I-II q. 104 a. 1 ad 1.   [154] II *Sent.* d. 44 q. 2 a. 1c.

[155] II-II q. 67 a. 3 ad 3: 'homo non potest esse simul accusator, iudex, et testis'.

[156] See II-II q. 60 a. 6c and ad 1. See also VIII. 3 n. 81 below.

or right (not in any way delegated by the state) of imposing relatively light penalties, 'penalties, such as a beating, which do no irreparable harm'.[157] But irreparable penalties are different. No penalty going beyond such a limited measure of reformative correction can rightly be imposed, under any circumstances, by any private person (even as head of a family). For such persons are not judges. They lack (Aquinas seems to be saying) the detachment which becomes possible in principle when the *persona publica* is differentiated from the *persona privata*.

That differentiation of *personae*, of roles, impressed Aquinas greatly. It is the basis, for example, of his rigorous teaching (rejected by distinguished colleagues) that judges, because they act as *personae publicae*, must in all cases proceed only on evidence legally admissible before them, and never on their private knowledge, even when that is certain and would entitle someone accused of a capital offence to be acquitted.[158] And the differentiation is also, for Aquinas, a principal component in that 'rule of law [rules] which is not the rule of men [rulers]'.[159] Not that Aquinas thinks the rule of law is *ultimately* a matter of institutional arrangements; rather, it is a matter of doing what can be done to see that the state is ruled by '*reason*, i.e. by law which is a prescription of reason {dictamen rationis}, or by somebody who acts according to reason' (rather than by 'men, i.e. according to whim and passion').[160] Still, there must be judges, people appointed to adjudicate, especially about disputed facts where the facts disputed and/or the dispute about them are issues of justice affecting the peace of the community. But Aquinas' principal appeal to the Aristotelian 'rule (government) of law' is for the purpose of arguing that as far as possible there should be laws to determine in advance what the judges are to decide; the fewest possible matters {paucissima} should be left to judicial discretion.[161]

---

[157] II-II q. 65 a. 2 ad 2; in the household the father has, not full governmental authority {perfecta potestas regiminis}, but only a rulership analogous to {similitudo} the government of a realm {regii principatus}: q. 50 a. 3 ad 3. See also v.7 at nn. 181–201 above.

[158] II-II q. 67 a. 2, q. 64 a. 6 ad 3: the judge in such a case should make exceptional efforts to obtain admissible evidence entitling the accused to acquittal. Also VIII. 3 n. 101 below.

[159] On 'the rule of law and not of men', see *Eth*. v. 11 n. 10 [1009]; see also VIII.1 at nn. 11–15 and a; VIII.2 below.

[160] Ibid. *Dictamen* in Aquinas signifies the content of rational (even if mistaken) practical judgement: see VIII.1 n. 4 below.

[161] I-II q. 95 a. 1 ad 2: for it is easier to find the relatively few people of practical reasonableness {sapientes} needed to enact decent laws {rectae leges} than the many

Indeed, one can say that for Aquinas the whole construction of a strictly 'public' realm is *by* law and *for* law. Both when working in the Platonic/Aristotelian paradigm of the *civitas*, as the civil and 'complete community',[162] and when shifting to the Jewish and perhaps Roman equivalent, a *populus*, Aquinas forcefully affirms the centrality of law in the political: 'it belongs to the very notion of *a people* {ad rationem populi} that people's [the members'] dealings with each other be regulated by just precepts of law'.[163]

And as we have seen, law—the central case of coercive law made and enforced by persons with public responsibility—appropriately requires of its subjects, not that they be or become persons of all-round virtue, but that they respect and uphold justice and peace. The justice and peace which the state's law rightly seeks to secure are, of course, often violated in private, within families or between the parties to private dealings. The public good of justice is not restricted to 'public spaces' or the transaction of public business. It can be desirable to get the rule of law into some private relationships which otherwise will become the occasion of injustice, wrong done by one person to another.

'Public good prevails over private good',[164] and private good should be 'related {ordinari} to public good as if {sicut} to an end'.[165] Such statements about the relationship between private and public or common[166] good are frequent in Aquinas' work. But they must be understood with precision, and read as compatible with what we have seen him clearly asserting: there are private

---

people needed to reach sound judgements {ad recte iudicandum} in court; legislation can be long-meditated, but many judgements have to be given in circumstances of some urgency {subito}; and legislative judgements, being concerned with matters both general and future, are less likely to be corrupted by affection, ill will, or some other desire arising in relation to present and pressing litigants and circumstances. Few people left to assess the justice of a case without close direction by law can be trusted to give a just judgement {iustitia animata iudicis non invenitur in multis}. Cf. VIII.3 at nn. 98–100 below.

[162] See nn. 3, 12 above.

[163] I-II q. 105 a. 2c: '. . . ut communicatio hominum ad invicem iustis praeceptis legis ordinetur'. Similarly, II-II q. 42 a. 2c: the unity [of a people, whether state or kingdom] attacked by desertion is a unity of law and common welfare {iuris et communis utilitatis}; II-II q. 161 a. 1 ad 5: 'civil life {vita civilis}, in which the subjection of one person to another is determined according to the legal order {secundum legis ordinem}. When commenting on Aristotle's characterization of the 'complete community' {koinōnia teleios} as one arranged to secure sufficiency in the necessities of life and, beyond that, in such a way that people live in a morally good way, Aquinas adds a restrictive qualification: 'in so far as people's lives are directed towards virtues through state laws {inquantum per leges civitatis ordinatur vita hominum ad virtutes}': *Pol.* I. 1 n. 23 [31].

[164] II-II q. 117 a. 6c.   [165] IV *Sent.* d. 19 q. 2 a. 1 ad 6.

[166] See e.g. III *Sent.* d. 30 a. 1 ad 4, IV *Sent.* d. 38 q. 1 a. 4 sol. 1 ad 3.

goods which prevail over public or other common good; the state's rulers cannot rightly intervene in private relationships and transactions to secure purposes other than justice and peace; individual good, the common good of a family, and the common good of the state are irreducibly diverse; and private persons need not regard their lives as lived for the sake of the state and its purposes.[167]

The human common good—now understanding that phrase without restriction to the state's or political community's—is promoted, and love of neighbour is intelligently put into practice, when the common good that specifies the *jurisdiction* of state government and law is acknowledged to be, neither all-inclusive nor (with one qualification) basic, but limited and (save perhaps in respect of restorative justice) instrumental.

Notes

a. *Difference between divine and human rule: the excised* ScG *text* . . .
'Quod lege dei non requiritur ab homine solum ut sit bene ordinatus ad alios, sicut legibus regum iustorum. Non solum autem divinum regimen tyrannorum regimini dissimile est, qui propriam utilitatem a subditis expetunt, sed etiam multum differt a regimine regum qui subditorum utilitatem intendunt. Reges enim ad socialem vitam inter homines conservandam constituuntur: unde publicae personae dicuntur, quasi publicum bonum procurantes. Propter quod leges ab eis positae homines dirigunt secundum quod ad alios ordinantur. Ea igitur quibus commune bonum non promovetur nec derogatur, humanis legibus neque prohibentur neque praecipiuntur. Deus autem non solum regendae multitudinis curam habet, sed etiam de unoquoque curat secundum id quod ei secundum se bonum est: est enim naturae conditor et gubernator, cuius bonum non solum in multitudine, sed etiam in unoquoque secundum seipsum salvatur. Praecipit ergo et prohibet non solum illa quibus homo ad alium

---

[167] Even when one recognizes that one's spouse or child has been sentenced by law justly and for the common good, one has no duty to stop wanting the punishment not to be imposed; one is fully entitled to hope that one's family's private common good will prevail in this way. In this precise sense, one can rightly prefer the private good of spouse, child, self, and family to the public and political common good: I-II q. 19 a. 10c; III q. 18 a. 6c: the preference does not contradict the public common good, and should not extend to willing to impede the public good (and see IX.2 at n. 45 below). (It is not the sort of preference one shows in choosing one option rather than another available option which one also regards as acceptable; still less is it the sort of preference one shows in ranking two commensurables.) The denial that one's life is lived for the sake of the political community is compatible with the recognition that suicide is characteristically a type of injustice, an injury to other people and to the public good {respublica}: II–II q. 59 a. 3 ad 2, q. 64 a. 5c and ad 1; III q. 47 a. 6 ad 3.

ordinatur, sed etiam ea quibus secundum se bene vel male disponatur. Hinc est quod Apostolus dicit, I Thess. [4: 3], "Haec est voluntas Dei, sanctificatio vestra".' *Opera* 14. 46* col. 1.

Although Aquinas eventually excised the (carefully revised) chapters which include this text, every part of the striking political thesis it articulates appears in the *Summa Theologiae*, if not always as clearly. The complex story of the composition of this part of *ScG* III is recounted in *Opera* 14 pref. pp. viii–xxi, and app. pp. 3*, 42*–44*. The critical editor who analysed the intricate series of changes judges that Aquinas' motive was concern for the internal logic of this *Summa* as a whole: see esp. pp. xi–xii. (The revision's goal was a treatment more economical and more tightly aligned with the general themes of the work. Divine law would now be explained, not by comparing and contrasting it with human law and government—which are nowhere the subject of discussion in *ScG*—but by appeal to other theological themes.) The shift in strategy affects material now mostly (but not entirely) found distributed from cc. 110 to 139.

b. *Purpose and scope of human law contrasted with divine law in* ST . . . The passage quoted in VII.2 at n. 24 above, from I-II q. 98 a. 1c, continues: 'The purpose of divine law is to lead one to the end {finis} of eternal fulfilment {felicitas}, an end which is blocked by any sin, and not merely by external acts but also by interior ones. And so what suffices for the perfection of human law, namely that it prohibit wrongdoing {peccata} and impose punishments, does not suffice for the perfection of divine law; what that needs is that one be made completely ready for participation in eternal fulfilment.' *ScG* III c. 121 n. 3 [2944] argues that divine law can rightly regulate our internal dispositions {interiores affectiones} as well as our external acts and dealings: 'Any law rightly made induces to virtue. But virtue consists in the rational regulation not only of external acts but also of internal dispositions. Therefore . . .'. Since *ScG* as a whole steers clear of political and legal questions, one need not take this argument as seriously offering a proposition—'any and every just law seeks to regulate the internal dispositions of its subjects'—which in relation to human law is unambiguously and repeatedly rejected by the *ST*: see I-II q. 91 a. 4c, q. 98 a. 1c (quoted in text at n. 24), and q. 100 aa. 2c and 9c. Rather, *ScG* III c. 121 n. 3 [2944] is employing a rapid theological argument: law is always in some way directed to virtue; but real, complete virtue—the sort that God wills people to have—involves internal dispositions; therefore divine law . . .

c. *Good of religious faith pertains to individuals in themselves* . . . The passage quoted in VII.2 at n. 32 above, from *ScG* III c. 80, reads: 'in rebus humanis est aliquod bonum commune, quod quidem est bonum civitatis vel gentis . . . Est etiam aliquod humanum bonum quod non in communitate consistit, sed ad unum aliquem pertinet secundum seipsum, non tamen uni soli util[e], sed multis; sicut quae sunt ab omnibus et singulis credenda et servanda, sicut ea quae sunt fidei et cultus divinus et alia huiusmodi'. So I-II q. 99 a. 3c, having restated the contrast between divine law and human law (the latter being 'primarily for relating people to each other {ad ordinandum homines ad invicem}), states that human laws have not been concerned to lay down anything about divine worship except in its bearing on people's common good {nisi in ordine ad bonum commune hominum}.

d. *Authenticity and date of* De Regno . . . The Leonine editor (Dondaine 1979: 421–4) plausibly concludes that it is substantially by Aquinas, and favours a later date before 1268. But, as he remarks: 'Inachevé, peut-être accidenté . . . cet opuscule se présente dans des conditions un peu difficiles; elles imposent prudence et discrétion dans le recours à son texte comme expression de la pensée de l'auteur': Dondaine (1979: 424). See earlier Eschmann (1949, p. xxx) (dating the work to 1260–5); (pp. xxii–xxvi) (holding that *De Regno* is a posthumously edited collection of unrevised and somewhat jumbled pages). Eschmann himself later rejected Aquinas' authorship of the work, though perhaps rather equivocally, and without clear explanation: see Eschmann (1958: 195–6); Weisheipl (1983: 434 n. 6); Dondaine (1979: 423). See generally Torrell (1996: 13 n. 65, 14 n. 67, 169–71).

e. *Public and private* . . . Since 'public' and 'private' are each analogous rather than univocal terms, the line between them can be drawn in other ways in other contexts. So e.g. in *Impugn.* c. 3, lines 235–78 [II c. 2 [56–7]], where the context is the admission of monks and friars to universities hitherto composed of other sorts of cleric, Aquinas undertakes a sketch of the difference between public and private: public societies {societates; communicationes} include the *civitas* or *regnum* (perpetual), traders for-gathering at large trade fairs or markets (temporary), and the university {studium generale}; private societies include families (perpetual), two friends or associates in a hostel (temporary), and colleges within the university. But his definitions of 'public' and 'private', in terms of the type of matters with which they are respectively concerned (*respublica* versus *negotium privatum*), are unhelpfully circular. So the issue in the text above is not to be settled by attending to the words 'public' and 'private', taken out of the context of the questions about coercion and adjudication, etc.

VIII

The State: Its Government and Law

VIII.1. *Law as Primary Proper Means of Co-ordinating Civil Society*

The government and laws of a state are the central case of government and law, and the most articulated form of human co-ordination. In reflecting on them, one is considering certain modes and forms of practical reason's directiveness towards common good. For practical reason—the propositional content of the practical understanding, reasoning, judging, choosing, and self-directing of practically reasonable persons—is brought to its most articulate and complex forms in the public reason of people who have reasonably judged themselves to be morally responsible for governing the *civitas*.

Aquinas proposes and argues for a definition of law: an ordinance of reason for the common good of a [complete] community, promulgated by the person or body responsible for looking after that community.[1] But in supplementing and explicating that definition, Aquinas immediately stresses that law—a law—is 'simply a sort of prescription {dictamen} of practical reason *in the ruler* governing a

---

[1] I-II q. 90 a. 4c: 'quaedam rationis ordinatio ad bonum commune, ab eo qui curam communitatis habet promulgata'. 'Promulgated' tacitly includes 'made'; see a. 3 obj. 1 and ad 1. ('Made' is in any case implicit in *ordinatio*, which refers both to the act of ordering or ordaining and to the propositional instrument for ordering or co-ordinating.) The addition of 'complete' is authorized by a. 2c.

perfect community',[2] and that 'prescriptions' are simply universal[3] propositions of practical reason which prescribe and direct to action.[4]

His explications also add that government (governing, governance) by law means, equally concretely, that these practical propositions conceived in the minds of those responsible for ruling must be assented to by the ruled,[5] and adopted into their own minds as reasons for action.[6] The assent may have been induced only by fear of sanctions, though such unwilling (reluctant) assent cannot be the central case of co-operation in government by law. Aquinas takes an early opportunity to supplement his definition by stating that it is characteristic of law {de ratione legis} that it be coercive (threatening force against violators).[7] In the previous chapter (VII.7) we saw how the irreparable character of necessary coercion is central to the rationale of public authority. But the present point is simply that law needs to be present in the minds not only of those who make it but also of those to whom it is addressed— present if not actually, at least habitually—as the traffic laws are in the minds of careful drivers who conform to them without actually thinking about them.[8] The subjects of the law share (willingly or unwillingly) in at least the conclusions of the rulers' practical thinking and in the plan which the rulers propose (reasonably

---

[2] I-II q. 91 a. 1c, q. 92 a. 1c; both looking back to q. 90 a. 1 ad 2.

[3] 'Universal' here means: referring to an indeterminate set of instances of a specified kind of action, as distinct from a particular precept directing an individual to do (or not do) this or that. So the following prescription, directive, precept, norm, or rule is universal in the relevant sense: 'There is to be no playing of [or: 'It shall be an offence to play'] bagpipes, trombones, or drums in student halls of residence located in suburban residential districts of London.'

[4] I-II q. 90 a. 1 ad 2 ('propositiones universales rationis practicae ordinatae ad actiones'); 92 a. 2c, q. 94 a. 1c. The common translation of *dictamen* by 'dictate' is unsound, in so far as 'dictate' suggests arbitrariness and even abuse of power. The word *dictamen* in Aquinas signifies the content of rational (even if mistaken) practical judgement {sententia vel dictamen rationis} (e.g. II *Sent.* d. 24 q. 2 a. 4c), and is thus frequently used by him to refer (1) to the content of one's conscience (e.g. 'conscience is a *dictamen* of reason': II *Sent.* d. 24 q. 2 a. 4c; likewise I-II q. 19 a. 5c; 'the judgement {iudicium} or *dictamen* of reason, the judgement which is conscience': II *Sent.* d. 39 q. 3 a. 3c), and (2) to the requirements of natural moral law and of 'natural reason' {naturalis ratio}: 'moral precepts are in accord with human nature because they are the requirements/prescriptions {de dictamine} of natural reason': IV *Sent.* d. 2 a. 4 sol. 1 ad 2; likewise I-II q. 99 a. 4c, q. 100 a. 11c, q. 104 a. 1c.   [5] I-II q. 92 a. 2c.   [6] I-II q. 90 a. 3 ad 1.

[7] I-II q. 90 a. 3 ad 2, q. 96 a. 5c. Both passages also link law's coerciveness with its *public* character; for the reasons, see VII.7 above. On law in a society of saints, see VIII.2 at n. 66, VIII.3 at nn. 91, 93 below.

[8] I-II q. 90 a. 1 ad 2 (propositions sometimes actually under consideration, sometimes held in the reason dispositionally {habitualiter}); q. 94 a. 1 ad [4]; cf. III. 6 n. 138 above.

and truthfully or unreasonably and falsely) as a plan for promoting and/or protecting common good.[9] For just as an individual's choice is followed and put into effect by the directive {imperium} of that individual's reason (III.3), so a legislature's or other ruler's choice of a plan for common good is put into effect by way of citizens taking the law's directive {imperium; ordinatio} *as if* it were putting into effect their own choice.[10]

The central case of government is the rule of a free people (III.4; VIII.2), and the central case of law is co-ordination of willing subjects by law which, by its fully public character (promulgation),[11] its clarity,[12] generality,[13] stability,[14] and practicability,[15] treats them as partners in public reason.[a]

Nobody is as directly responsible for looking after the state {cura communitatis}, and thus its citizens, as its legislators preeminently are.[16] But governing a complete community by law is in some respects a joint enterprise, a kind of co-ordination of the acts of the governed amongst themselves by co-ordination of each with the directives given by their rulers. Aquinas' general account of co-ordination was outlined in II.4 above. In VII.4 above, that account was supplemented by the thesis that co-ordination, in a group with a common good as far-reaching as the 'complete community's', calls for the law's *internalization*[17] by its subjects. One 'internalizes' the law when one willingly, promptly, readily—and not merely out of the 'extrinsic' motivations of fear of punishment or hope of reward[18]—complies with its requirements, not only according to the letter of the law but primarily according to the lawmaker's intention and plan for common good.[19] Such states of

---

[9] I-II q. 90 a. 1 ad 1, q. 91 a. 6c. And see II. 4 at nn. 49–52 above.

[10] See I-II q. 12 a. 1c, q. 17 a. 1c, q. 90 a. 1 s.c. and ad 2 and 3; III.3 at nn. 26–7 above.

[11] I-II q. 90 a. 4c.

[12] I-II q. 95 a. 3c (laws lacking clarity in expression {manifestatio} are harmful).

[13] I-II q. 96 a. 1.   [14] I-II q. 97 a. 2c.

[15] I-II q. 95 a. 3c ('disciplina conveniens unicuique secundum suam possibilitatem').

[16] II-II q. 50 a. 1c and a. 2c; VII. 5 at n. 80 above.

[17] I-II q. 93 a. 5c ('a kind of internal {interius} principle of actions') and ad 1 ('a kind of directive principle of human actions is *impressed* on people by promulgation'—a source of direction which *in respect of its interiority* is like an active *intrinsic* principle, e.g. the 'form' which governs the development of an embryo).

[18] See I-II q. 107 a. 1c. Every set of laws is addressed to two kinds of people: the obstinate and proud who are restrained and disciplined by law, and the good who are assisted by the law's guidance {per legem instructi} to fulfil their good intentions: q. 98 a. 6c.

[19] See I-II q. 96 a. 6. Some legislative intentions (e.g. that the law's subjects should become truly virtuous people) are not part of the legislation's obligatory content (see VII.4

---

affairs are the central case of law because they most fully instantiate the fundamental notion of law: a prescription of *reason*, by
means of which rational and indeed conscientious and reasonable
practical judgements about the needs of a complete community's
common, public good, having been made and published by lawmakers, are understood and adopted by citizens as the *imperium* of
their own autonomous, individual practical reason and will.

VIII.2. *Government: Limited and Ruling by Law*

'Government' or governance {principatus} is the holding and exercising of the whole range of authority—legislative, judicial, and in a
broad sense executive[20]—appropriate for securing justice and peace
in and for a political community. The preceding chapter argued
that Aquinas understands the state precisely as the type of community fitted to securing goods which are only well secured by
appropriately general and published laws enforced with impartial-
ity and coercive force: VII.6–7. The present section shows how
Aquinas holds that governments themselves are not above the
law, but are appropriately regulated and *limited* by law.

Aquinas's frequent observations on the quasi-political relations
between one's limbs, emotions, reason, and will amount, as we saw
(III.4), to a quietly insistent advocacy of legally limited government. Government which is not despotic is either regal or political.
What is common to the regal and the political forms of government
is that their subjects are *free* and *equal* people who *have the right
to resist* some of the government's directives (whether legislative,
executive, or judicial).[21] Such a right to refuse obedience is incon-
ceivable unless the governmental authority is limited. What sort
of limits does Aquinas have in mind?

In the case of 'political' forms of government, a broadly clear

---

at nn. 58–59 above); but there are also legislative intentions which are more binding
{magis obligant} than the enacted words interpreted without taking that intent into
account: IV *Sent.* d. 15 q. 3 a. 1 sol. 4 ad 3; *In Matt.* 1 ad v. 5 [49]. And there is a legislative
intent—what the legislature would have enacted (would have intended {intendisse}!) had
it envisaged the circumstances in question—which should be followed, at least where it is
obvious: I-II q. 96 a. 6 ad 2, II-II q. 60 a. 5 ad 2. To act on this intention is to prefer equity
{epi[ei]keia; aequitas} to the words or form of the law: ibid., II-II q. 157 a. 3 ad 1; *Eth.* v. 16
n. 1 [1078]; III *Sent.* d. 33 q. 3 a. 4 sol. 5c and ad 5, d. 37 a. 4c; n. 101 below.

20 See *Eth.* VI. 7 n. 4 [1198]; II-II q. 60 a. 6c.

21 I-II q. 58 a. 2c; *Virt.* q. 1 a. 4c (III. 4 n. 48 above); *Pol.* I. 5 n. 2 [90].

answer is readily found. Government is 'political' (as opposed to 'regal') 'when the one [person or body] who rules has power which is limited by certain laws of the state {potestatem coarctatam[22] secundum aliquas leges civitatis}';[23] some matters are within this person's or body's legal authority, and others are not.[24]

In 'regal' government, on the other hand, the ruler has 'plenary power'.[25] The word 'regal' {regalis} is, of course, from 'king' {rex}. But even the word 'king', in Aquinas' work, almost invariably includes anyone ruling with plenary presidential power, whether female[26] or elected[27] and perhaps holding office for a term of years. As contrasted with despotic government, 'regal' government, like 'political', is rulership over free people who have the 'right and authority {facultas} of repudiating in some cases the *king's* [i.e. the supreme authority's] precepts'.[28] As the legally limited powers of the US Congress and President exemplify 'political' government, so the legally unlimited legislative authority of the United Kingdom Parliament broadly exemplifies 'regal' government. For what defines government as 'regal', in Aquinas' sense, is not that it is monarchical, the rule of one person;[29] it could be the rule of an aristocracy or a democratic assembly as much as of a king or president. What makes it regal, rather than political, is that its authority is plenary.

But how can authority be both 'plenary' and limited, as Aquinas implies that regal authority can be?

One legal, or at least law-based, limit is this. Even such rulers as a Roman *princeps*, in an empire whose laws declare the *princeps* free from the laws {legibus solutus}, are properly subject to what Aquinas calls the law's *vis directiva*, the sheer directiveness of

---

[22] *Coarctata* is synonymous with *limitata*: see I q. 14 a. 1c; II *Sent.* d. 9 q. 1 a. 3c, IV *Sent.* d. 20 a. 1 sol. 2c; *Div.* c. 1. 1 [16].

[23] *Pol.* 1. 1 n. 5 [13]; also n. 7 [15], where the limits are described as created by laws made {positae} through 'disciplina politica'. The *politicus*, who unlike a *rex* governs in a 'political' regime, has power which is not free {libera} but rather 'according to law {secundum statuta}': *Pol.* 1. 10 n. 2 [152]; likewise *In I Tim.* 1. 4 ad v. 17 [46].

[24] *Pol.* 1. 1 n. 7 [15].

[25] In *Pol.* 1. 1 n. 5 [13] ('potestas plenaria'); n. 7 [15] ('praeest simpliciter et secundum omnia').

[26] Like the addressee of *Ep. Reg.*, Margaret of Constantinople, Countess of Flanders (rather than, as formerly seemed more probable, Adelaide Duchess of Brabant).

[27] Election is preferable to heredity: see *Pol.* II. 14 n. 3 [311] and 16 n. 3 [334]; I-II q. 105 a. 1c.

[28] *Virt.* q. 1 a. 4c: 'quantum ad aliqua praecepta regis'; similarly I-II q. 58 a. 2c.

[29] See *Pol.* 1. 5 n. 2 [90]: 'monarchia, id est principatus unius'.

their own laws. For laws, while in force and not dispensed from,[30] have a guiding and obligatory authority in practical reasoning, an authority independent of their *vis coactiva*, the compliance-motivating and enforcement-warranting force of any coercive sanction attached to them.[31] The failure of kings or emperors to conform to laws applicable to them will usually entail an injustice, an inequitable distribution of burdens.[32] But such inequity falls within one of the principal types of ground for calling laws 'unjust laws', *iniustae leges*—laws which by reason of their injustice can lack moral obligatoriness (VIII.3).[33] Thus holders of even 'plenary power' who demand the obedience of the subject, while themselves defaulting from their own duties under that very law, go beyond the limits of their authority, their rightful power.[34]

Moreover, even as between the holders of plenary, 'regal' power and their subjects, the enacted laws, e.g. on taxation, constitute 'a kind of covenant between king and people'.[35] Demands for payment

---

[30] On the power of rulers to grant dispensations from their own laws where application of the law would be inappropriate to a particular person or case and granting the dispensation is intended for the common good and done without favouritism, see I-II q. 97 a. 4c and ad 1 and ad 2. In conditions of sudden peril too urgent to permit an application to the appropriate authorities, anyone can 'interpret what is for the advantage of the community {interpretetur quid sit utile civitate}' and act outside the letter of the law, for 'necessity carries with it a dispensation {necessitas dispensationem habet annexam}, because necessity knows no law {necessitas non subditur legi}': I-II q. 96 a. 6c; IV *Sent.* d. 20 a. 1 sol. 2c {necessitas legem non habet}. But some laws cannot be dispensed from by anyone, since they 'embrace the very preservation of the common good, or the very order of justice and virtue'—e.g. laws against the destruction of the *respublica*, or the betrayal of the *civitas* to enemies, or 'doing something unjust or evil {aliquid iniustum vel male}' (understood: in the way that violations of the Decalogue's commandments against, for example, homicide are intrinsically 'unjust and evil'): I-II q. 100 a. 8c. See also n. 57 below.

[31] I-II q. 96 a. 5 ad 5. Aquinas quotes another Roman *legal* provision that whoever imposes laws on others ought to act according to the same law.

[32] Ibid., quoting Matt. 23: 3–4. See also *Eth.* v. 11 n. 10 [1009].

[33] I-II q. 96 a. 4c (nn. 102–15 below). Aquinas here sets out several other forms of injustice in law-making (see also the similar forms of injustice in respect of the judgements of courts: II-II q. 60 a. 2c); and in each case the free subjects of the holder of plenary governmental authority would have the *ius et facultas* of resisting the royal demands (or court orders: 'an unjust judgement is not a judgement': ibid.). But in these other cases one could not say that these limits are limits imposed by state law.

[34] One of Aquinas' early disciples, it seems, added to I-II q. 96 a. 5 ad 3 a text accepted by some later editors: 'And in the Codex [of Justinian, 1. 14. 4] . . . the Emperors Theodosius II and Valentinian write [in AD 429] to the prefect Volusian: "It is a saying worthy of the majesty of a ruler if the *princeps* acknowledges that he is bound by laws {legibus alligatum}; for *even our authority depends on that of the law* {de auctoritate iuris nostra pendet auctoritas}. Indeed, it is important for state-rule {imperium} to subject governance to laws {subiicere [submittere] legibus principatum}"'.'

[35] *In Rom.* 13.1 ad v. 6 [1041]: [statuta lex] 'est quasi quoddam pactum inter regem et populum'. The other references to *pactum* in this biblical commentary are to the divine covenants, old and new, made with God by Moses and Jesus on behalf of their peoples.

---

in breach of that implicit social contract exceed the ruler's rightful authority; for to speak of contract, covenant, or pact is to speak of mutual obligations and the conditioning of one side's obligation on the other's adherence to the contract.[36]

In any event, Aquinas gives the impression that he preferred the 'political' form of state government, limited by *laws made for the purpose of* regulating and limiting even the supreme rulers, to the regal.[37] More clearly, he affirms and repeats two closely related positions: (1) the peace and good government of states requires that there be a variety of different public offices, working in synchronic harmony rather than in unison; and that as many people as possible have a share of public office;[38] (2) the best form of government is one well mixed {bene commixta} with elements of royal, aristocratic, and democratic rule.[39]

In the *Summa Theologiae*, Aquinas' robust declaration that mixed government is best is followed, within a few sentences, by the concessive[40] affirmation that *regnum* is best 'if not corrupted'.[41] Indeed, there are many passages where he states that *regnum*—the rule of one person, elected or otherwise—is the best, or at least the best of the six forms of *politeia* discussed by Aristotle,[42] because it best secures the unity of decision without which co-ordination with all its advantages is unavailable and

---

[36] So subjects who have made a covenant {pactum} of perpetual subjection with the king whom they have appointed are released from their obligation under that pact by the king's failure to rule as the royal office requires: *Reg.* 1. 6 [1. 7] [49] [770].

[37] Even in the *De Regno*, which is addressed to a king and makes no mention of mixed government, Aquinas states that the government of a kingdom should be so arranged that opportunity for kings to become tyrannous is removed, and that the power of kings should be limited {temperetur} so that they will not easily fall into tyranny: *Reg.* 1.6 [1. 7] [42] [767]. Unfortunately the details he promises to give were not written or have been lost. But 'tempered authority' can hardly be unqualifiedly plenary.

[38] II-II q. 183 a. 2 ad 3; *Pol.* II. 5 n. 2 [208]. See also I q. 108 a. 2 on the appropriateness of a division of responsibilities (judicial, military, agricultural) and on the quasi-inevitability of a hierarchy of social classes (upper {optimates}, middle {medii; populus honorabilis}, and lower {infimi; vilus populus}.

[39] I-II q. 105 a. 1c (the principal passage is quoted in 1.3 at n. 6 above), q. 95 a. 4c; *Pol.* II. 7 nn. 4, 6 [245, 247].

[40] Aquinas is here (q. 105 a. 1 ad 2) replying to an objection which says that the Mosaic law restricted monarchy too much. Aquinas begins his reply by conceding that *regnum* is best (if uncorrupted), but then points out its dangers and defends the restrictions divinely imposed on it (according to the Old Testament). *Regnum* here essentially connotes the rule of *one*: see a. 1c.

[41] I-II q. 105 a. 1 ad 2. Though this passage seems implicitly to treat *regnum* as involving plenary power, it is not certain (*pace* Blythe 1986: 561) that Aquinas is treating it as 'regal' for the purposes of the 'despotic–political–regal' distinction.

[42] II-II q. 50 a. 1 ad 2.

---

peace is undermined or destroyed.[43]

There are two ways of reconciling the juxtaposed preferences for mixed government and for the rule of *one*. (1) The proviso, 'if not corrupted', is (as Aquinas underlines) most unlikely to be satisfied in a world in which very few people are thoroughly virtuous.[44] Thus, in at least the great majority of real-world cases, mixed government will be preferable to *regnum*. (2) 'Mixed government' is itself a type of *regnum*. Indeed, it is the best sort. For in such a regime, where one person is supreme ruler while others are ministers, and each adult member of the community is entitled to be elected ruler or minister and to vote[45] in such elections, the equality which is of the essence of 'political' justice and 'legal' rule[46] is respected while desirable *unity* of governmental decision-making is fully preserved *provided that there are clear laws* about rotation of office, about elections, and about the division of powers amongst ministers—and provided also that these laws are regularly followed by people who get power. Indeed, peace itself is advanced not only by unity of decision and co-ordination, but also by 'distinction of responsibilities and positions {officiorum et statuum}, in so far as many are thereby involved in *public* acts'.[47]

Aquinas plainly thinks there can and should be such laws, 'legal provisions about the establishment, appointment, and responsibilities of the rulers {quaedam praecepta de institutione principum et officiorum eorum}',[48] not least in relation to the supreme ruler(s).[49] In a 'political' form of 'monarchical' government, the elected president rules 'in accordance with the laws'.[50] The regular

---

[43] e.g. I q. 103 a. 4c; *Reg.* I. 2 [I. 3] [17–20][750–3]; *ScG* IV c. 76 n. 4 [4105].

[44] I-II q. 105 a. 1 ad 2. And the corrupted form of *rule of one* is typically the worst of all the corrupted forms of government: *Reg.* I. 4 [I. 5] [30] [761] ('optimum et pessimum consistunt in monarchia, id est principatu unius'), I. 7 [I. 6] [41] [767].

[45] Harmonious elections, in which voters are taking care to find office-holders of practical reasonableness, are the preferable mode of selecting secular rulers; but if such elections would subject the community to too much dissension, it is permissible to choose such rulers by lot: *Sort.* c. 5 [672]. (But in elections to ecclesiastical high office, voting cannot rightly be replaced by casting lots: ibid. [670].)

[46] *Eth.* v. 11 nn. 7–8 [1006–7]; *Pol.* I. 5 n. 2 [90] (n. 51 below); *ST* III q. 85 a. 3c.

[47] II-II q. 183 a. 2 ad 3.

[48] I-II q. 104 a. 4c: such constitutional provisions are one of the four sorts of legal provision that a people ought to have if law is to fulfil its role as 'a kind of art, so to speak, of establishing or arranging human living {quasi quaedam ars humanae vitae instituendae vel ordinandae}'.　　　　　　　　　　　　　　[49] See I-II q. 105 a. 1 obj. 1.

[50] *Pol.* I. 10 n. 2 [152]: '[when] someone elected ruler {in rectorem} rules a *civitas* . . . the ruler {rector civitatis} has power over the citizens according to law {secundum statuta}'. Likewise *In I Tim.* I. 4 ad v. 17 [46]; n. 23 above.

change-over in office which is characteristic, perhaps even of the essence, of 'political' government[51] cannot be accomplished without laws somehow specifying and delimiting the office(s), periods of office, and methods of appointment.[52] It is law that will establish the government as a democracy rather than an aristocracy, or vice versa;[53] Aquinas calls these constitutional provisions the *coordinatio* or *ordinatio* of the state[54] or the 'legally instituted *ordinatio* of the rulers'.[55]

This is not to say that Aquinas envisages (whether to approve or question) the possibility of constitutional provisions purporting to exclude certain matters from the power of an otherwise supreme legislature; or of judges applying such provisions against the state's otherwise supreme ruler(s).[56] He does not envisage the constitutional device of a separation of powers, i.e. a distribution of types of governing authority among institutions and persons of co-ordinate rank.[57] He does not make use of a distinction which might have helped to clarify the question whether 'political' as opposed to regal government necessarily involves mixed government, and whether *regnum* is necessarily regal as opposed to political: the distinction between (1) restrictions on, and divisions of, the subject-matter of legislative power and (2) requirements of manner, form, and procedure in the process of legislating or other governmental action. Certainly for such purposes as pardoning offences,[58] or temporarily or locally abrogating (dispensing from) a law, he

---

[51] *Pol.* 1. 5 n. 2 [90] ('political rule {politica} is the government of free and equal people {principatus liberorum et aequalium}; and so rulers and subjects take turns for the sake of equality and, moreover, many are appointed ruler (whether in one or various offices) {commutantur principantes et subiectae propter aequalitatem, et constituuntur etiam plures principatus vel in uno, vel in diversis officiis}'); 1. 10 nn. 2–3 [152–3] ('leadership of the political kind is changed about from one person to another {politicus principatus permutatur de persona in personam}'); III. 3 n. 10 [374].

[52] *Politics* 3. 10. 1287ª19; see also *Pol.* 1. 10 n. 2 [152].   [53] I-II q. 107 a. 1c.

[54] *Pol.* II. 7 nn. 2, 3, 4 [243–5].   [55] I-II q. 105 a. 1c.

[56] But in a diocese ruled by a bishop he takes it for granted that there may be a division of authority such that some matters are assigned to the responsibility of the cathedral chapter (governing committee), so that if the bishop presumed to intermeddle with these matters he would be *usurping* authority: II-II q. 62 a. 5 ad 5.

[57] Thus he accepts the approach of Roman imperial law (see *Codex* 1. 14. 5) that interpreting, and dispensing from, laws is a matter for the person or body who make them: see especially II-II q. 120 a. 1 obj. 3 and ad 3; also *ScG* III c. 76 n. 7 [2523]; I-II q. 96 a. 6 ad 2; so adjudication, which in applying law always in a sense interprets it, must be by public authority: q. 60 a. 6c. (Still, strictly speaking, one 'interprets' a law only when there is a doubt about its meaning; when that is clear, one's job is just to do what it says {in manifestis non est opus interpretatione, sed executione}: II-II q. 120 a. 1 ad 3.) Also nn. 19, 30 above, n. 81 below.   [58] II-II q. 67 a. 4c.

assumes that someone will have 'plenary authority in the state {in republica}'.[59]

As for the supreme legislative powers, Aquinas' position is clearer in its articulation than in its substance. Such powers are held and exercised either by the whole people {tota multitudo}—a free people[60]—or by some public *persona* responsible for the whole people {persona publica quae totius multitudinis curam habet};[61] in the latter case, the *princeps* who thus possesses legislative powers has them only as representing the people {inquantum gerit personam multitudinis}.[62] These statements leave unanswered a number of questions. One is the question debated by Aquinas' successors in later centuries: Is supreme state power held only by those to whom 'the people' have transmitted it?[b] The idea that all just goverment *represents* its subjects is clearly a moral construction—a way of summing up the implications of three moral truths: that government is for *common* good, not for the advantage of the rulers; that no one has any 'natural right to govern'; and that the subjects' obligation to obey is a duty owed not, strictly speaking, to the rulers themselves but rather to, if anyone, their fellow citizens.[63] To extend this idea of representation into an idea that authority must, or should, have been transmitted by some procedure of transference (however implicit or tacit) from the people to their representative(s) is to miss the point of the construction, and to convert it into a fiction or a sometimes inappropriate requirement for just government.

There is also the prior question how, in any case, a 'whole people' could make law by deliberation and enactment.[64] In suggesting that it can, Aquinas is certainly not suggesting that unanimity is required; indeed, the whole point of law-making, as of leadership

---

[59] I-II 96 a. 5 ad 3: in this sense or to this extent a *princeps* can be 'above the law'; similarly, *In Matt*. 20 ad v. 15 [1645] (bailiffs must reward only for merit, but kings may be gratuitous).

[60] I-II q. 97 a. 3 ad 3: 'a free group {libera multitudo} which can make law for itself'. It is not clear that this refers to 'democracy, which is the power of the people {democratia, quae est potestas populi}' (q. 104 a. 3 ad 2).

[61] I-II q. 90 a. 3c, II-II q. 57 a. 2c {cura populi}.

[62] I-II q. 97 a. 3 ad 3; also II-II q. 57 a. 2c.

[63] On passages such as *In Rom*. 13. 1 ad v. 7 [1042] ('ex necessitate iustitiae tenentur subditi sua iura principibus exhibere'), II-II q. 104 a. 6c and ad 1, and II *Sent*. d. 44 q. 2 a. 1c, which speak of the duty to obey just rulers, see n. 96 below. On the way in which the best have, and yet do not have, a right to rule, see n. 92 below.

[64] If (but only if) the people have power to make law by enactment, they also have a non-dependent power to make, interpret, amend, or unmake law by custom: I-II q. 97 a. 3c and ad 3.

and practical authority in general, is to attain co-operation in some pattern of conduct even when, *before and during* the co-operation, there is no unanimity about the merits of that conduct.[65] (Such unanimity would be lacking, and such co-ordination would be needed, even in a world of completely virtuous people.[66]) But Aquinas leaves unclear whether he has in mind an assembly of all adult citizens, or an assembly elected by all, or something else. An analysis of legislative authority shows that even a fully plebiscitary assembly or referendum procedure involves a representation, some collective public *persona* distinct from the whole people considered severally (one by one) as the persons to whom the legislation is addressed as subjects.[67] But Aquinas does not carry his discussion to the point where the issue would arise for clarification.

He accepts Aristotle's opinion that the members of a political community will be unfree {servi} if they lack the power most necessary {maxime necessaria} for freedom, namely to elect the rulers and correct them when they go wrong {corrigere eorum errores}.[68] The question whether a particular people is in reality (1) 'a free people' enjoying legislative authority, or (2) a community made up of 'free people'[69] or 'people free and equal' but subject to the legislative authority of some *princeps*, or (3) a people in some kind of unfreedom is one which Aquinas treats as settled somehow—on the basis, of course, of some normative practical and moral principle of promoting common good—by power, e.g. the power of a conqueror,[70] or by law. And law, even such basic constitutional law, is rightly subject to drastic change. If a people who have the legal-constitutional power to elect their rulers become so corrupt that they commonly sell their votes and elect rogues and criminals, the power may rightly be removable from the people and conferred on a few good citizens.[71] And if the people have the right to make provisions regarding their king or other presiding ruler, they can properly curb or wholly remove the authority (the

---

[65] Finnis (1980: 232–3).   [66] I-II q. 96 a. 4c; VII. 7 at n. 148 above.
[67] See Finnis (1980: 252–4).   [68] *Pol.* II. 17 n. 4 [344].
[69] Thus *Reg.* I. 1 [I. 2] [10] [746] contrasts the community of free people, ruled *by a leader* for their benefit, with a community of servants; likewise *Pol.* I. 1 n. 6 [14]; *Ps.* 45. 3 ad v. 3 (which adds that a *civitas* of slaves is not a city).
[70] See I-II q. 97 a. 3 ad 3. In II *Sent.* d. 44 q. 2 a. 2c he says that one who seizes power by force {per violentiam dominium surripit} does not thereby become truly ruler or governor {vere praelatus vel dominus} . . . unless later converted into a true ruler {dominus verus effectus sit} either by the subjects' consent or by a [higher] superior's authority.
[71] I-II q. 97 a. 1c.

rulership) which such a king or president has abused.[72]

So the idea of reciprocity, mutuality, and even 'pact'[73] between ruler(s) and ruled plays a significant part in Aquinas' theory of government. And he is willing to treat law-making as a kind of agreement {condictum} of the people, either actually (as in custom and informal usage, or plebiscitary 'convention') or representatively by acts communicating to the community the decisions of the ruler(s).[74] But this is far removed from the theory that some original or standing or foundational 'social contract' is or could be a fundamental ground or justification for legislative or other political authority, or for the (defeasible) obligation to respect such authority and obey its laws.

VIII.3. *Just and Unjust Laws: Authority and Obligation*

Most human laws, even just ones, do not simply reproduce the requirements of morality (i.e. of the natural moral law). But just human laws do have moral authority and thus, by entailment, moral obligatoriness. They have this authority because they have an intelligible relation to morality's permanent principles and precepts, a relation which Aquinas was the first to clarify and name.

In Aquinas' clarification and adjustment of the Aristotelian and Roman juristic categories and nomenclature, all human law is positive law.[75] But human positive law is derived from natural law and natural right—from morality's permanent principles and precepts—in two different ways. Some laws are derived by a kind of deduction, as conclusions from principles—the substance of a just law of murder, treason,[76] rape, fraud, or theft, for example; or the general provision for punishment of crime.[77] But many other laws, e.g. those stipulating penalties for specific classes of offence, are derived from morality not by deduction of conclusions, but by the

---

[72] *Reg.* I. 6 [I. 7] [49] [770].   [73] See nn. 35, 36 above.

[74] e.g. II-II q. 57 a. 2c and ad 2, q. 60 a. 5c, q. 66 a. 2 ad 1; *Eth.* v. 12 n. 15 [1030]. Note that *condictum* need not mean anything as formal as a contract; in the Vulgate it is used to signify (1) a unilateral divine promise communicated to Abraham (Gen. 18: 14) and (2) an adulterer's nocturnal appointment (Job 24: 16; *In Iob* 24 ad v. 16).

[75] See Finnis (1996a).   [76] See I-II q. 100 a. 8c.

[77] I-II q. 95 a. 2c; see IV.5 at n. 109, V.2 at nn. 31–2 above.

process which Aquinas identifies and names *determinatio*.[78]

Determinatio is best clarified by Aquinas' own analogy with architecture. The general idea or form of a dwelling-house (or a hospital), and the general ideas of a door and a doorknob (or a labour ward), must be made determinate as this particular design and house (or hospital), door, doorknob, etc.; otherwise nothing will be built. The specifications which the architect or designer decides upon are certainly derived from and shaped by the primary general idea, e.g. the commission to design a dwelling-house (or maternity hospital). But the specifications decided upon could reasonably have been rather different in many (even in every) dimension and aspect, and require of the designer a multitude of decisions which could reasonably have been more or less different. Stressing the designer's wide freedom within the ambit of the commission or other general idea, Aquinas says that laws whose derivation from natural law is of this second type have their force 'from human law alone' {ex sola lege humana vigorem habent}.[79]

This last statement really goes further than the analysis itself warrants. (More accurate is another of Aquinas' descriptions: such laws have their binding force not only from reason, but [also] from their having been laid down.[80]) The precise requirements imposed in laws made by *determinatio* would indeed have no moral force but for those laws' enactment, and the lawmaker had no moral duty to make precisely those laws. But once such a law has been made, its directiveness derives not only from the fact of its creation by some recognized source of law (legislation, judicial decision,[81] custom, etc.), but also from its rational connection with some principle or precept of morality.

And this connection is not simply with the general moral norm (to be considered shortly) that lawful and just authority should be respected. It is the connection of a law's *content* with morality's permanent principles and precepts as they bear on that law's

---

[78] I-II q. 95 a. 2c, q. 99 a. 3 ad 2, q. 104 a. 1c; IV *Sent.* d. 15 q. 3 a. 2 sol. 1c, d. 26 q. 2 (= *Supp.* q. 42) a. 2 ad 1, d. 34 a. 1 (= *Supp.* q. 50) ad 4, d. 36 a. 1 (= *Supp.* q. 52 a. 1) ad 3 and a. 5c; etc. [79] I-II q. 95 a. 2c.

[80] I-II q. 104 a. 1c: 'non habeant vim obligandi ex sola ratione, sed ex institutione'.

[81] A court's judgement {sententia iudicis} is like a kind of enacted special law {particularis lex} for the particular situation: II-II q. 67 a. 1c. Aquinas seems not to envisage a system ascribing formal precedential force to court judgements, and does insist (II-II q. 60 a. 5c) that judgements be in line with enacted ('written') law. But since the judge is an 'interpreter of justice' (II-II q. 67 a. 3c), and judgements are 'applications' of 'common law/ right' (I-II q. 96 a. 1 ad 1; IV *Sent.* d. 35 (= *Supp.* q. 62) a. 3 ad 1), a court's judgement can and should be the one that any other court would make in like case.

subject-matter. There is a sense in which the rule of the road—keep to the left/keep to the right—gets all its force from the authoritative custom, enactment, or other determination laying it down. But there is another and equally important sense in which such a rule of the road gets 'all its normative force' from the principles of practical reason which require us to respect (and our legislative representatives to promote) safety on the road, taking those principles in combination with non-posited facts about communication difficulties, traffic flows, braking distances, human reaction times, and so forth.[82] Though the lawmakers' *determinatio* is in a sense free, it also must be made with due consideration for the circumstances which bear on the appropriateness of alternative eligible laws.[83] Within limits, 'the way in which the natural [moral] law is to be observed is settled {determinatur} by positive law'.[84]

Law made by *determinatio* is purely positive law.[85] But Aquinas, in his later work, describes the whole of the law administered by a state's courts as 'law humanly posited'[86] or 'positive law',[87] even though part of it (e.g. the law about murder, theft, rape, and so forth) is wholly or substantially part of, or a deduced conclusion from, the permanent principles and precepts of natural law. For this part, which is both 'natural' and 'positive', he reserves the Roman juristic name *ius gentium*, the law that is substantially adopted by all peoples (and in that sense is positive law) because recognized virtually everywhere as what is required by reason (natural law).[88] For the purely

---

[82] So Aquinas was not altogether well advised to adopt Aristotle's dictum that in such cases (i.e. where there is what Aquinas calls *determinatio*) it is a matter of 'indifference' which law is adopted: see *Nic. Eth.* 5. 7. 1134^{b}20; *Eth.* v. 12 n. 5 [1020]; II-II q. 57 a. 2 ad 2, q. 60 a. 5 ad 1. The more limited and accurate statement is that in such cases the lawmaker has a number of options none of which is 'in itself repugnant to natural justice': II-II q. 57 a. 2 ad 2. Aquinas holds onto Aristotle's talk of 'indifference' by giving the term a special, narrow meaning: a *type of* conduct is 'indifferent' if it is not 'generically' (i.e. universally) either morally good or morally bad *as a type* (I-II q. 92 a. 2c), even though particular instances or ranges of instances of it may be bad in the circumstances of an individual or social (e.g. legislative) choice – and *no* particular act or choice is in all the circumstances morally indifferent or neutral; all are either good or bad: VI.2 n. 31 above.

[83] See e.g. II-II q. 77 a. 2 ad 2.   [84] IV *Sent.* d. 15 q. 3 a. 2 sol. 1c.

[85] e.g. II-II q. 57 a. 2c. See also x. 3 at n. 69 below.   [86] I-II q. 95 a. 2c.

[87] I-II q. 95 a. 4c. The 'written law' *contains* (though it does not establish) natural law/ right: II-II q. 60 a. 5c.

[88] *Eth.* v. 12 n. 4 [1019]; I-II q. 95 a. 4c ('dividitur ius positivum in ius gentium et ius civile'); II-II q. 57 a. 3c; it required no 'special creation {specialis institutio}' (ibid. ad 3) but is in fact adopted and thus is fully (though not merely) positive. Aquinas does not adopt the theory suggested in Justinian's *Digest* 1. 1. 5 and *Institutes* 1. 2. 2, that in whole or part the *ius gentium* is required by reason only in view of certain wrongful or other bad features of the human situation (e.g. wars).

positive part he sometimes adopts the Roman juristic name 'civil law' {ius civile}, the law (including criminal and other public law) that some particular *civitas* has made for itself by *determinatio*.[89]

Aquinas's emphasis on the positivity of all human law, and on the *sheer* positivity of that large portion of it which 'has *all* its binding force' from having been 'humanly made', brings into sharp focus the question of the lawmakers' authority. Clearly, to speak of *authority* is not simply to report the fact of *power*; people can seize, hold, and exercise power without authority.[90] The ambit of legis-lative authority is, in the central case (as we have seen), a matter for legal definition and delimitation. Morally speaking, talk of authority is tightly correlative with talk of obligation: to say that some person or body has authority to make laws is to say that, presumptively and defeasibly, laws made by that person or body will be morally binding on their subjects. This correlativity is based not on some linguistic 'given', but rather on the judgement that the same common good which calls for lawmakers with authority calls also, and to essentially the same extent, for the compliance of the law's subjects with their legal obligations.[c]

Few aspects of a community's common good are reliably attain-able without authoritative ordering (co-ordination) of people's con-duct (both actions and self-restraint). And this is not only because some people will violate or neglect certain moral responsibilities they owe to others unless those responsibilities are redefined as legally enforceable duties. It is also because, as the theory of *deter-minatio* implies, many problems of social life can be solved in more than one, perhaps many, different *reasonable* ways. So, in relation to this wide range of problems, agreement that some form of co-ordination is required will be much easier to reach than agreement about what the appropriate form of co-operation is. Even if disagreement about the appropriate form of co-ordination could in practice be settled by some other means, it rarely could be settled peacefully and fairly without an authoritative decision.

So, even in a paradise unflawed by any human vice, there would still have been need for government (not necessarily 'political' in our now-standard coercion-focused sense) and law (though not coercive law).[91] In his early treatment of this question he based

---

[89] I-II q. 95 a. 4c, II-II q. 32 a. 7 ad 2, q. 57 a. 3; *Eth.* v. 12 nn. 1–2 [1016–17].

[90] And their decrees can be *called* 'law(s)' and have something of the character of law: *Ver.* q. 23 a. 6 ad 2; I-II q. 92 a. 1c and ad 4; II.8 at n. 93 above.

[91] See VII.7 at nn. 148–9 above.

such government on the superiority in wisdom and intelligence that one or some would have, compared with others in their society.[92] But in his later treatment he adds the more fundamental consideration (to which he gives primacy) that social life needs common policy and common action which cannot be achieved in a group whose members have *many* ideas about priorities.[93] This need for authority can be verified easily in the life of even small groups of well-disposed but resourceful people—for example, our students in their hostel-corridor, considering whether to institute a curfew for themselves: III.3.

The authoritative decision, whether legislative, executive, or judicial, and whether by formal institutional decision or the informality of customary practice,[94] will not result in co-ordination unless it is accepted as settling the question, and accepted even by those who would have preferred a different form of co-ordination, a different decision, a different law. To treat the law as authoritative in one's practical deliberations, i.e. as morally binding, is to treat it as settling the question how to co-ordinate with others in one's actions and forbearances in the relevant area of conduct; or how to deal with others in one's judgements, orders, and actions as judge or administrator. Even when one regrets the law's resolution of a social problem, one may and ordinarily will consider that justice

---

[92] II *Sent.* d. 44 q. 1 a. 3c. Such superiority is *naturaliter* a basis for some being *rectores* or *domini* of others less intellectually capable: *Meta.* prol. n. 2; *ScG* III c. 81 n. 5 [2569]. But this must be understood with care. True, the conscientious voter necessarily votes for the better person available to hold office. But 'better {melior}' here means better in respect of the welfare {utilitas} of the community, and the absolutely (morally) better person may not be better in this respect, for someone else may be better for this community here and now because more competent (in learning or otherwise), or of better practical judgement {discretior}, or simply better at commanding a consensus and overcoming disunity. So conscientious voters may and should vote for a good {bonus} person whose tenure of office promises to benefit the community in one or more of these ways, and should also accept the results of any properly conducted {recta} election, even though their votes and/or the results go against someone who is simply speaking {simpliciter} better: *In Ioann.* 21. 3 ad v. 15 [2620].

[93] I q. 96 a. 4c: 'numerous people means numerous [simultaneous] intentions, while one person will have one [at a time] {multi enim per se intendunt ad multa, unus vero ad unum' (and in a paradise, all the many purposes {multa} which are proposed as purposes by the many people {multi} would be good options). On this reasonable *discordia*, see II-II q. 37 a. 1c. Of course, if there are significant differences in practical wisdom, an appropriate form of government will try to secure that the authoritative choice of schemes of co-ordination is made by the people of better judgement: I q. 96 a. 4c; see also I q. 92 a. 1 ad 2; cf. *Pol.* II. 1 n. 15 [183]; n. 92 above.

[94] On custom as a source of law and of interpretation, amendment, and abrogation of law, see I-II q. 97 a. 3c and ad 2 and ad 3. On custom as a most powerful support for law's project of protecting common well-being {communis salu[s]}, see q. 97 a. 2c and ad 1, suggesting that there therefore be great caution in changing the law.

---

and/or peace require some form of co-operation, including the framework or generic co-ordination (common to all areas of social problem) of accepting laws and judicial or other official decisions as authoritative. And one can readily acknowledge that the application of practical principles often calls for a *determinatio* which (by definition) could reasonably have been different. And so one understands too that civic friendship, and the principle of love of neighbour as oneself, and the Golden Rule of fairness, direct one to accept that the law's directive(s) presumptively settle what one morally should or should not do.[95] For if people do not do what they can to preserve justice and peace by such co-operation in co-ordination, not only will the political community tend towards disintegration and ruin, but one's fellow citizens—especially the weaker—will be harmed.[96] For there are many familial and individual goods which cannot flourish without the solid protection of the *respublica* and its law.

True, the law is not to be regarded as unchangeable or irreformable; the reasoning supporting a *determinatio* will quite often prove to have been less than perfect; or circumstances may have changed; and in such cases the law should be altered by appropriate means.[97] Moreover, even judges—who are morally and legally bound to apply law, not make it[98]—should depart from 'the letter of the law' when an application of the rule according to its terms would be contrary to natural right (so that the rule would have

---

[95] This obligation can even go beyond the letter of the law. So if the law of one's state (like Roman law: *Codex* 3. 43. 3) forbids gambling and gives the loser an action for restitution, one has an obligation (unless the law has been abrogated by desuetude) not only not to gamble but also to make restitution, on one's own initiative, of any winnings one makes by gambling; such restitution is to be to the loser, unless it was the loser who enticed one to make the gamble in question, in which case the restitution is to be made to charity—a moral obligation going wider than the legal remedy. See II-II q. 32 a. 7 ad 2; IV *Sent.* d. 15 q. 2 a. 4 sol. 3 ad 2.

[96] So obedience to just authority is required by the order of justice {ordo iustitiae}, for the sake of upholding the ordered well-being of human affairs {humanarum rerum status conservari} in one's *civitas*: II-II q. 104 a. 6c and ad 1. So too is due reverence or honour {pietas; observantia} to persons in authority, by virtue of their special responsibility {officium} for the common good, and the dignity of bearing that responsibility: II-II q. 102 a. 1c and ad 2, a. 3c and ad 2. In a sense, the obedience is owed to the king or other supreme authority (or more precisely, to the *office* of the ruler(s): II-II q. 102 a. 2 ad 3, a. 3c); but since just rulers rule not for their own benefit (rule which is by definition tyranny) but for the sake of the utility, the well-being, of their community (IX. 4 at nn. 81–2 below), the obedience ultimately is owed and directed, we may say, not to the ruler but to everyone living justly in the community.

[97] I-II q. 97 a. 1; still, caution in changing law is desirable: a. 2.

[98] II-II q. 60 a. 5c; and see VII.7 at nn. 158, 161 above.

---

been enacted differently if the legislature had foreseen the circumstances).[99] Still, picking and choosing amongst the law's requirements will inevitably undermine the law's protection of rights and interests, except where the decision to disobey on some particular occasion is motivated by concern for some competing moral responsibility[100] which just rulers would acknowledge as, in the common interest, fairly overriding their published law.[101]

As this last qualification illustrates, the moral authority of lawmakers and law-appliers, and of their laws and judgements, is neither unconditional nor indefeasible. Aquinas lists a number of limiting and defeating conditions, and is as fully conscious as any modern 'legal positivist' that 'human laws frequently work multiple wrongs on people {frequenter ingerunt calumniam et iniuriam hominibus}'[102] and can (like custom, which in turn the law shapes) have pervasive and lasting bad effects on the culture and inner life of a people.[103] Obviously, if the law purports to require its subjects to do things of the sort that no one should ever do, it cannot rightly be complied with; one's moral obligation is not to obey but to disobey.[104] And if it purports to authorize such acts (e.g. rape, theft, or infanticide), its authorization is morally void and of no effect.[105] But then there are conditions derived from the very nature and rationale of political authority and thus of positive law's moral obligatoriness. If the lawmakers (1) are motivated not by concern

---

[99] II-II q. 60 a. 5 ad 2, n. 19 above.

[100] It is not enough that one has some relevant moral *right*; if you *steal* from X the property which rightfully belongs to you and which X is wrongfully detaining, you do not harm X but you do act wrongly, 'against common justice {contra communem iustitiam}', by usurping and ignoring the legal process {usurpare iudicium, iuris ordine praetermisso} and probably also giving a corrupting example {scandalum proximorum}: II-II q. 66 a. 5 ad 3.

[101] On *epieikeia*, this liberty and responsibility of acting against the letter of the law, see I-II q. 96 a. 6, II-II q. 120 a. 1; and see nn. 19, 30 above. Aquinas' concern that *judges*, above all others, should do nothing that would result in a weakening of the law {disciplinae iuris enervationem: IV *Sent.* d. 19 q. 2 a. 3 sol. 1 ad 5} is manifested in his famous teaching about the judge's duty, under certain conditions, to condemn the innocent (VII.7 at n. 158 above), and other similar teachings about the judicial duty to adhere to law {secundum rigorem iuris} where others might properly resort to equity {per aequitatem} (IV *Sent.* d. 19 q. 2 a. 3 sol. 1 ad 5 on disclosure of secrets which should be kept secret).

[102] I-II q. 96 a. 4 obj. 3.   [103] See e.g. *Meta.* 2. 5 n. 3 [333]; *Ps.* 23. 5 ad v. 5.

[104] I-II q. 96 a. 4c and ad 2; II *Sent.* d. 44 q. 2 a. 2c.

[105] II-II q. 57 a. 2 ad 2 (theft and adultery). Courts should not guide their adjudication by enactments {scripturae leges} which are contrary to natural law/right {contra ius naturale}: II-II q. 60 a. 5 ad 1. One may presume that e.g. judicial orders are legally valid and morally acceptable, but if their invalidity is obvious they need not, and if their injustice is obvious they should not, be obeyed: II-II q. 64 a. 6 ad 3.

for the community's common good but by greed or vanity,[106] or (2) act outside the authority granted to them {ultra sibi commissam potestatem},[107] or (3) while acting with a view to the common good apportion the necessary burdens unfairly {inaequaliter},[108] their laws are unjust {iniustae leges} and *in the forum of reasonable conscience* {in foro conscientiae} are not so much laws[109] as acts of violence {magis sunt violentiae quam leges}.[110] Such laws lack moral authority, i.e. do not bind in conscience; one is neither morally obliged to conform nor morally obliged not to conform.[111]

This conclusion is subject to a proviso or exception: laws which are unjust by reason of one or more of these three enumerated types of defect in authority may, on occasion,[d] create an obligation in conscience just to the extent that disobedience would cause disorder or demoralization {turbatio}[112] or give the kind of 'example' that leads others into wrongdoing.[113] To avoid those sorts of unjust harm to public and private good one may have a moral obligation to *forgo one's right(s)* {iuri suo debet cedere}.[114] What, then, about the common situation, where enacted laws—imposing taxes, for example—are in some respects rather unjust, but obedience to them involves no choice of a kind that should never be made, and seems likely to make some contribution to the common good, while disobedience will probably impact unfairly on poorer and weaker members of the community?[115] Aquinas' response seems implicit in his general theory of justice and property (VI.2).

---

[106] This sort of motivation by concern for private rather than public good (and not any further injustice in the decision itself) is what makes a ruler, by definition, a tyrant: II *Sent.* d. 44 q. 1 a. 3c; IX. 4 n. 81 below.

[107] On such 'grants' or commissions, see VIII.2 at nn. 48–74 above; normally the grant will be by law, but the question whether a particular official's act is unjust by reason of being *ultra vires* cannot be answered without considering whether this 'going beyond' the law is authorized by *aequitas* and 'necessity' (see VIII.2 at n. 30, and n. 101, above).

[108] Laws which are *iniquae* are contrary to natural right 'either in every case or in most': II-II q. 60 a. 5 ad 2.

[109] See II.7 and II.8 at n. 93 above, on distinguishing central from deviant cases and focal from more peripheral meanings.

[110] I-II q. 96 a. 4c. Like all wrongful government {mala dominatio}, the making and enforcing of such laws is a kind of theft: *Dec.* 9 [1291]. Only in a small minority of texts (e.g. *Pol.* II. 13 n. 1 [297]) does he say that such laws are simply 'not law'.

[111] II *Sent.* d. 44 q. 2 a. 2c.

[112] *Turbatio* is usually translated as 'disorder', which seems to fit the context; but in (e.g.) II-II q. 33 a. 6c it seems to mean demoralization—the kind of upsetting of inner balance that makes a wrongdoer only worse.

[113] I-II q. 96 a. 4c and ad 3; II-II q. 104 a. 6 ad 3 (this possible obligation *propter vitandum scandalum vel periculum* is 'per accidens', i.e. collateral and not derived from the rational connection between the law's content and practical reasonableness).

[114] I-II q. 96 a. 4c.   [115] Cf. II-II q. 60 a. 5 ad 2 (n. 108 above).

Compliance with the legal authorities' unjust demands in these circumstances is morally appropriate provided it would not unfairly give a corrupting example, and would not cut into the necessities of life for oneself and one's household.

Notes

a. *Rule of Law . . .* So Aquinas has pointed to all the main features of the Rule of Law, as Fuller (1969: 242) acknowledged. See further VII.7 at nn. 159–61 above.

b. *Theories of transmission of authority . . .* Such an idea, that rightful authority is rightfully obtained only by transmission from the people, is expounded by followers and successors of Aquinas such as Cajetan (commentary on II-II q. 50 a. 1, in *Opera* 8. 375: 'royal government derives from a choice by the people, who have transferred their aspirations and their power to the king {regimen autem regium a *populi* quidem electione dependet, qui vota sua et *potestatem in eum transtulerunt*}'). See Journet (1954: 485–96); Finnis (1980: 247–8, 257–8).

c. *Correlativity of authority and obligation . . .* See Finnis (1987: 71–5).

d. *'Nisi forte' . . .* This phrase is often translated 'except perhaps', so that in I-II q. 96 a. 4c Aquinas is made to say 'such laws do not oblige in conscience, except perhaps for the sake of avoiding scandal or disturbance'. But just as in idiomatic English 'doubtless' and 'no doubt' are non-committal, concessive phrases, so *nisi forte* has an idiomatic meaning which ranges from 'except perhaps' through 'except, no doubt' to 'except of course'. For an example of the latter, see e.g. canon iii of the First Council of Nicaea (AD 325) in the mid-4th-century Latin version of Hilary of Poitiers. So Aquinas here and elsewhere should not be taken to be using *nisi forte* to indicate uncertainty.

IX

The Power of the Sword

IX.1. *Private Defence of Self and Others*

The 'power of the sword', as Aquinas understands it, is essentially the public authority of the state's rulers, and their judicial and military officers, to execute criminals and wage war.[1] On occasion a private person may be commissioned by proper political or judicial authority to participate in some such punitive or appropriately warlike activity.[2] But that is simply to say that, for certain purposes, a private person may be invested with public authority, and thus become, for those purposes only, a public person. Private persons in their private capacity have no right to punish even obvious malefactors or enemies of the state.[3]

Suppose I have not been invested with any such public authority, and am simply a private person. Can I rightly decide to kill someone who has threatened to (say) kill or rape me or my spouse, and who has made the threat credible by killing or raping others? On the grounds indicated before,[4] Aquinas is clear and firm that I can never rightly make such a decision, or act with any such intention.[5]

---

[1] See e.g. II-II q. 40 a. 1c (nullus habet coactionem nisi per publicam potestatem . . . non licet [principibus] violentia et coactione uti nisi secundum iustitiae tenorem: et hoc vel contra hostes pugnando, vel contra cives malefactores puniendo); q. 64 a. 3 ad 1 and a. 7c, q. 66 a. 8c.   [2] II-II q. 40 a. 1 ad 1.

[3] II-II q. 64 a. 3c, a. 5 ad 3; IV *Sent.* d. 37 q. 2 a. 1 (=*Supp.* q. 60 a. 1) (see VII.7 at n. 151 above).   [4] v.3 nn. 34–40 above.

[5] II-II q. 64 a. 7c: 'illicitum est quod homo intendat occidere hominem ut seipsum defendat [or ad 1: ut seipsum a morte liberet]'. The same goes for intending and choosing to kill to save someone else: see q. 60 a. 6 ad 2. Saving others is, of course, a legitimate and often obligatory purpose: n. 8 below.

The exceptionless moral norm for private individuals or groups is not: 'I may not choose to kill the innocent', but rather: 'I may never choose to kill any human being, innocent or guilty, harmless or harm-causing {nocens}'. Indeed, the same goes for intending and choosing precisely *to harm* anyone.[6]

Have I then no right to resist the vicious or insane[7] killer's attack? On the contrary, I can rightly resist the attack, preserving myself (or one or more others)[8] by using whatever means are reasonably necessary for, and part and parcel of,[9] repelling it. I do not lose this right just because I can foresee that these means will probably or even certainly[a] have as their side-effect the assailant's death.[10] For in doing what I do, I need not—and must not—be intending to kill (or indeed to harm). I can—and should—be intending and choosing no more than to do what it takes to stop the attack {repellendi iniuriam}.[11] That is the object {obiectum; finis} or purpose of my acting; and the effect on my assailant's life is a side-effect, outside the intention {praeter intentionem} or set of intentions from which the action gets its *per se* character as a morally assessable act.[12] Of course, these side-effects are not wholly outside my responsibilities of justice; if my efforts at self-defence against my assailant would bring death or destruction to people who are in no way harming me, and would thus be contrary to the Golden Rule, I ought to forbear, even if my forbearance costs me

---

[6] II-II q. 64 a. 3 ad 3, q. 65 a. 2c (quoted at n. 42 below); I–II q. 100 a. 3c.

[7] In II-II q. 64 a. 7 the aggressor is never described as unjust, but is simply an *invadens*. Of course, if the person in question (e.g. as executioner or bailiff) has a right to be threatening me with death, imprisonment, or divestment of property, my self-defence will itself be wrongful: II-II q. 41 a. 1 ad 3, q. 69 a. 4c and ad 2; n. 45 below. Note the interesting possibility that an executioner acting in good faith on the basis of a warrant which is not on its face unjust can be right to try to execute someone who, because unjustly convicted, acts rightly in using even lethal force to resist the executioner: read II-II q. 64 a. 6 ad 3 with q. 69 a. 4c.

[8] Whatever is said about the permissibility of self-defence extends also to the defence of others such as family, friends, travelling companions, and in general anyone undergoing undeserved attack: see II-II q. 108 a. 1 ad 2, a. 2 ad 2, q. 60 a. 6 ad 2, q. 65 a. 3 ad 3 ('ne *alium* feriat'); q. 188 a. 3 ad 1 (and passivity in the face of such injury to others is often vicious rather than virtuous).

[9] So a lie or an adultery, since it 'has no necessary bearing on preservation of life {non ordinatur ad conservationem vitae ex necessitate}', is not justified by my self-defensive intentions: II-II q. 64 a. 7 ad 4. To say otherwise would be to claim that a good end justifies a means which in truth, whatever its further intentions (ends), involves a wrongful intention (choice of means); and see v. 5 at nn. 133–41, v.6 at nn. 147–60 above.

[10] II-II q. 64 a. 7c.

[11] II-II q. 41 a. 1c, q. 64 a. 7c ('ad defendendum propriam vitam').

[12] II-II q. 64 a. 7c; v.3 at n. 37 above.

---

my life.[13] Indeed, if my assailant's attack, though utterly unjust, threatens only some rather slight injury or invasion of my rights, and I respond with lethal violence, I may well be violating the Golden Rule even if I have no motive of hatred or revenge and so no intent to kill or even to harm: my response will not have been proportionate to its legitimate purpose, its proper intention {proportionatus fini}.[14]

Aquinas' account of self-defence articulates the right with a clarity quite new in the tradition of moral reflection. It had always been understood that one can rightly repel force with force,[15] but the conditions had been articulated no more clearly than 'with the moderation of an irreproachable defence'.[16] Aquinas reaches his new statement by deploying (1) the fundamental clarification[17] differentiating the third type of order (morally significant deliberation and action) from the first (natural events) and the fourth (technical accomplishments); (2) the insight that among the many true descriptions of a segment of human behaviour (along with a segment of its effects), the description which is primary for the purposes of morally assessing that behaviour (with those effects) is the *intentional*, i.e. the set of nested ends and means included within the proposal adopted in the choice of the acting person;[18] (3) the further insight that aspects of the acting person's willing (e.g. care or negligence)[19] and of the behaviour's effects can and should also be morally assessed, but with standards somewhat different (though ultimately derived from the same master principle of reasonable respect for and love of human good, i.e. of neighbour as oneself).

It is no accident, then, that Aquinas' discussion of self-defence is the articulation of the morally significant distinction between intention and side-effects, the distinction which in recent times has become known—not without confusion—as the 'principle' or 'doctrine' of double effect. Exponents and opponents of the so-called doctrine have very often been unclear about its essential sources or foundations (recapitulated in this and the preceding paragraph), and

---

[13] See II-II q. 40 a. 1 ad 2 (we all ought to be ready for this sort of need for self-sacrifice); q. 64 a. 2 ad 1; n. 58 below. [14] See II-II q. 64 a. 7c.
[15] Justinian, *Digest* 1. 1. 3 and 10. 2. 4 and 45: 'natural reason permits one to defend oneself against danger . . . all statutes {leges} and all other laws {iuraque} allow the repelling of force'; likewise Innocent III (1209) in *Decretals of Gregory IX* 5. 12. 18.
[16] The formula is used by Innocent III (*Decretals of Gregory IX* 5. 12. 18).
[17] See II.1, 3 above. [18] See III.3 at n. 20 above.
[19] See V.3 at nn. 41–2 above.

therefore about its sense and application. It does no more than state the conditions on which one can rationally affirm that there are some kinds of acts (identifiable without using moral qualifications such as 'unjust', 'careless', 'excessively damaging') which must be excluded from one's further deliberations and choices, whatever the circumstances {in omnem eventum}.[20] Acts of these types are picked out by negative[21] moral norms which identify them by reference not to their side-effects but to the intentions which shaped them as options in deliberation, as actions executing the option chosen, including the effects *for the sake of which* the choice was made.

In this way all the basic aspects of human fulfilment, i.e. of a human person's full reality, are given their rationally proper place in deliberation, choice, and action. In the present context the basic good in question is the good of human life, as distinct from all subpersonal forms of existence. The norms in question state what is required in order to give that good, in every human being, the rationally appropriate reverence. That due reverence entails a zone of exceptionless immunity—immunity from *every* form of action done, by any private person whatsoever, with intent to destroy or even *to* damage that life.[22]

All the more striking, then, is Aquinas' acceptance that persons having public authority can rightly form and act upon an intent precisely to kill: 'to intend to kill another in self-defence is immoral for any human being *unless*, having public authority, someone who is intending to kill someone in self-defence refers this to the common good {refert hoc ad publicum bonum}, as is exemplified by the soldier fighting the enemy or the judicial officer {ministro iudicis}[23] fighting against bandits'.[24] Aquinas here alludes to the two types of public killing accepted in a tradition which he trusts[25] and is not concerned to challenge. Is it consistent with his general account of morality to hold that the circumstances or point of such lethal actions authorize the intention precisely to

---

[20] II-II q. 88 a. 2 obj. 2 and ad 2 (killing the innocent is *secundum se* wrongful in any eventuality). [21] See v.6 at nn. 146, 164 above. [22] See v.3 at nn. 36–40 above.

[23] Doubtless including 'policeman', but in IV *Sent.* d. 37 q. 2 a. 1 ad 2, *Pot.* q. 1 a. 6 ad 4, and II-II q. 64 a. 6 ad 3 the *minister iudicis* who is killing a thief {latronem} certainly (and in a. 3 ad 1 probably) is the executioner carrying out a capital sentence.

[24] II-II q. 67 a. 7c ('though even these persons will be acting immorally if they are motivated by some private passion {privata libidine}').

[25] See II-II q. 10 a. 12c, n. b below.

kill? Is it possible to envisage capital punishment without such an intention? Or killing in just war?

IX.2. *Public Defence of Justice: Capital Punishment*

To impose a sentence of capital punishment is, as Aquinas plainly says, to intend the death of the person executed.[26] But sometimes he seems to be saying that a judge can impose a sentence of capital punishment without intending the convict's death either as means or as end in any standard sense of 'means', 'end', or 'intend'.[27] Moreover, Aquinas' general theory of punishment (VI.5) gives some support to this notion. To impose a penalty as a means of reforming or deterring the offender, or deterring potential offenders, or educating or encouraging the community, is necessarily to choose the restriction, pain, or loss (e.g. of life or limb) *as a means* to the desired end(s), i.e. *as* a proximate object within the whole proposal intended and adopted in choosing and executing the penalty. But when punishment is imposed precisely as retribution in the sense explained in VI.5, it can seem plausible to say that what for the offender is a bad (the restriction, pain, or loss) is chosen by judge and executioner *as* a good—and not as a means to further good. This thought may take two forms.

In punishment precisely as retribution, the restriction, pain, or other loss is chosen as the suppression of the offender's will (which was indulged in the offence), and that suppression is not a mere means to some future good but rather is itself a good: the restoring of the order of justice disturbed in the offence. The choice to impose punishment is, then, 'referred to' the common good of justice, and as such is the choice of a good (and not of a bad as a means to that good).

Or again: Surgeons amputating gangrenous limbs do not choose

---

[26] II-II q. 64 a. 7c.

[27] e.g. II *Sent.* d. 37 q. 3 a. 1 ad 2: 'Just judges intend to establish an order of justice among [or: impose an order of justice on] those subject to them. Wrongdoers cannot be brought into such an order without being punished by some loss {defectum}. And so, although *such a loss* (which is the reason why punishment is called 'an evil') *is not intended by the judge (who intends rather the order of justice)*, still the just judge is spoken of as the punishment's author.' See also I q. 49 a. 2c; *Mal.* q. 1 a. 3 ad 10; *Ver.* q. 3 a. 4 ad 8. And if the judge can deliberate and act in such a way, so (Aquinas will think) can the judge's *minister*, the executioner: see II-II q. 64 a. 6 ad 3 (it is the judge not the executioner who kills when an innocent person is executed, unless the person's innocence and the order's injustice were obvious).

'to do evil that good may come'. They foresee and cause a loss of limb; the loss may even, where therapeutically necessary, extend to a joint or other part not yet actually infected. The loss is a bad in so far as the limb (or at least the part not yet corrupted) is or might in future be a useful part of the whole body. In the first (natural) and fourth (technical) orders, the damage may be (at least in part) more immediate than the healing of the whole body, and the loss is permanent. But in the third order of morally significant deliberation, the impact on the limb is 'referred to' the good of the whole body, which is not merely a 'further end' but rather the immediate object of the whole operation. When so 'referred' to the whole, the immediate damage and future loss are no more than side-effects of the chosen proposal to eliminate from the body a bad, a source of lethal infection.[28]

Each of these two lines of thought has left some trace in Aquinas' discussions of capital punishment.[29] But at the end of the day, Aquinas himself rejects their conclusion that imposing and carrying out capital punishment involves no intent to kill.[30] At the very moment when he is most keenly focusing on the distinction between what is and is not included within *intention* in relation to actions foreseen to have a lethal outcome, he accepts that the executioner is 'intending to kill {intendens hominem occidere}'.[31]

Can it then be justified? Can it be consistent with the respect for human life as a basic reason for action, the respect that is exceptionlessly required by general justice and love of neighbour? How can such a means—killing a human being precisely to destroy that person's life—be justified by any end?[32] Aquinas puts these questions to himself. His reply: when one does wrong, one deviates from reason's order and so too from human dignity—the dignity one has as 'naturally free and an end in oneself {naturaliter liber et propter seipsum existens}'—and lapses into the servitude of

---

[28] Thus what has sometimes been called the 'principle of totality' (see e.g. the texts of Pius XII and others in Gallagher 1984) is simply an application of the proper analysis of the third-order distinction between intention and side-effect: Grisez (1993: 542).

[29] As to the first, see II *Sent.* d. 37 q. 3 a. 1 ad 2; *ST* I q. 49 a. 2c, I-II q. 19 a. 10c; *Eth.* v. 16 n. 12 [1089]; *In Matt.* 11 ad v. 21 [946]. As to the second, see II-II q. 64 a. 2c and a. 3c, q. 65 a. 1c and ad 1 and 2; also q. 33. a. 7c.   [30] II-II q. 64 a. 7c.

[31] II-II q. 64 a. 7; see at nn. 23–4 above. See also *In Matt.* 25. ad v. 46 [2114]. If executioners have this intention, so too must the judges on whose orders they act: see q. 64 a. 3 ad 1; n. 27 above.

[32] II-II q. 64 a. 2 obj. 3: what is evil in itself cannot be made permissible by any end, but killing a human being is evil in itself, because we owe everyone the friendship which includes willing their life and existence.

subhuman animals {in servitutem bestiarum}.[33] So, having the status of beasts, criminals can be destroyed, not of course wantonly or pointlessly, but when doing so would serve to promote or protect human good. Execution of criminals is justified, he says, 'when they descend to the worst types of evildoing and become incurable' and 'their harming others is more likely than their reform'.[34] The utility of executing such people is twofold: it deters others or in some other way improves their conduct,[35] and it definitively removes from the social whole a part which is corrupt and very harmful to the whole.[36]

Aquinas' statements about killing the malefactor who is 'dangerous' and 'damaging {corruptivus}' to the community[37] can easily be misunderstood. He does not mean that people with lethally infectious diseases,[38] or others whose existence or condition is directly or indirectly a threat to others, but who are not guilty of serious wrongdoing, can be killed for the sake of the rest of the community,[b] or that it could ever be right to use innocent people coercively as guinea pigs in lethal experiments to save the rest. The danger, corruption, or infectivity which can justify capital punishment is nothing other than wrongdoing;[39] the common good to be preserved by such punishment is nothing other than justice.[40] This justice and common good would be damaged not healed or preserved or rescued by choosing to kill or harm innocent people:[41] 'It is not permissible to [choose/intend to] inflict harm upon anyone except by way of punishment for the sake of justice.'[42]

Still, the question remains. Why is it justified to choose and intend to inflict death or other irreparable[43] harm to the basic

---

[33] II-II q. 64 a. 2 ad 3.

[34] II-II q. 25 a. 6 ad 2, q. 66 a. 6 ad 2 (the harm threatened to others must be either irreparable or manifesting aggravated wrongfulness {horribilem deformitatem} e.g. theft of *public* property {rei communis}); q. 11 a. 3c (counterfeiting money).

[35] e.g. *ScG* III c. 144 n. 11 [3186]; II-II q. 99 a. 4c.

[36] e.g. II-II q. 64 a. 2c and a. 3c. Similarly, mutilation: II-II q. 65 a. 1 ad 1.

[37] II-II q. 64 a. 2c; also a. 3c.

[38] On the infectiveness of leprosy, see *In Matt.* 10 ad v. 8 [818]; plague {pestilentia est morbus infectivus}, see e.g. *Ps.* 1. 1 ad v. 1.

[39] II-II q. 64 a. 2c {propter aliquod peccatum}; a. 7c {bonum commune quod per peccatum corrumpitur}.

[40] II-II q. 33 a. 1c; I-II q. 96 a. 3c (justice and peace); q. 100 a. 8c (justice and virtue); IV *Sent.* d. 19 q. 2 a. 1 ad 6, a. 3 sol. 1 ad 4, d. 35 a. 3 ad 6.

[41] II-II q. 64 a. 6c; v. 6 n. 160 above.   [42] II-II q. 65 a. 2c.

[43] See VII.7 nn. 156–8 above. Aquinas is confident that punishment by death or other irreparable means such as mutilation, not to mention beating, slavery, exile, fine, and loss of status, can at least sometimes be inflicted without risk of a miscarriage of justice (punishing an innocent): II-II q. 108 a. 3 ad 1.

good of life and health, by way of punishment? Aquinas' argument that wrongdoing {peccatum} reduces one to the status of the beasts whose life we dispose of for our utility clearly fails. It proves too much; he himself permits capital punishment only for very grave wrongdoing. And he elsewhere denies both the premiss itself and other entailments of it. He explicitly denies the premiss, by affirming that though the wrongdoer's wickedness is hateful (and bestial), the wrongdoer retains the nature of a human person capable, right up to the moment of death, of being reformed, benefited by human goods, and befriended or loved.[44] And he denies the premiss implicitly, by arguing that those who have been condemned to death— even those justly condemned—retain important human rights (moral liberties). Though they do not have the right to *resist* their execution, they certainly have the right to seek to preserve their life by escaping. If sentenced to death by starvation, for example, they have the right to evade it by consuming smuggled food. In short, they are morally at liberty to avoid any act or omission which would contribute to their own death.[45] Aquinas' recognition that even those guilty of terrible crimes retain such rights or moral liberties, precisely in respect of their own just punishment, is incompatible with his thesis that they are, or can rightly be treated as, subhumans at the community's disposal.

Aquinas therefore fails to reply convincingly to the argument that capital punishment, since it involves the intent to kill as a means, is 'doing evil that good may come', i.e. the pursuit of a good end (the restoration of the order of justice) by inherently immoral means.[c] Does this mean that the punitive 'power of the sword'—a concept he takes from the Old and New Testaments[46]— is morally invalid? By no means. Even when the option of sentencing criminals to death or mutilation is set aside as immoral, there remains in relation to crime a twofold power of the sword.

There is first the power and responsibility which Aquinas made central in his contrast of private with public self-defence: the

[44] II-II q. 25 a. 6c and ad 1 and ad 2.

[45] II-II q. 69 a. 4c. If the judgement was just, they have no right to defend themselves by *resisting* the executioner; nor do others have the right to defend them by force: ibid. and ad 2 and 3, q. 10 a. 12 ad 2; IV. 1 n. 2, IX. 1 n. 7 above.

[46] *In Iob* 19 ad v. 29; *In Rom.* 13. 1 ad v. 4 [1035]. As Aquinas accepts, the New Testament already differs sharply from the Old by never treating capital punishment as the unique or required penalty for a given offence or kind of offence. The proper measure of punishment, even for murder, is established by *determinatio*, i.e. positive law, not deduction from any moral principles: see I-II q. 95 a. 2; IV *Sent.* d. 26 q. 2 a. 2 ad 1.

responsibility of the police {ministri iudicis} to struggle with criminals,[47] using even lethal force—where lethality is in the third order a side-effect—to overcome them, and bring them before the courts, restrain them during their trial, and contain them during the time of their punishment. On this amended version of Aquinas' ethic, we can say that the intentions of the police, prison warders, and so forth should never include an intent *to* kill (even as a means). But the distinction between the private right of defence of self or others and *public* authority would remain relevant. This public authority is not merely a moral liberty but essentially a responsibility (a liberty coupled with, and ancillary to, a duty). And it extends beyond reacting to current attack. The responsibility is—consistently always with moral limits—to detect and pursue and, where appropriate, to anticipate potential attack or other criminality, and to do all that is needed to suppress it and uphold or restore the order of justice.

Second, there is the administration of punishment as just retribution for the offence. As Aquinas concedes, imprisonment (perpetual if need be) or deportation {exilium} can be realistic alternatives to capital punishment as protectively detaching the guilty and menacing offender—even the murderer—from the rest of the community.[48] Of course, even these penalties, like any other, involve the choice of something *to* repress the offender's wayward will. Even when respectful of the basic good of life and health, such a measure involves an intent to do something which will, in some respects, be bad for the offender.[49] But even if imposing (passing or enforcing) sentences of exile, imprisonment, compulsory labour, or monetary exaction involves intending that the convicted offender be harmed, it does not involve the choice to harm any of the basic human goods identified by Aquinas. So it can be morally acceptable. It does not become morally unacceptable when the enforcement of the sentence (or of any other phase in the sequence beginning with detection, pursuit, and arrest) is violently resisted and is defended with all the force needed to overcome the

---

[47] II-II q. 64 a. 7c; nn. 23–4 above.   [48] I-II q. 87 a. 3 ad 1.

[49] Punishment is bad for those punished (*Mal.* q. 1 a. 1 ad 1 {poena est bona simpliciter sed est mala *huic*}) even though it is also good for them by restoring them to the equality and order of justice, and restraining or dissuading them from further wrongdoing (II-II q. 25 a. 6 ad 2; *Impugn.* IV c. 4 ad 3 [477]; and see II-II q. 83 a. 8 ad 3).

resistance, even force which though not intended to kill is foreseen to be lethal in its impact (side-effects).[50]

So the ruler, even if denied the use of capital punishment, can and should use coercive violence[51] against criminals, and in this way 'bears the sword' with justification.[52]

IX.3. *Public Defence of Justice: War*

'Just as the rulers of a city-state, kingdom, or province rightly defend its public order {rempublicam} against internal disturbance, by using the physical sword in punishing criminals . . . so too rulers have the right {ad [principes] pertinet} to safeguard that public order against external enemies, by using the sword of war.'[53] The decision to go to war always rests, therefore, with *public* authority; 'no private person has the right {non pertinet ad personam privatam} to initiate a war {bellum movere}'.[54] And the parallel between just punishment and just war goes further. The second condition for justly launching war is that there be *iusta causa*.[55] The phrase can mean 'just cause', or its meaning can be closer to 'cause of action' in Anglo-American law, i.e. a wrong giving ground for complaints and just claims for redress. Aquinas makes it clear that in this context he intends *iusta causa* to be much closer to the latter sense. We have no *iusta causa* for war unless those we are attacking {impugnantur}[56] deserve to be attacked by reason of their

---

[50] II-II q. 64 a. 7c.

[51] II-II q. 66 a. 8: 'violentia et coactio secundum iustitiae tenorem'.

[52] See Rom. 13: 4. As Pius XII (1955) was to explain (and Aquinas' own commentary: *In Rom.* 13. 1 ad v. 4 [1035] seems to accept; but cf. *In Matt.* 5 ad v. 21 (Busa 1992, RIL 087 no. 1)), this text is scarcely concerned with teaching about capital punishment, and teaches rather that state rulers have a coercive penal power not for wanton use but for the sake of (retributive) justice. [53] II-II q. 40 a. 1c.

[54] Ibid. But in so far as just war is a matter precisely of *defending* the common good, a judge 'or even a private person' engages in what can idiomatically be called 'war' by carrying through a just decision under threat of imminent death: II-II q. 123 a. 5c. In saying this, Aquinas is perhaps envisaging what one may call 'frontier justice', where the authorities are absent, or incapable of organizing resistance, when the natives (by assumption, unjustly) attack from without or bandits take over the town from within. But, though doubtless more common in his day than in our own, this sort of situation is not one that Aquinas identified for discussion.

[55] II-II q. 40 a. 1c, q. 83 a. 8 ad 3: 'it is permissible to attack enemies to restrain them from their wrongdoing'.

[56] See *In Eph.* 6. 4 ad v. 17 [366], contrasting self-defence with the use of arms to attack the enemy {impugnare adversarium}.

guilt in respect of some wrong which they refuse or fail to rectify.[57] This is the concept of guilt and desert which grounds retributive punishment.

Clearly, Aquinas' discussion of just war is focused upon the decision to initiate war. It goes without saying that a state actually attacked by outside forces (having itself done no wrong warranting war) can rightly defend itself;[58] such self-defence needs no *causa*.[59] His discussion, therefore, is seeking to explain when actions which today would often (sometimes questionably) be called 'aggression' can be justified. To the pre-conditions of *legitima auctoritas* and *iusta causa* he adds a third: proper intentions {*recta intentio*}. Here 'intention' covers the whole set of nested ends (ends and means) from the overarching intention to promote peace and the well-being of decent people (especially the poor), right down to the exclusion of cruelty,[60] fraud,[61] and, by implication, intent to kill or harm innocents.[62] Willingness to violate the laws or rights of war {*iura bellorum*} will render unjust the initiating or continuance of a war which would otherwise be just.[63] Conversely, soldiers of every rank who with decent intentions fight a just war are doing something not merely permissible but meritorious.[64]

Aquinas' discussion of just war highlights the analogy with

---

[57] II-II q. 40 a. 1c. The wrong might be persecuting or impeding true religious beliefs or practices: II-II q. 10 a. 8c (though war must never be waged to force conversion to religious faith, even the true faith: ibid. and ad 3).

[58] This is not an absolute right; there are circumstances, which everyone should inwardly prepare for, when a person or a community should refrain from self-defence and forcible resistance to evil: II-II q. 40 a. 1 ad 2. Aquinas does not identify them, but presumably they include cases where armed resistance would be hopeless and would cause unfair harm to the innocent; and see at n. 13 above.

[59] See Suarez (1621, d. 13 sect. iv para. 1): discussions of just war are primarily of 'aggressive war {bellum aggressivum}' (which can be morally proper and necessary: ibid. sect. i para. 5).

[60] II-II q. 40 a. 1c (defence of the poor and needy; exclusion of cruelty, etc.).

[61] Ibid. a. 3c (fraud); v.5 at nn. 100, 104, 128–9 above (lying).

[62] II-II q. 64 a. 6 (killing innocents). Though Aquinas does not spell this out, the exclusion of such states of mind as cruelty, lust for destruction and domination, implacability, etc. is required by fair concern to moderate even the unintended impact of military actions on the lives and property of non-combatants.

[63] II-II q. 40 a. 1c and a. 3c; vii. 1 n. 9 above. The distinction drawn in later centuries between *ius ad bellum* and *ius in bello* is a clumsy and somewhat misleading attempt to make the same point—misleading because a government's willingness to violate the moral or legal norms governing war-fighting entails that its decision to go to war is unjust.

[64] II-II q. 40 a. 2 ad 3. Indeed, devout men can rightly form religious associations precisely to fight (with appropriate public authorization), e.g. for the poor and oppressed: II-II q. 188 a. 3c and ad 2 and 4, a. 4 ad 2 and 5.

punishment—capital punishment—and downplays, without eliminating, the analogy with private defence of self or others. Just as
capital punishment involves the *intent* to kill, so too (he thinks)
does waging war as ruler, general,[65] or soldier.[66] But then the
questions we raised about Aquinas' justification of capital punishment arise in relation to war. Must it involve the intent to kill, and
can it be justified if it does? It seems clear that if choosing to kill—
killing with intent to kill—cannot be justified as a form of capital
punishment, it cannot be justified at all. For any attempted
justification would have to show that it can be right to choose
evil—the suppression of the basic human good of life—for the
sake of good, and this Aquinas, as we have seen, rightly rejects
(even in the context of a just war of self-defence) in relation to the
choice to lie to or defraud the enemy,[67] or kill innocent hostages.[68]

Moreover, it is possible for private persons to defend themselves
effectively without any intent to kill even when the means they
use are known to them to be lethal. So too it seems to be possible,
morally acceptable, and generally (though not universally) effective, to conduct warlike operations with lethal weapons and procedures without intending (choosing) precisely to kill. In war as in
private self-defence,[69] the intent can simply be to stop the enemy's
attack. Of course, this 'stopping the attack' goes far wider in war
than in personal self-defence. For: all enemy soldiers who have not
surrendered and are not trying to surrender can reasonably be
regarded, even when asleep, eating, or engaging in other non-
military activities, as participating in the enemy's overall attack,
or armed and unjustified resistance, which our own armed forces
can rightly seek to overcome without intending death or even,
precisely, irreparable harm.[70]

In the less precisely focused language of the orders of nature and
technique, weapons of war can be said to be 'designed to kill or

[65] The general intent of war-leaders is ultimate victory (I-II q. 18 a. 7c), but fully stated
their intention is to achieve this by fighting, and so it extends to the intention with which
an obedient soldier engages in battle: II-II q. 44 a. 6c; see also I-II q. 12 a. 2 and a. 4. The
soldier kills on the ruler's authority {auctoritate principis}: II-II q. 64 a. 3 ad 1; n. 31 above.
[66] See II-II q. 64 a. 7c; nn. 23, 24 above. The intent to kill need not, of course, be
unconditional but merely: to kill enemy combatants if they resist our advance.
[67] II-II q. 40 a. 3c; see also q. 110 a. 3 ad 4; n. 61 above.
[68] See II-II q. 64 a. 6; v.3 at nn. 36–41 above.
[69] Aquinas indeed seems to concede that there is only a relative, not a morally fundamental, difference between 'general or common' just war and a just 'war' fought by
private persons in defence of some common good: II-II q. 123 a. 5c; n. 54 above.
[70] See Finnis *et al.* (1987: 309–19).

destroy'. But the intentionality—the design—of actions is not in the first or fourth orders and is settled only by the practical reasoning adopted in the deliberations of the acting person. If, as Aquinas seems to assert and never denies, one can spear an assailant's heart in self-defence without intending to kill, it is possible to wage war, too—lethally and often successfully—without that intent. One could set ambushes and employ other ruses (short of lying and breach of promise).[71] What will be excluded are, for example, general 'take no prisoner' policies or any other policies making the killing of enemies an objective—say, to terrorize other soldiers, or put other psychological pressures on enemy leaders ('teach them a lesson'), or to maintain public support for the war effort at home—as well as policies of killing prisoners who can be restrained from resuming hostilities, and every policy of killing hostages as a means of persuasion and dissuasion; also every shaping of action by emotions of hatred, exultation in killing, and so forth.[72] And if we are right to abandon Aquinas' attempt to justify capital punishment, enemy leaders or others guilty of war crimes can be condemned not to death but to perhaps perpetual penal servitude. It is superficial to think that that is letting them off too lightly.[73]

And one should observe that, even if Aquinas is right to judge acceptable some intentional killing in capital punishment and war, the principles of his position impose many conditions on the circumstances, motives, and means. Those principles in no way entail that the instances of capital punishment, warfare, cold war espionage, and military (e.g. deterrent) strategy with which we are familiar are morally acceptable.[74] And the norm which synthesizes his position on killing—'killing the innocent {innocentes = non nocentes} is always wrong, as a matter of natural law'—is subject to no exceptions, whatever the circumstances.[75]

IX.4. *Defence of Self and Justice: Tyrannicide*

Aquinas' discussions of tyrannicide can be systematized on the basis of the distinction he so often draws between public authority

---

[71] II-II q. 40 a. 3c, q. 71 a. 3 ad 3; v.5 nn. 100, 104, 128–9 above, vi.3 n. 70 above.

[72] II-II q. 40 a. 1c.

[73] As Aquinas somewhere remarks, many offenders welcome a death sentence as the lesser penalty. [74] See Finnis *et al.* (1987, ch. xi).

[75] II-II q. 65 a. 6; I–II q. 88 a. 6 ad 3, a. 100 a. 8 ad 3; *Vercell.* q. 86; *In Heb.* 11. 4 ad v. 17 [604]; 1 *Sent.* d. 47 a. 4 ad 2; iii *Sent.* d. 23 q. 3 a. 1 sol. 3c; v. 3 at n. 36; Lee (1981).

and private defence of self or others. Suarez works out such a systematization in his polemic against the English king James I's doctrine of kingship.[76] In our own era, Aquinas' discussions are often said to have shifted from a youthful and incautious acceptance to a mature and cautious disapproval of tyrannicide.[77] But the evidence for the latter, as for Suarez's systematization, is virtually all in the *De Regno*, written (in Aquinas' middle period) for the conscience of a king, not his subjects, and never a fully reliable and satisfactory source for the opinion of Aquinas.[78] When the texts indubitably by Aquinas and securely datable are compared, there seems (as on so many other matters) no significant shift of that kind and no particular concern that tyrannicide be done on public authority. Indeed, as we shall see, the latest of his texts seem to abandon a distinction which he had earlier used to limit revolutionary action against unjust rulers.

On tyranny and tyrants Aquinas' views are clear enough. Tyranny cuts across the distinctions between rule of one, few, many, or the desirable mixture of one, few, and many.[79] It is government in the interests of the governing person(s) rather than, and at the expense of,[80] the good of the community as a whole.[81] That in turn entails that tyrants treat their fellow citizens and others as master treats slave: someone used for the benefit of the master.[82] Tyrants tend to be full of suspicion and fear of their own subjects, and to seek the atomization of social life, e.g. by prohibiting the feasts, celebrations, and other forms of social intercourse which encourage bonds {confederationes} between individuals and families and generate *familiaritas et fiducia*.[83] Not being for the common good of the political community and its members, the 'laws' of the tyrant are more a perversion of law {quaedam

---

[76] Suarez (1613: VI. IV).   [77] e.g. Gilby (1955: 290; 1958: 289).
[78] On the status of *Reg.* as a source, see p. 254 n. d above.
[79] I-II q. 95 a. 4c; on 'mixed' government, see VIII.2 at n. 39. See also II-II q. 140 a. 1c. A tyranny is standardly the rule of one person, but an oligarchy or democracy can be 'as one tyrant': *Reg.* 1. 1 [1. 2] [11] [747].
[80] *In Heb.* 1. 4 ad v. 8 [61]; *Reg.* 1. 3 [1. 4] [26] [758].
[81] II-II q. 42 a. 2 ad 3; II *Sent.* d. 44 q. 1 a. 3c; *Eth.* VIII. 10 nn. 5–6 [1676–7]; *Pol.* 1. 10 n. 4 [154], III. 6 n. 4 [394]; *Reg.* 1. 1 [1. 2] [11] [747]. Of course, the tyrant wants the citizens to be good, not 'good' properly speaking but 'good relative to {in ordine ad} that regime', i.e. obedient to it: I-II q. 92 a. 1 ad 4. The private benefit which is the tyrant's goal is often little more (or less) than great riches, stolen or otherwise unjustly exacted from subjects: see II-II q. 118 a. 8 ad 5; *Impugn.* c. 6 lines 10–14 [II. 5] [229].
[82] I-II q. 105 a. 1 ad 5; II *Sent.* d. 44 q. 1 a. 3c; *Pol.* III. 6 n. 5 [395].
[83] *Reg.* 1. 3 [1. 4] [27] [759]; also *In Iob* 15. 2 ad vv. 20–4.

---

perversitas legis} than laws in an unqualified sense {simpliciter};[84] a tyrannical regime is so completely defective {omnino corruptum} as a government that its decrees or purported laws and judgements are not really laws or judgements.[85] One is entitled to treat its laws, judgements, and directives as having, in conscience, the same status as a bandit's demand, except in so far as one's disobedience would have side-effects which one is not bound to accept (e.g. risk) or which one ought in fairness not to occasion (e.g. breakdown of law and order).[86]

It follows, as Aquinas observes, that if one is about to be arrested or in some other way unjustly attacked by the tyrant or the agents of a tyrannical regime, one has the right to defend oneself (and others in like danger), meeting force with force—if need be lethal in its effects.[87] One can respond to the attacks and threats of the regime just as one would respond to armed gangsters {latrones} in the face of their attacks and threats.[88] Here, then, is a private right which might extend as far as a kind of tyrannicide, in which the death of the tyrant is a side-effect (perhaps foreseen as certain) of force used in defence of self or others.

In the writings of his early and middle periods, Aquinas draws a distinction between tyrants who abuse an authority which they acquired legitimately and tyrants who are also usurpers. Tyrannical usurpers, at least until they have acquired a legitimacy through their subjects' acceptance {consensum} or through ratification by some higher authority, can be resisted and repelled by anyone able to do so effectively.[89] But legitimate rulers who govern tyrannously should rather be suffered patiently, unless and until other officials or citizens who have public authority to do so put an end to the regime, if need be by trying and executing the tyrant.[90] The harms

---

[84] I-II q. 92 a. 1 ad 5.

[85] I-II q. 92 a. 1 ad 4, q. 95 a. 4c, II-II q. 69 a. 4c; and see q. 70 a. 4 ad 2. Aquinas is speaking formally, i.e. about the tyrant's laws *qua* tyrannical, i.e. acts of usurpation or lacking just motivation. If a tyrant makes laws whose content is just, the common good will often require that they be obeyed: see VIII.3 at nn. 102–15 above.

[86] II-II q. 69 a. 4c, q. 104 a. 6 ad 3; and see II *Sent.* d. 44 q. 2 a. 2 ad 4.

[87] See II-II q. 69 a. 4c.   [88] Ibid.; also q. 66 a. 8 ad 3.

[89] II *Sent.* d. 44 q. 2 a. 2c (and ad 4 on the laudable killing of Julius Caesar); and see *Reg.* 1. 6 [1. 7] [46] [769] on the killing of Aioth. Suarez (1613, sect. VII p. 711) argues plausibly that Aquinas means that such resistance can be by any private person (provided that there is no superior authority to which appeal might have been made for relief from the usurpation; sect. VIII p. 712).

[90] *Reg.* 1. 6 (1. 7) [48–9] [769–70]: 'non privata praesumptione aliquorum, sed auctoritate publica'. The ruler's misconduct relieves subjects of obligations of fidelity to any

that so often follow from revolution, whether successful or unsuccessful, are such that acquiescence and passive disobedience should be assumed to be the morally better option.[91]

In the writings of his last period, however, Aquinas seems to have lost interest in the contrast between usurpers and other kinds of tyrant.[92] In either kind of tyranny, the injustice of tyrannical exercises of authority renders them devoid of authority in the conscience of the subject, and gives the tyrant the moral status of a brigand. Indeed, it is the tyrant (of either kind) who is guilty of sedition, not those who seek the regime's upset {perturbatio} and the people's liberation.[93] Still, though their intent to overthrow the tyranny violates no exceptionless moral-political norm, would-be liberators must as always consider also the unintended effects of their attempt.

Aquinas' thesis (not denied in his late writings) that the tyrant can be killed by public authority (as the emperor Domitian was put to death by the Roman senate[94]) stands and falls with his theory of capital punishment. If one sets that aside, as it seems one should, there remains considerable scope for acts of war against the leader or leaders of a regime which is not merely tyrannical but violent, and who cannot otherwise be stopped from pursuing their oppression. To say that Count von Stauffenberg could place his bomb under Hitler's map-table without the intent precisely to kill the

contract {pactum} of subjection (even perpetual subjection) that they may have entered into with the ruler: ibid. [49].

[91] *Reg.* I. 6 [I. 7] [44, 46–7] [768–9]. And the fillip given to Christianity by the patience of the early Christian martyrs reinforces the presumption against violent *coup d'état*: ibid. [46] [769].

[92] See e.g. II-II q. 42 a. 2 ad 3, q. 104 a. 6 obj. 3 and ad 3. Even in *In Iob* 34.1 ad v. 19 (probably a little earlier than *Reg.*) tyranny is treated as *per se* and without distinction a usurpation. Later authors in the tradition retained the distinction more or less in the form one may plausibly infer from II *Sent.* d. 44 and *Reg.* I. 6: the *usurper* is implicitly in a state of war against every part of the state and may be killed in defence of the state (if not also in retribution) by any part of the state e.g. a private individual; the *legitimate ruler* who rules with tyrannical violence may be overthrown only by the people as a whole or their agents (for the killing of such a tyrant by a private person could satisfy neither the conditions for initiating a just war or for imposing punishment, nor the conditions for justified private defence of self or others, a right which does not extend to anticipated rather than present attacks): see e.g. Suarez (1613: VI c. 4 paras. 6–13 pp. 710–16; 1621, d. 13 sect. VIII para. 2 pp. 854–5).

[93] II-II q. 42 a. 2 ad 3. For the phrase 'liberate the people' in this revolutionary context see ibid., obj. 3; *Reg.* I. 6 [I. 7] [45] [769] ('pro liberatione multitudinis'); II *Sent.* d. 44 q. 2 a. 2 ad 4 ('ad liberationem patriae').

[94] *Reg.* I. 6 [I. 7] [49] [770]. Domitian's assassination in AD 96, though involving many people in public life, scarcely had the prior senatorial authorization suggested to Aquinas by his sources.

tyrant certainly challenges the imagination. But what the plan required was that Hitler be incapacitated from participating in the ongoing Nazi tyranny whose murderous violence he directed. A rational analysis of deliberation and choice suggests that the attack on Hitler had (or could have had) precisely the same kind of intent as a soldier's using a rifle or grenade to stop the assault of enemy soldiers, or a howitzer to disrupt enemy formations assembling far behind the lines.

Stauffenberg and his associates undertook the burden and risk of widening their conspiracy so as to be exercising public authority over the political community whose criminal leader the bomb was intended to remove. Their whole project failed. Their mistakes, the unwillingness of some of them to lie to their torturers, and their lack of influence on post-war German politics have attracted some dismissive comment. Even within the horizons of a worldly politics, such dismissiveness seems superficial. The icon of the virtues in action is not so easily eliminated from the imagination and choices of other free persons. And even when, as often happens, heroically virtuous choices go unhonoured and unnoticed, there remain wider horizons in which they retain full meaning and value, horizons considered in the final chapter.

Notes

a. *The acting person's certainty—or the 'foreseeability'—that side-effects of a certain type will result does not make them intended* . . . II-II q. 64 a. 7 ad 4 does not imply that lethal means of self-defence may be adopted only if these particular means would in these circumstances result in death only 'sometimes'; no trace of any such limit is to be found in Aquinas' main discussion (a. 7c) of self-defence, and ad 4 is concerned with a topic which has nothing to do with the issue of certainty, risk, or improbability. More fundamentally, one must keep in mind the distinction between the types of order (11.1 above). When considering natural (first-order) events, Aquinas speaks of chance events as *praeter intentionem* (e.g. 1 *Sent.* d. 43 q. 2 a. 1c) and makes this in turn dependent upon the event being less likely than not {ut in paucioribus} (see *Phys.* 11. 8 n. 8 [214]). But when considering human acts for the purposes of a moral (third-order) characterization, what defines their intention(s) is not probabilities but the structure of ends and means as proposed in deliberation and adopted in choice: 'for from what is intended something may result, as a side-effect {praeter intentionem}, *always* or frequently . . . as when someone *intends* the enjoyment of wine's sweetness and drunkenness follows [as a side-effect though by no means fortuitously or occasionally or in a minority of cases]':

ScG III c. 6 n. 4 [1902]. As II-II q. 64 a. 7c makes clear in relation to self-defence, when the means are no more than is necessary for preservation (i.e. my action is *proportionatus fini* and *moderatae tutelae*), and I am not taking the occasion to seek revenge (ad 5), then there is no necessity for me to forbear 'in order to avoid killing the other'. This is not contradicted by the fact that where one's intent is illegitimate, one may be held responsible (culpable) for inevitable (foreseeable as certain) though unintended effects of one's action to the same extent as if they had been intended (I-II q. 20 a. 5c, q. 73 a. 8c; v.3 at n. 41 above).

b. *Threats to the community warrant intentional infliction of harm only if they also involve fault: the burning of heretics* . . . Aquinas holds that persons found guilty of obstinate or relapsed heresy—knowing, wilful, and pertinacious *departure from* the Catholic faith—may be eliminated from the community by capital punishment (ordered and administered exclusively by the state, but at the Church's invitation) (II-II q. 11 a. 3c, q. 39 a. 4 ad 3). (The Church thus has, in the phrase of Bernard of Clairvaux (*c*.1150), 'two swords', the spiritual sword which it wields itself by excommunicating the heretic, and the temporal sword—the physical sword {materiale gladium} of capital punishment—which it never wields itself but always only through the instrumentality of those secular states whose constitution requires or authorizes them to act at the Church's directive {ad eius iussionem} or nod {eius nutu}: IV *Sent*. d. 37 q. 2 a. 2 ex.; also a. 1c and s.c.)

The thesis is based on the premiss that heresy is not merely, as other unbelief (e.g. of Jews or pagans) can be, infectious and corrosive of the true faith of naïve or wavering people (II-II q. 10 a. 7c and 10c), and therefore contrary to the common good, but also a *culpable* infidelity consisting of, or closely analogous to, a breach of promise: q. 10 a. 8c. The thesis rested on the practice {consuetudo} of the Church in his era (cf. II-II q. 10 a. 12c), a practice which, as Aquinas says, had been rejected by the early Church and then adopted as a result of historical experience of successes in the 4th–5th century AD in forcibly repelling heresy: q. 10 a. 8 ad 1; *In Matt*. 13 ad v. 30 [1151]. More ample experience and reflection since Aquinas' era persuaded the Church that neither the practice nor the thesis could be defended (see Vatican II, Declaration on Religious Liberty, *Dignitatis Humanae*, 1965; x.5 at n. 137 below).

For the analogy with breach of promise was always unsound: the faith was usually adopted by proxy in infant baptism, and even when made by explicit act on conversion at or above the age of reason (see II-II q. 10 a. 12c on voluntary conversion by young Jews), this subscription to the faith was not accurately regarded as having the character of a commitment made to other people. Rather it was, as Aquinas himself says elsewhere, a matter which 'pertains to that person alone as an individual {ad unum aliquem pertinet secundum seipsum}': *ScG* III c. 80 n. 15 [2560], speaking of faith; see VII.2 at n. 32 above. And the medicinal (retributive/deterrent/eliminative) punishment of heresy was too tenuously distinguishable from compulsion of belief, a compulsion which Aquinas (like the Church) always vigorously rejected. Aquinas tried to insist on the distinction (IV *Sent.* d. 13 q. 2 a. 3 ad 5), but slipped into saying—inconsistently also with his own account of the nature of the assent of faith (e.g. II-II q. 1 a. 2c, q. 10 a. 8c)—that the punishment of heretics was justifiable as a matter of 'compelling them [back] to faith', 'physically compelling them to carry out what they promised and to hold fast to what they once accepted' (ibid.).

The requirement that faith be voluntary and free from coercive pressures (x.5 n. 130 below) is an implication of the basic good of religion as a personal search for, appropriation of, and adherence in practice to the truth about God as one can grasp it. Taken with the truth that faith as such pertains to the individual person and does not as such affect civil justice and peace, it yields the conclusion reached by Vatican II, that, provided public peace and justice are respected, all persons have a right, as against political authorities, to freedom from coercion in respect of all their expressions of religious belief: see x.5 at n. 137 below. This right is not the mere tolerance which Aquinas argues for in II-II q. 10 a. 11c.

c. *Capital punishment, because involving intent to kill, is wrong . . .* Aquinas rejects, and it seems rightly, the defence of capital punishment that formerly seemed to me (see Finnis 1983: 127–30; Finnis *et al.* 1987: 317; cf. 1991*a*: 56) to be available consistently with the principles of a sound ethics, namely that it need not involve the intent precisely to kill as a means or as an end.

Torture: Aquinas offers no arguments for or against the use of torture. In *In Iob* 10 ad vv. 4, 7 he speaks without comment of judges who, 'acting in accordance with justice', submit accused persons to torture {tormentum} in order to find out the truth. The popes in 1252 and 1259 had legislatively authorized judicial torture provided that it did not 'imperil life or limb', and it may be assumed that Aquinas' acceptance of the practice extended no further. But since the moral norm that excludes intentional killing excludes also intentional infliction of harm (IX. 1 at nn. 6, 22 above), the exclusion of capital punishment seems to entail and/or be entailed by the exclusion of the use of torture, private or public, to inflict such harm. (Indeed, Vatican II, Pastoral Constitution on the Modern World, 1965, sect. 27, goes further—in relation to torture—and teaches that 'such violations of the integrity of the person . . . as tortures {tormenta} inflicted on body or mind' are gravely wrong; John Paul II, Encyclical *Veritatis Splendor* (1993), sect. 80, treats that passage as articulating moral norms which are exceptionless; the *Catechism of the Catholic Church* promulgated by John Paul II in 1992 expressly repudiates and regrets past ecclesiastical authorizations and acceptance of the use of torture: sects. 2297–8.)

X

On our Origin and End

X.1. *Beyond Practical Reasoning*

This reflective account of Aquinas' social, political, and legal theory has mostly been within *moralis philosophia*. That is to say, it has been concerned with the (third) order that practical reasons can bring into one's deliberations and free choices, rather than with the (first) order of realities which are what they are quite independently of our reasoning about them (II.1). But no course of reflections could reasonably remain confined to the practical, to third-order considerations.

For the very fact that there *is* a third type of order—that rational order can indeed be brought into one's choices, that there *are* first principles of practical reason—is a first-order reality, a kind of given, something remarkable that is somehow independent of and prior to one's practical thinking. The projects or options which we conceive and deliberate upon—like the logic by which we guide our thought, and like our products and techniques—have their immediate explanation, their cause, in human thinking. But our capacities to make and to carry out a choice—like our capacity to think logically, and the availability and malleability of the materials out of which we make our products—are factors in the first order: they are what they are, independently of our thinking and willing. And the human goods known in practical understanding involve us in realities which, even though brought to fulfilment only by our creative thinking and free choices, in important respects are what they are independently of one's deliberation and choice: life, health, procreation, even the society of one's fellow human beings. Moreover, practical reasoning presupposes some non-practical, first-order awareness of possibilities; in turn, practical knowledge of human goods and excellences makes possible a much fuller knowledge of human nature. All these realities, like everything else in the first order, provoke the question: Why? What is their explanation? What other factors contribute to their being as they are and working out as they do? What must the world be like for such things to be the case? It would be very good to know!

Such questions, seeking explanations of origins, join up with our still-pending questions about ends, notably the question about *beatitudo perfecta*. For our inquiry into the unifying point of the various first practical principles led us to the concept of complete human fulfilment, yet it was evident that human choices and actions are incapable of actualizing such fulfilment. Why is human practical reason directed by so paradoxical an idea as incomplete fulfilment {beatitudo imperfecta}, a not fully fulfilling fulfilment?

Everyone knows that for Aquinas the answer to all these questions includes, and is shaped by, certain positions which he regards as truths about God. Not everyone, however, is clear that in Aquinas' view many of the truths about God, not least the truths relevant to our present concerns, are truly accessible to 'natural reason', that is, to philosophical reasoning based on ordinary experience of natural things, unaided by any divine revelation or inspiration. Such reasoning, though beginning with ordinary experience, reaches conclusions about realities not within that experience, and so (Aquinas notes) is often difficult; it can be pursued with some prospect of success only by those with philosophical aptitude and freedom from inner and outer distractions.[1] So it is appropriate, he thinks, that these truths available to natural, unaided reason should *also* have been conveyed by divine revelation.[2] Thus, as he stresses, a truth proposed to us in a non-philosophical way, by God or by a religious body which transmits God's revelation, may *also* be accessible to us by way of a purely philosophical reflection which takes no account of the events which believers point to as revelatory.[3] Indeed, as he points out,

---

[1] *ScG* I c. 4. [2] Ibid.; *ST* I q. 1 a. 1.

[3] I q. 1 a. 1 ad 2, q. 2 a. 2 ad 1; *ScG* I c. 3 n. 2 [14(b)], c. 4 nn. 1 and 6 [21, 26], c. 9 nn. 3 and 4 [55–7]. Not all the truths proposed by divine revelation, however, are of this kind; some are altogether inaccessible to philosophical reasoning; there is no ground whatever for

'almost the whole of philosophy's work {consideratio} is directed {ordinetur} towards a knowledge of God';[4] the work of Plato and Aristotle is some confirmation of this,[5] and the counter-example of their many sceptical successors, when considered carefully and without prejudice, does little indeed to disconfirm it.

But in a philosophical education, reflections about God come *last*,[6] as in this book. And they draw on our understanding of the other parts of philosophy, including *moralis philosophia* and natural science.[7]

In tracing some of Aquinas' fundamental reflections on first-order realities, we will not be straying from the subject of this book. For everyone is aware how close is the fit between first-order and third-order positions—how smoothly, for example, the thought that everything is no more than material particles evolving by blind chance towards eventual motionlessness fits with the thought that nothing really matters save getting pleasures while we may.[8] And though the natural sciences themselves have a self-correcting, critical method and integrity, it would be rash to assume that the tendency to rationalize one's wrongful choices plays no great part in the genesis, defence, and successful diffusion of wider 'scientific world-views' (not to mention loquaciously irrational 'post-modernisms').

Since the days when religious positions like Aquinas' were socially prevalent, thought about such matters has generally followed a clear historical course. After the Protestant rejection of Aquinas' conception of the ways in which divine revelation is transmitted, the Enlightenment rejected the very idea that there has been any such revelation. In doing so, it confidently main-

believing them save that God, directly or through the divinely established Church, has proposed them to us as true: *ScG* i c. 3 n. 2 [14], c. 5. Still, though not accessible to natural reason, these elements of what is proposed to us by divine revelation are not opposed to or incompatible with any truth accessible to natural reason; any conflict which there may appear to be between these elements of revelation and what we otherwise know by philosophy or natural science or *moralis philosophia* is certain to be resolvable by rational argument; so natural reason, while unable to establish these elements of revelation, is able to defend them against all rational objections: *ScG* i c. 7, c. 9 nn. 2 and 3 [52, 56].

[4] *ScG* i c. 4 n. 3 [23]; also i *Sent.* prol. q. i a. ic.

[5] See *ScG* i c. 3 n. 2 [14], c. 12 n. 6 [77].

[6] *ScG* ii c. 4 n. 5 [876]: 'in the teaching of philosophy {doctrina philosophiae}, which considers creatures in themselves and from them leads up to a knowledge of God, first comes reflection {consideratio} about creatures and last comes reflection about God'.

[7] *ScG* i c. 4 n. 3 [23], ii c. 4 n. 4 [875].

[8] Thus the radical materialism of Epicurus (*Ver.* q. 3 a. ic; *Fid.* i [599]) sustains (and is sustained by) his deliberate hedonism (see *Eth.* i. 5 n. 3 [57]; *Ps.* 32. 11 ad v. 11).

tained an idea of nature and of political entitlements held by virtue of moral 'Laws of Nature and of Nature's God'.[9] In the nineteenth and early twentieth centuries, many came to think that nature, natural law, and natural or human rights could be retained as truths and rational foundations quite independent of any rational affirmation of divine existence, nature, wisdom, and activity— affirmations to be removed from public discourse and education into the realm of private, 'personal' belief and unbelief. In the later twentieth century, however, public discourse and education are shaped ever more obviously around the belief that every 'value judgement'—every moral, social, or political judgement directing choice and action—is 'subjective', 'relative', 'personal', and 'autonomous'. 'Right' and 'wrong' are predicates to be treated as mere expressions of emotion, emotionally motivated decisions, and resultant social conventions.

So the *question* of right and wrong, and thus of truly inalienable human rights, is quietly[10] replaced by the question who is in charge, and by the determination to be among those who hold power, set the agenda, and possess the fruits of autonomous personal and group dominance. The moral, political, and juridical language of rights and responsibilities becomes the cloak which such self- and group-will needs for two reasons: to mask purposes which, if frankly expressed, would arouse resistance from competing wills; and to satisfy an uneasy conscience. For, although the publicly assumed and educationally promoted beliefs about theoretical truth treat practical reason as devoid of foundations other than human sentiment and interest, each person's practical reason in fact retains the capacity and the directiveness which contemporary beliefs deny it has.

We have the opportunity, and rational capacity, to retrace the steps which brought our public culture, education, and widespread individual belief to the present condition. And we have good reason to try. Such a retracing of steps, such a retractation of successive denials, might well take a form discernible by tracing Aquinas' reasons for his religious positions. Thus it might affirm not only practical reasonableness and natural law, as our previous chapters have done, but also the positions considered in the present chapter: the existence and providence of God, a public divine communication

---

[9] Thus the Declaration of Independence of the thirteen United States of America, 4 July 1776, first sentence.   [10] Or sometimes frankly, as by Nietzsche.

to humankind, and the human society divinely constituted to convey that communication through history and to be the community in which complete human fulfilment will finally be realized.

x.2. *Towards Explanation*

On scores of occasions, Aquinas describes a world-view which, in its modern forms, we all know well; he ascribes it to Democritus (a contemporary of Plato), Epicurus (a contemporary of Aristotle), and other early natural scientists or philosophers {naturales; philosophi} of fifth–fourth-century BC Greece.[11] The universe consists of nothing but an infinite number of minimal particles, quantitatively distinct but qualitatively identical, from whose purely chance arrangement emerge 'things' in all their diversity.[12] In the infinity of time, the universe must many times have composed and dissolved, by the chance conjunction and disjunction, the dispersion and concentration, in short the moving about, of these atoms.[13] Since there exists nothing but these material particles, there can be no non-material factor such as that which the tradition of Socrates, Plato, and Aristotle has called intelligence or understanding and distinguished from the senses, imagination, and sensation.[14] Rather, all human knowledge arises simply by the movement of sensory images which transit from the bodies we are aware of into our 'minds' (which are simply that part of our bodies which is affected by such movement of atoms to form and combine images).[15] About what has always existed and just *is* (atoms in flux), one should not ask questions;[16] in a strict and consistent version (e.g. Democritus') of the materialist world-

[11] See I q. 47 a. 1c; likewise q. 22 a. 2 ad 3, q. 84 a. 6c; I *Sent.* d. 39 q. 2 a. 2c; *Pot.* q. 3 a. 16c; and the texts (amongst many others) cited in the next ten footnotes.

[12] I q. 47 a. 3c; II *Sent.* d. 1 q. 1 a. 5c; *Ver.* q. 3 a. 1c (Epicurus); *ScG* I c. 43 n. 17 [371], II c. 39 n. 9 [1159]; *Sub.* 1; *Fid.* 1 [601] (Epicurus); *Phys.* I. 2 n. 2 [13], 10 n. 2 [76], II. 7 n. 6 [203], III. 6 n. 9 [334], 7 n. 6 [341], IV. 9 n. 5 [498], VIII. 1 n. 4 [968], 2 n. 11 [981], 3 n. 5 [995], and 20 n. 4 [1139]; *Cael.* I. 15 n. 6 [150] and 22 n. 7 [227]; *Meta.* I. 7 n. 2 [113], VII. 1 n. 17 [1261], VIII. 2 n. 2 [1692].

[13] I q. 44 a. 2c; *Pot.* q. 3 a. 17c; *Meta.* I. 13 n. 3 [203]; II *Sent.* d. 1 q. 1 a. 5c, d. 12 q. 1 a. 4c; *ScG* II c. 39 n. 9 [1159].

[14] I q. 75 a. 3c, q. 84 a. 6c; II *Sent.* d. 3 q. 1 a. 3c, d. 15 q. 1 a. 3c; *ScG* III c. 84 n. 9 [2591]; *Meta.* IV. 11 n. 2 [670], 12 n. 3 [674]. [15] I q. 84 a. 6c.

[16] See *Phys.* III. 3 n. 5 [295].

view, 'causal' explanations of the chance aggregates we call 'things'
are neither available nor needed.[17]

Democritus himself, so Aquinas thinks, was an earnest inquirer
disabled by the method of inquiry which corresponded to these
positions:[18] in so far as he took seriously his claim that everything
happens by chance (or sheer senseless, uninvestigatable necessity),
he was unable to understand growth or development {augmenta-
tio}[19] and, more generally, could not take into account the forms
and causes of the many intelligible realities that make up the
universe.[20] Natural science got going fruitfully[21] by inquiring after
what happens *really* (not merely what appears in human imagin-
ings or in the sensory impressions with which all science rightly
starts) and in the *order* of nature.

Still, a world-view like that of Democritus is widely held today.
It is widely assumed that the alternative can only be a scientific
method as unfruitful as Aristotle's is thought to have been (and in
some important respects certainly was), and/or an anthropomorphic teleology which naïvely projects onto the natural world
some conception of human advantage and human means–end
reasoning.

But any world-view like that of Democritus is radically inconsistent with contemporary natural science. Today's cosmology
explains the expanding universe by the big bang or some other
state of affairs, and gives an account of how what was earlier
merely potential has been actualized in an orderly, intelligible
way. Today's cell biology, like embryology, anatomy, physiology,
and pathology,[22] presents and re-presents in countless details an
understanding of recurrent patterns of process, of movement or
change from potentiality to act (actualization of potentiality).[23]
The same is true, in differing ways, of the many other natural
sciences. And these intelligible, often mathematically formul-
able, patterns of process—freed from the superseded patterns

---

[17] See *ScG* II c. 15 n. 10 [931].   [18] *Gen.* I. 3 n. 2.

[19] Ibid.; for followers of this philosophy and method did not know how to distinguish
potentiality (capacity) from actuation of potentiality: I q. 75 a. 1 ad 2.

[20] *Phys.* II. 4 n. 4. [169]; also I *Sent.* d. 39 q. 2 a. 2c.

[21] See *Meta.* II. 1 n. 4 [276]; *ScG* III c. 48 n. 12 [2258].

[22] Much of what occurs in accordance with natural order involves the destruction of
one system for the maintenance of another (not necessarily higher) order; the spider's
survival (and so far forth its good, end, flourishing) involves the fly's destruction (the loss
of all ends and even existence, as fly): see I *Sent.* d. 39 q. 2 a. 2c. See also n. 70 below.

[23] On 'act' and 'actuality' see v.8 n. m above.

and principles of Aristotelian natural science—instantiate quite
sufficiently the conception of natural order(s)[24] and intelligibility
(not unmixed with chance)[25] on which Aquinas builds the first of
his famous collection of five ways of showing that God exists.[26] In
sketching that argument, and others in that set, I shall try to
convey their gist, not their detail.

The patterns of functioning described in modern natural science
always involve a shift, a change or movement, *from* a state of
affairs P, some *potentiality (capacity) to* function in the relevantly
systematic way, *to* state of affairs A, the *actuation*/working out of
that potentiality, the unfolding of events in that systematic way.
This movement or change always invites explanation. The explanation of (i.e. that which explains) the movement or change must
be some other factor, call it X, which *by acting on* the subject-
matter in state P brings about the change from P to A. An explanation of A is provided by referring to factor X and to X's acting on the
subject-matter. It is not, of course, enough that X was merely
capable of acting on P; to explain the change from P to A, X
must be or at some time have been *actually* acting somehow on
P. Natural science anticipates, and typically finds, that X's activity
follows the same pattern of change or movement: from potentiality
(capacity) to actuation, call it from P_1 to A_1. The explanation (i.e.
the explanatory account) of state of affairs A will refer not only to P
but also to X, and thus not only to A_1 but also to P_1. And so on for
the further explanatory factor X_1 whose activity explains why X
not only can but actually does work to bring about the change from
P to A. And so too for X_2 as explaining X_1; and so on.

In the natural sciences, one makes progress by rejecting as
groundless any a priori assertion that A simply exists, is what it
is, and does what it does, without explanation, or by sheer chance.
One moves from the possibility to the actuality of providing explanations, and one does so by research to identify the P with which A
is correlated as potentiality is correlated with actuation, and the X
which explains why there was change from P to A, and the X_1
whose actuation and activity explains why X not merely could

[24] There need be no single natural goal, explanation, or rationale of things as a whole,
or even for organic life as a whole: *Eth.* VI. 6 n. 5 [1188]; see also the distinction between
two sorts of order in I q. 21 a. 2.

[25] I q. 22 a. 2 ad 1; *ScG* III c. 74; *Meta.* VI. 3 nn. 20–2 [1210–12]; II. 5 n. 59 and n. r above.

[26] The five ways are outlined in I q. 2 a. 3c; they are by no means the most carefully
elaborated or even the latest of Aquinas' many arguments for the existence of God, but do,
it seems, indicate all the kinds of arguments he thinks relevant and valid.

but actually did operate in the situation, and so on and on with cumulatively rich explanations.

As Aquinas strenuously argued, there is nothing incoherent or philosophically unacceptable about the supposition that the universe has existed for an infinite length of time.[27] So, where there are explanatory factors which have ceased to act when X acts, the explanation of A by such factors could be extended indefinitely. But extending *this* series of factors indefinitely still leaves any and every A (and, indeed, any and every explanatory factor in the series) radically under-explained; yet there is no rational ground for simply abandoning the search for explanation at this point in the inquiry. However much extended and multiplied, these explanatory and partially explained factors and states-of-affairs (A on to and/or back to X_n and beyond) amount to a vast state of affairs ('the universe', including its 'history'), one which as a whole as well as in every part instantiates the same pattern of change from potentiality to actuality. Moreover, besides that diachronic series of temporally successive factors and states of affairs, there is the synchronic series of factors ($X, X_1, X_2 \ldots$) which by their *simultaneous* action explain why P *is now* (or was at such-and-such a time) changing from P to A. And *this* series of simultaneously acting explanatory factors cannot be made adequately explanatory of A by being imagined to extend to infinity. So the universe (and every A within it)—whether taken diachronically (and as infinitely aged) or synchronically—is radically under-explained, and could not be what it is, unless there is some other, quite different sort of factor, some reality which (1) can contribute to the explanation of every X (and thus every A and the whole universe of Xs and As), but (2) can do so without changing, or in any way needing to change, from potentiality to actuality. Such a reality must be sheer actuality, without any mere potentiality.[28]

Essentially the same conclusion will be reached if one reflects that in saying of anything that it is acting (or is 'in act' or has actuality) we affirm that it exists.[29] In what we experience in

---

[27] I q. 46 a. 2; *ScG* II c. 38 n. 8 [1142]; II *Sent.* d. 1 q. 1 a. 5; *Aet* [295, 306]; *Quodl.* III q. 13 a. 2.

[28] I q. 2 a. 3c ('first way'); *ScG* I c. 13 nn. 3–32 [83–112]; *Comp.* I c. 3 [4]. See also Kretzmann (1997: 94–112); Grisez (1975: 52–67).

[29] Existing is the most fundamental act of any existing being: I q. 3 a. 4c, q. 4 a. 1 ad 3 ('Nothing has actuality except in so far as it exists; so it is precisely their existence that is the actuality of all things {ipsum esse est actualitas omnium rerum}'); q. 5 a. 1c; *ScG* II c. 53 n. 2 [1274].

nature, or point to in our natural-science explanations, there is
nothing that exists simply by virtue of being the sort of thing it
is. That is to say, everything whose existing reality (or once-
existing reality) is either a to-be-explained or an explanatory factor
in the natural sciences (or in everyday life) is such that it can,
without contradiction, be spoken of as *not* existing (now or at
some time past or future). That is to say, *what* it is does not, in
any of these cases, include *that* it is. So the existing of each and all
of these things which might well not have existed needs explanation; and once again, if one extends to infinity the sequence of
explanatory factors of this kind, one still leaves everything (and
each thing) radically under-explained. The one reasonable inference at this point is that, since there are these realities whose
existing needs explanation, there must be a reality whose existing
does not need explanation, a reality such that *what* it is includes
that it is, a reality such that existence is of its very essence[30] or
nature.[31] Once again, such a reality has to be pure actuality, without any shadow of mere potentiality-without-actuality (non-
existence).[32]

Indeed, if one considers the postulate that the universe has no
beginning and has existed for an infinite time—and if one takes this
postulate more seriously than the materialists do—one is bound to
postulate also that the universe (and everything in it) has as its
explanation precisely such a reality, i.e. some being for which non-
existence is impossible and existence/actuality is (by that being's
very nature) necessary. For, given the eternity of an infinite time,
any being or set of beings for which non-existence is a possibility
(as it is for everything in our experience or our natural science)
would certainly at some time not exist. So, on the supposition of its
having existed *from eternity*,[33] a universe of non-necessary beings

---

[30] *X*'s 'essence': what *X* is; identified by the answer to the question 'What is an *X*?'
[31] *X*'s 'nature': *X*'s essence considered precisely in respect of what *X* can do (in any
sense of 'do').
[32] See e.g. I q. 2 a. 3c ('second way'); q. 3 a. 4c, q. 44 a. 1; *Ent.* c. 4, line 54 [24], lines 94–
146 [26–7], c. 5, lines 30–42 [30]; *ScG* I c. 22 (with c. 14), II c. 15 n. 6 [927], III c. 65.
[33] '[T]he most effective way of proving that God exists is by supposing the eternity of
the world ([even though] Catholics [on the basis of revelation] consider this a false
supposition)—since on this supposition it is less obvious that God exists. For if the
universe {mundus} and change {motus} simply began {de novo incepit}, some cause
must obviously be posited as producing the universe and change from [or at] that beginning {quae de novo producat}; for everything which comes into being {quod de novo fit}
must take its origin from some innovating factor {aliquo innovatore}, since nothing
brings itself from mere potentiality into actuality or from non-existence into existence':
ScG I c. 13 n. 30 [110].

would at some time have ceased to exist, unless supported throughout by some reality *necessarily* existent *and* active in sustaining in existence the universe of non-necessary beings. But if the universe had ever ceased to exist, no universe would now exist unless brought into existence by a necessarily existent being capable of bringing into existence something otherwise absolutely non-existent. In short, postulating that the universe is eternal does not avoid the need to explain things' emergence *from nothingness*, the need which is obvious to everyone when considering the opposite hypothesis that the universe (including time) has a sheer beginning.[34]

The existence and actuality of such a necessary being makes it possible to explain not only the existence and ever-changing actuality of the universe in all its dimensions and parts, but also the orderliness of things.[a] As we have recalled, orderliness (though not without fortuity and disorderliness) is thoroughly characteristic of the world we know; there are countless systems (e.g. the countless natural, logical, voluntary, and technical systems involved in the vast scientific enterprise) which *work*, indeed work *well*, with enough *stability* to do what they characteristically do (and to make the repeatability of experiments a prime criterion in natural science). And this directionality of natural orders can now be understood as indeed directedness. For: the orderliness of all those things and processes that not only exist but also are naturally more than flux and chance is inexplicable unless the reality which is the fundamental explanation of their existence and actuality has been and is[35] projecting their order somewhat as an intelligible proposal is adopted and put into effect *intentionally*.[36]

Some such lines of thought, especially the first and the last,[37] are pursued by practically everyone[38] with varying degrees of clarity;

[34] See I q. 2 a. 3c ('third way', omitting the complexity introduced by the natural science of Aquinas' day, and read with I q. 46 a. 1 ad 2, q. 48 a. 2 ad 3; *ScG* I c. 15 nn. 4–5 [123–4], III c. 71 n. 3 [2469]; cf. *Cael.* I. 26 nn. 2–7 [254–9]). There is uncertainty in the manuscript tradition, and other readings and interpretations are common.

[35] The divine causing is as much now as at the universe's first moment: see I q. 8 a. 1c and 3c.

[36] See I q. 2 a. 3c ('fifth way'); q. 103 a. 1; *ScG* I c. 13 n. 35 [115]. So, as *Pol.* prol. nn. 1–2 [1–2] recalls, if one were to try to bring about what happens naturally, one would go about it in the way that nature does, and conversely, if 'nature' were to accomplish what one's human techniques accomplish, it would work in a way similar to those techniques {artes}. For the human intelligence which is the creative source of arts and techniques gets its 'light' from the divine intelligence which is the creative source of everything in nature.

[37] See I q. 2 a. 3c; *ScG* III c. 38 n. 1 [2161].

[38] *ScG* III c. 38 n. 1 [2161]: 'quasi omnibus hominibus'. See also III.5 at n. 106 above.

the conclusion, affirming such all-explaining sheer actuality, such non-dependent existence and causality, such necessity, and such ordering intentionality, also indicates, as Aquinas thinks, what everyone (or everyone who uses the word) really means by 'God'.[39]

Straining to ascribe everything to chance rather than a creative intelligence, materialists object that in some respects the pattern and evolution of things is wasteful, pointless, badly ordered, *unintelligent*. They do not attend to the fact that much which seems to them pointless or wasteful is still somehow a describable and to that extent stable and intelligible pattern. And in judging it defective or unintelligent because they do not understand its point, they resemble a country bumpkin {rusticus; idiota; ignorans} who, from the true premiss that he does not understand what is going on in a busy laboratory or hospital theatre, draws the conclusion that what is going on is random, unintelligible, pointless, or foolish, or perhaps just needlessly complex.[40] The intention of an intelligence capable of projecting and actualizing the entire cosmos and all its interlocking orders vast and minuscule (including human minds with all their capacities to understand and reason logically, mathematically, and interpretatively) is not an intention we could ever reasonably hope to understand *fully* by reasoning from those truths about it which, in our fruitful but laborious inferences from experience, we do manage to understand.

x.3. *God's Providence, Law, and Choice*

Arguments of the kind indicated in the last section not only show[41] the existence of God. They also make known the utter dependence

---

[39] See I q. 2 a. 3c; *Ver.* q. 3 a. 1c ('omnes loquentes de Deo'); q. 21 a. 4c. Also I q. 13 a. 8c and ad 2: 'everyone speaking about God means {intendunt} by that name something having a universal providence over things . . . The name is used [by those who speak of God] to signify something transcending all things {supra omnia existens}, something which is the source {principium} of everything and set apart {remotum} from all things.'

[40] See *Cred.* prol. [864]; *ScG* I c. 3 n. 4 [17]; I *Sent.* d. 39 q. 2 a. 2 ad 5; *Ver.* q. 5 a. 5 ad 6; also *ST* I q. 116 a. 1c and *ScG* III c. 92 n. 12 [2678] (grave-diggers who are not aware of their director's purpose of finding buried treasure in the graveyard). The flourishing of evildoers and the miseries of decent people in this world (see I *Sent.* d. 39 q. 2 a. 2 obj. 5; *In Iob* prol.) are in accordance with the abyss of the incomprehensible judgements of God {secundum altitudinem incomprehensibilium iudiciorum Dei}: *Quodl.* III q. 3 a. 3c; also I *Sent.* d. 39 q. 2 a. 2 ad 5.

[41] Aquinas says 'demonstrated' or 'proved': e.g. I q. 2 a. 2 ad 2 and 3, a. 3c, q. 13 a. 5c; III *Sent.* d. 23 q. 2 a. 2 sol. 2 ad 2; *Ver.* q. 10 a. 12 ad 1; *ScG* I c. 3 n. 2 [14], c. 9 n. 5 [58], c. 13 n.

of the entire universe on God's government of it and provision for its continuance. Only that government and that shaping and sustaining providence can explain the actuality, existence, specific reality, goodness, and orderliness of every being without exception. But before proceeding further in these reflections on the nature of God, we must take full account of the warning which Aquinas puts in the forefront of his inquiry: 'we cannot know what God is, but [only] what God is not; and so we cannot consider how {quomodo} God exists but rather the ways in which {quomodo} God does not exist'[42] 'and how other things are related to God'.[43] For we can have no understanding of *what* a being is in which *what* it is includes *that* it is. No genus or difference, no type, kind, or species which we know in our experience, can be predicated of God without a drastic shift in meaning which leaves of any concept which we apply to things in our experience no meaning, when predicated of God, save the minimum required to predicate of God what must be predicated to explain the very existence and orderliness of the universe.[44] Our truth-seeking, rational concern to find explanations requires us to affirm that God exists as pure act; but the content of the explanation itself requires us to acknowledge that this existence and act cannot be like any existence or act(uality) otherwise known to us.

Subject to this warning,[45] we should conclude that God, being pure actuality without shadow of potentiality, must be pure mind without mutability (or inertness!) or any trace of bodiliness—for the potentiality to be changed, e.g. by being divided or augmented, is intrinsic to being a body. The causing, ordering, and sustaining of the universe must, therefore, be an intellectual act which in one and the same timeless act both projects (by practical understanding) and effects (by willing), in every detail, this world with all its causal/explanatory systems, its unimaginable galaxies, subatomic particles, and fundamental forces—a world, too, of genomes, cells, and brains; of mathematics and logic which (even without aspiring

---

1 [81]; *Trin.* q. 2 a. 3c. But only a few people reach a knowledge of God by strict demonstrations: *ScG* III c. 39 n. 2 [2168]; and even fewer do so without making some mistake: n. 4 [2170]. And we may think that what is shown, though sound and true, is not a matter of logical necessity but of requirements of rationality in seeking explanatory knowledge ('rationality norms'): see Grisez (1975: 132–6, 168–72); Finnis (1992b: 17–23); I.4 n. 10 above.   42 I q. 3 introd. See also *ScG* I c. 14 nn. 2–3 [117–18].
43 *ScG* I c. 30 n. 4 [278].   44 See I q. 13 aa. 1–5; *ScG* I cc. 13 and 30–4.
45 Aquinas takes his own warning less austerely than Grisez (1975: 241–72).

to) fit that world; of loyalty, justice, and remorse; of computers, symphonies, chess, and constitutions.

The awesome difference in actuality, power, and excellence between the greatest human being and God exceeds immeasurably the difference in actuality, power, and excellence between the most transient and feeble speck and human persons at the height of their mature strength, genius, and virtue.[46] Polytheisms, idolatries, and gnosticisms propose a multiplicity of more or less creative and providential divinities, all falling short of God's simplicity of actuality, and reflecting rather the profusion of natures in the universe of experience. Pantheism proposes that the universe itself, precisely as informed by intelligibility and thus by mind, is divine. Though not as foolish, in principle, as atheism,[47] polytheism and pantheism alike are philosophically arbitrary and misguided.[48] They presuppose a semi-materialist underestimation of intellect's capacity to grasp (and project) multiple and changing realities (actual or possible) in a single act of mind. They veer towards the pernicious in the character they ascribe to a divinity or divinities falling short of the perfection of a pure and limitless act(uality), and imaging moral weaknesses of the people who project them. They are utterly inconsistent with a logically necessary implication of the arguments which justify affirming divine existence: that existence (pure act) is what divine being is. For, that being so, whatever we understand of something which can be or not be cannot be true of God, and the supposed divine principles posited by polytheism or pantheism, being intelligible to us, cannot be God. Pantheism and polytheism are rationally ineligible because they stray from the only way in which anything can be rationally affirmed of the divine: the way which Aquinas calls *remotio*—connoting both the utter separateness or transcendence (removed-ness) of God and the fact that affirmations about God can be made *only* by negating (removing) creaturely imperfections.[49]

In what ways, then, is Aquinas' social and political thought informed by affirmations about God? The answer, with which the rest of this chapter is concerned, has many elements and could

---

[46] See e.g. *ScG* I c. 3 n. 4 [17].

[47] Stupidity {stoliditas} of failing to see the evidence of God {manifesta Dei}: *ScG* III c. 38 n. 5 [2165]; also *Cred.* a. 1 [869].

[48] See e.g. II *Sent.* d. 18 q. 2 a. 2c; *ScG* I c. 20 nn. 34–7 [188–95] (philosophical bases and weakness of idolatry); *ScG* I c. 27 n. 9 [258] (and of pantheism).

[49] See I q. 12 a. 12c, q. 13 a. 10 ad 5; *ScG* I c. 14.

be expounded in many different ways. We can begin where Chapter
II's reflections on Aquinas' social theory began, with the ideas and
reality of *co-ordination* and *co-operation*.

When he is educating theological students in the language of the
Bible and of the Catholic theological tradition, Aquinas is willing
to speak of an 'eternal law'. For the universe is no mere jumble but
a vast community of beings, indeed a complete community {per-
fecta communitas}.[50] And the production and sustaining of the
universe is the supreme act of practical reason. In that act, God
envisages and freely chooses[51] the whole order of things, prescribing (so to speak) that order by impressing its principles (the 'laws of
physics', the 'laws of logic', and so forth) onto or into the various
orders of created entity and process. And this act is to the common
benefit of the whole (and thus of its parts). So we can think of this
supreme act of government as legislative, and its rational content
as a law which, like its author, is timeless (even though that content is freely chosen, not necessary, and regulates creatures which
are all within time).[52] This conception of an eternal law is promi-
nent in the *Summa Theologiae*'s treatise on law (and politics), and
can arouse the suspicion that Aquinas assimilates the government
of free people too closely to the ordering of physical and biological
nature.

But when developing his ideas more philosophically and without
the pressure to make use of every traditional theological form of
speech,[53] Aquinas strongly insists that law is something addressed
by one mind and will to others—by one freely choosing person *to
other freely choosing persons*.[54] This does not contradict the idea
of an eternal law governing even subrational creatures, but it
firmly relegates that idea to an extended, non-focal sense of 'law'.
The central case of law is an appeal to the mind, the choice, the
moral strength {virtus},[55] and the love[56] of those subject to the law.

---

[50] I-II q. 91 a. 1c.   [51] e.g. *Mal.* q. 16 a. 5c.
[52] I-II q. 91 a. 1, q. 93 aa. 1, 4, and 5; IV *Sent.* d. 49 q. 1 a. 2 sol. 5 ad 2.
[53] See *ScG* I c. 2 n. 3 [11], c. 3 n. 2 [14], c. 9 n. 2 (first sentence) [52a], nn. 3 and 4 [55–7], II
c. 4 n. 4 (last sentence) [875b]; cf. ibid. nn. 5 and 6 [876] on the overall intent.
[54] *ScG* III c. 114 n. 3 [2878] ('since law is precisely a rational scheme and rule for actions
{quaedam ratio et regula operandi}, it is only appropriate to give law to those who know
the rationale {rationem} of their actions'); n. 4 [2879] ('law is to be given to those with the
ability either to act or not to act; but this ability belongs only to rational creatures; so
only rational creatures are the subjects of law {sola igitur rationalis creatura est suscep-
tiva legis}'); n. 5 [2880], c. 115 n. 3 [2884]. Also c. 1 n. 10 [1867].
[55] *ScG* III c. 115 n. 4 [2885], c. 116 nn. 3, 4 [2890–1].   [56] *ScG* III cc. 116, 117.

It is always a plan[57] for co-ordination through free co-operation. So the rational plan of divine providence which in the *Summa Theologiae* is often called 'eternal law' is called in the *Summa contra Gentiles* 'divine law' but only in so far as that plan is made known or 'proposed to' us,[58] and thus shared in by us.[59]

For it is clear that the plan of divine government is partly unknown and partly known to us.[60] No reality in the universe can be, and be what it is, without God's causing it. That causing is entirely an act of mind. That act cannot be in any way imperfect; if it were it would not be what it must be if the universe is to have the explanation that it must have. So the plan of divine providence must extend to all things and all events in the entire history of the universe, in all their particularity, and—without subtracting from the strong freedom that persons can have in choosing[61]—must shape them all to the common good of the universe.[62] But we understand only certain general truths about the universe (and particular events only to the extent that they instantiate those general truths) and certain principles of practical reason picking out the basic human goods (and particular actions only in so far as they intend such goods and are assessable as fulfilling or departing from those standards of reasonableness).[63]

The principles of practical reasonableness are now understandable as having the force and depth of a kind of sharing in God's creative purpose and providence.[64] The good of practical reasonableness {bonum rationis} is now understandable as good not only intrinsically and for its own sake but also as a constituent in the good of *assimilatio* and *adhaesio* to the omnipotent creator's

---

[57] 'Plan' is an unsatisfactory term, since it suggests something in the fourth order. God and God's activity is not within any of the four orders. But our attempts to understand the divine law must be on the analogy of human legislating, which is primarily in the third order and only secondarily in the fourth.

[58] *ScG* III c. 121 n. 2 [2943]. The term 'divine law' is sometimes used in this way in *ST* e.g. II-II q. 109 a. 2 ad 3, a. 3 ad 3, q. 124 a. 5 ad 2, q. 141 a. 2 ad 1; but generally 'divine law' is used in *ST* with a much more restricted sense, to refer to the laws divinely revealed in the Old and New Covenants (see I-II q. 91 a. 4).

[59] I-II q. 91 a. 2c: sharers in providence, providing for ourselves and for [subrational] creatures.   [60] I-II q. 19 a. 4 ad 3.

[61] 1 *Sent*. d. 39 q. 2 a. 2c; *ST* I q. 22 a. 2 ad 4.

[62] So 'God permits some evils to occur, lest many goods be impeded': I q. 23 a. 5 ad 3; see also e.g. q. 2 a. 3 ad 1, q. 22 a. 2 ad 2.   [63] I-II q. 95 a. 2c.

[64] 'And so it is clear that the natural law is precisely the sharing out of the eternal law in the rational creature {participatio legis aeternae in rationali creatura}': I-II q. 91 a. 2c. It is *as* the natural law in this sense that the eternal law is the standard for human willing {regula voluntatis humanae}: I-II q. 71 a. 6c.

practical wisdom and choice. The truth of the practical principles is now understandable not only as the anticipation of the human fulfilment to which they direct us,[65] but also as their conformity to the most real of all realities, the divine creative mind, the mind which is nothing other than the very reality of that pure and simple *act*, God. Why are these principles *natural* law? Not because they are somehow read off from nature or human nature. Rather, for at least three reasons. They are not made by human devising {adinventio}[66] but rather are first-order realities, as are the other realities which pertain to our nature. Their reasonableness, moreover, is a sharing in the practical reasonableness, the wisdom, of the very author of our nature, the creator by whose wisdom and power the fulfilment which we can freely choose is (like our freedom itself) made possible. And no human choices or acts are against the natural law (or indeed against any divine law) except in so far as they are against human good.[67]

Our co-operation in carrying out the plan of providence through our adherence, as individuals or groups, to the natural law[68] is indeed a response of freedom to freedom. Aquinas makes clear the similarity between God's plan of providence and the just but '*purely* positive' laws of a decent human lawmaker (VIII.3). For God's choice to will this universe rather than some other is, like such a legislator's, a sheer *determinatio* in which practical rationality or wisdom leaves room for a preference which (as compared with other reasonable and available options) is both fully reasonable and yet not necessitated or required by reason.[69]

There are differences. The human lawmakers who, by *determinatio*, choose some rule of the road, rate of tax, or regime of property need not have chosen this one but, typically, were required by reason of the elements of the common good at stake to adopt *some* such rule, rate, or regime. But God, being pure act, is free from every trace of potentiality, lack, imperfection, or need.

---

[65] See III.6 n. t (p. 100) above.
[66] See I-II q. 91 a. 3c on human laws as particular arrangements devised {adinventae} according to human reasonings. [67] *ScG* III c. 122 n. 2 [2948].
[68] '. . . the "light" of natural reason by which we discern what is good and bad (which is a matter of natural law) is simply an "impression" of the divine light in us. And so it is clear that natural law is simply a sharing out of the eternal law in rational creatures': I-II q. 91 a. 2c; n. 64 above; Finnis (1980: 398–403). Indeed, the *ius naturale* is for us an unchanging bond or covenant {foedus sempiternum} with God: *In Rom.* 1. 8 ad v. 26 [149]; *In I Cor.* 11. 3 ad v. 13 [619].
[69] See *ScG* III c. 97 n. 12 [2734] (selection of particular wood for building the house) with nn. 13–14 [2735–6] and I-II q. 95 a. 2c (selection of particular shape of house).

God's perfection cannot conceivably be enhanced. So divine creation—whether creation of any universe or creation of this universe—cannot in any sense be required by any reason whatever.
In conceiving and willing the universe, God could have willed and
can will countless different sorts of universe and nature. There is
no conceivable 'best of all possible worlds'; to every intelligible and
excellent universe there could be added elements that would *in
some respect(s)* improve it.[70] Therefore, the divine creative act of
conceiving and bringing into being the entire universe must have
been, and be, an act of *free choice*, preferring one possible universe
(ours) to incommensurably good alternatives including not creating
anything at all.[71] Indeed, this supreme act of freedom must also be
a supreme act of liberality; since God, being pure actuality, can
have no lack or need of any kind whatsoever, all the good in the
created universe—creatures and everything from which any creature ever benefits—must be given out of God's sheer generosity
{liberalitas}.[72] The rationale of God's creative action can only be:
to *express* the glorious fullness of divine being *by* bringing into (and
maintaining in) existence beings which, by their actuality, their
variety of types and multiplicity of instantiations, their intelligibility, in some cases by their intelligence and freedom, and in all
cases precisely by their various perfections (flourishing) as individuals, groups, species, and universe, would have a kind of *likeness*

---

[70] I q. 25 a. 6; I *Sent.* d. 44 q. un. a. 1 and a. 2; *Pot.* q. 3 a. 16c. Even a universe free from
every evil would not be unqualifiedly better than ours, for in many respects it would be
less good than ours, in that it would lack all those countless sorts of beings whose
flourishing involves the consumption/destruction of other beings: see I *Sent.* d. 44 q.
un. a. 2 ad 5; also *ST* I q. 22 a. 2 ad 2. (Note that divine providence and government of
everything does not entail that God intends, whether as ultimate or as intermediate end,
the destruction and deformities involved in the workings of nature; rather, these evils are
permitted, not intended, and are means only in the sense that God turns them to good
effect: see *Ver.* q. 5 a. 4c and obj. 10 and ad 10; I-II q. 19 a. 9.) Moreover, if badness
(deficiency in goods) were subtracted from some parts of our universe, the perfection of
the whole would be much impaired, since its beauty in part derives from the co-ordination {ordinata adunatione} of good and bad, as a silent pause enhances the sweetness of a
melody: *ScG* III c. 71 n. 7 [2473].

[71] I q. 19 a. 10, q. 104 a. 3c; II *Sent.* d. 25 a. 1; *Ver.* q. 24 a. 3c; *ScG* I c. 81 nn. 2–4 [683–5],
cc. 86, 88, II c. 23, III c. 1 n. 1 [1862].

[72] I q. 32 a. 1 ad 3; *ScG* I c. 93 n. 7 [785], II c. 44 n. 15 [1217] ('God has brought things
into being out of sheer generosity {ex mera liberalitate}'). Being prior to any claim of
creatures, this is in no way a matter of distributive justice; but in its inherent appropriateness {decentia divinae bonitatis} the divine generosity {liberalitas} is analogous to
'general justice': I *Sent.* d. 43 q. 2 a. 2 ad 4; see also *ST* I q. 21 a. 3c, II-II q. 117 a. 5 ad 1. So
divine mercy, overcoming the deficiencies in creatures, is more fundamental than, and is
the very root of, the divine justice by which creatures have what they need to fulfil their
(freely given) natures: I q. 21 a. 4c.

{similitudo} to—be in a way a representation {repraesentatio}, an imitation {imitatio}, or image {imago} of—the divine goodness, precisely by these sorts of sharing in its effects.[73]

And what could be more *personal*[74]—somehow living, intelligent, loving, self-directing—than a being whose activity must be in some sense a deed of intelligence, free choice, and generosity? Our being persons—and above all,[75] our being in charge of our own acts so that nothing determines what option we choose save our very choosing—is a kind of imaging of the exemplary independence of God. And our being friends with other persons whose good we will for their sake (rather than to fulfil our own needs) is a kind of reflection of, and co-operation with, the liberality—that is to say, the love[76]—by which God enables us (and not out of any need of his[77] but rather for our sake)[78] to somehow share in the goodness of his actuality.

A strictly philosophical inquiry into the explicability of the universe thus yields the conclusion that there need be nothing arbitrary or anthropomorphic in people's belief that the ultimate source of the directiveness of their moral and other practical principles is a directing intelligence in whose illuminating power our own understanding somehow shares.[79] Nor in their belief that some kind of interpersonal co-operation with the divine is possible and, since possible, an important good and something supremely to be hoped for. Nor in their belief that their own projects—including the inquiries they wish to undertake, the relationships they wish to form, and the food-gathering and production on which they

---

[73] See I q. 65 a. 2c, q. 103 a. 4c; *ScG* I c. 29, c. 75 nn. 3–6 [641–4], II c. 35 n. 7 [1117], c. 38 n. 15 [1149], cc. 45–6, III c. 19 n. 4 [2007], c. 20 n. 2 [2010]; *Comp.* I cc. 102–7.

[74] See I *Sent.* d. 9 q. 1 a. 1c and ad 2.   [75] I-II prol. (II. 1 at n. 1 above); *ScG* III c. 111.

[76] For the rationale of liberality is love: I *Sent.* d. 10 q. 1 a. 1c, a. 2c, d. 18 q. 1 a. 4c and ad 4; see also d. 32 q. 1 a. 3c; *ScG* I c. 93 n. 7 [785].

[77] God, not being bodily or limited in being, cannot be masculine or feminine: see I q. 93 a. 6 ad 2; *In I Cor.* 11. 3 ad v. 10 [614]. But language needs ways to signify that God's being is personal. A neuter pronoun would suggest that God is indefinite or at least not personal in being (*Decret.* II, lines 194–204 [1195]); a feminine would suggest that God's activity and generosity takes the form of nurturing and developing something received. Still, precisely as persons, human females are as much 'in the image of God' as males: v.7 nn. 173–8 above.   [78] II-II q. 132 a. 1 ad 1; n. 85 below.

[79] As an instructive literary image of the intelligibility of natural law and of its (and practical reasoning's) first principles, Aquinas is fond of the Psalmist's answer to a question (Ps. 4: 6–7), 'Who will show us goods {bona}?' 'The light of your visage, O Lord, is imprinted upon us.' See e.g. I-II q. 19 a. 4c, q. 91 a. 2c; *Ver.* q. 16 a. 3c; *Ps.* 4.5 ad v. 5; *In Matt.* 21 ad v. 28 [1727].

rely—could not possibly succeed without the unfailing co-operation of the divine cause of nature's existence and orderly fecundity.[80]

Preserving the judgement that such an actuality must exist and be boundlessly intelligent and free, many have anticipated that so intensely personal a reality might communicate with other persons by some means even more intelligible and more personal than the unfolding of this ordered universe—by means, that is, of some act whose very point would be an interpersonal communication *to us*: most likely by some word(s).

x.4. *On the Point of Human Existence and Action*

But before going beyond philosophy's own resources to revelation and theology (critical reflection on the data of revelation), we should make a last survey of the harvest from Aquinas' philosophical arguments as they bear on the point of human existence, individual and social.

The search for an explanation of the universe and its myriad patterns of change yields the conclusion, with a necessity not 'conceptual' or 'logical' but rational,[81] that there must be a reality which is pure act without any admixture of mere potentiality. Being free from all mere potentiality, this reality—God—must be in some sense an incorporeal act of mind in which our universe in all its parts and times is conceived by a kind of practical understanding and chosen by a kind of willing. Being free from all mere potentiality, God's act of being includes (we must think and say) every kind of benefit of being, every kind of power (in act, not in potentiality), and every kind of perfection.

On the one hand, then, God cannot have chosen to create the universe to meet any need; lacking nothing, reality as a whole *could* not be improved by God's choice to create. On the other hand, creating, directing, and sustaining the universe need not, and could not, have been pointless, lacking in intelligibility; like every other aspect, so to speak, of the single divine act of being, the idea and act of bringing into being this universe cannot be deficient in intelligibility. The conclusion, as we have seen, seems inexorable:

---

[80] It is folly to think that God will preserve one without one's own care and action, and folly to think that one's own actions can succeed without the help of God's providence: *ScG* III c. 135 nn. 24–5 [3098–9].　　　　　　　　　　　　[81] See n. 41 above.

the point, the common good, of the universe must be the expressing, representing, and communicating (somehow sharing) of the divine perfection of actuality by bringing into being a universe of creatures which are each *like* {similis} God in having actuality, perfections, intelligibility, and so forth. While no creature by itself expresses God's reality, power, and goodness to more than a very limited extent, the universe taken as a vast system of systems and realities is certainly a significant *expression* of those divine qualities.[82]

In every case, creatures have their point—i.e. express God's perfections as he meant them to do—precisely by flourishing, by being fulfilled, or, in so far as they are naturally parts, by making their natural contribution to the fulfilment of some wider creaturely system. For by such flourishing, creatures and systems of creatures become more similar to {assimilantur} and more apt to represent {repraesentant} God, each in its own way; and all together they can express the inexhaustible divine perfection by their plurality and diversity {multiplicitas et varietas},[83] and their intelligibility each in itself and all as parts of the whole order.[84]

The flourishing of human beings is not as *mere* parts of a system. For we are persons, and when we are functioning well we act not simply by following the dynamisms of some system whose pattern is built into us, but rather by our mastery over our own acts. By thus having an authorship of one's own life through acts of free choosing, one acts on one's own account and, in a sense, for one's own sake, and in the plan of divine creation each of us is a *per se* end; the plan is directed towards one's personal flourishing, for one's own sake. Aquinas states all this most forcefully.[85] And he

---

[82] For the line of thought summarized in this paragraph, see I q. 50 a. 1c, q. 65 a. 2c, a. 103 a. 4c; more fully in *ScG* I c. 29, c. 75 nn. 3 and 4, c. 76 n. 8 [654], c. 78 n. 3 [662], II c. 35 n. 7 [1117], cc. 45–6, III cc. 19–22, c. 25, c. 34 n. 5 [2142], c. 51 n. 6 [2289]; and in *Comp.* I cc. 100–9; earlier, II *Sent.* d. 1 q. 2 a. 2c.

[83] *ScG* II c. 45 n. 2 [1220]; also n. 4 [1222] ('a created reality approaches the likeness of God more perfectly if it is not only good but also can act for the benefit of others . . . but it could not do so unless there were plurality and inequality {pluralitas et inaequalitas} amongst created realities'); n. 5 [1223] ('goods in plurality are better than one finite good, for they contain the latter and more besides').

[84] In the understanding of order, the relation of parts to the point of the whole is primary, and the relation of the parts to each other is secondary (though essential): see II.2 above; also *Eth.* prol. n. 1 [1]; *ScG* I c. 78 n. 4 [663].

[85] *ScG* III c. 111 (a point in the structure of *ScG* as important as the prologue to I-II in *ST*), c. 112 (masters of our own acts, authors of our own providence, principals, free people, governed for our own sakes, having a nature not instrumental but needed for its

adds that human existence, understanding, willing, and acting thus re-present and image God's actuality in a way that subpersonal creation cannot.[86] They do so in a specially close and vivid way when they have all the practical reasonableness, all the unfettered openness to human goods, that we have traced in outline in earlier chapters.[87]

Yet at the same time, if one understands that there is a God who is the universal and perfect cause of all goods, including persons and their forms of fulfilment, one can equally understand that God is more lovable than oneself—that one is to love God more than one's neighbour or even than oneself;[88] and that the master moral principle or first precept of the natural *moral* law (IV.5) can now be more adequately stated: one should love one's neighbour as oneself *by reason of* the divine goodness as it is participated, reflected, and imaged[89] in that neighbour as in every human being—a goodness that can be both respected and nurtured in those in and for whom one can do good.[90] In short, one is to love one's neighbour as oneself on account of, and (so to speak) for the sake of God {propter Deum},[91] the God whom we all should seek (and help each other to seek) to resemble and adhere to, and whose glory all human beings have the capacity to share.[92]

Practical reasonableness itself can also be seen now in a new light. It has a *further overarching point*, which subsumes, embraces, confirms, and explains all the other reasons for action, and which like all practical reasons is both individual and common, a reason both for individual and for interpersonal, group

own sake), c. 113 (each directed to God by what befits not only the species but also the individual, individually and personally).

[86] *ScG* II c. 46 nn. 3–6 [1231–3]. So the final perfection which is the ultimate point {finis} of the whole universe is the complete fulfilment of created persons who love God {sanctorum}: I q. 73 a. 1c; IV. 3 at n. 59, V. 7 at n. 167 above.

[87] Though immorality causes us to lose our likeness {similitudo} to God, it does not destroy our imaging {imago} of other aspects of God's goodness: I *Sent.* d. 3 q. 4 a. 1 ad 7.

[88] See III *Sent.* d. 29 q. un. a. 3c ('God is naturally loved, with a love of [natural] friendship, more than one loves oneself'). [89] II-II q. 44 a. 7c.

[90] I-II q. 100 a. 6 ad 1 ('love of God is reason for love of neighbour'); II-II q. 25 a. 1c ('God is reason for loving one's neighbour') and ad 1, q. 26 a. 3c; *Car.* q. un. a. 8c; *In Matt.* 6 ad v. 9 [584].

[91] e.g. I-II q. 99 a. 1 ad 2, II-II q. 19 a. 6c, q. 23 a. 5 ad 2, q. 44 a. 3c (*God is to be loved* is the point {finis} of *neighbour is to be loved*); *In Rom.* c. 13. 2 ad v. 9 [1057].

[92] II-II q. 47 a. 7c. So the point {ratio} of love of neighbours in this life is: 'association with them {consociatio} in the full sharing of *beatitudo*': II-II q. 26 a. 5c. See also *ScG* III c. 117 n. 2 [2895] (which adds that those who have a shared end ought to be united in affection).

choices and actions. This further, more ultimate point {finis} is: to be as *like* God as human persons can be. For that is how we can participate well in—and give our own life the characteristics of—that activity which not only is supremely intelligent,[93] free, self-possessed, and generous,[94] but also must make best sense of everything.

And is it also how we can participate in what Aquinas calls complete fulfilment {beatitudo perfecta}? Can we hope for the realization of what we have called integral human fulfilment— fulfilment of all human persons and communities? At this moment in his most elaborate and philosophical exploration of the point of everything, Aquinas switches to a new train of thought. Any created reality which is capable of understanding has the opportunity of participating in likeness to God in a uniquely close and fulfilling way, through understanding God: 'Since all creatures, even those without understanding, are ordered to God as to an ultimate end, all attain this end in so far as they share something of the likeness {similitudine} of God; intelligent creatures attain him in a more special way, by their own operation, in understanding him. So the intelligent creature's end must be: to understand God.'[95]

With this thought Aquinas begins a long argument (more than 100 pages in a standard English translation) in which the strategy of understanding the point of human existence from God's standpoint (so to speak) is supported by the classical strategy for identifying the unifying point of human existence: review our human desires and eliminate (as candidates for this integrating role) all those objects of desire (e.g. power, reputation, sensory pleasure) which cannot make fully satisfactory sense of one's own or one's communities' whole life. The conclusion on which these strategies converge is that perfect fulfilment {felicitas}, a condition in which all human desires are fulfilled and all human efforts find their completion, *consists in* an uninterruptable vision of God (and in God of the other truths that we naturally desire to know), a vision which

---

[93] Plato quite rightly adds, at this point in the argument, that we become like the God by being 'moderate': *Laws* 4. 716d; likewise *Republic* 6. 501b.

[94] *ScG* III c. 21: we tend towards the divine likeness in many ways, and most perfectly and ultimately inasmuch as we are the cause of other beings, and in this way one is most godlike in being a co-operator with God (n. 8 [2023]; similarly e.g. II *Sent.* d. 9 a. 1 ad 7; *Ver.* q. 9 a. 2c); also c. 22; *Comp.* I c. 103 [205–6]; *ST* I q. 103 a. 4c (we, like other created realities, are made like {assimila[n]tur} God in two ways: by being good and by moving other created realities towards goodness {ad bonitatem}). See also n. 107 below.

[95] *ScG* III c. 25 n. 1 [2055]; cf. II *Sent.* d. 1 q. 2 a. 2 ad 4 (understanding and loving God).

would be possible, by divine act, after one's bodily, active, and secular life {activa et civilis vita} is ended in death.[96]

This argument seems to me to succeed, but only when understood restrictively. It succeeds in showing that human *beatitudo perfecta* must be structured around seeing God (in a way that philosophy and faith can now only gesture towards), and be free from susceptibility to illness, injury, loss, or death. It succeeds in showing that such a *beatitudo* would be a further dimension of likeness, *assimilatio*, to God inasmuch as God's life is (a) the activity of an understanding totally intelligible to (and fitting object of) itself[97] and (b) a condition of complete *beatitudo*.[98] And it succeeds in showing that our *beatitudo* would also add to *assimilatio* a much closer relationship, a kind of joining up, cleaving, *adhaesio*, to God inasmuch as one would understand God and not only understand but also, inevitably, love him—something not possible for subrational created realities.[99] Complete fulfilment, thus understood, can have its beginning {inchoatio} in this life for all who are willing to live by their understanding (however implicit) that there is a God who is governing and providing for the universe, and who is able somehow, as part of that providence, to liberate human beings from whatever now makes their fulfilment incomplete.[100] For such willingness is a kind of love for this provident God, a kind of hope to be made like God by being freed from one's incompleteness and failings as a human person, and a kind of readiness to believe whatever God may choose to communicate. And one thereby accepts a new and most adequate reason for

---

[96] *ScG* III c. 25 n. 10 [2063], c. 63 nn. 1, 10 [2377, 2383].

[97] So Aristotle concludes that contemplative understanding must be for us the greatest source of *eudaimonia* because it makes us most like {syngenestate} the God: *Nic. Eth.* 10. 8. 1178^{b}24, 1179^{a}28.

[98] See also *Nic. Eth.* 1. 8. 1099^{b}17; *Eth.* 1. 14 n. 5 [169]: 'since *felicitas* is virtue's prize and point {finis}, it follows that it is something optimal and godlike {divinum} and blessed {beatus}—for we call something godlike not only in so far as it is from God but also in so far as it likens {assimilat} us to God by the excellence of its goodness'.

[99] *ScG* III c. 116 n. 2 with n. 1 and c. 115 nn. 3–5, c. 121 n. 1, c. 128 n. 2, c. 138 n. 1; *ST* I q. 108 a. 8c, I-II q. 1 a. 8c, q. 114 a. 10c, II-II q. 23 a. 7c; *Comp.* II c. 9 [581, 591]; *Ps.* 32.11 ad v. 11. So 'our ultimate end' can refer to our *adhaesio* to God (or possession of God in vision) or to that which one wishes to adhere to (or see), namely God himself: see IV *Sent.* d. 49 q. 1 a. 2 sol. 1c; I-II q. 1 a. 8c, q. 2 a. 7c, q. 3 a. 1c. In *ST* this *adhaesio* is more commonly rendered *coniunctio*; but see also II-II q. 140 a. 1c: 'divine law's purpose {finis} is that human beings may be joined to God {inhaerea[n]t Deo}'. See also v. 4 n. d above.

[100] On the beginning of *beatitudo perfecta* by a love of God (made possible by our ready—'natural'—understanding of God's existence, perfection, and providence) sufficient to motivate an at least anticipatory and implicit faith and hope for fulfilment in likeness and relationship to him, see II-II q. 2 a. 7 ad 3 with a. 8 ad 1, q. 4 a. 1c, a. 3c; *Ver.* q. 14 a. 2c.

following the rational principle of love of neighbour as oneself, inasmuch as one now understands that every human being is, like oneself, the object of this special, interpersonal divine providence and possible fulfilment in relationship with God.[101]

But only when understood in a quite restricted sense does the argument of Aquinas about the content of human fulfilment succeed. For, firstly, it does not show—perhaps does not really try to show, philosophically—that such fulfilment is no mere attractive possibility but also a reality. Perhaps the nearest Aquinas gets to offering such an argument is this: 'Since it is impossible for a natural desire to be in vain {inane}, which would indeed be the case if it were not possible to reach an understanding of the divine substance, which naturally all minds desire, it is necessary to say that it is possible for the substance of God to be seen intellectually . . . by our souls.'[102]

By saying 'it is necessary to say that it is possible . . .', Aquinas leaves open the possibility that the argument from natural desire implies that it will be fulfilled; but he stops short of asserting it. Having argued philosophically to the existence of a creator who lacks nothing in goodness, one has sufficient reasons to postulate that the structure of creation, including natural human desires, makes good sense. But precisely what, in the actual conditions of the universe taken as a whole, is necessary lest the natural desire be in vain is not something we are in a position to judge—certainly not with the resources proper to philosophy. For, confronting the deficiencies and evils which Aquinas fully accepts are to be found in the universe,[103] we all are in the position of *ignorantes* and must be careful not to incur his just criticism of those who (like the *rusticus* or *idiota* in the laboratory) regard as unintelligible what they do not understand.

Second, and in the long run more importantly, the arguments for a purely contemplative human fulfilment must be taken together with the reasons which Aquinas himself provides for significantly widening *beatitudo*'s content. Our most potent and maximal *adhaesio* to God would involve bringing the understanding

---

[101] See e.g. *In Rom.* c. 13. 2 ad v. 9 [1056]: 'all human beings are called our neighbours, because they either have *beatitudo* already or are on the way {tendunt} along with us towards it'.   [102] *ScG* III c. 51 n. 1 [2284].

[103] *In Iob* prol. reflects on materialist denials of divine existence and providence as responses to the apparent triumph of evildoers and the ruinous adversities of the innocent through both natural causes and the wickedness of others. And see at n. 40 above.

(contemplation) of a good to understanding's natural (i.e. reasonable) completion in love.[104] One's soul's condition after separation from one's body by death is imperfect;[105] indeed, a soul's existence in that condition is not really the existence of a person (but only of a kind of remnant of the person)—so that such a condition, albeit rich in understanding of God, can hardly be anybody's complete fulfilment.[106] And since God is not merely contemplative but also active in causing the universe and thereby bestowing on created realities their share of the goodness of actuality, so too our likeness or assimilation as created realities to God must include our being active in benefiting other beings.[107] How then could *beatitudo perfecta* fail to include, over and above contemplation and love of the God thus seen, a willing sharing of goods with other human persons, in friendship?

In his later works, Aquinas seems not to pose this objection squarely.[108] In his *Commentary on the Sentences* he had faced the problem more plainly, and had conceded (1) that contemplation as such is a solitary activity {propria assequenti . . . singulariter}, whereas practical understanding can be directed to a good or goods both individual and common {propria et communis} inasmuch as, like the leader of a group {rector multitudinis}, one can be directing both oneself and others to the good in question; and (2) that 'it is more perfect to have a perfection and convey it {transfundere} to others than merely to have it in and for oneself'; a contemplator

---

[104] e.g. *ScG* III c. 118 n. 2 [2902]. Indeed, 'contemplation' here must not be understood as a kind of 'gazing at', but rather as something like (as well as unlike) the inward understanding one has of one's own ideas and intentions, and of what one is doing *in* (say) moving one's hand in signing one's name; so (*ScG* IV c. 41 n. 13 [3800]) *beatitudo perfecta* is a sharing in and enjoyment of the divine contemplative and practical understanding, whereby God is united to human creatures in a manner higher and more unimaginable and inexpressible {eminentius et ineffabilius} than one's mind's unity with one's tongue in repartee.

[105] See *ScG* II c. 83 n. 11 [1660]; *ST* I q. 89 a. 1c.

[106] 'My soul is not me {anima mea non est ego}; and so, even if [my] soul attained salvation in another life, still neither I nor anybody else would have attained it' (*In I Cor.* 15. 2 ad v. 19 [924]); also *Ent.* c. 2, line 206 [12]; IV *Sent.* d. 44 q. 1 a. 1 sol. 2 ad 3; *Quodl.* VII q. 5 a. 1 ad 3; *ST* I q. 75 a. 4 ('[anima] non potest dici . . . persona . . . cum [anima] sit pars speciei humanae'); v.8 at n. 216 above. Still, Aquinas disconcertingly maintains that the restoration of one's whole self in bodiliness is not of the *esse* but rather of the *bene esse* of beatitude: I-II q. 4 a. 5c. See also IV *Sent.* d. 43 a. 1 sol. 1c. One's eventual bodily participation in *beatitudo* will be a kind of resultant {redundantia} of one's soul's immediate fulfilment and glorification by admission to an understanding and corresponding love of God's very being: I-II q. 4 a. 6c, II-II q. 26 a. 5c; *ScG* IV c. 86 n. 2 [4219].

[107] See n. 94 above; *ScG* II c. 45 n. 4 [1222] (n. 83 above), III c. 22 nn. 2, 5 [2025, 2028b]; c. 24 n. 8 [2053]; *Comp.* I c. 103; IV. 3 at n. 57, IV. 4 at n. 85 above. [108] Cf. I-II q. 3 a. 5.

{speculator} who helps others equally {aequaliter sibi} to contemplate is therefore more perfect than one who merely contemplates.[109] When he none the less concludes (leaving the problem unanswered) that *beatitudo* 'consists in' contemplation only {solum},[110] we must take the conclusion as tacitly hypothesizing—for the sake of argument—a condition of things in which the human person contemplating God could not benefit any other person in any way.

In the *Summa Theologiae*, finally, he directly raises the question whether *beatitudo* includes the fellowship of friends {societas amicorum}. His reply makes two points. If there were only one human soul to love God, that soul would not need friends to love. But on the supposition that human souls in the relevant condition will have human neighbours {proximi}, friendship will be, not a necessary or essential part of *beatitudo*, but rather a kind of concomitant (somewhat like pleasure is a concomitant of good action) which somehow adds to the goodness of *beatitudo* (is of its *bene esse*).[111] The idea of a more-complete complete fulfilment reveals the strain imposed by Aquinas' insistence that ultimate fulfilment wholly 'consists in' contemplation. Nor does he stay to explore what, in this condition of things, might be shared amongst friends and how they might benefit each other.[112]

In short, Aquinas' many statements about contemplation as the whole substance and content of complete fulfilment[113] must be taken as responses to a highly restricted question: about whether one would be fulfilled if (contrary to fact) one were reduced to being a disembodied and humanly solitary soul, gifted only, and alone of all human beings, with a direct understanding of God. To that question, the divine being's perfection of actuality and intelligibility, of intelligence, power, and *liberalitas*, leaves room for only one answer. But just how artificial this hypothesis of disembodied solitariness really is becomes clear in all that divine revelation teaches.

---

[109] IV *Sent*. d. 49 q. 1 a. 1 sol. 3 ad 1 and ad 2.

[110] Ibid. sol. 3c. In III *Sent*. d. 35 q. 1 a. 4 sol. 3c he has, however, stated that elements of the active life will remain in heaven; in *ST* II-II q. 181 a. 4c, too, he explicitly allows for this possibility, insisting only that if there are in heaven external acts (of a kind which the 'active life' has as its purpose) they will have as their purpose contemplation.

[111] I-II q. 4 a. 8c and ad 3; III *Sent*. d. 18 q. 1 a. 4 sol. 3c.

[112] See, however, I-II q. 68 a. 6 ad 2, II-II q. 121 a. 1 ad 3.

[113] Begin with I *Sent*. q. 1 d. 1 a. 1c!

x.5. *Revelation as Public Reasons: Church and States*

For the communication from God to human persons, when it definitively came, proved to be, as Aquinas sees it, radically public and social in its making, in its transmission, and in its account of the point and fulfilment of our life as individuals and groups.

The divine wisdom chose, Aquinas says, to reveal a number of things, some of them already accessible to philosophical or common-sense reasoning from experience,[114] and some which we have otherwise no ground in experience to accept. But all these things were *shown*, indeed visibly shown, by 'appropriate evidences {argumenta}' and an 'efficacy of proof' which—without threats or seductive promises, and in the midst of tyrannical persecutions—brought flocking to the Christian faith a great multitude of people, from most learned {sapientissimorum} to most simple, all accepting a faith which preaches truths mysterious and otherwise inaccessible, restricts our fleshly pleasures, and teaches the detachment from this-worldly concerns which Jesus from Nazareth showed.[115] This remarkable 'conversion of the world', beginning with the public transformation of Jesus's disciples and other simple and untutored people {illiterati et simplices}, was, Aquinas judges, the greatest and most clearly validating {certissimum} of the signs which were 'visibly showed' in confirmation of God's self-disclosure, surpassing even the argument provided[116] by other wonderful accompaniments such as miraculous cures and the raising of dead people to life.[117] But the revelatory power and credit-worthiness of Christ's teaching should be ascribed also to his persuasive authority and manifest personal virtue, and the

---

[114] People's knowledge of natural law by the light of natural reason is, at the same time, a means by which God 'comes to' people, a kind of revelation which, being by 'internal inspiration', is not 'public' in the strongest sense: see *In Matt.* 21 ad v. 28 [1727].

[115] *ScG* I c. 6 n. 1 [36–7] {read *contemptus mundi* with *Retra.* 1 [735]}; *Cred.* 1 [prol.] [867].

[116] *Pot.* q. 6 a. 9c; *ScG* IV c. 55 n. 11 [3941]; *ST* II-II q. 1 a. 2 ad 1, III q. 42 a. 1 ad 2, q. 43, q. 44 esp. a. 3; *Cred.* [prol.] [866]. The miracles which Christ worked confirmed his claim to be the son of and equal to God: *Quodl.* II q. 4 a. 1 ad 4. The accounts of them, e.g. in Matthew's Gospel, are rich in further meanings (since both the events narrated and the narrative itself were intended to symbolize aspects of the interaction between divine purpose and human responses), but are also, and primarily, *true history* {vera historia}: *In Matt.* prol. [10]. See also II. 5 at nn. 55–6 (and n. q) above.

[117] *ScG* I c. 6 nn. 1–4 [35–41]; *Rat.* c. 7 [996–7]; also generally confirmatory is the fulfilment of prophecies publicly made long before by the prophets of Israel: *ScG* I c. 6 n. 1 [35].

---

inherent excellence of what he taught—something he deliberately left to be judged from the public preaching and writing of those who had witnessed his own public life and works.[118]

What those apostles and their successors propose for belief, though it includes some propositions outrunning our experience and our comprehension, is a set of propositions, including reasons for choice and action, which reasonable people can accept and live by in their private and public choices and activity.[119] Some of these propositions (e.g. that God exists and is one and intelligent) are demonstrable by reason; some others (e.g. that Jesus lived, and spoke and acted with preternatural, credit-worthy authority) are fully open to rational discourse and assessment; the others (e.g. that in Jesus human nature was united to God in one person, and that after their death human persons will by divine power be resurrected body and soul) are mysterious but can be shown rationally to involve no contradiction or impossibility and so can, and should, be accepted as true on the authority of divine revelation.[120] The overarching judgement that all the propositions so authenticated are to be believed with confidence rightly takes its place alongside other important beliefs which, though neither self-evident nor deducible from the self-evident, are rationally foundational to a sound intellectual life and to fully appropriate public social institutions such as universities and states.[121]

God's self-communication included propositions about complete human fulfilment in eternal life; and about the community which Jesus established both to transmit that divine promise of eternal life and to help people help each other, through their own individual free choices, to become ready for that life (and indeed somehow already participants in it). This community, the Church, is both continuous with and a radical reconstituting of the people earlier formed under God's guidance to prepare gradually, over

---

[118] III q. 40 a. 1c and ad 1, q. 42 a. 1 ad 2, a. 4c.

[119] So, unless disbelief is question-beggingly presupposed (as in Hume's arguments against miracles), these are *public* and *publicly accessible* reasons.

[120] *ScG* I c. 7, c. 9 nn. 2–3 [52–6]; see also II-II q. 2 a. 10 ad 2. So a miracle such as the resurrection of Jesus leaves even a witness like Thomas (who touched the marks of the nails in the risen body of the crucified Jesus) in a position where reasonable faith ('this is God') not unreasonably goes further than bare reason ('this man has risen from the dead'): III *Sent.* d. 21 q. 2 a. 3 ad 2; see also II-II q. 1 a. 4c and ad 1.

[121] II-II q. 1 a. 4 ad 2, a. 5 ad 3, q. 6 a. 1 ad 1; *ScG* I c. 6 n. 1 [35–6]; on the public character of universities, VII.7 n. c.

centuries, for Jesus's definitive, final revelation.[122] Open to everyone, of whatever origin or status, the Church has its own governing arrangements, its own constitution and law (partly established definitively by Jesus and partly enacted subject to amendment and repeal by its current leaders), and its own mission and jurisdiction. Its concern is solely to serve as a way for human beings to make themselves ready for eternal life. So human associations are henceforth of two fundamentally distinct types.

On the one side is the 'temporal' or 'secular': the names connote a time-bound association and role; Aquinas uses them, in relevant contexts, as synonymous with 'worldly' {mundanus} and 'civil' or 'political' {civilis}. The contrast is with a 'spiritual' association organized, by divine inspiration, towards eternal participation (albeit in a somehow bodily way) in the non-bodily (spiritual, mind-like) life of God.[123] The spiritual association *par excellence* is a Church (in Latin *ecclesia*, transliterating the Greek synonym for Latin's *congregatio*); paradigmatically it is the society of 'the faithful' {congregatio fidelium}, the Christian people {populus christianus} to which 'every Christian person belongs' (save perhaps those who have wilfully separated themselves off into 'sects').[124] The Catholic (= universal[125]) Church is governed by the successors of the apostles, whom Christ appointed as its leaders.[126]

The sole organizing purpose of the Catholic Church is that there be *beatitudo perfecta* in eternal life for, so far as possible, all human persons, of every family, association, state, and people. It has no 'secular' purposes. Responsibility for human affairs is thus divided between, on the one side, the Church and, on the other side, secular societies, most notably states and families. The source of the division of responsibilities, as of the responsibilities (and

[122] On the law and constitution of Israel as essentially an educative, preparatory institution, see I-II q. 107 a. 1c, q. 91 a. 5 ad 2, q. 98 a. 2c and ad 1, q. 99 a. 6c; ScG IV c. 55 n. 12 [3942]. To serve God in the synagogue was to belong to the Church in which God is now to be served: IV Sent. d. 27 q. 3 a. 1 sol. 3c (= Supp. q. 66 a. 3c).

[123] See e.g. II-II q. 183 a. 1c, a. 2 ad 3; see also VII. 7 n. 142 above.

[124] Cred. 12 [a. 9] [972]; ScG IV c. 78 nn. 1–2 [4119–20] {populus fidelium; collectio fidelium}; II-II q. 147 a. 3c.

[125] Cred. 12 [a. 9] [982–4]. 'Universal' means extending throughout the world, non-discriminatory between sorts {conditiones} of human person, extending in time from the earliest foundation of Israel down to the end of this world, and solidly grounded {firma} on Christ: ibid. And 'only the Church of Peter has always been solid {firma} in the faith of the other apostles, since in all the other [churches] there is either no faith or a faith mixed with errors': ibid. The Church is to be, but has not yet been, established in every people, by preaching: I-II q. 106 a. 4 ad 4. (And see p. 54 n. 5 above.)

[126] ScG IV c. 76 nn. 8–9 [4109–10].

corresponding authorities), is the wisdom and will of God,[127] which is made plain to us in two ways: partly by the natural law which is accessible to unaided reason but has its ultimate source of normativity as being the mind (wisdom) of God as far as our reason can thus share in it; and partly by those provisions of the divine law which were revealed definitively in Jesus Christ.

The rationale of secular authority is, for a parent, to manage a household in which the children are nurtured and protected, fairly dealt with, and educated by instruction and discipline, in the hope that they will gain eternal life;[128] for the lawmakers and other rulers of a state, the secular mission to secure peace and justice within its territory.[129] The rationale for spiritual or ecclesiastical authority—its mission—is to bring to faith in the revelation as many people as can be persuaded freely to accept it[130] and to help all its members, explicit and implicit, so to live that their lives may by divine power extend, after their death, to eternal life with God.

The distinction of rationales is also a jurisdictional division. The Church's leaders have no jurisdiction over secular matters except in so far as the choice of a member of the Church,[131] albeit in a secular matter, is or would be seriously immoral and thus of a kind incompatible with genuine love of God (and so with eternal life with God), or without just cause would impede the Church's very mission. A parent has no jurisdiction over a child's free choices except in so far as they violate the moral rights of other members of the family or the parent's responsibility for the child's education and moral upbringing.[132] State government and law have no right

---

[127] 'Spiritual authority {potestas} and secular authority are both derived {deducitur} from divine authority': II *Sent.* d. 44 ex. ad 4.

[128] So the procreating which can be a motive for marital intercourse can best be regarded as an act of the virtue of *religio*: IV *Sent.* d. 26 q. 1 a. 4c (= *Supp.* q. 41 a. 4c).

[129] So the 'justice by which human society is governed in line with secular political good {ad bonum civile} can be sufficiently attained through the principles of natural right available to everyone {principia iuris naturalis homini indita}': *Ver.* q. 12 a. 3 ad 11.

[130] In no way by compulsion, only by persuasion {persuasione}: II-II q. 10 a. 8c and a. 12c; *Quodl.* III q. 5 a. 1 ad 2. As to those who have once accepted the faith, see IX.2 n. b (p. 293) above.

[131] Over persons not its admitted members the law and government of the Church have no jurisdiction at all: II-II q. 10 a. 9c.

[132] And except in those matters, 'a child is not bound to obey its earthly father': *Quodl.* II q. 5 a. 1c. Children are not bound to obey their parents in vocational decisions such as undertaking marriage or a state of dedicated virginity 'or other things of that kind': II-II q. 104 a. 5c; see also II-II q. 189 a. 6c; also II-II q. 10 a. 12c (children capable of making free choices have the right to choose whether or not to accept baptism); IV *Sent.* d. 29 a. 4; v. 7 at nn. 171–2, VII.6 at nn. 96–101 above.

to direct the Church's leaders, or its members in their religious affairs, except in so far as the state's peace and justice would otherwise be violated. So, although the Church's rationale is obviously superior to the state's—since for everyone, complete fulfilment in eternal life is more important than any other set of goods—it is also true that 'in those matters which pertain to political good {bonum civile}, *secular rather than spiritual* authority is to be obeyed {magis obediendum potestati saeculari quam spirituali}'[133] by the Church's members.

The state's leaders, if they are members of the Church, ought to obey the Church's leaders in all matters within the latter's authority.[134] (This whole teaching on Church and state is, after all, a teaching addressed precisely to the conscience of one who acknowledges the truth of the Church's claim to be founded by God as the primary means of transmitting divine revelation through the remainder of human history.) The Church's authority is of two distinct kinds.

On the one hand it is a legislative, executive, and judicial jurisdiction, like the governmental authority found in any other 'complete community'; so far forth, its binding force extends only to members of the Church,[135] and it can be concerned only with the organization of the ecclesiastical community to help its members towards eternal life with God. On the other hand, as successors of Jesus's apostles and thus as agents for transmitting God's revelation, which includes and confirms truths accessible to unaided reason, the leaders of the Church have a quite different kind of authority, essentially non-governmental in its content. This is their authority, from Christ, to identify and hand on (by teaching) truths of faith and morals, including propositions which are also part of the natural law. When given in a fully authoritative way, moral teaching of this sort gives sound guidance to everyone, even

---

[133] II *Sent.* d. 44 ex. ad 4. The following sentence, stating an exception in relation to the papacy, is generally and reasonably taken to refer to the fact that within the papal territories near Rome the Pope had secular as well as spiritual authority. With the position stated in the text and II *Sent.* d. 44, there is nothing really inconsistent in *Reg.* II. 3 [I. 14/15] [110–11] [819–20] and II. 4 [I. 15/16] [114] [822]; see Boyle (1974); Torrell (1996: 13–14).

[134] II *Sent.* d. 44 ex. ad 1; *Reg.* II. 3 [I. 14/15] [110–11] [819–20], II. 4 (1.15) [114] [822]; II-II q. 60 a. 6 ad 3.

[135] The Church's governing authorities have indirectly {indirecte} a kind of power over someone who is not a member of the Church, in so far as they can rightly forbid members of the Church to have dealings with the non-member on account of the latter's fault: *In I Cor.* 5. 3 ad v. 12 [259].

though only one who accepts the divine revelation as transmitted by the Apostles will accept that such acts of teaching—though they cannot *make* their propositional content true, and are essentially different from legislative acts—do guarantee the truth of their content and the certainty of judgements affirming that content. This has important consequences. A Church leader,[136] aware that a choice which he believes has been or may be made by some person or group is seriously wrongful in type, has the authority to state publicly that nobody should make such choices. Moreover, Aquinas saw no reason why such a public judgement should not be specific and even particular, identifying as immoral the act of some particular person, for example some king or other political ruler.[137]

At the same time, Aquinas does clearly state and affirm the distinction between ecclesiastical action and secular constitutional consequences.[138] One could articulate the consequences as follows. The ruler in question, if a member of the Church, could indeed be expelled from the communion, the active fellowship, of the Church. If, under and by virtue of the constitution of the ruler's political community, the ecclesiastical act of excommunication had the effect of invalidating the ruler's civil authority, that would be a proper effect and would involve no violation of the distinction between Church and state. For the proper rationale of the ecclesiastical act would be purely ecclesiastical, and secular consequences, if any, would result only by reason of the secular

---

[136] Say, the Roman Pontiff as successor to the first apostolic leader of the Apostles themselves: see e.g. *Impugn.* c. 3, lines 456–8 [II. 2] [66]; *ScG* IV c. 76 nn. 8–9 [4109–10]; *Reg.* II. 3 [I. 14/15] [112] [821]; *Graec.* II cc. 32–8; IV *Sent.* d. 24 q. 3 a. 2 sol. 3c.

[137] The two preceding paragraphs state the valid substance of the notion of the Church's 'two swords' (see IX.2 n. b above), stripped of its peculiar form of instantiation in the polities of Aquinas' era, which punished the ecclesiastical offences of heresy and schism as secular crimes, thereby prejudicing (1) the Church's character as an association which one adheres to by persuasion not compulsion (see n. 130 above), (2) the state's character as a body with compulsory jurisdiction limited to justice and peace (see VII.2–5 above), and therefore (3) one's right not to be coerced, by other people or associations, in respect of any of one's religious acts, subject always to '[a] the effective safeguarding and peaceful harmonizing of every citizen's rights, [b] adequate protection for that decent public peace which consists in an ordered living together in true justice, and [c] a due upholding of public morality' (see Vatican II, Declaration on Religious Liberty, *Dignitatis Humanae*, 1965, sects. 1, 2, and 7). And see IX.2 n. b (p. 292) above.

[138] For example, II-II q. 12 a. 2c: 'unfaithfulness by itself is not incompatible with the right to rule {non repugnat dominio}, since that right was established by the law of peoples which is a matter of human law or right {ius humanum}, whereas the distinction between the faithful and the unfaithful is a matter of divine law or right which does not suppress the human law or right {per quod non tollitur ius humanum}'.

constitution in force in the state in question. But Aquinas fails to articulate this principled distinction with clarity. Running together the ecclesiastical rationale and the secular constitutional result, he says that the Church has 'the authority of curbing secular leaders {potestatem terrenos principes compescendi}',[139] and that the secular rulers in such cases lose their authority 'by [the Church's] judgement {sententialiter}'.[140] Nor does he give attention here to the important difference between stating a true precept of moral principle and applying it to facts which may well be both complex and obscure.

Some of Aquinas' statements about proper relations between the Church and secular governments are distinctly time-bound.[141] But the right and responsibility of the Church's leaders to teach moral truths, not only as they apply to private life but also as they apply to political affairs or the actions of groups and associations entirely independent of the Church, and the responsibility of members of the Church, both in their public and their private lives, to put those truths into practice in the circumstances as they themselves judge them to be, are entailments of three positions central to Aquinas' social and political theory: (1) divine revelation can be seen to be true for reasons I shall summarily call public reasons, and therefore gives public reasons for private and public choices and actions; (2) its transmission was entrusted by its divine author to a non-secular, essentially non-state, association with its own autonomous constitution and government, as public and independent as any state can be; (3) the central subject-matter of divine revelation

---

[139] II-II q. 12 a. 2 ad 1. See also e.g. II-II q. 39 a. 4 ad 3 on the Church 'administering to [schismatics] the [medicinal] coercion of [i.e. by] the "secular arm" {brachii saecularis}'; IX.2 n. b (p. 292) above.

[140] II-II q. 12 a. 2c; and where, in such cases, the rulers in question are members of the Church, the Church is 'punishing them by judgement {sententialiter}, it being appropriate that they be punished by being unable [any longer] to rule their faithful subjects'. And if the rulers in question are not members, the Church—though accepting their secular authority as legitimate and binding on Catholics within their jurisdiction (II-II q. 10 a. 10), and though having no spiritual authority or judgement over them—can none the less, in an extended sense, 'have a temporal judgement over them' inasmuch as *members* of the Church, acting on their own authority, punish them temporally in the event of their wrongdoing: ibid. a. 9c.

[141] For example, the proposition that [some? all?] kings are vassals of the Pope (*Quodl.* XII q. 13 a. un. ad 2). Even when taken as a way of saying that in their relations with the papacy, kings have both duties and rights (Wilks 1963: 321), this feudal way of defining the relations between Church and state was dated even by the time Aquinas used it. Another example: II-II q. 10 a. 10 (the Church must prohibit acquisition by unbelievers of secular authority over believers, and may by an ordinance deprive unbelievers—who otherwise have legitimate authority over believers—of their authority).

is the complete human fulfilment attainable by our free co-operation with God's wisdom and *liberalitas*.

x.6. *Complete Fulfilment of Individuals in Society*

And that fulfilment is radically social. Though Aquinas never softens his thesis that it 'consists in' the intellectual vision of God, the narrow philosophical argument which advances that claim broadens out, in its theological (i.e. revelation-based) counterpart, to affirm a yet more complete fulfilment. The definitive expressing of God's goodness in heavenly human happiness—blessedness {beatitudo}—will include also the participation, body and soul, of many human persons,[142] in an order (peace) such that 'that *beatitudo* consists in two things {in duobus consistit}: seeing God and love of neighbour'.[143]

When Aquinas considers the appalling subject of the fate of those who will not in any way participate in complete human fulfilment, his account of their condition sometimes puts first their separation not only from God but also from every good human person.[144] One's social and political theory is bound to be affected markedly by one's rejection or, like Aquinas, acceptance of Christ's teachings about the permanent misery of those who have died in a state of willed refusal to adhere to God (even implicitly)[145] by hope[b] and love. But though that effect is likely to be most noticeable in assumptions about the seriousness of human wrongdoing and in accounts of human retributive justice, and though Aquinas casts his account of damnation in terms of divine 'punishment', the term is being used there in a highly extended sense and, like the imagery of a divine judgement and sentence, is liable to be badly misunderstood. For, as Aquinas makes clear, one's final destiny is settled

---

[142] IV *Sent.* d. 49 q. 2 a. 2 (= *Supp.* q. 92 a. 2) ad 6; I-II q. 3 a. 3 ad 3, q. 4 aa. 5, 6, and 8. How Aquinas personally envisaged heavenly fulfilment may perhaps be discerned from a poem plausibly attributed to him; it certainly conveys his teaching, is in line with his approach to poetry and prayer, and seems likely to be actually his: see n. c (pp. 333-4) below for the text (Verardo 1954: 288) and a translation which seeks to convey something of the Latin's texture. [143] *In Matt.* 5 ad v. 8 [433].

[144] See *Cred.* 15 [a. 12] [1017]; *In Matt.* 24 ad v. 5 [2008] ('maxima poena'); *In Ioann.* 15. 1 ad v. 6 [1994]; *Ps.* 2.9 ad v. 9; *ScG* III c. 144 n. 11 [3186]. On the separation, see *Quodl.* VIII q. 7 a. 1. [145] See text at n. 100 above; n. 154 below.

definitively at the time of one's death.[146] There is at this stage 'divine judgement' simply in this: the question whether there was such a wrongfully chosen refusal of adherence to God or not is answered with all divine clarity, insight, and objectivity. And there is 'punishment' and 'reward' (and on both grounds, consolation for those who have suffered evil in this life)[147] simply in this: the status of each person's soul will be fully in accord with a justice which takes into account absolutely everything and consists in the restoring of true equality between human beings within the vast community of persons created and preserved by divine mercy.[148] The later 'general' and 'final judgement' of all human persons, when human history is wound up and there is by extraordinary divine act a general reuniting of each human soul with the body whose particular form it is, will be no more (and no less) than a ratification and public manifestation of what was settled, for the fulfilled {beati} and the lost (damnati}, by their own free choices.[149] The *determinatio* of penalty which is central to human judging and punishment (or reprieve) of offenders has no counterpart in the resolution of the issue which for each of us—facing it, as we must, one by one, each as an individual—is the only issue that finally matters.

Until death, every member of the human race, without exception, is a member—some in potentiality {in potentia}, others in act(uality)—of the ordered multitude {multitudo ordinata} whose head is Jesus Christ:[150] the universal church of wayfarers {viatores} on the path to fulfilment with God. Just as one has duties of friendly co-operation and assistance to one's relatives and the members of one's household in domestic matters, and analogous

---

[146] III q. 59 a. 5 ad 1 and 3; IV *Sent.* d. 47 q. 1 a. 1 sol. 1c (= *Supp.* q. 88 a. 1c) and ad 1; *ScG* IV c. 91 nn. 1–2 [4246–7], cc. 93, 95; in the case of those souls which adhere to God, their admission to the vision of God will, however, be delayed if there remains in them some residue of immoral attachment to things other than God: see c. 91 n. 6 [4251], c. 94.

[147] See e.g. *In Matt.* 5 ad v. 5 [423]; and see VI. 5 n. 141 above.

[148] See I-II q. 87 a. 6, III q. 86 a. 4. What the lost undergo—their 'penalty'—consists essentially in their 'separation from God and the suffering resulting from that separation' (*Mal.* q. 2 a. 2 ad 8), a separation willed by God only because they have made themselves unsuitable for what they have lost (*Mal.* q. 1 a. 5c). [149] III q. 59 a. 5c and ad 1.

[150] And which therefore is called, by metaphor {in metaphoric[e] locution[e] . . . similitudinarie dictum}, the 'mystical body of Christ': III q. 8 a. 1 ad 2. This membership (albeit *in potentia*) of the pagan Indians in the 'body of Christ', precisely as a conclusion deducible from Aquinas' teaching in III q. 8 a. 3 that 'Christ is the head of all human beings', was fundamental to Las Casas' defence of the [West] Indians against the injustices involved in Spanish colonization in the 16th century: André-Vincent (1976).

duties to one's fellow citizens in the affairs of civil life, so one owes to everyone, including one's enemies, the duty to desire their eternal well-being, to pray[151] for it, and to work for it as befits one's situation.[152] The active life of those who, seeking to express God's goodness {gloriam Dei . . . quaer[entes]}, work for the well-being, including the eternal well-being, of their fellow human beings is in important ways *better* than a life spent in the sort of contemplation of God now available to us.[153] After their death, those who kept (or even at the last moment chose to set) their feet towards that true fulfilment will remain in that vast corporation, members of the completed Church,[154] a *congregatio* no longer of believers (explicit or implicit, in act or only in potentiality) but of people who actually understand and possess {comprehendentium}, no longer on the way {in via} but now in their homeland {in patria},[155] the divine city.[156] The members of that *congregatio* will enjoy the contemplative but loving vision of God. That 'seeing', that profound human understanding of God's very being, will not be to the exclusion of interest in human persons and other creatures; on the contrary, God's presence everywhere, and all-

---

[151] This may be a social act in more ways than one. For example: those people who have already begun, after their death, to understand (so far as is relevant to their fulfilment) the practical, creative understanding and intention by which God is constantly creating and sustaining everything can become aware of ('hear') the prayers which we address to them in God (who 'hears' them because nothing whatever in this world is hidden from that divine practical understanding without which nothing, including even our thoughts, could exist); and these people ('the saints') can add their own prayers to ours: IV *Sent.* d. 45 q. 3 (= *Supp.* q. 72) a. 1c. (On the utility of prayer, notwithstanding the all-embracing reach of divine providence, see *ScG* III c. 95.) So the fellowship {communio} among members of the Church is active even across the radical divide between the temporal world and the eternal.

[152] II-II q. 31 a. 2c and ad 1; III *Sent.* d. 29 q. un. a. 6c, d. 30 a. 2c.

[153] III *Sent.* d. 35 q. 1 a. 4 sol. 2c and ad 2. The fact that each of us can and should be active in work for the eternal well-being of others does not alter the fact that one can merit eternal life only by one's own, not other people's, act; for the shaping by which (given God's initiating and sustaining gift of his life—grace) one is made fit and ready for the gift of participation in divine glory must be self-shaping: IV *Sent.* d. 45 q. 2 a. 1 sol. 1c (= *Supp.* q. 71 a. 1c) and ad 1. See also n. 174 below.

[154] 'Outside the Church no avenue of salvation lies open for anyone': III q. 73 a. 3c; *Decret.* I, lines 690–1 [1182]. But the Church includes even those whose faith and hope are only implicit (whether because they have not heard, or have been unable to understand, the Gospel): see at n. 100 above and, on the salvation of 'barbarians' (here, non-Christians: *ScG* II c. 44 n. 1 [1203]), see II *Sent.* d. 28 a. 4 ad 4, III *Sent.* d. 25 q. 2 a. 2 sol. 2c and ad 3.

[155] III q. 8 a. 3, a. 4 ad 2. The explicit contrast between *in via* and *in patria* is used well over 200 times, everywhere in Aquinas, as his standard and favourite metaphor for the distinction between this life and eternal life with God.

[156] Citizenship in the city of God (and membership of the body of Christ which is the Church), unlike secular *civilitas*, will not be ended by death but rather perfected: III *Sent.* d. 33 q. 1 a. 4c.

---

governing power, will then be most perspicuous {clarissima perspicuitate} *in* and *through* an understanding of other people and their corporeal though transformed[157] environment.[158] And those who have this understanding will also *will* particular goods (whose relationship to what God wills for the good of the entire universe will now, unlike in their earthly life, be clear enough to them).[159]

For the character and life of that great society[160] of heaven, Aquinas the theologian uses the biblical metaphors. It will be the holy city Jerusalem[161] which—unlike, we may say, Plato's Socratic *polis*, *civitas*, or republic built only 'in thought'[162]—actually 'comes down'[163] from God into the final reality of human existence.[164] Its ruler {rector}—the originating source of its order—is the Lord, and to share in the vision of God is to participate like a citizen and member {quasi civis et socius}.[165] Though even then not fully equal to each other, and remaining widely diverse in individual character,[166] each and every member, female as well as male,[167] will in fact have the honour and status due to a king.[168] This 'kingdom of God is not distinguishable from *beatitudo [perfecta]*, except in the sense that the common good of a

---

[157] The transformation will be radical; in the new state of affairs, Aquinas thinks, 'nothing will act by virtue of nature, but only in accordance with the order {ordo} of divine justice . . . every natural [bodily] activity will cease': II *Sent.* d. 33 q. 2 a. 1 ad 3.

[158] IV *Sent.* d. 49 q. 2 (= *Supp.* q. 92) a. 2c; *ST* I q. 12 a. 3 ad 2; quoting Augustine, *De Civitate Dei* XXII. xxix. So 'the gifts of glory consist in three things: the fulfilment of one's soul in seeing God . . . the glorification of one's body . . . and a fitting environment {locus congruus}': II *Sent.* d. 22 q. 3 a. 1 ad 4.　　　　　[159] I-II q. 19 a. 10c and ad 1.

[160] Aquinas thinks that though great in size it will be much smaller than the 'fruitless multitude' of those who are lost (*In Rom.* 12. 2 ad v. 4 [973]); today it is very widely assumed that few if any will be lost. Both views, the latter more manifestly, seem to outrun the evidence in revelation.

[161] Jerusalem signifies the present Church but also our heavenly homeland {caelestis patria}: II *Sent.* d. 17 q. 3 a. 2 ad 6. See also *In Matt.* 21 ad v. 1 [1682]: 'moraliter Ierusalem interpretatur *visus pacis*, et significet *societatem bonorum*'.

[162] *Republic* 9. 592b.

[163] See *In Matt.* 4 ad v. 17 [362]: 'because we would not be able to ascend to God'.

[164] The polity {civilitas} of the Church will then be perfected, not abolished like the secular polity: III *Sent.* d. 33 q. 1 a. 4c.

[165] *Car.* a. 2c; similarly *Virt.* q. 1 a. 9c; *In Heb.* 11. 4 ad v. 16 [602]. Aquinas is attracted by the balance (so reminiscent of his theory of the families-based political community) in the Pauline statement that the blessed are 'fellow citizens and members of God's household {cives sanctorum et domestici Dei}' (Eph. 2: 19): e.g. *Car.* a. 2c; *Reg.* I. 9 [66] [785]; *In Matt.* 25 ad v. 14 [2032].　　　　　[166] See *In Rom.* prol. n. 1 [1]; *In Matt.* 20 ad v. 9 [1640].

[167] *ScG* IV c. 88 n. 3 [4229]. See also v. 7 n. 188 above.

[168] *ScG* III c. 63 n. 4 [2379b]; *Cred.* 15 [a. 12] [1013]; *Comp.* II c. 9 [582, 587]. Our homeland is a kingdom {regnum} precisely because of the indissoluble union of love {caritas} between its participants: *Decret.* II, lines 85–8 [1191].

whole group is distinguishable from the individual good of each of its members.'[169]

But Aquinas is also clear that the moral virtue most foundational to living out the practical truths disclosed or confirmed by revelation is a fitting, truthful humility.[170] Perhaps for this reason, perhaps also because the human good of the family is more fundamental than the goods of ruling, whether as king, president, director, or citizen, and perhaps because revelation disclosed that God's life itself is a quasi-familial communion of three persons, Thomas is fond of recalling that those who share in the vision of God are and will be 'sons and daughters {filii}'[171] or 'family members {familiares et domestici}'[172] in the divine household.[173]

Thus there will be completed {perficietur} the companionship and intimate sharing of life {societas et familiaris conversatio} which is the substance of friendship with God. By the divine gift[174] of somehow sharing in God's life {per gratiam}, all this can have its real beginnings here and now {hic in praesenti}, for any of us.[175]

---

[169] IV *Sent*. d. 49 q. 1 a. 2 sol. 5c. Cf. IV. 3 n. 48 above.

[170] See II-II q. 161 a. 1 ad 5 and a. 5, III q. 39 a. 3 ad 2; *In Ioann.* 10. 1 ad v. 1 [1368].

[171] III *Sent*. d. 19 q. 1 a. 4 sol. 1c. See also II-II q. 121 a. 1 ad 3.

[172] Cen. 361, 363–5; also 368. *Familiares* include trusted associates and close friends, as well as relatives.

[173] And they have there an ever-enduring right and status {perpetuum ius et dignitatem}: III q. 57 a. 6 ad 3.

[174] Apart from this sheer gift, no-one has—and none can by their natural powers do anything to earn—a right to participate in the divine family; it is only by *adoption* that anyone can do so: I-II q. 114 a. 3c; III *Sent*. d. 10 q. 2 a. 1 sol. 1c and ad 2, a. 2 sol 1c. Whatever God does as a matter of justice 'presupposes and is founded on the working of his mercy', i.e. pure generosity {liberalitas}: I q. 21 a. 4c; n. 72 above. For Aquinas a favourite image of the working of the divine gift within human freedom was, once again, political: 'the heart of the king is in the hand of the Lord, who will turn it just as he wills' (Prov. 21: 1), where 'king' signifies both power and the hardened sinfulness characteristic of the powerful—who while they live are none the less not beyond conversion under the influence of grace: e.g. III q. 86 a. 1c; *Mal.* q. 16 a. 5c; *Reg.* 1. 6 [1. 7] [51] [772].

[175] I-II q. 65 a. 5c. Not forgetting that that future glory and joy would be twofold, the fulfilment of sharing in God's life and the association with others {fruitio deitatis et communis sanctorum societas} (*In Heb.* 12. 4 ad v. 23 [706]), Aquinas will say (II *Sent.* d. 26 a. 1 ad 2): As *friend to friend, and not just as maker to product*, God leads them into a loving association so fulfilling that their *beatitudo* may share in his own glory and blessedness {non tantum diligit creaturam sicut artifex opus, sed etiam quadam amicabili societate, sicut amicus amicum, inquantum trahit eos in societatem suam fruitionis, ut in hoc eorum sit gloria et beatitudo quo Deus beatus est}.

Notes

a. *The fourth way . . .* There is reason to wonder about the explanation of not only the orderliness but also the orderedness of things, i.e. their levels of excellence as realities. For there is manifestly such an order of excellence (nobility): a molecule has all the perfections of an atom and further perfections, a cell has all the perfections of a molecule and more (organic integration and life), an animal all the perfections of a cell and many more (e.g. senses), and a human animal yet further perfections (especially intelligence and free choice, and therefore also a sense of humour {risibile: I q. 3 a. 4c, q. 44 a. 1 ad 1; *Ent.* c. 6, line 95 [37]; etc.} and a vocation for friendship; and fourth-order capacities such as language or musical composition and interpretation). At each level, going up, there is qualitatively more actuality, more being, greater natural goodness (perfection, excellence, worth); at each level, going down, there is less of these. But in none of the realities which we come upon in experience do we at any of these levels find a perfection which could not conceivably be enhanced in actuality, richness of being, and worth. (Indeed, since this ascent in perfection is by increase in complexity—see *Pol.* prol. n. 3 [3]—it could always be enhanced.) And if each such reality had what it takes to have *from/of itself* {ex se ipso} actuality, being, and goodness, there would be no reason for one reality to have *more* (or less) actuality, being, or goodness than any other. So the actuality, being, and worth of each such reality must in every case come from—be explained by—something else, something whose actuality, being, and inherent goodness (*1*) is unlimited (with the result that the question why *this* degree of perfection rather than *that* does not arise in relation to this reality) and (*2*) is somehow, and to varying degrees, shared (participated) in by every less perfect reality precisely as caused (explained) by this most perfect reality, God: *Pot.* q. 3 a. 5c; less perspicuously, I q. 2 a. 3c ('fourth way'); see also I q. 4 a. 2c, q. 44 a. 1c and ad 1; Geach (1961: 116, 124).

b. *Hell as a real possibility . . .* We should observe that if one goes to heaven no matter what one does, one can do nothing with the intention of sharing or helping others to share in God's kingdom and household, and so it becomes impossible to have that hope which Aquinas, in line with revelation and Christian tradition, considers a virtue as fundamental as faith and love. Those who lack this motive for choice and action—hope—will have many motivations towards either doing what they please, or adopting a rights-dissolving consequentialism in pursuit of some goal which, being necessarily other than the integral human fulfilment which is hope's specific object, will be arbitrarily narrowed to make the weighing of goods and bads seem possible.

c. *A prayer of longing for heaven which St Thomas Aquinas used to say silently, while contemplating . . .* See n. 142 above. For the translation of *agilitatis, subtilitatis,* and *impassibilitatis,* see III *Sent.* d. 16 q. 2 a. 2 obj. 4 and d. 21 q. 2 a. 3 ad 5c (which juxtapose all three with, as here, *claritas*), and ɪv *Sent.* d. 44. q. 2 a. 1 {impassibilitas}, a. 2 {subtilitas, agilitas}, a. 3 {agilitas}, a. 4 {claritas}, and *ScG* ɪv c. 86. In making sense of *infra de loci amoenitate*, anyone who has been to Aquinas' family castles (Roccasecca, Monte Sangiovanni) or to Monte Cassino, the three high places where he spent most of his first two decades, will understand the image of valleys, plains, foothills, and distant ranges all spread out in their richness and variety beneath the eye of the elevated observer.

O God of every consolation,
you who find in us nothing you have
not given,
on you I call:
After this life has reached its ending
may you be pleased to give me
knowledge of the first truth
and my will's fulfilment in your
majesty divine.

Te Deum totius consolationis
invoco,
qui nihil in nobis praeter tua dona
cernis,
ut mihi
post huius vitae terminum donare
digneris
cognitionem primae veritatis,
fruitionem divinae maiestatis.

Most generous rewarder:
Give my body, too,
the beauty of lightsomeness,
responsiveness of flesh to spirit,
fit readiness in glorified perfection,
assurance free from fear of harm.

Da etiam corpori meo,
largissime remunerator,
claritatis pulchritudinem,
agilitatis promptitudinem,
subtilitatis aptitudinem,
impassibilitatis fortitudinem.

And may you add to these
an overflow of riches,
inflow of delights,
confluence of goods,

Apponas istis
affluentiam divitiarum,
influentiam deliciarum,
confluentiam bonorum,

so that
I may rejoice
in your consolation above me,
your land's loveliness beneath me,
soul and body's glorification within
me,
friends human and angel delightfully around me.

ut gaudere possim
supra me de tua consolatione,
infra de loci amoenitate,
intra de corporis et animae
glorificatione,
iuxta de angelorum et hominum delectabili associatione.

Most merciful Father:
There with you
may I attain
in my reason, wisdom's light,
in my desire, possession of
true goods,
in my striving, triumph's honour—

Consequatur apud te,
clementissime Pater,
in eo
rationalis sapientiae illustrationem,
concupiscibilis desiderabilium
adeptionem,
irascibilis triumphi laudem;

With you:	ubi est, apud te,
all dangers gone,	evasio periculorum,
the dwellings various,	distinctio mansionum,
all wills harmonious;	concordia voluntatum;
where there is	ubi est
springtime loveliness,	amoenitas vernalis,
summer brightness,	luciditas aestivalis,
autumn's plenty,	ubertas autumnalis,
winter rest.	et requies hiemalis.
Lord God:	Da, Domine Deus,
Give life without death,	vitam sine morte,
joy without sorrow,	gaudium sine dolore,
where there is	ubi est
highest liberty,	summa libertas,
liberation from all cares,	libera securitas,
carefree tranquillity,	secura tranquillitas,
joyful happiness,	iucunda felicitas,
happy eternity,	felix aeternitas,
eternal blessedness,	aeterna beatitudo,
the sight and praise of truth:	veritatis visio atque laudatio,
God.	Deus.
Amen	*Amen*

References

For the works of Aquinas, see the List of Abbreviations and Conventions.

Anscombe, G. E. M. (1958), *Intention* (1957), rev. edn. (Oxford: Basil Blackwell).

André-Vincent, Ph.-I, OP (1976), 'L'Intuition fondamentale de Las Casas et la doctrine de Saint Thomas', *Nouvelle Revue Théologique*, 96: 944–52.

Baldwin, John W. (1959), *The Medieval Theories of the Just Price: Romanists, Canonists and Theologians in the Twelfth and Thirteenth Centuries, Transactions of the American Philosophical Society*, NS 40 4 (Philadelphia).

Barker, Ernest (trans. and ed.) (1948), *The Politics of Aristotle* (New York: Oxford University Press; first pub. Oxford: Clarendon Press, 1946).

Bataillon, Louis-Jacques (1983), 'Le Sermon inédit de saint Thomas *Homo quidam fecit cenam magnam*: Introduction et édition', *Revue des Sciences Philosophiques et Théologiques*, 67: 353–69.

Blythe, James M. (1986), 'The Mixed Constitution and the Distinction between Regal and Political Power in the Work of Thomas Aquinas', *Journal of the History of Ideas*, 47: 547–65.

Boyle, Leonard E., OP (1974), 'The *De Regno* and the Two Powers', in J. Reginald O'Donnell (ed.), *Essays in Honour of Anton Charles Pegis* (Toronto: Pontifical Institute of Mediaeval Studies).

Busa, Robert (1992), *Thomae Aquinatis Opera Omnia cum Hypertextibus in CD-ROM* (Milan: Editoria Elettronica Editel) (rev. edn. 1996).

Cai, Raphael, OP (1951a), *S. Thomae Aquinatis Super Epistolas S. Pauli Lectura*, 8th edn. (Turin: Marietti).

—— (1951b), *S. Thomae Aquinatis Super Evangelium S. Matthaei Lectura*, 5th edn. (Turin: Marietti).

—— (1952), *S. Thomae Aquinatis Super Evangelium S. Ioannis Lectura*, 5th edn. (Turin: Marietti).

Cathala, M.-R. (1935), *Sancti Thomae Aquinatis In Metaphysicam Aristotelis Commentaria* (Turin: Marietti).

Chenu, M.-D., OP (1963), *Toward Understanding Saint Thomas* (Chicago: Henry Regnery).

Donagan, Alan (1982), 'Thomas Aquinas on Human Action', in Norman Kretzmann, Anthony Kenny, and Jan Pinborg (eds.), *The Cambridge History of Later Medieval Philosophy: From the Rediscovery of Aristotle to the Disintegration of Scholasticism 1100–1600* (Cambridge: Cambridge University Press).

Dondaine, H.-F. (1979), 'Problèmes d'histoire littéraire', in *Opera* 42.

Eschmann, I. T., OP (rev. with introd. and notes) (1949), St Thomas Aquinas, *On Kingship to the King of Cyprus*, trans. Gerald B. Phelan (Toronto: Pontifical Institute of Mediaeval Studies).

Eschmann, I. T., OP (1958), 'St. Thomas Aquinas on the Two Powers', *Mediaeval Studies*, 20: 177–205.

Finnis, John (1980), *Natural Law and Natural Rights* (Oxford: Clarendon Press).

—— (1983), *Fundamentals of Ethics* (Oxford: Clarendon Press; Washington: Georgetown University Press).

—— (1987), 'Comment', in Ruth Gavison (ed.), *Issues in Contemporary Legal Philosophy* (Oxford: Clarendon Press).

—— (1989), 'Persons and their Associations', *Proceedings of the Aristotelian Society*, suppl. vol. 63: 267–74.

—— (1990), 'Allocating Risks and Suffering: Some Hidden Traps', *Cleveland State Law Review*, 38: 193–207.

—— (1991a), *Moral Absolutes* (Washington: Catholic University of America Press).

—— (ed.) (1991b), *Natural Law*, i and ii, International Library of Essays in Law and Legal Theory (New York: New York University Press; Aldershot: Dartmouth).

—— (1991c/1992a), 'Object and Intention in Moral Judgments according to St Thomas Aquinas', *The Thomist*, 55: 1–27; rev. in J. Follon and J. McEvoy (eds.), *Finalité et intentionnalité: Doctrine Thomiste et perspectives modernes* (Paris: Librairie Philosophique J. Vrin).

—— (1992b), *'Historical Consciousness' and Theological Foundations*, Étienne Gilson Lecture no. 15 (Toronto: Pontifical Institute of Mediaeval Studies).

—— (1994), 'On Conditional Intentions and Preparatory Intentions', in Luke Gormally (ed.), *Moral Truth and Moral Tradition: Essays in Honour of Peter Geach and Elizabeth Anscombe* (Dublin: Four Courts Press).

—— (1996a), 'The Truth in Legal Positivism', in Robert P. George (ed.), *The Autonomy of Law* (Oxford: Clarendon Press).

—— (1996b), 'Is Natural Law Theory Compatible with Limited Government?', in Robert P. George (ed.), *Natural Law, Liberalism, and Morality* (Oxford: Clarendon Press).

—— Joseph Boyle, and Germain Grisez (1987), *Nuclear Deterrence, Morality and Realism* (Oxford: Clarendon Press).

Fortenbaugh, William W. (1991), 'Aristotle on Prior and Posterior, Correct and Mistaken Constitutions', in David Keyt and Fred D. Miller (eds.), *A Companion to Aristotle's 'Politics'* (Oxford: Basil Blackwell).

Foster, Kenelm, OP (trans. and ed. with introd.) (1959), *The Life of Saint Thomas Aquinas: Biographical Documents* (London: Longmans, Green).

Fuller, Lon L. (1969), *The Morality of Law*, rev. edn. (New Haven: Yale University Press).

Gallagher, John, CSB (1984), 'The Principle of Totality: Man's Stewardship of his Body', in Donald G. McCarthy, *Moral Theology Today: Certitudes and Doubts* (St Louis: Pope John Center).

Gauthier, R.-A., OP (1954), 'Saint Maxime le Confesseur et la psychologie de l'acte humain', *Recherches de Théologie Ancienne et Médiévale*, 21: 51–100.

Geach, Peter (1961), 'Aquinas', in G. E. M. Anscombe and P. T. Geach, *Three Philosophers: Aristotle, Aquinas, Frege* (Oxford: Basil Blackwell).

Genicot, Léopold (1976), 'Le *De Regno*: Spéculation ou réalisme?', in G. Verbeke and D. Verheist (eds.), *Aquinas and Problems of his Time* (Leuven: Leuven University Press; The Hague: Martinus Nijhoff).

George, Robert P. (1993), *Making Men Moral* (Oxford: Clarendon Press).

Gilby, Thomas, OP (1955), *Between Community and Society: A Philosophy and Theology of the State* (London: Longmans, Green).

—— (1958), *Principality and Polity: Aquinas and the Rise of State Theory in the West* (London: Longmans, Green).

Gils, Pierre-M. J., OP (1992), 'S. Thomas écrivain' (1986), in *Opera* 50.

Goerner, E. A. (1979), 'On Thomistic Natural Law: The Bad Man's View of Thomistic Natural Right', *Political Theory*, 7: 101–22.

—— (1983), 'Thomistic Natural Right: The Good Man's View of Thomistic Natural Law', *Political Theory*, 11: 393–418.

Grisez, Germain (1965), 'The First Principle of Practical Reason: A Commentary on the *Summa Theologiae*, 1–2, Question 94, Article 2', *Natural Law Forum*, 10: 168–201; repr. in Finnis (1991b: i).

—— (1975), *Beyond the New Theism: A Philosophy of Religion* (Notre Dame, Ind.: University of Notre Dame Press).

—— (1991), 'Are there Exceptionless Moral Norms?', in Russell E. Smith (ed.), *The Twenty-Fifth Anniversary of Vatican II* (Braintree, Mass.: Pope John Center), 117–35, 154–62.

—— (1993), *The Way of the Lord Jesus*, ii: *Living a Christian Life* (Quincy, Ill.: Franciscan Press).

—— Joseph Boyle, and John Finnis (1987), 'Practical Principles, Moral Truths, and Ultimate Ends', *American Journal of Jurisprudence*, 32: 99–151; repr. with table of contents in Finnis (1991b: i. 236–89).

Grotius, Hugo (1625), *De Jure Belli ac Pacis Libri Tres* (1625; 5th edn. 1646), ed. B. J. A. De Kanter and Van Hettinga Tromp (Leiden: E. J. Brill, 1939), rev. R. Feenstra and C. E. Persenaire (Aalen: Scientia Verlag, 1993).

Hastings, Max (1989), *Overlord: D-Day and the Battle for Normandy* (London: Michael Joseph).

Hobbes, Thomas (1651), *Leviathan*, ed. J. C. A. Gaskin (Oxford: Oxford University Press, 1996).

Journet, Charles (1954), *The Church of the Word Incarnate*, i (London: Sheed & Ward).

Kretzmann, Norman (1997), *The Metaphysics of Theism: Aquinas' Natural Theology in* Summa contra Gentiles I (Oxford: Clarendon Press).

Langholm, Odd (1984), *The Aristotelian Analysis of Usury* (Bergen: Universitetsforlaget).

Lee, Patrick (1981), 'Permanence of the Ten Commandments: St Thomas and his Modern Commentators', *Theological Studies*, 42: 422.

Locke, John (1689), *The Second Treatise of Government* (*c*.1681, pub. 1689), ed. P. Laslett (1961, 1967, 1988); repr. corr. in *Political Writings of John Locke*, ed. David Wootton (Harmondsworth: Penguin; New York: Mentor, 1993).

McInerny, Ralph (1995), *Aquinas against the Averroists: On there being Only One Intellect* (Latin text from *Opera* 43, Eng. trans. McInerny, paragraphing as in the Leo William Keeler edn. (1936)) (West Lafayette, Ind.: Purdue University Press).

Maggiòlo, M., OP (1954), *S. Thomae Aquinatis In Octo Libros Physicorum Aristotelis Expositio* (Turin: Marietti).

Marc, Petrus, OSB (1966), Introductio, in *S. Thomae Aquinatis Liber De Veritate Catholicae Fidei contra Errores Infidelium* (*Summa contra Gentiles*), i (Turin: Marietti).

Maritain, Jacques (1951), *Man and the State* (London: Hollis & Carter, 1954).
—— (1986), *La Loi naturelle ou loi non écrite*, ed. Georges Brazzola: (Fribourg: Éditions Universitaires Fribourg Suisse).

Markus, R. A. (1970), *Saeculum: History and Society in the Theology of St. Augustine* (Cambridge: Cambridge University Press).

Miller, Fred. D. (1995), *Nature, Justice, and Rights in Aristotle's Politics* (Oxford: Clarendon Press).

Murphy, Mark C. (1996), 'Natural Law, Impartialism, and Others' Good', *Thomist*, 60: 53–80.

Noonan, John T. (1967), *Contraception: A History of its Treatment by the Catholic Theologians and Canonists* (1965) (New York: New American Library).

Owen, G. E. L. (1960), 'Logic and Metaphysics in Some Earlier Works of Aristotle'; repr. in Dühring, I. and Owen (eds.), *Aristotle and Plato in the Mid-Fourth Century* (1964); and in Owen, *Logic, Science and Dialectic* (Ithaca, NY: Cornell University Press, 1986).

Parmisano, Fabian, OP (1969), 'Love and Marriage in the Middle Ages', *New Blackfriars*, 50: 599–608, 649–60.

Pegis, A. C., J. F. Anderson, Vernon J. Bourke, and Charles J. O'Neil (eds.) (1955–7), Thomas Aquinas, *On the Truth of the Catholic Faith: Summa contra Gentiles* (Garden City, NY: Hanover House; repr. Notre Dame: University of Notre Dame Press, 1975).

Pera, Ceslas, OP (ed.) (1950), *S. Thomae Aquinatis In Librum Beati Dionysii De Divinis Nominibus Expositio* (Turin: Marietti).
—— (ed.) (1961), *S. Thomae Aquinatis Liber De Veritate Catholicae Fidei contra Errores Infidelium* (= *Summa contra Gentiles*), ii (books i and ii) and iii (books iii and iv) (Turin: Marietti).

Pirotta, A. M., OP (1936), *Sancti Thomae Aquinatis In Aristotelis Librum De Anima Commentarium* (Turin: Marietti).

Pius XII (1955), Address to the Italian Association of Catholic Jurists (5 Feb.), *Acta Apostolicae Sedis*, 47: 81.

Russell, Jeffrey Burton (1991), *Inventing the Flat Earth: Columbus and Modern Historians* (New York: Praeger).

Sidgwick, Henry (1902), *Outlines of the History of Ethics for English Readers* (1886), 5th edn. (London: Macmillan; repr. Indianapolis: Hackett, 1988).

Spiazzi, Raymundi M., OP (ed.) (1949*a*), *S. Thomae Aquinatis In Decem Libros Ethicorum: Aristotelis ad Nicomachum Expositio* (Turin: Marietti).

—— (1949*b*) (ed.), *S. Thomae Aquinatis In Aristotelis Libros De Sensu et Sensato; De Memoria et Reminiscentia Commentarium* (Turin: Marietti).

—— (1951) (ed.), *S. Thomae Aquinatis In Libros Politicorum Aristotelis Expositio* (Turin: Marietti).

—— (1952) (ed.), *S. Thomae Aquinatis In Aristotelis Libros De Caelo et Mundo; De Generatione et Corruptione; Meteorologicorum Expositio* (Turin: Marietti).

—— (1954) (ed.), *Divi Thomae Aquinatis Opuscula Philosophica* (Turin: Marietti).

—— (1955), *S. Thomae Aquinatis in Aristotelis Libros Peri Hermeneias et Poteriorum Analyticorum* (Turin: Marietti).

—— and M. Calcaterra, OP (eds.) (1954), *Sancti Thomae Aquinatis Opuscula Theologica*, ii (Turin: Marietti).

Strauss, Leo (1953), *Natural Right and History* (Chicago: University of Chicago Press).

Suarez, Francisco, SJ (1613), *Defensio Fidei Catholicae et Apostolicae adversus Anglicanae Sectae Errores* (A Defence of the Catholic and Apostolic Faith against the Errors of the Anglican Sect) (Coimbra), book vi (concerning the oath of allegiance exacted by the King of England [James I]); page references are to Williams *et al.* (1944).

—— (1621), *De Triplici Virtute Theologica, Fide, Spe, et Charitate* (Coimbra), dist. 13 *De Bello* (On War) trans. in Williams *et al.* (1944).

Synan, Edward A. (1978), 'Aquinas and his Age', in Anthony Parel (ed.), *Calgary Aquinas Studies* (Toronto: Institute of Mediaeval Studies).

—— (1988), 'St. Thomas Aquinas and the Profession of Arms', *Mediaeval Studies*, 50: 404–37.

Torrell, Jean-Pierre, OP (1985), 'Les *Collationes in decem praeceptis* de saint Thomas d'Aquin: édition critique avec introduction et notes', *Revue des Sciences Philosophiques et Théologiques*, 69: 5–40, 227–63.

—— (1996), *Saint Thomas Aquinas*, i: *The Person and his Work* (trans. by Robert Royal) (Washington: Catholic University of America Press).

Tugwell, Simon, OP (trans. and ed. with introds.) (1988), *Albert and Thomas: Selected Writings* (New York: Paulist Press).

Verardo, Raymundi A., OP (ed.) (1954), *Sancti Thomae Aquinatis Opuscula Theologica*, i (Turin: Marietti).

Voegelin, Eric (1957), *Order and History*, iii: *Plato and Aristotle* (Baton Rouge: Louisiana State University Press).

Weisheipl, James A., OP (1983), *Friar Thomas D'Aquino: His Life, Thought, and Works* (1974), corr. ed. (Washington: Catholic University of America Press).

Wiggins, David (1975), 'Deliberation and Practical Reason', *Proceedings of the Aristotelian Society*, 76: 29–51.

Wilks, Michael (1963), *The Problem of Sovereignty in the Later Middle Ages* (Cambridge: Cambridge University Press).

Williams, Gwladys L., Ammi Brown, John Waldron, and Henry Davis (eds.) (1944), *Selections from Three Works of Francisco Suarez SJ*, ii (Oxford: Clarendon Press).

Index Locorum

AQUINAS

II-II

ARISTOTLE

PLATO

INDEX

need(s) (*necessitas, indigentia, indigere*)
(*see also* poverty, *superflua*):
defined 191, 194, 201; *also* 81n.,
114n., 117, 119n., 164, 171, 189,
191–7, 200–3, 206–7, 240n., 245–6,
258, 309–12
negligence 141–2, 202n., 277
negotiatio (commerce) 200
negotiatores (merchants, traders) 227n.
neighbour: Ethiopians, Indians, and all
other (human) persons 126n., love of ~
as self 126–9, 131–2, 136–8, 140–1,
152, 154, 161–2, 164n., 192n., 194,
199, 227, 235, 239, 243, 252, 271,
277, 280, 314, 317, as point of
moral precept 127n.; *also* 112n.,
121, 200, 216–17, 223n., 240, 242n.,
314, 317n., 319
neighbourhoods 25–6, 117, 242, 246n.,
249
neighbourliness 112, 218
New Testament (*see* also Bible,
covenant) 11, 180n., 282
Nicaea, First Council of 274
Nietzsche, Nietzschean 139, 154, 297n.
'*nisi forte*', meaning of 274
noble, nobility (excellence, dignity) 109n.,
174n., 176n., 332
Noonan, John T. 145n., 180n.
norm (*praeceptum* (*q. v.*), *regula*) (*see also*
prudentia, rationality, '*semper sed . . .*
', specification, virtue): defined 87,
118, 124n.–5, 135, 138–40, affirmative
or negative 124n., 164n., 169n.,
deduction of 141, 143, 154, if negative
can be exceptionless 141, 148, 161–70,
182–3, 192n., 276, 278, 290, obscured
by depravity 168n., priority to virtues
156, 168, 187–8; *also* 99, 126–9,
131–2, 136, 142–3, 173, 185, 190, 193,
196n., 199n., 213, 256n., 267, 285n.

oath: often not binding on maker 16,
198n., 289n.–90n., or third
party 241n., lying on ~ 159n., 161n.
obedience (*obedientia, observantia*) 54,
264, 271n.; by children 11, 18, 171,
241n., 323n.; *also* 6, 73, 76, 101,
213n., 215, 234, 240, 258, 260, 266,
272–3, 286n., 288n.–90, 324
object (*obiectum, finis*) (*see also*
intention) 29–31, 45, 53, 81, 90–3; of
desire 315, of inclination 82, 85, 93,
246, of hope 332, of interest 93, of
justice 133, 138, 168, 170, 176, 217, of
love 141, as *materia circa*
quam 142n., 145, point 41, 119n., of

the *polis* 228, close-in (proximate)
purpose or point or means 70, 142–3,
145, 148–9, 151n., 153, 156n., 163,
166n., 180, 276, 279–80, subject-
matter 22, 41–2, 45, 100, 110n., 156,
178, 316–17, of will 53, 70n., 98,
111n., 143n., objective 31–3, 35–6,
41, 53–4, 59, 70, 77, 97, 222, 225,
232–4, 287, specifies act 142n.,
156n., 163, 166n.
obligation (*obligatio, obligare*), the
obligatory (*obligatorium*), defined 127,
affirmative v. negative 164, 169, ~ of
children to parents 11, 18, correlative
with authority 269, 274, defeasible
266, 272, to defend others 275, of
disclosure 155n., of fairness 161n., of
law(s) 260, 266–7, 269, 271, and
legislative intention 258, limits of
authority's ~ 239–40, 260, 272–3, of
marital *fides* 145n., 147n., mutual/
reciprocal 261, 289n., of non-
disclosure 158, 182, practices and ~
196–7, of promises 197n.–9, to repay/
return 164, 205, of restitution 202n.,
211n.–212, rooted in friendship and
practical reasonableness 197, 271, not
owed to rulers 264, unjust laws and ~
272–3; *also* 15–16, 215–17
oeconomica (household management):
defined 24, 52, 244n.; *also* 37n.,
119n., 122, 195n., 226n., 238, 244
Old Testament (*see also* Bible, covenant)
8, 11, 180n., 125n., 261n., 282, 308n.
operatio (act (*q. v.*), execution of
intention) 23–4, 26, 32, 107n., 109n.,
113n., 129n., 177n., 221n., 230
order, *see* four types of order(s)
ordinare (to set in order, to relate to) 35n.,
41n., 106n., 109n.–10n., 127n.,
146n., 170n., 217, 223n.–4n., 233n.,
237n., 240n., 251n.–3, 254, *ordinatus*
(to be related/ordered to) 25n., 223n.,
252, 256n., 262n., 276n., 328,
ordinabilis (to be relatable to) 118
ordinatio (order(ing), constitution,
arrangement) (*see also*
coordinatio) 17, 32, 255n., 257, 263
ordo (order, co-ordination (*q. v.*), direction,
arrangement, system, relationship)
(*see* also four types of ~): of acting
persons 32, 239n.–40n., directedness
to end(s) (*ad finem*) 142n., 151n.,
234n., 254, 288, fittingness of 111n.,
of law/right 213n., 251n., 272n., of
reasonableness 76n., 98, 103n.,
148n., types of 236n.